EDUCATIONAL ADMINISTRATION INNOVATION
FOR SUSTAINABLE DEVELOPMENT

PROCEEDINGS OF THE INTERNATIONAL CONFERENCE ON RESEARCH OF
EDUCATIONAL ADMINISTRATION AND MANAGEMENT (ICREAM 2017),
OCTOBER 17, 2017, BANDUNG, INDONESIA

Educational Administration Innovation for Sustainable Development

Editors

Aan Komariah, Taufani C. Kurniatun, Dedy A. Kurniady,
Rita Anggorowati, Ade Gafar Abdullah &
Asep Bayu Dani Nandiyanto
Universitas Pendidikan Indonesia

LONDON AND NEW YORK

CRC Press
Taylor & Francis Group
6000 Broken Sound Parkway NW, Suite 300
Boca Raton, FL 33487-2742

First issued in paperback 2020

© 2003 by Taylor & Francis Group, LLC
CRC Press is an imprint of Taylor & Francis Group, an Informa business

No claim to original U.S. Government works

ISBN-13: 978-1-138-57341-3 (hbk)
ISBN-13: 978-0-367-73378-0 (pbk)

Visit the Taylor & Francis Web site at
http://www.taylorandfrancis.com

and the CRC Press Web site at
http://www.crcpress.com

Educational Administration Innovation for Sustainable Development – Komariah et al. (Eds)
© 2018 Taylor & Francis Group, London, ISBN 978-1-138-57341-3

Table of contents

Foreword

Sustainable development is a principled development process (land, city, business, community, etc.) in meeting present needs without compromising the needs of future generations (Brundtland in UN, 1987). One of the essential factors required, to achieve sustainable development is improving the saturation of the environment without sacrificing the need for economic development and social justice. Sustainable development consists of three main pillars; economic, social, and environmental, which are interdependent and strong. Some people might see sustainable development is closely linked to economic growth and how to develop the economy over the long term, without depleting natural resources. Thus, sustainable development is an environmentally friendly development, efficient in the use of natural resources and providing long-term benefits for living things.

In the sustainable development context, which holds an important role to participate in the provision of educational processes in generating graduates who are able to be active in sustainable development. It is manifested through outstanding educational leadership, educational planning, educational practices, educational supervision and relevant human resource development as well as educational institutions appropriateness to the environment.

The very first International Conference on Research of Educational Administration and Management (ICREAM) 2017 presented various articles of research that discusses sustainable development in various countries. We hope that this conference can be followed by continuous study in accordance with the development of science and community needs.

Regards
Aan Komariah,
Taufani C. Kurniatun,
Dedy A. Kurniady,
Rita Anggorowati,
Ade Gafar Abdullah
Asep Bayu Dani Nandiyanto

Organizers

Chairperson
Prof. Aan Komariah, Universitas Pendidikan Indonesia, INDONESIA

Technical Chairperson
Dr. Taufani C. Kurniatun, M.Si, Universitas Pendidikan Indonesia, INDONESIA
Dr. Dedy Achmad Kurniady, M.Pd, Universitas Pendidikan Indonesia, INDONESIA

Committee
Dr. Ade Gafar Abdullah, M.Si
Herlina, M.Pd
Rita Anggorowati, M.Pd
Widia Murni Wijaya, SST., B.CS
Siti Nurlatifah, S.Pd

International Advisory Board
Prof. Simon Clarke (University of Western Australia, Australia)
Prof. David Giles (Flinders University, Australia)
Prof. Thomas F Nelson Laird (Indiana University, USA)
Tran Huu Luong, Ph.D (Ministry of Education and Training Vietnam)
Dr. Jose Da Silva Monteiro (Ministry of Education Democratic Republic of Timor Leste)
Assoc. Prof. Mariani Md. Noor (University of Malaya, Malaysia)

International Scientific Committee
Prof. Ngo Dinh Phuong (Vinh University, Viet Nam)
Prof. Sharil Marzuki (UPSI, Malaysia)
Prof. Datuk. Dr. Sufean Hussin (UM, Malaysia)
Prof. Djam'an Satori, MA (UPI, Indonesia)
Prof. Aan Komariah, M.Pd (UPI, Indonesia)
Prof. Dede Rosyada (UIN Jakarta, Indonesia)
Prof. Ibrahim Bafadal (UM, Indonesia)
Prof. Sugiyono (UNY, Indonesia)
Prof. Udin S Saud, Ph.D (UPI, Indonesia)
Prof. Johar Permana, MA (UPI, Indonesia)
Prof. Ace Suryadi (UPI, Indonesia)
Prof. Bejo Suyanto (UNJ, Indonesia)
Prof. Husaini Usman (UNY, Indonesia)
Prof. Kadim Masaong (UNG, Indonesia)
Prof. Arismunandar (UNM, Indonesia)
Prof. Ali Imron (UM, Malang, Indonesia)
Prof. Rusdinal (UNP, Indonesia)
Prof. Slameto (Universitas Satya Wacana, Indonesia)
Prof. Sonhadji (UM, Malang, Indonesia)
Prof. Ki Supriyoko (Uni. Sarjanawiyata Taman Siswa, Indonesia)
Prof. Baharuddin (UIN Maliki, Indonesia)
Prof. Ansar (UNG, Indonesia)

Prof. Nurhizrah (UNP, Indonesia)
Prof. Syaiful Sagala (Unimed, Indonesia)
Prof. Madha Komala (UNJ, Indonesia)
Prof. Fachruddin (Unnes, Indonesia)
Prof. Haryono (unnes, Indonesia)
Prof. Nurul Ulfatin (UM, Indonesia)
Prof. Sulthon Masyhud (Univ. Jember, Indonesia)
Prof. Bintang Sitepu (UNJ, Indonesia)
Prof. Bambang Budi Wiyono (UM, Indonesia)
Prof. Cut Zahri (Unsyiah, Indonesia)
Assoc. Prof. Khoa Tran (VNU, HaNoi Vietnam)
Assoc. Prof. Zuraidah Abdullah (UM, Malaysia)
Assoc. Prof. Thu Huong Nguyen Thi (VNU, Vietnam)
Assoc. Prof. Chhinh Sitha (Royal University, Cambodia)
Assoc. Prof. Nur Kholis, M.Ed (UIN Sunan Ampel, Indonesia)
Assoc. Prof. Udik Budi (UNY, Indonesia)
Assoc. Prof. Lantip Diaz Prasojo (UNY, Indonesia)
Assoc. Prof. Cepy Abdul Jabar (UNY, Indonesia)
Assoc. Prof. Arwildayanto (UNG, Indonesia)
Assoc. Prof. Nurhattati (UNJ, Indonesia)
Assoc. Prof. Rugaiyah Fitri (UNJ, Indonesia)
Assoc. Prof. Dwi Deswari (UNJ. Indonesia)
Assoc. Prof. Aceng Muhtaram Mirfani (UPI, Indonesia)
Assoc. Prof. Asep Suryana (UPI, Indonesia)
Assoc. Prof. Endang Herawan (UPI, Indonesia)
Assoc. Prof. Dedy Achmad K (UPI, Indonesia)
Assoc. Prof. Diding Nurdin (UPI, Indonesia)
Assoc. Prof. Nuraedi (UPI, Indonesia)
Assoc. Prof. Muhammad Faizal A, Ghani (UM, Malaysia)
Burhanuddin, M.Ed., Ph.D (UM, Malang)
Dr. Ed. Faridah, ST, M.Sc (UNM, Indonesia)
Dr. Megat Ahmad Kamaluddin Megat Daud (UM, Malaysia)
Dr. Imam Machali, S.Pd.I., M.Pd (UIN Sunan Kalijaga, Indonesia)

Educational Administration Innovation for Sustainable Development – Komariah et al. (Eds)
© 2018 Taylor & Francis Group, London, ISBN 978-1-138-57341-3

Scheming educational leaders' communication skills

R. Anggorowati
Universitas Pendidikan Indonesia, Bandung, West Java, Indonesia

ABSTRACT: The stipulation of communication as being one of the essential skills in life also applies to educational leaders who have the intention of leading their organization effectively. However, in the real-life situation, the educational leaders' communication skills have not been well-schemed. A reflective action research was used by doing informal, semi-structured interviews, questionnaires and observation in two national plus schools during a three-month period of time. This research suggests that the concept of building rapport, sensory acuity, calibration and active listening associated with Neuro-Linguistics Programming (NLP) can lead to behaviors that are more conducive to helping the educational leaders to work with their communication skills to support their leadership in their workplace.

1 INTRODUCTION

For the past few years, communication has been seen as being one of the most important skills that everyone, including educational leaders, should have. Leaders spend most of their time communicating. One of the major findings of the research on communication shows that every day a manager spends 70 to 90 percent of their time in communicating with their teams and others in the work place (Moran et al, 2014; Daft & Marcic, 2016).

Furthermore, effective communication also acts as an advantage for a leader to lead effectively. This is because one of the key points in becoming a good leader is the ability to change how people feel about themselves and inspiring them to achieve performance beyond their previous expectations – the concept of transformational leadership (Gill, 2011).

Beer (2009) stated that the way to build a resilient organization for sustained advantage is by making sure that every person in the organization has a high commitment. Building commitment can only be successful by making sure that everybody in the organization is involved. Covey (2013) stated that if there were no involvement, there will be no commitment.

How does one build involvement? By communication. Hence, every leader, including educational leaders, needs to be really aware of it and own the effective communication skills on a daily basis. Nevertheless, what really happens in the real-life situation is that the communication skills of educational leaders have not been well-schemed; thus the disparity between the required skills and practice in the field is becoming inevitable.

Various research on the importance of communication for leaders can be seen from the work of Men (2014), who suggested that leaders need to play a galvanizing role in internal communication and develop their leadership communication skills. In addition, Johansson et al. (2014) found that leaders' communication competence is related to employee engagement and organizational performance. Furthermore, Bornman and Puth (2017) found that South African employees perceive that leaders do not correctly utilize leadership communication and that leaders do not understand what it means to be a 'communicating leader'. They recommended organizations to implement training and development programs for all individuals in leadership positions, which will develop communicating leaders who are aware of what they are lacking and where they can improve themselves within their organizational environments.

Therefore, the Neuro-Linguistics Programming (NLP) approach, created in the 1970s, was chosen to be the technique used in this research, as it has been proven as acting effectively as

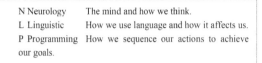

N Neurology	The mind and how we think.
L Linguistic	How we use language and how it affects us.
P Programming	How we sequence our actions to achieve our goals.

Figure 1.   Neuro-Linguistic Programming.
Source: O'Connor (2013).

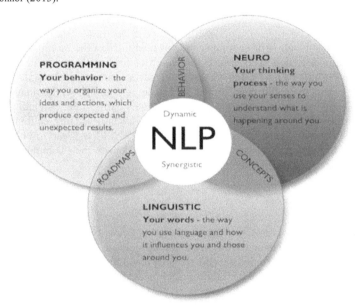

Figure 2.   NLP in brief.
Source: Sun (2016).

an emergent, contested approach to communication and personal development; this technique has become increasingly familiar in education and teaching (Tosey & Mathison, 2010). It is hoped that the result of this research will help in filling the gap that occurs in educational leadership in practice, and contribute to the growing literature in schools on the subject of relationship management.

The name 'Neuro-Linguistic Programming' comes from the three areas it brings together:

In short, as we can see in Figure 1, NLP can be framed as being an approach to communication, focusing more on the process of how the mind, and the way we will reflect on how we use the language, affect the sequence of our actions in achieving our goals.

Richard Bandler and John Grinder founded NLP during the 1970s in California, USA. It is explained as being an explicit and powerful model of human experience and communication and has been defined as 'the art of communication excellence' (Tosey & Mathison, 2006). The scheme of NLP in brief can be seen on Figure 2.

As one of the founders, Richard Bandler as cited in O'Connor (2013) stated that NLP is an attitude and a methodology, which leaves behind a trail of techniques. Furthermore, he believed that NLP helps every aspect of human life through a process which is called 'modeling'. With the intention of modeling, NLP studies how we construct our subjective experience – how we reflect on our values and beliefs and how we craft our emotional states – in the end, NLP studies how we compose our internal world from our experience and give it meaning. Thus, NLP studies experience from the inside within. NLP originally began by examining the best communicators and has progressed into the systemic study of human communication; this has grown by adding practical tools and methods generated by modeling extraordinary people. These tools were soon used internationally in sports, business, training, sales, law and education. However, NLP is not merely about a collection of techniques, but is also a way of thinking, and a frame of mind based on curiosity, exploration and fun.

When we are discussing NLP, we cannot separate the discussion from mind, as mind is something that has a close relationship when we are doing the process of thinking. The essential point to NLP is the appreciation and understanding, that each individual has available to them a number of different ways to represent their experiences of the world. In particular, a person draws upon five recognized senses (sense modalities) to be interconnected with the world and reality. NLP believes that as human beings, we have preferred modes for perceiving and understanding the modalities that we have: visual, Auditory, Kinesthetic, Olfactory and Gustatory (VAKOG). We grab our experience through our modalities and keep them as our internal representations; we then create our personal map of reality. However, we need to bear in mind that we do not know what reality is, as a map can never be completely accurate – otherwise it would be the same as the ground it covers. Some maps might be better than others for finding our way around. People navigate life like a ship through different kinds of area. Some areas might seem normal, and some might look dangerous. As long as the map shows the main hazard, we shall be fine. However, we might be in danger when the maps are faulty. This then leads the researcher to start thinking on how the approach could give some benefits in scheming educational leadership communication skills.

One research on communication in organizations, seen from the leadership point of view, was done by Fairhurst and Connaughton (2014). They found that leadership communication is transmissional and meaning-centered, but also relational, neither leader-centric nor follower-centric. This supports the NLP presupposition that *the map is not the territory*. O'Connor (2013) defined this as people responding to their experience, not to reality itself. Thus, NLP is the art of changing these maps so that we have greater freedom in action. In the educational leadership communication setting, this presupposition can be used as the gateway in changing every aspect of educational leaders' perception in seeing their subordinate, during their interactions while they are in the workplace.

From the vast number of NLP techniques, patterns and strategies – around 350+ according to Vaknin (2010) – this study will focus more on modeling, rapport, sensory acuity, calibration and active listening in building trust behaviors.

2 RESEARCH METHOD

A reflective action research with qualitative method was used by doing informal, semi-structured interviews, questionnaires and observation in two national plus schools in Bandung during a three-month period of time. This study involved two principals, two vice-principals, staff and teachers as practitioners. This is aligned with the work of Koshy et al. (2011), who proposed that action research ought to involve practitioners in systematic enquiries to improve practice. Such research is conducted 'on the job' and provides practitioners with opportunities to explore systematically issues that are important to them in their specific work context. Meyer (2000) stated that the strength of action research lies in its ability to help create solutions to practical problems in specific work-based situations.

During the research, I visited the schools on a daily basis to capture the experiences and perceptions of the intervention for those taking part. This study examined the responses of an extraction group of two principals, two vice-principals, staff and teachers, with their agreement and participation as unpaid volunteers. Pseudonyms have been used to ensure the anonymity of the respondents. This specific research enabled the production of descriptions and data collections of respondents' perception relating to their experiences of the intervention. The intervention and subsequent data collection took place at the same time and at the same place each week – every Wednesday and Thursday.

Semi-structured interviews were held informally, so the students felt relaxed and thereby provided more open and honest responses. As it was proposed by McKernan (2008), the observations were

Table 1. Description of respondents.

No.	Name	Age	Gender	Position
1	Andy	34	Male	Principal Secondary School
2	Rosa	38	Female	Principal Primary School
3	Anton	34	Male	Vice-Principal Secondary School
4	Ally	37	Female	Vice-Principal Primary School
5	Nanny	40	Female	School Admin Staff
6	Rose	41	Female	School Finance Staff
7	Pearl	36	Female	Primary Teacher
8	Andrew	36	Male	Secondary Teacher

conducted and written up soon afterwards; circumstantial evidence was also documented, as this is a useful method to record unanticipated behavior.

Questionnaires were also used as part of this research process in the form of tick boxes, formatted as yes and no questions to check on the respondents' perception and experience during the whole process. While the questions from the questionnaire could have been added to the interviews, it was essential to dig for more information and provide them with an opportunity to reflect and report their thoughts at a personal level, reducing possible interviewer bias or demand characteristics. We attempted to ensure neutrality and implemented a systematic data analysis to provide the necessary triangulation in rigorous research (Marshall & Rossman, 2016). It should be noted that the statistical representation of data was only conducted with the use of descriptive statistics. No statistical tests of difference or association were used. The research was divided into three phases.

In the first phase of the study, the observation of the educational leaders' behaviors was conducted by seeing how the principals and vice-principals communicate among themselves, as well as with the teachers and staff. The observations were continuous over a two-week period. All types of communication were recorded.

In the second phase, all educational leaders involved were given a workshop on NLP techniques for communication. The workshop lasted for two consecutive days.

In the third phase, the educational leaders were asked to practice all the communication skills with the whole school community, based on NLP on a daily basis. This phase started from week three to week twelve, and continued after the study had ended.

At the end of the research, we made sure that all the observed behaviors were noted and the participants were asked to fill out a questionnaire and do a non-formal in-depth interview to record how they felt, and their points of view and experiences on the process and techniques that they have been through in terms of practicing communication skills based on NLP. Table 1 provides a brief description on the participants. Note that the names of the respondents are pseudonyms.

3 RESULTS AND DISCUSSION

The educational leaders were learning and practicing how to do modeling, rapport, sensory acuity, calibration and active listening in building trust behaviors. They were being introduced to start to build rapport and good relationship with one to another. In NLP terms, pacing is the equivalent of understanding the *present state* in order to build a more appropriate and empowering *desired state* (O'Connor, 2013).

3.1 *Rapport*

Rapport is the quality of a relationship of mutual influence and respect between people (O'Connor, 2013). It is natural and cannot be manipulated. It is not the same as friendship as we do not have to get too personal with others. It does not come with agreement, but grows naturally. NLP supplies the skills to build a mutual respect in relationships.

During the process of research, the leaders are asked to begin with pacing another person. Pacing is a process of entering the other person's model of the world on their terms. It is a good way of building a sense of connectedness. Once the leaders have paced another person (in this case, a subordinate), established rapport and shown that he/she understands where they are coming from, then it is most likely they have a chance to lead them effectively. Leading is in a sense of when he/she could use the influence that she/he has built from pacing. The educational leaders should keep in mind that they cannot lead person unless they are willingly being led, and people are not willing to be led unless they have first been satisfactorily paced.

After successfully doing the pacing and leading process, leaders are asked to escalate their capabilities in order to make their subordinates *see* them based on their skills and interest. Every leader needs to be able to demonstrate their competency in order to build and maintain rapport when there is a shared task to be done.

The next step is in respecting and understanding the beliefs and values of other persons and paying attention to the subordinate as an individual. Every leader needs to have this skill. It does not mean that they have to agree with everyone's beliefs and values, but only to respect what is important to them. In this way, the subordinate will feel at ease, and be ready to engage in collaborative work.

The last step is shared values. It is hoped that the educational leaders start their roles by realizing that he/she is a part of humanity. Then they will position themselves as being at their most self and connected to others.

On the third phase, it was revealed that rapport building opens the gateway of better communication, as the way the leaders treat the subordinate meets the subordinates' expectation. They felt that they were being heard, respected and welcomed as a team.

As I quoted, Pearl said that, *"Now, Mrs. Rosa seemed to be opened and have time to listen me more. Especially when I talked about certain students who have learning differences. She listened me more and came with an idea that I could understand and adaptable in the classroom."*

3.2   *Sensory acuity and calibration*

Overall, sensory acuity means how good your senses are at doing what they should do. In the context of NLP, it refers to the ability to use our senses to make accurate observations about ourselves or other people. It is related with our sensitivity upon our senses. As NLP is based on how we use our senses, this skill really helped educational leaders to understand more about other people, including their subordinates around them. They need to be able to pay attention directed through their senses. By doing so, they will enrich their thinking and feelings. The educational leaders were introduced to the accessing cues and how to calibrate them to support their rapport building.

Calibration is a process of getting to know the *internal state* by observing other people's external behavior (Yuliawan, 2014). There are five things that every educational leader needs to observe from people in their surroundings:

(1) The way they breathe
(2) Inflection (change of voice)
(3) Muscle changes
(4) Lower lip changes
(5) Voice tone.

Table 2 shows the main accessing cues proposed by O'Connor (2013).

By practicing this skill, the educational leaders could actually focus on the fact – what really happened during the conversation, rather than the assumption and misleading paradigm. He/she could actually sense the connectedness with the subordinates and be able to communicate better than before.

My respondent, Andy, stated that, *"This assessing cues that support sensory acuity and calibration, were indeed helped me a lot in sharpen my sensitivity; which leads me to understand more on what my teachers and staffs trying to tell me."*

Table 2. Main accessing cues on NLP.

	Visual	Auditory	Kinesthetic
Eye movements	Defocused, or up to the right or left.	In the midline.	Below the midline, usually to the right.
Voice tone and tempo	Generally rapid speech, high, clear voice tone.	Melodious tone, resonant, at a medium pace. Often has an underlying rhythm.	Low and deeper tonality, often slow and soft, with many pauses.
Breathing	High, shallow breathing in the top part of the chest.	Even breathing in the middle part of the chest cavity.	Deeper breathing from the abdomen.
Posture and gesture	More tension in the body, often with the neck extended. Often thinner (ectomorphic) body type.	Often medium (mesomorphic) body type. There may be rhythmic movements of the body as if listening to music. Head may be tilted to the side in thought in the 'telephone position'.	Rounded shoulders, head down, relaxed muscle tone. May gesture to abdomen and midline.

3.3 *Active listening*

With rapport building, sensory acuity and calibration skills that they have mastered, the educational leaders are asked to practice their active listening on a daily basis. They were trained to always talk straight to the point, not circling around, and to make sure that they are listening more by showing a genuine gesture. Rogers and Farson (2015) proposed that active listening requires that the listener fully concentrates, understands, responds and then remembers what is being said.

Active listening should be followed by using reinforcement words and movement to show your enthusiasm. Leaders are asked to confirm by using the keyword used by the other person. Sometimes leaders are welcomed in clarifying and/or confronting things in a smooth way. This technique could also be used when the leaders need to, for example, convey their expectations, share the organizational values, or cascade the vision and mission.

One key point that every leader should never forget is that they need to show loyalty. Never talk behind someone else's back or spread out the private discussion materials in the forum. This could make the rapport break down and take you back to square one.

4 CONCLUSION

As was mentioned earlier in the Introduction, in NLP the map is not the territory. What we believe might be the real truth condition. If the educational leaders are able to be very skillful in maintaining good relations with the subordinates, then it frees them to really emphasize the human part of the relationship with the person. On a daily basis, common educational leaders will say that subordinates are having behavior problems and are not willing to work in a team. The leaders believe that the subordinates must be ignorant, or have less concentration, or be rebellious, or are not putting in enough effort. The leaders forget that what really happens is that they *are not* trying hard enough. Every change in the world needs to start with ourselves. It is stated that NLP is about adding choices, not taking them away. By enlarging the map with the subordinates' perspectives and doing some new techniques as an intervention – such as building rapport, sensory acuity, calibration and active listening – educational leaders like Ms. Rosa and Mr. Andy could gain more positive feedback and results from the subordinates.

Putting a higher notification that this research only took a small-scale exploration form of action research study, the evidences and experiences revealed a tentative conclusion about how educational leadership communication skills through the NLP scheme has been identified. It is my disputation to propose the type of evidence that I have provided here can help stimulate discussion between educational leaders, teachers and staffs, about building rapport, sensory acuity, calibration and active listening, which could support the communication skill. While this research study is small-scale, evidence in the form of observations, questionnaires and semi-structured interviews suggests that the concept of building rapport, sensory acuity, calibration and active listening associated with NLP can lead to behaviors that are more conducive to help the educational leaders to work with their communication skills in supporting their leadership in their workplace. Undoubtedly, further research into this specific phenomenon is required and links to concepts such as communication skills and organizational behavior are evident. I believe that NLP provides educational leaders, teachers and staffs with so many gateways to the world of educational organization management and, indirectly, to leadership and educational theory.

REFERENCES

Beer, M. (2009). *High commitment, high performance: How to build a resilient organization for sustained advantage.* San Francisco, CA: Jossey-Bass: A Wiley Imprint.

Bornman, D.A.J. & Puth, G. (2017). Investigating employee perceptions of leadership communication: A South African study. *Journal of Contemporary Management,* 14(1), 1–23.

Covey, S.R. (2013). *The wisdom and teachings of Stephen R. Covey.* New York: Free Press.

Daft, R.L. & Marcic, D. (2016). *Understanding management* (9th ed.).Stamford, USA: Cengage Learning.

Fairhurst, G.T. & Connaughton, S.L. (2014). Leadership: A communicative perspective. *Sage Leadership,* 10(1), 7–35.

Gill, R. (2011). *Theory and practice of leadership* (2nd ed.). London EC1Y 1SP: SAGE Publications Ltd.

Johansson, C., Miller, V.D. & Hamrin, S. (2014). Conceptualizing communicative leadership: A framework for analysing and developing leaders communication competence. *Corporate Communications: An International Journal,* 19(2), 147–165.

Koshy, E., Koshy, V. & Waterman, H. (2011). *Action research in healthcare.* London: Sage Publications Ltd.

Marshall, C. & Rossman, G.C. (2016). *Designing qualitative research.* Singapore: SAGE Publication, Inc.

McKernan, J. (2008). *Curriculum and imagination: Process theory, pedagogy and action research.* Abingdon: Routledge.

Men, L.R. (2014). Strategic internal communication: Transformational leadership, communication channels, and employee satisfaction. *Management Communication Quarterly,* 28(2), 264–284.

Meyer, J. (2000). Using qualitative methods in health related action research. *British Medical Journal,* 320(7228), 178–181.

Moran, R.T., Abramson, N.R. & Moran, S.V. (2014). *Managing cultural differences* (9th ed.). London and New York: Routledge Taylor & Francis Group.

O'Connor, J. (2013). *NLP workbook: A practical guide to achieving the results you want.* San Francisco: Conari Press.

Rogers, C.R. & Farson, R.E. (2015). *Active listening.* USA: Martino Publishing.

Sun, S.H. (2016). *Quora: What are the key differences between NLP and NAC?* Retrieved from https://www.quora.com/What-are-the-key-differences-between-NLP-and-NAC

Tosey, P. & Mathison, J. (2006). Neuro-linguistic programming and learning theory: A response. *Curriculum Journal,* 14(3), 371–388.

Tosey, P. & Mathison, J. (2010). Neuro-linguistic programming as an innovation in education and teaching. *Journal of Innovations in Education and Teaching International,* 47(3), 317–326.

Vaknin, S. (2010). *The big book of NLP expanded.* USA: Inner Patch Publishing.

Yuliawan, T.P. (2014). *The art of enjoying life.* Jakarta: Serambi.

Educational Administration Innovation for Sustainable Development – Komariah et al. (Eds)
© 2018 Taylor & Francis Group, London, ISBN 978-1-138-57341-3

The relationship between process and achievement indicator of student learning

F. Arfines, S. Susanto & S. Hawibowo
Universitas Gadjah Mada, Yogyakarta, Indonesia

ABSTRACT: A high grade point average (GPA) indicates a good achievement of student learning. Additionally, student engagement consists of the actual processes and the initiatives undertaken by the student inside and outside the classroom. Theoritically, there is a relationship between student engagement and academic achievement. This study aimed to find how strong is the relationship in the educational practice of undergraduate programs at Universitas Gadjah Mada. The instrument for measuring the student engagement was adapted from NSSE-National Survey of Student Engagement and prepared for an Indonesian student engagement survey entitled ISSLA-Indonesian Survey of Student Learning Activities. Statistical analysis was employed to interpret the data. The outcome of this study indicates that a high GPA correlates with a high student engagement, while a low GPA does not necessarily correlate with a low students engagement. This shows that different forms of student engagement relate to different learning outcomes, and may have not been considered when calculating the GPA.

1 INTRODUCTION

Higher education institutions play an important role to promote the advancement of a developing country. The main role of higher education is to produce graduates who will become great leaders or employees responsible for the country's economic and social development (Ali et.al, 2009). Therefore, institutions are required to pay greater attention to improving the teaching and student learning environment in order to provide a greater possbility for their academic achievements. These achievements are essential in producing best quality graduates with skills, knowledge, values, and attributes to play an important role in cultural, social, and economic development.

A high grade point average (GPA) indicates good achievement of the student learning process. It is theoretically a result of a good engagement in the learning tasks that are expected from the students. Student engagement is measured both by the time and energy students devote to educational activities, and how students use different facets of the institutional environment to facilitate and support their learning (Kuh, 2001). Students are more academically engaged when they are intellectually challenged, and produce creative works that lead to learning and personal development.

The National Survey of Student Engagement (NSSE) has been used in USA since 2000 and was adapted by the Indonesian survey entitled ISSLA-Indonesian Survey of Student Learning Activities in 2015. It focuses on higher education improvement, and supports higher education institutions to promote high levels of academic achievement by calling on undergraduate students to engage in complex cognitive tasks requiring more than mere memorization of facts. NSSE annually collects information at hundreds of universities about first-year and senior students' participation in programs and activities that institutions provide for their learning and personal development. The results provide an estimate of how undergraduates spend their time and what they gain from attending college (NSSE, 2010). The measurement includes four dimensions of engagement: academic challenge, learning with peers, experiences with faculty, and campus environment.

The survey items require students to assess their own level of engagement via behavioral indicators including participation in class discussions, preparation of drafts prior to submitting assignments, interactions with classmates outside of class on course-related items, and integration of resources for course assignments. Thus, highly engaged students are actively involved in their education, completing the tasks required to perform well in class, and therefore reaching their academic potential. Moreover, engaged students in the academic context are more mature (Montero & González, 2009) since they are able to cope with academic stress, which perhaps will lead in the future to more professionals having a sense of well-being.

The aim of this study is to investigate how the student active engagement correlates positively with GPA. This is a case-study in Universitas Gadjah Mada (UGM) which uses ISSLA 2015 data survey. ISSLA data are used by institutions to assess and improve undergraduate education by changing their practices and policies. The survey involved first-year and senior-year students, and the proposed hypothesis is that more active student engagement correlate with better academic achievements.

2 LITERATURE REVIEW

2.1 Student engagement

Student engagement represents two critical features of collegiate quality (NSSE, 2010). The first is the amount of time and effort students put into their studies and other educational activities. The second is how the institution deploys its resources and organizes the curriculum to get students to participate in activities.

Kuh (2001) provides an integrated definition encompassing the cognitive, affective, and behavioral aspects of engagement while highlighting the reciprocal responsibility of both the students and the institution to fostering engagement. As explained in this definition, student engagement is "the time and energy students devote to educationally sound activities inside and outside of the classroom, and the policies and practices that institutions use to induce students to take part in these activities".

Moreover, Krause (2007) adds that the engagement has become the focus of institutions to locate themselves in a competitive environment. The data of student engagement can be used by institutions to identify aspects of the undergraduate experience inside and outside the classroom that can be improved by changing the policies and practices to be more consistent with good practices in undergraduate education (NSSE, 2010). Meanwhile, the quality assurance mandate has drawn attention to the need for institutions to demonstrate that they add value and enhance the quality of the student experience by monitoring and evaluating cycles of continuous improvement.

2.2 Student academic achievement: Using the GPA

As mentioned earlier, grades are but one of many measures of academic achievement. GPA, however, is the best predictor of whether a student has succeeded while earning a bachelor or a master degree. Pascarella & Terenzini (2005) found GPA to be the critical predictor of persistence, even when variables like ability, motivation, socioeconomic status, and institutional characteristics were controlled. GPA predicted academic commitment regardless of students' social involvement and extracurricular college experience.

Furthermore, Kuncel et al (2005) state that achievement is generally measured by the test results of the student. The measurement of academic achievement has been carried out using various criteria of value, especially the GPA. It has been proved by the frequent use of GPA as variable measurement criteria of academic achievement in tertiary study.

Meta-analytic correlations have been reported between secondary and tertiary levels GPA. GPA is also consistently correlated with other variables such as intelligence, and is a significant predictor of work performance, and occupational status and prestige (Strenze, 2007). As a conclusion, GPA remains to be a useful and appropriate measure of academic achievement.

2.3 *Relationship between student engagement and student academic achievement*

According to Casuso-Holgado et al (2013), student engagement in learning process is positively correlated with the learning achievement of student. Alexander (2009) examined the relationship between student engagement and academic performance at historically Black public higher education institutions, specifically the relationship between NSSE benchmarks and self-reported academic performance. He discovered that while some independent variables had a statistically significant linear relationship with the dependent variable, others did not. Thus, student engagement has a multidimensional effect, and student engagement may or may not affect academic achievement.

In other cases, Carini et al (2006), Coates (2005), Connell et al (1994), Furlong & Christenson (2008), Marks (2000) stated that student engagement is highly correlated with GPA. Additionally, Kuh (2001a) has reported that positive correlations between national level benchmark scores and grade point averages (GPA) are an indicator that, 'higher engagement levels and higher grades go hand in hand'. The existence of strong positive correlations between NSSE benchmark scores and GPAs have been well documented (Kuh 2001a; Carini et al, 2006).

Coates (2005) associated student engagement with the high quality in learning outcomes. All these definitions could be said to have valid points for each school level. It is also important that student engagement in higher education is defined in a way to cover the processes of campus engagement and class engagement. Hu and Kuh (2002) adds that academic preparation, and those who had positive perceptions of their environment, were more likely to be engaged. Furthermore, Toppin & Chitsonga (2016) observed that the lack of preparation of first-year students caused them to be less persistent. Thus believing that the more time they spend in college, the more academically mature they become, and more able to critically think. In this respect, Mandernach (2015) defined student engagement as the quality and quantity of students' psychological, cognitive, emotional and behavioral reactions to the learning process as well as to in-class/out-of-class academic and social activities to achieve successful learning outcomes.

3 RESEARCH METHOD

3.1 *Design and participants*

This case was a cross-sectional study where no experimental treatment was given to the subject prior to the relationship of student engagement and GPA. In other words, this study was a descriptive research study using survey method. The respondents of this survey were eligible for participation if they were enrolled as UGM first-year students in 2014, and seniors in 2012.

3.2 *Research instrument*

In gathering the data, the writer used a questionnaire to elicit data about the GPA and student engagement level in learning process. The questionnaire has 47 items which the subject was expected to rate on a four-point Likert scale (with $1 = never$ to $4 = very\ often$).

3.3 *Setting and procedure*

The data was collected using online survey by accessing http://ugm.id/issla. The respondents were receiving email containing username and password to fill out the questionnaire. The survey was conducted on October 15–November 15, 2015. The data of this cross-sectional survey were analyzed by using the Statistical Package for Social Sciences (SPSS). After the scores from the Indonesian Survey of Student Learning Activities (ISSLA) and codes of independent variables were entered into the statistical software program, the data had been analyzed.

4 RESULTS AND DISCUSSION

4.1 *Results*

In total, 1422 students were analyzed. The distribution of the sample and descriptive statistics for each engagement indicator and academic results for the groups are shown in Table 1. The descriptive statistics show that senior-year students have higher averages for level of engagement and lower standard deviation than the first-year students. Similarly, the achievement of senior-year student is higher than the first-year student.

A Pearson's linear correlation analysis of the variables is presented in Table 2. Positive correlations are found in both first-year and senior-year. Table 3 indicates that GPA was the academic rate associated with student engagement for both first-year and senior-year students. It is found that student engagement predicts academic achievement for both first-year and senior-year students. The influential indicators also vary. For the first-year students, all indicators, except student faculty interaction, affect academic achievement, whereas for senior-year students there were only four indicators, i.e., collaborative learning, higher order learning, reflective integrative learning, and supportive environment, all of which affect academic achievement. Although collaborative, learning and higher order learning appeared to be the most significant indicators, the strength of the effect in all cases can be described as weak.

4.2 *Discussion*

The results of this study indicate that there is a correlation between student engagement and academic achivement. This result is in line with Mandernach (2015) who found the engagement level as a multi-faceted approach used to capture the interactive nature of the behavioral, affective and cognitive dimensions. It is also consistent with previous result that student engagement is regarded not only as an indicator of the education levels of societies and their education systems, but also as one of the indicators of the quality of education given in an institution (Kuh, 2001a). For this reason, the previous study revealed that there is a positive relationship between student engagement and learning outcomes or learning achievement (Carini, Kuh & Klein, 2006; Coates, 2005; Connell et al. 1994; Furlong & Christenson, 2008; Marks, 2000).

Table 1.   Descriptive characteristics of the sample.

Variable or Indicator	First-Year		Senior-Year	
	Average	SD[a]	Average	SD[a]
Number of respondents	1129 (79.40%)		293 (20.60%)	
Overall Student Engagement	180.08	51.70	223.54	28.31
Collaborative Learning	12.53	3.75	14.03	2.25
Higher-Order Learning	39.10	10.74	45.50	6.70
Learning Strategies	13.56	4.02	15.93	2.81
Reflective & Integrative Learning	16.70	4.81	19.08	3.39
Student-Faculty Interaction	6.53	1.82	7.50	2.27
Effective Teaching Practices	14.87	5.41	18.50	3.46
Quantitative Reasoning	6.07	2.13	7.19	2.13
Discussions with Diverse Others	9.63	3.72	11.72	2.64
Supportive Environment	42.71	15.12	55.55	9.85
Quality of Interactions	18.39	9.93	28.53	6.22
Academic Achievement				
GPA	1.76	.75	2.02	.82

a: Standard deviation

Table 2. Pearson correlation coefficient between engagement dimensions and academic results.

Variable or Indicator	Correlation index (CI) Academic Achievement[a]	
	First-Year	Senior-Year
Engagement Level		
Student Engagement	.000**	.020*
Collaborative Learning	.000**	.001**
Higher-Order Learning	.000**	.007**
Learning Strategies	.000**	.908
Reflective & Integrative Learning	.000**	.043*
Student-Faculty Interaction	.630	.125
Effective Teaching Practices	.000**	.775
Quantitative Reasoning	.000**	.614
Discussions with Diverse Others	.000**	.950
Supportive Environment	.000**	.015*
Quality of Interactions	.000**	.342

a: Grade point average
* = $p < 0.05$.
** = $p < 0.01$

Table 3. Regression analysis of student engagement as a predictor variable of academic achievement.

Predictor Variable	Unstandardized Beta	Std error	r^2
First-Year			
Student Engagement	.003	.000	.085
Collaborative Learning	.023	.006	.013
Higher-Order Learning	.011	.002	.025
Learning Strategies	.037	.005	.038
Reflective & Integrative Learning	.020	.005	.017
Effective Teaching Practices	.026	.004	.034
Quantitative Reasoning	.055	.010	.025
Discussions with Diverse Others	.051	.006	.063
Supportive Environment	.012	.001	.061
Quality of Interactions	.019	.002	.063
Senior-Year			
Student Engagement	.004	.002	.077
Collaborative Learning	.068	.021	.035
Higher-Order Learning	.019	.007	.021
Reflective & Integrative Learning	.029	.014	.011
Supportive Environment	.012	.005	.020

b: Dependent variable (Grade point average)
* = $p < 0.05$.
** = $p < 0.01$

The minor effect of student engagement on GPA indicates that there are many other factors relating to academic achievement. An individual characteristic is supposed give effect to academic achievement as Hu and Kuh (2002) statement about the examination of individual characteristics, and they found that students with parents who had more education were more academically prepared for their environment, and were more likely to be engaged. Though the relationship between engagement and achievement are not sufficiently strong to have a high predictive value. Other experts suggest that the more engaged students are the more likely they are to have the best academic achievements. Although there is a correlation between student engagement and academic achievement, it can be referred that student engagement is not the only factor affecting that achievement. There are factors that are outside the capacity of the instution that affect the GPA, such as the academic background of the student's parents, and the social envrioment around the student.

The next result shows that a high GPA does not necessarily indicate a high student engagement for both first-year and senior-year student. The criterion of academic achievement has not holistically emphasized the cognitive, affective and skill aspects. The engagement scale supporting the student-centered learning method, highlights the learning processes that include student experience and student learning activities. The cognitive ability is a good predictor of grades, but not learning and growth. This shows why students with high engagement will likely earn good grades, but will not necessarily report they have learned about life. On the other hand, students with low engagement may earn average grades but believe that they have made substantial progress as an individual (Hu & Kuh, 2002). In conclusion, a low engagement of student is not an indication of low achievement and vice versa.

Different forms of engagement are precursors to different outcomes. The engagement scale captures activity and experiences in learning process. It is important to understand what types of engagement are necessary to help students meet their goals especially for the first-year and senior-year student. As Alexander (2009) stated before, student engagement has a multidimensional effect. Therefore, student engagement affects academic achievement. Some of indicators may impact academic achievement in different context and construct. For example, quantitative reasoning did not predict GPA both for first-year and senior-year students, but may predict GPA of students from different study programs. Descriptive statistical data showed that student who had low GPA tend to have a high level of collaborative learning, discussions with diverse others, effective teaching practices, and supportive environment. For student-faculty interaction, first-year students were still adapting with the interaction habit with other student from different background. They still feel reluctant to interact with the faculty, but for senior-year students, the student-faculty interaction became more prevalent.

The senior-year students who are more engaged than the first-year students, were impacted by the experience in participating in learning activities. The result is consistent with previous study. Hu and Kuh (2002) noted sophomores, juniors, and seniors are likely to be more engaged compared with first-year students. When a student is academically prepared better, and the longer a student is experiencing college, the more likely a student would be more engaged at higher levels. Other studies also showed that that the length of the period of study can be an important factor in measuring the engagement level, with seniors being more engaged than first-year students (The National Survey for Student Engagement, 2000).

In addition, Toppin and Chitsonga (2016) also observed that first-year students often lack college preparedness. They added that persistence can improve their academic performance with time, and improve their cognitive ability, particularly in critical thinking, and thus gaining academic maturity. Further concerns are conducted by Montero and González (2009) that first-year students do not have the problem-solving skills to tackle engineering problem since they lack the experience to cope with open-ended situations. In this respect, the challenging activity can foster cognitive, affective and behavioral engagement in academic tasks and lead to student preparedness.

The engaged students in the academic context are showing maturity since they are able to cope with academic stress, which perhaps leads in the future to more professionals having a sense of well-being. It shows that senior-year students are more mature since they have been able to recognize and cope with their needs and problems. The key idea is that the student's encounters with everyday obstacles can shape their maturity. When students are highly engaged, they are not only less affected by several stressful episodes, but also have access to more constructive coping strategies (such as strategizing or help-seeking), leading to increased persistence and reengagement with difficult academic material.

The first-year student is in transition level from high school to higher education where many different things must be confronted in order to become more mature. More forms of engagement of first-year student indicate that students are adapting to new environments and habits while for senior-year year students the level of engagement is influenced by the challenging cognitive tasks (such as application, analysis, judgment, and synthesis) to make connections between their learning and the world around them. They reexamine their own beliefs and consider issues and ideas from others' perspectives. Another form of engagement was not predicting GPA because the internalization of the different form of engagement becomes their habit. Senior-year students are more mature since they have been able to recognize and cope with their needs and problems. The level of student engagement of first-year and senior-year has showed a process of becoming a mature student in academic setting.

Moreover, Krause (2007) also revealed the social interaction may sometimes reshape their identity when conflicts occur, bringing a postive step toward growth and maturity. In order to ensure that this form of engagement has a positive result, it needs support structures across the institution. The intellectually challenging activity will also help the growth and maturity of the student. A student can be serious about their focus and purpose of learning when they are challenged. They can also have the ability to cope with stressful events during their education if they have the right instituional and social support structure. Therefore, the academic maturity is believed to be a significant contributor to the learning outcomes.

4.3 *Study limitations*

This study has a limited sample based on the overall size of the student population in Universitas Gadjah Mada. This small sample is attributed to time restrictions and limited resources. Thus is should be considered that a larger sample size would provide more accurate result.

5 CONCLUSION

The hypothesis is that more engaged students are more likely to have better academic achievement. Low correlation scores between student engagement and GPA do not allow us to obtain a definitive answer, but the results have proved that academic engagement is one of many factors that have positively influenced students' GPA. It also reveals the conclusions that a high GPA indicates a high student engagement, but a low GPA is not necessarily an indication of low student engagement. It means that different forms of student engagement relate to different learning outcomes which may have not been measured in the GPA. Finally, these results suggest further researchers to investigate the relationship more comprehensively in order to understand the ways in which university students make a satisfactory progress toward a degree, by involving other academic variables like satisfaction, self-efficacy, motivation, commitment, academic maturity, learning style, etc.

REFERENCES

Alexander, M. J. 2009. A dissertation: *An Exploration of the Relationship between Student Engagement and Academic Performance of Undergraduate Students at a Public Historically Black Higher Education Institution in the Southeast.* Parkway: ProQuest LLC.
Ali, N., Jusoff, K., Ali, S., Mokhtar, N., & Syafena, A. 2009. The Factors Influencing Students' Performance at Universiti Teknologi MARA Kedah, Malaysia. *Management Science and Engineering* 3(4): 81–90.
Carini, R. M., Kuh, G. D., & Klein, S. P. 2006. Student engagement and student learning: Testing the linkages. *Research in Higher Education* 47(1): 1–32.
Coates, H. 2005. The value of student engagement for higher education quality assurance. *Quality in Higher Education* 11(1): 25–36.

Connell, J.P., Spencer, M.B., & Aber, J.L. 1994. Educational risk and resilience in African American youth: Context, self, action, and outcomes in school. *Child Development* 65(2): 493–506.

Furlong M.J. & Christenson S.L. 2008. Engaging students at school and with learning: a relevant construct for all students. *Psychology in the Schools* 45(5): 365–368.

Hu, S. & Kuh, G. 2002. Being (dis)engaged in educationally purposeful activities: The influences of student and institutional characteristics. *Research in Higher Education* 43(5): 555–575.

Krause, K. 2007. *New perspectives on engaging first-year students in learning*. Brisbane: Griffith Institute for Higher Education.

Kuh, G. 2003. What we're learning about student engagement from NSSE: Benchmarks for effective educational practices. *Change* 35(2): 24–32.

Kuh, G. & Hu, S. 2001. Learning productivity at research universities. *Journal of Higher Education* 72(1): 1–28.

Kuncel, N. R., Crede, M., & Thomas, L. L. 2005. The validity of self-reported grade point averages, class ranks, and test scores: A meta-analysis and review of the literature. *Review of Educational Research* 75(1): 63–82.

Malin, B., Marianne, O.P., and Petter J.G. 2010. Active and Emotional Student Engagement: A Nationwide, Prospective, Longitudinal Study of Swedish Nursing Students. *International Journal of Nursing Education Scholarship* 7(1): 1–18.

Mandernach, B.J. 2015. Assessment of Student Engagement in Higher Education: A Synthesis of Literature and Assessment Tools. *International Journal of Learning, Teaching and Educational Research* 12(2): 1–14.

Marks, H.M. 2000. Student engagement in instructional activity: Patterns in the elementary, middle, and high school years. *American Educational Research Journal* 37(1): 153–184.

Montero, E. & González, M.J. 2009. Student Engagement in a Structured Problem-Based Approach to Learning: A First-Year Electronic Engineering Study Module on Heat Transfer. *IEEE Transactions in Education* 52(2): 214–221.

National Survey of Student Engagement. 2010. *Major differences: Examining student engagement by field of study—annual results 2010*. Bloomington. IN: Indiana University Center for Postsecondary Research.

National Survey of Student Engagement. 2010. *National Survey of Student Engagement: About NSSE*. Retrieved from http://nsse.iub.edu/.

Pascarella, E., & Terenzini, P. 2005. *How College Affects Students: A Third Decade of Research*. San Francisco: Jossey-Bass.

Strenze, T. 2007. Intelligence and socioeconomic success: A meta-analytic review of longitudinal research. *Intelligence* 35(5): 401–426.

Toppin, I.N. & Chitsonga, S. 2016. Critical Thinking Skills and Academic Maturity: Emerging Results from a Five-Year Quality Enhancement Plan (QEP) Study. *Journal of Inquiry & Action in Education* 7(2): 81–93.

Educational Administration Innovation for Sustainable Development – Komariah et al. (Eds)
© 2018 Taylor & Francis Group, London, ISBN 978-1-138-57341-3

Good governance principles in a department: An implementation

V.L. Ayundhari, A.N. Hidayat & T. Adyawanti
Universitas Islam Nusantara, Bandung, West Jawa, Indonesia

ABSTRACT: Several matters in a department can arise, one of which is if the good governance principles do not run well. Investigating the implementation of the principles is therefore necessary. The purpose of this study is to draw an image of how these governance principles are implemented in a department. The researchers use qualitative approach by a means of case study method. The research subjects are the head, the secretary, and the lecturers. The data was obtained by communication, both verbally and face to face. A documentation study guide was used to complete the data obtained in interviews, conducted by collecting and analyzing documents, including formal archives, related to the governance implementation in the department. The research results indicate that the stakeholders hold credibility, transparency, accountability, responsibility, and fairness principles. Another finding is that the governance implemented in the department is rather deemed to be a way of distributing various activities.

1 INTRODUCTION

Governance has wide connections among management, leadership, mediation, property, and others. It also includes a number of areas and is used in a wider context such as good governance and its role in institutional administration (Barzelis et al., 2012). One such area is the governance that relates to a department. The department must set the planned governance, and implement the structures that have been compiled, constructed, and evaluated. Yet, the implementation of department governance has not been implemented to the fullest, so that the organized education quality is not all in accordance with the expected parties.

Also, most of the accreditation results are still not satisfactory. The atmosphere of department management is not yet conducive for every lecturer to perform their duties and improve his or her abilities. In addition, the lecturer's adequacy is still a crucial topic; as stated by Musliar, maintenance should be performed on higher education's quality and its graduates (Napitupulu, 2012). This relates to the role, duties, and responsibilities of a lecturer as the change agent and education provider in the classroom. Rustad also added (Pribadi, 2014) that as many as 75,372 lecturers in public and private universities have not been certified. The number of lecturers has not met minimum education requirements, which is to master's level, and ought to have functional position. This issue is then becoming one that lessens the accreditation value in a department. As was stated by Nicklin and Dickson (2009), accreditation strengthens professional development, organizational learning and capacity building. Brittingham et al. (2010) also elaborate that the value of accreditation signals to prospective employers that an educational program has met widely accepted educational standards.

To intensify the accreditation value, the head, the secretary, the lecturers and the staff of a department have to strive toward the activities related to the governance. They direct and perform it based on the accreditation. When the governance is only referred to as being accreditation-based, all-purpose and direction will only be oriented to it. As a result, the accreditation will be the identification of the head, staff, and lecturers of a department. Therefore, managing the governance based on accreditation is rather habituated among the head, staff, and lecturers. If it occurs, the department will be properly managed, and the accreditation value will increase. Conversely, if it is not enforced, the rate of success and existence of a department will be affected and not be unoptimized. The more governance is referred to as being accreditation-based, the better its accreditation value.

Also, many private universities running an Internal Quality Assurance System (IQAS) are countable still. Furthermore, many universities are not optimal in managing their courses, because the system is not earnestly implemented, either in the way of the department's governance or in its management. If a private university has IQAS, the governance of a department accreditation will be undoubted. There are also many uncertified lecturers in private universities. Many private universities reported that their department self-evaluation was below the standard, or only 60% (which should be 100%). Many private universities have no IQAS. Whereas universities with IQAS have been less seriously carrying out their internal accreditation, so that the accreditation conducted by the National Accreditation Association for Higher Education has given less optimal value.

The accreditation of a department is quite essential, because it is the responsibility of the government toward society to comply with the national standards in terms of providing so-called decent universities. In the process of gaining accreditation, there are seven standards to assess, including the governance itself. Governance is actually a complex and miscellaneous term. It involves many actors and sectors. There were several researches conducted about university governance, notably in a European context (Agasisti & Catalano, 2006; Amaral et al., 2009; Antonowicz & Jongbloed, 2015; Austin, 2009). Agasisti and Catalono (2006) said that to compete for and attract students, some higher educations have to reduce the quality and make the path to diploma easier.

However, the researches of governance at a departmental level are still scarce. Moreover, few studies on university or department governance are held in an Indonesian context. Thus, this study still has flaws in having no adequate previous literatures related to the department's governance.

We need good governance in order to have a high quality standard in running departments. Good governance can lead to good management, good performance, and good outcomes. The good governance will increase the accreditation value of a department, for it can assure and improve the quality of universities and programs (Eaton, 2013). This is essential in many circumstances. Yet, there is no fixed definition over what good governance is, but 'good' is related to principles of transparency, efficiency, participation, responsibility, rule of law, democracy, and justice (Dreschler, 2004). Governance implemented with participation of all sectors should be transparent and accountable. It is in line with the Committee of University Chairs (2014), that governance structures and norms should be consecutively attached to core values, such as autonomy, academic freedom, equality of opportunity, and full and transparent accountability.

Related to the above conditions, many more cases at private universities occurred, such as in interpreting improperly what governance is. As a result, the department activities are not managed according to the existing rules. It also has an impact on human resource management, which causes problems related to management processes, value systems, organizational structure, decision-making, the use of time allocation for human resources, the form of leadership, the level of leadership responsibility, the relationship among the head, the staff, and the lecturers, and to their superiors in a department.

Based on the above description, the research team conducted a study to get an overview of the implementation of governance principles in one of the Educational Management departments, Bandung, Indonesia.

2 METHOD

In this study, researchers used case study method. The approach is qualitative, and the subjects of this research are the head, secretary, lecturers, and staff in an Educational Management department in Bandung, West Java, Indonesia. Data collection technique used in this study is interviewing guides with the aim to obtain direct data from the research subjects. It includes interviewing colleagues or staff from work, or people the researchers already know (Biggam, 2012). The data was obtained by communicating both verbally and face to face. Researchers have been trying to uncover qualitative data in the form of words, to get an understanding associated with governance implementation in Educational Management departments. A documentation study guide is used to complete the data obtained in interviews, and conducted by collecting and analyzing documents, including formal archives, related to the governance implementation in the department. The documents are in the form of regulations, policies, activities, programs, work plans, and the progress that has been achieved. Observation guidance is performed by observing, collecting data, recording the activity of ongoing activity, behavior, attitude, incidents, development, and growth of governance implementation in the department.

3 RESULTS AND DISCUSSION

3.1 *Results*

The governance system in the Educational Management department has been running since the students began studying to obtain the degree certificate through an agreed mechanism, by maintaining and accommodating all the elements, functions, and roles of the head and staff in the department. The good governance implementation is supported by the system of values, norms, customs, and habits of the department. It is also evidenced by both the existence and implementation of established academic rules, transparent leadership election procedures, the rules among lecturers, students, and staff, as well as rewards and sanctions systems, guidelines and service procedures.

The governance system of the Educational Management department has achieved several good principles. The head, secretary, lecturers, students, and staff members are being united and responsible in realizing the vision of higher education, based on credible, transparent, accountable, responsible, and fair principles. These principles are more specifically described as follows.

1. *Credible:* Credible here means having the trust from the government, the private sector and stakeholders to achieve the stated objectives, among others: (1) being the coordinator of national scholarships, defined by Kemendikbud, for getting a master's degree; (2) obtaining support in ICT-based learning from the Ministry of Education and the Culture Academic Director; (3) being the coordinator of scholarships from the Ministry of Religious Affairs; (4) gaining the trust from the MORA scholarship in improving teachers' competence, the heads and supervisors of *madrassah*; (5) gaining the trust to organize the team of lecturers in executing several qualified projects; (6) gaining the trust from the Ministry of Education and Culture to become National Instructors in the socialization of Curriculum in year 2013; and, (7) being the founder of Madrassah Development Center, Ministry of Religion Affairs, West Java Province.

2. *Transparent:* Transparency is illustrated by consistently applying the principles of transparency. It can be seen through conveying important information to relevant parties, among others: the students' entrance selection process and employees' acceptance conducted online through a website, program performance reports' distribution to graduate program leaders and stakeholders, and the decision process for choosing the head of the department which is carried out by way of deliberation and consensus.

3. *Accountable:* Accountability is described by way of calling to account related parties for the performance of department management in order to increase the effectiveness and efficiency of achieving the vision, mission, and objectives. Strategic plan implementation in the department is made in the annual work plan, so the implementation of monitoring and evaluation of the strategic plan is carried out on a scheduled basis by using several existing systems and instruments, among others: (1) intensively supervise the mechanism according to the tasks and responsibilities in the organizational structure; (2) the department supervision is conducted by the quality assurance unit; (3) there is a mechanism of coordination meeting at the level of department and graduate program; (4) activity results are periodically disseminated to related parties; and, (5) there is periodically accounted financial management at the end of each semester.

4. *Responsible:* Responsibility is stated in the Teaching, Research, and Community Service implementation in accordance with the Ministry of Education and Culture policy through the principles of a 'fit' institution. The sundry rules in the department are based on the prevailing law

and regulations. Likewise, the internal rules at the department level do not hierarchically conflict with the internal rules, such as those that relate to the foundation, university, and graduate program. The hierarchy of internal rules starts from (1) the foundation's rules; (2) the Rector's decision; (3) the decision of the director; and, (4) the department's regulations. The department consistently enforces legislation, including those structured with structural oversight (inherent supervision) codes of ethics, in addition to the form of responsibility embodied in increasing the acceptability of education service delivery for the community.

5. *Fair:* Fairness is stated by providing equality and ensuring equity fulfillment toward the academicians' rights, such as in ensuring that the election process of the leaders is carried out in a fair way. In order to ensure the governance mechanisms, activities including planning, organizing, implementing, controlling and appraising are performed based on these following mechanisms: (1) the decision-making process relies on a participation pattern to obtain mutual satisfaction; (2) general policy-making mechanisms are at the university level, but certain policies in postgraduate programs involve the departments; and, (3) academic operational policy mechanisms and other activities are implemented by the department.

Program study leaders and other elements are elected every four years. This will motivate the lecturers to participate and contribute actively in building a better department. The head of the department's election is executed through the following stages: (1) the selection of prospective leaders; (2) the verification of leader candidates; (3) the determination of candidates are conducted at a plenary meeting, aimed at determining prospective candidates for being the leaders; and, (4) the election of candidates is consensus-based. The result of the leader election meeting is submitted to the Rector and later determined by Rector's decree.

Based on the above description, it can be concluded that the implementation of good governance principles in the department has performed well and is supported by the value systems, norms, and habits. The implementation upholds good principles as being credible, transparent, accountable, responsible, and fair. However, the service to the students has yet to be improved, with incidence of students failing to complete master's courses, or even dropping out, for finishing time is more than the limitation. The details are elaborated in the discussion below.

3.2 *Discussion*

The quality of governance implementation in the department should be improved by a means of giving services to students who have difficulties in completing lectures, especially the final project or thesis. The guidance that helps students related to the lectures completion and (or) thesis is called tutoring. Learning guidance is the assistance given to individuals when facing academic problems (Nurihsan, 2006). When facing academic problems, Obiozor et al. (2010) suggest that the students should discuss them in their classrooms and identify possible strategies to solve them, by taking advantage of the available abundant support services on campus which promote a meaningful teaching-learning process and student achievement. Other factors are learning motivation, learning skills, attitudes, study habits, and the ability to solve problems of learning (Prayitno, 1997). Proper way of learning, and difficulties associated with the demands of learning in an educational institution (Winkel, 1991).

All these statements are related to the problem in this study. It can be concluded that the learning guidance is the assistance provided by the counselor to students in the form of programmed and continuing guidance with the aim that students can complete their study on time.

The materials given in the learning guidance include attitudes and learning habits, discipline and practice, understanding the physical condition, social, cultural, learning orientation, motivation, and learning skills development (Prayitno, 1997). To achieve the objectives and the delivery of learning guidance materials, it is advisable to create a learning environment, to facilitate the students achieving the academic goals (Nurihsan, 2006), and to use some guidance and counseling services, such as orientation, information, channeling, learning, individual counseling, and counseling groups (Sukardi, 2003). In counseling support, individual and group works are both important. Later is applying the crisis approach (remedial, preventive and developmental), and then guidance, counseling, guidance group, group counseling, and teaching with nuanced guidance (Nurihsan, 2006). Corey and Corey (2006) categorized group works according to the content, purpose and expertise standards under four titles: task groups, psycho-education groups, counseling groups, and psychotherapy groups.

The head, secretary, lecturers, and staff members in the department expect their students to complete the study in a timely manner but not, for the student's guidance is needful. Students who do not finish the study on time are likely to have factors, such as having mostly low subject scores due to planned learning objectives which have not been achieved, the student qualification for certain subjects being low, the need for additional time for the delayed student due to time spent for completing several courses, the students who are below the average compared to other students, and the students who have difficulties completing their thesis due to having personal, learning, social, and career problems.

The lecturer or the counselor actually understand the qualification, causes and consequences for the students who have the above-mentioned problems. Yet, because the lecturers focus on the timely delivery of lecture materials or theses as planned, they may not know how to help and not pay attention to these problems. When the end of semester comes, attention is then given to specific students who do not complete or join the oral examination.

Remedials affect their psychological condition. The qualification of the student's learning result is generally expressed by the lecturers, such as defining student's flaws, the impact, and the effort to overcome problems and to improve the learning result. With the help of either lecturer or counselor, it is expected that students with learning difficulties who receive guidance can solve their problems. Robinson in Makmun (2004) suggests that students may have failed to learn, because they have difficulties of knowing, understanding, accepting, directing, and realizing their potential. Paulu and Darby (1998) also support that the students' personal difficulties and competing priorities can also create obstacles to completing homework successfully.

At the time of lecturing, lecturers can conduct activities related to the learning guidance of learning, such as collecting data about students themselves, providing information on various possible planning types that can help students' completion, identifying students who allegedly experienced difficulties, and making a recommendation of possible future efforts.

Learning guidance steps to help students to solve studying and thesis issues include identifying likely students, identifying problems, diagnosing, prognosing, improving or referring, conducting evaluation and following-up.

An overview can be gained of student progress in completing the course by observing the students when they are acting and interacting with their friends, professors or others at different times, opportunities, and analyzing subject grades, as well as adjustments. Meanwhile, an overview of student progress can be achieved by asking the students themselves and their friends, as well as asking the thesis completion directly to the supervisor. If within certain limits no change is encountered, the guided students need to be shown the alternatives for problem-solving. Suppose that there has been no positive effect, then looking for other troubleshooting routes is rather suggested, and investigating more troubleshooting as a whole, if necessary.

Guidance services provided by lecturers or counselors can be done individually or in a group service. While the service type can be done through activities, supplementary special services, and the overall activities of the curriculum and community. Guidance approaches that can be done by lecturers are directive and non-directive. Guidance techniques can be centered on two groups of activities: gathering complete and objective data, conditioning a good relationship with students by a means of providing information, course assistance in the process of making choices, decisions, and plans to solve the problems being faced.

4 CONCLUSION

The governance in the Educational Management department is sensed through the distributing activities, resources management, and a wide range of problems in managing the department. It is performed in planning, implementation, evaluation, control, and improvement. The governance implementation in the department includes the value system of the department, organizational structure, decision-making and resource allocation system, authority patterns and responsibility levels, the relationship between work units in the department, as well as the community governance outside the academic environment. The good governance principles implementation based on credibility, transparency, accountability, responsibility, and fairness principles are executed in the department. However, the department still needs to improve the management of student guidance services, notably for the thesis preparation.

REFERENCES

Agasisti, T. & Catalano, G. (2006). Governance models of university systems – Towards quasi-markets? Tendencies and perspectives: A European comparison. *Journal of Higher Education Policy and Management*, 28(3), 245–262.

Amaral, A., Neave, G., Musselin, C. & Maassen, P. (2009). *European integration and the governance of higher education and research, Vol. 26.*

Antonowicz, D. & Jongbloed, B. (2015). *University governance reform in the Netherlands, Austria and Portugal: Lessons for Poland.* Warsaw: Ernst & Young Usługi Finansowe Audyt. Retrieved from http://doc.utwente.nl/97592/1/Raport_SP_University_governance_ENG.pdf

Austin, I.O. (2009). *Understanding higher education governance restructuring: The case of the University of the West Indies.* Virginia Polytechnic Institute and State University.

Barzelis. A., Mejerè, O. & Saparnienè, D. (2012). *University governance models: The case of Lapland University.* 90–102. Retrieved from http://www.su.lt/bylos/mokslo_leidiniai/jmd/12_02_35/barzdelis_mejere_saparniene.pdf

Biggam, J. (2012). *Succeeding with your Master's dissertation: A step-by-step handbook.* Maidenhead: Open University Press.

Brittingham, B., Harris, M.J., Lambert, M., Murray, F., Peterson, G., Trapnell, J., …Eaton, J. (2010). *The value of accreditation.* Council for Higher Education Accreditation. Retrieved from https://www.acpe-accredit.org/pdf/ValueofAccreditation.pdf

Committee of University Chairs 2014. (2014). *The higher education code of governance.* Bristol: The Higher Education Code of Governance.

Corey, M.S. & Corey, G. (2006). *Process and practice groups.* USA: Thomson Brooks/Cole.

Dreschler, W. (2004). Governance, good governance, and government: The case for Estonian administrative capacity. *Trames*, 8(4), 388–396.

Eaton, J.S. (2013). *The changing role of accreditation: Should it matter to governing boards?* Retrieved from Association of Governing Boards (AGB) website https://www.agb.org/trusteeship/2013/11/changing-role-accreditation-should-it-matter-governing-boards

Makmun, A.S. (2004). *Psikologi pendidikan.* Bandung: Rosdakarya.

Napitupulu, E.L. (2012). *Program studi tak terakreditasi.* Retrieved from http://internasional.kompas.com/read/2012/11/09/16133757/958.program.studi.tak.terakreditasi

Nicklin, W. & Dickson, S. (2009). *The value and impact of accreditation in health care: A review of the literature.* Canada: Accreditation Canada.

Nurihsan, A.J. (2006). *Bimbingan dan konseling dalam berbagai latar kehidupan.* Bandung: Refika Aditama.

Obiozor, W.E., Onu, V.C. & Ugwoegbu, I. (2010). Academic and social challenges facing students with developmental and learning disabilities in higher institutions: Implications to African colleges and universities. *Journal of Academic and Social*, 1(1), 126–140.

Paulu, N. & Darby, L.B. (1998). *Helping your students with homework: A guide for teachers.* Washington D.C: Office of Educational Research and Improvement U.S. Department of Education.

Prayitno. (1997). *Pelayanan bimbingan dan konseling: sekolah menengah umum.* Jakarta: Coorporation of Cooperative of Karyawan Pusgrafin with Penebar Aksara Publishing.

Pribadi, A. (2014). *75.372 Dosen di perguruan tinggi negeri dan swasta belum layak disertifikasi.* Retrieved from http://wartakota.tribunnews.com/2014/01/27/75372-dosen-belum-layak-disertifikasi

Sukardi, D.K. (2003). *Manajemen bimbingan dan konseling di sekolah.* Bandung: Alfabeta.

Winkel, W.S. (1991). *Bimbingan dan konseling di institusi pendidikan.* Jakarta: Grasindo.

Educational Administration Innovation for Sustainable Development – Komariah et al. (Eds)
© 2018 Taylor & Francis Group, London, ISBN 978-1-138-57341-3

School mapping and distribution analysis based on a Geographic Information System (GIS)

Azizah & T.C. Kurniatun
Universitas Pendidikan Indonesia, Bandung, Indonesia

ABSTRACT: A Geographic Information System (GIS) can be used as a supporting system in the education sector for decision-making or problem-solving related to its geography. This study attempts to analyze the spatial distribution of the schools in Dramaga through school mapping. The objects of study are elementary and middle school levels. The objectives are to create school maps based on GIS, to analyze the coverage area of the schools and to calculate the social demands of education in the area. The school position data is collected by a GPS device and converted into points in shapefile format using ArcView 3.3. Based on data collections, there are 38 elementary and ten middle schools in Dramaga. All villages already had elementary schools, but it was found that two villages had no middle school. Opening a new school can improve the educational access, especially as is the case in two villages with no middle school.

1 INTRODUCTION

Educational planning and management in developing countries are facing some common problems such as overpopulated areas, unequal educational access and limited resources. Technology can be utilized to overcome these challenges. Such technology must be reliable in accommodating a community's needs for education. The Geographic Information System (GIS) is an adequate technology and system to meet the mentioned requirements. GIS can be optimized to be a decision support system in educational policymaking and planning.

GIS is a computer-based information system which attempts to capture, store, manipulate and display spatially referenced data (at different points in time), for solving complex research, planning and management problems (Fischer & Nijkamp, 1993). Attfield et al. (2001) explained the advantages of GIS in one publication, mentioning that GIS is a framework with collective tools that have the ability to integrate both spatial and numeric data; the output helps the stakeholders in their analysis, and in making decisions effectively and efficiently.

GIS can be applied to the education sector to promote the equality aspect of educational access. Shquair (2009) has discussed this topic in one publication. It is explained that the educational services are one of the most important public services that must be provided to members of any locality. Governments are therefore striving to provide educational institutions at all levels in order to accelerate progress and prosperity. This progress and people's development are measured by available services to the population, but not only the amount of these services, but also the quality of these services and their conformity to standards and specifications.

In order to meet the standards of human development, it is necessary for the government and decision makers to closely watch the existing education policy and its implementation condition (Agrawal & Gupta, 2016). The application of GIS technology will facilitate the assessment process on various administrative scales.

The government of Indonesia has set up the standards of minimum services for education, as directions for local administrators and schools to provide a quality of services that meets the standards. The regulation also provides basic reference in the assessment.

This study attempts to analyze the spatial distribution of the schools in Dramaga through school mapping. The objects of the study are elementary and middle schools, because both are the entry-level to formal education. The purposes are to create school maps of the area based on GIS, to analyze the coverage area of the schools and to calculate the social demands of education in the area. The regulation can be used as a benchmark to calculate the demand analysis. Demand analysis in this study includes: population to elementary school ratio, classroom necessity, elementary to middle school ratio and teacher to student ratio.

2 LITERATURE REVIEW

2.1 *School mapping*

School mapping plays the main role in this inquiry. This method is used in the distribution analysis of formal educational facilities, thus helping to evaluate the current status of how school coverage meets community demands. According to Al-Hanbali et al. (2005), school mapping is the art and science of building geospatial databases with relational databases of educational, demographic, social and economic information for schools and educational directorates to support educational planners and decision makers.

Furthermore, the general objective of school (education) mapping is to improve the education system at a local level, by providing information with a geographic dimension which will enable local-level planners to make better-informed decisions (Attfield et al., 2001).

Several studies about school mapping and GIS application in the education sector can be found in some countries. In a paper written by Olubadewo et al. (2013), there is a discussion about the spatial distribution of elementary schools in Kano State, Nigeria. The research also calculates the social demand to help the government develop a better educational plan based on the factual problems. Another case study can be found in the paper of Al-Rasheed and El-Gamily (2013), which studies the evaluation of schools based on the standard for the location of public schools, defined by the State of Kuwait Ministry of Education. The study also made an inventory of reserved lands for their future educational facilities planning.

Similar research was done by Lagrab and Aknin (2015) in the Mukalla District of Yemen. The study analyzed the spatial distribution of kindergarten facilities based on GIS, in order to test the efficiency of GIS technology to redistribute the existing kindergartens, choosing the best location in the future and applying the standard criteria for selecting the suitable locations for kindergartens.

3 RESEARCH METHODS

3.1 *Data collection*

A Dramaga sub-district map with its village boundaries is used as the basic map for this study. All thematic maps, such as population density maps and school maps, are modified from this map. The map is taken from Bogor Local Government and becomes a reference for the digitization process using GIS software (ArcView 3.3). The software converts the map into shapefile format and saves it as a theme, thus enabling the layering process. The layering process involves integrating some themes into one desired map. Each theme has an attribute table, consisting of basic information such as village name and numerical data.

3.2 *Field observation*

Based on the Ministry of Education database, 48 schools are operating in Dramaga sub-district. Basic information about the schools, such as name and school address, is used as guidance in the school location tracking survey. The school locations in all villages have been collected using GPS device Garmin GPSMAP® 60CSx. A school-locations tracking survey is completed to get the coordinate points, which consist of longitude and latitude. All school location data is transferred into a computer, converted into shapefile format and saved as certain themes. A theme is also completed for educational numeric data such as number of students, teachers, study groups and classrooms. Educational data such as number of schools, number of students, number of teachers, number of group studies and classrooms have been collected from the Educational Database of the Indonesian Ministry of Education.

3.3 *Study area*

This study takes place in Dramaga sub-district, Bogor Regency. It is located in the western part of Bogor Regency. Dramaga is well known as being one of the busiest and fastest growing areas in Bogor, impacted by the existence of the largest campus in the surrounding area, IPB. According to administrative divisions, Dramaga is divided into ten villages. The Dramaga sub-district area is 24.03 km^2 with a total population of 115,677 (based on BPS data in 2016). The most populated village is Babakan, with 16,260 residents. However, the highest population density area is Dramaga, where the population density is 11,740 residents/km^2, compared to other areas with densities under 7,000 residents/km^2. Figure 1 shows the population density map of Dramaga. The map uses graduated color in order to distinguish the density levels easily. According to Prahasta (2009), a graduated color map presents various color symbols based on its values.

4 RESULTS AND DISCUSSION

4.1 *School mapping*

Based on the Ministry of Education's database, there are 48 schools in Dramaga, which consist of 38 elementary schools and ten middle schools. The elementary school level is dominated by public state schools, in contrast to the middle school level which is dominated by 80% private schools. Figure 2 shows the map completed with school position points. School point locations are layered with village borderline polygons, to help determine in which village each school resides. As the map shows, elementary schools are well distributed in all villages. Each village has at least two elementary schools. Nevertheless, this condition is still below the standard, because the population to elementary school ratio is still low and needs to be improved.

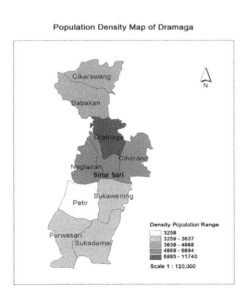

Figure 1. Population density map of Dramaga.

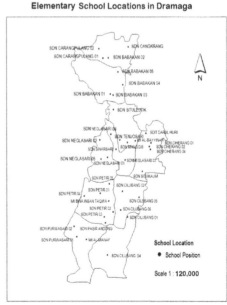

Figure 2. Elementary school locations map.

Middle School Locations in Dramaga

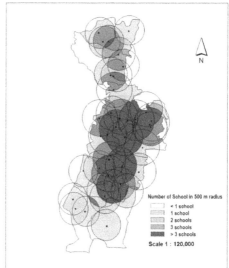

Coverage Area of Elementary Schools in Dramaga

Figure 3.   Middle school locations map.   Figure 4.   Coverage area of elementary schools.

To improve access to educational facilities, it is crucial to monitor how access varies across geography and sub-populations. Maps can be used to explore issues such as utilization and location of educational services, and the different levels of facilities (Bazemore et al., 2003). Based on field observation, the southern part of Dramaga is fairly steep terrain. It was found that some elementary schools have bad road access. An example is SDN Purwasari 02, where the school is located in steep topography and the main access road to the school is damaged, never having been fixed since the school was opened.

The Ministry of Education had set the standard for middle school facilities. It is specified that at least one middle school be provided for one sub-district, with the term of all elementary school graduates being accommodated by the middle schools available in the area. The result shows that the middle school capacity in Dramaga is lacking. There are only ten middle schools in the whole area, and two villages (Sukadamai and Ciherang) are found to be without a middle school.

4.2   *School coverage area analysis*

To understand how much area is well-covered by educational facilities, it is necessary to determine the coverage area of the schools. This study is using a buffer zone technique with 500 meters radius. According to Eray (2012), the buffer zone technique is useful to give information about the coverage area of a particular school. This technique is used to decide the correct school location based on residence zone or other school-related problems.

When the buffer zone of one school is overlapping with another, the density of school coverage is higher in that area. To determine the density easily, a thematic map is used with graduated color technique. Figure 4 shows the coverage area of elementary schools. The legend of the map shows that the colors refer to the density of schools. The darkest color dominates the map, indicating that some school locations are near to one another. As an example, SDN Babakan 01 and SDN Babakan 03 are in the same school area. Besides, school locations are mostly close to main roads, to make the schools easy to access. As is shown on the map, almost the whole area of Dramaga is well-covered by elementary schools, except for some small parts of Babakan, Purwasari and Sukadamai village.

Coverage Area of Middle Schools in Dramaga

Classrooms Necessity Map In Dramaga

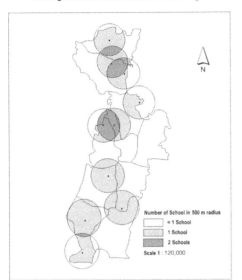

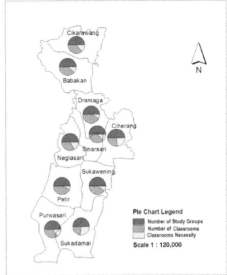

Figure 5.   Coverage area of middle schools.

Figure 6.   Classrooms necessity map.

Figure 5 shows the 500 meters buffer zone around the middle schools, to determine the area of influence for each school. Contrast this with the well-distributed elementary school. The coverage map shows that middle schools are not evenly distributed in all villages. Two villages with no middle school are inhabited by 15,875 and 8,946 residents. Sukadamai had a better condition, because the northern region is part of one school coverage area in the next village (Sukawening), due to the existence of SMP Taman Manggah Duah, located near the village border.

Some small parts of some villages had a better access to a middle school, as is proven by the overlapping segments in the map. The overlapping segments show where an area is inside the coverage of two middle schools. The darkest color is used to determine an overlapping area.

4.3   *Demand analysis*

Demand analysis is a modest calculation of some educational parameters. The purpose is to make the comparison easier. Thus, it generates information on which area needs an improvement or expansion. According to Ngigi et al. (2012), demographic data is used in demand analysis for various educational services within the study area. The maps generated in the GIS environment clearly illustrate the challenges facing the stakeholders, as well the disparities in the provision of quality education within the area.

Chapter II of the appendix of regulation in Ministry of Education Number 24/ 2007 (Ministry of Education, 2007) mentions that at least one elementary school with six study groups was provided for every 2,000 residents. Table 1 shows the result of demand analysis for each village division. Based on the calculation, the average population to elementary school ratio in Dramaga is 1:3,044. This ratio is above the standard and proves that there is overpopulation in elementary schools. To comply with the standard, an expansion of school facilities or the creation of new elementary schools is recommended. The ratio of elementary to middle school is quite high. This legitimizes the need to open some new middle schools, especially for two villages with no middle schools (Sukadamai and Ciherang).

Classrooms necessity is the gap between the amounts of existing study groups and the available classrooms. Figure 6 shows a map with pie charts that indicate the current state of classroom at

Table 1. Demand analysis results for each village.

Village	Pop. to elementary school ratio	Elementary to middle school ratio	Classroom necessity (unit)	Student to teacher ratio
Purwasari	2,552:1	2:1	10	24:1
Petir	2,085:1	7:1	8	22:1
Sukadamai	4,473:1	2:0	18	25:1
Sukawening	2,879:1	3:1	6	16:1
Neglasari	3,378:1	3:1	16	30:1
Sinarsari	3,242:1	3:1	8	22:1
Ciherang	3,175:1	5:0	22	23:1
Dramaga	3,552:1	4:1	7	23:1
Babakan	4,065:1	2:1	22	27:1
Cikarawang	2,410:1	4:1	11	18:1
Sub-District	3,044:1	4:1	117	23:1

Table 2. Number of elementary school graduates and the capacity of middle schools in Dramaga.

Village	Number of elementary school graduates (pupils)	Number of 7th grade classrooms available (unit)	Maximum capacity of 7th grade (seats)
Purwasari	154	1	32
Petir	246	2	64
Sukadamai	145	0	0
Sukawening	116	2	64
Neglasari	162	6	192
Sinarsari	134	1	32
Ciherang	194	0	0
Dramaga	125	10	320
Babakan	306	15	480
Cikarawang	89	2	64
Total	1,671	39	1,248

Source: Primary data of education, Ministry of Education.

both levels (elementary and middle schools). Elementary schools contribute to the gap greater than middle schools; to overcome the extra study groups, most of the elementary schools use double shift. Building new classrooms as much as is needed can clearly solve the problem. Based on calculations, the student to teacher ratio is the only indicator that meets the standard, with the others being below the standard.

Table 2 shows the comparison of data between the number of elementary school graduates and the capacity of middle school in Dramaga. In year 2016/2017, 1,671 pupils graduated from elementary schools, but the current capacity of middle schools was only 1,404 seats in the whole area. To cover up the gap, local government should consider adding 423 seventh grade middle school seats. According to the standard, one study group must have a maximum of 32 pupils; thus 423 seats are equivalent to 13 new classrooms. To improve middle schools access, opening a new school is highly recommended for two villages with no middle school.

5 CONCLUSION

GIS technology in the education sector is an appropriate approach to apply in developing regions. Its ability to integrate various data generates useful information in an interesting format. Furthermore,

GIS technology is not for evaluation purposes only, but can also be used for planning purposes. As illustrated in this study, GIS is used in assessing the current operational state of elementary and middle schools in Dramaga Sub-district of Bogor Regency. Results show that elementary schools are better distributed than the middle schools. Nevertheless, the elementary school to population ratio is still under standard. The cases of middle schools are of more concern, the study finding that two villages were with no middle school. Expansion of new schools in overpopulated areas can improve the educational access.

REFERENCES

Agrawal, S. & Gupta, R.D. (2016). School mapping and geospatial analysis of the schools in Jasra Development Block of India. *The International Archives of the Photogrammetry, Remote Sensing and Spatial Information Sciences, Volume XLI-B2, 2016*. Prague, Czech Republic.

Al-Hanbali, N., Al-Kharouf, R. & Alzoubi, M.B. (2005). Integration of geo imagery and vector data into school mapping GIS data-model for educational decision support system in Jordan. *ISPRS, Commission II, WG II/5*. Jordania.

Al-Rasheed, K. & El-Gamily, H.I. (2013). GIS as an efficient tool to manage educational services and infrastructure in Kuwait. *Journal of Geographic Information System*, 5(01), 75–86.

Attfield, I., Tamiru, M., Parolin, B. & De Grauwe, A. (2001). *Improving micro-planning in education through a geographical information system: Studies in Ethiopia and Palestine*. Paris: UNESCO.

Bazemore, A, Phillips, R.L. & Miyoshi, T.J. (2003). Using geographic information systems to define healthcare access in an urban community health center network. *ESRI International Health GIS Conference 2003*, Arlington, Virginia, May 4–7 2003.

Central Bureau of Statistic. (2017). *Dramaga sub-district in numbers year of 2016*. Bogor: BPS.

Eray, O. (2012). Application of Geographic Information System (GIS) in Education. *Journal of Technical Science and Technologies, 1*(2), 53–58.

Fischer, M.M. & Nijkamp, P. (1993). *Design and use of geographic information systems and spatial models in geographic information systems, spatial modelling and policy evaluation*. New York: Springer-Verlag.

Lagrab, W. & Aknin, N. (2015). Analysis of educational services distribution-based Geographic Information System (GIS). *International Journal of Scientific & Technology Research*, 4(03), 113–118.

Ministry of Education. (2007). *Appendix of Minister Regulation number 24 year 2007 about standard facilities and infrastructure of general education school*. Jakarta: Ministry of Education.

Ngigi, M.M., Musiega, D. & Mulefu, F.O. (2012). Planning and analysis of educational facilities using GIS: A case study of Busia County, Kenya. *Research Gate Publication*, April 2012.

Olubadewo, O.O., Abdulkarim, I.A.A. & Ahmed, M. (2013). The use of GIS as Educational Decision Support System (EDSS) for primary schools in Fagge local government area of Kano State, Nigeria. *Academic Research International*, 4(6), 614.

Prahasta, E. (2009). *Geographic information system: ArcView tutorial*. Bandung: Informatika Publisher.

Shquair, H.M.H. (2009). *Distribution and planning of the educational services in Salfeet governorate using Geographical Information Systems. (GIS)*. Palestine: An-Najah Al-Wathoniyah University.

Educational Administration Innovation for Sustainable Development – Komariah et al. (Eds)
© 2018 Taylor & Francis Group, London, ISBN 978-1-138-57341-3

Impact of authentic leadership and teacher participation in decision-making on school performance

H. Daryadi, A. Komariah & J. Permana
Universitas Pendidikan Indonesia, Bandung, West Java, Indonesia

ABSTRACT: This research is based on school performance achievement problems that have not been optimal in Sukabumi District, West Java Province, Indonesia. The method used is descriptive method with quantitative approach. The research was conducted on 74 schools in Sukabumi District, with as many as 74 principals and 148 teachers as respondents. Based on the results of the research, it can be concluded first that authentic leadership affects the performance of primary schools amounted by 55.1%. Second, that teacher participation in decision-making influences primary school performance by 59.7%. Third, that authentic leadership and teacher participation in decision-making affects the performance of primary schools by 67.6%, while the rest are influenced by other factors. The results showed that authentic leadership and teacher participation in decision-making had a simultaneous and significant influence on the performance of elementary schools in Sukabumi District.

1 INTRODUCTION

School performance problems are complex and vast, where school performance is the result of work or performance achievements of principals, teachers, students and stakeholders, all of whom are directed at improving the quality of education in the schools. Based on data from the National Accreditation Board (BAN) of Schools in Indonesia, from 1,552 primary schools in Sukabumi District registered, only about 285 schools are achieving predicate A (very good) in terms of school performance appraisal. It can be assumed that 285 schools with accreditation predicate A (very good) are schools that have excellent school performance. The rest of the schools, as many as 1,267 of the elementary schools, show good enough performance even still low.

School performance is a representation of the performance of all the resources that exist at the school, used to carry out the tasks in an effort to realize the purpose of the school. School performance is derived from the overall performance of interrelated school resources: principals, educators, education personnel, learners, and school committees. School performance is influenced by the managerial ability of the principal who is functioning to run all school resources in order to perform the task professionally. The results of the analysis of Clark et al. (2009) explain that school performance is strongly influenced by the principal's leadership. The paper explains that the principal who has work experience, experience studies and experience training, and professional development will be able to improve school performance.

The principal as a school leader is the person who manages the overall school management. The substance of education management includes curriculum management, student affairs, personnel, facilities and infrastructure, finance, and school relationships with the community. A principal must be able to manage the substance as well as possible so that educational institutions or schools can achieve their goals to the maximum effectively and efficiently. The principal is a school leader who has importance and influence, and role-plays in running school management to manage all the components of the school, which will affect the forward or backward, or whether or not it is a high-achieving school.

The principal, as the main figure in the improvement of school performance, should have strong leadership. According to Yukl (2009), it provides a definition of leadership in general as a process of influencing others to understand and agree with what needs to be done and how the tasks can be performed effectively, as well as being a process to facilitate individual and collective endeavors to achieve common goals. Leadership is the science or art of influencing a person or group of people to act as expected in achieving goals effectively and efficiently (Usman, 2014). The effective and efficient goals of the organization, according to Robbins and Judge (2015: 249), can be achieved through strong leadership, to challenge the status quo, create a vision of the future and inspire its members to achieve mission, formulate detailed plans, create efficient organizational structures, and oversee operations day-to-day. This strong leadership we can get from an authentic leader.

Authentic leaders are leaders who really have a desire to serve others through their leadership. Authentic leaders are leaders who have natural abilities, but they also acknowledge their shortcomings and always work hard to overcome these shortcomings. Authentic leaders lead with purpose, meaning and value. They build lasting relationships with people, because they are aware of the existence of followers. They are always consistent and disciplined. Authentic leaders have a high dedication to constantly develop themselves because they know that being a leader means a lifetime of dedication, so that they must constantly grow their personality.

The second most dominant factor in improving school performance is teacher participation in decision-making. According to Basaran (1996) and Göksoy (2014) the participation of teachers means carrying out the principal task of the teacher given by the principal and functioning as a teacher. However, key leadership qualities need to be supported by the active participation (participation) of teachers who participate in school performance development. Tarwo (2013) explains that teacher participation has a positive effect on school performance. That is, the better the participation of teachers, the more the school performance will increase.

Teacher participation in decision-making can encourage a conducive working climate, so the sense of ownership of a decision may increase. An increased sense of belonging creates a sense of responsibility, which in turn increases the dedication of the school's citizens. Teachers want to participate in decision-making because they want to show that they have an opinion and even want to be rewarded for being able to give ideas. Involvement of teachers in the decision-making process by the principal is a form of appreciation. A teacher feels appreciated for her existence and is considered indispensable. Awarding a teacher through involvement in the form of participation gives satisfaction to the teacher concerned. Thus, teacher satisfaction is realized because of the teachers' participation in decision-making and their satisfaction in decision-making. In the end, teachers are encouraged to implement the school principal's decisions as well as possible.

Based on the above description, the researchers are therefore interested in conducting research in some primary schools in Sukabumi District that have a very good accreditation value. Is there a synergy between the principal's leadership role and teacher participation in decision-making on school performance improvement? Thus, the results of this study can be induced to other schools in order to realize good school performance, so that the value of accreditation in schools in Sukabumi District, especially primary schools, can be increased.

2   METHOD

The method used in this research is descriptive method. Descriptive research is a study that describes something that happened or tests the relationship between something without direct manipulation of the conditions experienced (McMillan & Schumaker, 2012). The descriptive research process is in the form of collection and compilation of data, as well as the analysis and interpretation of data. Descriptive research can be compared by comparing similarities and differences in certain phenomena. The descriptive method is done by collecting, classifying, and analyzing/processing data, and making conclusions and reports with the main purpose to make representations about a situation objectively in a description of the situation.

Sources of data taken in this study are from the State Elementary School in Sukabumi District, which has predicate accreditation Very Good. A school population accredited A (Very Good) of 285 schools.

The sample technique used in this study is proportionate stratified random sampling technique. This technique is used when the population has members/elements that are not homogeneous and stratified proportionally (Sugiyono, 2014). The reason for the use of proportionate stratified random sampling technique is because the population is stratified, the samples are also stratified, and the strata are determined according to the school accreditation. Determination of the number of samples in this study uses the formula of Riduwan (2014):

$$n = \frac{N}{N.d^2 + 1}$$

Description:

n = Number of samples

N = Number of population

d^2 = Precision set

So, the sample calculation can be done as follows:

N = 285 with precision 10%.

$$n = \frac{285}{285.0,1^2 + 1}$$

$$n = \frac{285}{3,85} = 74,026 \quad \text{rounded up to 74 schools}$$

So, the number of samples is 74 schools. From the number of samples, then searched stratified sample by using the proportional allocation formula of Sugiyono (2014), that is:

$$ni = \frac{Ni}{N}\, n$$

Description:

ni = Number of samples

n = Total sample size

Ni = Number of populations according to stratum

N = Total population

The sample is stratified based on the school distribution data spread over 47 districts of seven areas in Sukabumi, using the proportion of schools from the seven existing regions by considering the number of schools that have accreditation A.

3   LITERATURE REVIEW

3.1   *School performance*

In general, the definition of performance is a quantitative and qualitative measure that describes the level of achievement of a predetermined goal or goals by taking into account the input indicators, processes, and outputs. Sagala (2009) suggests performance as being a measure of the success of an institution, encompassing all activities through measurement of the objectives that have been established and implemented. He added that there are three important elements that exist in the performance of institutions, goals, and instruments used. The school's performance reflects 'the effectiveness and efficiency of school processes' (Maslowski, 2001). Effectiveness, in a general sense, refers to the category of school goal attainment, while efficiency indicates whether this goal is achieved in a timely and costly manner. School performance is the quality of school services that are capable of producing quality educational output and in accordance with the needs of the community/users (Jaedun, 2008). Meanwhile, according to Bergeson et al. (2007), in understanding performance in relation to school institutions, school performance is the result of work that can be achieved by all school residents in institutions with the authority and responsibility to achieve institutional goals (school).

3.2 *Authentic leadership*

George (2003) explains that authentic leaders are leaders who really have a desire to serve others through their leadership. Authentic leaders are leaders who are guided by the quality of the heart, sincerely and wholeheartedly. Authentic leaders are leaders who have natural abilities, but they also recognize their own shortcomings and always work hard to overcome those shortcomings. Authentic leaders lead with purpose, meaning and value. They build lasting relationships with people, because they are aware of the existence of followers. They are always consistent and disciplined. Authentic leaders have a high dedication to constantly develop themselves because they know that being a leader means a lifetime of dedication, so that they must constantly grow their personality. The term 'authentic' means trustworthy, genuine, and legitimate. Something can be said to be authentic if it is in accordance with the facts of what is seen, heard and felt, so that it can be trusted. Authentic is when something is bona fide (honest, trustworthy), genuine (genuine, original), real (riel, real, true), true (true, correct), undoubted (no doubt), and unquestionable (undeniable).

3.3 *Teacher participation in decision-making*

Participation can be seen as action to engage or participate. The term 'participation' can be interpreted in several senses, although all ultimately lead to one conclusion that participation is the involvement of group members in achieving group goals. Irene (2009) explains that participation is the involvement of someone or some people in an activity, either mental or physical involvement, by using all their capabilities in all of the activities carried out, and supporting the achievement of goals and being responsible for all their involvement. Furthermore, Davis and Newstrom (1989) state that 'participation is mental and emotional involvement of persons in group situations that encourages them to contribute to group goals and share responsibility for them'. This means that participation is the mental and emotional involvement of individuals within a social group that encourages the ability to develop in accordance with the group's objectives.

4 RESULTS AND DISCUSSION

4.1 *Results*

From the calculation of hypothesis testing through correlation and regression analysis, both simple and double, it can be concluded that 'Authentic Leadership and Teacher Participation in Decision-Making influence simultaneously and significantly the Performance of Primary School in Sukabumi Regency'.

Here is the amount of contributions from each of these variables:

1. Authentic Leadership contributes 0.551 or 55.1%. So, the Performance of Primary School in Sukabumi District is influenced by 55.1% by Authentic Leadership while the rest is influenced by other factors.
2. Teacher Participation in Decision-Making contributes 0.597 or 59.7%. So, the Performance of Primary School in Sukabumi District is influenced by Teacher Participation in Decision-Making by 59.7%, while the rest is influenced by other factors.
3. Authentic Leadership and Teacher Participation in Decision-Making Affects the Performance of Primary Schools in Sukabumi District by 67.6%, while the rest is influenced by other factors.

Table 1. Recapitulation of hypothesis testing results.

Variable	Correlation coefficient (R)	Value of regression equation	Sig	Coefficient of determination	Other variables
X_1 to Y	0.742	$\hat{Y} = 86.245 + 1.176X_1$	0.000	55.1%	44.9%
X_2 to Y	0.773	$\hat{V} = 99.675 + 2.251X_2$	0.000	59.7%	40.3%
X_1 and X_2 to Y	0.822	$\hat{Y} = 79.615 + 0.624X_1 + 1.446X_2$	0.000	67.6%	32.4%

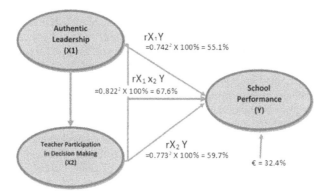

Figure 1. Result of interpretation of research X_1, X_2 to Y.

The recapitulation of hypothesis testing results from each variable of Authentic Leadership and Teacher Participation in Decision-Making, on the Performance of Primary School in Sukabumi District is shown in Table 1.

Table 1 describes the structure of Authentic Leadership and Teacher Participation in Decision-Making on the Performance of Primary Schools in Sukabumi District in Figure 1.

4.2 Discussion

The principal is a school leader who has a very important, influential, and role-playing position in running school management, managing all the components of the school, which will affect its advance or retreat, whether or not a school is achievable. This is in line with Mulyasa's opinion (2014), which states that the success or failure of education and learning in schools is strongly influenced by the ability of principals to manage each component of the school (who is behind the school). However, the leadership quality of the principal needs to be supported by the active participation (participation) of teachers who participate in developing school performance. Tarwo's (2013) results show that teacher participation has a positive effect on school performance. This means that the better the participation of teachers, the better the school performance.

In addition, there are research results that reveal the presence of influence between authentic leadership as well as teacher participation in decision-making on school performance. First, authentic leadership affects school performance. As Khan (2010) points out, authentic leaders have a positive effect on employee attitudes and behaviors that ultimately lead to improvements in organizational performance. Second, teacher participation in decision-making has a very important role in improving school performance, as shown by the result of research Sarafidou and Chatziioannidis (2012) that if teachers participate to give a contribution, active participation in all decision-making in the school can influence school performance.

Referring to the results of previous research experts, this study also found that Authentic Leadership and Teacher Participation in decision-making affect the school performance. The results of correlation calculations reveal that there is a simultaneous and significant influence of Authentic Leadership Principals and Teacher Participation in Decision-Making on school performance.

The correlation resulting from the calculation is positive, meaning that the higher the principal's authentic leadership and teacher participation in decision-making, the more there will be an impact on improving school performance. Conversely, the lower the authentic leadership of the principal and the participation of teachers in decision-making, the more there will be an impact on school performance degradation.

5 CONCLUSION

Authentic Leadership and Teacher Participation in Decision-Making have a simultaneous and significant influence on the Performance of Primary Schools in Sukabumi District. This has the meaning that the better the Headmaster's Authentic Leadership and Teacher Participation in Decision-Making, the more will be the impact on the improvement of Primary School Performance. The principal is able to become an authentic leader through improving his self-discipline, and there is an increase in teacher participation through teacher empowerment, especially in the academic field. Forms of activities include: involvement in the formulation of school vision, mission and objectives; formulate school programs; develop lessons; create teaching aids and appropriate teaching materials; develop student interests; and conduct technical guidance on students. In addition, teachers are always expected to engage in non-academic decision-making, including: doing extracurricular activities and social activities; building relationships with parents/students; building student character; and making school discipline rules. This is a form of teacher appreciation, which has an impact on improving teacher quality.

REFERENCES

Bergeson, T., Shannon, S. & Ed, D. (2007). *The nine characteristics of high performing schools.*
Clark, D., Martorell, P. & Rockoff, J. (2009). *School principals and school performance.* Calder Working Paper No 38.
Davis, K. & Newstrom, J.W. (1989). *Human behavior at work: Organizational behavior.* New Delhi: Tata McGraw-Hill.
George, B. (2003). *Authentic leadership: Rediscovering the secrets to creating lasting value* (1st ed.). San Francisco: Jossey-Bass A Wiley Imprint.
Göksoy, S. (2014). Participation of teachers in school administration and their organizational citizenship behaviors, 4(7), 171–182.
Irene, S.A.D. (2009). *Desentralisasi dan partisipasi masyarakat dalam pendidikan.* Yogyakarta: FIP UNY.
Jaedun, A. (2008). *Model asesmen kinerja sekolah berbasis peserta didik*, (November), 13–14.
Khan, S.N. (2010). Impact of authentic leaders on organization performance. *International Journal of Business and Management*, 5(12), 167.
Maslowski, R. (2001). *School culture and school performance.* Culture. Retrieved from http://doc.utwente.nl/36122/1/t0000012.pdf%5Cnhttp://eric.ed.gov/?id=EJ276371
McMillan, J.H. & Schumaker, S. (2012). *Research in Education: A conceptual introduction* (4th ed.). New York: Longman USA.
Mulyasa, E. (2014). *Manajemen dan kepemimpinan kepala sekolah.* Bandung: PT Remaja Rosda Karya.
Riduwan, M.B.A. (2014). *Metode dan teknik menyusun tesis.* Bandung: Alfabeta.
Robbins, S.P. & Judge, T.A. (2015). *Perilaku organisasi (Organizational behavior).* Jakarta: Salemba Empat.
Sagala, S. (2009). *Manajemen strategik dalam peningkatan mutu pendidikan.* Bandung: Alfabeta.
Sarafidou, J. & Chatziioannidis, G. (2012). Teacher participation in decision making and its impact on school and teachers. *International Journal of Educational Management*, 27(2), 170–183. Retrieved from https://doi.org/10.1108/09513541311297586
Sugiyono, D. (2014). *Metode penelitian administrasi (dilengkapi dengan metode R&D).* Bandung: Alfabeta
Tarwo, W. (2013). *Pengaruh perilaku kepemimpinan kepala sekolah dan partisipasi guru terhadap kinerja sekolah (studi pada SMP di Komisariat 1 dan 3 Ciamis).* Ciamis: Universitas Galuh.
Usman, H. (2014). *Manajemen: Teori, praktik, dan riset pendidikan Edisi 4.* Jakarta: Bumi Aksara.
Yukl, G. (2009). *Kepemimpinan dalam organisasi Edisi 5.* Terjemahan Budi Supriyanto. Jakarta: Pt. Indeks.

Early childhood education learning and human resource management strategy

I. Diniati
Universitas Pendidikan Indonesia, Bandung, West Java, Indonesia

ABSTRACT: Early Childhood Education is the first school environment education provided for children. It is the most decisive and important foundation for children's success to enter the next stage of education, as well as forming their character. Therefore, it needs more attention in terms of management and learning implementation that must be done professionally, be standardized, and sustainable. This study aims to determine the Early Childhood Education learning and human resource management in one of the kindergartens in Indonesia. The research method used is qualitative with case study approach. Results show that the school's educators and education personnel planning, recruitment, selection, coaching, development, assessment, appreciation, and dismissal are done very well. The school's learning management (such as regarding curriculum, activities development and procedures) is also done very well, and although done autonomously, still refers to the standards. Despite being under the supervision of a foundation, the school has authority to independently run its management under the accountability of a principal. In order to improve its quality of human resource management, all personnel should always develop and improve their competence for the school in order to grow and develop properly.

1   INTRODUCTION

Education is one of the most important aspects of human life, where every human being that begins from childhood requires education as a basic foundation to tread to the next life. One way to achieve that goal is through the education process, which means a guidance provided by an adult to an immature child to achieve his or her maturity (Langeveld, 1980).

Early Childhood Education is the first school environment education provided for children. It is the most decisive and important foundation for children's success to enter the next stage of education, as well as forming their character. Therefore, it needs more attention in terms of management and learning implementation, which must be done professionally, be standardized, and sustainable.

Even though nowadays there are already several institutions of Early Childhood Education, they are still not meeting the criteria of good and professional management. Besides, the low level of governmental guidance and attention in allocating the education budget for children is also the cause of the low level of the educational institution management's quality and professionalism.

Based on the phenomenon, the researcher is interested in revealing the management's quality and professionalism level of one of Early Childhood Education institutions in Indonesia.

2   METHOD

The method used in this research is qualitative approach. Qualitative approach is a research procedure that serves to generate descriptive data in the form of written or spoken words from people, and behavior that can be known (Moleong, 2000).

Meanwhile, the type of research used is case study, which is an exploration of a certain phenomenon or social unit such as individual, group, institution, and community (Sturman, 1997). According to Bromley (1990), it is a systematic investigation of events needed to describe and explain a phenomenon. Case studies can also be used appropriately in many areas, besides being a detailed investigation of one setting, one single subject, one collection of documents, or one particular event (Bogdan & Biklen, 1998).

The research location took place in At-Taqwa Kindergarten in Bandung, West Java, Indonesia. The reason of this selection is because it has rapidly developed and is in great demand by the surrounding community, and even by people living quite far from the neighborhood where this school is located. The interesting thing about this school is that the researcher recognized its stability, and even its tendency to improve, both in terms of its quality and quantity, compared to other nearby kindergartens.

Meanwhile, the data collection technique used in this research is participant observation, in-depth interview, as well as document review. Those techniques are used because the meaning of a phenomenon can be well understood by interacting with the research subject where the phenomenon takes place (Sugiyono, 2005).

3 RESULTS AND DISCUSSIONS

3.1 *Early childhood education human resource management*

1. Educator and education personnel planning

The human resource planning for teachers and employees is implemented independently by the school. In this case, the principal plays an important role in making human resource planning policies that will be used as a manual when recruiting employees. In planning human resources, the school considers that the existence of the school's vision and mission is instrumental in maintaining the continuity of value that has been instilled by its founders. By sticking to these values, it is expected to have different characteristics from any other surrounding schools.

Regarding the procurement of human resources (both educator and education personnel), the principal is tasked to identify the school's need for human resources. The identification of these needs is primarily determined by rationalizing the number of learners by the number of teachers. It is then mapped out which group or class experienced the lack of teachers. Typically, the shortage happens due to: (1) Previous employee has resigned; (2) Previous employee has moved; (3) The number of students increases; and (4) The presence of the school's new program.

In this mapping process, if it is identified that the school apparently requires new resources, then the principal will hold a recruitment drive. The school foundation or committee does not interfere with the planning process. They have no responsibility in managing the school operations because that would be considered as inhibiting the smoothness of the planning timeline.

This planning process is carried out routinely every year, considering the change of position and function transfer, as well as teacher rolling conducted right before the beginning of the new school year, through deliberation at a teacher work meeting.

2. Recruitment and selection

a. Recruitment

Recruitment is entirely the responsibility of the school. The purpose of the recruitment is to obtain a new employee who not only has the scientific capacity in accordance with the required formation, but who is also a Muslim and has a great Islamic faith.

Recruitment is done at any time depending on the needs. The principal as a person who knows the needs of employees, will immediately conduct deliberations with other teachers for the preparation of new employee procurement. Then the school will inform the public that they have opened new employee vacancies.

The general requirements announced in the recruitment of new employees are: (1) Muslim and has a great Islamic faith; (2) Wearing hijab (for women teacher); (3) Can read and write Al-Qur'an; (4) At least a high school graduate, preferably bachelor degree in Early Childhood Education/Psychology/Arabic Education; (5) Physically and mentally healthy; (6) Mastering computers (at least MS Office); and (7) Applying for an application addressed to the principal by enclosing their curriculum vitae, a copy of their last diploma, a copy of a valid identification card, a copy of the family registers, two color photographs, a health certificate from a doctor, and a written statement of work permit from parents/spouse (especially the husband, if already married).

In the procurement of human resources, something that is considered difficult to obtain is a prospective teacher or employee who has a great Islamic faith in accordance with the school's vision and mission. This is because the school strongly upholds the principle to get educators with great Islamic faith. The reason is because having great faith is the power to spiritually encourage people to have noble morality and to prevent them from developing bad character. The consequence of character is that people can control and supervise their every motion so that it becomes a starting point for them to behave (Maragustam, 2015). Therefore, the educators will be great guardians and role models for children.

b. Selection

The selection process for a new employee candidate is carried out by the school with the principal as the person in charge. After posting the vacancy to the audience and the school having received the application, the candidate's application file will then be selected by the administration. If there are quite a lot of applications entered, then the applications will first be sorted. After a candidate is administratively passed, he or she will be called to perform a written test, writing and reading the Al-Qur'an, and micro-teaching. Finally, there is an interview if all the previous tests have been successfully done. This selection process from start to finish is done directly by the principal, assisted by senior teachers and special administrative personnel for file selection. An exception is for a non-urgent interview stage, which sometimes involves the assistance of the school's foundation.

The material subject in the written test and interview includes knowledge of children's education/pedagogy (especially early childhood), Islamic religious test (Pillars of Faith, Prayers, etc.), personality tests (psychology), early childhood teaching skills (micro-teaching), and also problem-solving or case studies in teaching and learning activities (of Early Childhood Education in particular).

In the end, the final decision is in the principal's hands, although sometimes it is decided by the foundation. However, usually the decision is based on input and recommendation from the principal.

If it is already decided, the new candidate will be given a three-month trial. Having passed the trial, he or she will then be awarded a one-year teaching contract. After completing the one-year contract, he or she can then be given permanent employment. This applies both to teacher and education personnel.

3. Development of educators and education personnel

Development programs are usually held annually by the foundation. However, due to structural and foundation changes, currently the guidance and development is done directly by the school, besides following the government programs. Development programs implemented are generally related to skills and curricula.

One of the national programs is sustainable education, targeting the community of teachers who have already registered in the Principal Data of Educators (*Dapodik*) and then the Sustainable Professional Development Management Information System (*SIM PKB*). In the implementation, the government will call teachers to engage in education and training for those who already registered in *Dapodik* and have conducted the Master Competency Test (*UKG*) for certification candidates.

Teachers must follow all the training courses if they have scored below the average resulted in their *UKG* tests.

Meanwhile, the school's internal development program could be followed daily in the form of for instance, enrichment seminars, workshops, discussions (success story or experience sharing), related to the psychology and education of children in particular. The development of educational qualification should also be followed by educators and education personnel who still do not have a bachelor degree diploma.

The purpose of these coaching and development implementations is to increase operational input toward the teaching and learning process in school, broadening the teachers' information, as well as advancing their knowledge of good, new, up-to-date, and creative learning models and medias, in order to avoid child boredom with study at school.

Besides from the government and school, there are also development programs held through a forum called Kindergarten Teacher Association of Indonesia (*IGTKI*) and Teacher Special Activities (*KKG*) in the form of seminars and workshops, in addition to the enrichment carried out by the teachers' individual awareness.

The educators' and education personnel's development program is also conducted by the school in collaboration with related parties, in order to improve the teachers' and school managers' professionalism. Examples of such cooperation are with the professor of the early childhood teacher education program at Universitas Pendidikan Indonesia for educators and education personnel with regard to parenting, as well as doctors of Daarut Tauhid Islamic Boarding School regarding health substance. In addition, there was also cooperation with Danone water companies regarding a drinking water program.

4. Assessment and evaluation of educators and education personnel

The assessment is divided into administrative supervision and teacher supervision. Administrative supervision is performed with a predetermined schedule by the supervisor in each class, while teacher supervision is done each semester by the supervisor along with the principal. The principal's assessment is done by the supervisor, while the teacher's assessment is held by the principal along with senior teachers.

The assessment is done for the purpose of the educators' and education personnel's development and self-evaluation, by assessing their performance through observation on classroom learning process as well as on performing their individual duties and functions. This observation is done as effectively as possible, ensuring that it will not disrupt the learning process by using the components of the assessment determined by the government.

The observation results are recorded, to be later discussed per each component in a meeting. Some required development will be discussed individually with the person in question. The objective is to ensure that the person is aware of his or her shortcomings and to promptly correct them. However, if all assessments meet the standards, the individual discussion is no longer necessary.

Educators and education personnel who are considered very well, are rewarded. Other rewards besides salary, benefit, and incentive given at the end of the school year, are in the form of free Islamic Pilgrimage or *Umrah*, participation in certain activities, government automatic career development (by Principal Data of Educators or *Dapodik*), or other simple souvenir gifts.

One of the criteria to get the reward for career development from the government is a period of working. For example, the period of working before 2005 can follow the certification of Teacher Professional Education and Training (*PLPG*), which affects the rights of allowance from the government. After passing the certification, the school will reapply for equivalence (to civil servants), which again affects the rights of allowance from the government.

Meanwhile, the criteria to get reward from the school besides period of work, is working attendance (discipline), and skills in dealing with students, parents and even fellow educators and education personnel. These skills can be assessed through peers, students, and especially parents' feedback, as an additional value that affects the receipt of rewards, aimed at making them more passionate about work and self-development.

As for those considered less good educators and education personnel, in terms of handling children or reading and writing Al-Qur'an, they are usually directly guided to correct these deficiencies. This is not in the form of punishment, but rather as compulsory education aiming at achieving better performance. Except for performance that is already outside the criteria of the school, they will be immediately terminated in accordance with the initial employment agreement.

5. Termination of educators and education personnel

Termination of educators and education personnel could be based on several reasons, including: (1) Due to his/her own request, for rational reasons accepted by school; (2) Due to retirement or completed tenure; (3) Due to a decrease in performance, despite coaching given by the school (but this rarely happens); (4) Due to being less sensitive to children; and (5) Due to nonlinear creed with the school's vision and mission.

So far in this school, there has never been a termination due to a negative cause. Generally, educators or education personnel resign due to mutation or family interest. Otherwise, the prospective resources were dismissed after their three-month period trial due to being considered less sensitive toward children, or due to their nonlinear creed with the school's vision and mission.

Termination procedures in the trial period are done through several stages, which are verbal warning, written warning, and then employment termination. As for wishing to quit upon their own applications, it is mandatory to file a letter of resignation at least one year before the effective date of termination.

3.2 Learning management of early childhood education

1. Curriculum

The curriculum used is Education Unit Level Curriculum (*KTSP*) of At-Taqwa, where the school has the authority to set its own curriculum containing various local content, referring to the vision and mission of the institution. The curriculum is an educational unit standardized, that is autonomous but refers to the curriculum of the Ministry of Education and Culture (the government) in its process. This school's *KTSP* curriculum is composed by the principal and teachers, with the principal as a person in charge. The formulation is based on the curriculum of 2013, as well as the Indonesian Laws of National Education System (*UU Sisdiknas*).

The featured programs offered by the school are an Islamic religious education and additional activities supporting the main learning and teaching activities or extracurricular. Some examples of extracurricular activities are music, role play, art (motion, sound, and picture), English conversation, Indonesian martial arts called *Pencak Silat*, marching band, *Angklung* traditional musical instrument, *Mobis* creativity educational toys, and choir.

2. Development of learning activities

Learning activities are developed in accordance with the school's vision which is 'Actualizing the Islamic generation of monotheism (*Tawhid*), achievers, creative, competitive, and with noble characters', as well as the school's mission which is: (1) Holding the concept of *Tawhid*, whom always afraid of Allah, through the development of Islamic knowledge from various aspects; (2) Being achievers through knowledge development based on Al-Qur'an and *Hadith* (reports describing words, actions, and habits of Prophet Muhammad); (3) Being creative through skill development in line with child development level; (4) Being competitive through the performance arena; and (5) Having noble character applied in daily habituation of good attitude and behavior.

The purpose of this learning activities development is to integrate Islamic religious ability with the general ability to be balanced, but still emphasizing on six substances, including independence, socialization, cognitive, motor, language, and art. These six aspects are developed from the four scopes of spiritual, social, knowledge, and skill.

Mulyasa (2012) stated that learning should be emphasized on appreciation alongside with connotative and affective values implementation, manifested in daily behavioral skills. It is why the development of learning activities are carried out by way of habituation conducted in daily routine, such as saying greetings to teachers as well as praying before and after learning. Besides, there are other programmed activities referring to the established curriculum implemented annually, per semester, weekly, and daily, other than incidental additional programs.

In addition to the development of habituation, there is also the development of basic skills in accordance with the school's vision and mission, including:

a. The religious moral ability to instill the values of religious life, faith, and devotion of students to *Allah*. The school provides facilities such as places and equipment of worship, pictures, and story books containing religious moral elements.

b. Language skills so that students are able to express their thoughts in simple language as well as allowing them to communicate using decent and correct language.

c. Cognitive ability that serves to support problem-solving existing in the learning process, as well as the ability to manage their learning acquisition results. Cognitive ability also requires students to be able to think carefully, have mathematical logic skill, knowledge of space and time, and an ability to understand the concepts of shape, color, size, and pattern.

d. Physical abilities to practice motor skills development, namely gross and fine motor skills. Motor skills development refers to physical movement development control through the synchronized activities in the nerve center (Hartini, 2017). Thus, the gross motor skills are exercised by walking on a straight line, walking on a boardwalk, walking on tiptoe, and walking on heels while lifting weights. As for fine motor skills, they are learned by drawing, folding, stringing beads, cutting, weaving, and image coloring. Other physical abilities performed in order to develop both gross and fine motor skills are maintaining physical health such as exercising, measuring the height and weight of students, having meals together with healthy menus (nutrition program), as well as medical examination by doctors from Daarut Tauhid Islamic Boarding School.

e. Art skills in order to drive students to be creative and appreciate their own creativity. The school provides many facilities for students to be creative in arts, such as marching band, musical and dancing skill trainings, as well as role playing activities (drama).

Meanwhile, the school's learning principles are learning and habituation while playing. The learning process is also customized to the needs of students, both physically and psychologically. The approach used in the learning process is thematic, where the theme and sub-theme is used by teachers to teach students about the purpose of learning objectives to be achieved, besides developing students' various potentials such as in dancing, singing, or drawing.

In the next academic year, the school will try to gradually change the learning pattern from group method to center method, aiming to explore students' potential without doing much drilling and by reducing the teacher-centered method. Besides, it will furthermore improve the students' ability in language, attitude, and relation-building in order to socialize faster. This is because generating friendship and affection is one social skill exploring strategy (Mursid, 2015). Meanwhile, some types of center that will be or have been opened are the center of preparation, natural materials, block building, micro play or role play, and art.

3. Learning procedure

a. Classroom management

The classroom is arranged into two groups for playgroup (older and younger group) and five study groups for kindergarten. The total number of study groups is seven, which is divided into three age groups (Playgroup, Kindergarten A, and Kindergarten B). On Fridays, older and younger playgroup classes are merged. Each study group has two to three responsible teachers, including an additional extracurricular teacher, adjusted to the children's age group.

Available rooms include six classrooms, a library, a teacher and education personnel office, a principal office, three stockrooms, three student toilets, a teacher toilet, a pantry, as well as playground, music space, student health unit, field for sports and ceremonies, mosque, and parking lot.

Each classroom is flexibly arranged according to learning necessity, where students sometimes sit on chairs (arranged in rows or circle), on the carpet, or even outside the classroom. However, the main activity is held inside the classroom so that it will not disturb other classes. The field outside the classroom is fairly wide so that the children are free to run, play, or observe as much as they can. This playground is safe, fenced, and free from vehicles. Because experts believe that children's cognitive development is determined more on how long they spent time outdoors than indoors (Baber, 2016).

Inside the classroom, the walls are used as a place to hang media as well as learning resources. Educational toys and learning media are arranged in accordance to their function, so that they are easy to be used whenever needed by students. There is also ample storage in each and every class for students' creations (if not taken home). They are even put on a display for an exhibition at the end of every school year.

b. Procedure of activities

The learning activity process is implemented in three stages, namely: (1) the starting point of play, which is the preliminary activities carried out to motivate students to follow learning activities, such as introduction to the environment; (2) the main point (core of play), is activities designed to achieve standard of competence carried out through the process of exploration, experimentation, playing, and closed by eating together; and (3) the closing point of play, is activities undertaken to close the learning process. It is carried out by implementing dialogs of reflection (feedback) with the children, in an attempt to deduce learning outcomes.

c. Assessment of learning process

Students' assessment is carried out directly in between learning processes. The data needed for assessment is collected through interaction, observation, and assignment of student work-sheet/creation/performance (such as recitation of prayers, verses and letters of Al-Qur'an, and children's songs), depending on each theme and activity. This data collecting is very important because it reflects the development and learning process of children in their classroom (Sandall et al., 2004).

The assessment element given is based on the content in the curriculum. Meanwhile, the tools used for assessing the students are guidebook to conversation, anecdotal record for typical events observation, students' guidebook, as well as students' progress report books. Aspects evaluated are every child's attitude and behavior, the way of communicating, time-based problem-solving, and other activities or performances such as singing, practicing sport, role playing, or dancing.

4   CONCLUSIONS

The school's educators and education personnel planning, recruitment, selection, coaching, development, assessment, appreciation, and termination are done very well. Its learning management such as curriculum, activities development and procedures are also done very well, and although done autonomously, still refers to the standards set by the government. Despite being organizationally under a foundation, the school has authority to independently run its management under the accountability of a principal. Strategic principals are expected to be more capable of being active and cautious in decision-making, giving due consideration to the inside and outside of the school (Chan, 2017). Thus, the principal has the most important role in managing Early Childhood Education learning and human resources management.

In addition to being a very well-managed school, one of the main advantages for this school compared to other schools is the predicate of an integrated Islamic school with the best characterized teachers. Therefore, the teachers can educate children to have not only good cognitive and psychomotor abilities, but also affective ability through character modeling.

REFERENCES

Baber, M.A. (2016). Appropriate school starting age: A focus on the cognitive and social development of a child. *Journal of Education and Educational Development*, 3(2), 280–290. doi:10.22555/joeed.v3i2.1065

Bogdan, R.C. & Biklen, S.K. (1998). *Qualitative research for education: An introduction to theory and methods*. Boston: Allyn and Bacon.

Bromley, D.B. (1986). *The case-study method in psychology and related disciplines*. Chichester: John Wiley & Sons.

Chan, C.W. (2017). Leading today's kindergartens: Practices of strategic leadership in Hong Kong's early childhood education. *Educational Management Administration & Leadership*, 1–13. doi:10.1177/1741143217694892

Hartini, S. (2017). Developing the quality of early childhood mentoring institutions. *Jurnal Pembangunan Pendidikan: Fondasi dan Aplikasi*, 5(1), 87–100. doi:10.21831/jppfa.v5i1.15508

Langeveld, M.J. (1980). *Pedagogik teoritis*. Bandung: Bapemsi.

Maragustam, M. (2015). Paradigma holistik-integratif-interkonektif dalam filsafat manajemen pendidikan karakter. *Jurnal Studi Agama dan Masyarakat*, 11(1), 122–144. doi:10.23971/jsam.v11i1.409

Moleong, L. (2000). *Metodologi Penelitian Kualitatif*, Remaja Rosdakarya, Bandung.

Mulyasa, H.E. (2012). *Manajemen PAUD*. Bandung: Remaja Rosdakarya.

Mursid, M. (2015). *Pengembangan pembelajaran PAUD*. Bandung: Remaja Rosdakarya.

Sandall, S.R., Schwartz, I.S. & Lacroix, B. (2004). Interventionists' perspectives about data collection in integrated early childhood classrooms. *Journal of Early Intervention*, 26(3), 161–174.

Sturman, A. (1997). *Case study methods*. Oxford: Pergamon.

Sugiyono. (2005). *Metode penelitian pendidikan: pendekatan kuantitatif, kualitatif dan RD*. Bandung, Alfabeta.

Educational Administration Innovation for Sustainable Development – Komariah et al. (Eds)
© 2018 Taylor & Francis Group, London, ISBN 978-1-138-57341-3

Assessment as a strategy to boost Vietnamese teacher education provision quality

A. Duong
The University of Sydney, Australia

ABSTRACT: Teacher education in Vietnam includes training programs from early childhood, primary to secondary education. This paper focuses on the quality of teacher education preparation which requires attention from the government toward fundamental and comprehensive educational reform. Despite efforts in innovative curricula, teaching methods and creating opportunities for students to join scientific research activities, it is shown that the competence of pre-service teachers needs further development. The research reported here performs strategic SWOT analysis involving qualitative methods to examine the situation in Vietnam and categorize solutions for improving teacher education quality. It could be achieved by redesigning the curriculum as disciplines by balancing theoretical and practical knowledge; creating more internship opportunities for students from the second to the final year; and boosting assessment in teacher education. Assessment could be conducted by surveying students' and graduates' satisfaction of the curricula and schools for their teachers' professional and pedagogical competences. Besides strengthening students' achievements during their studies by the successful provision of formative assessment, it may hold the key toward improving the quality of teacher education overall.

1 INTRODUCTION

Assessment plays a crucial role in the 21st century as it bridges the gap between teaching and learning, in which it requires learners to master up-to-date skills for both social and career life. It is necessary for teaching and learning to focus on the ongoing process toward competencies through updated learning and instructing methods. Learning involves not only obtaining new knowledge but also connecting new knowledge and students' previous knowledge (Yue et al., 2008). In that sense, it emphasizes the way we measure the gained knowledge during the learning. The rapid change in the context of assessment drags on the adjustment of the way to give feedback in higher education (Boud & Molloy, 2012).

Teacher education in Vietnam requires several years' training in being a teaching professional, following 12 years of schooling. Depending on different levels of education, there will be certain requirements for training in pedagogy. For example, teacher training programs for high school teachers, in Vietnam in general, consists of three years' training with expertise units in which they are majored; then students may have approximately one year studying pedagogical units and teaching practices.

There have been many actions taken by the Ministry of Education and Training (MOET) on how to gain better quality for teacher education. Or even, they have piloted several projects at various school levels under partnerships among MOET and UNESCO and NGOs (Live & Learn, 2016). They have tried to innovate the curriculum, teaching pedagogy and organizing extra activities for students toward their future career. However, effort seems to be spent more on this sector in which teacher education institutions are the main driving force (MOET, 2011).

Assessment is considered to be an effective way to positively affect students' learning and senses of agency in education (Borgioli et al., 2015). They nurture the belief that assessment practices will assure the values of teaching and learning from students' participation, identity, power and even agency in classes. This idea is consolidated by Roscoe (2013) when she concluded that a balanced and integrated assessment system will fundamentally change tertiary classrooms.

According to MOET's report in August 2017, Vietnam currently has 58 universities, 57 colleges and 40 vocational schools which run teacher education courses (of which there are 14 universities, 33 colleges, and 2 vocational schools that are teacher education institutes). It has attracted a lot of attention from the public, so far, to the quality of teacher training because it is widely believed that teacher quality could have a strong effect on students' engagement and achievements in class (NSW-DEC, 2013).

The aim of this paper is to identify the strengths and challenges of sustainable development for teacher education and search for solutions to improve the quality of teacher education, especially to enhance graduates' competences before entering their teaching career.

2 LITERATURE REVIEW

Studying in higher education means that students are expected more and more to distinguish themselves in the dynamic and competitive environment (Caeiro et al., 2013; Jenkins, 2010; Stewart, 2011; Tollefson, 2000). Assessment helps them to be self-driving and self-regulating (Black & Wiliam, 2009; Clark, 2012; Nicol & Macfarlane-Dick, 2006) on their learning journey. One emerging issue for modern training is how to engage students and have certain groups of competences for future careers and life (Hoang, 2016).

Assessment is a broad term including testing or other methods such as observations, interviews, and behavior monitoring, to provide professional judgment of gathered information in reliance of student performance toward targeted goals to monitor progress and make educational decisions (Kizlik, 2016; Overton, 2012; Tognolini & Stanley, 2011). Assessment can also involve 'the focused and timely gathering, analysis, interpretation, and use of information that can provide evidence of student progress' (The New Zealand Curriculum, 2007). There may be various kinds of assessment which are in common assessing the same material from different but interrelated perspectives (Tognolini & Stanley, 2011). In the past, educators concentrated mostly on assessment of learning while that context has been shifted into assessment AS/ FOR learning later on (Arieli-Attali, 2010; Hayward & Spencer, 2010; Leirhaug & MacPhail, 2015; MacCann & Stanley, 2009).

Formative assessment is defined by Black and Wiliam (2003) as the flexible and continuous assessment of education quality. Decades later, it has been widely known as a method to keep up with learning purposes (Filsecker & Kerres, 2012). Formative assessment is said not to have any significant influence on student achievement (Kingston & Nash, 2011), but it tells a different story if teachers reinforce the need for feedback during learning (Filsecker & Kerres, 2012). Assessment results enable students to be aware of where they are in terms of their progress, what their strengths or weaknesses are, what their approximate zones of development are, what they have done and what they can do with the support of teachers or classmates.

As a result, Vietnamese schools and tertiary institutions should enable students to be perfect masters or skillful employees in the future to create the qualified workforce for society. However, it is believed that further research should be done on how formative assessment is implemented efficiently under perspectives of teachers and students although benefits from formative assessment remain doubtful.

Sometimes, in contrast, it was clear that many classroom assessments did not support learning, and was often used more to socialize children than to improve achievements (Torrance & Pryor, 1998). Such studies were beginning to direct attention to the classroom processes – that are the ways teachers put formative principles into practices focused on learning through daily actions.

Formative assessment in cultural higher education context

The goals of higher education has been shifted into producing highly knowledgeable individuals, also stressing on real situation skills such as problem-solving skills, professional skills, and authentic learning (Dochy et al., 1999). It means that education should create a learning culture where students and teachers would have a shared expectation before starting a unit. Especially, formative assessment should go in line with specific social and cultural contexts because assessment concentrates genuinely on competitive examination cultures of standardized assessment in East Asian societies (Broadfoot, 1999; Zeng, 2001).

Substantial changes in the learning atmosphere via classroom practice influence the learning culture (Sadler, 1998). Real practice, however, shows that teachers often follow the structure and progression of the subject discipline rather than with those matters of student development (Yorke, 2003). Understanding the cultural context of the students and the nature of their learning experience is important to comprehend the added possible challenge to the instructors. That is why cultural differences in pedagogy may be due to students' culture and their inability or unwillingness to respond to self-assessing and peer-assessing.

The Zone of Proximal Development first introduced by Vygotsky (1978) mentioned a lot to maintain student motivation in applying assessment in training. In this way, formal formative assessments can be defined as those that take place in a specific curricular assessment framework. Assessment itself encourages students to demonstrate their natural abilities and student learning is regulated to achieve superior performance. Previous studies have observed that students' creativity and innovation is encouraged while connections to the real world are established (Yin, 2005).

In the implementation of formative assessment, teachers are recommended to treat students' answers as very first draft rather than as the final product (Leung & Mohan, 2004). This idea comes up with interview results of Vietnamese teachers in which they promote additional opportunity for dialog between teacher and students to be better able to self-regulate learning and improve their product.

3 RESEARCH METHODS

The research utilizes the theory of motivation and socio-culture in identifying the zone of proximal development of students and enhancing students' achievements. Social interaction and communication are an essential channel for students to self-assess and peer-assess, to define their strengths and weaknesses. Students could learn from each other to attain higher competencies.

This paper uses document analysis method by looking at several reports and papers on teacher education in Vietnam; information is taken from the websites of the Ministry of Education and Training; also, some university websites are used, such as at Hanoi National University of Education, VNU HN University of Education, Vinh University, Hanoi Metropolitan University, and Thai Nguyen University of Education. A study of lecture observation is also explored to examine the context of teacher education and the impacts of assessment on students' achievements.

Besides, the research applied strategic management methods like SWOT analysis, which proposes strategic management solutions based on information about the inside and outside atmosphere of an organization (Sammut-Bonnici & Galea, 2015). From internal and external knowledge obtained from qualitative method, the research has discovered the strengths and weaknesses, opportunities and challenges of current policies in Vietnamese education.

4 RESEARCH FINDINGS

According to the Strategy for Education Development in period 2011–2020, Vietnam aims at positively providing students with ethical values, a healthy lifestyle, creative thinking, a practical skills approach to reality, foreign language skills, and information technology capabilities to provide a qualified workforce for society. The science of assessment and evaluation in education has just been focused for several decades and seldom could it adequately 'translate' theories, documents, and methodologies into the practice of measuring and evaluating the quality of education.

Meanwhile, education systems are confronted with the problem of an unqualified workforce in which 65% of graduates have to take additional courses to meet employers' demand (Sai & Duong, 2016) and 50% of graduates cannot find a job in their majors (Tran, 2014). Current problems may be caused by declining academic standards, an increasing number of visiting lecturers, large-size classes, and weakening values of some degrees due to an oversupply of graduates (Atkinson & Minnich, 2014; Beattie et al., 2006; Black & Wiliam, 2005; Hattie & Timperley, 2007; Shepard, 2016).

Teacher education in Vietnam revealed couples of setbacks and needed certain improvements (Pham, 2015). In order to have qualified graduates, is it a requirement to have excellent input of students and high-skilled lecturers? If so, how could we assure these elements? If not, what are the conditions we must retain?

4.1 *Grading system*

There is a link between curriculum, instruction and assessment in education (Roscoe, 2013); the role of the curriculum has been strengthened in the reform of education periodically. However, curricula in teacher education in Vietnam show that teaching, learning and assessment are mostly based on grading/marking mechanisms. An historical demonstration for this point is the presence of the thousand-year-old Literature Temple in Hanoi where scholars with doctoral degree are honored by having their names listed on turtle steles.

There are three main elements of grading system for a student in a semester, including participation (10–20%), mid-term examination (20–40%) and final examination (50–70%) (Kieu et al., 2016). At the same time, obstacles for implementing active pedagogies identified consist of large-size classes (over 50 students), limited facilities and heavy curriculum requirements. It is found from curricula in some teacher education programs that there is only 5–10% of time for internships (in the sixth and eighth semester only i.e. the third and final year), equivalent to 5–10 over 95–200 credits in total.

4.2 *Confucianism influences*

Vietnam is an Asian country which is strongly influenced by external cultures such as Western, Chinese and Russian, especially in the education sector. Outstanding from those cultures is Confucianism which educates the moral value (Tran, 2014). It maintains two fundamental principles: the necessity of correct behavior and the importance of loyalty and obedience.

Findings from an observational study being conducted by the researcher in 2017, indicate that pedagogical standards are strictly obeyed in teacher education in Vietnam accordingly. It is the fact that pedagogical standards are examined carefully through verbal and non-verbal language in class in a pedagogical practice lecture.

Sometime students may feel stressed and they may be devoid of motivation in their prospective teaching careers. It is observed from a lecture that by a combination of dynamic, joyful and flexible activities organized by the lecturer, students are involved in learning activities and change their viewpoints on human development, career meanings and bring about the feeling of happiness for themselves. Assessment practices in lectures may also be recognized to create impacts on equity in teacher higher education. This is especially concerning students' participation, identity, power and agency in classes. It could be said that lecturer's behaviors and attitudes, and assessment techniques play a core role in engaging students in learning.

4.3 *The role of accreditation*

In order for an education institution to be widely recognized, it must be accredited nationally or internationally. According to the Plan implementing accreditation in the training quality of teacher education institutions in 2017 (No.118/KHBGD&DT dated 23/02/2017 by MOET), there will be 35% of universities and 10% of colleges accredited at the end of 2017. It means that we are paying more attention to the conditions to assure the consistent quality; that means, assessment becomes the key factor (Masters, 2013; Yorke, 2003).

4.4 Study load for internship

According to Pavlova (2013), the most pedagogical and effective way in teaching is welcoming different opinions and allowing enough space to develop students' ideas in practice. The research realizes some requirements we need to meet to innovate our education system, such as:

1. developing students' content knowledge and practical pedagogical skills by increasing the time for internship right from the third or fourth semester;
2. strengthening scientific research skills for students – this requirement is rather difficult to attain but some of universities have already created the scientific research competitions for students to show their abilities such as Vinh University, Hanoi University of Education, and VNU – University of Education.

Take the case in Malaysia for example, the connection between theory and professional learning during fieldwork is highlighted in teacher education (Gallant & Mayer, 2012). Consequently, research skill is not compulsory but necessary to achieve higher competencies in teaching.

4.5 Feedback from stakeholders in curriculum development

Qualified teachers, definitely, play a knot to generate competent graduates. While the importance of curriculum could not be denied, facilities and teaching methods could help make sure that we are creating the next generations of qualified teachers. Nguyen (2016) has emphasized that the CDIO approach in technology teacher education universities needs to meet the demand of integration. In that context, updating the curriculum is proved to be a part of innovation.

Similarly, it could involve graduates, employers and other stakeholders in the process of designing the curriculum periodically by surveying their feedback for the current curriculum or graduates' performance. Besides, we could research and invest in assessing the current model of teacher education and propose to link assessment more directly into the education process. Assessment could be done on, for instance, teacher performance, student performance, facilities and infrastructure, training program, feedback from employers, competency and employability of graduates.

4.6 The impact of formative assessment

With clear guidelines and assessment criteria, students will be involved and actively take part in each activity in classrooms to show their best capacities in achieving the learning goals. In other words, teachers hold the key to paving the way for students' development by giving feedback for each of their performances during the learning journey. Furthermore, the role of feedback is critically recognized in formative assessment (Cauley & Mcmillan, 2010; Filsecker & Kerres, 2012). Times have changed, resulting in innovations in society, and education is also mentioned in the list of innovations.

Teachers are able to determine what standards students already know and should know so that they can make some modifications or changes to the set goals. Students are more motivated to learn and take responsibility for their learning. Especially, students can become users of assessment alongside the teacher and learn valuable lifelong skills such as self-efficacy, self-evaluation, self-assessment, and goal-setting (McMillan & Hearn, 2008; Tollefson, 2000).

Findings from observation study of a lecture also illustrate the fact that assessment of students' competencies from the start to the end of a course remain important as well. During the process of learning, students should be provided with feedback on their current performance and expected changes to shift their learning forward. This process is called formative assessment and involves the steps of sharing learning expectations, questioning, giving feedback, self-assessment and peer-assessment (Black & Wiliam, 2009). By these activities, students will be engaged in active efforts to show their competencies. Students are the ones who directly identify their weaknesses, recognize their strengths and design steps to walk closer to their expected learning outcomes. Formative assessment supports teachers and students to do that job.

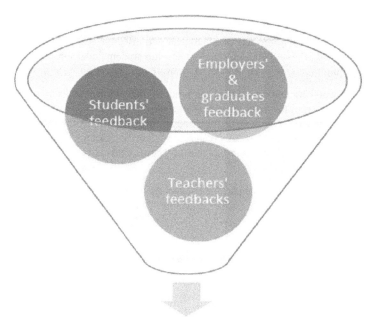

Assessment

Figure 1.   Requirements of reviewing teacher education programs periodically (MOET, 2012).

5   CONCLUSION

Some Vietnamese educators have suggested solutions for innovating teacher education programs such as training using a credits system (Dinh, 2014) or developing teachers' competencies (Pham, 2015); it still shows little progression.

However, graduates need to take part in additional training following university if they are to meet the demand from employers once commencing their jobs (Sai & Duong, 2016). Therefore, this research hopes to clarify that formative assessment assists bridging the gap between classroom activities, students' practices and intended performance goals.

MOET also specified the key role of assessment in the regulations on criteria for evaluating the quality of the training program of high school teachers at tertiary level (MOET, 2012). Nevertheless, there are only two standards mentioning curriculum and assessment: Standard 2 (Designing and updating the curriculum) and Standard 7 (Surveying for graduates' employments and employment consultation). That is why we need to strengthen the focus on assessment more and more and translate it into practice so that training programs are accredited and quality-assured.

Additionally, the guideline for evaluating the quality of the training program does not specify the time spans or study load for internships, which is a core element for teacher education at the moment. The researcher considers this element as the backbone of education and focuses on the performance of to-be-teachers in the future. They could train their practices and adjust their pedagogical methods during the internship or practical training (Hamano, 2008). It is believed that this period could make the difference and distinguish the graduates with high competence from the ones with low competence.

Next, surveying for graduates' feedback on the curriculum and surveying for employers (schools/education institutions) for their teachers' competences (including content knowledge and pedagogical skills) is considered as the most effective solution to increase the quality of the training program. Because these groups were directly involved in the process of educating, they are the

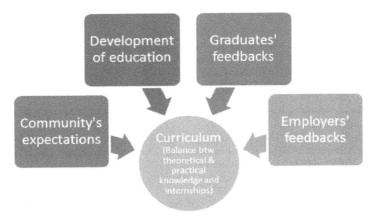

Figure 2.   Factors to contribute to updated curriculum for teacher education programs.

ones who know clearly the strengths and weaknesses of the program. The graduates will give the comments on teaching methods, curriculum and employability orientation while the employers give feedback on the competency of graduates (Figure 2).

Conducting a survey for feedback from employers or schools who have graduates as their teachers has not yet been implemented widely and systematically in Vietnam. It shows the fact that there are not many reports on surveying for employers' feedback published at the moment. It is hoped to be conducted shortly to have proper and practical feedback for educators or curriculum developers. As a result, it becomes a means for training institutions' accountability once it is made public, raising the qualifications of teacher education outputs.

Education is a form of human ethical training. Teacher students' abilities could be even demonstrated through interactions and ethical issues between them and their pupils in some internship activities. In other words, assessment becomes sensitive and culture matters when it comes to education, especially teacher education.

REFERENCES

Arieli-Attali, M. (2010). *Formative assessment with cognition in mind: The Cognitively Based Assessment of, for and as Learning (CBAL TM) research initiative at educational testing service*, (October 2013). Retrieved from http://doi.org/10.13140/2.1.3555.7129

Atkinson, J. & Minnich, P.C. (2014). Supporting formative assessment for deeper learning: A primer for policymakers. Robert Linquanti, WestEd.

Beattie, G., Shovelton, H., Blindern, P.O., Duit, R., Treagust, D., Givry, D., ... Driver, R. (2006). An experimental investigation of some properties of individual iconic ... *Cognition*, 43(2), 1086–1109. Retrieved from http://doi.org/10.1002/tea

Black, P. & Wiliam, D. (2003). In praise of educational research: Formative assessment. *British Educational Research Journal*, 29(5), 623–637.

Black, P., & Wiliam, D. (2005). Changing teaching through formative assessment: Research and practice. *Formative assessment: Improving learning in secondary classrooms*. The King's-Medway-Oxfordshire Formative Assessment Project. Paris, France. Retrieved from www.oecd.org/edu/ceri/34260938.pdf

Black, P., & Wiliam, D. (2009). Developing the theory of formative assessment. *Educational Assessment, Evaluation and Accountability*, 21(1), 5–31. doi:10.1007/s11092-008-9068-5

Borgioli, G., Ociepka, A. & Coker, K. (2015). A playbill: Rethinking assessment in teacher education. *Journal of the Scholarship of Teaching and Learning*, 15(3), 68–84.

Boud, D. & Molloy, E. (2012). Rethinking models of feedback for learning: The challenge of design. *Assessment & Evaluation in Higher Education*, 38(6), 1–15. doi:10.1080/02602938.2012.691462

Broadfoot, P. (1999). *Education assessment and society*. Open University Press.

Caeiro, S., Filho, W.L., Jabbour, C. & Azeiteiro, U.M. (2013). *Sustainability assessment tools in higher education institutions.* doi:10.1007/978-3-319-02375-5

Cauley, K.M. & Mcmillan, J.H. (2010). Formative assessment techniques to support student motivation and achievement. *The Clearing House: A Journal of Educational Strategies, Issues and Ideas,* 83(1), 1–6. doi:10.1080/00098650903267784 http://doi.org/10.1080/0969594X.2013.790308

Clark, I. (2012). Formative assessment: Assessment is for self-regulated learning. *Educational Psychology Review,* 24(2), 205–249.

Dinh, Q.B. (2014). *Solutions for innovation teacher education programs as learning credits,* Scientific research project at MOET level, No B2011 – 17 – CT03.

Filsecker, M. & Kerres, M. (2012). Repositioning formative assessment from an educational assessment perspective: A response to Dunn & Mulvenon (2009). *Practical Assessment, Research & Evaluation,* 17(16), 1–9. Retrieved from http://pareonline.net/pdf/v17n16.pdf

Gallant, A. & Mayer, D. (2012). Teacher performance assessment in teacher education: An example in Malaysia. *Journal of Education for Teaching,* 38(3), 295–307.

Hamano, T. (2008). Educational reform and teacher education in Vietnam. *Journal of Education for Teaching,* 34(4), 397–410.

Hattie, J. & Timperley, H. (2007). The power of feedback. *Review of Educational Research,* 77(1), 81–112. doi:10.3102/003465430298487

Hayward, L. & Spencer, E. (2010). The complexities of change: Formative assessment in Scotland. *The Curriculum Journal,* 21(2), 37–41. doi:10.1080/09585176.2010.480827

Hoang, T. (2016). Three issues in current Vietnamese education. Retrieved from http://ired.edu.vn/vn/doc-tin/74/ba-van-de-cua-dai-hoc-viet-nam-hien-nay

Jenkins, J.O. (2010). A multi-faceted formative assessment approach: Better recognising the learning needs of students. *Assessment & Evaluation in Higher Education,* 35(5), 565–576. doi:10.1080/02602930903243059

Kieu, T.K., Singer, J. & Gannon, T. (2016). Education for sustainable development in Vietnam: Lessons learned from teacher education. *International Journal of Sustainability in Higher Education,* 17(6), 853–874.

Kizlik, B. (2016). Measurement, assessment, and evaluation in education. Retrieved from http://www.adprima.com/measurement.htm

Leirhaug, P.E. & MacPhail, A. (2015). 'It's the other assessment that is the key': Three Norwegian physical education teachers' engagement (or not) with assessment for learning. *Sport, Education and Society,* 20(5), 624–640. doi:10.1080/13573322.2014.975113

Leung, C. & Mohan, B. (2004). Teacher formative assessment and talk in classroom contexts: Assessment as discourse and assessment of discourse. *Language Testing,* 21(3), 335–359.

Live & Learn. (2016). *Climate change education in secondary schools across Viet Nam.* Retrieved from www.livelearn.org/projects/climate-change-education-secondary-schools-across-vietnam

MacCann, R.G. & Stanley, G. (2009). Item banking with embedded standards. *Practical Assessment, Research & Evaluation,* 14(17), 8.

Masters, G.N. (2013). *Design principles for a learning assessment system. Reforming educational assessment: Imperatives, principles and challenges.*

McMillan, J. H. & Hearn, J. (2008). Student self-assessment: The key to stronger student motivation and higher achievement. *Educational Horizons,* 87(1), 40–49. Retrieved from http://www.eric.ed.gov/ERICWebPortal/contentdelivery/servlet/ERICServlet?accno=EJ815370

MOET. (2011). *Decision No. 6290/QĐ-BGDĐT about development of pedagogical education and universities of education from 2011 to 2020.* Retrieved from www.moet.gov.vn/?page_6.4&opt_brpage&view_3858

MOET. (2012). *Regulations on criteria for evaluating the quality of the training program of high school teachers at tertiary level.* Retrieved from https://thuvienphapluat.vn/van-ban/Giao-duc/Thong-tu-49-2012-TT-BGDDT-Quy-dinh-tieu-chuan-danh-gia-chat-luong-chuong-trinh-164169.aspx

Nguyen, M.T. (2016). CDIO approach in technology teacher education universities meeting the demand of integration. *Journal of Vocational Education Science,* Vol 37+38, October + November, 2016.

Nicol, D.J. & Macfarlane-Dick, D. (2006). Formative assessment and self-regulated learning: A model and seven principles of good feedback practice. *Studies in Higher Education (2006),* 31(2), 199–218. doi:10.1080/03075070600572090

NSW Department of Education and Communities, Centre for Education Statistics and Evaluation, Office of Education. (2013). *Great Teaching, Inspired Learning: What does the evidence tell us about effective training?* (p. 4).

Overton, T. (2012). *Assessing learners with special needs: An applied approach.* Pearson Education.

Pavlova, M. (2013). Teaching and learning for sustainable development: ESD research in technology education. *International Journal of Technology and Design Education,* 23(3), 733–748.

Pham, T.K.A. (2015). Hanoi National University of Education, Teacher education program in Vietnam: Drawbacks and development orientation. *Proceedings of the International Conference on Developing teacher education programs: Opportunities and Challenges*, Thai Nguyen Teacher Education University.

Roscoe, K. (2013). Enhancing Assessment in Teacher Education. *The Canadian Journal for the Scholarship of Teaching and Learning*, 4(1), 5.

Sadler, D.R. (1998). Formative assessment: Revisiting the territory. *Assessment in Education: Principles, Policy & Practice*, 5(1), 77–84. doi:10.1080/0969595980050104

Sai, H.C. & Duong, A.T. (2016). Solutions for improving students' competences under alumni's perspectives at Vietnam National University Hanoi, Vietnam. *The International Journal of Humanities & Social Studies*, 4(5), 300–306.

Sammut-Bonnici, T. & Galea, D. (2015). SWOT analysis. In *Wiley Encyclopedia of Management*. John Wiley & Sons, Ltd.

Shepard, L.A. (2016). The role of assessment in a learning culture. *Educational researcher*, 29(7), 4–14.

Stewart, T. (2011). Effects of implementing a formative assessment initiative. Retrieved from http://digitalcommons.wku.edu/diss/12

The New Zealand Curriculum. (2007). The New Zealand Curriculum.

Tognolini, J. & Stanley, G. (2011). Tognolini and Stanley 2011. In P. Powell-Davies (Ed.), *A standards perspective on the relationship between formative and summative assessment* (pp. 25–32). England: British Council.

Tollefson, N. (2000). Classroom applications of cognitive theories of motivation. *Educational Psychology Review*, 12(1), 63–84. doi:10.1023/A:1009085017100

Tran, K. (2014). Developing tertiary education in Vietnam. *Journal of Vietnamese Social Science*, 10(83), 54–62.

Vygotsky, L.S. (1978). Interaction between learning and development. *Readings on the Development of Children*.

Yin, Y. (2005). *The influence of formative assessments on student motivation, achievement, and conceptual change*. Stanford University.

Yorke, M. (2003). Formative assessment in higher education: Moves towards theory and the enhancement of pedagogic practice. *Higher Education*, 45(4), 477–501.

Yue, Y., Shavelson, R.J., Ayala, C.C., Ruiz-Primo, M.A., Brandon, P.R., Furtak, E.M., …Young, D.B. (2008). On the impact of formative assessment on student motivation, achievement, and conceptual change. *Applied Measurement in Education*, 21(4), 335–359. doi:10.1080/08957340802347845

Educational Administration Innovation for Sustainable Development – Komariah et al. (Eds)
© 2018 Taylor & Francis Group, London, ISBN 978-1-138-57341-3

Leadership character values for realizing good governance in Bekasi City

Fadhilah & E.S. Nurdin
Universitas Pendidikan Indonesia, Bandung, West Java, Indonesia

ABSTRACT: Good leadership values are reflected in the vision and mission of the reformed government. The multiplicity of phenomena of money politics in the system of leadership and public services are the background of this research problem. The research objectives are to formulate a model of Good Governance leadership in public service, and to find the factors which become the affordances and constraints in the implementation of Good Governance leadership in Bekasi City according to the perspective of General Education, by using the *kualitatif* method and phenomenological-hermeneutic analysis. Findings and conclusions of this research are generally that the quality of leadership in public service is relatively good. However, there are still some weaknesses in terms of less responsiveness. Some efforts made by the Office of Investment and One Stop Service of Bekasi City leadership in responding to the needs of the community to obtain a fast and transparent permit service shows the implementation of the values of transformational leadership character that is needed and must be developed in order to implement the principles of Good Governance in public service.

1 INTRODUCTION

Leadership becomes the gateway to achieving the goals of an organization. Good leadership is reflected in the personalities of its leaders as well as their impact on the working climate, in order to accomplish the organization's vision and mission. In relation to government organizations, good leadership will lead to the achievement of the country's objectives.

In the Reformation Era, one of the main objectives of the state administration includes addressing the problems of corruption occurring in public service activities through bureaucratic reform. Therefore, ethical standards of public service are required as a guide leader in carrying out tasks of leadership.

The success of a leader in managing the government and the private sector including through the organization of public services to the community, the best behaved well, dedicated and trial on community interests (Sinambela, 2006). Therefore, ethical standards of public service are required as a guide leader in carrying out tasks of leadership.

Keban, (2004) asserts that the basic values (core values) that became standards of public administration are: freedom, equality, justice, truth, kindness and beauty.

In this case, good leadership is needed in order to implement the principles of 'Good Governance' (UNDP, 1997). Such principles are reflected in the values of leadership character, in line with the vision and mission of the reformed government to create a clean government, free of corruption, collusion and nepotism.

Since the enactment of Law Number 32 Year 2004 (2004) regarding regional government, some changes have been made in terms of leadership style and system; they have become more democratic, and are no longer top-down and centralized like the ones during the New Order era. However, in practice it is still difficult to implement the principles of Good Governance. This is evidenced by numerous phenomena of corruption cases and money politics in the sectors of public services involving a number of government officials, both at the central and regional government levels.

Moreover, the opinions of the public concerning public services in general suggest that the services are still convoluted and time-consuming. In addition, some public service costs are considered to be less transparent.

The main theory used as the foundation of analysis in this study consists of several theories that essentially support the efforts for implementing Good Governance in Indonesia, especially in the sector of public services. Such theories include leadership theory, concept of government ethics, Good Governance concept, organizational behavior theory, and the concept of value/character education.

One of the definitions of leadership, among others, is suggested by Danim (2012). He states that 'leadership is any action taken by an individual or group to coordinate or give direction to another individual or group incorporated in a particular container to achieve previously defined objectives'. Danim also cites other definitions of leadership as follows.

According to McFarland, 'leadership is a process in which leaders are seen as figures who give command, influence, or guidance, or a process which affects the work of others in choosing and achieving the established goals. Pfiffner suggests that leadership is the art of coordinating and giving direction to individuals or groups to achieve desired goals. Sutisna argues that leadership is the ability to take initiative in social situations to create new forms and procedures, to design and organize deeds, and in doing so it evokes cooperation towards the achievement of goals' (Danim, 2012, p. 6).

Based on the definitions of leadership above, it can be concluded that leadership is the ability of individuals (leaders) to influence others through guidance, direction, coordination and cooperation, in a job or relationship with other individuals (groups) to achieve certain goals. According to Sutisna, it can be concluded that leadership is the art of creating/designing actions that can motivate others to attain particular goals.

When it comes to the definition of leadership, numerous leadership theories come to light, among which are 'eight types of leadership theory'. The eight genres of leadership theory are presented as follows:

1. The genetic theory (great man theory); this assumes that a leader is born, not formed. A leader is a 'big man', born because he/she is needed as a hero, and is prepared to rise to leadership.
2. The trait theory; this is similar to the genetic theory and suggests that leaders possess the traits/characteristics required for leadership.
3. Contingency theory; this emphasizes the relationship between environment and leadership style appropriate for a particular situation.
4. Situational theory; this points out the need for the action of leaders in accordance with certain situations.
5. Behavioral theory; this is contrary to the assumption in the genetic theory. This theory postulates that a leader is the result of formation or process of learning/observation, not merely because of being born.
6. Participative theory; this states that an ideal leadership style is concerned with the involvement/contribution of others, and the encouragement of members to participate in decision-making.
7. Transactional theory (management theory); this focuses on the role of supervision, organization and group performance, and the need for rewards and punishment systems.
8. Transformational theory/relational theory; this focuses on good cooperation between leaders and followers in the completion of basic tasks and functions, based on ethics and high moral standards (Danim, 2012, p. 8–9).

Each theory of leadership in its implementation shows different leadership styles. In general, the leadership theories considered ideal are the Transactional and Transformational theories (Bernard & Avolio, 2003).

In connection with the background of the problems mentioned above, in order to achieve the goal of reformed government free of corruption, collusion and nepotism, it is necessary to implement the values of both types of leadership in accordance with the situation, and conditionin the field based on government ethics (Ndraha, 2003) and the principles of Good Governance (UNDP, 1997).

Good leadership in public services is needed to achieve the goals of reformed government through the implementation of values of leadership character, based on government ethical standards and the principles of Good Governance. According to The Liang Gie (1994), the ethical principles of government administration comprise of six basic principles: Responsibility, Dedication, Loyalty, Sensitivity, Equality, and Equity.

According to the UNDP concept, the principles of Good Governance consist of five aspects: *Legitimacy, Direction, Performance, Accountability,* and *Fairness.* The five principles have their own indicators. Legitimacy is based on the principle of participation and orientation to mutual agreement. Leadership requires a good Direction, from a strategic and visionary leader. The Performance aspect emphasizes the principle of responsiveness and the principle of Effectiveness and Efficiency. The responsive attitude of the institution and its processes manage to serve all stakeholders. The principle of Effectiveness and Efficiency emphasizes the processes and outcomes of institutions that meet the priority needs and use the best resources. The Accountability aspect involves decision makers in government, private sectors, and civil society organizations that are publicly accountable, as well as external or internal stakeholders, based on the transparency principle in accordance with the freedom to obtain accurate information The Fairness aspect emphasizes the principle of equality in human rights for all people, men and women (UNDP, 1997). The UNDP Principles of Good Governance are translated by The National Development Planning Agency of Indonesia (2007) into 14 principles with their respective indicators, as shown in the Table below.

Table 1. Principles of Good Governance (UNDP, 1997) are translated by The National Development Planning Agency of Indonesia (2007).

No	Principles of *Good Governance*	Minimum indicator
1	Foresight	– Forward planning with vision and strategy – Clarity of objectives in any policy and program – Support from the Individual to actualize the vision
2	Openness and transparency	– Availability of adequate information on each process of formulation and implementation of public policy – Access to information that is ready, easy to reach, free to obtain, and on time
3	Society participation	– Understanding of the state administrators regarding participatory process/method – Decision–making based on mutual consensus
4	Accountability	– Congruence between implementation and its standard procedures – Sanction imposed on mistake/negligence in the execution of activities – Measurable outputs and outcomes
5	The supremacy of law	– The presence of firm and consistent legislation – Fair and non–discriminatory law enforcement – Lawsuit against any offender – Awareness and obedience to the law
6	Democracy	– The existence of people's basic rights such as the right to gather, associate and express opinions – Equality before the law – Equal opportunity to participate in decision-making of public policy – Equal opportunity to gain public information Equal opportunity to try and achieve something – Equal opportunity to be innovative, creative, and productive

(Continued)

Table 1. (*Continued*)

No	Principles of *Good Governance*	Minimum indicator
7	Professionalism	– High performing – Principle abiding – Creative and innovative – Qualified in their field
8	Responsiveness	– The availability of complaints services, in the form of crisis centers, Community Service Units (UPM), suggestion boxes, and readers' letters that are easily accessible to the public – Standards and procedures in following up on reports and complaints
9	Effectiveness and Efficiency	– Quality and right-on-target public administration with optimal use of resources – Monitoring and evaluation for improvement – Reduction of overlapping organizational functions/work units
10	Decentralization	– Clarity of divisions of tasks and authorities between levels of government and inter-level positions in the region in accordance with the government Regulation on Division of Affairs, the revised version No. 25 of 2000 – Clarity of support provision for community services
11	Partnership with private businesses and society	– The understanding of the government apparatus about partnership patterns – The existence of a conducive environment for people with disabilities – Open opportunities for the community/business community to play a role in the provision of public services – The empowerment of local economic institutions, and micro, small and medium enterprises
12	Commitment to gap reduction	– The policies which are oriented to meet the needs of society in a balanced manner (cross subsidies, affirmative action) – The availability of special services/facilities for poor people – Equality and gender equity – Empowerment of disadvantaged areas
13	Commitment to the environment	– Regulations and policies to protect and conserve natural resources and the environment – Reduced levels of pollution and environmental damage
14	Commitment to a fair market	– Development of society's economy – Guarantee of a healthy competition climate

To implement the principles of Good Governance, in the perspective of the theory of organizational behavior, a social learning process is required to bring changes to the behavior of individuals in groups (social) or organizations. The definition of learning according to Robbins is 'any relatively permanent change of behavior that occurs as a result of experience'. Any behavioral change is the result of learning, and learning is a behavioral change (Robbins, 1996). According to Robbins, there are patterns of individual behavior in a particular organization, namely: classical conditioning, operant conditioning (effective operant), and social learning (Robbins, 1996). The conditioning theory can be applied in efforts to change the system of public service leadership in a better direction through bureaucratic reform.

The problems that arise in the field related to the implementation of the principles of Good Governance in public services are analyzed integrally and holistically, based on the concept of leadership and the theory of *General Education Model* by Hanstedt (2012), and *primarily the six basic meanings* according to Phenix (1964, p. 6–8), that apply in human life, namely:

1. The Empiric Meaning; the ability to understand things through the process of investigation and empirical analysis.
2. The Symbolic Meaning; the ability to communicate/use language and numeracy.
3. The Aesthetic Meaning; the ability to capture the beauty of visual arts and natural phenomena.
4. The Synnoetic Meaning; the ability to decide if an action is appropriate based on consideration of emotion (psychological) and thought/ratio.
5. The Ethic Meaning; the ability to distinguish moral behavior (good and bad).
6. The Synoptic Meaning; the ability to give meaning to history, religion and philosophy.

The concept becomes the basis for formulating a good leadership model in accordance with the vision and mission of reformed government, as well as the principles of Good Governance in public service. In this case, the necessity of the implementation of the values of transactional and transformational leadership character, in accordance with the situation and conditions in the field, which enables the individual to cultivate self-potential, is derived from those six types of values/basic meanings.

2 RESEARCH METHOD

Using the qualitative method and phenomenological-hermeneutic analysis, Kuswara's study (2009) holistically aims to find the phenomenon behind the factors that become the affordances and constraints in the implementation of good leadership values in public services, based on the perspective of General Education/Values and Character/General and Character Education.

The data was obtained through direct observation process and in-depth/intensive interviews with six officials at the Office of Investment and One Stop Service of Bekasi City and 25 community members, as the public service users. Through rigorous scientific reduction of phenomenologist-hermeneutics (interpretation), this research is conducted to uncover the essence of various meanings related to the affordances and constraints of Good Governance implementation in public services in Bekasi City. Data analysis is done according to Character Education perspective.

3 FINDINGS & DISCUSSIONS

The result of this qualitative research and analysis of phenomenology-hermeneutics on the phenomenon of the implementation of Good Governance principles from the aspect of leadership in the public service sectors in Bekasi City can be seen implicitly from the interview result with six government officials at the Office of Investment and One Stop Service, Bekasi City, including the Head of Planning Subdivision and the Head of General and Personnel Subdivision, as shown below (Table 2).

Based on the data recapitulation in Table 1.b above regarding the implementation of Good Governance leadership values in the Office of Kota Bekasi, it is generally considered good. As for the participation of the community, it is of fair quality.

The quality of public services at the Office of Investment and One Stop Service of Bekasi City can be seen from the data of Satisfaction Indicators in Table 3 below.

Based on Table 2 above, it can generally be concluded that the quality of service is relatively good. However, there are still some weaknesses in terms of certainty of time, clarity of procedures and details of service/ licensing fees, and completeness of facilities. Based on the results of intensive interviews during the study, there are factors that arise from the problems of individual characters of the leaders of state apparatus, as well as the culture of the community as public service users.

Table 2.   Implementation of Good Governance principles from the aspect of leadership in Bekasi City.

		The rating on the implementation of *Good Governance* values			
No	*Good Governance* values	Poor	Fair	Good	Excellent
1	Foresight	0	1	5	0
2	Openness and transparency	0	2	4	0
3	Society participation	0	4	2	0
4	Accountability	1	1	4	0
5	The supremacy of the law	0	2	4	0
6	Democracy	0	2	4	0
7	Professionalism	0	2	4	0
8	Responsiveness	0	2	4	0
9	Efficiency and effectiveness	0	2	4	0
10	Decentralization	0	0	6	0
11	Partnership with private business world and society	0	1	5	0
12	Commitment to gap reduction	0	2	4	0
13	Commitment to the environment	1	0	5	0
14	Commitment to a fair market	0	2	4	0

Source: Research data after being processed, 2017.

Therefore, the Office of Investment and One Stop Service of Bekasi City continuously strives to improve the quality and capacity of leadership and staff/technical performance by providing technical guidance in accordance with the needs, and makes a breakthrough (innovation) to respond to the needs of public service users in order to get faster and more transparent services through simplification (public service through an online system). This is intended to minimize the possibility of a case of 'illegal charges', which has put public services in a bad light (Jeremy, 2003) due to their slow process. As a consequence, public services are taken advantage of by panders. According to the results of interview with some officials of the Office of Investment and One Stop Service and some public service users concerning the lack of maximum implementation of the principles of Good Governance in public services, in addition to factors caused by facilities and infrastructure, there are also character factors (Character Matters) (Lickona, 2012) of individual employees or character of leadership.

It can be anticipated if there is good coordination and cooperation, and increase the awareness and responsiveness of leadership toward the needs of the public users of public services who want to get the services as soon as possible. Responsiveness can be developed by cultivating a sense of empathy, which is a social and moral value that is very important for the state apparatus in serving the interests of society.

Transparent leadership character in serving the public interest can be enhanced by referring to the standard operating procedure and the mental guidance of the state apparatus continuously and incidentally.

Some efforts made by the Office of Investment and One Stop Service of Bekasi City leadership in responding to the needs of the community to obtain a fast and transparent permit service shows the implementation of the values of transformational leadership character that is needed and must be developed in order to implement the principles of Good Governance in public service. On the other hand, discipline enforcement for employees who violate the ethics of public service is the implementation of transactional leadership (Danim, 2012) in carrying out the duties and responsibilities of leadership in order to achieve the objectives of the organization (Kumorotomo, 1999). In addition, a remuneration system is required as a strategy to improve productivity and employee performance. Thus, both leadership characters (transactional and transformational) are needed in the leadership of public services for the implementation of Good Governance in accordance with the objectives of the reformed government.

Table 3. Quality of public service implementation at the Office of Investment and One Stop Service, Bekasi City Based on public service principles (Minister for the Utilization of the State Apparatus Decree Number 63/2004) N = 25.

No	Principles of public service	Public assessment on the quality of the implementation of public service principles			
		Poor (%)	Fair (%)	Good (%)	Excellent (%)
1	Simplicity (not complicated: one door/one roof service, or still separated between different work units)	4/25 = (16%)	8/25 = (32%)	12/25 = (48%)	1/25 = (4%)
2	Clarity in terms of: A) technical and administrative requirements/public service procedures;	1/25 = (4%)	8/25 = (32%)	14/25 = (56%)	2/25 = (8%)
	B) officials responsible for public service and problem solving	3/25 = (12%)	7/25 = (28%)	13/25 = (52%)	2/25 = (8%)
	C) details of public service fees and payment procedures	3/25 = (12%)	6/25 = (24%)	16/25 = (64%)	0/25 = (0%)
3	Certainty of time (time required in accordance with the Standard Operational Procedures (SOP) of public service)	2/25 = (8%)	11/25 = (44%)	10/25 = (40%)	2/25 = (8%)
4	Accuracy: public service products are received correctly, accurately and legitimately	0/25 = (0%)	10/25 = (40%)	14/25 = (56%)	1/25 = (4%)
5	Security (processes and products of public services provide a sense of security and legal certainty)	2/25 = (8%)	7/25 = (28%)	15/25 = (60%)	1/25 = (4%)
6	Responsibility (service that can be accountable in accordance with the rules and legislation)	2/25 = (8%)	6/25 = (24%)	14/25 = (56%)	3/25 = (12%)
7	Completeness of facilities and infrastructure (adequate facilities in the activities of public service delivery)	5/25 = (20%)	8/25 = (32%)	10/25 = (40%)	2/25 = (8%)
8	Ease of access (ease of place/location and use of facilities in public service procedures)	8/25 = (32%)	3/25 = (12%)	12/25 = (48%)	2/25 = (8%)
9	Discipline, courtesy (disciplined attitude and polite public service apparatus)	3/25 = (12%)	2/25 = (4%)	17/25 = (68%)	3/25 = (12%)
10	Comfort (convenience of situation and condition of indoor/public service process environment)	1/25 = (4%)	5/25 = (20%)	16/25 = (64%)	3/25 = (12%)

Source: Research data after being processed, 2017.

4 CONCLUSION

Based on the background of the problems and discussion above, in order to improve the quality of public service at the Office of Investment and One Stop Service, Bekasi City, the development of values of leadership character, especially the value of community participation, responsiveness, and visionary is needed to improve the quality of public services to meet the needs of public service users.

Referring to Phenix's (2012) suggestion about the six basic values, good leaders must maximize their own potential that comes from the six basic values/meanings in human life.

REFERENCES

Bernard. B.M. & Avolio, B.J. (2003). Predicting unit performance by assessing transformational and transactional.

Danim, S. (2012). *Kepemimpinan pendidikan*. Bandung: Alfabeta.

Gie, T.L. (2014). Etika administrasi pemerintahan. In *Studi tentang Etika Umumnya dan Etika Administrasi Pemerintahan Khususnya* (pp. 1–34). Jakarta: Universitas Terbuka. ISBN 9789790117204.

Hanstedt, P. (2012). *General education essentials*. AA (Association of American Colleges and Universities). Jossey-Bass a a Wiley Imprint.

Jeremy, P. (2003). *Strategi memberantas korupsi (Confronting corruption: The elements of national integrity system= Elemen sistem integritas nasional)*. Jakarta: Yayasan Obor Indonesia.

Keban, Y.T. (2004). *Enam dimensi strategis administrasi publik*. Yogyakarta: Penerbit Gava Media.

Kumorotomo, W. (1999). *Etika administrasi negara*, PT. Jakarta: Rajagrafindo Persada.

Kuswara, E. (2009). *Metodologi penelitian komunikasi fenomenologi, konsepsi, pedoman dan contoh penelitiannya*. Bandung: Widya Padjadjaran.

Law Number 32 Year 2004 About Local Governance (State Gazette of the Republic of Indonesia Number 125 2004 Year, an additional Sheet of the Republic of Indonesia Number 4437).

Lickona, T. (2012). *Character Matters* (Persoalan Karakter), *Bagaimana membantu anak mengembangkan penilaian yang baik, integritas, dan kebijakan penting lainnya*, penerj. Juma abdu Wamaungo dan Jean Antunes Rudolf Zien, Bumiaksara, Jakarta, cetakan pertama.

Ndraha, T. (2003). *Kybernology (Ilmu pemerintahan baru 1 dan 2)*. Jakarta: Penerbit Rineka Cipta.

Phenix, P.H. (2012). *Realms of meaning*. Copyright in United States of America.

Robbins, S. (1996). Perilaku Organisasi. Jakarta: Prenhallindo.

The United Nations Development Program (UNDP). (1997). *Governance and sustainable human development.*

Educational Administration Innovation for Sustainable Development – Komariah et al. (Eds)
© 2018 Taylor & Francis Group, London, ISBN 978-1-138-57341-3

Preparing our future educational leaders: The story behind the construction of a unique postgraduate program in educational leadership and management

D.L. Giles
Flinders University, South Australia

ABSTRACT: We are in a time when there is an unprecedented demand for educational leaders. In the urgency of preparing our future leaders, universities can overlook the importance of practicing and emergent leaders *knowing about* leadership as well as constructing their leadership practice knowledge from experiences of *being in* leadership. Similarly, leadership preparation is inadequate when the focus of the learning is risk-aversion, managerial imperatives, and programs that strip the intricacies and uncertainties of *being in* a particular leadership context. Decontextualized leadership programs are harmful at best and lessen the space for critical dialogue surrounding the adaptive nature of leadership and the formation of organizational cultures which respond to the everyday realities of a local context. This presentation draws upon an ongoing phenomenological research agenda which focuses on the centrality of relationships in the preparation and formation of leaders, leadership and organizational cultures. Moving from previous research findings on the essential nature of relationships in leadership, the presentation considers a unique Educational Leadership and management program that has been re-constructed and is now taught in Australia and China with significant success.

1   THE BROADER SOCIO-POLITICAL CONTEXT OF EDUCATION

The current ideological context of education shapes not only the discourse on education but also the nature of professional development for leaders and managers. This ideology is widespread and systemic at political and local levels. The ideological presence is at times subliminal to our everyday experience and often becomes our new 'common sense'. A basic tenet of this ideological position is that human beings are fundamentally self-accumulating and selfish; predisposed to maximising their private good in the face of a public good. The role of Government in this ideology is both minimalistic and authoritarian, and primarily revolves around compliance and adherence to the ideological implications for life and practice. Those administering educational policy and funds, not necessarily experienced educators rather graduates of business and economic programs constructing policies for the distribution of funds in education seek to do so with the utmost efficiency and effectiveness required of a managerialist ideology. The performativity, accountability, risk-minimization, administration, and industrial relations within education are engineered in favor of the ideological priorities.

While educational organizations have some flexibility in terms of their operation, much of the expected practice is shaped by the ideological position. The purpose of education within an economic rationalist ideology shifts from an educated citizen towards the equipping of young adults as economic units within a capitalist society. Not surprisingly, the administration of educational endeavours shifts towards quantitative and evidence-based priorities consistent with business acumen.

Rather than speak of educational learning experiences, it seems befitting to refer to educational activity, and indeed leadership, as a transaction. Pedagogically, the 'expert' teacher transacts with students for a demonstrable outcome. Students interact with teachers for clarity of expectation towards an explicit outcome. Organisational leaders transact with teachers for improved performance as measured by students' results. In this objectified scenario, the transactional nature of education is a matter of efficiency and effectiveness. The value-added aids to learners' social capital and economic position contrasting with an egalitarian view that an individual's education is a matter of empowerment and social justice.

2 RUNNING COUNTER TO THE DOMINANT IDEOLOGY OF THE DAY; THE ONTOLOGICAL NATURE OF RELATIONSHIPS IN EDUCATION

The purpose of ontological research is to explore and uncover shared understandings about a phenomenon of interest that have been taken for granted in our everyday lived experiences within the dominant ideology (Giles, 2008; Giles, Smythe & Spence, 2012; Giles, 2009). This article draws upon an ongoing ontological research agenda focused on the centrality of relationships in the formation of leaders, leadership and organizational cultures. Such research brings into question what we have taken for granted in the meanings of our lived experiences of being *in* leadership.

3 FINDINGS FROM PHENOMENOLOGICAL AND ONTOLOGICAL INQUIRIES

Recent phenomenological research exploring the nature of relationships (Giles, 2008) had four ontological findings, which, I argue, are significant to any discussion on the ongoing formation of leadership and organizational cultures. Indeed, an ongoing research agenda is further detailing shared and cross cultural understandings of the implications and application of these findings to the framing of leadership and organizational cultures, as well as being central to the construction of a postgraduate educational leadership program for practicing and emergent leaders. The four very powerful ontological findings from the phenomenological research on the everyday nature of relationships are briefly summarised as follows:

We are always, already in relationships (Giles, 2011a).

To be human is to relate. Ontologically we are not just beings in the world; we are beings *together* in the world. Our relationships continue in the presence or absence of others. In addition, relationship can start but the relationship never ends. Relationships have an enduring quality. Implications exist for leadership and organisational cultures.

Relationships exist in the space between us.

Objectively and historically, we have thought of relationships as being about the individuals (or objects) involved. Ontologically, we have taken for granted that relationships exist in the space 'between' those relating. The moral and ethical responsibility for the nature of a particular relationship belongs to all those involved in the relationship.

Relationships are always mattering whether we are aware of this or not (Giles, 2011b).

The ontological nature of being in the world is relational such that relationships are always mattering to our everyday experiences. From the outset, 'who we are' and 'how we are' is felt and read by others. The 'reading' of another begins before words are spoken and continues on within the lived experience of being in relationship. As humans we show our 'way of being' in everyday experiences. Our way of being has a communicative aspect. Leaders and teachers embody their way of being such as who they are and how they are is read and felt by others. I argue that, within an organization, the collective expression of how relationships are mattering is representative of the 'mood' of the organization.

Being in relationships is like being in a 'play of relating' (Giles, 2010).

The experience of being 'in' relationship remains uncertain. We engage with many uncertainties that we have limited to no control over; relationships included. It is as if we are caught up in a 'dramatic play' without a script to read from or refer to. Caught up in the play, and becoming aware of the movement of those relating reinforces the need to attune to the nature of the relationships and they're relating. We never seem to have complete control over our relationships. Being in the play then, involves the growth of relational sensibilities that enable of wisdom in particular experiences to grow.

The findings of these ontological inquires influences my thinking and research on the formation and practices within leadership. The nature of the relationship that exists between a leader and their colleagues influences the experience of those within the organization. Organization cultures involve the relational spaces between individuals that influence the mood of the organization. In summary, relationships are integral to being human and yet the nature of particular relationships and our way of relating can be taken for granted.

4 THE ONTOLOGICAL NATURE OF RELATIONSHIPS IN EDUCATION LEADERSHIP: RELATIONAL LEADERSHIP

In addition to the ontological findings above on the relational nature of education, further research using interview data from leaders in education explored the ontological nature of leadership through an exploration of everyday lived experiences of *being in* or *being with* leadership. Using the leaders' narratives enabled an ontological framing of the nature of leadership. In addition to confirming previously held ideas, that leadership is inherently relational, and relationships are the essence of leadership, I constructed an ontological description of "*relational leadership*".

Ontologically, the essence of relational leadership was constructed as follows: *Relational leadership*

- lives 'towards' a deep moral commitment to critical, humane and connected inter-relationships,
- lives 'out' a way that authentically models and embodies care-full relationships (individually and organizationally)
- 'attunes' to the subtleties of the immediate, dynamic & relational context through refined relational sensibilities
- Enacts a refined *phronesis* shown in relational sensibilities such as attunement, tact, nous, resoluteness, improvisation, moral judgment etc. (Giles, 2014; Giles & Palmer, 2015; Giles, Bills & Otero, 2015; Giles & Bills, 2017)

It is important to note that the expression, *relational leadership*, is not to be seen as another style of leadership, rather the purpose of the expression was to provide a reminder of the ontological nature of leadership; that leadership is always relational, and relationships are the essence of leadership.

The research findings describing everyday experiences of being *in,* or being *with* a leader, revealed the presence of taken for granted relational sensibilities (Giles, 2010; Giles & Palmer, 2015; Giles, 2014; Giles et al., 2015) that were inherently involved in leaders' everyday experiences of relating (Bills, Giles, & Rogers, 2016; Giles, 2015a). For example, where a leader show a 'resoluteness' within the complexities of a particular context, such resolve can be seen and felt by others. However, if the resoluteness was merely an act of 'power' over others, this too is felt and changes the nature of the future relating with this leader. Importantly, if a leader does not take the time to reflect on their everyday experiences then there is a lost opportunity for the growth of wisdom. In my view, relational sensibilities are not only integral to the nature and experience of leading but also contributes towards the development of the leader's practical wisdom.

5 PREDOMINANT FEATURES OF MANY EDUCATIONAL LEADERSHIP AND MANAGEMENT COURSES

Having described ontological understandings of relationships and 'Relational Leadership', I consider the significance of such findings for the design and delivery of courses and programs for educational leadership. In addition, I describe a particular educational leadership course which has intentionally engaged in the application of ontological findings and approaches to the study of the lived experiences of leaders. (For more specific comment, see Giles et al., 2016; Giles, 2017; Giles, et al., 2012, 2016).

We are in a time when there is an unprecedented demand for educational leaders. During these times, we can make the mistake of attempting to *fast track* leaders' professional learning or, similarly, concern, we can create leadership courses that *decontextualize* the learning. Courses like this are inadequate when they focus amounts to risk-aversion, managerial imperatives, and programs that strip the intricacies and uncertainties of *being in* a particular educational context. The provision of very generalized information about leadership alongside a priority for upskilling managerial skills should not be called educational, instead they should be called *training* programs given their reductionist approach to leadership preparation.

In the urgency of preparing our future educational leaders, universities too can overlook the important difference of *knowing about* leadership alongside constructing practice knowledge related to knowing, doing and being *in* leadership. There needs to be space for critical dialogue surrounding the adaptive nature of leadership and the everyday realities of *being a leader* in a local context.

5.1 *Preparation and development*

Just as educational practices have been influenced by the dominant ideology so too has the preparation and discourse of leaders and managers in education. It would seem that the preparation and development of educational leaders and managers is often a matter of up-skilling and increasing an individual's knowledge and understandings of important processes. The concern for capacity building and the development of competencies is seen as a priority for individuals and organisations alike.

Many, however, would argue that this form of professional development is technicist in nature in that an individual's technical skills and abilities are the priority. Similarly, this instrumental approach to professional development is conveniently measureable and thereby linked to individual performance and compliance, without serious consideration and critique of the problematic nature of a leader's lived experiences (Giles et al., 2016).

Providers of professional development typically use 'best practises' that have worked in the past. Pragmatic solutions to common problems are addressed with reference to a champion in the field. These heroes share their solutions as practices that are meant to be widely applicable and often without regard for the local context. The concern here is that generic professional preparation of this type can become formulaic, where emergent leaders are expected to follow the hero in 'doing as they say not doing as they do'. Local contexts are always different, idiosyncratic and culturally unique. While technical and instrumental approaches to leadership preparation can assist, critical education calls for leadership to engage in the reciprocity of their leadership and their immediate context (Giles et al., 2016).

6 THE FLINDERS STORY OF ONTOLOGICALLY RE-PURPOSING AN EDUCATIONAL LEADERSHIP COURSE

6.1 *What don't we stand for: managerialist approaches*

Whereas management focuses on doing things right (a matter of efficiency and effectiveness), leadership should focus on doing the right things. Since the 1980s, with the rise of the dominant ideology, managerial priorities appear to be advanced at the expense of much needed Educational Leadership. Education and leadership are always contextual; Leadership occurs in context and context influences leadership. While similarities exist across contexts, humane and relational leadership attend to the special character of the local context. The moral imperative of education is being lost to technicist and instrumental priorities in education. Purpose-driven educational models need to be constructed and modelled for their authenticity (Giles et al., 2016).

6.2 Re-purposing

This paper shares some of the story behind the repurposing of an Educational Leadership course at Flinders University. As faculty researching and teaching Educational leadership and management, we collaboratively developed a stance on the inclusion of ontological, phenomenological and Appreciative Inquiry approaches in educational leadership courses (Chapman & Giles, 2009; Giles, 2014; Giles & Alderson, 2008; Giles, & Kung, 2014; Kung, Giles, & Hagan, 2013; Giles & Kung, 2010). We recording this process of shaping the 'special character' of in our first book (Giles et al., 2012) entitled "Co-constructing a relational approach to Educational Leadership and management". A more recent 2nd addition, entitled "Teaching within a relational approach to educational leadership" (Giles et al., 2016) was published last year. Further description will be available when the Giles (2017) text on relational leadership is published.

This article tells of the efforts of a team of academics who are known as the leadership workgroup within the College of Education, Psychology and Social work at Flinders University. As a team we are responsible for the teaching, research and administration that relates to the post-graduate educational leadership courses and topics within the school. The team is made up of part-time teaching staff, lecturers and professors with interests across the educational sector and a corresponding breadth of research interests. We share the view that organisational leadership is critical to educational organisations.

In 2011, and with the arrival of additional personnel, we revisited the rationale for our educational leadership course. We reflected on what we had stood for in the past? We considered how this might change in the future? On the one hand this was internally driven with personnel changes and, on the other hand, the opportunity arose from external requests about the nature of our course. With partnership opportunities afoot, and with a consensus to authentically engage with others, we embarked on a single meeting that went for more than a year (Giles et al., 2014, 2016). We asked questions about new topics that were being developed. How did they fit within the structure of the course? Why was this new content relevant and what synergies exist between the topics? How is the content and intent of our course modelled by academic staff?

These questions are easier to write now as we have walked a distance together. A lack of consensus amongst the academic team could have resulted in an eclectic course designed to graduate students without an integrative philosophy. We asked ourselves, what is the rationale for our course as a whole? After eight months we intentionally sought to develop and record shared understandings for our practise that was a result of rich dialogic and collegial activity. The goal was not to get the 'right' rationale nor was it to recall the 'loudest'. We were committed to developing shared understandings that were inclusive of our different experiences and convictions about leadership.

While the documents might have an appearance of permanence, it is just that, an appearance. The position taken was that the document is metaphorically like a signpost that points to what is critically important to us. Our experiences and understandings shape the special character that is known as Educational Leadership at Flinders University.

6.3 A relational approach

First and fore most leadership practice is a relational endeavour. To be human is to co-exist (Nancy, 2000). Relationships and leadership coexist and confluence (Gergen, 2009). Our relational approach is underscored by a social constructionist philosophy which highlights the relational nature of education by drawing attention to the ongoing formation of human beings as a dynamic and social process of becoming. The preparation and development of educational leaders and managers should be re-languaged as a process of formation. The idea here is that leadership formation relates to an individual's *being* and *becoming*.

Leadership is a phenomenon that exists in everyday experiences. Embracing leadership as a phenomenon problematizes leadership as uncertain and dynamic; characteristics that are readily found in leadership stories. Leadership is uncertain, 'always in the making', can never be taken for granted and never be considered as a prescription or be prescriptive. While definitions and concepts are convenient tools for thinking, ontological inquiries appear to privilege more holistic considerations of the reciprocity within leadership. If leadership formation is an ongoing process, how do the lives of academics model this? How does the organisational culture value and support the holistic formation of emergent, inspiring and current leaders? When leadership is considered in a holistic manner the dialogue cannot avoid moral imperatives that relate to an ethic of care and critical concerns for social justice. Means and ends cannot be separated.

The notion of leadership formation is consistent with critical and humanistic perspectives where an individual's formation is a growth process rather than a matter of deficits and compliance. Our position is that leadership formation should explicitly build upon strengths. 'Strengths-based' approaches point to the priority of identifying, enhancing and leveraging students' strengths. While the conversation around strengths appears to be antithetical to academic pursuit and deconstructive activity, strengths-based approaches are essential to holistic leadership formation. A consideration of strengths should be within the context of the moral imperative 'of' education and the critical humanistic agenda 'for' education. Where strengths advance an emancipatory agenda for education, strengths engender a dignity and appreciation of diversity for a public good.

One particular strengths-based strategy is the life-centric process called 'Appreciative Inquiry'. Appreciative Inquiry is a research approach that involves systematic exploration of experiential narratives. Originally conceptualised by Cooperrider and Srivastva (1987), the approach involves a positive disposition in the investigation of 'what is working' for individuals and groups. In the Flinders course, students engage in appreciative inquiries that explore the 'life' within their own professional practise and that of the organisations with which they are associated.

6.4   *A relational pedagogy*

Our commitment to a strengths-based, social constructionist lens involves turning back on the assumptions that underpin traditional pedagogies and re-purposing educational endeavor sustaining a contemplation of leadership as ongoing, active and always in-*form*-ation (Bell & Palmer, 2015).

Both staff and students bring their previous learning to timetabled workshops, distance modules and supervisory sessions that have been co-constructed. The learnings are drawn together in relational re-co-constructing processes that are at the heart of educative endeavours. Relational spaces are dialogic in nature, offering multiple emerging storylines that may simultaneously converge and diverge but that always sustain the rich diversity of meaning foregrounding the roles of context, history, locality and culture in our considerations of educational leadership.

In the living out of our aspirations, the team have engaged with students more holistic pedagogical tools. Among these are narratives, strengths-based planning tools, peak event analysis, phenomenological writing and thematic, reflective journaling. At the heart of each of these tools is a dialogic process of inquiry.

Our prioritisation of relationships is a recognition that relationships are essential to our humanity. These generative spaces open opportunities for a re-fresh-ing of our views, strategies and aspirations. Thus relational pedagogy is more than a prioritisation of relationships. Relational pedagogies are an active re-co-construction that reshapes who we are and how we are together. It invites us to enter the play and to improvise.

6.5   *Essential themes*

In the re-purposing of an educational leadership course, several essential themes were identified and articulated which underpinned our redevelopment at a topic level. These themes situate our distinct contribution to leadership formation in education. The themes are as follows (Giles et al., 2012, 2016):

- The ongoing professional learning of leaders
- Leadership formation as a critical and humanistic endeavour
- The relational and contextual nature of leadership
- Strengths-based & sustainable approaches to leadership.

6.6 The ongoing professional learning of leaders

The *ongoing professional* learning of educational leaders is a *vitally important priority* for leadership, management, sustainability of schools, educational organisations and the wider community. Professional learning for those in leadership is an *ongoing, continuous process*. The process of formation experientially does not start and stop. Instead professional learning involves an accumulating set of experiences that afford opportunities for reflective and contemplative consideration. In a similar way, we argue that professional learning is *always holistic* in that a leader's knowledge, understanding, skills and dispositions, are directly related to the leader's way of being in practice. The development of practical wisdom, a matter beyond the accumulation of skills and knowing, involves reflective and contemplative considerations that are integral to the experience of leading and formed over a long period of time.

We privilege the expression, leadership formation, over and above the language of preparation and development. The use of the word *formation* captures the notion that leaders and leadership reside within a continuous process of *form*-ation and re-*form*-ation; being and becoming. The leaders' and managers' holistic formation is set within an educational context. As such the formation has a moral imperative where the change processes are directional in as much as they are for the sake of others. Personal formation then is both a private and a public good.

While leaders hold positional power, deeper transformative change processes are more readily found where individuals and groups are shown what the particular change looks like as it is embodied by those in leadership. Educational leadership programs for emergent and practicing leaders should draw upon leaders' prior experiential learning. Past experiences provide phenomenological data that can be interpreted and analysed to show how leaders have been *in* leadership in concrete, specific and local situations. Interpretive and hermeneutic activity can show inter-relationships between leadership and context, with the hope of deepening sensitivities to the subtleties of practice.

6.7 Leadership formation as a critical and humanistic endeavor

The formation of educational leaders is a *critical & humanistic concern* with implications for leadership, educational processes, as well as the partnering of educational organisations within their community. We use the word *critical* here as a Frierian expression. For us the contribution of critical theory is a call to individual empowerment on the one hand and a greater social justice on the other. Similarly, we refer to leadership formation as a humanistic endeavour to signal the holistic, relational and *person*-al nature of educative experiences.

As a critical & humanistic endeavour, our course is intentionally orientated towards *sustainable* and *socially just* practices. In so doing we challenge, and ask our students to challenge *deficit theorising* of education generally, and leadership practice and students' learning, more specifically. Freire's notion of *conscientization* involves the bringing to awareness of values, beliefs and ideologies that are systemic to, and hegemonic within, social and political constructs. Learning, indeed education, from a critical perspective is consistently concerned with the leader as an agent of change. The leader is also the articulator of continuity, which is aimed at, and central to, challenging socio-cultural power structures. Of importance here for Freire, is that change processes are initiated from within the leader as the basis of the courage and tenacity required to challenge socio-political power structures. The leader as a person is critical to the task of leadership. While leadership is a professional role, from a critical perspective, leadership is an embodied praxis.

Leaders need to be able to conduct personal and organisational *enquiries,* along with the ability to read meaning from the data and formulate possibilities for action. Leaders need to be able to employ interpretive and *self-reflective and self-assessment processes* which deepens their sensitivities and awareness to the nature and movement of their relational context. Critical and humanistic practices are invariably located within a wider educational community and beyond to include para-educational organisations. To this end, educational leaders need to be able to *network* with other leaders in an ongoing and critical dialogue. This may be initiated in educational leadership and courses where inter-relationships are valued within and beyond the course.

6.8 The relational and contextual nature of leadership

Our programme of professional learning for educational leaders advocates and promotes the *relational nature of education and leadership*. Leadership is a relational endeavour that is experienced locally, in situ, and in the complex and dynamic demands of *context*. Situational demands influence, enable, limit and constrain a leader's practice. We see as the essence of educational leadership, being that of relationships and leadership. When leadership inquiries start from the phenomenon of leadership, the relational and contextual nature of leadership is always evident. Drawing upon ontological research findings, our course privileges relational leadership as a reminder of the essence of leadership over conceptualizing adjectival leadership styles alone.

Relational leadership and relational sensibilities go hand in hand. In the experience of leading, relational leaders show a range of sensibilities. Wise leaders develop practical wisdom show sensibilities that include tact, nous, improvisation, attunement, moral judgement and the like. This approach collapses the false dichotomies that separate knowledge and skills, vision and values into a singular and holistic mode of inquiry.

The challenge for providers of educational leadership is to develop these sensibilities within current and future leaders. While the pursuit of best practice is academically fruitful, experiential learning and a consideration of relational sensibilities shows leadership practice to be beyond recipes and beyond rules of engagement. The point here is that leadership relates to a way of being, which is immersed in a dynamic and emergent context. Leaders who are aware of the contextual complexity of the education sector appreciate the macro and micro subtleties of the local, political, economic, cultural and ideological influences on education. A leader's ability to repurpose and re-culture an organisation is contingent upon their abilities and sensibilities to read the immediate and multi-layered context.

6.9 Strengths-based and sustainable approaches to leadership

The formation of educational leaders should be underpinned by *strengths-based approaches* that provide a life-centric way of examining professional practice in context. Strengths-based approaches are always holistic in nature. Strengths based approaches affirm the individuality of individuals as a strategy for inter-dependence and the development of a sense of community. One particular strategy that students are coached in is Appreciative Inquiry. This approach engages with lived experiences in a grounded manner and is applicability to both individual and organizational formation.

Strengths-based strategies invariably focuses attention on the critical matter of sustainability in that it focuses on strengths and is predisposed towards an agenda that is hope-full and grounded. While some would advocate appreciative inquiry as a future's focused capacity building strategy, we suggest that the power of appreciative inquiry is individuals' reconstructed positive and personal narrative. Empowered through the identification and development of personal strengths, individual's self-efficacy and agency are enhanced. The sustainability of educational leaders personally and professionally is merged within a strengths-based holistic inquiry.

7 CONCLUSION

In addition to the declining numbers of educators who are willing to step into a leadership positions, there is also an urgent need for Educational Leadership and management courses that can support the formation of these leaders. The notion of re-purposing is a call to reinstate a purpose of education that is shared by teacher and leaders as well as forming the foundation of a special character statement which speaks of the unique contribution of a particular course and program.

Courses for aspiring, emergent and organizational leadership need to have courses that are contextualized. In this way, the courses engender relevance and meaningfulness as well as drawing these leaders into a deepening critique of the relational nature of their local context. It is in the local context where a leader's way-of-being shows how personal and professional challenges of leadership are experienced. Priority must be given to the ontological nature of leadership as this is experienced by the leaders 'being and becoming in' leadership.

REFERENCES

Bell, M. & Palmer. C. 2015. Shaping a strengths-based approach to relational leadership. In H. Askell-Williams. *Transforming the Future of Learning with Educational Research.* Hershey, PA: IGI Global.

Bills, A. M., Giles, D., & Rogers, B. 2016. 'Being in' and 'feeling seen' in professional development as new teachers: the ontological layer(ing) of professional development practice. *Australian Journal of Teacher Education, 41*(2).

Chapman, L., & Giles, D. L. 2009. Using appreciative inquiry to explore the professional practice of a Midwife Lecturer. *Studies in Continuing Education 31*(3): 297–305.

Gergen, K. 2009. *Relational being: Beyond self and community.* New York: Oxford University Press.

Giles, D. L. 2008. *Exploring the teacher-student relationship in teacher education: A hermeneutic phenomenological inquiry.* Unpublished doctoral thesis, Auckland University of Technology, Auckland.

Giles, D. L. 2009. Phenomenologically researching the lecturer-student teacher relationship: Some challenges that were encountered. *Indo-Pacific Journal of Phenomenology, 9*(2), online.

Giles, D. L. 2010. Developing pathic sensibilities: A critical priority for teacher education programmes. *Teaching and Teacher Education 26* (8): 1511–1519.

Giles, D. L. 2011a. Relationships always matter in education: Findings from a phenomenological inquiry. *Australian Journal of Teacher Education 36* (6): 80–91.

Giles, D. L. 2011b. 'Who we are' and 'how we are' are integral to relational experiences: exploring comportment in teacher education. *Australian Journal of Teacher Education 36*(1): 60–72.

Giles, D. 2014. Appreciatively Building Higher Educator's Relational Sensibilities. *The Journal of Meaning-Centered Education.* Volume 2, Article 1, Retrivied from http://www.meaningcentered.org/appreciatively-building-higher-educators-relational-sensibilities.

Giles, D. L. 2015a. A storyline of ideological change in a New Zealand primary school. *International Journal of Organisational Analysis 23*(2): 320–332.

Giles, D.L. 2015. *Exploring teacher-student relationships with hermeneutic phenomenology.* Germany: Lambert Press.

Giles, D.L. 2017+. *Relational Leadership: a phenomenon of inquiry and practice.* [Publication under review London: Routledge].

Giles, D. L., & Alderson, S. 2008. An Appreciative Inquiry into the transformative learning experiences for students in a family literacy project. *Australian Journal of Adult Learning 48*(3): 465–478.

Giles, D. L., Bell, M., Halsey, J., & Palmer, C. 2012. *Co-constructing a relational approach to educational leadership and management.* Melbourne: Cengage.

Giles, D. L., Bell, M., Halsey, J., Palmer, C., Bills, A. & Rogers, B. 2016. *Teaching within a relational approach to educational leadership* (2nd edition). Melbourne: Cengage. URL: Giles et al, 2016.

Giles, D.L., Bills, A., & Otero, G. 2015. Pedagogical approaches for developing relational sensibilities in educational leaders. *Reflective Practice 16*(6): 744–752.

Giles, D.L. & Bills, A. 2017. Designing and using an organisational culture inquiry tool to glimpse the relational nature of leadership and organisational culture within a primary school.' *School Leadership and Management 37*(1&2): 120–140.

Giles, D. L., & Kung, S. 2010. Using Appreciative Inquiry to explore the professional practice of a lecturer in Higher Education: Moving towards life-centric practice. *Australian Journal of Adult Learning 50*(2): 308–322.

Giles, D. L., & Kung, S. 2014. Revisiting student's learning experiences appreciatively: Findings from a course evaluation using an Appreciative Inquiry process. *Journal of Applied Research in Higher Education 6*(2): 215–230.

Giles, D. & Palmer, C. 2015. Exploring a Principal's Practice during a Period of Significant Organizational Change: Relational Leadership and Sensibilities in Action. *The Journal of Meaning-Centered Education.* Volume 3, Article 1, http://www.meaningcentered.org/exploring-a-principals-practice-during-a-period-of-significant-organizational-change-relational-leadership-and-sensibilities-in-action.

Giles, D. L., Smythe, E. A., & Spence, D. G. 2012. Exploring relationships in education: A phenomenological inquiry. Australian Journal of Adult Learning 52 (2): 214–236.

Kung, S., Giles, D.L., & Hagan, B. 2013. Applying an Appreciative Inquiry process to a course evaluation in Higher Education. *International Journal of Teaching and Learning in Higher Education 25*(1): 29–37.

Educational Administration Innovation for Sustainable Development – Komariah et al. (Eds)
© 2018 Taylor & Francis Group, London, ISBN 978-1-138-57341-3

The role of parents in Sundanese language preservation

D. Haerudin
Indonesia University of Education, Bandung, West Java, Indonesia

ABSTRACT: This paper presents one of the results of research on 'A Need Analysis of Mother Tongue Program Development 2013.' The study aimed to describe the efforts of parents in the preservation of the Sundanese language as a native language and a local language. The description of this paper includes the use of Sundanese language in everyday life at home and in its surrounding environment; in communication with teachers at school; the importance of instilling manners of speaking (*undak-usuk/unggah-ungguh*) into children; the importance of Sundanese language teaching in schools; the importance of children learning local culture; the types of culture that children learn; the efforts of parents to encourage children to learn the culture; and the opinion that the local language is used as the language of education at the elementary level. The research used descriptive method. The data collection technique in this study was a questionnaire technique questionnaire. The instrument used to collect data was a list of questions or questionnaires that would be distributed to each respondent. The data analysis technique used in this research was descriptive statistical analysis techniques. This study concludes that the preservation of Sundanese should begin in houses, where parents use it in communicating with members of the family. Parents must motivate, encourage, and facilitate children, or other family members, to have an understanding of the importance of Sundanese language as the local language, as well as having proper Sundanese language skills.

1 INTRODUCTION

There are various problems underlying this study. They include the weak language skills of young children, the fact that Sundanese is not introduced in the family environment, and the low of public attention to the Sundanese language. Public indifference toward local language marks the start of the decline of the position and the function of Sundanese language among communities. This will decrease the number of speakers (Brock, 2015), the value strength, and the significance of the local language. Likewise, the Sundanese language, in turn, will be abandoned by the community, especially the younger generation, because they do not understand the language's position and functions.

Kartini (1982) states that the Sundanese language is more widely used in rural areas (outside the city) than in urban areas. On the results of the study, it is also explained that the use of Sundanese language in West Java is also influenced by pressures. The definition of pressure in the study refers to the speaking partner, who is the higher-ranking or older (Panicacci & Dewaele, 2017).

To address the problems certainly requires the cooperation of all parties, especially the family environment (parents) and educational institutions. It is important to expose knowledge and understanding of the cultural richness embodied in language and literature, as a valuable treasure and universal source of local wisdom (Cornhill, 2014).

Therefore, this paper presents one of the results of research on 'A Need Analysis of Mother Tongue Program Development 2013.' One of the results is the efforts of parents to empower Sundanese language in the districts of Bungbulang, Garut Regency, and Pasir Jambu, Bandung Regency.

2 LITERATURE REVIEW

2.1 *Sundanese as a local language*

The local language, as stated in the conclusion of National Language Politics 1975, in Alwasilah (1989), has several functions. The functions are to be a symbol of regional pride, a symbol of regional identity, a means of communication in the family environment and the local community, a benefactor of the national language, the language of instruction in elementary schools in a certain area, a development tool, and a benefactor of local culture. A similar idea is also stated by Hult and Källkvist (2016) and Grünigen et al. (2012).

In detail, the function and the status of local languages cover the following. Firstly, the survival and development of local languages that continue to be maintained by the speech communities is part of Indonesian cultural life that is guaranteed by the Constitution of 1945. Secondly, the local languages are cultural treasures that can be used for the sake of not only development and standardization of our national language, but also for the sake of promotion and development of local languages, and therefore they need to be maintained. Thirdly, the local languages are the epitome of socio-cultural values that reflect and tie the culture of the speech community. Fourthly, the local languages are varied, not only in their structure but also in the number of their native speakers. Fifthly, certain local languages are used as a calculation tool, either orally or in writing, while other local languages are only used orally. Sixthly, in terms of growth and development, a local language influences and, at the same time, is influenced by the national language, other local languages, and particular foreign languages. The phenomenon occurs because of the increase of Indonesian language users, the increase of the smoothness of the relationship between regions, and the increase of population outflow, as well as the number of marriages between ethnic groups.

Sundanese language, like other local languages, is under the protection of the state. The Constitution of 1945 (*Undang-Undang Dasar*, 1945), Chapter IV, Explanation of Article 36, states, 'In regions that have their own languages which are well-maintained by their people (i.e., Javanese, Sundanese, Madurese, and so on), the languages will be respected and well-maintained by the state also. The languages are the part of the live Indonesian culture'.

Local languages grow and develop in West Java, as contained in Local Regulation number 5 of 2003, Chapter I, Article 1 (7), are Sundanese, Cirebon, and Betawi-Malay. Sundanese is also the second language with the largest number of speakers in Indonesia. The speakers are spread over almost the entire region of West Java, except in the Cirebon territories that use languages of Cirebon, and some parts of Bogor, Depok, and Bekasi, which use Betawi-Malay.

2.2 *The empowerment of Sundanese in the family environment*

Language is powerful – having power, useful, and valuable – when it is controlled and used by its speakers in everyday life (Menegatti & Rubini, 2013). The people of a nation, especially the children/youth that control local language, will inherit their cultural norms (i.e. identity). Likewise, the Sundanese language will be beneficial if it is maintained and developed by the speech community. The Sundanese, in fact, are full of cultural norms.

Language is the most prominent distinguishing feature because language makes each social group feel itself to be a distinct entity from the other groups (Reyes, 2017). A child has the potential of language skills since the day she/he is born. Mastering language is highly dependent on the language heard in everyday life. Therefore, family determines a child's first language skills. Sundanese introduced to children from an early age within the family becomes the mother tongue of the child.

Douglas (2008) proposed the First Language Acquisition Theory in his book *Principles of Language Learning and Teaching* that children actually have a prominent ability to communicate. Babies chatter and weep, with or without sound, sending so many messages and receiving more messages. In their research, they state that when children are aged one year, they try to imitate words and pronounce sounds they hear.

At 18 months old, the number of words is multiplied, and they begin to appear in 'sentences' with two or three words. The sentence is commonly called 'telegraphic' (telegram style) utterances. At two years old, children understand language that is more sophisticated, and they expand their speaking skills, even to form negative statements and questions.

At 3 years old, children can receive a quantity of extraordinary linguistic inputs. Their speech and comprehension abilities increase rapidly when they become manufacturers of nonstop chattering. Their conversation is incessant. Language becomes a blessing and a curse for the people around them! Their creativity only brings smiles to their parents and siblings.

Language fluency and creativity of a child continues until school age. At school age, when studying the social functions of language, children not only learn what they have to say but also what they cannot say. Introduction of Sundanese, in its capacity as a local language, actually is not only important in the family environment, but also in the formal context of the school environment.

This is consistent with the results of the Seminar on National Language Politics in 1975. The formulation of the seminar states that the development of the teaching of local languages is aimed at improving the quality of teaching of the local language that its speakers have: (1) local language skills; (2) good knowledge of local language; and (3) positive attitude toward local language and its literature. The teaching of local language is the means to (a) support the development of national culture elements; (b) direct the local language development; and (c) standardize the diversity of local languages'.

The teaching of local language (Sundanese) in school has an important function in the social life of Sundanese culture because it is an effective way to preserve, foster, and develop the language, literature, and social culture of Sundanese (Grünigen et al., 2012). Although it already has the legitimacy from the government, the teaching of local language (Sundanese) in West Java still faces various problems. Sudaryat (2001) mentions that the problems are (1) the lack of professional teachers; (2) the lack of interest and attitude of students; (3) the failure of the learning process; (4) the content of curriculum and teaching materials; and (5) the teaching environment.

One aspect of the issues raised is the environment in which children learn. Family is an environment that helps to determine the success of learning (Zolkoski & Bullock, 2012). It means that family support also greatly influences the children's success in learning language. Therefore, parents have an important role in supporting the success of local language mastery. There are fewer researches related to parental supervision of Sundanese. Therefore, this research is expected to provide useful information for the public.

This study aims to describe the use of Sundanese language in everyday life at home and its surrounding environment; in communication with teachers at school; the importance of instilling manners of speaking (*undak-usuk/unggah-ungguh*) into children; the importance of Sundanese language teaching in schools; the importance of children learning local culture; the types of culture that children learn; the efforts of parents to encourage children to learn the culture; and the opinion that the local language is used as the language of education at the elementary level.

3 RESEARCH METHOD

This research uses descriptive method. The steps cover a) collecting factual information in detail and describing the symptoms that exist; b) identifying the problems that exist; c) making comparisons; and d) determining things to be taken or the implications of those experiences for future planning and decision-making with regard to policies of Sundanese language guidance.

The respondents of the research were parents of students. The data was collected in two districts: the Bungbulang District of Garut Regency, Pasir Jambu and Ciwidey Districts of Bandung Regency. The data collection technique in this study was a questionnaire technique questionnaire. The instrument used to collect data was a list of questions or questionnaires that would be distributed to each respondent. The data analysis technique used in this research was descriptive statistical analysis techniques. The descriptive statistical analysis is to analyze the data by describing or depicting data that has been collected as it is.

4 RESULTS AND DISCUSSION

Respondents of this study were 138 parents of students, consisting of 55 men, 65 women, and 18 who did not mention their sex. The age of respondents is ranged between 20–25 years (3), 25–30 years (24), 30–35 years (44), 35–40 years (10), 40–45 years (30), 45–50 years (3), 50–55 years (2), 50–60 years (1), over 60 years (1), and did not answer (32). Respondents came from two Regencies: 28 people from Garut (Bungbulang District); and Bandung (56 people from Pasir Jambu and 54 people from Ciwidey).

The instrument used to collect data about the role of parents in maintaining Sundanese is related to (1) the language used by parents in everyday life at home; (2) the language used by parents in daily life in the neighborhood around the house; (3) the language used by parents to communicate with teachers in schools; (4) the transformation of language manners (*undak-usuk/unggah-ungguh*) in children; (5) the importance of Sundanese language teaching in schools; (6) the importance of learning local culture; (7) the type of culture that children learn; (8) the efforts of parents to encourage children to learn local culture; and (9) the use of local language as the language of education at elementary level.

The data obtained from 138 respondents are as follows.

1) *The language used by parents in everyday life at home*
   There are 112 (81%) respondents who use local languages as a daily language in home. One (0.72%) respondent uses the national language. 12 (8.69%) respondents use a mixture of languages. 13 (9.42%) respondents did not answer.

2) *The language used by parents in everyday life in the neighborhood around the house*
   There are 125 (90.57%) respondents who use local language as their daily language in the environment around the house and 13 (9.42%) respondents who did not answer.

3) *The language used by parents to communicate with teachers in schools*
   There are 95 (68.84%) respondents who use the local language to communicate with teachers in school. Two (1.45%) respondents use the national language. 28 (20.29%) respondents use a mixture of languages. 13 (9.42%) respondents did not answer.

4) *Instilling manners of speaking (undak-usuk/unggah-ungguh) into children*
   There are 110 (79.71%) respondents who teach manners of speaking (*undak-usuk/unggah-ungguh*) to their children. 15 (10.87%) respondents do not teach. 13 (9.42%) respondents did not answer.

5) *The importance of Sundanese language teaching in schools*
   120 (86.95%) respondents agree that the local language should be taught in school. 18 (13.05%) respondents did not answer. There are various reasons for parents who agree that Sundanese need to be studied in schools. 38 (27.54%) respondents argue that it is because Sundanese is everyday language. 30 (21.74%) respondents argue that it is important for the preservation of the local language. 20 (14.49%) respondents state that it is to assist students to learn subjects quickly. 28 (20.29%) respondents state that it is because there are many children who cannot speak Sundanese well. 19 (13.77%) respondents state that children now feel no prestige to speak Sundanese. 12 (8.69%) respondents argue that it is important to make their children know manners. 27 (19.56%) respondents did not answer.

6) *The importance of learning local culture*
   There are 138 (100%) respondents who agree that their children should learn local culture.

7) *The types of culture that children should learn*
   Several respondents emphasized that there are certain types of culture that need to be learned by children. Practicing dance is mentioned by 92 (66.66%) respondents. Batik is proposed by 84 (60.86%) respondents. Practicing local music is agreed by 58 (40.03%) respondents. Practicing drama is mentioned by 54 (39.13%) respondents. Practicing a speech in the local language is proposed by 82 (59.42%) respondents. Reading poetry/singing local songs is agreed by 44 (31.88%) respondents. Learning etiquette/manners is mentioned by 15 (10.86%) respondents. Sundanese traditional games is proposed by 19 (13.77%) respondents.

8) *The efforts of parents to encourage their children to learn the local culture*
Parents do many things to make their children learning the local culture. Urging children to learn is proposed by 24 (17.39%) respondents. Urging children to read textbooks is mentioned by 2 (1.49%) respondents. Listening/watching news/information is only supported by 2 (1.49%) respondents. Introducing the local culture from an early age is considered important by 20 (14.49%) respondents. Attending local art performances is accepted by 21 (15.22%) respondents. Attending local contests is proposed by 32 (23.19%) respondents. Introducing Sundanese children's traditional games is supported by 20 (14.49%) respondents. Telling Sundanese stories is considered important by 19 (13.77%) respondents. Taking Sundanese courses is proposed by 17 (12.32%) respondents. No answer was given by 9 (6.52%) respondents.

9) *The local language should be used as instructional language of education in elementary school*
Parents mostly agree (106 respondents (76.81%)) that the local language should be used as the instructional language of teaching and learning activities at the elementary level. There was disagreement from only 5 (3.62%) respondents. Last, 27 (19.56%) respondents did not answer.

The reasons for parents' agreement cover many things. It is believed by 76 (55.07%) respondents that students understand teaching materials/learning more easily. One (0.72%) respondent perceives that children can be a champion/the first rank. Sundanese language clarifies/helps students to understand lessons; that is believed by 5 (3.62%) respondents. The Sundanese language course should be in curriculum; this is an idea of 5 (3.62%) respondents. There is only a small share of school hours for Sundanese lessons; there are 19 (13.77%) respondents who believe that thought. Sundanese language is very important for the preservation of culture; the view is held by 21 (15.22%) of respondents. The Sundanese language course should be mixed with Indonesian; the opinion is proposed by 15 (10.87%) respondents. Last, 17 (12.31%) respondents did not answer.

Respondents of this research still have concern and play an important role in preserving and empowering Sundanese in the region. The data shows 81% of parents using Sundanese language as the communication tool with family members at home. The condition supports efforts to conserve the local language (Sundanese), which is initiated in the family. The habit of using the local language with children at home also means the development of children as members of the family in learning to understand their identity as Sundanese. Parents place the local language according to its function. The functions of local languages (such as Sundanese, Javanese, Balinese, Madurese, Makassarese, and Batak) are to be (1) a symbol of regional pride; (2) a symbol of regional identity, (3) and a means of communication in the family environment and the local community (Alwasilah, 1985).

Parents do not use Sundanese language only at home but also in the surrounding environment. The data shows that 90.57% parents use Sundanese language every day as a means of communication with neighbors in their neighborhood. The condition describes the positive language behavior because the use of Sundanese in the neighborhood influences children's behavior and speech behavior. If members of society around the house are accustomed to using Sundanese in daily communication, it will impact on their children's attitudes to speak Sundanese language as the local language.

As noted by Coates (2015), the language attitude is marked by three characteristics: 1) language loyalty; 2) language pride; and 3) awareness of the norm. Language loyalty, according to the concept, is the attitude that encourages a society to maintain the independence of the language, or even to prevent the entry of foreign influence. Language pride is an attitude that encourages a person or a group to make a language into a symbol of personal or group identity, and to differentiate themselves from other people or groups. Awareness of the language norms encourages careful, lighter, polite, and decent use of language (Muñoz, 2014). Such awareness is a factor that will determine the speech behavior in the form of language use. Language fidelity, language pride, and language awareness are positive characteristics of language.

Parents generally always use Sundanese language to communicate with teachers. The data shows 68.84% parents using Sundanese language when communicating with teachers at school or in other places. Teachers as educators have a conservative role and provide a role model. Teachers show good speaking attitudes, not only to the students, also to the parents of the students. Likewise, the use of Sundanese with teachers in schools has become a habit for most people in the research. The parents try to show his or her identity. It means that parents have implemented one of the functions and position of Sundanese as a local language. As contained in the formulation of National Language Politics, 1975, 'the survival and development of local languages that continues to be maintained by the speech communities is parts of Indonesian cultural life that are guaranteed by the Constitution of 1945'.

Parents always seek to instill language manners (*undak-usuk/unggah-ungguh*) into children. The data shows 79.71% parents have attempted to instill or teach *undak-usuk/unggah-ungguh* of Sundanese to their children from an early age. It illustrates that generally the parents understand the importance of speaking manners. The use of speaking manners can create harmony in communication, maintain pragmatic attitude in speaking, instill mutual respect between people, and generate understanding of manners in civil society (a society that upholds values, norms, and laws, which are supported by the mastery of civilized faith, science, and technology). This is in line with the opinion of Yudibrata (1989), in the book *Bagbagan Makena Basa Sunda*, who states that pragmatically Sundanese is used for specific purposes in one situation. Rules of Sundanese use (*undak-usuk*) constitute the basic principles of how to implement the use of language. By learning *undak-usuk* of Sundanese, children understand and use language skillfully in communication. Pragmatic or the rules of language use propose training to be able to speak, to write, to read, and to listen; not teaching theories/knowledge/language systems that are formal and abstract.

Parents consider that it is important that the Sundanese language be taught in schools. The data shows that 86.95% parents state the need and the importance of the Sundanese language being taught in schools. This indicates that parents have a high sense of viewing the Sundanese language as a local language and mother tongue. In addition, they have an intelligent insight. They state that as the everyday language, Sundanese needs to be studied formally in school so that children have the ability to speak Sundanese well, including knowing manners, being capable of speaking subtle language, and not feeling embarrassed to speak Sundanese. This is in line with the objective of Sundanese language learning in school, as expressed in Sundanese Curriculum 2013, that students obtain experience and compose Sundanese language; appreciate and be proud of Sundanese language as the local language in West Java, which is also the mother tongue for most people; understand Sundanese in terms of form, meaning and function, and able to use it appropriately and creatively in various contexts (goals, purposes, and conditions); be able to use Sundanese to improve intellectual ability, emotional maturity, and social maturity; have the ability and discipline in Sundanese language (speaking, writing, and thinking); be able to enjoy and take advantage of literary works to improve the knowledge and ability of Sundanese language, personal development, and to expand the horizons of life; appreciate and be proud of Sundanese literature as a treasure of culture and the people of Sunda.

Parents state that children should learn local culture. The data shows 100% parents agree that their children should learn important local culture. The reasons are, among others, that children must have an identity (*kasundaan*), understand the environment in which they live – the Land of Sunda; and, the next generation of Sundanese culture in the future.

As for matters related to the types of culture that children should learn, parents suggest different types. They are, among others, 1) practicing dance and batik; 2) playing local music; 3) playing drama; 4) practicing speech in the local language; 5) reading poetry/singing local songs; 6) learning etiquette/manners; and 7) traditional Sundanese games (*kaulinan urang Sunda*).

Parents make some efforts so that their children want to learn the Sundanese culture, such as persuading children to read Sundanese textbooks; facilitating children to listen to/to watch news/information about Sundanese culture; introducing regional culture from an early age; registering their children to participate in art events, in contests and in games; fostering their children to listen to the stories in Sundanese language; and registering their children on courses of arts.

Parents agree that the local language should be used as the language of education at the elementary level. The data shows 76.81% parents support the Sundanese language as the language of instruction in schools. The reasons for parents' agreement cover many things. Some believe that students understand teaching materials/learn more easily. However, some parents claim that the Sundanese language should only be used as a medium to clarify/to help children to understand subjects, in addition as a medium of cultural preservation. That is, the Sundanese language is not used as a language of education, but the Sundanese language is used when the child does not understand materials. Local languages can be used in early grades of elementary school. As noted in the conclusion of National Language Politics of 1975 in Alwasilah (1985), that local languages can be used as media of instruction in elementary schools, especially the early grades. In addition, local language has several functions. The functions are to be a symbol of regional pride, a symbol of regional identity, a means of communication in the family environment and the local community, a benefactor of the national language, the language of instruction in elementary schools in a certain area, a development tool, and a benefactor of local culture.

5 CONCLUSIONS

The parents in the study area use Sundanese language in everyday life at home, in the neighborhood around the house, or when communicating with teachers in schools. The parents seek to provide examples of usage of speaking manners (*undak-usuk/unggah-ungguh*) in everyday life to their children. They agree that Sundanese language and culture are important to be taught in schools. They expect their children to learn the kinds of culture, such as practicing traditional dances, batik, folk music, drama, speech in the local language, read poetry/sing local songs, learning etiquette/manners, and traditional games. Parents make some efforts so that their children want to learn the Sundanese culture, such as persuading children to read Sundanese textbooks; facilitating children to listen to/to watch news/information about Sundanese culture; introducing regional culture from an early age; registering their children to participate in art events, in contests and in games; fostering their children to listen to the stories in Sundanese language; and registering their children on courses of arts.

REFERENCES

Alwasilah, A.C. (1985). *Sosiologi bahasa*. Bandung: Angkasa.
Brock, U.B. (2015). Language-in-education policies and practices in Africa with a special focus on Tanzania and South Africa. In *Second International Handbook on Globalisation, Education and Policy Research* (pp. 615–631). Netherlands: Springer.
Coates, J. (2015). *Women, men and language: A sociolinguistic account of gender differences in language*. Routledge.
Cornhill, D. (2014). *Tribal knowledge in early childhood education: A Ngāti Te Ata Waiohua case study*. Doctoral dissertation, Auckland University of Technology, Auckland, New Zealand.
Douglas, B.H. (2008). *Prinsip-prinsip pembelajaran dan pengajaran bahasa (edisi kelima)*. Jakarta: Kedutaan Besar Amerika Serikat.
Grünigen, R.V., Kochenderfer-Ladd, B., Perren, S. & Alsaker, F.D. (2012). Links between local language competence and peer relations among Swiss and immigrant children: The mediating role of social behavior. *Journal of School Psychology*, 50(2), 195–213.
Hult, F.M. & Källkvist, M. (2016). Global flows in local language planning: Articulating parallel language use in Swedish university policies. *Current Issues in Language Planning*, 17(1), 56–71.
Kartini, T. (1982). *Kedudukan dan fungsi Bahasa Sunda di Jawa Barat*. Jakarta: Pusat Pembinaan dan Pengembangan Bahasa.
Menegatti, M. & Rubini, M. (2013). Convincing similar and dissimilar others: The power of language abstraction in political communication. *Personality and Social Psychology Bulletin*, 39(5), 596–607.
Muñoz, C. (2014). Exploring young learners' foreign language learning awareness. *Language Awareness*, 23(1–2), 24–40.
Panicacci, A. & Dewaele, J.M. (2017). Do interlocutors or conversation topics affect migrants' sense of feeling different when switching languages? *Journal of Multilingual and Multicultural Development*, 1–16.

Reyes, A. (2017). *Language, identity, and stereotype among Southeast Asian American youth: The other Asian*. Routledge.

Sudaryat, Y. (2001). *Makalah Konferensi Internasional Budaya Sunda (KIBS) I*. Bandung: Panitia KIBS.

Undang-Undang Dasar. (1945) Negara Republik, Indonesia.

Yudibrata, K. (1989). *Bagbagan Makéna Basa Sunda*. Bandung: Rahmat Cijulang.

Zolkoski, S.M. & Bullock, L.M. (2012). Resilience in children and youth: A review. *Children and Youth Services Review*, 34(12), 2295–2303.

Educational Administration Innovation for Sustainable Development – Komariah et al. (Eds)
© 2018 Taylor & Francis Group, London, ISBN 978-1-138-57341-3

Teachers' teaching performance: Pedagogical competence, work motivation, school culture and profession allowance

D.L. Hakim, U.S. Sa'ud, A. Komariah & C. Sunaengsih
Universitas Pendidikan Indonesia, Bandung, Indonesia

ABSTRACT: The present study is concerned with the factors affecting vocational high school (SMK) teachers' teaching performance. The factors affecting teachers' teaching performance include: teachers' motivation, personality and emotion, competence, interest, work environment, school facilities and infrastructures, policy, administration, teachers' level of education, teaching supervision, development program, school culture, mental and physical condition, headmaster's leadership model, welfare guarantee, headmaster's managerial capability, training, and economic incentive. With these considerations, this study aims to empirically describe the effects of pedagogical competence, work motivation, school culture, and profession allowance variables, both individually and simultaneously, in relation to teachers' teaching performance. The study employs survey method, under quantitative approach, as the research methodology. The population for the study is teachers with teaching certifications in 50 SMKN in West Java. The findings show that pedagogical competence, work motivation, school culture and profession allowance variables have positive and significant influence upon teachers' teaching performance. Further, work motivation, school culture and professional allowance are important factors in increasing teaching performance.

1 INTRODUCTION

In order to improve education quality in general, since 2005 the Indonesian government has made a commitment to make educational quality improvements in developing teachers' professionalism. To that end, the Law No. 14/2005 on Teachers and Lecturers has been passed, followed by the Government Regulation No 19/2005 on teachers' certification. Teachers' certification is the appreciation that the government presents to professional teachers to recognize them. The certificate is only provided to teachers who have met certain standards. This is in line with the government's expectation that certification will improve teachers' performance, which in turn will also improve the quality of education. This certification program is particularly important for teachers because it entails profession allowance. Certified teachers will receive a certain amount of profession allowance from the government. It means that the objective of this certification is not only to improve the teachers' professional quality in education but also to improve their life quality in general. It aims to increase the teachers' quality of life and their dignity, which will affect their performance in performing their duties and responsibilities in achieving the objectives of national education (Sukanti, 2013). Teachers' teaching performance is one element of the education process that has the most significant influence over the improvement of education quality. In order to measure how comprehensively the organizational objectives and goals are achieved, performance indicators can be used as a reference. Performance improvement can be seen daily from how many performance indicators are completed. The same also applies to teachers' performance. To improve teachers' performance, well-planned and well-organized performance management is required. Such management will improve teachers' performance in terms of their knowledge, skills, attitude, and other supporting competences (Benson et al., 2011). Through education, training, and performance development, the teachers' actual quality in performing their duties and tasks can be ensured, so that its influence on students' learning achievement will be significant. Based on this consideration, the teachers' teaching performance evaluation is an important way to optimize teachers' implementation of skills and responsibilities in performing their duties.

The teachers' teaching performance is affected by several factors, including teachers' pedagogic competence, work motivation, school culture, and profession allowance. These factors are deemed significant for the improvement of the teachers' teaching performance in schools. Research by Barrera-Osorio and Raju (2017) shows that there is no positive effect of teacher incentive programs on teacher performance in Pakistan, so it needs to be investigated for cases in Indonesia.

Competence is inseparable from a teacher. Comprehensive competence is embedded in a teacher in performing his duties. The teachers agree that it is necessary for them to have pedagogic competence, personal competence, professional competence, and social competence (Celik, 2011). One of the most important competencies is pedagogic competence of the teacher. The teachers' ability to understand students and manage the teaching-learning process, and their capability to implement these abilities harmoniously are part of pedagogic competence (Mensch & Ennis, 2002). In regard to teachers as the facilitators of students' learning, pedagogic competence is an absolute requirement. Knowledge transformation and transfer in the teaching-learning process will be more optimal if the teachers possess the capability to manage the instruction process (Learning, 2010). Therefore, teachers have to possess added value in the form of pedagogic competence.

In addition to pedagogic competence, work motivation is one of the important factors affecting the teachers' teaching performance. Their working capacity is surely affected by how great is their intention or urge to perform the work; this is motivation (Learning, 2010). Their motivation will surely affect their performance. Good or bad performance depends on how high or how low is their motivation. Basically, teachers' performance and teachers' work motivation are interrelated, and they affect each other. The teachers with good motivation will also show good performance, and the teachers with good performance will be able to motivate. The teachers with good performance will be able to motivate, not only themselves but also the students and other teachers. Since teaching is a learning experience organized in a certain period of time, the teachers can serve as motivators to encourage students to think creatively, imaginatively, and synthetically (Bennell, 2004). One thing to be realized is that the education process is not a naturally occurring process. It needs good planning, organization, and management, with the teachers as the primary pillar. Therefore, the teachers need high motivation to have good teaching performance.

Besides motivation, school culture is another factor that has significant influence on the teachers' teaching performance. Conducive school culture will facilitate the teachers to give good teaching performance. School culture may begin from the teachers' pedagogic competence and their motivation. The teachers' pedagogic competence and motivation will determine the situation and habits built in the school. In every aspect of human life, there are habits that are continuously performed. The habits may turn into a character, which will turn into a culture. School culture reflects how all *civitas academica* socialize, act, and solve problems in the school environment. In a school with good culture, the habit of self-development is thriving, in which everyone in the school continuously improves themselves and the quality of their performance. This habit will become a tradition and will no longer be considered a burden of work. However, in the field, school components still think that habits, values, attitudes, and behaviors of following the rules and developing oneself are a burden. A school culture is the guidance for school members to handle and solve every matter in the school environment (Serrat, 2009). School culture is a variable that affects how school members act and behave. This clearly shows that school culture will affect the teachers' teaching performance.

Profession allowance is another factor that affects the teachers' teaching performance. Profession allowance is a continuous allowance the government provides for teachers when the teachers have acquired their teaching certificate. In other words, the government is obligated to provide teachers who possess an educator certificate with the incentive of profession allowance, the amount of which is equal to one month's salary, every month (*Law of the Republic of Indonesia no. 14 Year 2005 on Teachers and Lecturers*). The government provides this allowance with an expectation to significantly improve teachers' performance, which will also improve the quality of education. However, teachers should not receive teaching certification just because of the profession allowance. The primary objective should be the improvement of their competence. Therefore, the teachers should prepare themselves as best as they can to meet the required competence standards in order to get the certification (Hammond, 2002). However, there are still teachers who pursue certification without any consideration for their quality of teaching. The certification and profession allowance they receive do not improve their professionalism. This is one of the factors that hinders the development of the students' learning achievement.

Considering these factors, it is not easy to comprehensively realize a quality improvement in the teachers' teaching performance. The findings of previous studies indicate that the certification program that the government implements does not automatically improve the teachers' teaching performance in school. Empirically, there are teachers who do not meet the standardized criteria, for instance, in terms of education qualification. Today, out of 2.92 million new teachers, only 51% have a bachelor's degree, while the rest have a lower level of education. In terms of certification requirement, only 2.06 million teachers (70.5%) meet the requirements, while 861,670 teachers do not satisfy the certification requirement. Those teachers who do not meet the certification criteria, who have low motivation, who think school culture is a burden, and who pursue certification only for the allowance, remind us that it is difficult for them to satisfy the criteria for being professional teachers.

Based on this background, it is clear that teachers, who are central figures in the teaching-learning process, have significant influence over the success of education in schools. This has piqued the researchers' interest to analyze and examine the effect of certified teachers' teaching performance, focusing on the correlation between the teachers' pedagogic competence, work motivation, school culture, and profession allowance in relation to the teachers' teaching performance in the electrical engineering departments of public vocational schools in West Java. The null hypothesis in this study is that there is positive and significant correlation between the teachers' pedagogic competence, work motivation, school culture, and profession allowance in relation to the teachers' teaching performance. The objective of this study is to gather and analyze empirical data, find the model of analysis, and measure the significance of the teachers' pedagogic competence, work motivation, school culture, and profession allowance, simultaneously, in relation to the teachers' teaching performance in public vocation schools in West Java. To achieve these objectives, survey method of quantitative approach is employed. The result of this study is expected to provide a basis for a government policy development to improve the teachers' recruitment pattern and to provide allowance for the teachers in order to promote their academic competence through formal and non-formal education.

2 RESEARCH METHODOLOGY

The present study employs survey method with quantitative approach. The survey in this study involves cause and effect description and hypothesis testing. Meanwhile the quantitative method is employed as the research framework, from subject selection, data collection technique, data collection procedure, to data processing. This study also implements an inferential statistics model with parametric statistical method. This model is chosen because the present study focuses on how to discover the correlation between variables. In other words, it aims to discover the cause-effect correlation and its direct and indirect effects. The researchers analyze the correlation between the teachers' pedagogic competence (X1), teachers' work motivation (X2), school culture (X3), and profession allowance (X4) and their simultaneous effects upon teachers' teaching performance (Y). The study is implemented in all public vocational schools (50 schools) in West Java, focusing on the technology and engineering departments, electronics engineering programs, and industrial electronic engineering competence. The sample is selected through probability sampling, using random sampling technique, resulting in 101 certified teachers as the sample.

3 RESULTS AND DISCUSSION

The gathered data was measured and the following results were obtained.

From Table 1, it can be seen that the correlation between X1, X2, X3, X4 variables and Y variable is 0.775; it means that the correlation or effects of Teachers' Pedagogic Competence, Teachers'

Table 1. Correlation between variables.

		Teachers' teaching performance	Teachers' pedagogic competence	Teachers' work motivation	School culture	Profession allowance
Pearson correlation	Teachers' Teaching Performance	1.000	.362	.727	.698	.661
	Teachers' Pedagogic Competence	.362	1.000	.267	.277	.291
	Teachers' Work Motivation	.727	.267	1.000	.991	.910
	School Culture	.698	.277	.991	1.000	.895
	Profession Allowance	.661	.291	.910	.895	1.000
Sig. (1-tailed)	Teachers' Teaching Performance	.	.005	.000	.000	.000
	Teachers' Pedagogic Competence	.005	.	.031	.026	.020
	Teachers' Work Motivation	.000	.031	.	.000	.000
	School Culture	.000	.026	.000	.	.000
	Profession Allowance	.000	.020	.000	.000	.
N	Teachers' Teaching Performance	101	101	101	101	101
	Teachers' Pedagogic Competence	101	101	101	101	101
	Teachers' Work Motivation	101	101	101	101	101
	School Culture	101	101	101	101	101
	Profession Allowance	101	101	101	101	101

Work Motivation, School Culture and Profession Allowance on Teachers' Teaching Performance is strong. The Sig. (2-tailed) value $= 0.000$. This Sig. (2-tailed) value is lower than $\alpha = 0.05$. This indicates that the hypothesis 'there is positive and significant correlation between Teachers' Pedagogic Competence, Teachers' Work Motivation, School Culture and Profession Allowance variables and Teachers' Teaching Performance variable' is accepted. The significance of the variables' effect can show that the simultaneous effect of the variables is represented by the coefficient of determination (r^2) of $0.775^2 = 0.600$ or 60.0%. It means that Teachers' Pedagogic Competence, Teachers' Work Motivation, School Culture and Profession Allowance variables have 60% influence on Teachers' Teaching Performance. The remaining 40% is affected by other factors. This indicates that if these four variables are implemented simultaneously and properly, they can significantly improve teachers' teaching performance. These findings show that motivation has the highest influence of all the factors. Therefore, performance is not only about the results achieved but also has to do with the source of those results. In other words, performance is a result of the competence, motivation, culture, and profession allowance implemented simultaneously and harmoniously in their daily work. The primary objective of a good teacher performance system is to ensure that the students receive the greatest benefit from the education system managed by those teachers, to provide fair, effective, and consistent evaluation, and to promote the teachers' professional development (Larsen, 2009).

Teachers' teaching performance has the most significant influence on education quality improvement. Education reformation efforts to produce high quality education have been performed for a long time. It is natural that the government plans teachers' rights and obligations very well. Teachers' performance development management should be managed and implemented seriously so that the teachers can earnestly carry out their duties. The government's policy concerning this matter should be implemented continuously and consistently.

4 CONCLUSION

Teachers' pedagogic competence, teachers' work motivation, school culture, and profession allowance have positive and significant effect on teachers' teaching performance. The findings of this study indicate that teachers' teaching performance is determined by the teachers' pedagogic competence, the teachers' work motivation, school culture, and profession allowance. Therefore, the higher these variables are, the better the teachers' teaching performance will be. Teachers' motivation has the most significant influence on the teachers' teaching performance (i.e. 0.727). In other words, the teachers' work motivation in public vocational schools in West Java generally has the highest significance in comparison to other variables. These general criteria indicate that vocational schoolteachers possess all dimensions contained in the teachers' work motivation, including discipline, passion, ambition, competitiveness, creativity, and achievement. Among all these dimensions of motivation, the teachers' motivation to achieve has the lowest score, even though it is still regarded as being a good criteria.

REFERENCES

Barrera-Osorio, F.B. & Raju, D. (2017). Teacher performance pay: Experimental evidence from Pakistan. *Journal of Public Economics,* 148(2017) 75–91.

Bennell, P. (2004). *Teacher motivation and incentives in Sub-Saharan Africa and Asia. Knowledge and Skills for Development, Brighton.*

Benson, V., Anderson, D. & Ooms, A. (2011). Educators' perceptions, attitudes and practices: Blended learning in business and management education. *Research in Learning Technology*, 19(2), 143–154.

Bishay, A. (1996). Teacher motivation and job satisfaction: A study employing the experience sampling method. *Journal of Undergraduate Sciences*, 3(3), 147–154.

Celik, S. (2011). Characteristics and competencies for teacher educators: Addressing the need for improved professional standards in Turkey. *Australian Journal of Teacher Education*, 36(4), 73–87.

Hamid, S.R.A., Hassan, S.S.S. & Ismail, N.A.H. (2012). Teaching quality and performance among experienced teachers in Malaysia. *Australian Journal of Teacher Education*, 37(11), 85–103.

Hammond, D.L. (2002). Research and rhetoric on teacher certification: A response to 'teacher certification reconsidered.' *Education Policy Analysis Archives, 10.*

Kemendikbud. (2015). Lomba kreativitas pembelajaran guru pendidikan khusus jenjang menengah tingkat nasional.

Larsen, M.A. (2009). Stressful, hectic, daunting: A critical policy study of the Ontario teacher performance appraisal system. *Canadian Journal of Educational Administration and Policy*, 95, 1–44. Retrieved from http://search.ebscohost.com/login.aspx?direct=true&db=eric&AN=EJ863211&site=ehost-live

Learning, D. (2010). Innovative teacher professional development. *International Review of Research in Open and Distance Learning*, 11, 81–95. Available at: http://www.irrodl.org/index.php/irrodl/article/viewArticle/758.

Mensch, J.M. & Ennis, C.D. (2002). Pedagogic strategies perceived to enhance student learning in athletic training education. *Journal of Athletic Training*, 37(4 suppl), S-199–S-207.

Serrat, B.O. (2009). A primer on organizational culture. *Sustainable development*, 1–6.

Sukanti. (2013). Pengembangan profesi guru secara berkelanjutan. 1–47.

Undang-Undang Republik Indonesia No. 14 Tahun 2005 Tentang Guru dan Dosen.

Educational Administration Innovation for Sustainable Development – Komariah et al. (Eds)
© 2018 Taylor & Francis Group, London, ISBN 978-1-138-57341-3

Managing heutagogy for sustainopreneurship in the technology and information era

A.K. Hia, A. Komariah, Sumarto & D.A. Kurniady
Universitas Pendidikan Indonesia, Bandung, Jawa Barat, Indonesia

N. Waruwu
Universitas Negeri Jakarta, Jakarta, Indonesia

ABSTRACT: The main problem in the training is the lack of ability of the participants to plan, organize, implement, and conduct an independent evaluation of the learning process to run business for sustainability. The availability of information technology has not been enabled to encourage the changes of training practices for pensioners. The creation of economic value, fulfillment of obligation to maintain balance, diversity, sustainability of value for the next generation and the environment are sustainability process. The aim of this study is to find how heutagogy for pensioners for sustainable entrepreneurial in the era of technology and information. Research method in research is verificative survey. The number of samples was 45 pensioners. The results showed that self-learning practice from pedagogy to andragogy then to heutagogy can encourage more sustainable behavior change. Principles of sustainability in learning such as holistic, diversity, sustainability and balance are developed by optimizing information and technology functions. The management of training should take account of the characteristics of the pensions and optimize the function of Information and Communications Technology (ICT) to promote the sustainability of the entrepreneurial learning process.

1   INTRODUCTION

Technology and information has driven changes including how to learn and manage training. The integration of technology and information support the learning process in training. Sayago et al. (2013) suggests advanced adults who successfully learn by using ICT. However, little is known about ICT in adult learning.

The main problem in training is ability of the participants to plan, organize, implement, and conduct an independent evaluation of the learning process to run business for sustainability. Today we are in the era of technology and information stalled in providing a wider and unlimited learning space. But information is not accessed and used as material for discussion, scientific development and praxis including. The training management system has not been designed to enhance literacy ITC to improve sustainopreneurship behavior. Learning practices, for pensioners to encourage sustainopreneurship, have not been a sustainable process. The learning process for sustainable has stopped after completion of entrepreneurship training, and also has not been directed to independent learning practices to build sustrainopreneurship through the availability of Information and Communications Technology (ICT). This was due to the knowledge of pensioners that become the action orientation was inhibited. Little & Knihova (2014) stated that: "Learning architecture and design ought to be enhanced by the thoughtful use of various new tools, strategies and delivery platforms working in harmony". Kopnina (2013) stated the perspective of eco-centric in environment ethics generally marginalized. Espinosa (2015) conveyed that the current challenge is how sustainability. Previous, Hill and Johnston (2003) suggested that human beings must learn to see themselves as natural beings acting within nature. Belanger (2003) suggested that articulating a

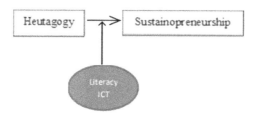

Figure 1.   The relation process of heutagogy, sustainopreneurship, and literacy ICT.

framework of "environmental" lifelong learning creates a contemporary vision that recognizes the important role that many adult education initiatives play within the environmental education scene. Bhatia (2015) delivered: "The improvements in the quality of life have led to enhancement of the life span of elderly population through programs that design for the senior citizens with the aim of enriching their life".

Today Implementation and development of the concept of sustainability in training is still limited, especially for pensions. Douglas (1996) has put forward: "integrated environmental business management curriculum model which is firmly embedded in current industrial and policy-making practice to promote economic and sustainable development". Ari (2013) points out that sustainability of training is extremely important for the successful training. Baumgartner and Winter (2013) stated: "Sustainability issues are integrated into corporate strategies, actions, and behavior".

Learning activities for sustainopreneurship is a continuous process. In fact, awareness of social, environmental, and cultural responsibility is limited to pseudo-consciousness. The existing learning process has not directed the formation of behavior sustainopreneurship. ICT can be enabled to optimize learning outcomes. This effort is to improve the quality of life through business activities in the retirement group, and this is a process that needs to be supported by self-directed learning that utilizes ICT. Described as follows in figure 1.

The learning process for adults has limitations, ICT integration into the learning system can improve the effectiveness of learning in the group of adults who are pensions. The goal to establish sustainable entrepreneurial behavior will be more effective with the ongoing learning process. Available information can be used as a material for reflection and constructing reality for adults. The results of these reflections serve as a basis for strengthening values, shaping attitudes and behaving sustainability in entrepreneurship as known as sustainopreneurship.

Discourses on heutagogy, sustainopreneurship behavior in administrative perspective with studies in retirement groups are limited. This paper presents issues relating to sustainopreneurship among retired. Process to develop sustainopreneurship behavior through education and training by optimizing ICT is an important part but currently it is getting less attention. The aim of the study is to analyze influence of heutagogy to sustainopreneurship behavior moderated by ICT literacy.

2   LITERATUR REVIEW

2.1   *Manage heutagogy*

Various aspects of the characteristics, experience, needs and interests of adults learning are different. Participants as subject of learning. A set of activity design involves the participants. In the implementation of learning, real experience, reflection, social interaction using a varied approach and generalization of concepts or ideas sourced from diverse experiences. Pedagogy, andragogyto heutagogy in adult learning are growing up. The theory of self-adult learning conveyed by Knowless (1984) described self-study as a learning process beginning with planning, implementation and evaluation.

In the era of technology and information, the practice of heutagogy has grown, including among adults. Hase and Kenyon (2001) promoted that, heutagogy which is the study of self-determined

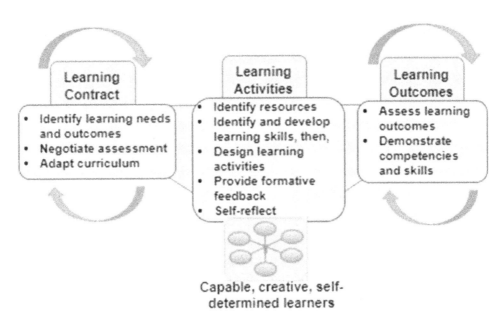

Figure 2.   Heutagogy learning process, Blaschke and Hase (2016).

learning, may be viewed as a natural progression from earlier educational methodologies and may well provide the optimal approach to learning in the 21st century. Heutagogy is a holistic framework for creating twenty-first-century self-determined learners. Msila & Setlhako (2012) stated: " heutagogy underscores the idea of learning how to learn". Jones et al (2014) suggested heutagogy: determined by the learner heutagogy. Blaschke and Hase (2016) also recomended one of the differences between andragogy and heutagogy is that heutagogy further expands upon the role of human agency in the learning process.

Heutagogy is related to ICT development. Karakas and Manisaligil (2012) suggested how changes in independent learning landscape in the digital age. Virtual collaboration expands access to knowledge and innovation together. Technological convergence can facilitate the increased activity of learning activities through technology. Global connectivity, connecting the internet that provides access to the world. Online communities engage in meaningful conversation and engage in problem-oriented, non-partisan social activism. The learning process in heutagogy is described as follows in figure 2.

Input, process, and output as unity system in the training, Need assesment, curriculum is design based on needs of the learners. In the learning process, reflection and discussion as well as feedback becomes an indicator of the success of the learning process. The success of learning is demonstrated by the skills and competencies, Evaluation involves participants for assessment.

2.2   Literacy ICT

In the ICT era, the availability of information is overwhelming. UNESCO (2006) said that: "Literacy refers to a context–bound continuum of reading, writing and numeracy skills, acquired and developed through the process of learning". Agnaou (2004) said literacy depends on the social context. Nanda and Ramesh (2012) expressed ICT literacy is using digital technology, communications tools, and/or networks to access, manage, integrate, evaluate, and create information in order to function in a knowledge society, as stated in a report on digital transformation a framework for ICT Literacy. Adetimirin (2012) on literacy cited the literacy international panel report in 2002 that ICT literacy can be defined as the use of digital technology, communications tools and networks to access, manage, integrate, evaluate and create information in order to function in a knowledge society. Wawan (2016) suggested the ability to use digital technology, communication tools, and/or networks to identify, locate and retrieve information, determine quality, relevance, usefulness, and manage information and then summarize information presented as knowledge submitted for self-development.

2.3 *Sustainopreneurship*

The creation of economic value is inseparable from the individual's responsibility to social, cultural, and environmental concerns including responsibility for the life of the next generation. Terry (2006) expressed responsibility for the social responsibilities of management. Problems such as social problems, culture, environment will caused the destruction of the structure of the business world and society. Kaufmann (2009) conveyed on entrepreneurial social responsibility. A view of the environment affects activity to create economic value. Schaltegger (2000) suggested that eco-preneurs destroy methods of production, products, market structure and consumption patterns and replace them with superior products and environmental services.

In addition to eco-preneurship and social, there is spiritual entrepreneurship. Agbim (2013) explained that the growth of entrepreneurship is caused by the reality of man. Entrepreneurship is multi dimension.

The subject matter of entrepreneurial responsibility continues growing up. Schaltegger and Wagner (2011) described entrepreneurship as systems, institutions, and individuals. Cohen and Win (2007) stated the concept of sustainability in entrepreneurship that opens the opportunity to bring products and services into the future. Sustainopreneurship concept introduced by Schaltegger, S. (2000) that the existence of vision, passion and unlimited. Abrahamsson et al. (2007) described sustainopreneurship as bringing value to markets, communities and the environment. It is psychological ide.

One of the basic concepts used to all about explain entrepreneurial behavior is Ajzen (2002). Affirmed by Ajzen (2014) that: Theory of Planned Behavior (TPB) is alive and well and gainfully employed in the pursuit of understanding of human behavior. Rueda et al. (2015) showed TPB can be used to measure entrepreneurial behavior. Attitudes, subjective norms and self-efficacy are used as indicators of entrepreneurial intention.

Earlier Attitude changes were described by Fishbein and Yzer (2003) as the influence of behavioral beliefs and outcome valuations, norms and self efficacy. The behavior itself is influenced by skill, intensity and environmental support (Fishbein & Yzer, 2003). The demand for sustainable practices in the business world has an impact on the provision of education or training for entrepreneurship. Demands that can promote high sustainability. Littledyke et al. (2013) stated that "Education for Sustainability (EfS) has international priority". Filho (2011) provides limits on the application of educated sustainability concepts, expressed "sustainability as a method, a strategy and as a way of thinking, allows a better understanding of the implications of sustainability principles, and smoother implementation of them into practice". Davim et al. (2016) affirmed sustainability in the education is growing on teaching, research, and community involvement, as well as college operations, although much works are still remains to be done.

3 RESEARCH METHOD

Sample research is pensions. Total pensions are 40 who learn entrepreneurship in Institute Training and Consulting PT. Meta Bright Vision (MBV), Bekasi. Instrument that used to measure heutagogy by Blaschke and Hase (2016) such: The design element in self-determined learning are: exploration, creation, collaboration, connetion, sharing and reflection. In literacy ability, researcher used measurement by Wawan (2016) indicating Define, Access, Evaluate, Integrate Manage Create Communicate. Sustainopreneurship behavior measured by the concept of Ajzen (2002), Fisbein & Yzer, (2003) those are intensity, skill and environmental support with dimensions as suggested by Schalteger (2000). Data collection using interviews, observation to know the training process. Questionnaires are used to determine changes in entrepreneurial behavior and ICT literacy by using Likert scale. Qualitative analysis with procedure of collection, reduction, presentation, conclusion interactively. Quantitative analysis (test for entrepreneurial behavior).

4 RESULTS AND DISCUSSION

Sustainopreneurship behaviors learning influenced by 1) positive attitudes toward social, environmental and cultural issues, 2) awareness of norms and 3) confidence gained through the learning process in training. These three factors lead to the formation of sustainopreneurhsive behavior. Environmental support is becomes important aspects. sustainability, technology and training. There is strong connection among them.

Therefore, self-learning management needs to be implemented based on heutagogy learning process as proposed (Blaschke & Hase, 2016). Management of heutagogy training is a system designed to improve behavior while encouraging comprehensive self-learning (heutagogy) among pensions by optimizing ICT. The finding show that ICT strengthens the relationship heutagogy and sustainopreneurship behavior. ICT lead to the formation of more positive attitudes, better understanding of norms due to available information, and increasing pension confidence by providing a number of examples of successful business behaviors that can drive changes in social, cultural and economic environments simultaneously.

Pensioners have more positive attitudes toward environmental, social and economic issues. The behavior of pensioners in a business was more controllable. Value creation processes pay more attention to the employees, the development of innovative cultivation, and the waste generated from the running business processes. ICT literacy strengthened the process of exploring, creating, collaborating, connect, reflecting, sharing knowledge, skills, beliefs about the importance of sustainopreneurship behavior. The emphasis on the management of self-learning towards sustainopreneurship behavior is the process of learning to understand the vision and mission on social issues, culture, environment, economy.

Participants who studied in the heutagogy directed themselves to self-planning the learning process, understanding the goals, determining the way, and achieving the best to establish sustainopreneurship behavior. Learning planning focused on how plans increase intensity (strengthens positive attitudes, encourages critical understanding of existing issues and enhances confidence) environmental skills and support. Availability information technology helped participants to learn with the necessary information.

The participants of self-study attempted to learn how to organize business organization and activities so that skills, intensity and support increase. For example through existing media, the pensioners organized movements to build support for sustain preneurship behavior. Hase & Kenyon (2003) explained how self-directed learning improves workplace capability and reduces complexity. The availability of ICTs made it easier for pensions to manage the complexities to learn to behave sustainably including members of the organization.

The pensioners learn to build attitudes, skills and entrepreneurial behavior by ICT. The pensioners directed itself to learn exercise supervision, control both the learning process towards the establishment of sustain behavior or on the results of any business activities undertaken whether in accordance with the purpose or not. Hase (2009) confirmed some of the challenges and opportunities of heutagogy and e-learning in the workplace. The formation of sustainopreneurship behavior is a process that involves direct business activities and self-directed learning process supported by ICT.

The planning, organizing learning, the leading function in learning and evaluation of learning outcomes have integrated in the business management process. Those activities are mutually supportive in improving skills, intensity and environmental support of sustainopreneurship-based behaviors such as the concept of Fisbein & Yzeir (2003), Ajzen (2002), Ajzen (2014). The participants were provided with the understanding and ability to manage heutagogy as an integrated process in business activity. Participants generate information to strengthen their attitudes, broaden understanding of norms relating to their responsibilities and increase confidence. Participants learn to manage the post-training, self-learning process with the goal of behavior change for themselves as well as for other members of the organization.

In the heutagogy learning process the participants were directed to understand the importance of the company's vision and mission. Vision and mission oriented towards solving social, cultural, environmental, and economic problems become the foundation of values for planning, managing, organizing, implementing and evaluating the learning process of heutagogy. Learning process such as needs analysis, determination of joint assessment, curriculum, learning process, how to improve sustainopreneurship behavior be more effective and efficient.

The ability to define, access, evaluate, manage, integrate and create by generalizing and adapting, implementing, designing, create the relevant informations for the purpose of promoting sustain-ability in an effort to strengthen sustainopreneurship behavior. Information create more positive attitude toward business practices in principle of balance, diversity, overall and business sustain-ability. The entrepreneurs have a positive attitude towards the business function both environment and for the social life of the community such as labor absorption and environmental improvement through business waste reduction. People-oriented business practices, work teams, innovation, growth, stability, and aggressiveness has continued to be "passed on to the next generation".

An important factor in supporting the success of independent learning reinforced by the ICT literacy was the ability of the participants to plan, organize, implement and evaluate how the learning process Participants were able to optimize ICT management, ICT literacy in order to support the formation of intensity, skill and support through information provided in existing communication technology. In line with Canter (2012) which stated: "The new concept stems from heutagogy but it enriched it by bringing new facets and connects it with lifelong e-learning". The participants learn to manage the learning process based on lifelong learnings using ICT.

5 CONCLUSION

The implementation of entrepreneurship education for retirement in accordance with the needs of pensions. Success to improve entrepreneurial behavior for sustainability cannot be separated from principles such as holistic, diversity, sustainability and balance. The function of ICT is to ensure the process of reflection for sustainability is supported by knowledge.

Managerial implications: The management of training should take account of the characteristics of the pensions and optimize the function of ICT to promote the sustainability of the entrepreneurial learning process.

REFERENCES

Abrahamsson, A. 2007. Researching Sustainopreneurship – conditions, concepts, approaches, arenas and questions: An invitation to authentic sustainability business forces. *13th International Sustainable Development Research Conference, Mälardalens Högskola, Västerås, 10–12, pp. 1–22.*

Adetimirin, A. E. 2012. ICT Literacy Among Undergraduates in Nigerian Universities. *Education and Information Technologies, 17(4), 381–397.*

Agbim, K.C et al. 2013. The Relative Importance of Spirituality in Entrepreneurship Development Among Graduates of Nigerian Tertiary Institutions. *International Journal of Business and Management Invention 2(4), pp. 25–35.*

Agnaou, F. 2004. Gender, Literacy and Empowerment. *New York: Routledge.*

Ajzen, I. 2002. Perceived Behavioral Control, Self-Efficacy, Locus of Control, and the Theory of Planned Behavior. *Journal of Applied Social Psychology, 2002, 32, 4, pp. 665–68.*

Ajzen, I. 2005. Attitudes, Personality and Behavior. *N.Y Open University Press.*

Ajzen, I. 2014. The Theory of Planned Behaviour is Alive and Well, and Not Ready to Retire: A Commentary on Sniehotta, Presseau, and Araújo-Soares. *Health Psychology Review, 7199 (May), 1–7.*

Ari, M. 2013. Sustainability of Training of Trainers on Technical and Vocational Education (TVE) by The Help of Wimax Supported Online E-Laboratory Application. *Computer Applications in Engineering Education, 21(3), 439 447.*

Baumgartner, R.J & Winter, T. 2013. The Sustainability Manager: A Tool for Education and Training on Sustainability Management. Corporate Social Responsibility and Environmental Management Corp. *Soc. Responsib. Environ. Mgmt. 21, 167–174.*

Belanger, P. 2003. Learning environments and environmental education. *New Directions for Adult and Continuing Education*, 2003(99).

Bhatia, P. G. 2015. Lifelong Learning – Learning to Learn. *The Business & Management Review, 5(4), 29–30.*

Blaschke, L. M., & Hase, S. 2016. The Future of Ubiquitous Learning. *The Future of Ubiquitous Computing, (November), 25–41.*

Canter, M. 2012. E-Heutagogy for Lifelong E-Learning. *Procedia Technology, 1, 129–131.*

Cohen, B & Winn, M.I. 2007. Market imperfections, opportunity and sustainable entrepreneurship. *Journal of Business Venturing 22, pp. 29–49.*

Davim, J.P & Filho, W.L. 2016. Challenges in Higher Education for Sustainability. *Springer International Publishing Switzerland.*

Douglas, W. 1996. Greening of Business Germany: *Towards, 4, 12–18.*

Espinosa, A. 2015. Governance for Sustainability: Learning from VSM Practice. *Kybernetes Vol. 44, No. 6/7, pp. 955–969*

Filho, W.L. 2011. World Trends in Education for Sustainable Development. Frankfurt. *Deutsche National.*

Fishbein, M & Yzer, M.C. 2003. Using Theory to Design Effective Health Behavior Interventions. *Communication theory. 32. pp. 164–183.*

Hase, S. 2009. Heutagogy and E-Learning in The Workplace: Some Challenges and Opportunities. Impact: *Journal of Applied Research in Workplace E-Learning, 1(1), 43–52.*

Hase, S. 2016. Self-determined Learning (heutagogy): Where Have We Come Since 2000? Technology Journal of Applied Research, (May). Retrieved from *https://www.sit.ac.nz/Portals/0/upload/documents/sitjar/ Heutagogy - One.pdf.*

Hase, S & Kenyon, C. 2001. Moving from Andragogy to Heutagogy: Implications for VET, 28–30.

Hase, S & Kenyon, C. 2003. Heutagogy and Developing Capable People and Capable Workplaces: Strategies for Dealing with Complexity. *Proceedings of The Changing Face of Work and Learning Conference, 1–7.*

Hill, L. H., & Johnston, J. D. 2003. Adult education and humanity's relationship with nature reflected in language, metaphor, and spirituality: A call to action. *New Directions for Adult & Continuing Education*, 2003(99).

Jones, C., Matlay, H., Penaluna, K., & Penaluna, A. 2014. Claiming the future of enterprise education. *Education + Training*, 56(8/9).

Kaufmann, H.S. 2009. The Contribution of Entrepreneurship to Society. *Int. J. Entrepreneurship and Small Business, Vol. 7, No. 1, pp. 59–73.*

Karakas, F. Manisaligil, A. 2012. Reorienting Self-Directed Learning for The Creative Digital Era. *European Journal of Training and Development 36 (7), pp. 712–731.*

Knowless, M. 1984. Andragogy in Action. California; Jose Bass.

Kopnina. H. 2013. Evaluating Education for Sustainable Development (ESD): Using Ecocentric and Anthropocentric Attitudes Toward the Sustainable Development (EAATSD) Scale. *Environ Dev Sustain. 15:607–623.*

Little B. & Knihova L. 2014. "Modern trends in learning architecture", *Industrial and Commercial Training, 46 (1), pp. 34 – 38.*

Littledyke, M. & Littledyke, R. A. 2013. A systems approach to education for sustainability in higher education, 14(4), 367–383.

Msila, V. & Setlhako, A. 2012. Teaching (still) Matters: Experiences on Developing a Heutagogical Online Module at UNISA. *Procedia – Social and Behavioral Sciences, 69 (Iceepsy 2012), 136–142.*

Nanda, A. & Ramesh, D. B. 2012. Assessment of Information and Communication Technology (ICT) Literacy among Teachers and Practitioners in the Field of Disability. *International Journal of Information Dissemination and Technology, 2(1), 54.*

Rueda, S., Moriano, J. A., & Liñan, F. 2015. Validating a Theory of Planned Behavior Questionnaire to Measure Entrepreneurial Intentions. *Developing, Shaping and Growing Entrepreneurship, (January 2016), 60–69.*

Sayago, S., Forbes & P. Blat, J. 2013. lder People Becoming Successful ICT Learners Over Time: Challenges and Strategies Through an Ethnographical Lens. *Educational Gerontology*, 39: 527–544.

Schaltegger, S. 2000. Vom Bionier zum Sustainopreneur, *Presentation at Rio Impuls Management Forum 2000.*

Schaltegger, S. 2011. Vom Bionier zum Sustainopreneur. *Sciences-New York, (November), 1–12.*

Schaltegger, S. & Wagner., M. 2011. Sustainable Entrepreneurship and Sustainability Innovation: Categories and Interactions. *Business Strategy and the Environment Bus. Strat. Env. 20, 222–237.*

Terry, G.R. 2006. Principle of Management. *Michigan University.*

UNESCO. 2006. Education for All. Literacy for life. Paris. *UNESCO Publishing.*

Wawan. 2016. Pengembangan Model Pembelajaran Mandiri untuk Meningkatkan Kemampuan Pengembangan Diri melalui Pendidikan Literasi TIK (Studi pada Pelatihan Tutor PAUD di Kota Cimahi), UPI. *Dissertation unpublished.*

Educational Administration Innovation for Sustainable Development – Komariah et al. (Eds)
© 2018 Taylor & Francis Group, London, ISBN 978-1-138-57341-3

The implementation of character education in learning processes at primary school

A.N. Hidayat, K. Muttaqien & V.L. Ayundhari
Universitas Islam Nusantara, Bandung, West Java, Indonesia

ABSTRACT: This study aims to get an image of character education implementation in learning processes at primary school. Case study method, data collection techniques in interviews and observation, as well as the data analysis were done qualitatively. The results show that before teaching, teachers should shape the students to performing tasks, and practicing science, building relationships with students, understanding the conditions and their personal characteristics, and utilizing existing resources as well. The character values developed in learning are faith and devotion to the God Almighty, being independent of others, willing to sacrifice, being cooperative and responsible, discussion method, subjects-integrated, habituation, manners of the heart activity, classroom-based character education, school culture, and education character objectives as the spirit and the foundation of education. Observing the way of thinking, acting, speaking, along with attitudes, worship motivation, asking friends, teachers and parents is used to conduct the assessment.

1 INTRODUCTION

Character education should denote particular values about the nature of children and how they learn (Kohn 1997). These 'good' values are better implemented since elementary school, as character education takes precedence over learning activities and spends the longest in this level. So the execution of character education in elementary school is very appropriately integrated to learning in time. The teacher have important role. Benninga et al (2003) described that "Logically, experts agree that character education is the responsibility of adults". "Some characteristics of the management process of character education in an educational unit are "...integrating the values of characters in whole learning activities" (Culbertson, 1982). Lickona et al (2002) also strengthened the view as stated in the third principle that all aspects of schooling including instructional process is a comprehensive approach to achieve effective character education. The implementer here is the teacher as the organizer of teaching and learning process in school (Makmun 2004). When giving moral education concept, for instance. It should be involved in the education of teachers (Berkowitz & Oser, 1985; Lickona, 1991). Young teachers are suggested to put in elementary and secondary schools, because the concept of moral and character is easy to introduce to children. Therefore, teachers should do their best and as accurately as possible integrate the values of the characters in learning activities, so as the children become more preponderant and will foster character development in their later childhood. Battistich (2013) also elaborates schools are better dealing with problems that often occur today, among others: aggresive and antisocial behavior, drug use, precocious sexual activity, criminal activities, academic under-achievement, and school failure. He also adds that character education has the important additional benefits of helping youth to develop positive personal and social attitudes and skills. When students interact in social activities and develop their sensitivity, the positive impact can also be seen on the learning (Brooks, 2005). As a result, the characters' degradation can be slowly but surely diminished.

Examining good things from character education values, Pike (2010) however state "character education is regarded as indoctrinatory and an infringement of children's rights". It may lead to some disagreement to what is being perceived as shared value. But Fathurahman (2012) believe the goal of character education will be achieved if supported by national education system in a determinitive and supportive policy.

Several studies related to the integration of character values on learning, among others: Mulya and Jayadiputra (2012); Mulya and Hidayat (2013). The results showed the researchers have implemented learning with character values, and the character values development related to work at the time of learning and scouting. It results discipline, professionalism, and responsibility values. Kamaruddin (2012) combines subjects such as character values through the game. When educators ask the questions, students have to pass the ball until it goals. To win the game, the students realize they need unity in the team. Mulya and Karwati (2014) have developed and integrated religious values in learning through the habituation and provision of religious duties. Karwati and Efendi (2015) instilled character values performed by principals through various school activities like creating a conducive atmosphere while implementing learning and extracurricular. Karwati and Mulya (2016) also conducted character education during the learning process and non-extracurricular activities. Meanwhile in the higher level of education, Hidayat and Kingking (2017) have identified the character values to integrate and undertaken them in teaching educational psychology subject. The results also have been evaluated by observing student behavior. They communicate and discuss the change afterward. Among all study results, integrating character education values with learning is still less discussed; in the context of Indonesian elementary schools in particular.

Based on the above-mentioned premises, the researchers are triggered to conduct further research about character education in elementary school. This study result is to materialize a proper model which later can be implemented by elementary school teachers to carry out character education in the learning process. Hence, "How is the implementation of character education through learning in Primary School?" is formulated as the research problem.

2 METHOD

The approach used in this research is the qualitative or naturalistic approach. Case study method is aimed to reveal the implementation of character education through learning and whether it is performed often or not.

This research reveals a patch-up data in the field. The researchers did not give treatment but attempted to understand the actions, views, and interpretation of the principal, teachers, and students when interacting with the environment. The researchers also gave meaning when the interaction occurred in the class with the intention of cognizing the atmosphere of character education in learning. This research uses the qualitative approach with the consideration: to describe the behavior and the factors that influence the research subjects as a whole, to reveal the actual data, to create the conditions and activities that are being done, to direct and to understand the conducted research objectives dealing with current problems. The research result can be used, as the nature's setting is rather limited. This research uses the descriptive method to search, compile, analyze, and interpret data. Data were collected using the interviewing guides, observation guidelines, and documentation study guides.

This research is conducted in three stages: preparation, execution, and ending. At the preparatory stage, the researcher sought to get an idea of the researched problem, improved the design, the research focus and the resource persons. To achieve the result of this phase, the researcher set and formulated the research design, prepared, revised, reproduced the instrument, and recognized parties that were corresponded to the research.

The second stage aims to obtain complete data by fostering a conducive relationship, so as to get the actual one. Conducting triangulation by a means of interviews, learning observation, and documentation studies to the research participants. The data has been obtained, selected, and reduced so it can be utilized to sharpen the focus of the problem.

In the third step, the researchers tested the truth of the obtained data through member checking. This is largely determined by credibility, fidelity, transferability, and confirmability. To actualize these, the activities done were in form of recapitulating the information revealed from the field completely, compiling the results of data analysis, selecting and summarizing the research result systematically, formulating research conclusions, and preparing the research report as a whole.

3 RESULTS AND DISCUSSION

3.1 *Results*

Based on the interview results with teachers, it shows that before teaching, teachers should shape the students to performing tasks, and practicing science, building relationships with students, understanding the conditions and their personal characteristics, and utilizing existing resources as well.

The teachers' observation results on both class V and VI show that to improve children's development notably religious aspects, the teachers at the beginning always ask the children about who have performed the prayer and read Qur'an in the previous day. The teachers also explain the importance of prayer, Qur'an, and life purpose.

Teachers' interview results show that the character values developed during the learning process are faith and devotion to God the Almighty. The students are also being independent, sincere, cooperative, responsible, and helping each other.

School principals and teachers in the interview also said that the method used during the course of character education is discussion method. They also integrated the character values over subjects, implemented conditioning and habituation for children.

When interviewing teachers, it is indicated that they implemented classroom-based character education, school culture, manners of the heart activity, and education character objectives as the spirit and the foundation of education. Meanwhile, observing the way of thinking, acting, and speaking, along with attitudes, worship motivation, and asking friends, teachers, and parents is used to conduct the assessment.

From the results of the research above, it can be concluded that both principals and teachers jointly implemented the character education through guidance and counseling-based learning (Kemendikbud, 2016), development (Muro & Kottman 1995), and classroom (Kemendikbud, 2016).

3.2 *Discussion*

This discussion describes the conclusion of character education implementation through learning in Elementary School based on guidance and counseling, development, and classroom.

Before carrying out counseling-based character education and counseling through learning, it is better to conduct planning first as Rahayuningsih and Sholikhan (2016) did. Many things that schools need to prepare to achieve effective learning. Some of them are learning curriculum, lesson plans, school schedules, and the establishment of programs that support learners. The teachers should also seek to understand the children needs that unmet and unresolved. This can be done by asking the teacher, the first-grade parents, because parents are the children's first and main environment so that parents have a very essential role towards the learners character building (Rahayuningsih and Sholikhan 2016). Or by giving direct interviews to some children who can represent the classroom, one year in advance.

In the implementation of guidance and counseling-based character education through learning, the teacher should create safe and comfortable environment when the children move into a new classroom and express themselves (Freeman, 2014). This can be achieved by building a harmonious relationship with the students like listening to their stories, interpreting their expression, appreciating the success they have just made, responding positively and justifying what they do. Teachers should be able to reveal their abilities, their merits compared to friends, family or society, and experiences dealing with personal, social, learning and career. During the learning, the teacher should identify the case, and the students' problems that occurred in the classroom he or she taught. Teachers in assigning tasks should also be able to develop their character for the better.

Cook and Kaffenberger state the role of guidance and counseling in learning as a whole is without question, as guidance and counseling have a positive effect on high school students' academic achievement (ACA 2006). The results of Morey, et al. (ACA 2006) and Praport (ACA 2006) concluded that guidance and counseling helped to reduce chaos in the classroom. Similarly, the findings is suggest that guidance and counseling can help to improve social skills.

At the end of the guidance and counseling-based character education implementation through learning, teachers should assess changes over the children's behavior when interacting with their friends in school. The teachers should also quickly convey the result of positive assessment to them. However if the result is less good, it would be more appropriate to deliver the result individually; to ask them why, and what factors become obstacles.

Prior to developing character education-based through learning, teachers should comprehend what kind of developmental tasks which are capable and (or) less to be performed by the students, since developmental problems may hinder the achievement of subsequent developments. It also affects other developmental aspects (Syaodih, 2005). Guidance services as a teacher-assisted effort for children are better implemented at one blow with the occurred learning process (Syaodih, 2005).

In the implementation of education character-based through learning, teachers should integrate both developmental tasks and developmental aspects to subject matter, along with the assigned tasks as well. But the teacher should reveal and collect the information about developmental tasks that have been completed by the children before, as well as what developmental aspects that developed well or not. If this is already known, the teacher will easily combine it with the subject matter.

At the end of developing character education through learning, teachers should reveal and observe the students' developmental tasks that have and (or) not mastered; developmental aspects that develop well and (or) less. This can be observed when students interacting with friends at school. The results should be delivered as soon as possible to them and discussed with the principal and other teachers. It would also be better if reported and discussed with their parents.

Before classroom-based character education through learning is done, teachers should understand the characteristics of each individual, and determine the character values to be integrated into lessons. To understand the developed characters and values, it can be expressed by approaching, listening, appreciating and validating what the children tell, and observing the behavior by reading their body language in everyday life. If the teacher is teaching the first grade of elementary school, he or she can ask what are the students' superior characteristics and values to their parents. But if the teacher is teaching at the second and fourth grade of elementary school, he or she can ask to the prior teachers—analyzing their report cards, list of values, absences, sociometric results and record of events. The results are then analyzed together with other teachers. The teacher should be able to foster a harmonious relationship with the children, meaning he or she is expected to communicate instructionally with them better. As for the skills that must be possessed are attachment, empathy, summarizing, asking questions, honesty, assertiveness, confrontation, and solving problems (Surya, 2013). The main principle of good character is respect, truth, fair, and responsibility (Skaggs & Bodenhorn, 2006)

When conducting classroom-based character education through learning, every teacher at the beginning of the lesson should check the students who performed prayer in the previous day, especially the obligation to perform 'shalat' and Qur'an reading. If there is a student who did not do the worship, the teacher can ask why to the students. Let us say the student had problems when performing, the teacher then helped to solve it. For a child performing the service, the teacher should respect and validate it. In addition to checking children who performed worship, teachers should also be able to integrate the character values with the subject matter in each learning. The teacher should take the core of the subject matter and then mix with the developed values in the class wherein he or she teaches. At the time of teaching, the teacher should be able to maintain a harmonious relationship with the students. For that, the teacher should always approach, give meaning, appreciate and validate everything done by the students afterward (Bertolino & O'Hanlon 2002). One other thing is, the teacher should observe and record the student who has symptoms of having problems. The problems can be solved during the learning, but after the learning completed is also possible. During the learning, teachers should maintain a relationship with children like trying hard to not offend them, because it will affect the character education implementation itself.

At the end of the character education-based classroom implementation through learning, the teachers should conduct some evaluation by observing and analyzing the children responses about all developed grades by a means of revealing the children's view toward the improved character values done by them. The implication of the results of the Skaggs and Bodenhom's research (2006) argue that "Adminstrators and the school personnel who are considering implementing a character education program may wonder how to choose the best Character Education for their community". Teachers should also assess changes that occur over students both individually and classically. This can be done by seeing them acting, thinking, and feeling. To obtain more accurate evaluation result, teachers can interview students, their friends, and parents. The result of classroom-based character education evaluation should be better succeeded. Or if there is any improvement in general, it should be delivered in front of the class. But if it is less successful, the result should be submitted individually and carefully outside of the learning time, so that their learning motivation would not decline. Subsequently, the character education evaluation result will be more useful for further character education implementation if discussed in class, group, and individual with other teachers. When developing the character, the parents should spend more time and efforts to understand inner potential of their children by a means of providing appropriate environment and daily life materials. Children's interrelationship with parents would be elevated through the character education into family environment. Milliren & Messer (2009) also convince character education can become an everyday opportunities. Home can be the best place to get the opportunity. This statement strengthens that the character development is really supported by harmonious relationship between parents and children. If the coaching of character values and relationships within the family has become a culture, the values that exist in the family will increasingly have a positive effect over the children because cultural value of the area are very strong dan dominant in shaping a person's character. Cultural values will be reflected in very word, action and will be ingrained in humans, including in thinking and making decisions, so the existence of cultural values inherent in human beings will form a strong foundation of character and inherent to any time (Ferdiawan & Putra, 2013).

4 CONCLUSION

Character education is one of the aspects of development worth to investigating further. Children in primary school age are the right subject for the investigation since in this time of development children are at their sensitiveness in term of receiving stimulation. Educators have a very important role to develop character values of children through various learning including modeling, habituating, repeating good deeds in daily life and integrating the values into learning strategies.

REFERENCES

American Counseling Association. 2006. *Effectiveness of School Counseling.* (n.d.). Retrieved from ACA website http://www.counseling.org.

Benninga, J. S., Berkowitz, M. W & Smith, K. 2003. The Relationship of Character Education Implementation and Academic Achievement in Elementary Schools. *Journal of Character Education.*

Battistich, V. 2013. *Character Education, Prevention, and Positive Youth Development.* University of Missouri, St. Louis.

Berkowitz, M., & Oser, F. (eds.). 1985. *Moral education: Theory and application.* Hillsdale, NJ: Lawrence Erlbaum.

Bertolino, B., & O'Hanlon, B. 2002. *Collaborative, Competency-Based Counseling and Therapy.* Boston: Allyn & Bacon.

Brooks, D. 2005. Increasing Test Score and Character Education *The Natural Connection.* Retrieved from http://www.youngpeoplespress.com/Testpaper.pdf.

Culbertson, J. 1982. *Character Education: Teaching Values for Life.* Chicago: Science Research Associates. Inc.

Fathurahman, P. 2012. Model of the character education in developing countries. *Journal of Applied Sciences Research* 8(3): 1813–1816.

Ferdiawan, E., & Putra, W. E. 2017. ESQ Eucation for children character buiding based on phylosophy of Javaness in Indonesia. *Procedia-Social and Behavioral Sciences* 106 (2013) 1096–1102. Retrieved from www.sciencedirect.com

Freeman, G. G. 2014. The Implementation of Character Education and Children's Literature to Teach Bullying Characteristics and Prevention Strategies to Preschool Children: An Action Research Project. *Early Childhood Education Journal,* 42: 305–316.

Hidayat, A. N., & Kingking, M. 2017. *Integrasi Nilai-Nilai Karakter dalam Pembelajaran Mata Kuliah Psikologi Pendidikan pada Mahasiswa Tunanetra Program Studi PLB FKIP Uninus Bandung.* Independent Research Report. Bandung: Unpublished.

Kamaruddin, S. A. 2012. Character Education and Students Social Behavior. *Journal of Education and Learning* 6 (4): 223–230.

Makmun, A. S. 2004. *Psikologi Kependidikan.* Bandung: Rosdakarya.

Milliren, A., & Messer, M. H. 2009. Invitations to character. *Journal of Invitational Theory & Practice,* 15, 19–31.

Mulya, D. B., & Hidayat, A. N. 2013. *Pengelolaan Sosial Budaya Sekolah Berbasis Karakter (PLSBSBK) di SMKN 4 Padalarang Kabupaten Bandung Barat.* Dikti Research Report. Jakarta: Unpublished.

Mulya, D. B., & Jayadiputra, E. 2012. *Pengelolaan Sosial Budaya Sekolah Berbasis Karakter (PLSBSBK) di SMAN 1 Cisarua Kabupaten Bandung Barat.* Dikti Research Report. Jakarta: Unpublished.

Mulya, D.B., & Karwati, E. 2014. *Pengelolaan Lingkungan Sosial Budaya Sekolah Berbasis Karakter (PLSBSBK) di MAN 1 Cililin Kabupaten Bandung Barat.* Dikti Resesrach Report. Jakarta: Unpublished.

Muro, J. J., & Kootman, T. 1995. *Guidance and Counseling In Elementary School and Middle School.* Iowa: Brown and Benchmark Publisher.

Karwati, E., & Efendi, G. Y. 2015. *Pengembangan Karakter Anak Melalui Pengelolaan Iklim Sosial Budaya Sekolah (PKSMPISBS) di SMPN 2 Ngamprah Kabupaten Bandung Barat.* Dikti Research Report. Jakarta: Unpublished.

Karwati, E., & Mulya, D. B. 2016. *Pengembangan Karakter Anak Melalui Pengelolaan Iklim Sosial Budaya Sekolah (PKSMPISBS) di Madrasyah Tsanawiyah Negeri 2 Bandung Barat.* Dikti Research Report. Jakarta: Unpublished.

Kemendikbud. 2016. *Penguatan Pendidikan Karakter. Tingkat Sekolah Dasar dan Sekolah Menengah Pertama.* Jakarta: Kemendikbud.

Kohn, A. 1997. How Not To Teach Values: A Critical Look at Character Education. *Phi Delta Kappan* 78 (6): 429–39.

Lickona, T. (1991). *Educating for character: How our schools can teach respect and responsibility.* New York: Bantam

Lickona, T., Schaps, E & Lewis, C. 2002. Eleven Principles of Effective Character Education. *Special Topics, General.* 50.

Pike, M. A. 2010. Christianity and character education: faith in core values? *Journal of Beliefs & Values*: Studies in Religion & Educati 31(3): 311–312.

Rahayuningsih, S., & Sholikhan. 2016. Disciplinary Character Education At Early Age. *IQSR Journal of Research & Method in Education,* 6 (5) Ver, II.

Skaggs, G., & Bodenhorn, N. (2006). Relationships between implementing character education, student behavior, and student achievement. *Journal of Advanced Academics* 18 (1): 82–114.

Surya, M. (2013). *Psikologi Guru.* Bandung: CV Alfabeta.

Syaodih, E. (2005). *Bimbingan di Taman Kanak-Kanak.* Jakarta: *Departemen* Pendidikan Nasional.

Educational Administration Innovation for Sustainable Development – Komariah et al. (Eds)
© 2018 Taylor & Francis Group, London, ISBN 978-1-138-57341-3

Analysis of factors affecting teacher competence in the northwest mountains of Vietnam

S.C. Hong, T.T. Thuy, L.T. Hung & L.T.H. Ha
Vietnam National University, Hanoi, Vietnam

ABSTRACT: The study investigated the impact of different factors on teaching competencies in secondary education. The study was conducted with a survey of 1,256 junior and senior high schoolteachers in the Northwest mountains of Vietnam. The data obtained was tabulated, analyzed and interpreted by using the statistical techniques of mean, standard deviation average rating, T-test and Analysis of Variance (ANOVA), to reveal the variables that most affect teacher competence in the Northwest mountains, and to identify seven factors that most affect the competence of teachers. These identified factors are internal factors (gender, age, major, experience, and race), and external factors, namely the distances to school, school facilities, and culture.

1 INTRODUCTION

Vietnam is experiencing rapid demographic and social change. From about 60 million in 1986, Vietnam's population reached 94 million in 2016 (World Bank, 2017). The Northwest has a population of 4,268,400, accounting for 4.7% of the country's population. The average population density of the Northwest is 84 persons/km^2 (population density in the Northern Midlands and Mountains is 120 persons/km^2), of which the highest is in Hoa Binh province with 175 persons/km^2 and the lowest is in Lai Chau with 44 persons/km^2. The region is the locality of more than 40 ethnic groups in a multi-ethnic nation with 54 ethnic groups; each has its own lifestyle, culture and language. The ethnic minorities in the Northwest mountains have much lower assets and income than do those ethnic minorities in other regions (Nguyen et al., 2017). The Northwest region ranks as having the lowest GDP per capita. There is still a big gap in living standards between those of the Northwest provinces and the national average (only 40%–60% of the national average in 2012). The Northwest has the highest poverty rate in the whole country, especially in Son La province, and Lao Cai province is three times higher than the national average. Dien Bien province with 38.6% is four times higher than the 9.8% of the country (GSO, 2013). Being aware of the role and position of the Northwest region, over the past years the government has continuously paid attention to the leadership and direction of investment in developing the region.

Development of education in the Northwest region will contribute to raising the intellectual level and at the same time create a source for on-the-job training, especially high-level human resources for ethnic minorities. However, over the past years, education in the Northwest has still had many problems, for instance a shortage of teachers, facilities, and schools. Recently, ethnic minority teachers have been limited (24% in total) with limited pedagogical capacity. The non-ethnic minority teachers did not know the psychological, physical, and cultural characteristics of the ethnic minority students, so they did not speak the ethnic languages and they encountered many difficulties in teaching. To enhance the quality of the teachers, the government has paid attention to teachers' professional development by finding the characteristic of the cultural region and other factors affecting teacher competence.

The study investigated the impact of different factors on teaching competencies in secondary education. The study was conducted with a survey of 1,256 junior and senior high schoolteachers in the Northwest mountains of Vietnam. The data obtained was tabulated, analyzed and interpreted by using the statistical techniques of mean, standard deviation average rating, T-test and Analysis of Variance (ANOVA), to reveal the variables that most affect teacher competence in the Northwest mountains. Seven factors were identified that most affect the competence of teachers. These factors identified are internal factors (gender, age, major, experience, and race), and external factors, namely the distances to school, school facilities, and culture.

2 LITERATURE REVIEW

2.1 *Teacher competence*

The concept of competence has been contested in the literature since it first emerged in the late 1960s, drawing on behavioral psychology and conceiving teacher competences as being observable events in teachers' performance (Harris, 1997; Zuzovsky & Libman, 2006; Valli & Rennert-Ariev, 2002).

The understanding of the concept of a competence in the literature has undergone significant changes since its introduction into discussions of teaching 'expertise'. Originating from behavioral psychology, the concept of teaching competencies as a set of 'discrete', 'theory-free', practical skills spread within many countries, beginning in the late 1960s. The idea was that observable events in teachers' performance in practice could serve as a basis for defining them as being 'competent' teachers. Accordingly, adequate teacher preparation had to be effective in shaping future teachers' performance in their daily teaching (described in van Huizen et al., 2005). The belief underlying this paradigm was that teaching expertise could best be mastered by applying a range of methods or class management techniques learned from experienced teachers.

The concept of competence, in teaching, thus encompasses the following features:

- it involves tacit and explicit knowledge, cognitive and practical skills, as well as dispositions (motivation, beliefs, value orientations and emotions) (Rychen & Salganik, 2003);
- it enables teachers to meet complex demands, by mobilizing psycho-social resources in context, deploying them in a coherent way;
- it empowers the teacher to act professionally and appropriately in a situation (Koster & Dengerink, 2008);
- it helps ensure that teachers undertake tasks effectively (achieving the desired outcome) and efficiently (optimizing resources and efforts);
- it can be demonstrated to a certain level of achievement along a continuum (González & Wagenaar, 2005).

Attempts to define the knowledge base for teachers have provided important insights into areas of teacher knowledge such as subject matter and pedagogical content knowledge, curricular knowledge (Shulman, 1986, 1987), and teachers' practical and personal knowledge, that have informed and continue to inform innovation in teacher education and development programs.

Other aspects of teacher knowledge and understanding seem to remain insufficiently addressed in teacher education, and in research, despite repeated emphasis of their importance. For example, teachers are increasingly considered to need an understanding of how their values and teaching contexts affect their practice (Stooksberry et al., 2009); an awareness of their moral impact (Beyer, 1997; Hansen, 2001); to be able to manage change (Fullan, 1993b); or even act as 'brokers of contradictory interests', vested in education by its various stakeholders (Fang, 1996, p. 54).

A similarly broad understanding of teacher competence is visible in a few other recent competence frameworks (Koster et al., 2005; Tigelaar et al., 2005). They adopt a concept of competence as 'an integrated set of personal characteristics, knowledge, skills and attitudes that are needed for effective performance in various teaching contexts' (Stoof et al., 2002; Tigelaar et al., 2005).

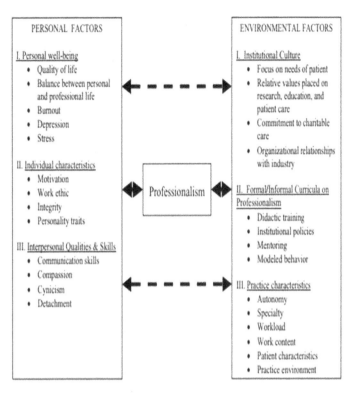

Figure 1.   Model of personal and environmental factors contributing to a physician's professionalism.

2.2 *Factors affecting teacher competence*

Regarding the professional competence, West and Shanafelt (2007) showed the factors affecting professional competence in medical education, including personal factors and environmental factors (Figure 1).

Al-Hinai (2007) also points to a number of factors that influence the professional development of the teacher, which emphasizes external factors such as tradition, culture, social structure, and the effects of international factors.

Drawing ideas from a number of sources on the issue of teachers' professionalism (Whitehurst, 2002; Alatis, 2007; Bransford et al., 2005; Sweed, 2008; Kealing, 2008), the writers believe that the acquisition of teachers' professional characteristics does not come from one source. The writers believe that at least six aspects play a significant role in teachers' professionalism. These are general knowledge ability, focused-training, teaching experience, knowledge of subject matter, certification, and academic degree.

Teaching experience is also believed to be one of the important aspects that make up teachers' qualities (Johnston et al., 2005; Yeh, 2005). The role of teachers' experience on the acquisition of professional qualities has been studied by Johnston et al. (2005). Their study revealed that teachers' experience plays a crucial role in the development of teachers' professionalism acquisition. Alatis (2007) also argues that experience contributes to teachers' theory building. Alatis mentions several aspects that make up teachers' theory building. These are teachers' experience as language learners and as teachers, professional development (training), classroom practices, and teaching reflection. These all become the teachers' collection of cognitive information. The collection of cognitive information then shapes the teachers' characteristics and their characteristics are represented in their daily teaching activities, along with their teaching career development.

A teacher's knowledge of subject matters is the essence that directly affects students' achievement (Whitehurst, 2002; Grossman et al., 2005). As Grossman et al. argue, this comprises of two major aspects (the knowledge of subject being taught and the knowledge of how to teach the subject). A teacher's knowledge of subject matters is gained from many different sources such as from academic institution, training, and self-development.

It is common sense that good teachers are the ones who are talented in teaching and educating learners, and good teachers might not be made through certification. Thus, good teachers are communities certified teachers. However, from the authority point of view, the certification program can be seen as one of the government policies aiming at improving teacher quality (Tamir & Wilson, 2005). Teacher certification has long been an issue in education (Darling-Hammond et al., 1999; Whitehurst, 2002).

3 RESEARCH METHOD

This study was conducted in seven provinces in the Northwest mountains of Vietnam (Hoa Binh, Lao Cai, Yen Bai, Lai Chau, Son La, Dien Bien, and Ha Giang) from March to April 2017. Four schools were selected in each province (two junior schools and two senior high schools). The number of teachers in each school is 35–40 people. The research instrument used was a questionnaire prepared following the Likert scale. Each statement consists of five answer choices. The statement consists of a choice of answers with values: strongly agree (5), agree (4), disagree (3), disagree (2), and strongly disagree (1). In addition, the study employed the qualitative research through interviewing seven teachers from seven schools of the Northwest region, to understand the cultural region affecting teacher competence. Each teacher was interviewed in 30 minutes.

Before being used for research, the instrument for each variable was tested to determine its validity and reliability. The trial was conducted on 50 teachers in three schools. After the validity and reliability was established, a grains invalid statement was issued from the instrument, thereby leaving only the grains statements that are valid and reliable. Having obtained a valid and reliable instrument, the instrument was then used for real research. Validity and reliability of the instrument was conducted to test whether the gage (instrument) that is used qualifies as being a good measuring tool, and qualifies as a measuring tool to measure what is being measured.

SPSS 22.0 software was used for analyzing data to obtain descriptive and inferential statistics. Descriptive statistics measure both the central tendency and the dispersion of the data, including means and standard deviations. The data obtained was tabulated, analyzed and interpreted by using statistical techniques mean, standard deviation average rating, T-test and analysis of variance to reveal the variables that most affect teacher competence in the Northwest mountains. Seven factors were found that most affect the competence of teachers. These factors were identified as being internal factors (gender, age, major, experience, and race), and external factors, namely the distances to school, school facilities, and culture.

4 RESEARCH FINDINGS

A survey of 1,256 teachers was from 36 secondary and high schools in seven Northwestern provinces. There were 71.6% female teachers and 28.4% male. The teachers' education background was: Professional education (0.2%); College of teacher education (11%); BA in teacher education (71.6%); and postgraduates (11.3%).

The number of teachers surveyed was divided equally between the two natural sciences and the social science groups, 47.1% and 52.9%, respectively. The ratio of Mathematics and Language Arts teachers was approximately 17%, followed by Foreign Language teachers accounting for 11%. The rate was 6–8% for the sciences: Chemistry, Biology, History, and Geography. In line with the structure of the curriculum, the number of teachers teaching specialized subjects such as Physical Education, Technology, Computer Science, Music, and Art accounts for a very small proportion of the total number of local teachers.

Table 1.   Descriptive statistics factors affecting teacher competence.

Factor		N	Percent (%)
Gender	Male	353	28.4
	Female	891	71.6
Education background	Professional education	3	0.2
	College of teacher education	136	11.0
	BA in teacher education	963	77.5
	Postgraduate in education	140	11.3
Age	Under 30	180	14.3
	From 30 to under 40	837	66.6
	From 40 to under 50	183	14.6
	Over 50	56	4.5
Major	Natural Science	546	47.1
	Social Science	614	52.9
Experience	Under 5 years	128	11.0
	From 5 years to under 15 years	711	61.0
	From 15 years to under 25 years	259	22.2
	More than 20 years	67	5.8
Race	Kinh people	985	80.0
	Non-Kinh people	247	20.0
Religion	Non-religious	1, 169	97.8
	Religious	26	2.2
Distance to school	Under 1 km	161	14.5
	From 1 km to under 5 km	579	52.1
	From 5 km to under 10 km	140	12.6
	From 10 km to under 20 km	168	15.1
	Over 20 km	64	5.8
Income	Under 3 million VND	22	1.8
	From 3 million to under 4 million VND	119	9.6
	From 5 million to under 7 million VND	287	23.2
	From 7 million to under 10 million VND	447	36.1
	Over 10 million VND	363	29.3

In this survey, 11% of the surveyed teachers have less than 5 years of work experience. Most of the experienced teachers have from 5 to less than 15 years, accounting for 61%, from 15 years to less than 25 years, accounting for 22%, and 5.8% of teachers have over 25 years of teaching experience.

A number of factors to be taken into account that affect the professional competence of teachers include internal factors (gender, age, major, experience, and race), and external factors (ethnicity, religion, geographic distance, income, and working conditions). The following Table describes the factors that affect the professional competence of teachers.

This study examined nine competencies of teachers. The factors that impact on them include: (1) Knowledge of the content and how to teach it; (2) Knowledge of students and how they learn; (3) Plan for teaching and learning; (4) Implement effective teaching and learning; (5) Create and maintain supportive and safe learning environments; (6) Assess, provide feedback and report on student learning; (7) Engage in professional learning; (8) Communicate with students, colleagues and parents; and (9) Develop the school and community.

4.1   *Internal factors*

T-tests were used to test two groups of male and female teachers for nine component competencies to test the difference in mean scores for the two groups. The results are shown in Table 2.

Table 2. T-test sex differences in component capacities.

Code	Competence	t	Sig.
NL3	Plan for teaching and learning	−3.446	.001
NL4	Implement effective teaching and learning	−4.188	.000
NL6	Assess, provide feedback and report on student learning	−3.929	.000
NL7	Engage in professional learning	−2.969	.003
NL8	Communicate with students, colleagues and parents	−2.769	.006

Table 3. T-test major differences in component capacities.

Code	Competence	t	Sig.
NL1	Know the content and how to teach it	−1.985	.047
NL2	Know students and how they learn	1.985	.047

From the results of the above Table, we find that in the nine component competencies, there are five component competencies that show the gender difference significantly in self-assessments of teacher competencies: NL3 Plan for teaching and learning (t = −3.446, sig. = .001), NL4 Implement effective teaching and learning (t = −4.188, sig. = .000), NL6 Assess, provide feedback and report on student learning (t = −3.929, sig. = .000), NL7 Engage in professional learning (t = −2.969, sig. = .003), NL8 Communicate with students, colleagues and parents (t = −2.769, sig. = .008). So, there is a difference between male and female teachers in some specific capacities, as shown above.

As for the ethnic composition, in the survey we present the ethnic composition. However, because of the small number of ethnic minority teachers, we coded in two groups: ethnic minority groups and ethnic minority groups. T-tests for two groups of Kinh teachers and ethnic minority teachers did not find any difference between the two groups. This result is also consistent with the results of in-depth interviews in this study. When interviewed, most teachers shared no discrimination between Kinh and ethnic minority teachers, so there was no difference in competence between the two groups.

Regarding the educational level, the educational level of the surveyed teachers was divided into intermediate, college, university and postgraduate levels. The ANOVA test with the four result groups shows that there is no difference between the groups in terms of educational attainment in the teacher's professional capacity assessment. According to the results of in-depth interviews, young teachers are highly educated. However, teachers share despite high training but lack experience compared to some teachers with long experience despite being trained. Create an intermediate or college degree. Based on this result, we continued to test the difference between groups with years of work experience. The study was divided into five groups of five years of experience: less than 5 years, from 5 years to less than 10 years, from 10 years to less than 15 years, from 15 years to less than 20 years and over 20 years. An ANOVA test was applied for the difference between groups of years of work experience in the assessment capability (F = 3.044, sig. = .028 < .05). Tukey's test results show that the more years a team is working, the more appreciated it is in its assessing capacity.

In terms of teaching specialization, when surveying, we let teachers write down the specialized information they are teaching. After data processing, the teachers' teaching expertise was categorized as naturalistic teachers and social teachers. The T-test results in Table 3 show that there is a difference between the natural teacher group and the social teacher group in the two component competencies NL1 Know the content and how to teach it, NL2 Know students and how they learn (t = −1.985, sig. = .047), in which the mean score of NL1 with the teacher group is 3.99 and the natural teacher group is 4.06, and the NL2 group are respectively 3.99 and 4.06. The average scores of the two groups showed that group teachers had NL1 and NL2 higher than the social group teachers.

Table 4. ANOVA test for group differences on internet distance to school in component capacities.

Code	Competence	F	Sig.
NL1	Know the content and how to teach it	3.975	.003
NL2	Know students and how they learn	3.975	.003
NL3	Plan for teaching and learning	6.721	.000
NL4	Implement effective teaching and learning	4.265	.002
NL5	Create and maintain supportive and safe learning environments	3.571	.007
NL6	Assess, provide feedback and report on student learning	4.657	.001
NL7	Engage in professional learning	4.693	.001

4.2 External factors

In addition to the subjective factors of the teacher itself, the study also examined other external factors such as geographical distance, regional culture, family economics, and school facilities.

Regarding distance to school, we are particularly interested in this effect because the Northwest is a mountainous tributary. Difficult travel is also one of the factors that affects the professional capacity of the teacher. In this study, we surveyed the distance by asking, 'How far do you come from school?' After processing the data, we divided the responses into five groups: Less than 1 km, from 1 km to less than 5 km, from 5 km to less than 10 km, from 10 km to less than 20 km, and from 20 km or more. ANOVA test results show that there are differences between teacher groups at different distances.

The results of Table 4 show that there are differences between groups of teachers with different distance to school. The remaining seven competencies differed between teacher groups located at different distances (sig. < .05). Tukey's test showed that for groups of geographical distances it was found that almost all groups with distances of less than 1 km had higher scores than those with distances of 10 km to 20 km, and 20 km or more. The result of in-depth interviews showed the factor affecting teacher competence. Some teachers said that when they have to go far away, they have difficulties in tracking students. A teacher in Luc Yen district, Yen Bai said,

'Because school does not have dormitory, many students far away have to live near the school. Therefore, the teachers have to pay attention to the students outside the school hours, but due to the condition I am far away from school, I have not been able to watch the children out of the classroom. There is also a school for teachers in the school, but only the unmarried teacher'.

Teachers not only had difficulties in distance to school but also had difficulties in the cultural region and custom of the location in Northwest mountains. The factors were studied through in-depth interviews with teachers. Most teachers think that there is not much difference in regional culture reflected in the professional capacity of the teacher. However, there are a small number of teachers who share the difficulties of customary practices that affect the teaching of teachers. In the case of Cao Phong district in Hoa Binh province, a physics teacher with 15 years of experience said,

'In the district, most of the children are ethnic Muong, when there are jobs like funeral or weddings children. Often, they follow the tradition of the Muong people, having a large number of members and relatives. There are times when I go to class only a few children go to school. Because of that I had difficulty in teaching'.

Apart from the cultural and customary factors in the Northwest region, the areas of economic development characterized by local characteristics such as specialized farming and exploitation of resources, are especially also influencing factors on teacher competence. For example, in the Cao Phong district of Hoa Binh province, the area specializes in growing oranges. Here most households plant oranges and live on it. A teacher in Thach Yen High School said,

'Many students have left school during their study to go to plan orange because they think that after graduating they do plan orange too, they leave school soon to do that. Therefore my school dropout rate is very high. I also spent a lot of time moving around the family but they did not let their children go to school but it seems to be not significant'.

Table 5. ANOVA test for group differences on income in component capacities.

Code	Competence	F	Sig.
NL1	Know the content and how to teach it	2.743	.027
NL2	Know students and how they learn	2.743	.027
NL5	Create and maintain supportive and safe learning environments	2.591	.035
NL8	Communicate with students, colleagues and parents	5.067	.000

Table 6. T-test teaching subject differences in component capacities.

Code	Competence	t	Sig.
NL7	Engage in professional learning	−2.393	.030
NL8	Communicate with students, colleagues and parents	−2.086	.037
NL9	Develop school and community	−2.084	.037

As a result, survey results and in-depth interviews have pointed out the geographic distance, culture, and customs of the region affecting teacher competence in the Northwest region.

Income is one of the factors that affects the overall work capacity of employees. With teachers, if the income is stable to meet the needs of life, they will devote themselves to teaching and education. In this study, we looked at teachers' income levels by subgroups: Less than 3 million VND, from 3 million to under 5 million VND, from 5 million to under 7 million VND, from 7 million to 10 million VND, and over 10 million VND. The data processed by the ANOVA test showed that among the nine component competencies, there were four component competencies with different income groups in terms of self-assessment of professional competence (see Table 5). NL1 Know the content and how to teach it ($F = 2.743$, sig. $= .027$), NL2 Know students and how they learn, NL5 Create and maintain supportive and safe learning environments ($F = 2.591$, sig. $= .035$), and NL8 Communicate with students, colleagues and parents ($F = 5.067$, sig. $= .000$).

Tukey's test for comparing income groups with each other found that the results showed that the higher the group of teachers with higher incomes assessed their occupational competencies than the lower-income groups. This shows that the income factor affects the professional capacity of the teacher. Therefore, the state must have policies related to salaries to ensure the life of teachers' peace of mind to work, dedicated to the profession.

In terms of material facilities, in this study we focus on the survey of schools having internet access for teaching and learning. With the trend toward international integration and the impact of the 4.0 industrial networks, the requirements for information technology for education are indispensable. We surveyed the use of information technology and whether the schools have internet facilities to serve and support the teaching of the teacher. A T-test was applied for two internet-based and non-networked schools, showing the difference between two groups of teachers in the assessment of professional competence (see Table 6), of which three compositional qualification groups had statistically significant differences, including NL7 Engage in professional learning ($t = -2393$, sig. $= .030$), NL8 Communicate with students, colleagues and parents ($t = -2.086$, sig. $= .037$), NL9 Develop school and community ($t = -2.084$, sig. $= .037$).

In addition to the internet connection factor, we also examined the teacher's frequent use to see how teachers use computers and networks on a regular basis to influence professional competence. An ANOVA test was applied for four groups: Rarely, Occasionally, Frequently, and Very Frequently. The results are shown in Table 7.

There are NL3 Plan for teaching and learning ($F = 2.688$, sig. $= .045$) and NL6 Assess, provide feedback and report on student learning ($F = 2.967$, sig. $= .031$) are significant. The assessment is statistically significant for the difference between groups in the use of computers and the internet

Table 7. ANOVA test for group differences on internet connections at school in component capacities.

Code	Competence	F	Sig
NL3	Plan for teaching and learning	2.688	.045
NL6	Assess, provide feedback and report on student learning	2.967	.031

(sig. < .05). This is also consistent with the interview that the study conducted. A teacher with experience of 20 years at Lao Cai High School No. 3 shares:

'I have taught for 20 years, before without computer I usually write lesson plans. However, in recent years I have been exposed to computers and I used to write lesson plans, plan teaching. Particularly, I am able to manage grades, tests of student grades on the computer and enter scores online into the system. I find the network and computer to help teachers more convenient in teaching their work'.

5 CONCLUSION

This study found the factors affecting the professional capacity of the Northwestern teachers in the Northwest from the overview of research models in the world and the practical context of Northwestern Vietnam. Impact factors include two main groups: (1) Teachers themselves (sex, education, professional skills, experience, ethnicity, and religion); and (2) External factors (geographical distance, economic conditions, culture, and customs). The results show the factors that affect the professional capacity of teachers in the Northwest. Some component capacities are strongly influenced by a variety of factors, such as the ability to understand the subject syllabus, teaching methods and assessment, and the ability to understand the development of psychophysiology, cognitive and student learning activities, capacity for assessment, and communication skills. In particular, research results point to a number of factors that affect multiple component capacities such as sex, geographical distance, and participation in training courses.

This result shows that when designing activities or assigning tasks, or organizations in education, attention should be paid to gender issues and geographical distance issues. In addition, with the selection of subjects needed to be surveyed to suit the practical needs of teachers in the Northwest.

This study investigated the factors influencing the professional capacity of teachers in the Northwest. From these results policy makers and educational administrators can refer to appropriate policies to improve the quality of teachers who contribute to team capacity development solutions for teachers in the Northwest mountains.

REFERENCES

Alatis, J.E. (2007). What language teaching is. A project of the National Capital Language Resource Center. Retrieved from http//www.nclrc.org/essentias

Al-Hinai, M. (2007). The interplay between culture, teacher professionalism and teachers' professional development at times of change. In T. Townsend, & R. Bates (Eds.), *Handbook of Teacher Education: Globalization, Standards and Professionalism in Times of Change* (pp. 41–52). Springer.

Beyer, L.E. (1997). The moral contours of teacher education. *Journal of Teacher Education*, 48(4), 245–254.

Bransford, J.D. et al. (2005). Introduction. In L. Darling-Hammond & J.D. Bransford (Eds.), *Preparing Teachers for a Changing World* (pp. 1–39). San Francisco: Jossey-Bass Publisher.

Darling-Hammond, L. & Berry, B. (2006). Highly qualified teachers for all. *Educational Leadership*, 64(3), 14.

Fang, Z. (1996). A review of research on teacher beliefs and practices. *Educational Research*, 38(1), 47–65.

Fullan, M.G. (1993a). *Change forces: Probing the depths of educational reform* (1st ed.). Routledge.

Fullan, M.G. (1993b). Why teachers must become change agents. *Educational Leadership*, 50(6), 12–17.

González, J. & Wagenaar, R. (Eds.) (2005). Tuning educational structures in Europe II. Universities' contribution to the Bologna Process. University of Deusto & University of Groningen. Retrieved from http://tuning.unideusto.org/tuningeu/

Grossman, P. et al. (2005). Teaching subject matters. In L. Darling-Hammond & J.D. Bransford (Eds.), *Preparing Teachers for a Changing World* (pp. 201–274). San Francisco: Jossey-Bass Publisher.

Hansen, D.T. (2001). Teaching as a moral activity. In V. Richardson (Ed.), *Handbook of Research on Teaching* (4th ed.). Washington: AERA.

Harris, A. (1997). The deprofessionalization and deskilling of teachers. In K. Watson, C. Modgil & S. Mogdil (Eds.), *Teachers, Teacher Education and Training* (pp. 57–65). London: Cassell.

Johnston, B. et al. (2005). The professional development of working ESL/EFL teachers: A pilot study. In D.J. Tedick (Ed.), *Second Language Teacher Education* (pp. 53–72). New Jersey: Lawrence Erlbaum Associates Publisher.

Kealing, J. (2008). Training teachers for change? Assessing language teacher participation in workshops and their subsequent adaptation of new teaching practices and attitude. A paper presented at The Seventh International Conference on Teachers' Competencies and Qualifications for ELT in Indonesia held at Bandung Institute of Technology.

Koster, B., Brekelmans, M., Korthagen, F.A.J. & Wubbels, T. (2005). Quality requirements for teacher educators. *Teaching and Teacher Education*, 21(2), 157–176.

Koster, B. & Dengerink, J.J. (2000). Professional standards for teacher educators: How to deal with complexity, ownership and function. Experiences from the Netherlands. *European Journal of Teacher Education*, 31(2), 135–149.

Medley, D.M. (1977). Teacher competence and teacher effectiveness. A review of process-product research. Retrieved from http://files.eric.ed.gov/fulltext/ED143629.pdf

Mumtaz, S. (2000). Factors affecting teachers' use of information and communications technology: A review of the literature. *Journal of Information Technology for Teacher Education*, 9(3), 319–342.

Nguyen, C.V., Tran, T.Q. & Vu, V.H. (2017). Ethnic minorities in northern mountains of Vietnam: Employment, poverty and income. *Social Indicators Research*, 134(1), 93–115. doi:10.1007/s11205-016-1413-3

Pantic, N. (2011). The meaning of teacher competence in contexts of change. In search of missing elements of a knowledge base for teacher education–moral purposes and change agentry. Utrecht University.

Rychen, D.S. & Salganik, L.H. (2003). *Key Competencies for a successful life and a well-functioning society*. Göttingen: Hogrefe & Huber.

Shagrir, L. (2015). Factors affecting the professional characteristics of teacher educators in Israel and in the USA: A comparison of two models. *Compare: A Journal of Comparative and International Education*, 45(2), 206–225.

Shulman, L.S. (1987). Knowledge and teaching: Foundations of the new reform. *Harvard Educational Review*, 57(1), 1–22.

Stooksberry, L.M., Schussler, D.L. & Bercaw, L.A. (2009). Conceptualizing dispositions: Intellectual, cultural, and moral domains of teaching. *Teachers and Teaching: Theory and Practice*, 15(6), 719–736.

Sweed, J. (2008). Attitude and teacher development. A paper presented on The Seventh International Conference on Teachers' Competencies and Qualifications for ELT in Indonesia held at Bandung Institute of Technology 15–17 April 2008.

Tamir, E. & Wilson, M. (2005). Who should guard the gates? Evidentiary and professional warrants for claiming jurisdiction. *Journal of Teacher Education*, 56(4), 332–342.

Tigelaar, D.E.H., Dolmans, D.H.J.M., Wolfhagen, I.H.A.P., & van der Vleuten, C.P.M. (2004). The development and validation of a framework for teaching competencies in higher education. *Higher Education: The International Journal of Higher Education and Educational Planning*, 48(2), 253–268.

Valli, L. & Rennert-Ariev, P. (2002). New standards and assessments? curriculum transformation in teacher education. *Journal of Curriculum Studies*, 34(2), 201–225.

van Huizen, P., van Oers, B. & Wubbels, T. (2005). A Vygotskian perspective on teacher education. *Journal of Curriculum Studies*, 37(3), 267–290.

West, C.P. & Shanafelt, T.D. (2007). The influence of personal and environmental factors on professionalism in medical education. *BMC Medical Education*, 7(1), 29.

World Bank. (2017). *International Bank for Reconstruction and Development, International Development Association, International Finance Corporation, Multilateral Investment Guarantee Agency: Country partnership framework for Socialist Republic of Vietnam*. Retrieved from http://documents.worldbank.org/curated/en/173771496368868576/pdf/05-04-2017-Vietnam-CPF-to-SECPO-05052017.pdf

Yeh, H. (2005). Teacher study groups as a vehicle to strengthen EFL teachers' professional identity and voice. *Asian EFL Journal*, 7(4), 50. Retrieved from http://www.asian-efl-journal.com.international.php

Zuzovsky, R. & Libman, Z. (2006). standards of teaching and teaching tests: Is this the right way to go? *Studies in Educational Evaluation*, 32(1), 37–52.

Educational Administration Innovation for Sustainable Development – Komariah et al. (Eds)
© 2018 Taylor & Francis Group, London, ISBN 978-1-138-57341-3

Assessing collaborative problem-solving competency through an integrated theme based on teaching chemistry

L.T. Hung, V.P. Lien & N.T.P. Vy
Vietnam National University, Hanoi, Vietnam

ABSTRACT: This research focuses on building a problem-solving collaboration competency assessment tool in teaching chemistry. Categories of problem-solving collaboration competency assessment are detailed from the 2015 PISA problem-solving collaboration competency framework. From those assessment categories, this research proposed appropriate assessment tools that can be used in teaching, such as a student activity observation survey, academic record, teamwork minutes, teamwork assessment rubric and so on. On this basis, the research aimed at designing and implementing a problem-solving collaboration competency assessment for a particular integrated theme based on teaching chemistry. The analysis result shows the reliability of the categories makes sure Cronbach alpha index and concordance level with rating scale model. The result of the verified analysis t-test (control experiment test) demonstrates multi-subject teaching efficiency in boosting students' competency.

1 INTRODUCTION

Currently, society is developing more and more in accordance with the need for international integration and cooperation to solve domestic as well as regional problems. According to the 2011–2020 educational development strategy regarding general education in Vietnam, to meet the demand for human resources with a competence for integration, it is intended to develop the general competences and specific competences of each subject.

It was found that CPS competence is one of the most important competences that needs to be developed for students for the following reason: if the student only develops problem-solving ability, it is not enough to use the knowledge, skills and attitudes to engage in problem-solving. At present, practical issues are often quite complex, requiring the cooperation of individuals to exchange ideas and solve problems. In particular, in the context of integration, the need for cooperation is even more important. That is why we chose to research and develop CPS competence for pupils through teaching chemistry in order to improve creativity and positive cooperation for students. In terms of this competence, there are a number of studies (O'Neil et al., 2003; Grinffin et al., 2012, 2015; OECD, 2015), which have formed the general framework for CPS competence, definition, structure and assessment criteria.

However, the selection and application of these theoretical frameworks in the assessment of competency in teaching has many challenges. In this study, we will focus on the study of theoretical framework OECD force in PISA 2015. By using the expert approach, we developed specific indicators and criteria for assessing CPS in teaching chemistry and chose a lesson-based integrated curriculum to conduct a pedagogical experiment with a special topic from a chapter covering nitrogen and phosphorus at Viet Duc High School in Ha Noi, Vietnam.

2 THEORETICAL FOUNDATION

There are many different definitions of CPS which is one of the twenty-first century skills (ATC21S™ project). It can be defined as a joint activity where small groups execute a number of

Table 1. Matrix of CPS skills (PISA, 2015).

	(1) Establishing and maintaining shared understanding	(2) Taking appropriate action to solve the problem	(3) Establishing and maintaining team organization
(A) Exploring and understanding	(A1) Discovering perspectives and abilities of team members	(A2) Discovering the type of collaborative interaction to solve the problem, along with goals	(A3) Understanding roles to solve problem
(B) Representing and formulating	(B1) Building a shared representation and negotiating the meaning of the problem (common ground)	(B2) Identifying and describing tasks to be completed	(B3) Describe roles and team organization (communication protocol/rules of engagement)
(C) Planning and executing	(C1) Communicating with team members about the actions to be/being performed	(C2) Enacting plans	(C3) Following rules of engagement, (e.g. prompting other team members to perform their tasks)
(D) Monitoring and reflecting	(D1) Monitoring and repairing the shared understanding	(D2) Monitoring results of actions and evaluating success in solving the problem	(D3) Monitoring, providing feedback and adapting the team organization and roles

steps in order to transform a current state into a desired goal state (Hesse et al., 2015). CPS is also conceptualized as a complex skill requiring both social and cognitive competencies. It arises from the links between critical thinking, problem-solving, decision making and collaboration – all of which are hypothesized to contribute to the skill (O'Neil et al., 2003). The few existing definitions of collaborative problem-solving have the following in common: (i) they postulate the existence of a group consisting of at least two individuals; (ii) they assume that there is a problem and a shared goal, which needs to be achieved; and (iii) not only cognitive but also social and communication skills need to be used to solve the problem (Greiff, 2012).

We can see that "the primary distinction between problem-solving by an individual and collaborative problem-solving is its social nature – the need for communication, exchange of ideas, shared identification of the problem and its elements, and negotiated agreement on connections between problem elements and relationships between actions and their effects. CPS makes each of these steps observable, as they must be shared with a partner or other members of a group if a solution is to be successfully identified" (Care & Grinffin, 2014).

According to the OECD (2015), CPS is an important and necessary competence of both the educational environment as well as the labor force demand. NLG is defined as "CPS competency is the competence of an individual to effectively engage in a process whereby two or more agents attempt to solve a problem by sharing the understanding and effort required to come to a solution and pooling their knowledge, skills and efforts to reach that solution" (PISA, 2015).

In our opinion, CPS competence is a complex of the knowledge, skills and attitudes of the learner needed to solve the problem that cannot be solved alone and the need to cooperate with others who work together to achieve common goals. From that point of view, to assess CPS, teachers need to assign tasks that can only be solved with the participation of many members.

After studying the literature in several research fields, we decided to build an assessment toolkit based on the PISA 2015 structure because we found it reasonable to assess. Three core collaborative problem-solving competencies are: (i) establishing and maintaining shared understanding; (ii) taking appropriate action to solve the problem; (iii) establishing and maintaining

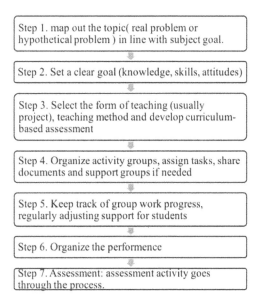

Figure 1.   Steps in planning the integrated curriculum.

team organization. These three competencies arise from a combination of collaboration and individual problem-solving processes, so the group must perform these problem-solving processes concurrently with a set of collaborative processes (PISA, 2015). According to PISA 15, Whether the process of problem-solving or individual problem-solving process is based on the same cognitive development foundation. The individual problem-solving processes are exploring and understanding, representing and formulating, planning and executing, and monitoring and reflecting (PISA, 2012).

These three major CPS competencies are crossed with the four major individual problem-solving processes to form a matrix of specific skills in the design of the assessment toolkit. We placed 12 criteria on top to build three indicators for each criterion. Each indicator is specified with the three levels: low, middle and high level with the current measurable action. We suggest some assessment tools and assessment methods for each indicator.

When using this framework for teaching and assessing, teachers should apply the method, the tool so that it is suitable for the content lesson and students' ability.

3   MAP OUT THE INTEGRATED THEMES

The nitrogen-phosphorus chapter has a number of compounds that are highly applicable in their lives, so we can easily build up the relevant topics covered in this chapter such as: the effect of nitrogen-phosphorus concentration on the growth of Hoan Kiem Lake algae, chemical fertilizers and the environment.

3.1   *Develop curriculum-based assessments*

Before the project, the following were determined:

1. Background knowledge about nitrogen-phosphorus
2. Level of interest of students in topics related to environmental pollution of Sword Lake
3. Ability to solve P related problems in student practice, e.g. What is the ghost phenomenon?

Table 2. Guide to assess CPS competence for Criterion A1.

Criteria	Indicator	Level			Method/Assessment tool
		Low	Middle	High	
(A1) Discovering perspectives and abilities of team members	Recognizing strengths and weaknesses of others?	Do not learn the pros and cons of team members	Using some methods of understanding the pros and cons of members	Discovering the pros and cons of team members	Methods – Observations – Peer assessment – Self-assessment Tool – Observations checklist – Study records – Group work protocol
	Assigning work consistently with members' capacity; Searching, sharing documents with team members	Do not assign job specifically; Do not search for documents	Assigning work based on member capacity; General resources are not yet available	Job assignment in line with member capacity; There is a wealth of resources shared with team members	

Table 3. Matrix of assessment indicators.

Observation note	Peer review cards	Test	Product group
A1.1 Explore pros and cons of team members involved in dealing with N, P pollution	A1.3 Search and share documents related to pollution N, P at Hoan Kiem Lake		A3.1 Identify the problem
A1.2 Effective job matching	B3.3 Implement the rules of the group		A3.2 Analysis of a number of reasons
A2.1 Give some form of cooperation	C1.1 Join group meetings		A3.3 Find out the main cause
A2.2 Select different types of group meetings	C1.2 Study and present views on issues related to nitrogen-phosphorus pollution		B1.1 Describe the relationship of the problem to the subject knowledge
A2.3 Frequency, efficiency of group work	C1.3 Positive change to find common ideas		B1.2 Describe the importance of the problem in life
B3.1 Elected by team leader	C2.1 Propose solution for pollution treatment N, P		B1.3 Identify the relationship between theoretical knowledge and social knowledge related to the problem
B3.2 Develop common principles for group work	D1.2 Detection of Common misconceptions		B2.1 Identify and describe the objective of the subject's knowledge and social knowledge needed to solve the problem
C2.2 Modify N, P pollution treatment solution based on member comments	D1.3 Accept, regulate self-esteem by common sense		B2.2 Identify and describe the goals of the subject's skills and problem-solving skills
C2.3 Unanimous choice of solution	D3.2 Share views and adjust group activity guidelines		B2.3 Identify and describe the attitudes goals for the lesson and attitudes to the problem to be solved
C3.1 Record, monitor teamwork process	D3.3 Adapt to the principle of group activity		D2.3 Evaluate the results of the problem-solving activity
C3.2 Reminders, suggestions for non-active members			
C3.3 Adjust the rules in line with reality			
D2.1 Track problem-solving process			
D2.2 Adjustment			
D3.1 Provide feedback to each member			

During and after the project: Use the evaluation of 36 indicators identified in the assessment through the teaching project "Effect of concentration of N, P on the growth of green algae, blue algae in Hoan Kiem Lake". Conduct an assessment tool matrix with the following four assessment tools: observation cards, peer review cards, tests and product groups. Selection of indicators based on the following principles:

– Observation note: The indicators included in the observation sheet items are easy to expose and can be assessed through group assessment and teacher assessment. This will make it easier for teachers to observe if there are too many students in the classroom.
– Peer review cards: Selection of personal indicators, not high knowledge, usually indicators of consciousness, so the team members can easily measure the indicator of the village body, as well as team members.

After conducting the scoring of the criteria by the tools, the selection of points for each criterion is the same, we gained the score of CPS. Score each maximum of two points so we will have a maximum score of six points. Overall score NL solved the problem to a maximum of 72 points. Based on Table 4 levels of PISA. The research team divides into five levels as the level 1 of the group is not yet competency-aligned with level 0 of each guideline.

Score	Level
0–14.4	Competence not formed = Level 0
14.5–28.8	Low level = Level 1
28.9–43.2	Medium level = Level 2
43.3–57.6	Good level = Level 3
57.7–72	High level = Level 4

Table 4. Level of CPS competence 4.

Integrated goal			Integrated contend		
Chemistry	Physic	Biology	Chemistry	Physic	Biology
Presents the stage of compounds containing N, P in the lake			Physical properties of compounds containing N, P		Metabolic processes in the body
Explain the conversion of N, P in the lake water	Presenting mechanical methods to prevent waste	Explain the process of aerobic and anaerobic respiration in organisms	Chemical properties of compounds containing N, P	Mechanical methods to present waste.	Respiration of bacteria
Explain the effect of concentration of N, P on the development of cyanobacteria and green algae. Assessing effectiveness of chemical, physical and biological method to N, P pollution treatment in Hoan Kiem Lake					

3.2 *Lesson plan*

Teaching in the form of project-based teaching with the topic "Effect of nitrogen-phosphorus concentration on the growth of Hoan Kiem Lake algae".

Unit Summary: Nitrogen and phosphorus pollution is an alarming problem today. Although N and P pollution is not directly harmful to human health, it is the source of water pollution and the health of organisms living in the lake. Through this project, students are required to combine learned knowledge and social knowledge to understand the state of N and P pollution in Hoan Kiem Lake and how to handle it.

Task.

Group 1+2:

Assessing the situation and proposing solutions to treat N and P pollution in Hoan Kiem Lake by chemical and biological methods.

Group 1+2:

Assessing the situation and proposing solutions to treat N and P pollution in Hoan Kiem Lake by chemical and physical methods.

Integrated goal:

Process.

Step 1. First lesson (15 mins): Introduction Project (5 mins); group formation, building ideas and planning (10 mins): In the group splitting step, there are many ways to draw groups, group them by seating position or let students select their own groups. After setting up the group, The teacher gives student grades and tutorials on group assessment and peer evaluation.

Step 2. Teamwork (two weeks): Students work in groups, teacher asks students to exchange information regularly on group work to timely adjust and support. Ask students to show proof of teamwork online, meeting with teachers. For each activity observation the teacher group can be combined with the group activity report to measure the A1.1, A1.2, A2.2, A2.3, C2.2, C2.3, Report C3, D 2.3. At the same time, students can measure all remaining indicators in the rubric.

Step 3. Second lesson (90 mins).

+ Performent: Groups perform their products in class within 30p. Teacher can evaluate the indicators to be evaluated through product grouping based on the rubric of the prepared product reviews. At the same time, the groups also cross-assess, and the teams evaluate the results of their problem-solving themselves.

+ Feedback, reviews (30 min): Teacher comment and give groups self-assessment time. By observing, the teacher can evaluate indicators D 2.1, D 3.1.

Step 4. Test (20 min).

Teachers take tests to measure the level of knowledge, skills and attitudes of each student. Although these indicators have been measured in the product group, the test may give details at the student's individual level.

We can see that project activity that may be covered by the rating 36 indicators CPS competence is also contain the number of the work to shape that competence for students. Results for the force training between both class is equivalent, matching choice as the provider level and experience.

4 RESULTS AND DISCUSSION

With the experimental class (Class 11A3 of Viet Duc High School in Ha Noi, Viet Nam), we conducted an integrated project. In the other class (Class 11 A2), we introduced knowledge related to the integration topic with the normal method. In the course of the experiment, use of methods and tools to measure the levels of student performance indicators in the experimental class were used. After the test, students in the two classes took exams to assess their level of knowledge. After analyzing the results, some conclusions were drawn on the following issues.

Table 5.   Reliability of toolkit.

Cronbach's alpha	N of Items
.719	36

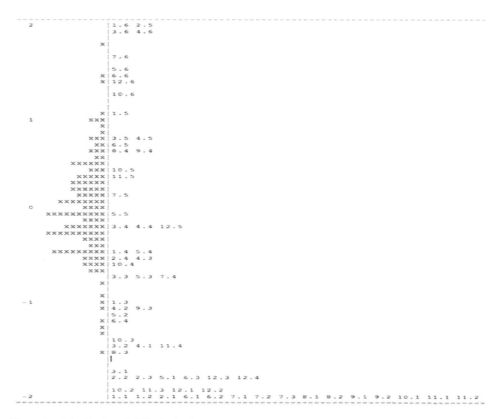

Figure 2.   Distribution of difficulty level.

4.1   *Reliability of the toolkit*

As a result, we have a common confidence coefficient for the overall measure of Cronbach's alpha reliability of 36. The reliability indicator, Cronbach's alpha = 0.719, is within acceptable tolerability. Although the total reliability of 36 criteria was satisfactory, the reliability of the 12 criteria was only 0.664. Therefore, we need to consider correlation of sum to eliminate bad items. When analyzing the 12 groups of criteria separately, it can be seen that the criteria B1, D1, D3 have a total variable correlation of < 0.3, which is low, so we need to revise the indicators in these three criteria to get good results After reviewing, the team found that criteria D1, D3 were the two criteria measured primarily by self-assessment so it is important to re-examine the student's self-assessment.

Conformance testing of the 12 criteria by means of Conquest software, resulted in an average value of INFIT MNSQ fit within the range of 0.59–1.44, which is appropriate. Below is a table of MNSQ values for the 12 criteria. Conventional criteria for numbers 1–12 are easier to analyze during data analysis. The results for these criteria are consistent with the suitability of the toolkit.

Table 6. MNSQ value of the 12 criteria.

Criteria	1 (A1)	2 (A2)	3 (A3)	4 (B1)	5 (B2)	6 (B3)
MNSQ	0.86	0.83	0.92	1.36	1.14	0.93
criteria	7 (C1)	8 (C2)	9 (C3)	10 (D1)	11(D2)	12 (B3)
MNSQ	0.94	0.97	0.90	1.25	0.90	0,96

4.2 Difficulty level and capacity of the candidate

For each criterion maximum 6 points for six levels. In order to assess the difficulty level distribution of each of the 12 criteria and competitor's competencies, we used the Conquest software to compare the results with the logistic log. The results are as follows: This is in the range of -1.5–1.7 logistic units, but the difficulty of the criteria is from -2 to 2, so the criterion is outside the competency range. In the following, we conducted the analysis of the criteria level.

The criteria level can be classified into three groups:

Group 1: High difficulty levels like 1.6, 2.5, 3.6, 4.6.
Group 2: Levels appropriate for students.
Group 3: Difficult levels below the student's ability level: 1.1, 1.2, 6.1 …

From the above distribution, it can be seen that the questions in Group 1, where the difficulty level is outside the competitor's ability is usually level 5 or 6 of the criteria. Conversely, the criteria below the competitor's competencies are usually levels 1–2 of the criteria, which is suitable. However, criterion 12 should be revisited because of the low level of 3.4. Criterion 12 (D3) involves monitoring, providing feedback and adapting to group norms and organization, which is primarily due to student self-evaluation, which may be due to poor student judgment. The results are not suitable.

4.3 The reliability of the test

The reliability of the test (Cronbach's alpha $= 0.606$) is acceptable. Conducting the analysis of the test, we can see that if some questions are eliminated it will be more reliable, such as Question 3, 7, 8 and 10. These questions need to be revised. Questions 7 and 8 are used to measure B1. This is consistent with the low reliability of criterion B1, so it is important to consider revising Question 7.8 to obtain a higher degree of reliability for criterion B1.

4.4 CPS competence point

Calculation: Each indicator has three levels of points 0, 1 and 2, so the maximum is two points. Therefore, the maximum score for 36 indicators is 72 points.

After scoring and inputting the necessary data into the computer after I have processed that data using Excel and SPSS software to calculate the values.

This table above show that the student grade is in the range of 35–56 points (average: 46, median: 45 and mode: 44 is approximately equal). From this it can be seen that the capacity difference between the HS is relatively large.

With the score obtained, the research team divided into five levels of competency to obtain the distribution chart of the CPS competence as shown in Chart 1. The graph shows that the HS is mainly level 3 (65%), level 2 (30%) and level 4 (5%). Show that most of the students have formed the CPS competence in average, quite. Because the survey sample is small, larger samples can be obtained for subjects covered with competence levels.

Table 7.　Describe CPS competence score.

Valid	40
Missing	0
Mean	461.250
Std. Error of Mean	90525
Median	450.000
Mode	44.00.00
Std. Deviation	572.528
Variance	32.779
Range	24.00.00
Minimum	35.00.00
Maximum	59.00.00

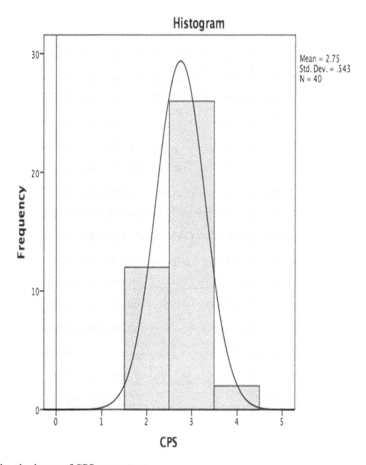

Figure 3.　The plot layout of CPS competence.

4.5　*The impact of subject-based teaching t-tests between the control and experimental classes*

After conducting the pedagogical experiment and conducting the test on two classes, the two-tailed result was $0.028 < 0.05$, indicating that there was a difference between the two results. Therefore, the difference here is due to the impact of subject teaching which helped grade 11 A3 students achieve better results than 11 A2.

The correlation between test scores and CPS competence scores. By using SPSS software in relation to test scores and CPS competence scores, we can see Sig. $= 0.287 > 0.05$, indicating that there is no correlation between the test scores and NL. Thus, if the teacher only pays attention to the results of learning knowledge, it is impossible to assess the level of student achievement.

The correlation between product group scores and CPS competence scores. To examine the correlation between the product group score and the IBA of the HS, the Pearson correlation to obtain a two-tailed value of $0.00 < 0.05$ and a correlation coefficient of 0.655 was used. These two values are interrelated. This is also understandable as the HS group activity can express quite clearly the ability to cooperate as well as solve their own problems.

From the two correlations above, it can be seen that the students' performance evaluation through the activity or through the group's product score of the learning theme yielded significant results in the evaluation of the CPS competence.

5 CONCLUSION

Through the pedagogical experiment process, the reliability of the assessment tools has been verified, as well as the correlation between the rating score and the tool score with other assessment channels such as the test and observation. The reliability of the toolkit is acceptable, but some indicators need to be adjusted to make the tool better. Most students have formed CPS with mostly medium and good results.

REFERENCES

Andriása Dam, Joensen, Stuart Edwards, Manolis Mavrikis, Katerina Avramides, Kristen Weatherby, Peter Blatchford and Peter Kutnick for their input and assistance (2017), Solved! Making the case for collaborative problem-solving, Nesta

Care, P.G. (2015). *Assessment and Teaching of 21st Century Skills. Methods and Approach (Eds).* Dordrecht: Springer.

Care, P.G. (2014). An approach to assessment of collaborative problem solving. *Research and Practice in Technology Enhanced Learning,* 9(3) 367–388.

Greiff, S. (2012). *From interactive to collaborative problem solving: Current issues in the Programme for International Student Assessment, University of Zagreb.* Faculty of Humanities and Social Sciences. Department of Psychology.

Grinffin, E.C. (2015). *Assessment of collaborative problem solving.* European Schoolnet Academy.

Heyse, J.E. (1996). *Berufliche Weiterbildung undberufliche Kompentenzentwicklung.* Arbeitsgemeinschaft. Qualifikation Entwicklung Management (Hrsg.): Kompetenzentwicklung 1996, Waxmann, Münster. S. 15–152.

OCCD. (2012). *Definition and selection of competencies: Theoretical and conceptual foundation.* DeSeCo Annual Report 2001.

OCCD. (2015). Pisa 2015 released field trial cognitive items, GB(2014) 2 Field Trial Analysis Plan for the Cognitive Assessment from the 37th meeting of the PISA Governing Board).

Weinert, F.E. (2001). Concept of competence: A conceptual definition. In D.S. Rychen, & L.H. Salganik (Eds.), *Defining and selecting key competencies: 46.*

Worf, A. (1995). *Competence-based assessment.* Buckingham, Philadelphia: Open University Press.

Educational Administration Innovation for Sustainable Development – Komariah et al. (Eds)
© 2018 Taylor & Francis Group, London, ISBN 978-1-138-57341-3

An academic quality development model based on transformational leadership

B. Ismaya, U.S. Sa'ud, A. Komariah & D. Nurdin
Universitas Pendidikan Indonesia, Bandung, West Java, Indonesia

ABSTRACT: Transformational leadership helps higher education to frame its attitudes to move its university forward. It is considered that who demonstrate these leader higher education characteristics of transformational leadership have effects on satisfaction leader University UII Yogyakarta and better performance at university. Therefore, this study purposes to discover the level of transformational leadership that higher education demonstrates during its administrative practices on a daily basis. The results reveal that the university demonstrates a high level of characteristics of transformational leadership in terms of idealized influence, inspirational motivation, individualized consideration and intellectual stimulation behaviors.

1 INTRODUCTION

Leadership is a process by which one person influences the thoughts, attitudes and behaviors of others. Leaders set a direction for followers and help them see what lies ahead. Without effective leadership a group of human beings quickly degenerate into argument and conflict, as people generally see things in different ways and tend to lean toward different solutions. Leadership is the ability that enables other people to do something significant which they might not otherwise do. It is energizing people toward a goal (Singh, 2015).

Leadership involves a type of responsibility aimed at achieving particular ends by applying the available resources (human and material) and ensuring a cohesive and coherent organization in the process (Ololube, 2013).

Leadership is arguably one of the most observed, yet least understood phenomenon on earth (Burns in Abbasialiya, 2010). Over time, researchers have proposed many different styles of leadership as there is no particular style of leadership that can be considered universal.

Great man theory assumes that the capacity for leadership is inherent, that great leaders are born, not made. This theory often portrays leaders as heroic, mythical and destined to rise to leadership when needed. The term great man was used because, at the time, leadership was thought of primarily as a male quality, especially military leadership (see also, Ololube, 2013).

Similar in some ways to the great man theory, trait theory assumes that people inherit certain qualities or traits which make them better suited to leadership. Trait theories often identify particular personality or behavioral characteristics that are shared by leaders. Many have begun to ask of this theory, however, if particular traits are key features of leaders and leadership, how do we explain people who possess those qualities but are not leaders? Inconsistencies in the relationship between leadership traits and leadership effectiveness eventually led scholars to shift paradigms in search of new explanations for effective leadership (Amanchukwu et al., 2015).

There are four interrelated behaviors viewed as essential for leaders to move followers into the transformational style: idealized influence, inspirational motivation, intellectual stimulation and individualized consideration. Idealized influence constitutes the charismatic factor of transformational leadership in which leaders become role models for ethical behavior by their followers (Avolio & Bass, 2004). Moreover, transformational leadership theory is all about leadership that

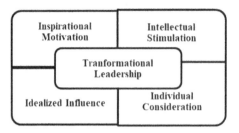

Figure 1. Transformational leadership model.

creates positive change in the followers whereby they take care of each other's interests and act in the interests of the group as a whole (Warrilow, 2012, p. 356).

Transformational leadership is about building relationships among people and creating real, significant change by emphasizing values and creating a shared vision among those in the organization. Transformational leaders generally rise during times of turmoil and change in an organization. The first priority of a transformational leader is to identify and understand the needs of the individuals in the organization and then elevate those needs. By focusing on their requirements, the transformational leader motivates individuals to achieve at higher levels and to produce the type of work they did not think they could. This increases the employees' beliefs in themselves and their abilities. Transformational leaders inspire employees to "transcend their own immediate self-interest" and focus on the common interests of their colleagues and the organization as a whole (Jason Martin, 2015, p. 35). The transformational leadership model can be seen in Figure 1.

The theory of transformational leadership states that, as an agent of change, transformational leaders are able to obtain performance beyond expectations by setting challenging goals to steer and motivate themselves and other members in the group for higher levels of performance (Bass & Avolio, 1993; Masi & Cook, 2000; Bass et al., 2003; Avolio & Bass, 2004; Northouse, 2010).

Doody and Doody (2012) defined transformational leadership as "a process that motivates followers by appealing to higher ideas and moral values where the leader has a deep set of internal values and ideas and is persuasive at motivating followers to act in a way that sustains the greater good rather than their own interests". Northouse (2013) defined transformational leadership as "the style of leadership in which the leader identifies the needed change, creates a vision to guide the change through inspiration, and executes the change with the commitment of the members of the group".

Transformational leadership style boosts consciousness of collective interest among the organization's members and helps them to achieve their mutual goals. Theories of transformational leadership emphasize emotions, values and the importance of leadership focused on encouraging creativity and new ideas in employees (García-Morales et al., 2012). Leadership plays a crucial role in firms' innovation, because leaders can introduce novel ideas into an organization, establish specific goals and encourage innovation initiatives from subordinates (Noruzy et al., 2013).

According to Suresh. A. Rajini (2001), there are four factors to transformational leadership, (also known as the "four I's"): idealized influence, inspirational motivation, intellectual stimulation and individual consideration. Each factor will be discussed to help managers use this approach in the workplace. The factors are:

1. Idealized influence describes managers who are exemplary role models for associates. Managers with idealized influence can be trusted and respected by associates to make good decisions for the organization. Leaders have high standards of ethical and moral conduct.
2. Inspirational motivation describes managers who motivate associates to commit to the vision of the organization. Managers with inspirational motivation encourage team spirit to reach goals

Salis's hierarchy quality concept is stated below
Picture II.2. Hierarchy quality concept

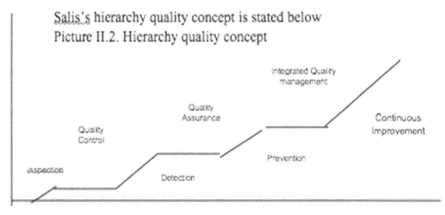

Source: adopted from Sallis (2012:60)

Figure 2. Sallis' hierarchy quality concept.

of increased revenue and market growth for the organization. Leaders communicate high expectations to followers, inspiring followers through motivation to commitment and engagement in a shared vision of the organization.
3. Intellectual stimulation describes managers who encourage innovation and creativity through challenging the normal beliefs or views of a group. Managers with intellectual stimulation promote critical thinking and problem solving to make the organization better.
4. Individual consideration describes managers who act as coaches and advisors to the associates. Managers with individual consideration encourage associates to reach goals that help both the associates and the organization. Effective transformational leadership results in performances that exceed organizational expectations.

According to Bass (1993), the aim of transformational leadership would be to transform people and organizations in a literal sense, to alter them in mind and heart, enlarge vision, insight and understanding, clarify reasons to make behavior congruent with values, concepts and bring about changes which are permanent, self-perpetuating and momentum building.

According to Bass and Avolio (1993), transformational leadership happens when leader become wider and uphold the interests of the employees, once they generate awareness and acceptance for the purpose and assignment of the group, so when they blend employees to appear beyond their own self-interest for the good of the group (Nanjundeswaraswamy & Swamy, 2014).

The main program of quality management in higher education is building a quality culture in the learning community processes of which procedures include quality control (QS), quality insurance (QS), Quality Management (QM) and Total Quality Management (TQM). Higher education management must also be supported by solid organization culture and human resources. As pointed out by Salis (200:18), the quality concept can be drawn as shown in Figure 2.

In addition, Satori (2014) draws sequence process quality hierarchy starting from quality control up to forming quality culture, as in Figure 3.

Based on the literature review, it can be concluded that it is essential in the higher education context that quality management activity becomes an essential stage in building quality culture. However, this quality culture will not succeed properly unless it is supported by the organization leadership. Therefore, successful higher education in applying quality insurance is supported by solid leadership that impacts on ethos of organization.

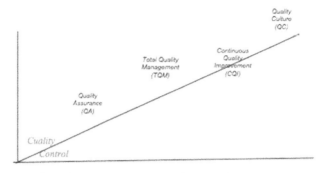

Source: elaborated from lecturing session Thursday, 25 September 2014

Figure 3. Quality hierarchy based on Satori 2014.

Related to the concepts mentioned, Weiss and Molinaro (2005) explained that a *high-performance organization* is characterized by the following aspects:

a. A clear idea of who the customer is and a comprehensive business strategy that drives customer leadership.
b. Efficient internal work processes that flow smoothly up and down and across the organization.
c. Employees who are engaged with the culture and values in the work environment. The employees understand the big picture and know how their work contributes to the organization's success with customers.
d. Performance measures and rewards are aligned to the business strategy and are implemented in an engaging manner.

Even Weiss and Molinaro (2005, pp. 138–139) added that three fundamental tools are needed for effective organizational leadership: (1) develop an enterprise-wide perspective and work in the interest of the whole organization; (2) build relationships and influence key stakeholders; and (3) increase collaboration and integration across the organization.

Sa'ud (2006) in his paper about quality insurance, stated that continuous quality improvement needs to be carried out in insurance design whether internally driven and or involving the external sector. Quality insurance approach is main so that education can organize source optimally to ensure academic service quality and education accountability for stakeholders.

2   RESEARCH METHODOLOGY

This study was conducted using a qualitative research design. This kind of research is used to gain in-depth knowledge in a study (Denzin & Lincoln, 2005; Marshall & Rossman, 2006). More specifically, the study employed an ethnographic research design in collecting data. Ethnographic designs, as Creswell (2002) described them, "are qualitative research procedures for describing, analyzing, and interpreting a culture-sharing group's shared patterns of behavior, beliefs, and language that develop over time." As such, by using this research design and utilizing in-depth interviews, the study explored "culture-sharing" behaviors, beliefs and language among teachers in a Turkish context. Teachers' views were obtained through interviews with semi-structured questions, as recommended by Bogdan and Biklen (1998), to "get the subjects to freely express their thoughts around particular topics."

2.1   *Sample*

The participants of this study comprised eight leaders in higher education in the Universiti Islamic Indonesia Yogyakarta. The participants were chosen by using a purposive sampling method described as the best for use with small numbers of individuals or groups which may well be sufficient for understanding human perceptions, problems, needs, behaviors and contexts, which is the main justification for a qualitative research audience (Bailey, 1994).

2.2 *Data collection and analysis*

The data were collected by using the "repertory grid" technique, which is a constructed interview method. This technique can best be characterized as a semi-structured interview (face-to-face, computerized or phone interview) in which the respondent is confronted with a triad of elements and then asked to specify some important ways in which two of the elements are alike and, thereby, different from the third (Bailey, 1994; Kerkhof, 2006).

In this study, the data were collected by using the following procedure. First, in an email, the teachers were informed about the purpose of the study, and asked if they would participate in this research voluntarily. Those who were invited to take part in the research consented after being assured of the confidentiality of the data being gathered from them. It was promised that their identities would be kept secret and their names would not be mentioned in any part of the study or shared with anyone else. Second, an interview was planned on an agreed-upon day with those who accepted the invitation, and the participants were visited on that date. The interviews were both recorded and noted with their permission and each took approximately 50–60 minutes.

In order to analyze the data, the content analysis technique was employed. This type of analysis usually aims to analyze similar data on a topic and comment on it (Büyüköztürk et al., 2008; Mayring, 2000; Yildirim & Şimşek, 2000). The first step taken in the data analysis process was the data organization procedures recommended by Bogdan and Biklen (1998). In organizing the data, the researcher revisited each interview and listened to each audiotape while reviewing the transcripts to ensure the accuracy of the data. Each participant's interview transcript was later analyzed according to the data analysis procedures described by Bogdan and Biklen (1998), which call for development of coding categories, mechanical sorting of the data and analysis of the data within each coding category. In this respect, each participant's interview was coded separately according to the participant's views on principals' transformational leadership behaviors as well as on various emerging themes and, later on repeated themes among the interviews were grouped into coding categories. It was done in three steps: category definition, exemplification and codification regulation. First, the answers to each question were separated into meaningful categories, named and coded. For example, the questions were conceptualized and named with four separate statements as transformational behaviors. These are idealized influence, inspirational motivation, individualized consideration and intellectual stimulation. In the second step, the conceptualized statements were brought together. In the third step, it was intended to avoid repetition. In the last phase, the identified results were explained and related to each other. It was also intended to build a cause-and-effect relationship among the separate parts. In this sense, the views of teachers were coded as T1, T2, T3 and T4.

The constant comparative approach (Glaser, 1992) was used in the process of organizing and analyzing the data. The use of the constant comparative method results in the saturation of categories and the emergence of theory. Theory emerges through continual analysis and doubling back for more data collection and coding (Bogdan & Biklen, 1998; Glaser, 1992). In this method, each set of data collected (interview transcripts) were reviewed in search of key issues, recurrent events or activities in the data that became categories of focus. The data for each participant were reviewed multiple times for confirmatory and contradictory statements until the data were organized into satisfactory categories and sub-codes to address the research question.

2.3 *Research questions*

In order to fulfill the aforementioned purpose, the following semi-structured questions were raised:

1) How does UII leader apply aspect "Influence Charisma Ideal" in giving information and awareness at organization vision and mission led?

2) How does the UII leader apply "inspiring motivation" in inspiring, motivating and modifying leaders' organization behavior in developing academic quality?
3) How does the UII leader carry out the "stimulated intellectual" aspect in encouraging creativity and innovation among lecturers and staff in developing critical thinking and problem solving to better build higher education toward developing leading academic quality?
4) How does the UII leader perform the "individual consideration" aspect in reflecting, thinking and identifying employee needs, recognizing employee capacity, delegating its authority, giving attention, building guidance, and training followers specially and personally to achieve a directed organization that is led?

2.4 *Practical contribution*

Understanding the functionality of transformational leadership improves its practical application.

Organizations that wish to foster transformational leadership styles might incorporate the insight of the transformational leadership functionality in the selection and development processes of their future leaders.

The Delta Concept looks toward specific competencies important for transformational leaders. Furthermore, it points toward potential strategies for developing these competencies. The elaboration of these topics is subject to further research.

The following will initially consider these topics and highlight further research perspectives. Overall *The Delta Concept* underlines the dynamic and contextual perspective of transformational leadership.

Transformational leaders need to exercise influence in a contextualized way. This incorporates inherently an interactive perspective.

As demonstrated in this research, social processes are of relevance in the transformational leadership functionality. It is likely that social skills in general are of great importance for transformational leaders. This is supported by considering the specific processes in more detail. For instance, familiarizing can be linked to a competence related to immersion and analysis of new contexts, relationship building is linked to communication skills and display of interest and respect, and transformational learning is linked to self-reflection and critical thinking.

In *The Delta Concept*, the influencing process builds on interaction of leaders and followers. This involves competences relating to channeling creativity, consolidating points of view and increasing motivation.

With this overall interactive and dynamic perspective, it is likely that uncertainties arise for transformational leaders. Comprehensively dealing with these uncertainties might be a vital task and competence of transformational leaders.

The SEED data suggests that effecting transformational leadership is linked to learning processes – this has been made explicit in *The Delta Concept* with the process of transformational learning. It is likely that familiarizing, relationship building and influencing respective learning processes are also present. It is subject to further analysis to derive learning compounds relevant within the transformational leadership functionality.

With regard to potential strategies of facilitating the learning of transformational leadership skills, the SEED Program suggests that *exposure* to a new context is an efficient and effective approach. This might be an integrative part of respective future designs of transformational leadership learning programs.

3 CONCLUSION

A leader who has the ideal influence is described by his ability to grow trust and subordinate admiration of the leader so that subordinates will follow the steps made by the boss. In this study, the ideal effect can be described from the attitude of the leader who became an example for his subordinates.

In the inspirational motivational character, the leader expresses the achievement of the goal by using symbols that appeal to subordinates and expresses the goals in simple ways. Leaders are also expected to encourage enthusiasm and optimism of each subordinate to implement the system of academic quality development.

A leader who has the characteristics of intellectual stimulation in this study is defined as a leadership characteristic in an effort to foster creativity and innovation among lecturers and staff by developing critical thinking and problem solving to make higher education better toward academic quality development. Leaders strive to promote the rationality of subordinates by collecting ideas of academic quality improvement in their institutions.

On the characteristics of individual considerations, leaders are able to act as trainers or mentors to encourage everyone to commit to a common goal, to give back and to connect the needs of the individual with the organization's mission. In addition to individual character, the leader seeks to spend time directly in advising subordinates and accompanying and supervising subordinates, as well as reflecting, thinking and constantly identifying the needs of his subordinates regarding his subordinate abilities, delegating his authority, paying attention, fostering subordinates Specialized and personal to achieve organizational goals.

REFERENCES

Bailey, K.D. (1994). *Methods of social research* (4th ed). New York, NY: The Free Press.
Beauchamp, M.R., Barling, J. & Morton, K.L. (2011). Transformational teaching and adolescent self-determined motivation, self-efficacy, and intentions to engage in leisure time physical activity: A randomised controlled pilot trial. *Applied Psychology: Health and Well-Being*, 3, 127–150. doi:10.1111/j.17580854.2011.01048.x
Bogdan, R. & Biklen, S.K. (1998). *Qualitative research for education* (3rd ed.). Boston, MA: Allyn & Bacon. Inc.
Büyüköztürk, Ş., Kılıç Çakmak, E., Akgün, Ö.E., Karadeniz, Ş. & Demirel, F. (2010). *Bilimsel Araştırma Yöntemleri (5. Baskı)*. Ankara: PegemA Yayıncılık.
Creswell, J.W. (2005). *Educational research: Planning, conducting, and evaluating quantitative and qualitative research*. NJ: Upper Saddle River.
Denzin, N.K. & Lincoln, Y.S. (2005). *The SAGE handbook of qualitative research* (4th ed.). Los Angeles, CA: SAGE Publishing House.
Doody, O. & Doody, C. (2012). Transformational leadership in nursing practice. *British Journal of Nursing*, 21(20), 1212–1218.
Glaser, B.G. (1992). *Basics of grounded theory analysis*. Mill Valley, CA: Sociology Press.
Italiani, F.A. (2013). "Pengaruh Gaya Kepemimpinan Transformasional Dan Transaksional Terhadap Kinerja Pegawai Departemen Sdm Pt. Semen Gresik (Persero) Tbk". Jurnal Ilmu Manajemen | Volume 1 Nomor 2 Maret 2013.
Italiani, F.A. (2014). "Pengaruh Gaya Kepemimpinan Transformasional Dan Transaksional Terhadap Kinerja Pegawai Departemen Sdm Pt. Semen Gresik (Persero) Tbk". Jurnal Ilmu Manajemen | Volume 1 Nomor 2 Maret 2014.
Kerkhof, Ad., Apter, A. & Grimland, M. (2006). The phenomenon of suicide bombing: A review of psychological and nonpsychological factors. *Crisis Journal*. 27(3), 107–118. doi:10.1027/0227-5910.27.3.107
Krause, P. (2009). *Patterns of executive control over public spending*. Paper presented at the LSE Conference "Emerging Research in Political Economy and Public Policy" London, 11 March 2009. Retrieved from http://www.lse.ac.uk/europeanInstitute/events/2008-09/Krause.pdf (on December 2012).
Marshall, C. & Rossman, G.B. (2006). *Designing qualitative research* (4th ed.). Thousand Oaks, CA.
Mawn, L. (2012). *Transformational leadership in higher education lecturing*. Bangor University.
Mayring, Ph. (2000). *Qualitative Inhaltsanalyse. Grundlagen und Techniken* (7th edition, first edition 1983). Weinheim: Deutscher Studien Verlag.
Nordin, N. (2013). Transformational leadership behaviour and its effectiveness outcomes in a higher learning institution. *Journal of Integration Knowledge*.
Northouse, P.G. (2013). *Leadership theory and practice* (6th ed). Los Angeles, CA: SAGE Publishing House.
Robbins, S.P. & Mary, D.C. (2010). *"Manajemen"*. Edisi Kesepuluh. Jakarta: Penerbit Erlangga.

Sedarmayanti. (2011). *"Membangun Dan Mengembangkan Kepemimpinan Serta Meningkatkan Kinerja Untuk Meraih Keberhasilan"*. Bandung: PT Refika Aditama.

Seltzer, J. & Bass, B.M. (1990). Transformational leadership: Beyond initiation and consideration. *SAGE Journal of Management* 6(4), 693–703.

Smith, M. (2011). Are you a transformational leader? *Nursing Management (Springhouse)*, 42(9), 4450.

Sukmana, E. & Sudibia, G.A. (2015). *"Pengaruh Kepemimpinan Transformasional, Motivasi Dan Burnout Terhadap Kinerja Karyawan Outsourcing Rri Mataram"* E-Jurnal Manajemen Unud, 4(8), 2333–2349. ISSN: 2302-8912.

Tim Dosen Administrasi Pendidikan Universitas Pendidikan Indonesia. (2009). *"Manajemen Pendidikan"*. Bandung: Alfabeta.

Ward, C. (2011). Transformational leadership styles among leaders in Singapore schools: A study of gender differences. *International Leadership Journal Global Leadership*.

Warrilow, S. (2012). Transformational leadership theory. Ezine articles Retrieved from http;//ezinearticles.com? transformationalleadershiptheory. (Accessed November 28 2012)

Yıldırım, A. & H. Şimşek. (2010). *Sosyal Bilimlerde Nitel Araştırma Yöntemleri* (9. baskı). Ankara: Seçkin Yayınevi.

Educational Administration Innovation for Sustainable Development – Komariah et al. (Eds)
© 2018 Taylor & Francis Group, London, ISBN 978-1-138-57341-3

Reasons for home schooling in Indonesia

T. Istiwahyuningsih & N. Suharto
Universitas Pendidikan Indonesia, Bandung, Indonesia

ABSTRACT: This article examines motivations for home schooling in Indonesia and compares them with the different researches in the United States where various aspects of home schooling have been explored extensively. Evidence includes a qualitative interview with Center for the Development of Early Childhood Education and Community Education officer in West Java and document analysis found in published books and online news and articles. Previous studies identified two distinct groups of home schoolers: ideologues and pedagogues. The findings suggest that most families in this study expressed motivation distinctions between the ideologue-pedagogue dichotomy for starting home schooling. However, contrary to findings from previous research, a finding shows a mixture of both ideological and pedagogical reasons for practising homeschooling.

1 INTRODUCTION

One of the most frequent forms of informal education held in the community is the home schooling. The implementation of home schooling in Indonesia has been done for a long time and continues to grow rapidly. Even the enthusiasm of the community to choose home schooling is quite high. This is evidenced by the rapid development of the number of home schoolers from year to year. According to Secretary-General of Home Schooling and Alternative Education Association (Asah Pena), Budi Trikorayanto, the number of home schoolers recorded in Asah Pena throughout Indonesia reached 30,000 in 2014 and was estimated to increase each year (Kompas, 2015).

Very little has been written on the topic of learning at home in the Indonesian context. Sumardiono (2007) mentioned that there were no books in Indonesian language that specifically discuss about home schooling. He, as one of the home-based educators and the author of *Home Schooling: Lompatan Cara Belajar* (Home Schooling: A Leap for Better Learning) and *Apa Itu Home Schooling* (What is Homeschooling) admitted that most of the information in his books were derived from the internet. He pointed out that the internet provided abundant information of home schooling. He explored various aspects of home schooling such as its theory and practice especially in the United States. There was also a small but growing body of work written by the Indonesian press, Kompas, that focuses on home schooling issues such as its practitioners, motivations, registering, equity, discrimination and legality since 2006.

According to data reported in BPS-Statistics Indonesia publication (2017), the estimated population of Indonesia in 2017 is about 258.7 million. Among the number, "not/never attending school" and "not attending school anymore" groups based on age group are as follows: 0.91% of the population aged 7–12; 5.12% aged 13–15, 29.16% aged 16–18 and 76.07% aged 19–24. More detailed data are listed in Table 1.

According to statistics, those who conduct home-based education are included in the groups of "not/never attending school" and "not attending school anymore". Undoubtedly, these data do not represent the true size of the population. According to the interview with an officer in Center for the Development of Early Childhood Education and Community Education in West Java, the reason is many parents involved in home schooling do not register their children to provincial ministries of education. In addition, learners from formal schools who are migrating to home school and have never registered before to provincial ministries of education do not have national student numbers so they are categorized as "not attending school anymore" group. As a result, the lack of data related to the exact number of homeschoolers has caused their rights have not been fulfilled.

Table 1.   Percentage of population aged 7–24 years by sex, school age group and school participation 2016.

Sex and School Age Group	Not/Never Attending School	Attending School	Not Attending School Anymore
Male			
7–12	0.77	99.05	0.18
13–15	0.77	93.82	5.41
16–18	0.79	69.62	29.59
19–24	0.73	23.64	75.63
7–24	0.76	70.71	28.53
Female			
7–12	0.73	99.12	0.14
13–15	0.56	95.98	3.47
16–18	0.77	72.11	27.12
19–24	0.81	24.23	74.95
7–24	0.73	71.55	27.72
Male + Female			
7–12	0.75	99.09	0.16
13–15	0.66	94.88	4.46
16–18	0.78	70.83	28.38
19–24	0.77	23.93	75.30
7–24	0.75	71.12	28.13

Source: National Socioeconomic Survey, BPS-Statistics Indonesia 2017.

By contrast, Arai (2000) examines that in the United States there exists a relatively large body of literature about various aspects of home schooling. There are numerous "how-to" manuals and an extensive array of support and teaching materials. Some common criticisms of home schooling have also been explored extensively.

Broadly speaking, there are two basic types of parents who engage in home education: The Ideologues and the Pedagogues (Van, 1988). The Ideologues explain that they are teaching their children at home for two reasons: They object to what they believe is being taught in public and private schools and they seek to strengthen their relationships with their children. These parents have specific values, beliefs, and skills that they want their children to learn, and they do not trust any available school can teach these things adequately. Essentially, the Ideologues want their children to learn fundamental religious teaching and a perspective that places family at the center of society and truly stresses individual freedoms. The Pedagogues educate their children at home primarily for pedagogical reasons. They criticize that the schools teach the students incompetently. These parents are highly independent and work hard to take responsibility for their own lives. They appreciate their children's intellect and creativity and believe that children learn best when education taps into the child's authentic desire to learn.

There is tremendous variation within both of these general classifications. Further, the substantive decision of parents to home school their children is often motivated by specific and unique conditions that also vary widely from family to family. In some cases, parents have to deregister their children from school. The decision to withdraw their children from school was generally created by two circumstances: first, parents began to home school when they came to believe that schools their children attended taught a curriculum that directly contradicted their own values and beliefs; second, parents removed their children from school because they believed that their children would be harmed academically and emotionally by the organization and pedagogy of formal schools. Van (1988); Knowles (1991); Mayberry and Knowles (1989) all reported that characterizing people as either ideologues or pedagogues was helpful in identifying parents' motivations for home schooling.

However, educational researchers may cite a third reason for selecting home schooling: leadership development such as entrepreneurship, conflict management, and problem solving (Seago, 2012).

Much of the academic study on motivations for home schooling derives from the United States context, and most notably from Knowles (Knowles, 1991; Mayberry & Knowles, 1989). Mayberry and Knowles (1989) informed variety in the exact causes of Ideologues' disappointment with the curricula. In part, these parents' dissatisfaction was based on religious grounds (Cortese, 2003). Many reported that public schools did not present either adequate or the right kind of religious teaching and learning. Several parents explained that the liberal humanism of public schools was contradictory to their religious faith. Home schooling for these people was a way to confirm that their children were educated in a manner appropriate with their belief system. However, not only people with religious convictions objected to the public-school curricula. Other parents, especially those with gifted or bright children, considered that the formal school curricula were not challenging enough to stimulate their daughters or sons. Mayberry and Knowles (1989) explained that these parents criticized that the lack of challenge would be very detrimental to their children if they came to dislike school because it was boring. Rather than risk jeopardizing their children's potential, these parents decided to provide proper challenge at home.

Mayberry and Knowles (1989) stated that negative aspects of socialization process concerned the majority of Pedagogues. These parents believed that bullying at school such as the malicious teasing, pranks, and exclusionary behavior, especially during unsupervised times (e.g., recess, lunch hour, and after school) could be extremely damaging to their children's sense of self. They usually weighed this risk against the many positive aspects of class time. But in the end, they decided that the only way to preserve their children's self-concept and confidence was through home schooling.

For other parents, the public education structure is believed as a pedagogically poor condition. The hierarchical learning conditions where the teacher is the possessor of knowledge and students are merely receptacles contradict their values (Meighen, 1988). These people believe that institutionalized learning – which demands students to learn particular subjects in particular ways at particular stages in their educational period – restrain creativity and can actually decrease the desire to learn (Holt, 1989; Jeub, 1994).

Despite their differences, the ideologues and the pedagogues also shared some reasons for rejecting to send their children to school. Four major similarities have been identified. First, Mayberry and Knowles (1989); Knowles (1991); Mayberry (1988, 1993) have all pointed to family unity or strengthening the bonds among family members as a very important reason for home schooling. By keeping their children at home, most parents felt they could produce a more closely knit, loving family.

Second, Mayberry and Knowles (1989) and Van (1988) have suggested that many parents, regardless of whether they object to the ideological or the pedagogical dimensions of public schooling, view home schooling as a way to practice an alternative lifestyle, particularly by resisting the globalization influences such as materialist and consumerist values of contemporary societies.

A third major reason for home schooling among U.S. parents, regardless of whether they are ideologues or pedagogues, is unpleasant views about school. Parents in Knowles (1991) study said that school was a waste of time, or they felt different, singled out at school. Many of these parents had also had positive experiences of learning outside of school, and they wanted to reproduce these experiences for their children.

Finally, along with the majority of researchers in the field, Marshall and Valle (1996) found that parents used home schooling to assert their responsibility for their children's education. Many of these parents claim that they have a right and a responsibility to protect their children from harmful influences.

2 METHOD

The data were collected through a qualitative interview with Center for the Development of Early Childhood Education and Community Education officer in West Java, interviews with 3 families engaged in home schooling and document analysis found in published books and online news and articles which contained 7 parents' testimonies about their motivations for home schooling.

131

Obviously, these sampling procedures are not thorough enough to give statistical generalizations about the practice of home schooling in Indonesia. However, the goal was to provide an additional consideration of reasons for home schooling in Indonesia in the context of results from the United States studies. The basic information gathering consisted of questions about parents' motives for home schooling and how they arrived at the decision to home school.

3 RESULTS AND DISCUSSION

Parents engaged in home schooling are diverse, with differing educational and class backgrounds. From the interview with an officer in Center for the Development of Early Childhood Education and Community Education, most of the parents have undergraduate degrees. One of the parents in the data is employed as a teacher.

Most families come from middle to upper class backgrounds, although there are families with financial difficulties. The families also vary in the length of time that they had been home schooling ranging from 1 to 5 years whereas in one case there has been doing it longer for 13 years.

Not all the participants expressed a strong spiritual or religious commitment. Two families said religion played an important role in their decision to teach at home – in one case the parents who embrace Islamic religion expressed that they wanted their children to be *hafiz*. It is an Arabic word used to identify the one who entirely memorizes and recites the Qur'an, the holy book of Muslims, which is over 600 pages with more than 6,000 verses. Being *hafiz* is still one of the most rewarded honorifics in Muslim society.

For most participants in this study, the decision to educate their children at home was not planned early before; rather, the decision took years. Typically, the process began with a condition which their children found difficulties adjusting the environment in formal school. Attending formal school even caused them frustrated and ill. This condition caused parents' dissatisfaction with some element of the public school, which led to an investigation of alternatives. Most families reported that at this point they were not even aware of home schooling as an option. However, in two cases parents opted for home schooling before their children even attended school. The following comment was from one parent who had made the decision early.

"After doing some research on it, reading some books and finding information in the internet about homeschooling practice especially in the United States, I and my wife were so determined that we were going to home school our children."

Knowles (1991) found that many people chose to home school because of bad school experiences. In this research, four parents specifically connected their children's bad personal experiences at school with their decision to home school. Several people found school socially difficult at times and saw these experiences as influencing their choice to keep their children at home. Negative memories of school appeared to be a major motivation for home schooling among parents in this study. The following comments were from parents of two different families.

"Choosing to home school my son was a suitable decision. At the beginning of his first junior high school he felt stressed because of many duties and pressure from his classmates. He was so troubled with socialization with his friends. These conditions even caused him ill and absent at school."

"My son hated to go to school because he got bullied by friends and teachers. His teacher was ferocious and authoritarian. He got bored and did not like the strict school rules. Many of his friends also spoke abusively."

There was also a parent who did not seem to differentiate as clearly between ideological and pedagogical objections to schooling. Most families felt that the overall environment of schools was detrimental to their children's well-being. For example, several families mentioned strict curriculum and teacher's labeling to the children as well as a lack of individual attention.

"There are lots of problems in school. Frankly we are often not comfortable with public schools, for example: school hygiene, unhealthy food sellers, ranking and labeling, teachers comparing students with other students or their siblings, no freedom in choosing books to study, a compulsory to wear a uniform by having to wear white socks and black shoes only. According to the teacher's confession my son likes to argue teacher. What really struck me is the teacher's additional sentence: 'The child does not need to be smart, the important thing is to obey.' It's really confusing."

In addition, Center for the Development of Early Childhood Education and Community Education also listed some reasons of parents to provide education to their children through home school, including:

1. Parents idealism

Many parents of home schoolers who choose this educational path for their children are motivated by their desire to provide the best education in their own way.

"The first reason (for choosing home schooling), I am not pleased with the existing curriculum (in Indonesia) The second reason, I want to have a closer bond with my children. We as the parents should be the ones who are responsible for educating both of our children."

2. Children's busy activities

Children who start their careers at young ages usually have high level activities such as celebrities and athletes. They prefer to follow home schooling so that the learning time can be arranged in accordance with the availability of time they have.

"My son cannot wake up early in the morning. If you go to formal school you must wake up early in the morning, while his shooting schedules are at night."

3. Personal faith and norms

Often it is difficult for families to find a school that teaches values according to what they believe. Meanwhile, parents want to provide education in accordance with their beliefs. On the other hand, there are times when parents also feel worried about the socialization of children outside the home. To prevent children from bad socialization that are not in accordance with the norms and values, they prefer to educate their own children at home.

"When my first daughter was toddler, we conducted home schooling by adjusting the child's activities. There were no strict learning schedules, but we had daily targets. The targets were to recite *juz amma* (Chapter 30 of the Qur'an), prayer and *iqro'* reading (Arabic reading). At the age of 8 she voluntarily requested a scheduled study. Her younger sister is now following her schedules, too."

4. Children with special conditions

Children who have special conditions in this context include gifted or bright children and children with limitations. Gifted or bright children are usually not accommodated maximally in formal school. Learning in the classroom and in large numbers usually are not demanding enough to challenge them. If forced to learn in large class conditions and not handled specifically, usually the children will easily get bored which in the end their talents are not optimized, even the academic achievement can decline.

"I could see my son's brilliance when he was 3 years old. Physics and mathematics books were the daily obligatory readings. My son failed to pass kindergarten A to kindergarten B because at that time he refused to follow the activities in the classroom, finally I home school him. He had succeeded in passing the university enrollment test at the age of 14."

Children who have special educational needs due to severe learning difficulties, physical disabilities or behavior problems generally go to Special School. However, some parents prefer home schooling.

"My daughter is free from all kinds of rules that govern special needs children in such a way as in Special Schools (SLB) that make them like a manufacturer's goods: uniform and mass product."

5. Directing children's talents and interests to skilled individuals

The parents want to prepare their children with adequate skills so that they can be professional workers in the future based on the children's preference fields. The following comments were from parents of two different families.

"The underlying reason for the decision is very simple, we want children to get education that correspond to their interests and talents. We never worried about the future of homeschooling children because nowadays a lot of works would prioritize skills rather than certificates from formal schools."

"We consider that there are so many professions today that did not exist or imagined 20 years ago, such as animators, game testers, social media specialists and so on. So what will happen in the professional world 20 years ahead? There could be more diverse ways for our children to be beneficial to the society according to their interests and talents along with technology."

Finally, some parents felt quite strongly that home schooling was part of living an alternative lifestyle. These parents thought that home schooling resonated nicely with their other values. This finding is consistent with those of Mayberry (1988) and Knowles (1991).

4 CONCLUSION

The parents chose to home school their children for a variety of reasons. Previous studies have found two distinct groups of home schoolers: ideologues and pedagogues. It is suggested that most families in this study express motivation distinctions between the ideologue-pedagogue dichotomy for starting home schooling. However, contrary to findings from previous research, one family in this study expressed a mixture of both ideological and pedagogical reasons for practising home schooling.

These studies show that many home schoolers are motivated by parents' commitment in teaching spiritual and religious values in their children's education, their desire to direct their children's talents and interests to skilled individuals, their desire to assert their rights to determine their children's education, their children's negative experiences in the previous formal school, and the children's needs of school time adjustment for their professional career.

The reason for practising home schooling that belongs to neither ideological nor pedagogical reasons is opportunity or time reason although the number may not be significant in Indonesia. Children who start their careers at young ages have high level activities such as celebrities and athletes. They prefer to follow home schooling so that the learning time can be arranged in accordance with the availability of time they have.

REFERENCES

Arai, A. Bruce. 2000. Reasons for Home Schooling in Canada. *Canadian Journal of Education 25*, 3: 204–217.
BPS-Statistics Indonesia. 2017. *Statistical Yearbook of Indonesia 2017*. Jakarta: BPS-Statistics Indonesia.
Cortese, Anthony J. 2003. *Walls and Bridges: Social Justice and Public Policy*. State University of New York: United States..
Holt, J. 1989. *Learning All the Time*. Reading, MA: Addison-Wesley.
Jeub, C. 1994. Why parents choose home schooling. *Educational Leadership, 52*(1), 50–52.
Knowles, J. G. 1991. Parents' rationales for operating home schools. *Journal of Contemporary Ethnography, 20*, 203–230.
Marshall, J. D., & Valle, J. P. 1996. Public school reform: Potential lessons from the truly departed. *Education Policy Analysis Archives, 4*(12). Retrieved September 6, 2001, from http://epaa.asu.edu/epaa/v4n12.html
Mayberry, M. 1988. Characteristics and attitudes of families who home school. *Education and Urban Society, 21*, 32–41.
Mayberry, M. 1993. Effective learning environments in action: The case of home schools. *School Community Journal, 3*, 61–68.
Mayberry, M., & Knowles, J. G. 1989. Family unity objectives of parents who teach their children: Ideological and pedagogical orientations to home schooling. *Urban Review, 21*, 209–225.
Meighen, R. 1988. *Flexischooling: Education for tomorrow, starting yesterday*. Nottingham, Eng.: Education New Publishing Cooperative.
'Model Pendidikan: Peminat Bertambah'. *Kompas*, 16 March 2015, p. 12, Retrieved from http://www.kompasdata.id/Search/NewsDetail/12590294
Seago, J. (2012). A Third Reason to Home School: Leadership Development. *Home School Researcher*, 28(1), 1–7.
Sumardiono. (2007). *Homeschooling: Lompatan Cara Belajar*. Jakarta: Elex Media Komputindo.
Van, G. J. A. (1988). Ideology, curriculum, and pedagogy in home education. *Education and Urban Society, 21*, 52–68.

Educational Administration Innovation for Sustainable Development – Komariah et al. (Eds)
© 2018 Taylor & Francis Group, London, ISBN 978-1-138-57341-3

Students' perceptions of exercise-based mathematics learning in primary education

Iswan & Herwina
Muhammadiyah University of Jakarta, Jakarta, Indonesia

ABSTRACT: The majority of primary school mathematics teachers have been implementing exercise-based learning based on a certain coursebook suggested by the government for years. Teachers may state that the book has simple and practical learning instruction and is well trusted because it has been written by educational experts and accredited by the national government. However, students' perceptions of such learning instruction are seldom studied. This study investigated the opinions of Grade 5 students regarding the exercise-based mathematics learning based on a certain course book. There were 60 students from Cirendeu Public Primary schools involved in this qualitative study. The findings revealed that a majority of the students perceived the exercise-based mathematics learning positively because they found that the materials are interesting, understandable and motivating. In contrast, the students were also concerned about the image design and character that should be modernized.

1 INTRODUCTION

The national curriculum in Indonesia positions mathematics as the one of required subjects aimed at upgrading individuals to possess the skill to understand and implement mathematics concepts; to promote logical thinking of patterns and properties; to solve problems; to communicate the ideas through symbols, tables and diagrams and that a positive attitude toward mathematics benefits real life (Depdiknas, 2007). In summary, students should be able to think mathematically, to implement mathematical knowledge in problem solving and decision making, and dealing with daily life. However, a gap exists between the national education purpose in the curriculum and the facts in the classroom. Mathematics classes are dominated by conventional learning in which the teacher controls and takes the biggest role in the learning instruction.

In fact, 85% of 25 million children in Indonesia are primary school students with 145,000 public primary schools and 1,235,000 teachers (Sembiring et al., 2008). Starting from 1973, national modern mathematics were applied in primary schools, but the implementation became problematic. Teachers' unreadiness for change created a new teaching attitude which claimed that modern mathematics was too difficult, and teachers only needed to follow the textbooks page by page (Sembiring et al., 2008). Currently, the majority of students are spoon-fed and do not get used to thinking creatively and critically. Teachers claim that this condition also happens because of the number teaching classes that they have. The limited number of teachers must teach 10–12 mathematics classes and even more with a large number of students (30–40 students). The national government seems unready to recruit more teachers as civil servants. Still many non-civil servant teachers exist in Indonesia but with very low teaching fees and require other jobs to fulfill their life needs. The win-win solution that the government can offer now is that besides facilitating teachers with continuous professional development, the national government has also been continuously standardizing the mathematics textbooks of primary schools. Although some primary schools gradually changed their teaching approach to the ideal one, the fact is that the majority of primary schools with conventional learning are dominant and therefore, further studies must be considered.

2 THEORETICAL FRAMEWORK

Students' learning achievement is dominantly influenced by the learning instruction. The development of students' cognitive, affective and psychomotor aspects is influenced by the way that they learn (learning styles) and the teacher teaches (Damrongpanit & Auyporn, 2013). Furthermore, the ideal learning process should fulfill four essential components, namely: 1) students' background knowledge of the lesson; 2) students' efforts; 3) teachers' ways to educate, examine and evaluate; 4) the teaching quality (Dimitric, 2003). Mathematics learning with those kinds of principles is highly possible to achieve. Exercise-based learning is considered as a type of teacher-centered classroom management and. According to Rogers and Frieberg (1994), teacher-centered classes have the teacher as the sole leader who manages the learning instruction, has the responsibility for preparing the lesson and as the class organizer, becomes the rule maker and gives lack of responsibilities to students. These principles are mostly implemented in exercise-based learning. In other words, the teacher is the class controller and director of learning instruction who has a clear idea of how far the students are involved with and engaged in the learning (Wagner & McCombs, 1995).

In fact, the debates between the teacher-centered and student-centered approaches in mathematics classes are unavoidable. Absolutists claim that teachers should have the core role in teaching. In contrast, the fallibilists perceive that the student should be dominant in the class (Kurniati & Surya, 2017). Interestingly, one study revealed that in Chinese primary schools, where the classroom situation is almost the same as Indonesia, the teacher-centered class might contribute a positive impact to mathematics learning (Ningning et al., 2014). However, they claimed that an eclectic approach with both student-centered and teacher-centered approaches should be well-implemented in the learning process. The awareness of the issues of diversity in the class should also be taken into account. Katwibun (2013) stated that a teacher can teach more effectively in a mathematics classroom with diverse students if diversity understanding and cultural learning approaches are well-implemented.

Furthermore, he explained that the diversity in mathematics classes can be grouped into three roles, namely: (1) race/ethnicity; (2) socioeconomic status/class; and (3) language. Related to student background, the types of student can be categorized into the groups of introverts (unstable and stable ones) and extroverts (unstable and stable). Stable introverts are passive, careful, thoughtful, peaceful, controllable, reliable, even-tempered and calm but the unstable introvert tends to be moody, anxious, rigid, sober, pessimistic, reserved, non-sociable and quiet. The stable extroverts seem social, outgoing, talkative, easy-going, lively, carefree and responsible, but the unstable ones are touchy, restless, aggressive, excitable, changeable, impulsive, optimistic and active (Eysenck, 1982). The newest Indonesian national curriculum (K-13) promotes student-centered learning with learning activities such as a problem-based learning model, a discovery/inquiry learning model and project-based learning (Kurniati & Surya, 2017). However, the fact that most teachers and students rely on the coursebooks shows that a deeper insight/perception about whether this kind of approach is effective or not is necessary.

3 METHOD

This is a qualitative descriptive study conducted at Cirendeu Public Primary school number 2 in South Tangerang. The were 60 students from two classes of the fifth grade, selected using purposive sampling in which the author took participants with various scores classified as low, middle and high scores. The author adapted and formulated the questionnaire model with 20 questions separated into three sections. In section one, five statements are related to the students' personal data about what they think of mathematics. Section two consists of seven statements related to students' perceptions of the teacher's teaching method. Section three has nine statements related to the students' learning experience of mathematics classes. The students responded to the questionnaire by giving a score of "1" for strongly agree, "2" for agree, "3" for disagree and "4" for strongly disagree.

Table 1. Students' perceptions of mathematics.

Statements	Score
I personally like mathematics	174
I can do better in mathematics	120
I play games related to mathematics	130
The harder the lesson, the more I am curious about the lesson	169
I sometimes remember the mathematics lesson outside the class	169

Table 2. Students' perceptions of the student-centered class.

Statements	Score
I like learning through discussion (in pairs or small groups) with classmates in class	121
I prefer if the teacher gives me various ways to answer questions	122
I prefer that the teacher encourages us to make and discuss mistakes	152
I prefer that the teacher guides us to invent and use our own methods	132
I ask my teacher if I do not understand	120
I ask my friend(s) if I do not understand	112
I look for different ways to solve problems	160

4 FINDINGS

The data of questionnaire revealed that commonly students of Cirendeu Public Primary school number 2 in South Tangerang has negative perception of mathematics but fortunately believes that they can be better in mathematics and possesses good motivation. It can be seen from Table 1 that the high score of the questionnaire value for statements 1, 4 and 5 shows their negative attitude toward mathematics. However, the low score in statements 3 and 5 suggests that they still have motivation and will be interested in a different learning approach.

Related to their perception of exercise-based learning it shows that they are used to being in a teacher-centered class (passive students) but tend to change the approach into a student-centered class (active students). It may be seen from Table 2 that the low score of statements 1, 2, 4, 5 and 6 suggests their positive perception of a student-centered class. Unfortunately, the high score of statements 3 and 7 shows that the students are still low risk takers and lack creativity.

In Table 3, the low score of statements 4 and 7 shows that the students are used to being passive. In contrast, the high score of other statements shows that they do not enjoy exercise-based learning (teacher-centered class). This phenomenon is closely related to the data from Table 2 in which the students tend to have a student-centered approach.

5 DISCUSSION

The newest national curriculum called K-13 promotes student-centeredness. In fact, Cirendeu Public Primary school number 2 in South Tangerang still implements a teacher-centered approach in their mathematics classes. Based on the findings, it can be seen that although the students are used to being in teacher-centered learning, they want to be involved more in the classroom instruction. In line with Kurniati and Surya (2017), where the teacher implements a teacher-centered approach in the class, the students become passive and perceive mathematics negatively. Based on the questionnaire about students' perceptions of the student-centered class, the low scores of statements 1, 2, 4, 5 and 6 indicate that the students have good motivation to learn mathematics and

Table 3. Students' perceptions of exercise-based learning (teacher-centered class).

Statements	Score
I prefer that the teacher explains the lesson carefully and orders us to learn from that	144
I prefer to work on practice exercises	160
I prefer that the teacher clearly gives the method to answer questions	157
I enjoy that teacher orders us which questions to work on	133
I prefer to follow the textbook page by page	152
I enjoy listening to the teacher's explanation	166
I like adopting the method from the board or textbook	135
I enjoy working on the questions that my teacher tells us to	159
I enjoy working by myself	148

control, and want a student-centered approach in their mathematics class although the high scores of statements 3 and 7 reveal their passive learning habit as an impact of teacher-centeredness on their learning experiences. The students are low risk takers and uncreative in solving their learning problems. The teacher becomes their spoon feeder.

Although the questionnaire about students' perceptions of the teacher-centered class also indicates that the students do not really matter to follow the teacher's order about which questions to do and copying the teacher's method to work on the questions (statements 4 and 7), the high scores of statements 1, 2, 3, 5, 8 and 9 show the students' rejection of most teacher-centered instructions. They want to cooperate with friends, to be creative and to get more sources of knowledge instead of the teacher's explanation only. Ningning et al. (2014) suggested that a mathematics class requires both student-centered and teacher-centered approaches in the classroom. To achieve learning effectiveness, the teacher should have been trained to acknowledge more effective approaches. The teacher can guide and organize collaborative activities and can be an evaluator and a problem solver of students' mathematics problems.

Furthermore, modifying the two approaches (eclectic approach) should also cover good classroom management (Garret, 2008). To be a successful teacher, it should be maintained how the teacher considers the learning instruction and classroom management. Katwibun (2013) also claims that the students' background produces diversity in the classroom. The class will be a new small community with different race/ethnicity, socioeconomic status and language (mother tongue). To bear in mind the groups of introverts (unstable and stable) and extroverts (unstable and stable) also determines the type of class that the teacher adopts (Eysenck, 1982). Based on this study, even though the factors of classroom management, diverse class, and students' characteristics were not thoroughly examined, the data indicate that the students admitted the failure of the traditional class in their learning and hoped for a different approach, namely a student-centered one.

6 CONCLUSION

Based on the discussion, it can be concluded that the students of Cirendeu Public Primary school number 2 expect a student-centered class in mathematics learning instruction. Based on the data regarding students' perception, although the students are still passive in learning, they tend to be more involved in the classroom instruction such as having a class discussion and collaborative learning. The limitation of this study is that it only represents the students' perceptions of an exercise-based method (teacher-centered) in mathematics learning. In other words, the findings cannot be generalized into a larger context that most possibly has different aspects to consider. Besides, this study only covered the students' perceptions without the teachers' perceptions. Moreover, the students cannot be critical enough to evaluate the class because they are still primary school students.

REFERENCES

Damrongpanit, S. & Auyporn, R. (2013). Matching of learning styles and teaching styles: Advantage and disadvantage on ninth-grade students academic achievements. *Journal of Academic Journal: Educational Research and Review, 8*(20).

Depdiknas, R.I. (2007). *Standar Kompetensi Dan Kompetensi Dasar Tingkat SD/MI.*2007.11.

Dimitric, R.M. (2003). Components of successful education. *Journal of the Teaching Mathematics, 6*(2), 69–80.

Eysenck, H.J. & Eysenck, M.W. (1985). *Personality and individual differences: A natural science approach.* P594. New York, NY: Plenum.

Garret, T. (2008). Student-centered and teacher-centered classroom management: A case study of three elementary teachers. *Journal of Classroom Interaction, 43,* 34–37.

Katwibun, D. (2013). The need for preparing mathematics teachers for diverse classrooms in Thailand. *Journal of Social and Behavioral Sciences, 93,* 756–761.

Kurniati, I. & Surya, E. (2017). Student's perception of their teacher teaching styles. *International Journal of Sciences: Basic and Applied Research (IJSBAR).*

Ningning, Z., Martin, V., Annemie, D., Guoyuan, S. & Chang Z. (2014). Does teacher-centered teaching contribute to students' performance in primary school? A video analysis in Mainland China. *International Journal of Research Studies in Education, 3*(3), 21–34.

Rogers, C. & Freiberg, J. (1994). *Freedom to learn* (3rd ed.). Upper Saddle River, NJ: Merrill Publishing.

Sembiring R.K., Hadi S. & Dolk M. (2008). Reforming mathematics learning in Indonesian classrooms through RME. *Journal of ZDM Mathematics Education, 40,* 927–939. doi: 10.1007/s11858-008-0125-9

Wagner, E.D. & McCombs, B.L. (1995). Learner centered psychological principles in practice: Designs for distance education. *Educational Technology, 35*(2), 32–35.

Educational Administration Innovation for Sustainable Development – Komariah et al. (Eds)
© 2018 Taylor & Francis Group, London, ISBN 978-1-138-57341-3

The relationship between organizational culture and granting of compensation with local teacher performance

L.G. Kailola & C. Purwanti
Universitas Kristen Indonesia, Jakarta, Indonesia

ABSTRACT: The purpose of this study was to determine whether there is a relationship between organizational culture and the provision of compensation with local teacher performance. The population of this study were the teachers at Global Jaya International School (GJIS), Bintaro Jaya, Tangerang, which amounted to 87 teachers. The sampling technique involved a random sampling method. The result is 40 teachers who netted into a sample of research and 20 teachers to test the research instrument. The research survey method used a correlational approach, which consisted of 40 questions for each variable. The calculation of validity was achieved using the product moment correlation formula and the reliability with Cronbach's alpha test. The coefficient of double correlation of organization culture (X1) and compensation (X2) with teacher performance (Y) was 0.954 with a determination coefficient (R square) of 0.910. This shows that: (1) there is a positive and significant relationship between organizational culture (X1) and local teacher performance in GJIS; (2) there is a positive and significant relationship between provision of compensation (X2) with local teacher performance in GJIS; (3) there is a positive and significant relationship between organizational culture (X1) and compensation (X2) together with local teacher performance in GJIS.

1 INTRODUCTION

Indonesia, as a member of the world community, cannot avoid the current era of globalization. This era of globalization is characterized by rapid progress in all sectors, not only in economics and technology, but also in education. The world of education in Indonesia is also experiencing very rapid growth in which many new schools are emerging alongside the existing ones. As more schools are available, tight competition among schools is inevitable. To win this competition, every school will try to improve its quality.

There are several important aspects to improve the quality of a school including human resources in the school environment. Teachers are the most important resource for schools, because they have the potential to aid schools in achieving their goals.

On the other hand, as a human being, the teacher also has various needs to fulfill. The desire to fulfill these needs are seen as drivers to do something, including work. Schools must be able to create a conducive atmosphere to know the needs and expectations of teachers that can motivate them to improve their performance.

Improvement of school quality can be done in various ways including teacher performance improvement. High teacher performance is needed by a school because teacher performance is the main capital of schools to grow and compete. Teacher performance in classroom learning tasks influences many things such as work environment, school facilities and infrastructure, organizational culture, learning design, work motivation, compensation, work discipline, work ethic and smooth communication between colleagues.

Organizational culture is an important factor in improving teacher performance. Organizational culture includes rules, guidelines and procedures in the work so that every member of the organization can carry out their duties as well as possible. A good organizational culture will provide high teacher performance, create job satisfaction and a work ethic.

Another factor that determines teacher performance is compensation. Providing appropriate compensation to teachers can improve teacher work performance and motivation. Therefore, the compensation plan should be set based on fair and reasonable principles, in accordance with the labor law, or in accordance with the rules of work of the respective institutions.

Problems regarding a teacher's inadequate performance are experienced by teachers in several schools, both national and international. Global Jaya International School (GJIS), which is one of the international schools in Banten province, is inseparable from the above issues. This requires a comprehensive review to find the root of the real issues that affect the performance of local teachers in GJIS. Through this research the extent of giving compensation to local teachers in GJIS, whether it is fair and reasonable, can be identified. Does this provision of compensation affect the performance of local teachers in GJIS? And, is there any relationship between organizational culture with the improvement of local teachers' performance. Knowing this relationship is expected to be a guideline for GJIS to continue to develop a program of improvement in its efforts to achieve its vision and mission.

2 LITERATURE REVIEW

2.1 Teacher performance

According to the Indonesian dictionary, performance can be interpreted as achievement that appears as a form of success in one's work. The success of performance is also determined by the work and ability of a person in the field. The success of work is also related to one's job satisfaction (Mangkunagara, 2000). To achieve maximum performance, a teacher should strive to develop all the competencies they have and take advantage of and create situations in the school environment in accordance with applicable rules. According to Anwar Prabu Mangkunagara (2000) defines performance (work performance) as a result of work in quality and quantity achieved by an employee in performing their duties in accordance with the responsibilities given.

2.2 Organizational culture

Organizational culture is the value and informal norms that control individuals and groups in interacting with each other within the organization (George & Gareth, 1996). Organizational culture is a set of basic assumptions and beliefs adopted by members of the organization, developed and inherited to address external and internal problems (Handoko, 2008). Organizational culture is a set of values that helps members of the organization know acceptable and unacceptable actions (Gregory & Richy, 1999). An organization is a collection of people working together to achieve a common goal. An organization is the arrangement of personnel to facilitate the achievement of some predetermined objectives through the allocation of functions and responsibilities (Sukardono, 1996).

Organizational culture is a philosophy of ideology, values, assumptions, beliefs, expectations, attitudes and norms that are shared and bind a society. Organizational culture is a way of thinking and doing something that is traditionally embraced by all members of the organization and new members must learn or at least partly accept them to be accepted as part of the organization (Handoko, 2008). Culture can be viewed as a norm that refers to a form of statement of what can and cannot be by members of the organization, and assumptions that refer to what is right or wrong, reasonable or unreasonable, and possible or impossible.

2.3 Compensation

Compensation is something that employees receive as a reward for their work (Hasibuan, 2007). Hasibuan states that compensation is all income in the form of money, goods directly or indirectly received by employees in return for services provided by the organization. Compensation is everything that workers earn in return for their contribution to the organization. Compensation management is seen as an important part of the organization and is a management strategy to increase motivation, which in turn is expected to improve employee performance. If employees are not satisfied with what they receive in the form of salary, it may affect their performance. Conversely, if they feel satisfied, they will try as much as possible to improve work productivity. It can be said that compensation can encourage workers to work more effectively, productively and efficiently.

3 METHODOLOGY

3.1 Research methods

The method used in quantitative research. Type of research using survey method with correlation approach.

3.2 Research design

The constellation model of the relationship between independent variables with associated variables can be described as follows:

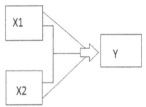

Y: Teacher Performance
X2: Compensation
X1: Organizational Culture

3.3 Sampling technique

3.3.1 Population
The population in this study were local teachers from GJIS totaling 87 people.

3.3.2 Samples
Samples are some of the study population were selected as representative a representative of the whole to be studied (Sugiyono, 2006). From the number of members of the population taken at random by using the formula Slovin.

$$N \cdot d^2 + 1$$

$$n = \frac{87}{87 \cdot 0.05^2 + 1}$$

$$n = 71$$

Table 1. Number of teachers from the local population.

Unit	Number
Primary	48
Secondary	39
Total	87

Source: Data for Global Jaya International School.

143

Based on the above formula, if the population of local teachers in GJIS totals 87 people, the number of samples obtained was 71. The total sample is 25% of the total population. So, if a population is 87, then the sample size is $87 \times 25\% = 22$.

Based on the above formula, it can be determined that the required sample size is between 22–71. Therefore, a value in the middle of this was selected, which is 40 people.

3.4 *Data analysis technique*

Data were analyzed using statistical tests of correlation and regression. Before using correlation and regression test, it requires normality, linearity, and homogeneity test as well.

4 RESULTS AND DISCUSSION

Hypothesis 1: Relationship between organizational culture (X_1) with the teacher performance (Y)

Based on Table 2 obtained t_{count} equal to 10.24 and the value probability (sig.) 0.000. Unknown t_{table} on two-way test with significance level of 0.05, the number of respondents 40 people and degrees of freedom (df) $n - 2 = 38$ is 2.024. Because t_{count} (10.24) is greater than t_{table} (2.024) and a probability value (0.000) is smaller than the significance level of 0.05, then proved that the hypothesis H_0 is rejected and H_1 accepted, which means there is a positive and significant correlation between organizational culture with performance local teachers at Global Jaya International School.

Hypothesis 2: The relationship between compensation (X_2) and teacher performance (Y)

Based on Table 3 was obtained t_{count} for 16.6 and value probability (sig.) 0.000. Unknown t_{table} in the two-way test with significance level of 0.05, the number of respondents 40 people and degrees of freedom (df) $n - 2 = 38$ is 2.024. Because t_{count} (16.6) is greater than t_{table} (2.024) and a probability value (0.000) is smaller than the significance level of 0.05, then proved that the hypothesis H_0 is rejected and H_1 accepted, which means there is a positive and significant relationship between compensation with performance local teachers at Global Jaya International School.

Table 2. Significance tests correlation coefficient between organizational culture variables (X_1) variable teacher performance (Y).

Coefficients[a]

Model	Unstandardized coefficients		Standardized coefficients		
	B	Std. Error	Beta	t	Sig.
(Constant)	34.313	8.779		3.908	.000
Orgn. Culture	.685	.067	.857	10.237	.000

[a] Dependent Variable: Teacher Performance.

Table 3. Significance tests correlation coefficient between compensation (X_2) variable teacher performance (Y).

Coefficients[a]

Model	Unstandardized coefficients		Standardized coefficients		
	B	Std. Error	Beta	t	Sig.
(Constant)	1.109	7.403		.150	.882
Compensation	.983	.059	.938	16.608	.000

[a] Dependent Variable: Teacher Performance.

Table 4. Multiple correlation coefficient significance test.

ANOVA[a]

Model	Sum of squares	Df	Mean square	F	Sig.
Regression	9185.180	2	4592.590	186.748	.000[b]
Residual	909.920	37	24.592		
Total	10095.100	39			

[a] Dependent Variable: Teacher Performance.
[b] Predictors: (Constant), Organization Culture, Compensation.

Hypothesis 3: The relationship between organizational culture and compensation combined with teacher performance

From Table 4, it can be seen that the value of F_{count} amounted to 186.75 and a significant probability value (Sig.) of .000. To determine the significance of regression equation and compensating cultural organization (X_2) with the teacher performance (Y) need to compare the F distribution tables using a numerator degrees of freedom = 1 and db denominator $(n - 2) = 38$ with a significance level of 0.05. Retrieved F_{tables} 4.098 and F_{count} amounted to 186.75. This shows that F_{count} (186.75) greater than F_{table} (4.098) and a probability value (0.000) is smaller than the significance level (0.05). It can be concluded hypothesis H_0 is rejected and H_1 accepted, which means there is a positive and significant relationship between organizational culture and providing compensation with the performance of the local teachers at Global Jaya International School.

5 CONCLUSIONS

The present study showed and proved that to improve and maintain the performance of local teachers in GJIS, the application of a good culture of organization and a good system of compensation is required. The school creates induction programs at the beginning of each school academic year, workshops and teacher training. Give compensation by adjusting due to increase of the rate of inflation annually. It makes the local teacher will feel treated fair and reasonable.

REFERENCES

Daryanto, S.S (2005). *Indonesian dictionary complete.* Surabaya: Apollo.
Devies, Ivor K. (1987). *Management of learning.* Jakarta, Indonesia: PT Rajawali Pers. Djarkasih. Jakarta: Publisher.
Earl Babbie. (1982). *Understanding sociology.* California: Wadsworth Publ. Comp. Chiff Englewood: Prentice Hall.
Flippo, E.B.F. (1997). *Personnel management.* New York, NY: McGraw-Hill Inc.
George, J.M. & Gareth R.J. (1996). *Understanding and managing organizational behavior.* New York, NY: Adison Wesley Publishing, Co.
Gibson, I. & Donnelly. (1994). *Organizational behavior process structure.* Interpreting Djarkasih. Jakarta: Erland.
Gregory, M. & Richy, W.G. (1999). *Organizational behavior* New Delhi, India: AITBS Publishers & Distributors.
Handoko, T.H. (2008). *Management.* Yogyakarta: BPFE UGM.
Hasibuan, M.S.P. (2007). *Human resource management.* Jakarta, Indonesia: Earth Literacy.
Law of the Republic of Indonesia No.14 of 2005 on Teachers and Lecturers. Jakarta, Indonesia: Ciputat Press.
Mangkunagara, A.P. (2000). *Human resource management.* Jakarta, Indonesia: Youth Rosdakarya.
Regulation Legislation National Education System No.19 of 2005. Yogyakarta: Student Library.
Robbins, S.P. (1996). *Organizational behavior.* USA: Prentice-Hall International.
Sugiyono. (2006). *Statistics for research.* Bandung, Indonesia: Alfabeta.
Sukardono, G. (1996). *Organizational change and impacts.* Jakarta, Indonesia: Atma Jaya University.

Educational Administration Innovation for Sustainable Development – Komariah et al. (Eds)
© 2018 Taylor & Francis Group, London, ISBN 978-1-138-57341-3

Capacity building of programs in primary schools: Teachers' reflections

L. Kaluge & L. Kustiani
Universitas Kanjuruhan Malang, Jawa Timur, Indonesia

ABSTRACT: This study investigated programs in primary schools for capacity building to develop schools and teachers. Two research questions were posed related to aspects of capacity development and comparisons of the programs in basic education. The design for this study was a descriptive survey. A sample of 1,448 teachers was cluster randomly selected, from 18 districts in seven provinces, for filling out the questionnaires. The findings revealed the ten aspects of capacities across five main programs that have a positive affect for teachers and schools. The programs resembled each other in some respects, however, were differentiated due to particular uniqueness. Based on the findings, it was recommended that for capacity building, teachers in primary schools should be exposed to continuous professional development and training programs to enable them be more effective and adaptable to the changing world of education.

1 INTRODUCTION

Capacity building is a change process of people capacities, both institutional and societal over time. The elements of capacity development cover knowledge management, leadership, establishing networks, developing internal cooperation and enriching information (Millennium-Declaration, 2000; Stöcklin, 2010; UNDP, 2006). Essentially, the capacity development process occurs inside those concerned, as an endogenous process. Those from outside only support them through facilitating processes to accelerate their development, helping them access the resources and input they need. CIDA (CIDA-Policy-Branch, 2000) stated that the purposes of capacity building for making people able are: (1) to practice their essential functions in problem solving, formulating and accomplishing objectives, and (2) to understand and handle the need for self-continuous development in the wider environment.

Schools are the landscapes of capacity development, the places where teachers strive for meaningful educational efforts. In the context of professional teaching, teachers are professionally trained, socialized into the complex task of teaching and in fact, equipped professionally with the requisite teaching (Stoll & Temperley, 2009; Wing, 2004). The primary and ultimate goals of teaching and learning involve acquisition and transfer of skills and knowledge for the individual learner (Marsh & Farrell, 2014; Murray et al., 2008). Schools have sets of goals which they strived to achieve. The goals of schools as organizations come under the words "teaching and learning" for consideration.

There are more than ten different projects operating in Indonesia since the first decade of 2000. In terms of program characteristics, five were selected and typically related to capacity building in primary schools (Anam, 2006; Muljoatmodjo, 2004; Winkelmann, 2001). These programs were the Regional Educational Development and Improvement Program – funded by the Indonesian Government (REDIP-G), Decentralized Basic Education Project (DBEP), Creating Learning Community for Children (CLCC), Basic Education Project (BEP) and Science Education Quality Improvement Project (SEQIP). Among the programs, there were variations in conducting the programs from the national level down to the school.

At the national level, the CLCC and REDIP-G prepared human resources to run the programs. The other programs did not require the existing resource persons at the national level for conducting the capacity building. The capacity building activities were mostly in training and workshops. CLCC focused on supporting the implementation of active-joyful-effective-learning (UNESCO-UNICEF, 2000; UNICEF, 2003), while REDIP-G focused on the provision of knowledge and skills of their field workers and prepared the guidelines for the parties involved in the program (MONE-JICA, 2004). REDIP-G took a substantial period of time due to the initiation process to transfer the know-how from the REDIP-JICA Program. The trainers or facilitators of the training or activities at this national level also varied from the program manager or officers in REDIP-G or program experts and also master trainers in the CLCC.

At the provincial level, there were only two programs conducted regarding capacity building in the area of school-based management, namely CLCC and BEP. The CLCC focused the objectives of training on multiple subjects covering school-based management, active-joyful-effective-learning and community-participation as an integrated package of training. The BEP focused on the provision of knowledge and skills to allow the participants to be able to list the school eligible for obtaining school block grants (ADB, 2002). The content of the training included materials relevant to the needs of achieving the objectives of the training or capacity building to enable participants to master the content and the process of working later on. The modes of training were mostly lecturing, discussion, simulation and modeling.

At district level, there were four programs that provided capacity building. Those programs were REDIP-G, DBEP, CLCC and BEP. The SEQIP focused on the teaching-learning process as capacity building. All programs were directed to guide or provide participants with the capability or competencies for implementing the programs as expected at the sub-district or school levels (Muljoatmodjo, 2004). The participants of the training varied from the district representatives to the school representatives such as school principals and school committee members. The training or the capacity building was conducted in various modes from lecturing to brainstorming, focus-group discussion, participatory discussion as well as workshops.

At cluster level, capacity building in the area of school-based management was conducted by the DBEP only. At this level of capacity building the main objective was preparing the training participants with the capability to develop all matters related to good practice (Muljoat-modjo, 2004). The training was facilitated by qualified resource persons from school principals, school committees and school supervisors. The training was organized by the district manager

At school level, the training or the capacity building in the area of school-based management was offered by DBEP and CLCC (ADB, 2002; Muljoatmodjo, 2004; UNICEF, 2004). The following is the information on the capacity building of the three programs. The outcomes of the training were in line with the objectives of the training, which were eventually directed toward the optimal achievement of students. The content of the training was to support the implementation of the program at school level. The facilitators or resource persons of the training comprised of the district coordinator of the program.

This study picked up aspects of capacity development classified into four groups related to instructional matters (teaching plan, active learning process, resource use, evaluation and classroom climate), training benefits for teacher professionalism, school discipline, accountability and community satisfaction. Tracing back to the existing information on the individual good practices from the schools was the focus.

2 RESEARCH METHODS

There were two main questions to be answered. First, to what extent are the aspects of capacity building perceived by teachers? Second, what were the different and similar effects of the programs for capacity building in basic education?

The data used in this study were obtained from a project on mainstreaming good practices in basic education operated by the South East Consortium for International Development (SECID) in Indonesia, funded by the European Commission.

The data represented schools, districts and provinces. For the mapping study, the selection of the target location of the study was based on six criteria. The first was the availability of the program offering good practices within the nine programs discussed in the earlier parts in a province and its respective districts. The second was the number of programs offered in a certain province, district and/or sub-district. The third was the availability of the schools where good practices from the programs were implemented. The fourth was the number of schools in the sub-district, number of sub-districts in the district and number of the districts in the province which implemented good practices from certain programs. The fifth was specifically the sub-district or district which offered some good practices from which people can learn and benefit from. The sixth was the readiness of the provinces, districts, sub-districts and schools to be visited.

Seven provinces were used as data sources. The total respondents were 1,448 teachers representing primary schools (SD – *Sekolah Dasar*) from 18 districts in seven provinces.

The data were processed statistically by using descriptive and regression analyses. Comparing the projects was useful in order to answer the research questions, then identifying the salient good practices of each one.

3 RESULTS AND DISCUSSION

3.1 *Results*

There were two main research questions to be answered. The first question asked about the extent the aspects of capacity building were perceived by teachers.

Table 1 presents the results that among the nine aspects of capacity building, all were reliable as shown by Cronbach alpha coefficients above 0.6. The average scores were above two, meaning that these aspects seemed to perform in schools generally important. The standard deviation and variances showed how the data spread as variables. Capacity in using teaching resources, community satisfaction and school accountability were the lowest aspects meaning that in future those aspects need special attention to improve.

The illustration in Table 2 needs further explanation as follows. The standard errors are in brackets. The regression model is horizontally presented from left to right, with CLCC on the position of constant (grand mean), whereas the remaining programs were treated as dummy variables. CLCC contained the base coefficient in regression terms for other programs. The coefficients of the other programs were the regression estimation (b) and the distance from the grand mean.

Table 1. Scale description and reliability.

	Mean	Std. Deviation	Variance	No. of Items	α
Teaching plan	3.23	.64	.41	4	.84
Active instruction	3.27	.45	.20	9	.81
Using teaching resources	2.33	.36	.13	12	.72
Teaching evaluation	3.02	.51	.26	5	.70
Classroom climate	3.26	.46	.22	6	.66
Training usefulness	3.62	.45	.20	8	.89
School discipline	3.18	.60	.36	4	.85
School accountability	2.70	.53	.28	6	.74
Community satisfaction	2.52	.59	.35	6	.79

Table 2. Regression summary of the five primary programs.

	Programs					R^2	F
	CLCC	REDIP-G	DBEP	BEP	SEQIP		
Teaching plan	3.123 (.048)	.627* (.165)	.049 (.075)	.118* (.059)	−.015	.014	5.01
Active instruction	3.270 (.029)	−.155 (.100)	−.066 (.045)	−.004 (.036)	−.173* (.040)	.019	7.01
Using teaching resources	2.270 (.021)	−.104 (.070)	−.039 (.032)	−.010 (.025)	−.099* (.029)	.012	4.25
Teaching evaluation	3.148 (.030)	.137 (.101)	−.300* (.046)	−.106* (.036)	−.329* (.041)	.062	23.8
Classroom climate	3.173 (.028)	.226* (.097)	.088* (.044)	.109* (.035)	−.007 (.040)	.014	5.03
Training usefulness	3.590 (.037)	−.282* (.128)	−.127* (.058)	−.096* (.046)	−.379* (.052)	.041	15.3
School discipline	3.260 (.035)	.240* (.121)	−.153* (.055)	−.069 (.043)	−.268* (.049)	.029	10.9
School accountability	2.738 (.030)	.310* (.105)	−.077 (.047)	−.062 (.038)	−.279* (.043)	.045	16.7
Community satisfaction	2.546 (.115)	.067 (.115)	−.018 (.052)	−.041 (.041)	−.226* (.047)	.022	7.98

The second research question was about the difference and similarity effects of the programs for capacity building in basic education. Table 2 shows that on the nine aspects of capacity building, as expressed by the R^2, teaching evaluation, school accountability and training usefulness had the highest contribution (between 6.2 to 4.1%) as perceived by teachers. In creating dummy variables for all the programs, CLCC was treated as the base. CLCC was pre-eminent in training usefulness, active teaching-learning, using teaching resources, teaching evaluation, maintaining school discipline and community satisfaction. REDIP-G was superior in teaching plan, classroom climate and school accountability. The rest were indifferent compared to these two exemplary programs.

3.2 *Discussion*

There were plenty of evidences to affirm that good practices of capacity development existed somewhere being developed by various projects. At the school level, the aspect of instructional matters – teaching plan, active learning process, evaluation, and classroom climate – took place as good practices above the middle scores. The only exception was using the teaching resources, seemed teachers did not need to improve their capacities on this. This means that the teacher was inseparable from the learners (Tarpey & Poultney, 2014). The instructional aspects were the pivot of formal education. Soemarman (2010) stated that teaching is an attempt to help someone acquire or change some skill, attitude knowledge, ideal or appreciation.

Learning is conceptualized in terms of behavioral change (Soedijarto, 2009) and defined as a relatively enduring change in behavior that is a function of prior behavior (Cerubini, 2008). The changes in behavior are usually described as intended outcomes. They are the expectations of the teacher after the process of interaction with the learners (Zürcher & Arlianti, 2013). It must not be imagined that this interaction only produces the intended outcomes, of course unanticipated consequences may follow and unexpected barriers to goal attainment may arise.

Regarding the training benefits for teacher professionalism, the teachers' reflections appeared to be very high. The importance of training and development of human resources, that afforded at the upper level was regarded as the citadel of knowledge and the foundation of intellectualism, the most ground for the intellectual incubation of leaders of tomorrow (Byrne-Jiménez & Orr, 2012;

Peshak & Kincaid, 2008). A system which certified only competent people in character and learning should have presenters who were equally well developed, trained and retrained academically and professionally.

School discipline and accountability got scores above the mid-point. Pathways to capacity in education also include discipline and trust (Cosner, 2009; Slater, 2008). The collegial trust concerns principals set, enforce, and school-wide discipline. One of the key terms here is the concept of interaction, assimilation and reaction. In the process of interaction, what is exchanged is information, and the information is assimilated. For this process to be concrete, Susilowati and Salim (2009) stated that the concept of participation is required.

The aspect of community satisfaction was good at the middle position. It supported the practices inside the schools as part of the pathways (Slater, 2008; Tarpey & Poultney, 2014). The community as stakeholders within the context of collaborative initiatives, satisfaction expressed the well done communication. Human resources development is the framework for helping and developing teachers to develop their personnel and organizational skills, knowledge, abilities and the work attitude that will elicit sustainable development.

Both CLCC and REDIP-G were excellent in using their trickling down strategies. The pre-eminence of CLCC was known and imitated by many projects. On the other hand, CLCC itself kept on improving through self-evaluation from year to year (Browne-Ferrigno & Muth, 2004; Peshak & Kincaid, 2008). REDIP-G was good in creating guidelines from district down to school level and controlled the schools through formal supervisors. REDIP-G also spent much time in developing the capacity of the trainers and participants because a lack of their capacities would cause the project to suffer seriously (Leeman et al., 2015).

4 CONCLUSION

Aspects of capacity building in primary education programs were revealed here. There were varieties among the programs in the past, they showed their good practices that should be maintained and developed further to the current situation. Changes had and might happen in any location and at any time. Practices in formal education (Browne-Ferrigno & Muth, 2004) always open the space for capacity building that kept on needing the appropriate adjustment.

This study revealed that capacity building affected the life of education at primary schools and was perceived positively by teachers as good practices. Nine common elements were explored important roles, none was failed. Even there were differences among projects and with different accentuation, the meaningful of the efforts could not be denied. The aspects such as the enabling factors of social and local capacities were still needed for further study in order to pursue elementary educational betterment.

REFERENCES

ADB. (2002). *Loan Agreement (Special Operations): Decentralized Basic Education Project.* Dated 20 February 2002. No. 1863-INO (SF). Jakarta.
Anam, S. (2006). *Sekolah Dasar: Pergulatan Mengejar Ketertinggalan.* Solo: Wajatri.
Browne-Ferrigno, T. & Muth, R. (2004). Leadership mentoring in clinical practice: role socialization, professional development, and capacity building. *Educational Administration Quarterly,* 40(4), 468–494.
Byrne-Jiménez, M. & Orr, M.T. (2012). Thinking in three dimensions: Leadership for capacity building, sustainability, and succession. *Journal of Cases in Educational Leadership,* 15(3), 33–46.
Cherubini, L. (2008). Teacher candidates' perceptions of school culture: A mixed methods investigation. *Journal of Teaching and Learning,* 5(2): 39–54.
CIDA-Policy-Branch. (2000). *Capacity development, why, what, and how.* Gatineau, Quebec.
Cosner, S. (2009). Building organizational capacity through trust. *Educational Administration Quarterly,* 45(2), 248–291.
Leeman, J., Calancie, L. & Kegler, M.C. (2015). Developing theory to guide building practitioners' capacity to implement evidence-based interventions. *Health Education & Behavior,* 44(1), 59–69.

Marsh, J.A. & Farrell, C.C. (2014). How leaders can support teachers with data-driven decision making: A framework for understanding capacity building. *Educational Management Administration & Leadership*, 43(2), 269–289.

Millennium-Declaration. (2000). *Capacity Development*. Retrieved from *http://www.un.org/millenium/ declaration/are_55e.htm* (Accessed 4/8/2008).

MONE-JICA. (2004). *The study on regional educational development and improvement program (phase 2) in the Republic of Indonesia: Progress report 4 summary*. February 2004. Jakarta.

Muljoatmodjo, S. (2004). *Task 1 most critical and important capacity gaps in basic education*. Progress Report 1 for UNICEF. Jakarta, Indonesia: UNICEF.

Murray, J., Campbell, A., Hextall, I., Hulme, M., Jones, M., Mahony, P., Menter, I., Procter, R. & Wall, K. (2008). Mapping the field of teacher education research: Methodology and issues in a research capacity building initiative in teacher education in the United Kingdom. *European Educational Research Journal*, 7(4), 459–474.

Peshak, H. & Kincaid, G.D.K. (2008). Building district-level capacity for positive behavior support. *Journal of Positive Behavior Interventions, 10*(1), 20–32.

Slater, L. (2008). Pathways to building leadership capacity. *Educational Management Administration & Leadership,* 36(1), 55–69.

Soedijarto. (2009). Some notes on the ideals and goals of Indonesia's national education system and the inconsistency of its implementation: A comparative analysis. *Journal of Indonesian Social Sciences and Humanities,* 2(2), 1–12.

Soemarman, T. (2010). *Maximizing Training - memaksimalkan pelatihan demi hasil yang optimal*. Malang: Penerbit Dioma.

Stöcklin, S. (2010). The initial stage of a school's capacity building. *Educational Management & Leadership,* 38(4), 443–453.

Stoll, L. & Temperley, J. (2009). Creative leadership teams – capacity building and succession planning. *Management in Education,* 23(1), 12–18.

Susilowati, E.S. & Salim, Z. (2009). The paradox of education, productivity and career development. *Journal of Indonesian Social Sciences and Humanities,* 2(2), 69–94.

Tarpey, C. & Poultney, V. (2014). Maximizing leadership capacity and school improvement through re-alignment of children's services. *Management in Education,* 29(2), 63–68.

UNDP. (2006). Capacity Development. In *Capacity Development Practice Notice*. Retrieved from *http://www.undp.org/ oslocentre* (Accessed 10/5/2009).

UNICEF. (2003). *CLCC-Creating Learning Communities for Children: A project proposal to AusAID*. September 2003. Jakarta, Indonesia.

UNICEF. (2004). *CLCC-Creating Learning Communities for Children: Second progress report to the Government of New Zealand*. June 2004. Jakarta, Indonesia.

UNICEF-UNESCO. (2000). *CLCC–Creating Learning Community for Children: Improving primary schools through school-based management and community participation* (A Joint UNESCO-UNICEF-GOI Pilot Project: Evaluation Report). Nov-Dec. 2000. Jakarta, Indonesia.

Wing, K.T. (2004). Assessing the effectiveness of capacity-building initiatives; seven issues for the field. *Nonprofit and voluntary Sector Quarterly,* 33(1), 153–160.

Winkelmann, C. (2001). Das Science Education Quality Improvement Project (SEQIP) der GTZ in Indonesien. S. 26 – Pacific News Nr. 16 – (Juli/August). Retrieved from http://www.pacific-geographies.org/wp-content/uploads/sites/2/2017/06/SEQIP-GTZ.pdf (Accessed 20/8/2017).

Zürcher, D. & Arlianti, R. (2013). Ex-post evaluation 2012/13 – brief report: Science Education Quality Improvement Project (SEQIP), Indonesia. Eschborn, Germany: Deutsche Gesellschaft für Internationale Zusammenarbeit (GIZ) GmbH.

Educational Administration Innovation for Sustainable Development – Komariah et al. (Eds)
© 2018 Taylor & Francis Group, London, ISBN 978-1-138-57341-3

Determinant factors of academic service quality in vocational schools

A.P. Kartiwi
Universitas Muhammadiyah Sukabumi, Sukabumi, West Java, Indonesia

ABSTRACT: Vocational School has never been the first choice for the community to send their children after graduating from junior high school. The academic service quality is one of the decisive factors in improving the schools' credibility. It is densely related to the students' satisfaction as the consumers of education. Therefore, it is necessary to conduct research to verify the determinant factors in improving the academic services quality. This research was conducted in two vocational schools in the Palangkaraya city aimed to compare the determinant factors of academic service quality. The method used was descriptive survey with a sample of 171 students. As the results of the research, it was revealed that one of the vocational school had high determinant factor in the physical facility and empathy as the lowest. While at the other school, the highest determinant factor was responsiveness and the lowest was empathy.

1 INTRODUCTION

One of the goals of education is to prepare learners to enter the community (Jayakumar, 2008; Scardamalia, 2000). To be able to live in society one must have skills that will then be used to survive (Wagner, 2014). School is an institution where learning and learning process takes place (Parsons, 1959; Senge et al, 2012). Vocational schools have always been the second choice for parents to send their children to school after graduating from junior high school. The paradigm of society still finds vocational schools to be secondary schools for children with less academic ability and are considered to be low quality schools (Bowles & Gintis, 1976; Nurmi et al, 2002; Bonna et al, 2002).

Vocational secondary school is a high school that has a special curriculum that aims to provide certain skills to learners to be independent or continue to a higher level in accordance with the field of expertise. (Indonesia, 2003; Murniati and Nasir, 2009) The principle of vocational education is "learning by doing" in which learners not only study inside the class but also try to practice it directly in the work environment (Wibowo, 2016; Colley et al, 2003).

As a school service organization can not be separated with the concept of quality (Sallis, 2014; Eisemon, 2014; Hopkins, 2015). The meaning of quality education relates to what is produced and who the user of the education is. The definition refers to the value provided by education and the processors and the audience of educational outcomes (Sallis, 2014). The definition of quality for the service organization should facilitate and fully support all the core performances that have been achieved, which should be achieved, and which may be possible. The form of performance given by the service organization to the consumer is the service (Carnochan et al, 2014).

Service is an intangible experience received by the consumer (Parasuraman et al, 1988; Sallis, 2014). In the world of education, services are provided to consumers by school personnel, the intended consumers are learners (Wei et al, 2014). Here are five key dimensions related to service quality (SERVQUAL) called the service quality dimensions covered by Human Resources and physical support:

(1) Tangibles, is the appearance of physical facilities, equipment, personnel and communication materials

Table 1. Classification average score respondents.

No	Mean Score	Criteria
1	1.00–1.80	Very Low
2	1.81–2.60	Low
3	2.61–3.40	Medium
4	3.41–4.20	High
5	4.21–5.00	Very High

(Moser, 2017)

Table 2. Population and sample.

School	Population	Sample
SMKN 1	825	89
SMKN 2	575	85
Total	1400	174

(2) Reliability, is the ability to carry out or deliver services properly and reliably as promised
(3) Responsiveness, is the desire to help customers and deliver or provide services quickly.
(4) Assurance, is the knowledge, ability and character of employees in the process of service.
(5) Empathy, is a caring attitude, understanding and giving special understanding to the customer.
   (Seth et al, 2005; Parasuraman et al., 1988; Mosahab et al., 2010; Hasan et al., 2009)

Dimensions that can ensure the quality of service can be delivered accurately, accurately, quickly in accordance with customer expectations, so that service performance can be said to be having a high quality. In this research, the five dimensions will be used to find out the description of the quality of academic services found in Vocational High School in Palangkaraya City, and to find the determinant factors in the quality of academic services.

The problems discussed in this research are the quality determinants of academic services in Vocational High Schools in Palangkaraya City.

2 RESEARCH METHODOLOGY

The method used is descriptive survey with comparative form. Data collection tool used is in the form of questionnaire. This method is used to describe the respondents' feedback to the analysis tool then the results will be compared between the two research objects. (Moser & Kalton, 2017; Ragin, 2014).

School academic services are measured using five dimensions, ten indicators and twenty-point statements. The average results of the respondents' feedback will then be compared with the average classification table average score of the following respondents.

Respondents in this study were students in two research objects namely SMKN 1 and SMKN 2. This study is using probability sampling, with a simple random sample method. Determine the sampling size using Taro Yamane formula. (Moser & Kaltoon, 2017; Bryman, 2015). The population and sample of this study are described in the table as follows.

Based on the table 2, the overall population of this research is 1400 students with sample of 174.

3 RESEARCH FINDINGS & DISCUSSIONS

SMKN 1 and SMKN 2 are the first vocational schools established in the city of Palangkaraya. Given the need for potential human resources by local governments, the development of vocational

Table 3. Respondents' result.

No	Indicators	SMKN 1		SMKN 2	
		$\bar{x}$	Criteria	$\bar{x}$	Criteria
Tangibles 3.47					
1	Physical appearance	4.17	High	3.15	Medium
2	Personnel Equipment	3.70	High	2.89	Medium
	Mean	3.93	High	3.02	Medium
Reliability					
1	Fast Response	2.81	Medium	2.91	Medium
2	Trusted	3.45	High	2.80	Medium
	Mean	3.13	Medium	2.85	Medium
Responsiveness					
1	Responsive	2.85	Medium	4.07	High
2	Ability to provide good service	3.10	Medium	3.93	High
	Mean	2.97	Medium	4.00	High
Assurance					
1	Knowledge	2.65	Medium	2.78	Medium
2	Character in service process	3.00	Medium	3.00	Medium
	Mean	2.83	Medium	2.89	Medium
Empathy					
1	Caring attitude	1.36	Very Low	2.64	Medium
2	Understanding the need for students	2.35	Low	1.88	Low
	Mean	1.85	Low	2.26	Low
	Service Quality	2.94	Medium	3.00	Medium

high schools is further strengthened. This can be seen from the increasing number of majors in public vocational schools in Palangkaraya.

Application of ISO 9001: 2000 is expected to increase service quality of vocational schools in Palangkaraya, standards were implemented including the standard functions, duties and obligations of the principal and teaching staff, managerial, service management to the completeness of the school facilities.

Based on the research, quality of services provided in an educational institution especially vocational schools can be influenced by several factors including.

Here is the description of the average score on the respondents' answers to each indicator proposed in each aspect.

Based on tabulation it is known that the highest determinant factor at SMKN 1 is Tangible and the lowest determinant factor is Empathy. While at SMKN 2, the highest determinant factor is Responsiveness while the lowest one is Empathy.

Overall, based on the results of data processing in two research objects it is noted that the quality of academic services in vocational schools in Palangkaraya are in the medium category, with the highest determinant factor is Responsiveness and the lowest determinant factor is Empathy.

4 CONCLUSION

Result of the research revealed that the lowest factor is empathy. This illustrates the lack of school personnel's willingness to provide the best service in a professional manner to school consumers i.e. students. The quality of academic services on both subjects was not significantly different.

Recommendations to both schools in order to improve the motivation of personnel is by providing quality academic services for students and applying quality management in a more professional way so that the school would be more trustable both by the students and parents as consumers.

REFERENCES

Bonnal, L., Mendes, S., & Sofer, C. (2002). School-to-work transition: apprenticeship versus vocational school in France. *International journal of manpower*, 23(5), 426–442.

Bowles, S., & Gintis, H. (1976). *Schooling in capitalist America* (Vol. 57). New York: Basic Books.

Bryman, A. (2015). *Social research methods*. Oxford university press.

Carnochan, S., Samples, M., Myers, M., & Austin, M. J. (2014). Performance measurement challenges in nonprofit human service organizations. *Nonprofit and Voluntary Sector Quarterly*, 43(6), 1014–1032.

Colley, H., James, D., Diment, K., & Tedder, M. (2003). Learning as becoming in vocational education and training: class, gender and the role of vocational habitus. *Journal of vocational education and training*, 55(4), 471–498.

Eisemon, T. O. (2014). *Benefiting from basic education, school quality and functional literacy in Kenya* (Vol. 2). Amsterdam: Elsevier.

Hasan, H. F. A., Ilias, A., Rahman, R. A., & Razak, M. Z. A. (2009). Service quality and student satisfaction: A case study at private higher education institutions. *International Business Research*, 1(3), 163.

Hopkins, D. (2015). *Improving the quality of education for all: A handbook of staff development activities*. London: Routledge.

Indonesia, P. R. (2003). Undang-undang Republik Indonesia nomor 20 tahun 2003 tentang sistem pendidikan nasional.

Jayakumar, U. (2008). Can higher education meet the needs of an increasingly diverse and global society? Campus diversity and cross-cultural workforce competencies. *Harvard Educational Review*, 78(4), 615–651.

Mosahab, R., Mahamad, O., & Ramayah, T. (2010). Service quality, customer satisfaction and loyalty: A test of mediation. *International business research*, 3(4), 72.

Moser, C. A., & Kalton, G. (2017). *Survey methods in social investigation*. London: Routledge.

Murniati, A. R., & Nasir Usman, M. P. (2009). *Implementasi manajemen stratejik dalam pemberdayaan sekolah menengah kejuruan*. Bukit tinggi: Perdana Publishing.

Nurmi, J. E., Salmela-Aro, K., & Koivisto, P. (2002). Goal importance and related achievement beliefs and emotions during the transition from vocational school to work: Antecedents and consequences. *Journal of Vocational Behavior*, 60(2), 241–261.

Parasuraman, A., Zeithaml, V. A., & Berry, L. L. (1988). Servqual: A multiple-item scale for measuring consumer perc. *Journal of retailing*, 64(1), 12.

Parsons, T. (1959). The school class as a social system. *Schools and society: A sociological approach to education*, 32–40.

Ragin, C. C. (2014). *The comparative method: Moving beyond qualitative and quantitative strategies*. California: Univ of California Press.

Sallis, E. (2014). *Total quality management in education*. London: Routledge.

Scardamalia, M. (2000). Can schools enter a knowledge society. *Educational technology and the impact on teaching and learning*, 6–10.

Senge, P. M., Cambron-McCabe, N., Lucas, T., Smith, B., & Dutton, J. (2012). *Schools that learn (updated and revised): A fifth discipline fieldbook for educators, parents, and everyone who cares about education*. New York: Crown Business.

Seth, N., Deshmukh, S. G., & Vrat, P. (2005). Service quality models: a review. *International journal of quality & reliability management*, 22(9), 913–949.

Wagner, T. (2014). *The Global Achievement Gap: Why Even Our Best Schools Don't Teach the New Survival Skills Our Children Need and What We Can Do About It*. New york: Basic Books.

Wei, X., Wagner, M., Christiano, E. R., Shattuck, P., & Yu, J. W. (2014). Special education services received by students with autism spectrum disorders from preschool through high school. *The Journal of special education*, 48(3), 167–179.

Wibowo, N. (2016). Upaya Memperkecil Kesenjangan Kompetensi Lulusan Sekolah Menengah Kejuruan dengan Tuntutan Dunia Industri. *Jurnal Pendidikan Teknologi dan Kejuruan*, 23(1), 45–59.

Educational Administration Innovation for Sustainable Development – Komariah et al. (Eds)
© 2018 Taylor & Francis Group, London, ISBN 978-1-138-57341-3

Gender role on the effects of human capital and social capital on academic career success

N. Kholis
Universitas Islam Negeri (UIN) Sunan Ampel, Surabaya, Jawa Timur, Indonesia

ABSTRACT: This study examines the degree to which gender moderates the effects of human capital and social capital on academic career success, i.e., having higher academic ranks and leadership positions. 469 lecturers (men = 55.7%, women = 44.3%) from 18 universities in Indonesia returned survey questionnaires with analyzable quality. To examine the effects of career predictors on outcomes, hierarchical regression analyses were performed. Results show that older men and women tended to have higher academic ranks. Then, women tended to hold leadership positions when they are older, whereas men already had leadership positions at their younger age. Next, both committee appointment and intra-organizational networking were essential for achieving a leadership position. Inter-organizational networking was not important for women's leadership position and was even counterproductive for men's leadership position. The findings suggest that factors that contribute to men's academic career success are not necessarily applicable to women's academic career success.

1 INTRODUCTION

What factors lead some academics to achieve higher academic ranks and leadership positions? Past research revealed some factors associated with career success, such as demographics, human capital, motivational, and organizational variables (Judge et al., 1995), and social capital (Seibert et al., 2001). Although these studies were conducted in the nonacademic environment, they are fundamental in understanding predictors of academic career success.

Predictors of academic career success include accumulative advantage, sponsored mobility, and contest mobility (Miller et al., 2005), and demographic and human capital variables (Bayer and Astin, 1975). However, the understanding of careers in academia is limited compared to that of careers in the industrial and business sectors (Baruch and Hall, 2004). Additionally, bringing gender and/or the Asian and Indonesian context into the study of academic career even complicates the understanding of career (Leong and Leung, 2004). Therefore, a contextualized exploration and testing of career success predictors is needed to better understand career success in academia.

Accordingly, this study proposes and tests a model of academic career success. Some predictors included in this model are derived from past research and some are specific to Indonesian context. The results from the test of the hypothesized model should provide important evidence regarding the predictors of academic career success.

2 LITERATURE REVIEW

2.1 *Conceptual model of academic career success*

Career success may be defined as the positive psychological or work-related outcomes or achievements individuals have accumulated as a result of their work experiences (Ng et al., 2005). Two typical dimensions of career success have been conceptualized: objective and subjective (De Pater, 2005, Heslin, 2005). Objective career success is the public aspect of a person's career, measured against objective, verifiable and measurable criteria such as income or salary level, advancement

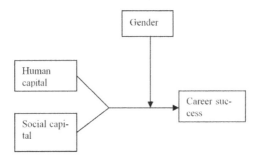

Figure 1.   Moderating role of gender on the effects of human and social capital factors on career success.

or promotion rank, and occupational status (Kern et al., 2009). Subjective career success, on the other hand, is individuals' feelings of accomplishment and satisfaction with their careers (Judge et al., 1995). Although measuring the subjective aspect is important in academic career research, this study is focused on using objective dimension of career success.

Figure 1 shows the hypothesized model of academic career success, with the role of gender as moderator.

2.2   *Academic career success*

Consistent with Bayer and Astin (1975) and Tiao (2006) we include academic rank and leadership positions as indicators of objective career success in academia. As the figure shows, we hypothesize that human capital and social capital variables affect academic career success, yet gender moderates the effect.

Achieving the highest academic rank is one of the important goals for a person working in academia. The highest academic rank (professor) enhances personal and university reputation. Reaching top academic rank is difficult for many academics. Those who hold the highest academic level can be considered as successful in their academic career.

Another success indicator in academia is holding a (higher) leadership position. A leadership position, especially the highest one, carries with it social and financial enhancement; and this might not be easily reached by many employees. Thus, the ability to reach such a position denotes a sense of success.

2.3   *Predictors of academic career success*

1. Gender

Gender is one of the common constructs used in understanding and explaining career success in academia (Benschop and Brouns, 2003). Various studies found that men hold higher academic ranks (Wright and Guth, 2009) and occupy higher leadership in universities (Eggins, 2009). Similarly, Indonesian studies revealed that more men occupy higher academic ranks and leadership positions and that women representation tend to decrease in the higher positions (Kholis, 2012a). Thus, it is proposed that women academics have lower academic rank and leadership positions than men.

2. Human capital variables

Human capital is defined as the knowledge, talents and skills that individuals acquire during their life such as education, training and development and work (Becker, 1993). The investment made by individuals in education, training and work experiences partly determines their career successes. Promotion to a higher academic rank in Indonesia requires a combination of proven academic work: education and teaching, research, publications, and community services, scholarly presentations and committee appointments (Coordinating Minister, 1999).

Career research found that human capital variables such as education and work experience are strong determinants for career success in terms of salary and career progression (Tharenou et al., 1994, Ng et al., 2005). In academic settings, human capital variables, e.g., publications were also found to be the main influence for career advancement (Bayer and Astin, 1975) and the speed of promotion (Lyness and Thompson, 2000).

However, the ability to accumulate human capital (i.e. credit points) may differ from men to women. Several studies indicate that women academics publish less than men (D'Amico and Canetto, 2010, Reed et al., 2011, Kholis, 2012b). The lack of credit point accumulation in publication may be due to women academics still holding more family care responsivities, resulting in conflicting time for family and professional activities. Indeed, a study shows that women were more likely to mention lack of energy and time for accumulating credit numbers than men.

Additionally, although women had equal educational qualifications and competence to men, they were less likely to hold a leadership position (Kholis, 2017). Thus, gender is assumed to interact with human capital variables in achieving academic rank and leadership position. It is predicted that human capital affects academic rank and leadership position, and this effect is stronger for men.

3. Social capital variables

Social capital can be defined as valuable assets such as 'information, referrals, resources, and support' (Ibarra, 1997) that individual accumulates by means of their relationship ties with others or their positions in a particular social structure. In academia, social capital factors such as networking and involvement in external organizations are important for personal and professional development as well as getting access to opportunities for promotion (Turner, 2002). Via networking and external organizational involvement, an academic may often be invited to teach at other universities, to present a paper, to do joint-research, to submit an article for publication, and to perform a community development activity. These can all be converted into credit numbers necessary for academic advancement.

Research has found that networking can help in publishing and gaining referees for the promotion process (Todd and Bird, 2000, Buddeberg-Fischer et al., 2009), speeding up the promotion process (Sabatier et al., 2006). Furthermore, apart from formal requirements, such as academic rank, leadership selection processes, especially the higher ones, involve political activity (Davey, 2008). In a political domain, voters, who may have been accrued from networking and involvement in external organizations, are very important for candidates to win. In fact, networking is a proven strategy by which women can reach top leadership positions in universities (Tiao, 2006). Furthermore, active involvement in various organizations increased political participation (Worng et al., 2007) and enhanced individuals' capacity for, e.g., playing political action (Putnam, 1995) in the leadership selection process.

However, men and women's intensity in building networks and being involved in external organizations may be different, partly due to organizational constraints and family responsibility. Externally-connected-to-campus organizations are dominated by men especially in their leadership, hindering women from being more actively involved in them. Furthermore, with more caring responsibilities (Eagly and Carli, 2007), women typically have less time for networking and therefore have limited access to male networks (White, 2003). Nonetheless, despite having similar networking behavior to men, women are unlikely to receive the same level of career benefits as men (Wang, 2009). In addition, although men and women reported similar degrees of network support, the benefits of informal networks appear to be greater for men (Kirchmeyer, 1998).

These studies show the existence of gender effect on the relationship between social capital and career success, and we can expect that this holds for careers in academia too. Therefore, we propose that social capital affects academic rank and leadership position, and this effect is stronger for men.

3 RESEARCH METHOD

3.1 *Sample and procedure*

Respondents were 466 lecturers from 18 universities in Indonesia (men $= 261$; women 208). The vast majority of respondents had a Master's degree (68.8%), and the second largest group had a Doctoral degree (22.5%). While more women had a Master's degree, more men had a PhD degree. A few respondents held undergraduate degrees (6.7%). On average, male respondents were older ($M = 42.2$, $SD = 8.80$) than female respondents ($M = 40.0$, $SD = 8.17$), $t(466) = 2.80$, $p < 0.01$, by up to two years. Furthermore, most of the respondents were married (92.5%) and were parents/had children (84.0%). Female respondents spouses had a higher educational level ($M = 3.39$, $SD = 0.95$) than male respondents ($M = 2.83$, $SD = 0.93$), χ^2 (2, $N = 425$) $= 35.73$, p < 0.01.

The questionnaires were mailed to the targeted universities, which were obtained from university databases and then selected on the basis of the availability of the data collector. The questionnaire was a paper-based survey. The number of questionnaires mailed to each of the universities was not the same as this was dependent on the size of the university, and the readiness as well as the capability of the collectors. The data collectors randomly distributed the questionnaires to existing lecturers within the university in which they work. Answering questionnaires was voluntary and therefore it was assumed that respondents did so frankly and without pressure. Each of the answers to the questions in the questionnaires carried the same weight. Of the questionnaires that were mailed, 466 were returned with analyzable quality, representing a response rate of 62.5%.

3.2 *Measurement*

Respondents were asked to give their actual age (in years) and to indicate their gender (1 = Male, 2 = Female); their highest educational level (1 = undergraduate, 2 = Graduate diploma, 3 = Master, and 4 = PhD); marital status (1 = Married, 2 = Single); parental status (1 = Do not have child(ren), 2 = Have child(ren). They were also asked to select their spouse's education (1 = Until high school, 2 = Diploma, 3 = Undergraduate, 4 = Postgraduate, and 5 = Doctorate).

Human capital variables include thesis supervision, publications and committee appointment. To measure thesis supervision respondents were asked to put the number of theses they supervised based on the thesis category: 1 = None, 2 = Bachelor, 3 = Master, 4 = Doctorate. Publications were comprised of two variables: book and journal publications. For book publications, respondents were asked to give the number of books they have published during their academic career. Filling in zero or leaving it blank in this item was considered as not having a book publication.

For journals, they were asked to indicate the types of journal and the number of articles they published over the last five years. The coded items were 1 = No publication; 2 = Popular magazine or newspapers; 3 = Indonesian non-accredited journal; 4 = Indonesian accredited journal; and 5 = International journal. Finally, respondents were asked to provide the number of committee appointments based on the positions in the committee in the last year: 0 = None, 1 = Member, 2 = Coordinator, 3 = Treasurer, 4 = Secretary, 5 = Head, and 6 = Supervisor.

Social capital covers extra-organizational involvement, intra-organizational networking, and inter-organizational networking. For extra-organizational involvement, respondents were asked to indicate their degree of involvement in one or more organizations of which they are members, i.e. informal organizations connected to campus; professional union; community organization; political party; and religious organization. The types of organizations included were specifically chosen and used for this study. A 5-point response format was used (1 = Very inactive; 5 = Very active). The final scale used here has been analyzed using Exploratory Factor Analyses (EFA) with Principle Components Analysis (PCA) and Confirmatory Factor Analyses (CFA) and has met satisfactory requirements, with an alpha of 0.84.

Intra-organizational networking was assessed with 12 items. Six items were developed by Bozionelos (2003) and measure intra-organizational resources containing two dimensions: expressive network resource with three items, e.g., 'There are individuals in the organization with whom

I share emotional support, feedback and work confirmation'. The other dimension is labeled instrumental network resource also with three items, e.g., 'I keep in touch with a number of people in the organization who are at higher hierarchical levels than I am'. Six items were added to cater to networking behavior outside the organization (inter-organizational networking). The additional six items were developed based on extant literature (Wolff and Moser, 2009, Bartol and Zhang, 2007).

An example item of inter-organizational networking is 'There are individuals I personally know outside my current organization who can influence decisions in the organization where I currently work'. The scale was measured using a 5-point response format ranging from 1 = Strongly disagree to 5 = Strongly agree, with high scores meaning wider networks. The 12 items were subjected to PCA and CFA. The scale reliability of intra-organizational networking was $\alpha = 0.91$, while that of inter-organizational networking was $\alpha = 0.81$. For measuring academic rank, respondents were asked to give their current academic ranks. Their answers were coded hierarchically according to the rank orders of lecturers set out by the Indonesian government, being 1 = Expert Assistant; 2 = Lecturer; 3 = Head Lecturer; 4 = Professor.

To collect information about leadership position, respondents were asked to give the name of the position they currently hold. Blank or no response was considered as not having a leadership position, and coded zero. The leadership positions that they provided were then grouped into three leadership levels, and coded 1 = Low position (department and unit levels); 2 = Middle position (postgraduate and faculty levels); and 3 = High position (university level).

3.3 *Analyses*

Hierarchical regression analyses were employed. It was important to examine the standardized regression coefficients of the separate equations because they reveal the degree of change in the dependent variable with each unit change in the predictor variable (Cohen and Cohen, 1975). This is a critical property when comparing variable relationships across gender where predictor variables often have different ranges. This process revealed the contributing variables to success indicators for men and women. The standardized beta weight (β) of significant independent variables was used to explain the relative contribution to the dependent variables.

Academic rank and leadership position were regressed on age, gender, human capital variables and social capital variables. At step 1 age was entered as a control variable. Gender was entered in step 2 as a factor. Variables of human capital and social capital were entered in step 3. Finally, to test for indirect effects of interactions of gender with age, with human capital and with social capital, these were added in step 4 as additional independents.

4 RESULTS AND DISCUSSION

The results of hierarchical regressions predicting objective academic career success (academic rank and leadership position) are discussed in this section. (Due to limited pages Tables of descriptive statistics and the regressions are not provided here). The regression analyses show that each set of hypothesized variables (gender, age, human capital, social capital) explained a significant amount of variance in academic rank and leadership position. Age explained 48%; gender added 1%; human capital variables added 8%; and social capital variables added 1% of the variance in academic rank.

For leadership positions, age explained 6%; gender added 2%; human capital variables increased 19%; and social capital variables added 3% of variance. In the final, full model regression, age predicted academic rank ($\beta = .44$, $p = .00$): older lecturers tend to have higher academic ranks. Age did not predict leadership position ($\beta = -.09$, $p = .56$). Gender did not affect academic rank ($\beta = -.05$, $p = .87$) and leadership position ($\beta = -.38$, $p = .34$). The prediction that 'women have lower academic rank and leadership position than men' was not supported. For women, having lower academic rank and leadership is not because of their gender but because of their age.

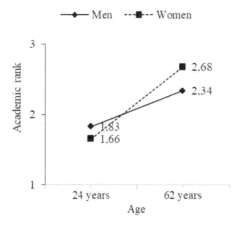

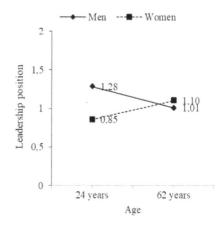

Figure 2. Interaction effects of gender and age on academic rank.

Figure 3. Interaction effects of gender and age on academic rank.

The interaction effect of gender and age was marginally significant for academic rank ($\beta = .39$, $p = .06$) and leadership position ($\beta = .45, p = .09$). Figure 2 shows that both older men and women have higher academic rank; but the age effect is stronger for women.

Furthermore, Figure 3 suggests that younger men have higher leadership position than older men; but on the contrary, older women have a higher leadership position than younger women. Thus, age matters more for women's higher academic rank and leadership position than for men's.

None of the human capital variables predicted academic rank; yet, committee appointment significantly affected leadership position ($\beta = .37, p = .02$): the more the lecturers are appointed to committees, the more likely they are to hold a (higher) leadership position. No interaction effects of gender and human capital variables on academic rank and leadership position were observed. The assumption that 'human capital affects leadership position, and this effect is stronger for men' was partially supported for leadership position with respect to committee appointment.

None of the social capital variables predicted academic rank; neither were their interactions with gender. The hypothesis that 'social capital positively affects academic rank, and this effect is stronger for men' was not supported. Intra-organizational networking significantly predicted leadership position ($\beta = .38, p = .02$): the more the lecturers build networks within their organization, the more likely they are to hold a (higher) leadership position. Inter-organizational networking negatively predicted leadership position ($\beta = -.46, p = .00$): the more the lecturers build networks outside their organization, the more likely they are to have a lower leadership position or not to have a leadership position.

The interaction effect of gender and intra-organizational networking on leadership position was marginally significant ($\beta = -.58, p = .07$). The effect is depicted in Figure 4, which indicates that intra-organizational networking is more beneficial for men's leadership position than for women's.

The interaction effect of gender and inter-organizational networking on leadership position was also significant ($\beta = .69, p = .02$). The effect is shown in Figure 5, which suggests that inter-organizational networking is counterproductive for men's leadership position. Inter-organizational networking does not affect women's leadership position. Therefore, the hypothesis 'social capital affects leadership position, and this effect is stronger for men' was partly supported with respect to the importance of intra-organizational networking for men's leadership positions. However, this hypothesis was refuted with respect to the negative impact of inter-organizational networking for men's leadership positions.

In this study gender is not a direct predictor of academic rank and leadership position. Previous studies found that men hold higher academic rank and leadership positions (Bayer and Astin, 1975, Sabatier et al., 2006, Sanders et al., 2009), but in this study that is explained by age rather than

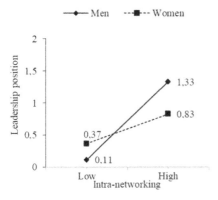

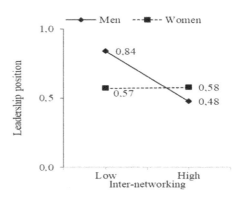

Figure 4. Interaction effects of gender and intra-networking on leadership position.

Figure 5. Interaction effects of gender and inter-networking on leadership position.

gender. Regardless of gender, therefore, older female and male lecturers tend to have a higher academic rank.

In addition, age effects on academic rank and leadership positions were stronger for women than for men. Women tend to reach higher ranks at higher ages compared to men. Perhaps, early in their career women spent more time on care responsibilities than men, so that they have less time for accumulating credit numbers necessary for academic advancement, e.g., writing articles. With less intensive care responsibilities later on, women may have more time for academic activities leading to achieving a higher academic rank, and by the time they reach the higher rank they are older. Women of childbearing age suffer from motherhood bias in getting promoted (King, 2008), the negative effects of which are less when they are older (Heilman and Okimoto, 2008).

While women need to be older to reach a higher leadership position, more men already have a (higher) leadership position at their younger age. Younger men may have already fulfilled the requirements for a leadership position at an earlier stage due, for example, to having higher education and academic rank. On the contrary, younger women may not be appointed for higher leadership positions because they lack the necessary requirements. In addition, younger men held leadership positions more often than older men, whereas for women the opposite was the case. Older men may have occupied leadership positions in the past, meaning that they are no longer eligible to run for future leadership. This is true for the higher leadership positions, i.e. rector or dean, in which the limit of their appointment is eight years (2 terms) (Indonesian Govt., 1999). Then, the selection of a higher leadership position may require younger age to allow for high mobility and productivity, so that those closer to the retirement period may not be nominated.

The tendency of older women to hold leadership positions more often than younger ones indicates that being older means an increased ability to meet the leadership requirements, such as higher academic rank. Furthermore, because women have never been appointed for a leadership position at younger age, they may be selected for one at an older age. Due to more performance-based than expectation-based evaluation for a leadership position, women may need longer to prove themselves capable of being a leader (Lyness and Heilman, 2006). Thus, age matters more for women's academic rank and leadership positions than for men's.

Concerning human capital, the study found that committee appointment is an important predictor of leadership position. The importance of committee appointment in the leadership position may be understood with respect to the nature of leadership election process, which involves a degree of politics (Davey, 2008, Tiao, 2006). High involvement in committees may increase the candidates' visibility and make their qualities readily observable, leading to success in an election process. Meeting the standard requirements coupled with visibility-increasing activities enhances the likelihood of being appointed to a (higher) leadership position.

This explanation is heightened by the fact that social capital variables, especially intra-organizational networking, have a positive effect on leadership position. Since the selection of leaders involves political activity, building an internal network could lead to success in the election process. Network building is important for gaining recognition, popularity, increasing political support (Worng et al., 2007) and enhancing individuals' capacity for playing political action (Putnam, 1995) leading to the attainment of top leadership positions in universities (Tiao, 2006).

This study found that intra-organizational networking is more beneficial for men's leadership position than for women's. A possible explanation is that work networks are dominated by men, often called 'old-boys' networks (Wenniger and Conroy, 2001), or that more men than women are decision makers because a larger number of leaders are men (White, 2003), or that men have more access to influential individuals and powerful associations within organizations (Forret and Dougherty, 2004). Alternatively, men may use networks more strategically for supporting their career goals, such as gaining leadership positions, whereas women may use networks for other purposes than their career goals. Thus, men may use networks differently from women. The important of networks for men's leadership position may also be connected with the fact that more men meet the requirements for higher leadership positions (e.g., higher education).

Contrary to our expectation, the study found that inter-organizational networking is counterproductive for men's leadership position. A possible explanation is that intensively building networks outside the organization may reduce lecturers' popularity internally or their intentions to apply for a leadership position; thus decreasing the likelihood of being appointed as leaders. The tasks attached to a lower leadership position may be less demanding, providing spare time and energy for the holders to build networks outside their organization.

5 CONCLUSION

In summary, age is a more important predictor of academic rank than gender. Human capital in terms of committee appointment is important for attaining higher leadership position. Furthermore, social capital factors in terms of intra-organizational networking are essential for gaining a higher leadership position. Finally, inter-organizational networking is not important for women's leadership position and is even counterproductive for men's leadership position. It is suggested that factors contributing to academic career success may be different for men and women. This study contributes to better understanding of career success predictors in academia particularly in Indonesian academia. A more comprehensive study needs to be conducted with a larger number of predictors to allow for more conclusive results.

REFERENCES

Bartol, K. M. & Zhang, X. 2007. Networks and leadership development: Building linkages for capacity acquisition and capital accrual. *Human Resource Management Review,* 17, 388–401.

Baruch, Y. & Hall, D. T. 2004. Preface for the JVB special issue on careers in academia (2 14 2003). *Journal of Vocational Behavior* 64: 237–240.

Bayer, A. E. & Astin, H. S. 1975. Sex differentials in the academic reward system. *Science* 188: 796–802.

Becker, G. S. 1993. *Human Capital: a theoretical and empirical analysis with special reference to education,* Chicago, University of Chicago Press.

Benschop, Y. & Brouns, M. 2003. Crumbling ivory towers: Academic organizing and its gender effects. *Gender, Work & Organization,* 10: 194–212.

Bozionelos, N. 2003. Intra-organizational network resources: Relation to career success and personality. *International Journal of Organizational Analysis,* 11: 41–66.

Buddeberg-Fischer, B., Stamm, M. & Buddeberg, C. 2009. Academic career in medicine – requirements and conditions for successful advancement in Switzerland. *BMC Health Services Research,* 9.

Cohen, J. & Cohen, P. 1975. *Applied multiple regression/correlation analysis for the behavioral sciences,* Hillsdale, NJ: Lawrence Erlbaum Associates.

Coordinating Minister 1999. The Minister decree on the functional positions of lecturers and their credit numbers.

D'amico, R. & Canetto, S. S. 2010. Similarities and differences in women's and men's publication and citation record among academic psychologists. *Journal of Women and Minorities in Science and Engineering* 16: 343–361.

Davey, K. M. 2008. Women's accounts of organizational politics as a gendering process. *Gender, Work & Organization* 15: 650–671.

De Pater, I. E. 2005. *Doing things right or doing the right thing: A new perspective on the gender gap in career success.* Dissertation, Universitiet van Amsterdam.

Eagly, A. H. & Carli, L. L. 2007. *Through the labyrinth: The truth about how women become leaders,* Boston, Harvard Business School Press.

Eggins, H. 2009. Women in higher education, research and innovation: Gains and further challenges. *In:* Hughes, S. (ed.) *2009 World Conference on Higher Education.* Unesco Paris: The UNESCO Forum on Higher Education, Research and Knowledge.

Forret, M. L. & Dougherty, T. W. 2004. Networking behaviors and career outcomes: Differences for men and women? *Journal of Organizational Behavior* 25: 419–437.

Heilman, M. E. & Okimoto, T. G. 2008. A potential source of bias in employment decisions. *Journal of Applied Psychology* 93: 189–198.

Heslin, P. A. 2005. Conceptualizing and evaluating career success. *Journal of Organizational Behavior,* 26, 113–136.

Ibarra, H. 1997. Paving an alternative route: Gender differences in managerial networks. *Social Psychology Quarterly* 60: 91–102.

Indonesian Govt. 1999. Government regulation no. 60 year 1999 on higher education.

Judge, T. A., Cable, D. M., Boudreau, J. W. & Bretz, R. D. J. 1995. An empirical investigation of the predictors of executive career success. *Personnel Psychology,* 48, 485–519.

Kern, M. L., Friedman, H. S., Martin, L. R., Reynolds, C. A. & Luong, G. 2009. Conscientiousness, career success, and longevity: A lifespan analysis. *Annals of Behavioral Medicine* 37: 154–163.

Kholis, N. 2012a. Career advancement in Indonesian academia: A concern of gender discrimination. *Jurnal Kependidikan Islam* 2: 13–28.

Kholis, N. 2012b. Gendered career productivity and success in academia in Indonesia's Islamic higher education institutions. *Journal of Indonesian Islam* 6: 341–366.

Kholis, N. 2017. Barriers to womens career advancement in Indonesian academia. *YICEMAP.* Yogyakarta: Atlantis Press/Advances in Social Science, Education and Humanities Research (ASSEHR).

King, E. B. 2008. The effect of bias on the advancement of working mothers: Disentangling legitimate concerns from inaccurate stereotypes as predictors of advancement in academe. *Human Relations* 61: 1677–1711.

Kirchmeyer, C. 1998. Determinants of managerial career success: Evidence and explanation of male/female differences. *Journal of Management* 24: 673–692.

Leong, F. T. L. & Leung, K. 2004. Academic careers in Asia: A cross-cultural analysis. *Journal of Vocational Behavior* 64: 346–357.

Lyness, K. S. & Heilman, M. E. 2006. When fit is fundamental: Performance evaluations and promotions of upper-level female and male managers. *Journal of Applied Psychology* 91: 777–785.

Lyness, K. S. & Thompson, D. E. 2000. Climbing the corporate ladder: Do female and male executives follow the same route? *Journal of Applied Psychology* 85: 86–101.

Miller, C. C., Glick, W. H. & Cardinal, L. B. 2005. The allocation of prestigious positions in organizational science: accumulative advantage, sponsored mobility, and contest mobility. *Journal of Organizational Behavior* 26: 489–516.

Ng, T. W. H., Eby, L. T., Sorensen, K. L. & Feldman, D. C. 2005. Predictors of objective and subjective career success: A meta-analysis. *Personnel Psychology* 58: 367–408.

Putnam, R. D. 1995. Tuning in, tuning out: The strange disappearance of social capital in America. *PS: Political Science and Politics* 27: 664–683.

Reed, D., Enders, F., Lindor, R., Mcclees, M. & Lindor, K. 2011. Gender differences in academic productivity and leadership appointments of physicians throughout academic careers. *Acad Med* 86: 43–7.

Sabatier, M., Carrere, M. & Mangematin, V. 2006. Profiles of academic activities and careers: Does gender matter? An analysis based on French life scientist CVs. *Journal of Technology Transfer* 31: 311–324.

Sanders, K., Willemsen, T. M. & Millar, C. C. J. M. 2009. Views from above the glass ceiling: Does the academic environment influence women professors' careers and experiences? *Sex Roles* 60: 301–312.

Seibert, S. E., Kraimer, M. L. & Liden, R. C. 2001. A social capital theory of career success. *The Academy of Management Journal* 44: 219–237.

Tharenou, P., Latimer, S. & Conroy, D. 1994. How do you make it to the top? An examination of influences on women's and men's managerial advancement. *Academy of Management Journal* 37: 899–931.

Tiao, N.-C. 2006. *Senior women leaders in higher education: Overcoming barriers to success.* Doctor of Education Dissertation, Eastern Michigan University.

Todd, P. & Bird, D. 2000. Gender and promotion in academia. *Equal Opportunities International* 19: 1–16.

Turner, C. S. V. 2002. Women of color in academe: Living with multiple marginality. *The Journal of Higher Education,* 73.

Wang, J. 2009. Networking in the workplace: Implications for women's career development. *New Directions for Adult & Continuing Education*: 33–42.

Wenniger, M. D. & Conroy, M. H. 2001. *Gender equity or bust!: On the road to campus leadership with women in higher education,* San Francisco, Jossey-Bass Publishers.

White, K. 2003. Women and leadership in higher education in Australia. *Tertiary Education and Management* 9: 45–60.

Wolff, H. G. & Moser, K. 2009. Effects of networking on career success: A longitudinal study. *Journal of Applied Psychology,* 94, 196–206.

Worng, Y.-L. I., Nath, S. B. & Solomon, P. L. 2007. Group and organizational involvement among persons with psychiatric disabilities in supported housing. *The Journal of Behavioral Health Services & Research* 34: 151–167.

Wright, F. & Guth, J. 2009. Women in the higher education sector. *The Industrial Law Journal* 38: 139–142.

Educational Administration Innovation for Sustainable Development – Komariah et al. (Eds)
© 2018 Taylor & Francis Group, London, ISBN 978-1-138-57341-3

Brain Jogging exercise and athletes' self-confidence

Komarudin
Universitas Pendidikan Indonesia, Bandung, West Java, Indonesia

ABSTRACT: Confident athletes believe in their own ability, while less confident athletes often doubt their own ability to show their best performance. Hence, appropriate practice methods are needed to increase athletes' confidence. This research aimed at investigating the effect of Brain Jogging exercise on athletes' self-confidence. The research design chosen was one group pretest-posttest design. The population comprised soccer athletes from the Universitas Pendidikan Indonesia Student Activity Unit. Twenty samples were chosen using a non-probability sampling technique. They were given Brain Jogging as a biweekly treatment for 11 meetings. The evaluation instrument used in this study was The State Sport Confidence Inventory. The t-test was used to analyze the data. The results revealed that Brain Jogging exercise improved the athletes' self-confidence. Brain Jogging exercise is a psychological exercise method suitable for improving athletes' self-confidence, especially soccer athletes.

1 INTRODUCTION

Self-confidence is a person's belief in himself that he has the ability to perform tasks (Whiteman, 2016). It is a variable closely related to one's sports performance so that it determines athletes' achievement and performance in sports (Hays, 2009). A confident athlete is able to control himself and his surroundings so that the athlete feels secure and acts firmly, persistently and confidently in performing his tasks (Mowlaie, 2011). On the other hand, a less confident athlete always doubts his own ability, which may bring him fear and anxiety in showing his best performance. Short (2003) claimed that self-confidence has an impact on an individual's behaviors and attitudes. Therefore, self-confidence needs to be continuously habituated using appropriate methods and Brain Jogging seems to offer an answer.

Brain Jogging in Indonesia was developed by Kuswari. This exercise was widely known in Western Europe (Germany, Netherlands, France and Spain) as "Life Kinetic". Kuswari labeled this activity as Brain Jogging as the movements in this exercise are dominated by jogging. Brain Jogging is the combination of motor activity and cognitive challenges and the training of visual perception, especially the perception of the peripheral visual field. Moving limbs in different and unusual combinations, catching and throwing objects, thus training the visual perception and limb-eye coordination, is a basic characteristic of the training (Demirakca, 2016). The essence of Brain Jogging is combining different motor activities (often disrupting basic movement techniques) which activate and shape associative cortical fields and at the same time, improve the efficiency of an athlete's thought processes (Duda, 2015). This exercise has been used by many people including professional athletes to train their mental qualities and their brains. Some beneficial purposes of Brain Jogging are stress reduction, better relaxation, better concentration and memory, better and faster learning, improvement of mental and physical performance, fewer errors and increased self-confidence (Lutz, 2017).

To date, much research has been conducted to analyze the role of physical activities in improving athletes' self-confidence. Whiteman (2016) revealed that brain activity patterns can predict a person's confidence state. What is more, they have discovered that this brain activity can be manipulated to increase self-confidence. Physical activity and exercise positively impact older adults at

Table 1. The means and standard deviation of athletes' self-confidence.

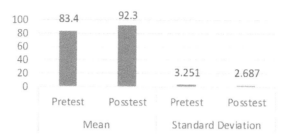

Table 1. The means and standard deviation of athletes' self-confidence.

any age and with various physical and psychological conditions (Bherer, 2013). In addition, the sport confidence model identified three types of sport confidence (i.e. physical skills and training, cognitive efficiency and resilience) that are important for success in sport (Machida, 2016). Therefore, self-confidence related to sports is an important factor to determine sportsman performance (Heper, 2014). The study confirmed that self-confidence affects athletes' performance. Further, it also claimed that physical activities are of self-confidence components deemed influential in sports achievement. However, the research on the combination of physical activities, cognition and perception fused in one Brain Jogging exercise aimed at improving self-confidence is not popular in Indonesia. This situation has attracted the researcher to further investigate the effect of Brain Jogging exercise on the improvement of athletes' self-confidence.

2 METHOD

The one group pretest-posttest design was chosen as the experimental research design. The population of this study comprised 45 soccer players in the Indonesia University of Education, out of which 20 samples were chosen by using a non-probability sampling technique. The researcher chose only those who actively practice and regularly take part in soccer competitions. The pretest was then administered to the selected sample to identify their initial self-confidence state. They were then given Brain Jogging as the treatment in this study. The treatment was conducted weekly at 11 meetings. The treatment number was adopted from Demirakca (2016). Upon completion of the eleven-meeting treatment, the posttest was then administered to analyze the effect of Brain Jogging on the athletes' self-confidence. As previously mentioned, the instrument used to assess self-confidence is The State Sport Confidence Inventory (Vealey, 1986). This instrument has been tested and all the items are valid and have a reliability level of 0.80. The t-test (paired t-test) using SPSS version 21 was used to analyze the data (Santosa, 2013)

3 RESULTS

The results of the study are presented in the form of data description consisting of means, standard deviations and pretest and posttest results. The results are described in Table 1.

Based on Table 1, the mean from the pretest is 83.400 with a standard deviation of 3.251, while the mean from the posttest is 92.300 with a standard deviation of 2.697. It was observed that the posttest score was higher than the pretest score. This implies that Brain Jogging affects athletes' self-confidence. Prior to the data analysis, the pretest and the posttest scores had been confirmed to be normally distributed and homogenous. As a result, the data were then analyzed by using parametric statistical analysis (paired sample t-test). The result is described in Table 2.

Table 2. T-test computation result.

Mean		−8.9
SD		4.12821
Std. Error Mean		0.9231
95% Confidence interval of the difference	Lower	−10.83206
	Upper	−6.96794
t		−9.641
df		19
Sig. (2-tailed)		0.000

Based on Table 2, the significance level is 0.000 < 0.05. This means that the null hypothesis is rejected. This result leads to the conclusion that Brain Jogging significantly improved the athletes' self-confidence.

4 DISCUSSION

Brain Jogging significantly improved the athletes' self-confidence. To confirm the finding, it is stated that self-confidence is grounded in perceptions of ability, thus the competitive orientations should reflect an athlete's belief that attainment of a certain type of goal demonstrates competence and success (Vealey, 1986). As a result, successful sportsmen have higher levels of self-confidence than less successful ones and they show this in a more comfortable way. The other explanation is that these highly confident sportsmen believe in their abilities to win and be successful or to perform better (Ibrahim, 2016).

Confident athletes have high perceived strength adequacy of physical fitness and perceived strength have high goal oriented grades (Heper, 2014). High athlete's perception on his own ability, physical fitness and strong vision will make this athlete to perform better in his tasks. In Brain Jogging, the motion of the athlete is so complex that it demands good motion coordination skills, it is very challenging for athletes to try to repeat every move until the athlete is able to perform every motion successfully. In fact, doing every movement in Brain Jogging must be done repetitively, which demands good concentration and coordination.

Brain Jogging is a fun physical activity that provides many benefits to all areas of life. It is also a program that improves mental and physical performance. It is not only fun, but it is the perfect way to improve performance. An essential aspect of this combined training is that the exercises are not trained until automatized. As soon as a participant's performance reaches about 60% correct trials, the task demands are changed, and new combinations of symbols and movements are introduced (Demirakca, 2016). Athletes practicing Brain Jogging will improve their condition and this is a good foundation in sport, respect for one's competence, adequate preparation and good physical condition (Roxel, 2005). Physical condition trained through physical activity is one method that can increase athletes' self-confidence

It was also believed that self-confidence is an important factor in determining one's performance in sports. Confident athletes will perform, have a good emotional condition, have a good strategy and are able to control their performance well (Heper, 2014). To this end, some exercises or psychological intervention methods can be applied to improve athletes' self-confidence (Machida, 2016). One of these intervention methods is Brain Jogging.

5 CONCLUSION

It may be concluded from the experiment that Brain Jogging has a significant effect on athletes' self-confidence. As a result, Brain Jogging fits as a psychological exercise method that can improve athletes' self-confidence.

REFERENCES

Bherer, L., Erickson, K.I. & Ambrose, T.L. (2013). A review of the effects of physical activity and exercise on cognitive and brain functions in older adults. *Journal of Aging Research Volume,* Article ID 657508, 8 pages.

Demirakca, T., Cardinale, V., Dehn, S., Ruf, M. & Ende, G. (2015). The exercising brain: Changes in functional connectivity induced by an integrated multimodal cognitive and whole-body coordination training. *Hindawi Publishing Corporation Neural Plasticity*, Volume 2016, Article ID 8240894, 11 pages.

Duda, H. (2015). Application of life kinetic in the process of teaching technical activities to young football players. *Journal of Kinesiology and Exercise Sciences*, 71(25), 53–63.

Hays, K., Thomas, O., Maynard, I. & Bawden, M. (2009). The role of confidence in world-class sport performance. *Journal of Sports Sciences*, 27(11), 1185–1199.

Heper, E., Yolacan, S. & Kocaeksi, S. (2014). The examine goal orientation and sports self confidence level of soccer players. *Procedia – Social and Behavioral Sciences*, 159, 197–200.

Ibrahim, H.I., Jaafar, A.H., Kassim, M.A.M. & Isa, A. (2016). Motivational climate, self-confidence and perceived success among student athletes. Retrieved from www.sciencedirect.com.

Komarudin. (2015). *Psikologi Olahraga*. Bandung, Indonesia: Rosdakarya.

Lutz. (2017). *Perform better with life kinetic life: Brain based training model for elite performance.* Los Angeles, CA: Kinetic Presentation NSCAA Convention 2017.

Machida, M., Otten, M., Magyar, T.M., Vealey, R.S. & Ward, R.M. (2016). Examining multidimensional sport-confidence in athletes and non-athlete sport performers. *Journal of Sports Sciences*, 1466-447X (Online) Journal, 18 April 2016.

Mowlaie, M. (2011). The mediation effects of self-confidence and sport self-efficacy on the relationship between dimensions of anger and anger control with sport performance. *Procedia – Social and Behavioral Sciences*, 30, 138–142.

Roxel, A. (2005). *Sports psychology*. Manila: UST. Publishing House.

Santoso, S. (2013). *Menguasai SPSS 21 di Era Informasi*. Jakarta: PT. Elex Media Komputindo.

Short, S.E. & Sullivan, P.J. (2003). Building, maintaining, and regaining team confidence in sports. *Journal of Physical Education, Recreation & Dance,* 74(1).

Vealey, R.S. (1986). Conceptualization of sport confidence and competitive orientation: Preliminary investigation and instrument development. *Journal of Sport Psychology*, 8, 221–246.

Whiteman, H. (2016). *Training the brain to boost self confidence*. Medical News Today.

Educational Administration Innovation for Sustainable Development – Komariah et al. (Eds)
© 2018 Taylor & Francis Group, London, ISBN 978-1-138-57341-3

Management capacity strategy in primary education policy implementation in rural areas

A. Komariah, D.A. Kurniady, A. Sudarsyah & C. Sunaengsih
Universitas Pendidikan Indonesia, Bandung, Indonesia

ABSTRACT: Management capacity in the level of policy implementation is one of the important points of various policies and strategies that the government issues. Management capacity is the frontline to determine how a policy should be implemented to improve the quality of education. The main problem of policy implementation lays in the weak management capacity in responding to stakeholders' needs and knowledge advancement. In its implementation, the policy and strategy cannot always be executed as planned. The present study employs descriptive method using qualitative approach. It is conducted in primary schools in rural areas of Sumedang Regency. In general, the steps of the study include: (1) preliminary study, (2) descriptive study, and (3) data analysis. The result of this study shows the description of management capacity strategy to implement primary education policies in rural areas.

1 INTRODUCTION

Management capacity in the policy implementation level is one of the important points of government's strategies and policies. With its management capacity, an institution can ensure that all providers of formal primary education in the nation will operate under certain minimum quality standard. Basically, one of the factors that cause the failure of organizational change is the error of capacity management or development within the organization. Most organizations rely on organizational resources rather than on capacity management. That is not wrong, but the question of how to manage it is more important than the question of what to manage (Horton, et al. 2003).

The direction of primary education is the objective that the government wishes to achieve through the obligatory 9 years primary education in all regions of Indonesia. According to the Strategic Plan of Education and Culture Ministry, the 2015–2019 period focuses on regional competitiveness. An organization can be significantly successful if it performs its own capacity management development changes. The development effort that used to focus on efficiency or operational needs should be changed into development effort that focuses on management capacity development (Matachi 2006). Hence, management capacity development that begins with programs, planning, cooperation, and connectivity between the human resources within the organization, both internally and externally, becomes a crucial thing.

In the implementation, strategy and policy direction cannot always be executed as planned. Indonesia's geographical condition, which consists of many islands, provides benefits as well as challenges. For certain areas, particularly the rural ones, it becomes a problem. The existing primary education policies seem only beneficial for those with access. Government's strategies and implementation need strong managerial. Nowadays, all matters pertaining to education implementation are being scrutinized and focused on. The government (both central and regional) and school stakeholders (students' parents, businesses, industry, education critics and experts, public organizations, and society) pay great attention towards school condition; particularly concerning the fact that school management is unable to provide the best service, the effect and result of which have not been actually felt by the stakeholders.

School management capacity is considered the root of the problem. Government's and public's expectation towards school management has not been met, particularly concerning the school's learning capability to respond to various situations and conditions. Reformation of such extensive and complex basic services requires real capacity improvement to strengthen the existing management and governance. Management capacity in this sense is not just the capacity of Education Office of the Province, Regency, District, and the school, but also the capacity of other parties involved with the process pertaining to policy and strategy implementation and expectation, delegating responsibilities, and ensuring accountability and quality improvement. Highly committed leadership is required to ensure that this extended management mechanism will continue efficiently and effectively (ACDP 2014b).

The primary objectives of the present study are to discover the general overview of management capacity in implementing primary education policies in Rural Areas of Sumedang Regency, as well as the overview of the primary education policies implementation in rural areas of Sumedang Regency. Considering these objectives, qualitative method is used. For the preliminary study, various data are gathered comprehensively, particularly the descriptive data. Since qualitative analysis is used, the gathered data are interpreted and analyzed before a conclusion is drawn.

The present study is limited to only examining organizations' management capacity, particularly in education organizations, in implementing primary education policies. However, the findings and experiences of the researchers in the last two decades shows that in an organization, management capacity is vital for the organization, and that management capacity development lies heavily on leadership capacity. This study is expected to further test management discipline and to apply it properly, as well as to increase practitioners' confidence towards education institutions.

2 METHOD

The study employs qualitative descriptive approach. Based on the concept of qualitative data analysis, the gathered data are interpreted and analyzed through several steps. First, field notes are taken (results of observation and interview); based on these field notes, a more comprehensive and structured report is made. The researchers then make a summary of the field notes, consisted of observation, interview, and document study results. The next step is member check on the summary of field notes (observation and interview) with the relevant subjects of the study, and audit-trail of the documents. Then, data triangulation is performed to ensure data validity; and summary report is revised to ensure that it reflects what the sources intended. The final step of data gathering is to provide general and specific commentaries for certain parts of the summary report. The data is analyzed through data reduction, data display, and data verification. The study is conducted in primary schools in rural areas of Sumedang Regency.

3 RESULT AND DISCUSSION

The results show an overview of education management capacity in rural areas primary schools in figure 1.

Knowledge building through enhancing skills, and fostering a learning community scores 2.45, which puts it in the sufficient category. The other three variables: leadership building through developing shared directions and taking a key influence in what happens in the region, valuing community and the importance of place and local initiatives, and providing supporting information through capturing and utilizing quality information are all in sufficient category, with scores of 2.03, 2.08, and 2.19, respectively. Meanwhile, network building through partnerships and alliances scores the lowest, with 1.91 score.

These findings indicate that a design and real steps to execute management capacity in the field are necessary. Management capacity in the field requires a framework of clear and detailed strategy, which should be adjusted with the actual implementation of policy and the characteristics

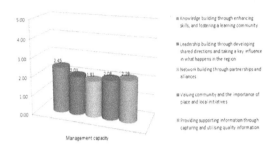
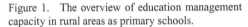
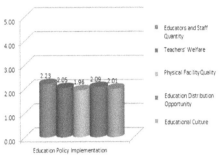

Figure 1. The overview of education management capacity in rural areas as primary schools.

Figure 2. The overview of education policy implementation.

of primary education in Sumedang Regency. The design of management capacity strategy should include the components, work mechanism/procedure, requirements, and achievement indicators.

The overview of education policy implementation based on the study is as follow in Figure 2.

The diagram shows that the quality of education facilities and infrastructure has the lowest score (1.96), while educators and staff quantity, teachers' welfare, education distribution opportunity, and educational culture are in sufficient category. The score for each aspect, respectively, is 2.23, 2.05, 2.09, and 2.10.

The complicated problems of elementary education in rural areas particularly concern with the availability of educators or teachers. This is the problem that we have to tackle. Teachers' reluctance to teach in rural areas is one of the main reasons for this problem. It is common for teachers to submit a request of transfer from rural areas to urban areas after teaching for certain period of time. Hence the quantity of teachers in urban areas is significantly greater than that in rural areas. Another reason is the gap of income between rural and urban areas teachers. This gap in income has forced teachers in rural areas to have other jobs besides teaching. The cause for this gap is the limited fund that the government provides (ACDP 2014a).

In addition, one of the determining factors of successful education implementation is the quality of physical facilities and infrastructure of education. However, it is difficult for rural schools to obtain high quality facilities. As we know, adequate physical condition will support the education process. With adequate physical condition and facilities, the education process will be more comfortable. Therefore, educational facilities and infrastructure should be sufficient to meet educational needs and science and technological advancement (Lunenburg 2010). The data from the National Education Ministry shows that there are many primary schools and secondary schools that do not meet the standard of minimum service requirement. Currently, there are 41.31 percent or 74.806 schools below the standard of minimum service requirement. 50.39 percent (91.243 schools) have just met the standard of minimum service requirement. In addition, only 8.03 percent (14.545 schools) that have met the national standard, and only 0.33 percent (595 schools) that met international standard (Kompas, 13/6/2011/ELN). This data is clearly reflected in the field, particularly if we see the primary schools in rural areas (Kemendikbud 2012).

Education distribution is another matter that should not be neglected. Education should be distributed evenly in the national education system to reach all citizen of Indonesia, including those in rural areas. However, until today, most of the people in rural areas only have the opportunity to get primary school level of education. Secondary schools are out of their reach, due to both its long distance and high cost. This is in line with the data from National Education Department's Research and Development Agency and the Department of Religious Affair's Directorate General of Religious Education Development. In 2000, both agencies reported the Pure Participation Score for primary school age students in 1999 is 94.4% (28.3 million students), which are high. Meanwhile the Pure Participation Score for Junior High School students is only 54.8% (9.4 million students).

Moreover, early childhood education is very limited in rural areas, even though that level of education is important for preparing the students for the next level of education. Considering all these data, it is important to have appropriate education distribution strategy and policy (Kemendikbud 2015).

Besides these four aspects, educational culture is also an important aspect. In rural areas, education is not a priority for the people. Most of them choose to work instead of continuing their education. This is because of socio-cultural factors pertaining to the society, including their tradition, public opinion, and habits in the society, which makes them do not feel reluctant to not continue their education (Übius & Alas 2009). Most of the parents choose to employ school-aged children, or to make them work, to help with the economy. This condition becomes a particular resistance for government's efforts to realize the 9 years Obligatory Education Program. This is an effort to expand public access towards education, which will make them understand the importance of education for children. Improving public awareness and comprehension of the importance of education is expected to reduce the drop-out rate and increase children's interest to go to school.

4 CONCLUSION

Based on the findings and discussion, the researchers conclude that management capacity in educational policy implementation in rural areas primary schools belongs to the category of sufficient. It means that management capacity in the aspects of Knowledge building through enhancing skills, and fostering a learning community, Leadership building through developing shared directions and taking a key influence in what happens in the region, Network building through partnerships and alliances, Valuing community and the importance of place and local initiatives, and Providing supporting information through capturing and utilizing quality information have not been optimally implemented. The implementation of primary school policies in rural areas schools is also below expectation as indicated by the level of policy implementation aspects (educators and staff quantity, teachers' welfare, facilities and infrastructure quality, education distribution opportunity, and educational culture), which belongs to sufficient category.

REFERENCES

ACDP, 2014a. *Dukungan Bagi Perencanaan dan Pemantauan Standar Pelayanan Minimum Pendidikan Dasar*, Jakarta. Available at: www.acdp-indonesia.org.
ACDP, 2014b. *Studi Perencanaan Strategis Percepatan Pendidikan Dasar di Pedesaan dan Daerah Terpencil di Tanah Papua, 2014 Analytical and Capacity Development Partnership (ACDP) Studi Perencanaan Strategis Percepatan*, Jakarta. Available at: www.acdp-indonesia.org.
Horton, et al. 2003. *Evaluating Capacity Development; Experiences from Research and Development Organizations around the world.* Netherlands-Canada: ISNAR, IDCR, ACP-EU, CTA
Kemendikbud, 2012. *9 Kebijakan Pembangunan Pendidikan Dasar di Daerah Perbatasan,*
Kemendikbud, 2015. *Rencana Strategis Kementerian Pendidikan dan Kebudayaan 2015–2019,*
Lunenburg, F., 2010. School Facilities Management. *National Forum of Educational Administration & ...,* 27(4), pp. 1–7. Available at: http://assets.efc.gwu.edu/resources/repository/120/Lunenburg_School_Facilities_Management.pdf.
Matachi, B.A., 2006. *Capacity Building Framework*, United Nations Economic Commission for Africa.
Übius, Ü. & Alas, R., 2009. Organizational Culture Types as Predictors of Corporate Social Responsibility. *Engineering*, 1(1), pp. 90–99. Available at: http://www.ktu.edu/lt/mokslas/zurnalai/inzeko/61/1392-2758-2009-1-61-90.pdf.

Educational Administration Innovation for Sustainable Development – Komariah et al. (Eds)
© 2018 Taylor & Francis Group, London, ISBN 978-1-138-57341-3

Middle school location in the Indonesian coastal zone based on an accessibility level analysis

T.C. Kurniatun, E. Rosalin, L. Somantri & I. Risnandar
Universitas Pendidikan Indonesia, Bandung, West Java, Indonesia

ABSTRACT: This study aimed to analyze the needs for facilities and infrastructure of junior high schools and the determination of their locations based on a social demand approach and Geographic Information System (GIS) details in coastal areas of Indonesia, especially in the Agrabinta Cianjur District, West Java. This research commenced from the limited educational facilities and skills condition, especially related to schools and new classrooms for junior high schools. The methods used in this research were an explorative method followed by a descriptive method. The data analysis techniques used in this research were ratio analysis, projection analysis of infrastructure and GIS needs. The results of this study illustrate the causes of non-conformity of school sites based on geographic characteristics of the region.

1 INTRODUCTION

Conceptually, the approach in educational planning, especially related to the fulfillment of government obligations is relevant to the social demand approach. In general, this social-needs approach is usually carried out in countries that have gained independence from colonization and developing countries (Comb, 1970; Longe, 2003; Adekoya & Gbenu, 2008). This planning approach requires educational planners to predict future needs by analyzing demographics, geographic information, participation in education, student flow and community interest regarding types of education (Adekoya & Gbenu, 2008; Udin & Makmun, 2005, Timan, 2004; Ibia, 2010).

In an effort to plan education with the current social demand approach, the role of the Geographic Information System (GIS) is essential, especially to determine the location of schools as educational facilities and infrastructure. As explained, GIS data and spatial analysis provide input for policy making (Flemming, 2014; Burrough & Mc Donnell, 2005; Agrawal & Gupta, 2016). GIS analysis related to school location in a region should consider the population distribution, location of the school not too far away (within 30 minutes) and easy access from the settlement even on foot (Jayadinata, 1999; Iskandar, 2009).

Based on these facts, this study aimed to analyze the needs of schools and the determination of appropriate school locations in the coastal areas of Indonesia, especially Cianjur Regency, West Java Province, based on a social demand approach and GIS in the framework of nine-year compulsory education.

2 RESEARCH METHOD

This study used an explorative method followed by a descriptive method which in its application using the study of tendency and content analysis. The location of this research observation was the Agrabinta District of Cianjur Regency. This represented a location having coastal characteristics in West Java Province Indonesia.

The data analysis technique in this research was using GIS analysis technique done by using MapInfo Professional 10.5 software. To know the level of suitability of school location in the

Agrabinta Sub-district of Cianjur Regency, data processing analysis using scaling technique and buffering analysis (De Chiara & Koppelman, 1975). The focused analysis in questions were:

1. Distribution analysis of school sites based on their area is analyzed by nearest neighbor analysis (Clark & Evans, 1954). The calculation formula uses the scale "R" as follows:

$$R = 2D \frac{\sqrt{n}}{a}$$

    R = Nearest neighbor scale
    D = Observed neighboring distance average
    n = Number of objects/symptoms/sectors
    a = Total area

From the results of these measurements, the value of "R" ranged from zero (0) to 2.1491 with a pattern interval as follows:

Interval value	Pattern
0.00–0.70	Cluster
0.71–1.40	Random
1.41–2.1491	Dispersed

Next step was to look for many classes that formed as well as the class interval which would be able to measure the level of suitability of school location with the formula Sturges (Sudjana, 1988), with the following formula:

$$K = 1 + 3.322 \log N$$

Description: K = The number of classes formed
    N = Units of overlaid map
    K = 1 + 3.322 log 6
    K = 1 + 3.322 × 0.699
    K = 3.02 rounded up to three classes
The next step was to find the interval of each class by using the following formula:

$$IK = Range / K$$

Description: *Range* = Minimum Score – Maximum Score: K = The number of classes

2. Road Conditions Quality Analysis.

    The scores for the road condition analysis were: asphalt road of good condition was given a score = 5; asphalt road that was slightly holed was given a score = 4; asphalt road that was damaged got a score = 2; and stone/ground road got a score = 1 (Ministry of Education & Ministry of Public Works, 1997/1998). There were seven schools with asphalt road access, eight schools with slightly perforated asphalt road access, 19 schools with asphalt road access in a damaged condition and six schools with access roads.

3. Location Suitability Decision Analysis.

    After all schools got scores based on each research variable, the location conformity was obtained by summing the scores obtained for each school. Schools with a score of 4–9.3 were in an inappropriate class, while schools with scores of 9.4–14.6 were in an appropriate class and schools with scores of 14.7–20 were in the appropriate classes.

3 RESULTS AND DISCUSSION

3.1 *School distribution based on population distribution in the Agrabinta District of West Java, Indonesia*

A school distribution map for the Agrabinta District was made based on the survey results by plotting the location using the Global Positioning System (GPS). From the location plotting activities the coordinate data of all schools were obtained and then incorporated into the map of the district of Agrabinta using MapInfo Professional 10.5 software. Based on the survey results the coordinates for each school were obtained. From these coordinates, the location of the school was analyzed based on its proximity to the settlements. This is in line with the principle of accessibility related to school location standards (De Chiara & Koppelman, 1975). Placement of school sites in residential areas can also be seen by buffering the map of the distribution of settlements. The results show that in the Agrabinta District there are still many difficult settlement of education service. Assessment of settlements that are not receiving educational services are seen from settlements that are not covered by polygon resulting from buffering on the school distribution buffer map in Agrabinta District. Therefore, the distribution of schools based on the distribution of settlements in the Agrabinta District can be suggested as being uneven.

Then the distribution of school location based on the area in the Agrabinta Sub-district was done by calculating using nearest neighbor analysis from Clark and Evans (1954). The analysis of distribution pattern of school location based on its region was done by using Equation 1, with the result of the calculation being as follows:

$D = 1,542.292939$ m (nearest neighbor for elementary school)

$n = 31$

$a = 257,600,000$ m^2

$\quad = 2 \times 1,542.294939 \times 0.000347$

$R = 1.0703$

$$R = 2 \text{ x } 1,542.294939 \frac{\sqrt{31}}{257,600,000}$$

The results of the nearest neighbor analysis for SMP are as follows:

$D = 6,401.0357$ m

$n = 5$

$a = 257,600,000$ m^2

$\quad = 2 \times 6,401.0357 \times 0.000139$

$R = 1.7795$

$$R = 2 \text{ x } 6,401.0357 \frac{\sqrt{5}}{257,600,000}$$

Based on the calculation, the scale value of R of primary school is 1.0703. That means that the distribution of primary schools in Agrabinta Sub-district belongs to the class spread uneven (random). In contrast to the value of the R scale of junior high school and high school which respectively reached the numbers 1.7795 and 1.7935. The figures indicate that the distribution of junior high schools and senior high schools in the Agrabinta Sub-district belongs to the dispersed class.

Based on the results of the analysis of the school spread above, the researchers concluded that the distribution of school locations in the Agrabinta District were considered as being uneven. The calculation is in accordance with that of Ramdan (2014). In the research, both researchers mentioned that the pattern of distribution of school location could be calculated by using the nearest neighbor analysis. The calculation will help in knowing the suitability level of the school location.

However, the assessment of the location of school distribution based on the distribution of settlements conducted by researchers is different from Satria (2013). In his research on the evaluation of the distribution of school locations, the assessment of school distribution based on the distribution of settlements is only done through field surveys. Although using the same standard of De Chiara

Table 1.   School location suitability level based on road condition scoring, road network and distribution of Agrabinta District, Cianjur Regency.

| No | School name | Score | | | Total score | Conformity class |
		Road condition	Road network	Settlement		
1	ES 1	5	5	5	20	Appropriate
2	ES 2	1	1	5	12	Quite Appropriate
3	ES 3	2	4	5	12	Quite Appropriate
4	ES 1	2	4	5	12	Quite Appropriate
5	ES 1	2	4	5	12	Quite Appropriate
6	ES 1	4	4		18	Appropriate
7	ES 1	1	1	5	8	Inappropriate
8	ES 1	2	2	5	10	Quite Appropriate
9	ES 1	2	2	5	14	Quite Appropriate
10	ES 1	2	1	5	13	Quite Appropriate
11	ES 1	4	2	5	12	Quite Appropriate
12	ES 1	2	4	5	16	Appropriate
13	ES 1	2	4	5	16	Appropriate
14	ES 1	2	4	5	12	Quite Appropriate
15	ES 1	1	1	5	8	Inappropriate
16	ES 1	1	1	5	8	Inappropriate
17	ES 1	2	2	5	14	Quite Appropriate
18	ES 1	5	5	5	20	Appropriate
19	ES 1	2	2	5	10	Quite Appropriate
20	ES 1	2	4	5	12	Quite Appropriate
21	ES 1	2	2	5	14	Quite Appropriate
22	ES 1	5	5	5	20	Appropriate
23	ES 1	2	2	5	14	Quite Appropriate
24	ES 1	1	2	5	13	Quite Appropriate
25	ES 1	4	4	5	18	Appropriate
26	ES 1	2	2	5	14	Quite Appropriate
27	ES 1	4	2	5	16	Appropriate
28	ES 1	2	2	5	14	Quite Appropriate
29	ES 1	2	2	5	14	Quite Appropriate
30	ES 1	1	4	5	15	Appropriate
31	ES 1	4	4	5	18	Appropriate
32	JS 1	5	5	5	20	Appropriate
33	JS 1	5	5	5	16	Appropriate
34	JS 1	4	4	5	18	Appropriate
35	JS 1	2	2	5	14	Quite Appropriate
36	JS 1	2	2	5	14	Quite Appropriate
37	JS 1	4	4	5	14	Quite Appropriate
38	JS 1	5	5	5	16	Appropriate
39	JS 1	4	4	5	14	Quite Appropriate
40	JS 1	5	5	5	16	Appropriate

Source: Field Survey Results (2017).

and Koppelman (1975), Satria (2013) did not conduct buffering analysis. According to him, conducting a direct survey and data collection alone is enough to assess whether the existing school spread is uneven or not.

3.2   *School location suitability level in the Agrabinta District, Cianjur Regency, based on accessibility level*

Roads and networks are the main factors affecting the accessibility level of a region. Therefore, scoring of road networks, road conditions, residential areas and disaster-prone areas (Ministry of

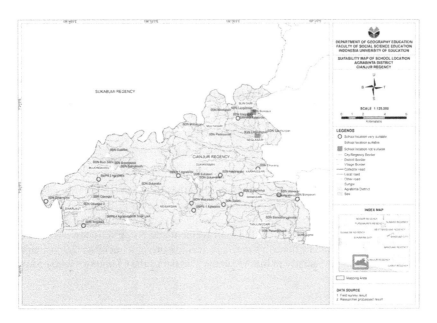

Figure 1.   School site suitability map.

Education & Ministry of Public Works, 1997/1998) was conducted. The results of scoring the roads and networks show that the level of suitability of school locations are as follows.

Referring to the Table 1 scoring of road conditions in the Agrabinta District, it can be alleged to be less good. From the results of the survey conducted, most of the road conditions leading to schools in the Agrabinta District are in a damaged condition. Only a few roads in Agrabinta are in good condition, one of them is the Agrabinta Road which is the main link between the Agrabinta Sub-district and other sub-districts.

After all the maps are overlaid, the level of suitability of the school locations in the Agrabinta District can be known. Based on field survey results and map analysis from 40 schools in the Agrabinta District, there are seven schools located on the main road network, 14 schools located on local road networks, 14 schools located on neighborhood road networks and five schools located on road network trails. In addition to using scoring tables, assessment of the road network can also be done through maps (Rofi'ah, 2013).

Referring to the scoring results obtained maps of the suitability of school locations based on the level of accessibility of school locations in Figure 1.

Road network parameters, road conditions and population distribution will determine the degree of accessibility for students to the school locations. Based on the above table, some school locations that meet the appropriate criteria and are adequately suited are influenced by a good level of accessibility to the schools. In contrast, some inappropriate school locations are caused by low levels of accessibility to schools. However, the main factor related to school location placement should be based on the population distribution in a region. For each type of service center, such as a school, to survive it requires a minimum population (threshold population). If the number of people served is less than the minimum population, the service provider will die or the dwarf grows. Based on this, we can conclude that some suitable school locations in the Agrabinta District, due to the location of the schools, are in the area of population dispersal. While some school locations are not suitable because the location of the school is not in the area of population distribution.

Based on the result of the score of 40 school units in the Agrabinta District, there are 15 schools with a similar grade level. Then 22 school units are in the appropriate suitability class, and the remaining three schools are in the inappropriate suitability class. In line with the results of Rahardjo's research (2012) it can be seen that in the coastal area of South West Java there are four types of beaches: (a) volcano beach, (b) organic beach, (c) sea-deposition beach and (d) land-deposition beach. Of the four types of beaches, the volcanic coast dominates the entire coastal area, followed by coastal sedimentation and organic beaches, respectively. In the forms of the concave beach (bay), the rate of development of the region is relatively more advanced when compared to the shape of the convex-coastal (cape). The Argabinta District tends to have a concave beach character so that the area is relatively more advanced. Thus, the location is not suitable among others due to the topography of the hilly, not caused by the coastal character itself.

4 CONCLUSION

Based on the results of the study, it can be concluded that the level of suitability of school locations in the Agrabinta District is quite good. Nevertheless, from the side of its distribution, schools in District Agrabinta seemingly uneven, so there should be a policy of even distribution of education services can be realized significantly. In addition, the improvement and construction of accessible support facilities such as roads should be done in a real way. It is important to increase the participation rate of the school population, especially in the Agrabinta District of the Cianjur Regency of West Java.

REFERENCES

Adekoya, S.O.A. & Gbenu, J.P. (2008). *Fundamentals of educational planning (revised and enlarged)*. Lagos, Nigeria: Micodex Nig. Ltd.
Agrawal, R.D. & Gupta B. (2016). School mapping and geospatial analysis of the schools in jasra development block of India s. In *The International Archives of the Photogrammetry, Remote Sensing and Spatial Information Sciences, Volume XLI-B2, 2016 XXIII ISPRS* Congress, 12–19 July 2016, Prague, Czech Republic.
Burrough, P.A. & Donnell, R.A.M. (2005). *Principles of geographical information systems.* Oxford, United Kingdom: Spatial Information System and Geostatistics. India.
Chiara, J.D. & Koppelman, L. (1975). *Urban planning and design criteria* (2nd ed.). New York, NY: Van Nostrand Reinhold.
Clark, P.J. & F.C. Evans. (1954). Distance to nearest neighbor as a measure of spatial relationship in populations. *Journal of Ecology, 35*, 445–453.
Comb, P.H. (1970). *What is educational planning.* Paris, France: United Nations Educational, Scientific and Cultural Organization.
Depdikbud & Departemen Pekerjaan Umum. (1997/1998). *Pedoman dan Mekanisme Penentuan Lokasi Sekolah.* Jakarta: Depdikbud, Direktorat Jendral Pendidikan Dasar dan Menengah & Departemen Pekerjaan Umum, Direktorat Jendral Cipta Karya.
Flemming, C. (ed). (2014). *The GIS guide for elected official.* California: Esri Press.
Ibia, E. (2010). *The adoption of the principles of social demand approach (SDA) as a strategy towards ensuring the success of the Ube programme in Nigeria.*
Iskandar. (2009). Metodologi Penelitian Pendidikan dan Sosial. Jakarta: Gaung.
Jayadinata, J.T. (1999). *Tata Guna Tanah dalam Perencanaan Pedesaan Perkotaan dan Wilayah.* Bandung: ITB.
Longe, R. (2003). Introduction to educational planning. In J.B. Babalola (Ed.). *Basic text in educational planning* (pp. 11–12). Ibadan: Awemark Industrial Printers. Olaniyonu, S. O. A.
Rahardjo, A. (2012). *Analisis Tata Ruang Pembangunan.* Yogyakarta: Graha Ilmu.
Ramdan, M.A. (2014). *Evaluasi Sebaran Lokasi dan Daya Tampung Sekolah di Kecamatan Lebakgedong Kabupaten Lebak.* Bandung: UPI.
Rofi'ah, H. (2013). *Evaluasi Terhadap Lokasi Gedung SLTA di Kecamatan Sambeng Kabupaten Lamongan.* Surabaya: Universitas Negeri Surabaya.
Satria, D. (2013). Evaluasi Sebaran Lokasi Fasilitas Pendidikan Terhadap Tempat Tinggal Peserta Didik SMP dan SMA di Kota Solok. Padang: Universitas Negeri Padang.
Sudjana. (1988). *Statistika I.* Bandung: Tarsito.
Timan, A. (2004). *Perencanaan Pendidikan.* Buku Ajar. Malang: Jurusan AP FIP UM.
Udin, S.S. & Makmun, S. Abin. (2005). *Perencanaan Pendidikan.* Bandung: Remaja Rosdakarya.

Educational Administration Innovation for Sustainable Development – Komariah et al. (Eds)
© 2018 Taylor & Francis Group, London, ISBN 978-1-138-57341-3

Phenomenological study on educational financing based on students' learning needs

D.A. Kurniady & R. Anggorowati
Universitas Pendidikan Indonesia, Bandung, West Java, Indonesia

ABSTRACT: Quality education is determined by the presence of skilled and reliable human resources in carrying out its duties and functions as the executor of activities in the educational process and adequate funding support. Based on the description, the focus of the problem to be disclosed is with regard to how the financing design can support the development of the quality management system. Using the case study method of phenomenology with adapting the Interpretative Phenomenological Analysis on the data collected, the result shows that an educational organization should always undertake development strategies tailored to the demands and needs of the environment in order to survive and compete with other educational organizations. To achieve this, it is necessary to provide adequate financing support in order to achieve what has been established or planned. Therefore, it is necessary to clarify what programs and activities classified as the focus of financing in conducting education, to achieve the target or quality of the pre-determined.

1 INTRODUCTION

The success of the National Education program will be greatly supported by various resources that have global competitiveness in order to face the challenges of the future as a result of globalization from various aspects of life, especially in education (Larbi & Fu, 2017; Bryson, 2018). Creating resources, especially human resources with global competitiveness, can be created through an educational process that meets the expectations and demands of users or education service providers (Kotabe & Kothari, 2016; Tommasetti, Troisi & Vesci, 2017). Quality education is determined by the existence of skilled and reliable human resources in carrying out its duties and functions as the executor of activities in the education process and adequate funding support (Bratton & Gold, 2017).

Based on the description, the focus of the issues to be disclosed is with respect to financing patterns that match the learning needs of learners so as to provide benefits and enhance competitiveness globally. The state of art of national education financing can only be disclosed through data documented in various reports and research results. The two main aspects of financing are revenues and allocations are not easily traced completely. Finance policy and educational policy in the budgeting process, allocation and distribution can not always be traced consistently (Bowe, Ball & Gold, 2017). There is a general trend, that between the financing policy and the education policy each runs independently, since creating coordination and synchronization of policies at the national level does not seem to be easy.

Furthermore M. Fakry (2000), explains that, theorists of financing education has long developed various models of educational financing to meet the needs of education equally and fairly. This concept is called the Foundation Program developed especially in the USA in funding education for each state. In the context of regional autonomy and its relation to efforts to develop regional education financing system, firstly it must first be built on the foundation and principle as a grip. The principles that can be raised in relation to the implementation of regional autonomy are as follows:

(1) Equality and equity to obtain educational opportunities not only among autonomous regions in one province but between provinces and between autonomous regions throughout the republic of Indonesia.
(2) Equalizing power at the level of autonomous regions at the district and municipal levels, at the provincial level for all autonomous regions of the province, and the central level for all autonomous regions in each province throughout the territory of the Republic of Indonesia.
(3) The financial balance of the province, as well as at the central level should serve as the glue of the unity and unity of the nation and as an infrastructure to exercise equalizing power in the education financing system throughout the territory of the Republic of Indonesia.
(4) At the provincial level the education financing system should be based on the principle of partnership between the source of funds for the province and the district and municipal funding sources.
(5) The regional capability and purchasing power of the local people should be the basis for determining the pattern of distribution of funds to finance education in the area.

The above principles contain elements of foundation programs and equalization programs for later use as the basis for the distribution of financial resources to finance various types and levels of education in accordance with the educational needs or the need for education and the community. In connection with this, M. Fakry (2000) explains that there are two main models of educational financing with the pattern of regional autonomy that are: (1) Flat Grants; and (2) Equalization Grants, in the form of:

a. *The allocation to the regions is the same regardless of the variation in the type and level of education for each region.*
b. *The allocation for each region is not the same as considering the variation of educational needs according to level and certain types of education.*

This variation can be caused by the variation of regional capability and purchasing power of the people, can also be caused by variations in the types and levels of education or educational needs of the students.

One of the main tasks of the school is to carry out learning activities, in which there are various activities and people involved (both educators, educators and learners) in order to achieve learning objectives in accordance with the learning needs of learners. In order for the learning process to be carried out to provide assurance for every component within the school, the school must have a quality management plan, quality guidance, and standard operational procedures established by top management and should be known by all Residents of the school.

To see the quality of a school institution we can actually see a comprehensive, starting from the availability of curriculum, the competence of graduates to be achieved, educators and education in accordance with the field of expertise (professionalism), the availability of supporting infrastructure, a conducive organizational culture, good leadership, and transparent financial management (Meyer, Kamens, & Benavot, 2017). If the elements show performance and refer to the rules set, then a quality school can be realized. Qualified in this case is the conformity between the programs established by the school with the expectation of education service users.

2 RESEARCH METHODOLOGY

This study uses the paradigm of qualitative research approach as it is conducted in the actual setting of phenomenon. The study of phenomenology was chosen to capture the direct experience experienced consciously by the person who experienced it.

This research is located in Bandung City with selected research sample based on requirement and purpose of this research. Selected location is tailored to the purpose and purpose that allows researchers to conduct research. In this research is expected to be obtained a number of participants who will provide sufficient data so that will get some findings relating to the financing of primary school education and learning needs of learners. The participants involved in this research are the principals and supervisors in Bandung, Indonesia. The pseudonym identity will be presented to maintain the principle of anonymity and the confidentiality of respondents.

In data collection, the researcher uses in-depth interview technique, focus group discussion by applying IPA (Interpretative Phenomenological Analysis) in performing data analysis. The essence of IPA lies in the focus of analysis, where the focus directs our analysis's attention to the statements submitted by respondents/participants to make sense of their experiences.

3 RESULTS & DISCUSSION

3.1 *Financing designs which support quality system development*

A financing design that can support the development of a quality system in an educational organization needs to refer to a defined strategic plan, looking at what vision, mission, and goals each organization wants to achieve in the budget for each educational organization. It is intended that the required funds can be clearly defined for what the funds are used, and the organization is not confused in meeting the various prerequisites that evolved during implementing the development of the quality standard of education in its environment. Since education organizations in their quality improvement plans only focus on efforts in teaching and learning activities, which are related to the development of educators and educators, facilities and infrastructure, and curriculum, not touching on what processes and procedures that will need to be developed accordingly with policies developed within an educational organization. Surely this is related to the concept of effectiveness and efficiency in the acquisition and use of funds.

A financing design that can accommodate the needs of an educational organization can be implemented by identifying cost drivers or cost drivers that are factors that impact the change in total cost levels.

Cost drivers relate the factors that become the cost, which in this study where took place in Indonesia, the cost refers to the 8 (eight) components of the National Education Standards, to the object cost of the product or service where the cost is charged to achieve learning outcomes in accordance with the learning needs of learners.

The product or service, is the result of an activity that uses the resources as the cause of the cost. The activity in question is all actions, actions or specific work undertaken during the education process that is directed to the learning outcomes in accordance with the learning needs of learners. The cost driver is used to measure the amount of activity performed and how many hours the activity is carried out against a cost object. In cost theory is called the consumption cost driver or activity consumption cost driver. While resources are economic elements that are needed or used in the execution of activities, such as the number of people, the amount of material used, place, work time, and power and services. Where it is in cost theory is called the driving cost of consumption of resources or resource consumption cost drivers. The activities and the use of these resources need to be grouped into learning and teaching processes, which in theory are called cost shelters or cost pools (Blocher, Stout, Juras & Cokins, 2015).

On the basis of this, the recommended cost calculation model that can be implemented in the primary school environment is the calculation of activity-based or activity-based costing. The rationale for why it is determined, because the product or service is the result of the activity, and the activity uses the resources that cause the cost, so that the funds can be used effectively and efficiently or clearly the basis of its use, in creating the educational process in accordance with learners' needs. To clarify how to run the recommended financing management, please refer to the following figure which briefly explains the relationship between cost, shelter, cost objects and cost drivers in the primary school environment, as follows.

The key element before determining how much the school costs to incur is to establish the components that are the source of the cost. In order to create alignment in the implementation, the school must have standard reference components of the generally accepted cost.

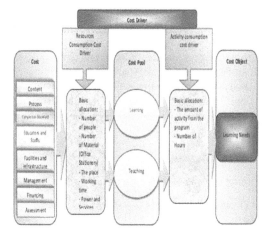

Figure 1. Funding patterns in primary schools (Adapted from Blocher, Stout, Juras & Cokins, 2015).

Therefore, the components that can be used as sources of cost can refer to Indonesian Government Regulation no. 19 of 2005 on National Education Standards which enables the knowing of activities which become the burden of education costs and Government Regulation no. 48 of 2008 on Education Funding to determine the type or group of costs, and this should be done by the school because it has become a standard standard for every national education delivery.

The cost component is used as benchmark source of cost of expenses according to Government Rule No. 19 of 2005 includes: 1) Content Standards; 2) Standard Process; 3) Graduate Competency Standards; 4) Standards of Educators and Education Personnel; 5) Standard of Facilities and Infrastructure; 6) Management Standards; 7) Financing Standards; and 8) Education Assessment Standards. After establishing the components that are the focus of educational financing, the school must then define the activities that drive cost (Cost Driver) in implementing the educational process. The type of activity that becomes a cost burden. The outcome of expenditure financing can be tailored to the goals and objectives to be achieved by the school.

This depends on the vision, mission and goals set by the government, especially the Education and Culture Department and the school concerned. The illustrations described are examples of how schools manage their finances, and what outcomes should be achieved so that learning and teaching processes are able to accommodate learners' learning needs, defined as cost objects or cost objects.

With the clarity of programs and activities to be funded, schools can allocate and distribute the availability of funding sources obtained by schools. However, if there is a lack of available funds, schools can explore funding sources through inter-school collaboration (represented by school committees) and education service users (such as world business industry, alumni who succeed in their career ladder or who are concerned about education, and other parties). This is done with the aim that the various prerequisites or procedures established in the quality management system to be implemented can be accommodated well. Regarding the quality management system to be designed, can be seen in the next section.

3.2 Development of quality management systems within educational organizations

In developing the quality management system can follow the stages as follows:

(1) Identification of all processes of Quality management/arrangement within the organization,
(2) Set the name of the process that is the focus of quality improvement as outlined in the quality management plan (target/quality target), e.g. Curriculum Evaluation & Development, etc.
(3) Set the input and output of each Quality process.

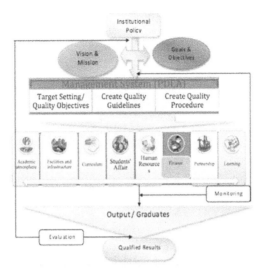

Figure 2.   Quality management position analysis.

(4) Allocate the required resources in a Quality process
(5) Assign customers (in this case learners) to each process including their needs and requirements
(6) Set the owner of the process (eg, curriculum evaluation to be the responsibility of the study program head)
(7) Determine the sequence and interaction of existing Quality structuring processes (with procedures for interaction)
(8) Authorize, document and distribute those Quality processes.
(9) Determine the criteria and methods necessary to ensure the effectiveness of the operation and control of those processes.
(10) Define the result characteristics of a process, success criteria (via evaluation)
(11) Set the communication process.

The whole process can be seen in the figure 2 as follows.
Figure 3 shows the position analysis in quality management.
The picture illustrates that in implementing the quality management system the educational institution needs to have the vision, mission and objectives as the basis for achieving the expected output. Furthermore, the school develops its quality management system based on its vision, mission and objectives in a quality management system by designing a quality management plan (targets/quality objectives) and quality manuals that serve as reference for improving the quality of educational organizations. Each unit that exist within the educational organization such as: 1) the academic section; 2) facilities and infrastructure; 3) curriculum; 4) student affairs; 5) HR; 6) funding (if necessary); 7) partnership; and 8) learning (relating to curriculum, syllabus, course, and problem). Based on the above described description, the educational organization must undertake or establish continuous improvement and development for the achievement of its quality management guarantee effort by doing or creating:

(a) The commitment of all citizens of the educational organization concerned to carry out the vision, mission, and objectives that have been set, in carrying out quality improvement.
(b) Academic culture and academic atmosphere (academic atmoshpere) are conducive.
(c) Building perceptions among all human resources (principals, teachers, staff nonguru, students) that it is the obligation of every citizen of the organization to always improve its performance.
(d) Facilities that can support the achievement of quality objectives.

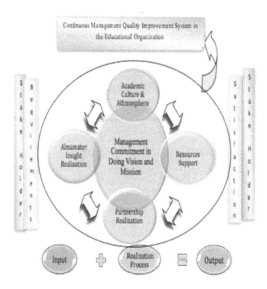

Figure 3. Continuous management quality improvement.

Some of these descriptions are expected to give confidence to organizations and stakeholders that the Education Organization is able to provide products/outputs that are consistent in meeting the requirements required by stakeholders to meet the level of satisfaction they expect.

4 CONCLUSION

Based on the description that has been presented, an educational organization should always make the development of strategies tailored to the demands and needs of the environment in order to survive and compete with other educational organizations.

To achieve this, it is necessary to provide adequate financing support in order to achieve what has been established or planned. Therefore, it is necessary to clarify what programs and activities are the focus of financing in conducting education, to achieve the targets or pre-determined quality. In order for the education organization's continuity to be achieved, it must always make constantly improvement in the various components of management education so as to meet the needs of the stakeholders as the benchmark or standard in order to achieve global competitiveness, supported by adequate financing pattern in accordance with the vision, mission, and goals that have been set. Therefore, the steps that should be taken by every educational organization would be to determine the needs and expectations of stakeholders or communities and other interested parties, to establish quality policy and organizational quality goals and to determine the processes and responsibilities needed to achieve the quality objectives. Moreover, the educational organization will need to determine and provide the resources needed to achieve the quality objectives, establish methods to measure the effectiveness and efficiency of each process, apply these measures to determine the effectiveness and efficiency of each process and determine the means of preventing non-conformities and eliminating the cause. Last but not least, the educational organization will need to establish and implement continuous improvement process of quality management system by preparing Standard Operating Procedures and Manual Procedures Implementation of internal quality assurance that explains about 3 things: (a) academic quality policy, (b) academic quality assurance system, and (c) organization, responsibility and authority.

REFERENCES

Blocher, E.J., Stout, D.E., Juras, P.E. & Cokins, G. 2015. *Cost management, a Strategic Emphasis 7th ed.* New York: McGrawHill Education.

Bowe, R., Ball, S.J., & Gold, A. 2017. *Reforming Education and Changing Schools: Case studies in policy sociology.* UK: Routledge.

Bratton, J. & Gold, J. 2017. *Human Resource management, 6th Edition: Theory and Practice.* UK: Macmillan Publishers Limited.

Bryson, J.M. 2018. *Strategic Planning for Public and Nonprofit Organizations: A Guide to Strengthening and Sustaining Organizational Achievement 5ed.* New Jersey: John Wiley & Sons, Inc.

Gaffar, M. F. 2000. *Pembiayaan Pendidikan: Permasalahan dan Kebijaksanaan Dalam Perspektif Reformasi Pendidikan Nasional. Konvensi Nasional Pendidikan Indonesia IV (*Education Financing: Issues and Policy in the Perspective of National Education Reform. 4th Indonesian National Education Convention). Unpublished. Jakarta 19–22 September 2000.

Kotabe, M. & Kothari, T. 2016. Emerging market multinational companies' evolutionary paths to building a competitive advantage from emerging markets to developed countries. *Journal of World Business*, 51 (5): 729–743.

Larbi, F.O., Fu, W. 2017. Practices and challenges of internationalization of higher education in China; international students' perspective: A case study of Beijing Normal University, *International Journal of Comparative Education and Development*, 19 (2/3): 78–96.

Meyer, J.W., Kamens, D.H., & Benavot, A. 2017. *School Knowledge for the Masses, World Models and National Primary Curricular Categories in the Twentieth Century.* UK: Routledge.

Tommasetti, A., Troisi, O., & Vesci, M. 2017. Measuring customer value co-creation behavior: Developing a conceptual model based on service-dominant logic, *Journal of Service Theory and Practice* 27 (5): 930–950.

Educational Administration Innovation for Sustainable Development – Komariah et al. (Eds)
© 2018 Taylor & Francis Group, London, ISBN 978-1-138-57341-3

Revitalization of vocational education through a dual expertise program

A. Kurniawan
Universitas Pendidikan Indonesia, Bandung, West Java, Indonesia

ABSTRACT: In an effort to prepare graduates or competent human resources that can synergize with the world of industry, especially to be able to compete with foreign workers, quality vocational education is the answer for those challenges. This can only be done by revitalizing the vocational education policy. The research method used in writing this article is a descriptive method of analysis by examining and analyzing all sources and data collected related to a dual expertise program. The result of this program in 2016, a total of 12,827 teachers will continue the advanced stages of the dual expertise program by 2017. The impact of this program is expected to fulfill the needs of productive teachers in vocational high schools.

1 INTRODUCTION

According to Indonesian law on the education system: Vocational education is a secondary education that prepares students primarily to work in a particular field. However, according to Wibawa (2017), vocational education is a higher education for particular applied skills. There are many definitions of vocational education, but in general vocational education is middle/higher education that supports the acquisition of specific applied skills. A general definition of vocational education is education designed to prepare skilled workers for industry, agriculture, commerce and so on, which is usually provided at the upper secondary level. Programs of vocational education include general studies, practical training for the development of skills required by the chosen occupation and related theory (UNESCO, 1973).

In most industrialized countries, some two-thirds of the workforce that constitutes the backbone of the economy are intermediate-level workers and employees who have learned a substantial part of their occupational skills and knowledge through the support of teachers, trainers and instructors in the domains of non-academic technical vocational education and human resources development (European Centre for the Development of Vocational Training, 1998; UNESCO-UNEVOC International Centre for Technical and Vocational Education and Training & UNESCO Institute for Statistics, 2007).

The role of vocational education teachers is vital to prepare the students for the real conditions of work and to linearize the world of work qualifications. This is the underlying reason for the importance of practical implementation in the industry as efforts to establish hard skills and soft skills in job readiness. By gaining experience of this practice, students can combine theory with practice that has been done. Of course, the implementation of the curriculum involving practice in this industry is not an easy task, especially when the purpose of the teaching is not in line with the program objectives of the study (Chang & Hsu, 2010). Therefore, the program needs to have a purpose and a clear mission for the development of learners in the future, balancing the academics and industry practitioners. Integrating academic and vocational education is a better way of educating students and alerting them to the complexities of the world and the nature of the physical, social, political and economic realities confronting them (Kincheloe, 1995).

2 RESEARCH PROBLEM

The first challenge is globalization, especially the enactment of the ASEAN Economic Community (AEC) by the end of 2015 is possible increasing the mobility and free labor competition among all ASEAN member countries. It is estimated that from 2010 until 2025 the demand for skilled workers in the ASEAN region will increase about 41% or about 14 million people. Half of that number is a necessity for Indonesia, followed by the Philippines with a need of skilled workers amounting to 4.4 million people. In accordance with the AEC scenario, in 2025 in Indonesia, there will be an increase of 1.9 million employment opportunities (about 1.3% of total employment). The second challenge is the change in job structure in the labor market caused by a decline in the level of work of vocational high school graduates and increasing the work of high school graduates. The decline in the level of employment allegedly occurred due to a lack of ability of vocational high school graduates in response to changes in job structure in the labor market. The level of work of vocational high school graduates is slightly increased (indicated by a small decrease in the percentage of unemployed graduates), but the increase in the level of this work is much lower than that of high school graduates (indicated by the very large decrease in the percentage of idle graduates) (MoEC, 2016).

3 VOCATIONAL CONDITION

According to the Ministry of Education and Culture (MoEC), in the period 2009–2014 the Indonesian government built about 3,000 new vocational high schools, and by early 2016 the number of vocational high schools had reached 13,167 schools (3,349 state vocational high schools and 9,818 private vocational high schools) as described in

Comparable with the increasing number of vocational high school students, the government increased the quantity of teachers to meet effective teaching conditions. However, in accordance with the large number of private schools, the majority of vocational teachers mostly teach in private vocational high schools. The increased number of vocational teachers can be seen in Figure 2.

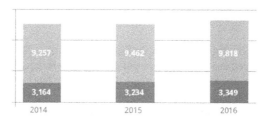

Figure 1. Number of schools.
(Directorate of Vocational High School, 2016).

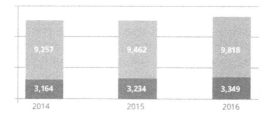

Figure 2. Development of vocational high school teachers 2014–2016.
(Directorate of Vocational High School, 2016).

However, the rise in the number of vocational high school teachers is not equal with the increase of quality teachers who are competent in teaching. Only 22% of vocational teachers are qualified as productive subject teachers (commonly called productive teachers). Productive teachers are teachers who have a certificate of competence that is appropriate to the subject being taught. A certificate of competence matched with vocational subject taught, ensures that teachers are able to teach competency that matched with his majors where he is placed. Certification can also guarantee that teachers competency is matched with applicable standards among professionals.

The majority of vocational teachers are from the normative and adaptive subject group teachers (also called normative teachers and adaptive teachers). Normative and adaptive teachers are teachers who teach citizenship, math, language and others that are not relevant to the vocational program. This leads to a complete lack of teachers and educators with the competency to teach in an area of expertise. If this continues, vocational high school students do not really receive a teaching process that is matched with the competency program.

4 POLICY

The President has issued the Presidential Instruction of the Republic of Indonesia Number 9 of 2016 on the revitalization of vocational high schools in order to improve the quality and competitiveness of Indonesian human resources. The instructions are implemented through the dual expertise program by the Directorate General of Teachers and Education Personnel, Ministry of Education and Culture. This is a policy to increase the number of teachers with competency according to the standard of teaching specific areas of expertise in vocational high schools, referred to as productive subject teachers in vocational high schools.

According to Thomas R. Dye as quoted in Tilaar and Nugroho (2016), the public policy process includes the following: identification of policy problem, agenda setting, policy formulation, legitimating of policies, policy implementation and policy evaluation.

If it is associated with public policy process theory as proposed by Thomas R. Dye, then the dual expertise program can meet the criteria of that theory. This we can look at from the steps taken in this policy process.

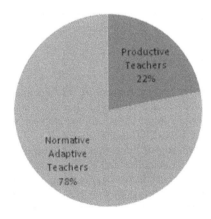

Figure 3. Comparison of productive and normative-adaptive teachers in vocational high schools. (Directorate of Vocational High School, 2016).

Figure 4. Public policy process by Thomas R. Dye.

a. Identification of policy problem

Based on the latest data from the Directorate General of Teachers and Education Personel, currently there is a problem with a lack of productive vocational high school teachers. For state vocational high schools, the lack of productive teachers amounts to 41,861 teachers, while the lack of productive teachers in private vocational high schools is 50,000 people, so the total lack of productive teachers in vocational high schools amounts to 91,861 people.

b. Agenda setting

Between 2016 and 2017, the Ministry of Education and Culture planned to increase productive teachers for short periods, to reach an additional 15,000 productive teachers. The recruitment of 15,000 productive teachers was conducted through the dual expertise program.

c. Policy formulation

The dual expertise program formulation policy involves many parties such as academics, the World Industrial World, Professional Certification Institute (PCI), Provincial Education Office, Ministry of Research, Technology and Higher Education, Ministry of Manpower, The Ministry of Industry and the Ministry of SOEs.

d. Legitimating of policies

To support the policy, the President issued the Presidential Instruction of the Republic of Indonesia Number 9 Year 2016 on the revitalization of vocational high schools in order to improve the quality and competitiveness of human resources in Indonesia.

e. Policy implementation

This dual expertise program will be held for two stages with a total target of 30,000 teachers. The period 2016–2017 is the first stage with 15,000 teachers, and the next year with 15,000 teachers. The process and training stage (training) is through the "ON-1 IN-1 ON-2 and IN-2" pattern and ends with certification of expertise from PCI. To obtain a certificate of expertise and certification through Professional Teacher Training and Training (PTTT) in LPTK to obtain an educator certificate.

f. Policy evaluation

Implementation of monitoring and evaluation of this dual expertise program is conducted by parties inside and outside the MoEC. In the MoEC it is handled by the Bureau of Planning and Foreign Cooperation, the Finance Bureau and the Inspectorate General. Meanwhile, parties outside the MoEC include the National Development Planning Agency, the Ministry of Finance, the State Audit Board and the Office of the Presidential Staff.

5 DUAL EXPERTISE PROGRAM

Based on recent data from the Directorate General of Teachers and Education Personnel, there is currently a lack of teachers in vocational productive subjects. For state vocational high schools, this lack reached 41,861 teachers, while in private vocational high schools it reached 50,000 teachers, bringing the total lack of teachers to 91,861.

As a form of solution, the Ministry of Education and Culture devised a policy to add productive teachers for a short period between 2016 and 2017, to reach an additional 15,000 productive teachers. The recruitment of 15,000 productive teachers was conducted through an expertise certification program and certification of educators for high school/vocational high school teachers (later called as dual expertise program).

There are at least two main objectives of dual expertise program:

a. To improve the competency of high school/vocational high school teachers that administer adaptive subjects (English, math, physics, chemistry, biology, social science and entrepreneurship), to acquire additional competency skills and be able to be productive subject teachers in vocational high schools.

b. To fulfill the needs of productive teachers in vocational high schools especially for the five priority areas: maritime/marine, agriculture, creative economy, tourism and technology and engineering. To accommodate the needs of the productive teachers in five groups of priority

Table 1. Potential teacher candidates for the dual expertise program.

No	Subjects	Needs	Available	Excess
A	High school Teachers (SMA)	47624	58234	10610
1	Civic education	8494	8648	154
2	Biology	8082	9832	1750
3	Physics	8082	9206	1124
4	Chemistry	8082	9168	1086
5	Geography	7139	9432	2293
6	Economics	7139	7742	603
7	Other foreign languages	303	767	464
8	Anthropology	303	3439	3136
B	Vocational school Teachers (vocational high school)	15291	10513	4781
1	Civic education	5097	5068	30
2	Mathematics	5097	818	4280
3	Art and culture	5097	4627	471
C	High school (SMA) and vocational high school) Teacher affected by 2013 curriculum		13993	13993
1	Information and communication Technology		8320	8320
2	Natural sciences		907	907
3	Social sciences		651	651
4	Entrepreneurship		2691	2691
5	Computer skills and management of information		1424	1424

Source: MoEC (2016).

areas. There are 51 competency skills targeted by the dual expertise program, some of these competencies are: agribusiness, fishery, hotel accommodation, design and production of wood-work, design and production of textile craft, culinary art, multimedia, nautical merchant ships, nautical fishing vessels, Karawitan Art, production techniques and broadcasting of radio and television programs and travel agency.

This dual expertise program planned to be implemented in two phases with a target of 30 thousand teachers. The period 2016–2017 represents the first phase with 15,000 teachers, and the next year another 15,000 teachers. Targeted teachers must have certain criteria, all of their age between 45 to 55 years old and identified that they are the excess of teachers.

6 PLANNING

Why productive teachers are important? Because fulfillment of productive teachers has an impact on high vocational graduates. It is expected to be achieved if the teachers has high competency. According to the MoEC, teachers who want to join the program must meet certain criteria, be aged between 45 to 55 years old. These teachers also identified that they are the excess of subject teachers, i.e. adaptive vocational high school teachers (civic education, mathematics, art and culture, natural sciences, social sciences, entrepreneurship and computer skills and management of information); and high school teachers (civic education, biology, physics, chemistry, geography, economics, other foreign languages, anthropology, information and communication technology) detected through basic data of education (Dapodik).

This program has certain criteria for accepting participants. Teachers must have an interest in one particular skill competency program which is determined. Dual expertise program enrollment can only be accessed online and that has been configured based on teachers' data in the basic data of education. This strict registration system means that teachers who do not meet the requirements, e.g. not identified as excess teachers cannot enroll in this program.

7 IMPLEMENTATION

The Ministry of Education and Culture making the arrangement and fulfillment of productive vocational teachers to support the improvement of the quality of vocational education as well as education and job skills training. Through the Directorate General of Teachers and Education Personnel, the Ministry of Education and Culture took strategic steps in 2016, by designing a dual expertise program, formerly known as the Teachers Transfer Function Program. In the dual expertise program, a teacher of high school/vocational high school could have two certifications: educator certification and expertise certification. In doing so, teachers of high school/vocational high school who already have expertise certification are expected to meet the lack of productive teachers in vocational high schools.

The goal of the dual expertise program is to obtain a certificate of expertise as a teacher, which will last for 12 months through four phases with phases ON and IN. For the ON phase, participants learn to be independent in their original school, and are given modules and mentoring. As for the phase IN in the industries and at The Center for Development and Empowerment of Teachers and Education Personnel (P4TK).

a. Phase ON-1: This began in early December 2016 and lasted for three months at the participant's original school. Teachers still teach subjects which they held since the beginning. In this phase, participants undertook independent learning. Participants continued to teach subjects which they held since the beginning. In this phase, the participants perform self-learning with a module given by the Directorate General of Teachers and Education Personnel. Participants undertake guided self-learning on professional competency and pedagogy (learning the theory and practice with the teacher assistant).

b. Phase IN-1: This phase lasted for two months in March and April 2017. This phase was held in the referral vocational high school, Education – Educational Personnel Institutions (LPTK), and in technical training institutions of the Ministry of Education and Culture, at P4TK. In this phase, participants followed the strengthening of productive materials (theory and practice). They also undertook self-guided reflection learning (three modules), guided by speakers and instructors consisting of teachers, widyaiswara, lecturers and industry practitioners.

c. Phase ON-2: This lasted for three months from May to July 2017. This phase is the phase of the practice of productive subjects. Participants, teaching productive materials in the original school or school where apprentice (referral vocational high school). They doing self-learning guided on the productive expertise competency (learning the theory and practice with the teacher assistant).

d. Phase IN-2: This involved sharpening the productive material which lasted for one month, August 2017. In this phase, participants followed a sharpening drill (theory and practice). They doing independent learning reflection guided under the guidance of speakers and instructors. This phase is held at referral vocational high school, education - educational personnel institutions (LPTK), P4TK and the world of business and industry. Referral vocational high school that becomes apprentice or practice of the participants should have some requirements. These requirements are that participants should have dual expertise program competency, have a practice room/adequate workshop (amount and completeness), have permanent teachers for productive subjects dual expertise program targeted at least two people, and preferred has certified partnership with local industry.

e. After finishing the ON and IN phases, the participants attended job training with work practice in the world of business and industry for two months in September and October 2017. At this phase the participants must truly practice appropriate expertise areas of expertise taken in that industry.

f. To get certification of expertise, participants followed a sharpening of expertise competency which has been assigned, as well as the expertise competency test. The expertise certification issued by the PCI.

g. To get certification of educators, participants followed the teacher certification program through a pattern of education and training of the teaching profession (PTTT) in the form of test theory and practice of learning. Competency was tested in order to obtain the certification of educators, i.e. professional competence, pedagogical, personality and social. Certification of educators was issued by the LPTK which organizes PTTT. The process to obtain dual certificates, i.e. certification of expertise and certification of educators occurred during November and December 2017.

8 EVALUATION

According to the Directorate General of Teachers and Education Personnel (2017), in 2016 there were 16,487 teachers enrolled online in double expertise program. Then filtered as many as 15,170 teachers prospective participants of multiple skills programs that meet the requirements that have been determined. As many as 998 teachers resigned so that only 12,827 teachers attended the debriefing and signed the integrity pact. A total of 12,827 teachers continued to the advanced stages of the dual expertise program by 2017. Fifty-one expertise packages were opened, but there were non-registrants in two expertise packages: Seaweed Cultivation, and Cooling Technique and Air System.

9 IMPLICATIONS

The dual expertise program actually planned to improve vocational high school/high school teachers that administer certain subjects in order to acquire additional expertise competency and that are capable of being productive teachers in vocational high schools. Therefore, these teachers were given additional authority to teaching as productive teachers in different vocational high schools with previous expertise competency but relevant educational backgrounds.

This granted authority carry out after the teachers follow the phases of the education process and training held by Ministry of Education and Culture. Teachers who have completed these phases with graduate status receive a letter of completion of education. The teachers are subsequently eligible for the next phase, namely certification of expertise and certification of educators. Certification of educators and certification of expertise acquired by the teachers is formal proof that the teacher has been professionally trained as a productive high school vocational teacher.

With authority to teach productive subjects in vocational high schools, teachers identified as excess or teachers affected by the 2013 curriculum can obtain their teaching hours again. This is good news for those who previously had not fulfilled their teaching hours. For teachers, a minimum of 24 hours of teaching is mandatory in order to obtain the right of profession allowance.

10 CONCLUSION

The implementation of quality vocational education must be in parallel with the development of science and technology, as well as the dynamics of labor needs. Teachers as learning activity implementers in school has responsibility to be able to adapt with a variety of rapid developments and high standard of industrial demands. The purpose of dual expertise program is to improve the competency of high school/vocational high school teachers that administer adaptive subjects to acquire additional expertise competency, capable of being productive subject teachers and fulfilling the needs of productive teachers at vocational high school.

REFERENCES

Biro Komunikasi dan Layanan Masyarakat. (2016). *Media Komunikasi dan Informasi, Jendela Pendidikan dan Kebudayaan, Edisi VII November 2016.* Jakarta: Kementerian Pendidikan dan Kebudayaan.

Chang, T. & Hsu, J. (2010). Development framework for tourism and hospitality in higher vocational education in Taiwan. *Journal of Hospitality, Leisure, Sport and Tourism Education.*

Direktorat Jenderal Guru dan Tenaga Kependidikan. (2017). *Laporan Akuntabilitas Kinerja Instansi Pemerintah T.A 2016 (Performance accountability report of government agencies in 2016).* Jakarta: Kementerian Pendidikan dan Kebudayaan.

Kementerian Pendidikan dan Kebudayaan. (2016). *Revitalisasi Pendidikan Vokasi (Vocational Education Revitalization).* Jakarta: Kementerian Pendidikan dan Kebudayaan.

Kincheloe, J.L. (1995). Tail and trouble. Integration of academic and vocational education. *Counterpoints: Studies in the Postmodern Theory of Education, 7.*

Tilaar, H.A.R. & Nugroho, Riant. (2016) Kebijakan Pendidikan: Pengantar Untuk Memahami Kebijakan Pendidikan dan Kebijakan Pendidikan *Sebagai Kebijakan Publik (Education policy: Introduction to understanding education policy and education policy as public policy).* Yogyakarta: Pustaka Pelajar.

UNESCO. (1973). *Technical and vocational teacher education and training.* Paris, France.

UNESCO-UNEVOC International Centre for Technical and Vocational Education and Training & UNESCO Institute for Statistics. (2007). *Participation in formal technical and vocational education and training programmes worldwide: An initial statistical study.* Bonn, Germany: UNESCO.

Wibawa, B. (2017). *Manajemen Pendidikan: Teknologi Kejuruan dan Vokasi (Education management: Vocational and vocational technology).* Jakarta, Indonesia: Bumi Aksara.

Educational Administration Innovation for Sustainable Development – Komariah et al. (Eds)
© 2018 Taylor & Francis Group, London, ISBN 978-1-138-57341-3

Management of pedagogical capacity building activities for preschool teachers in Vietnam

H.T. Lan
National College for Education, Cau Giay, Vietnam

ABSTRACT: Management of pedagogical capacity building activities for preschool teachers in Vietnam is an urgent issue in the context of Vietnamese society today. This article presents the contents and measures to manage pedagogical capacity building activities for preschool teachers, contributing to the provision of preschool education with high quality human resources to meet the requirements of education renovation in Vietnam.

1   INTRODUCTION

Among the factors that make up the quality of education and human resources for the development of a nation, teaching is seen as a key factor with its decisive role. Therefore, in the education development strategy, many countries all over the world pay special attention to fostering teachers and managing pedagogical capacity building activities of teachers in general and preschool teachers in particular – known as one of the determinants of education success in the development of Vietnam in the integration period.

In the current context, it is important to implement Resolution No. 29-NQ/TW at the eighth meeting of Party's central committee at term XI (dated 04/11/2013) on "Radical changes in education and training to meet the requirements of industrialization and modernization in a socialist-oriented market economy in the course of international integration", with the aims of "Building open, practical education, good teaching, good study and good management; providing a reasonable structure and method of education; associating with the establishment of a learning society; ensuring the quality improvement conditions; standardization, modernization, democratization, socialization and international integration of the education and training system". In order to perform the task of fostering preschool teachers well, the strict management of pedagogical capacity building activities for preschool teachers, the objective evaluation and the effectiveness of preschool teacher training activities are applied as an important link in improving the quality of teachers in Vietnam.

2   CONTENTS

2.1   *Pedagogical capacity structure of preschool teachers in Vietnam*

According to psychologists, capacity is the integration of personal characteristics and psychological attributes that are consistent with specific requirements of a given activity or criterion and bring results in practice [1]. The capacity of teachers in general and preschool teachers in particular includes a wide range of competencies: professional capacity, teaching capacity, scientific research capacity and some other supplementary skills such as informatics, foreign languages, community activities and so on. These factors have organic relations with each other to create the capacity structure of the teacher.

According to the terminology glossary of the Vietnam–Belgium Education Project, "capacity is the totality of abilities observed in an individual versus the training criteria. Capacity is expressed through knowledge and behavior".

Thus, in addition to the standards of moral quality and political thought, the teacher must be a good educator in which pedagogical capability has a significant and decisive influence on his or her professional personality.

For preschool teachers, the pedagogical capacity structure is considered in terms of functions, tasks and main activities. Their pedagogical capacity includes: teaching capacity, education capacity and pedagogical organization activities.

1. Group teaching capacity:

In this capacity group, it is necessary for preschool teachers to regularly foster and develop many competencies including:

a) Ability to understand students in the process of teaching and education. This is the ability to "penetrate" into the inner world of students, to deeply understand the physiology of each preschool age, as well as observing subtle psychological manifestations of the children when they are engaged in study and play. The ability to understand children is the result of a persistent, responsible, loving and responsible labor process, by which the preschool teachers not only master the expertise but are also well-versed in child psychology, psychology pedagogy, some psychological qualities such as "sharp-wittedness", the ability to observe, the ability to analyze and synthesize and so on.

b) Level and deep social knowledge of teachers. This is a basic capacity of pedagogical capacity, known as one of key capacities of teaching art as preschool teachers have the task of developing the senses and educating the children's personality through various means, in particular the knowledge, attitudes, skills, attitudes and so on that human beings discover. Through play activities, the teachers organize children to recreate knowledge-taking ways of humanity in order to retain what needs to develop the children's psychology, personality, create the foundation, background to build the qualities and capacity of the new man. The work of the preschool teacher is also the work of an educator, an absolutely diverse, complex and hard work in terms of action. Due to specific career characteristics, preschool teachers must undertake many roles: a teacher, a physician, an artist, an actor and so on, which forces them have a deep understanding not only in the area of expertise but in social life as well. Knowledge and deep understanding of society is a prerequisite for creating the prestige and respectable image of a preschool teacher.

c) Ability to design and build lessons. It is the pedagogical competence of the teacher with learning materials to make it suitable to the age, psychological characteristics and experience of the children in accordance with the pedagogy. In the trend of teaching from an operational point of view, teachers must have a wide range of capabilities analysis, summarization, systemization of knowledge, presentation, leading, argument, creation of charisma and emotion to encourage children to attend periods, and experience and accumulate knowledge in an active way. Teachers need to master teaching techniques so that the study and play always create excitement and stimulate creative, independent and positive thinking of the children.

d) Language capability. In teaching and education as well, the teacher's language is often directed toward solving a certain task such as: explaining, analyzing, communicating new knowledge, assessing and so on, promoting the children's attention and thinking to the learning activity. The language capability of the teacher is often expressed in both its content and form, and contains a great density of information, which expresses knowledge, wisdom and deep thoughts. When the teacher communicates and conveys knowledge to the children, however, he or she must use a clear, simple, understandable vocabulary to create strength, appeal and attraction for the children through each learning activity and play in the kindergarten.

2. Education capacity:

a) Building children personality development project. This is the ability to understand based on education purposes, training requirements to visualize, predict personalities, qualities needed to educate each child for his or her own natural growth.

b) Pedagogical communication. Pedagogical communication is demonstrated in the following skills: communication orientation; communication positioning; control; mastery of emotional states; use of means of communication. In addition, the pedagogical capability is not only reflected in the interaction between the teacher and his or her children and in all aspects of pedagogical activity but also in close contact with colleagues, parents and social organizations. Through communication, the teachers contribute their energies to aligning school education with family and social education.

c) "Conversion" of children. In order to understand and create pedagogical influences that are positively related to the development of children's personality, the teachers must have the capacity to "convert" the children. This is the capacity to directly influence the children in terms of emotion and reason. Therefore, it is crucial for the teachers to always exemplify building a fair, objective, trusted, loving, intimate, serious and good relationship with their children. They must keep an exemplary, polite, courteous posture and style of work, and convert the children by means of their righteousness, generosity and pedagogical art.

3. Ability to organize pedagogical activities:

Pedagogical activities organization capability is demonstrated by the teacher's ability to plan instructional activities, organize group activities for children, incorporate the teacher's activity and establish mutual relationships with the children. At the same time, the teachers are capable of finding ways to encourage children to actively participate in learning, dealing with pedagogical situations and taking responsibility for decisions in the classroom.

2.2 *Management of pedagogical capacity building activities for preschool teachers in Vietnam*

Management, in Latin (*manumagere*), literally means manual control, which is characteristic of the process of steering and guiding all departments of an organization through the establishment and change in resources (human, finance, materials, intellectual and intangible values).

From this point, it is possible to propose the concept that management is the organized, targeted impact of the management subjects on the entity and management objects to use the organization's resources and opportunities in the most effective way to achieve the objectives set out in the context of changing environmental conditions.

Management of pedagogical capacity building activities for preschool teachers is understood as the process of planning, organizing, directing, checking and evaluating the implementation, update, consolidation, development and systematic provision of knowledge, skills and expertise for preschool teachers during the performance of duties of any teacher at the preschool. Management tasks must ensure the implementation of management functions in the process of fostering and enhancing the pedagogical capacity of preschool teachers, from planning, organization and control to checking and evaluation to make the fostering activities achieve the set out objectives and effectiveness.

2.3 *Measures for the management of pedagogical capacity building activities for preschool teachers in Vietnam*

Measure 1. Recruitment and training:
Input quality is one of the factors that make up any preschool teacher's capacity. It is important for the managers of pedagogical schools to develop a high quality pedagogy program in order to select well-qualified preschool teachers. They can select students in the gifted bachelor classes in basic sciences, train the pedagogical capacity to meet the requirements of teacher criteria and standards, and establish a team of preschool teachers who are able to ensure quality, enhance the level of qualifications, capacity, ethical qualities, pedagogy, responsibility, devotion to the profession and

spirit of international integration; perform the task of teaching, imparting knowledge, promoting the initiative and creativity of preschool children in an effective manner.

In order to fulfill this, it is compulsory to first reach a consensus among party committees, leaderships, agencies, committees, departments under the Ministry of Education and Training, Department of Education and Training of various provinces and cities, officials and teachers at preschools. Research and discussion should be well organized to raise awareness among management staff at all levels about training, fostering and recruitment, thereby making them see the current status of Vietnamese preschool teachers compared with the demand for education reform, as well as international integration and inadequate development of schools. The knowledge that is equipped beforehand without regular updates, supplementation and development will soon become outdated, fail to keep up with changes in the knowledge economy and globalization in education.

Managers need to identify the content, target audience, have the right orientation, and then propose any policies to attract and encourage the preschool teachers to participate in professional qualifications, science and technology, informatics and foreign language fostering activities.

It is also necessary to promote the awareness of each preschool teacher. This is very important because teachers are the ones who directly make the change in the quality of training. They themselves have to realize their role and responsibility for improving the quality of the team of preschool teachers by self-cultivation, training of moral quality, striving to improve their professional qualifications, professional pedagogy, scientific research ability and promote self-learning ability and self-study.

International cooperation should also be expanded through the following activities: organizing conferences and seminars on fostering of pedagogical capacity for preschool teachers in response to education reform, inviting central leaders, the Provincial People's Committee, Department of Home Affairs, Department of Education and Training for joint participation to evaluate and give strategic orientation on the team development. From this point, the managers are able to identify any difficulties, obstacles when implementing management measures of pedagogical capacity building for preschool teachers so that all levels, branches and schools are responsible for coordination and resolution.

Measure 2. Management of the plan for pedagogical capacity building activities for preschool teachers:

Managers in planning should set out major orientations in pedagogical capacity building activities for preschool teachers in the direction of building an open education system, lifelong learning and a learning society, basically, synchronously and systematically. From this point, it is possible to develop a plan for the implementation of pedagogical capacity building activities for preschool teachers (defining the contents, programs, forms and methods) to bring high results with reasonable expenses.

For example: The management plan for pedagogical capacity building activities for preschool teachers in Vietnam is shown in the following points:

1. Determining the need for capacity building.
2. Object of capacity building.
3. Objectives of capacity building.
4. Determine the program contents of capacity building.
5. Define evaluation standards and scales.
6. Identify necessary resources (human, material, finance).

The management plan for pedagogical capacity building activities for preschool teachers must be conducted comprehensively from the raising of awareness of the position, importance and requirements of teachers' fostering, meeting the education reforms to determining the content, developing the plan, organizing the implementation, managing the direction, checking and evaluating the conditions to ensure the task of capacity building and capacity building management of preschool teachers throughout the country. In order to make the above thought, besides the preferential policies for teachers and investment in the development of pedagogical schools, especially schools with preschool education, many countries around the world have put the task of managing the plan for pedagogical capacity building activities for preschool teachers become the target of the industry to contribute to meet the professional standards of preschool teachers.

Measure 3. Renovation of any direction in the management of pedagogical capacity building activities for preschool teachers in Vietnam:

Directing the management of pedagogical capacity building activities for preschool teachers is the process of targeted impact of the collective and individual managers on faculties, departments, preschool teachers, aiming to implement plans, contents and programs on fostering and raising the quality of teachers, meeting the requirements of education reform.

Since pedagogic schools in Vietnam are varied in the profession, the responsibility for the profession quality is borne by the department. Therefore, it is necessary to renovate the direction in the management of pedagogical capacity building activities for preschool teachers in a flexible, practical and focused manner. It is important to promote decentralization, increase responsibility, create motivation and activeness for units, and lead the implementation of any plan for fostering and management of pedagogical capacity building activities for preschool teachers in a periodical manner.

The role of managerial level in the ministry, branch and the school should be promoted along with clear demonstrations of functions, tasks and responsibilities to direct the fostering of preschool teachers. Decentralization of management authority should be implemented in a clear way to create initiative in the performance of tasks, enhance the independence and responsibility of the management level in the directing task.

Measure 4. Checking and evaluation of pedagogical capacity building activities for preschool teachers in Vietnam:

Checking and evaluation is not only an important function of management but an effective management measure, which also ensures a regular and stable backward link in management. Checking and evaluations in education are considered legally-mandated activities, which are regulated in the legal documents of the State, the Ministry of Education and Training.

Thanks to checking and evaluation in the management of pedagogical capacity building for preschool teachers, the school leaders have sufficient information on the implementation of the fostering plan by the management level and can evaluate any changes in the capability of the preschool teachers after the training time, detect any shortcomings in the course of implementation to make necessary supplements and adjustments.

The checking and evaluation also have great influence on the behavior and sense of preschool teachers in order to enhance their sense of responsibility in the work of fostering their professional qualifications and qualities.

Checking and evaluation results are one of the foundations to help schools properly evaluate the process, capacity and qualifications of the teachers to make any plans to assign, arrange and use preschool teachers in an effective and consistent manner to maximize the strength of each individual, promptly plan the source and build a team of key individuals in charge of fostering the teachers of the school itself and the whole region.

After each training session, it is necessary to organize the implementation and checking of results achieved from the training plan, and to summarize to draw on experiences for further activities.

For managers, it is necessary to master the requirements, strategic objectives of socio-economic development, education development in general and preschool education in particular in the country and in the world to create a basis of assessing the current status of teachers' capability in an accurate manner in line with the objectives, contents and methods of fostering teachers. All forces, both international and domestic, should be engaged to take part in the fostering and management of capacity building activities in general and pedagogical capability in particular for preschool teachers.

Checking and evaluation can be carried out through the following activities:

Professional analysis reports and forecasts, which give more holistic and deeper viewpoints for every content and management field to the managers.

Operational testing, known as an effective tool, demonstrated through regular and independent assessments conducted by the specialized inspection and quality assurance department at the school.

Personal observation, an important checking method, should not be underestimated. Observation may help the manager to capture reality in an honest, natural way.

Checking the implementation of plan for pedagogical capacity building activities for preschool teachers:

1. Check the development of the plan for fostering preschool teachers at all levels, from strategic plans at the school level to detailed plans of professional groups and training plans and self-training of teachers themselves to ensure the unification of content, forms and methods of fostering. From this point, plans shall be well prepared to supplement the necessary conditions to ensure that the fostering of pedagogical capacity for teachers in each stage is implemented in a more effective manner.
2. Check the implementation of the management decisions to direct the pedagogical capacity building activities for preschool teachers.
3. Check the level of awareness, level of participation and coordination of staff involved in fostering pedagogic capacity of teachers.
4. Check the necessary conditions for fostering activities: The system of guidance documents, fostering contents, fostering program, subjects participating in fostering, implementation time and conditions of facilities to serve the capacity building of preschool teachers.
5. Evaluate the results through any changes in qualities, qualifications, professional capacity and pedagogical capacity. In order to address the above issues, it is necessary to review the views on teacher assessment to ensure objectivity, honesty and overcome the achievement at first.
6. Evaluate each period for cyclical training content and specialized training. The evaluation of the fostering effectiveness of preschool teachers must assess career progression by organizing preschool teachers to participate in career experience and applying knowledge acquired in teaching activities.

By summarizing the checking results, the evaluation board reviews, analyzes, assesses objectively and announces the evaluation results to each preschool teacher so that they can grasp their advantages to continue promoting and overcoming the existing problems.

The inspection, examination and evaluation must be conducted regularly in order to create long-lasting effects in promoting teachers to study by themselves, raise their knowledge and capability to satisfy any requirements of innovation in preschool education in the country.

Measure 5. Supplementation and perfection of mechanisms and policies on preferential treatment of wages, preferential allowances, motivation and creation of a favorable environment for preschool teachers to actively participate in fostering activities:

In the current market economy, the current salary of preschool teachers is very low, which is insufficient for them to guarantee their daily lives. The working time is often eight hours per day. Some teachers are not dedicated in teaching, reduced sense of learning, fostering professional qualifications, find ways to "work part-time" to earn income, stabilize family life. On the other hand, due to the lack of preferential treatment in studying and fostering of pedagogical capacity, some teachers, who tend to be mature in knowledge and occupational skills after studying the courses of pedagogical capacity building; find ways to stay in universities or look to foreign companies to work without returning to the old school, leading to a "brain drain" situation. Therefore, in order to create motivation and a favorable environment for teachers to actively participate in fostering pedagogical capacity, there must be an impact on changing the working environment, policies and mechanisms of employing teachers in preschool institutions today.

Salaries and other policies are some of the main motivational factors for the contribution and innovation of preschool teachers. In the course of implementing the policy for preschool teachers, special attention should be paid to the policy of training and fostering elite teachers to become key officials and improve professional qualifications and professional capability to meet the requirements of the development of educational human resources of the school as well as the locality. Currently in Vietnam, the policy on training and fostering of pedagogical capacity for preschool teachers has not been paid timely attention. Therefore, managers should have a policy to provide financial support for teachers to study at higher levels. It is important to train teachers through direct training at preschool institutions. Managers and school leaders need to make long-term roadmaps and plans to increase investment in fostering pedagogical capacity for teachers that is regarded as investment for the most sustainable, meaningful development for the schools.

It is necessary to honor, commend and reward any teachers who have outstanding achievements in training courses to improve pedagogic capacity in a timely manner. The Party's and the State's remuneration policy toward teachers must be strictly implemented according to regulations.

3 CONCLUSIONS

Management measures to improve the pedagogical capacity of preschool teachers are urgent and should be implemented synchronously in the trend of international integration education in order to raise awareness and quality, professional qualifications, pedagogical capacity, ensure a quality team and meet the increasing requirements of society. However, based on the peculiarity of the area, specific conditions and time, the competent units shall consider, select and prioritize to apply a certain measure in an effective and suitable manner.

REFERENCES

Dang, T.H. (2012). Capacity and capacity-based education. *Journal of Educational Administration*, 12.
Government. (2005). *Decision no. 09/2005 dated January 11, 2005 promulgating the Project on building and improving the quality of teachers and educational administrators in the period 2005–2010*.
Planning for success: Teaching active learning classes with UniSa University of South Australia, Prepared by staff at learning Connection of use in 2006.
Proceedings of the International Scientific Conference. 2016. *Development of teachers to meet the requirements of renovating general education*, Publishing House of Hanoi National University of Education.
Tran, T.B.M. (1997). *Training and use of teaching staff*, Hanoi: Education Strategy and Curriculum Institute.

Educational Administration Innovation for Sustainable Development – Komariah et al. (Eds)
© 2018 Taylor & Francis Group, London, ISBN 978-1-138-57341-3

The implications of Thailand's one tablet per child policy

A. Leksansern & P. Niramitchainont
Mahidol University, Thailand

ABSTRACT: This research aimed to study and analyze the implications of the Thai government's one tablet per child policy, and recommend guidelines and preventive measures for implications of educational populist policy in the future. This research implemented both qualitative and quantitative research; documentary research, focus group discussion by the Future Wheel method and cost-benefit analysis techniques, with a questionnaire and in-depth interviews being conducted. The key informants and respondents are 12 stakeholders from the one tablet per child policy, which has had some impact so far. The results revealed that the one tablet per child policy had negative impacts and low values. The preventive measures for implications of educational populist policy should promote the equity and equality in education for learning achievement and lifelong learning skills.

1 INTRODUCTION

Both the overall and specific areas of corruption in Thailand have a structure and relationship that is more diverse and complex (Case, 2017). Furthermore, the dynamic aspects of society affect the types of corruption so that it is always changing. This creates complications for observation, monitoring and crime identification for punishment. The government has shown its determination to eradicate corruption by developing the Third Phase of the National Corruption Prevention Strategies for 2017–2021. The second strategy of the Third Phase of the National Corruption Prevention Strategies is to increase the political intent to battle corruption. Regarding this strategy, the citizens have expressed their concerns on fighting governmental and official corruption. The third strategy of the Third Phase of the National Corruption Prevention Strategies is to prevent policy corruption.

Currently, policy corruption is the most common type of corruption found. Policy corruption includes political party's policies and the non-transparent use of power which negatively impacts the development of the country's economy and society. Policy corruption is a type of corruption that tremendously ruins the national economy in a short amount of time (Jiang, 2017; Rothstein & Varraich, 2017).

In Thailand, populist policies have been used since 1975 in the form of the fluctuating money project, but it was clearly used as a policy during the regime of Thaksin Shinawatra to govern the nation. This gave Shinawatra a lot of popular votes, which resulted in him being prime minister for a second term. In his second term as prime minister, he still used populist policies. Populist policies are policies that give politicians a lot of votes from the citizens and are memorable. Citizens love these policies since they could make their lives easier so that the citizens' standard of living improved. In exchange for better living standards, the government has to increase their income for these policies. This could mean taking out loans, using natural resources and increasing taxes. This will affect the nation's public debt, government's finances and inflation. Therefore, populist policies look good in the short-term, but they have long-term negative impacts on the economy (Thammajaiwannakitwannasin et al., 2011; Academic and Law Office, Office of the Secretary of the House of Representatives, 2015).

The one tablet per student or one computer per student project is one of the Peu Thai Party's populist policies that the party used for campaigning. It was one of the party's rushed policies that aimed to give more than 800,000 primary one students from all schools opportunity and equality for education. The project aimed to give tablets or computers to students so that students could use them to access knowledge and news that they are interested in. Furthermore, it was supposed to improve the quality of education by helping students to be able to read, write and think while they are enjoying learning anywhere anytime. The project ended in its second year due to management problems with the private company that provided the tablets, unfair bidding and ineffective usage in some areas (Wonganant, 2012).

Hence, this study's objectives were to study and analyze the impacts of the Thai government's one tablet per child project and to propose preventive measures for possible impacts for educational populist policies and various expansion methods of educational populist policies.

Some studies have been done across the world regarding to this issue. Despite all the pros and cons, examining the impact of technology in educational field used were always have its own benefits and challenges (Tang & Hew, 2017; Khan et al., 2018; Butcher, 2013).

This study will be useful to the governmental sector, such as the government, various ministries, agencies that develop policies and national finance agencies; private sector; academic sector; public organizations, media and the civil society sector. Furthermore, politicians will be aware of the severity of the impacts of educational populist policies, stakeholders and areas of impacts. This will ensure that the required support will be provided to every group of stakeholders and impact management. In case the government proposes populist policies in the future, they will review the context, readiness and national tax to assess the feasibility of public welfare development policies.

The research objectives were: To study and analyze the impacts of the one tablet per child project and to study and propose preventive measures for possible impacts of educational populist policies and various expansion methods of educational populist policies.

2 RESEARCH METHOD

This study used both quantitative and qualitative data collection techniques, which included documentary research, focus groups, questionnaire, in-depth interviews, cost-benefit analysis and the Future Wheel method. There were 12 key informants for the study on the impacts of the tablet project. In order to cover all aspects of the study, purposive sampling was used. Reviewing literature developed the criteria for informant selection. Some of the informants were selected using the snowball sampling method. The details are as follows:

- Officials from the Bureau of Technology for Teaching and Learning Office under the Basic Education Commission, Ministry of Education who supervise the computers (tablets) project.
- Officers from the Project Management Office that managed the learning by using a portable computer project under the Ministry of Information and Communication Technology.
- Two officials from the Office of the Provincial Primary Education Area 2.
- A researcher from the application and integration of tablet computers for teaching at the primary level, according to the government's phase I policy.
- Two representatives from the portable computer (tablet) company.
- A primary year one student.
- Two teachers that teach primary year one.
- One parent.

The documentary research was conducted to analyze situations relevant to teaching that used portable computers or tablets during the years 2012–2015. The process involved a spread out questionnaire to inquire key stakeholders about the approach and measures used to deal with populist policies. Focus group discussions with key stakeholders were conducted using the Future Wheel method to study and analyze both positive and negative impacts at the personal, community, societal, public management, national financial, national security and national economy levels. If the data were not clear, then in-depth interviews were conducted with the stakeholders to clarify the data. Then, a cost-benefit analysis was conducted to compare whether the benefits were worth the cost of the project. The data were analyzed using content analysis.

3 RESULTS AND DISCUSSION

3.1 *The impacts of the Thai government's tablet for learning project*

Operations for the tablet for learning project started with tablets being distributed to all primary one students under the Ministry of Education during the 2012 academic year. A total of 860,000 tablets were distributed under the project, which cost a total of 2,178 million Thai baht. Each tablet cost about 2,000 baht. In the first year of the project, the Ministry of Information and Communication Technology was in charge of acquiring all the tablets. In 2013, it was concluded that a total of 1.8 million tablets would be bought for 5,093 million baht. This means that more tablets would be acquired, and more money spent than in the first year of the project. This increase in purchase is due to the extension of the project to also cover secondary school year one students.

The details of the project are as follows: 1) Zone 1 Tablet or tablet for primary one students in the central and southern region needed 431,105 tablets; 2) Zone 2 Tablet or tablet for primary one students in the northern and northeastern region needed 373,637 tablets; 3) Zone 3 Tablet for students and teachers at the secondary year one level in the central and southern region needed 426,683 tablets; 4) Zone 4 Tablet for students and teachers at the secondary year one level in the northern and northeastern region needed 402,889 tablets.

The project faced many problems during its second year resulting in its termination. For instance, the project was terminated because the companies that were supposed to deliver the tablets to Zone 1 and Zone 2 were unable to deliver the tablets on time; hence, the contract was cancelled. Therefore, a new company got the contract. For Zone 3, the bid for the contract was unfair resulting in a lawsuit. In the end, the company that won the contract won the lawsuit and was able to continue purchasing and delivering the tablets until the contract was fulfilled. The company for Zone 4 was unable to deliver the tablets, so a price bid for a new company had to be held. Before the bid was held, the project was terminated with the budget for 2014. Hence, for the fiscal year 2013, only Zone 4 did not receive the tablets. It could be seen that there were many problems with the project since the purchasing stage, delivering stage that was slow, and the performance of the tablet that was as low as its price. Furthermore, there were researches by the Office of the Inspector General of the Ministry of Education, Office of the Secretary of the Council for Education, Srinakharinwirot University, and other agencies that got this result.

The implementation of the Future Wheel technique to study the impacts of the tablet for learning project found that there were both negative and positive impacts, which are as follows:

3.2 *Individual level*

The individual level was positively impacted in three aspects, which were: 1) there was a change in the students' learning from technology; 2) there was more opportunity for students to access knowledge and learning; and 3) teachers were able to innovate teaching by using new teaching media.

There were three impacts that were negative, which were: 1) teachers still lack technological knowledge; 2) teaching with tablets added further to teachers' workload; and 3) parents and the general public still lack the knowledge needed to advise children on the usage of tablets.

In terms of worth, it was not worth it since the teachers who were responsible for the tablets and their usage were not equipped with the knowledge to teach students using the tablet. Hence, primary one students did not get sufficient knowledge from learning through the tablet. Furthermore, in 2012, a total of 2,178 baht were granted to purchase 860,000 tablets. This means the tablets cost about 2,532 baht (approximately USD 80.67) each. Since the government wanted to equally distribute the tablets for equal opportunity to education for all students and to promote development of new learning media, each student received a tablet.

3.3 Community and social level

The community and society were positively impacted in two aspects, which were: 1) the people's and every sectors' awareness in using technology for learning; and 2) there was an increase in teachers and parents involvement with students' learning.

There were three impacts that were negative, which were: 1) schools were not readily equipped with teachers that can use tablets; 2) the schools had insufficient funds to spend on training teachers so that they would be able to effectively teach with tablets; and 3) there was an argument between those who supported and those who were against the project on replacing books with tablets.

In terms of worth, it was found that the project created technological awareness, but people were not ready for this technology. This resulted in disparity between students whose parents were knowledgeable with technology being able to advise them on usage, while the other group of students were unable to get help from their parents, as their parents were not knowledgeable in technology.

3.4 Government and fiscal management level

The government was positively impacted in one aspect, which was the government was able to improve education quality and create equal learning opportunities for students in every area. This promotes learning and the development of personnel in every sector. In addition, it also promotes equal access to learning and helps reduce the disparity between different areas.

There were three impacts that were negative, which were: 1) this was an rushed project that the stakeholders were not ready to effectively, continuously, and sustainably managed the project; 2) it uses a lot of budget, but lacked worth assessment; and 3) it was a policy proposed by a political party, which means it might not be continued once the government changes.

In terms of worth, it was found that using 2,178 million baht to buy 860,000 tablets without planning resulted in many problems. The problems were cancellation of the purchasing contract, tablet maintenance and teaching readiness, which resulted in the project being terminated. This means that the money spent during the project was wasted. It could be said that this project was not worth the money spent.

3.5 National security, economy, and reputation level

There were two positive impacts, which were: 1) the country's overall economy was stimulated so that the market was expanded; and 2) competition between technological companies.

There was one negative impact, which was that making a huge investment when there was there was no basic infrastructure could affect the economy, since Thailand still lacks quality equipment and stable hi-speed Internet connections.

In terms of worth, it was found that the project used a large budget and personnel from various sectors including central, local and school sectors. Furthermore, the project was rushed, so stakeholders did not participate in the project resulting in the project not being able to create enough worth for the economy and society.

3.6 The preventive measures for possible impacts for educational populist policies

The preventive measures for possible impacts for educational populist policies are as follows.

1. Educational policies should be continuous and should not change with the government since developing education is a long-term issue that needs to be continuous. Therefore, those working on educational policies should be local organizations that play a role in stimulating schools to improve. These local organizations should be able to prevent politicians from influencing the education sector. Hence, right now, Thailand should decentralize management power for education to local organizations under the Ministry of Education. Education for each area should be supervised by its governing body. Furthermore, these organizations should be given the opportunity to decide how to use the budget to improve the quality of education.

2. The government sector should have measures to prevent educational populist policies since populist policies are usually very hard to implement due to their quick development, lack of participation and usage for votes. In addition, populist policies are usually not implemented resulting in the policies being terminated. If this happens to educational policies, then it would affect the country's development of education.

4 CONCLUSION

In general, the tablet for learning project had negative impacts and was not worth the money in terms of economy and society when compared with other beneficial policies.

The project purchased 860,000 tablets, where each tablet cost approximately 2,532 baht for all primary one students to improve their opportunities for learning from more diverse sources, to decrease educational disparity and encourage teachers to use technology as a medium for teaching. However, the project was rushed, and stakeholders were not ready resulting in flaws in terms of technological systems and human resources. This resulted in further negative impacts. This is because the educational applications and Wi-Fi system in Thailand still does not support the use of tablets for learning. Furthermore, both parents and teachers were not ready for educational applications and tablet maintenance resulting in primary one students not being able to fully use the tablets to help them learn. Hence, the investment made in the tablets was wasted since there were many problems with purchasing contracts and continuing the project under the next government. This caused the project to be terminated.

This coincides with a study on assessing the results of decentralization and educational management in areas under the General Secretary of the Education Council (2006), which found that the obstacle to decentralizing power to local agencies is the lack of educational resources. These resources include both personnel and equipment. The tablet project was similar since it also lacked resources. The resource that is still lacking is technology.

It was also found that personnel, teachers, students and parents are still not equipped with the technological skills and that the various current equipment does not support teaching via tablets.

REFERENCES

Academic and Law Office, Office of the Secretary of the House of Representatives. (2015). *Thailand reform issues: Populist policies that will affect public debt and an increase in the responsibility of populist projects.* Bangkok: Office of the Secretary of the House of Representatives Printing.

Butcher, J. (2013). Can tablet computers enhance learning in further education? *Journal of Further and Higher Education, 40*(2), 207–226.

Case, W. (2017). *Populist threats and democracy's fate in southeast Asia, Thailand, the Philippines, and Indonesia.* UK: Routledge.

Jiang, G. (2017). Application of social censure on corruption. In *Corruption control in post-reform China* (pp. 137–180). Singapore: Springer.

Khan, Md.S., Shamim, Md.R.H. & Nambobi, M. (2018). Learning styles and online tools: How to construct an effective online learning environment. In A.V.S. Kumar (Ed.) *Optimizing student engagement in online learning environments.* USA: IGI Global.

Office of National Anti-Corruption Commission. (2016). *National anti-corruption strategies phase 3 (2017–2021).* Retrieved from https://www.nacc.go.th/ewt_news.php?nid=12661

Rothstein, B. & Varraich, A. (2017). *Making sense of corruption.* Cambridge, UK: Cambridge University Press.

Tang, Y. & Hew, K.F. (2017). Is mobile instant messaging (MIM) useful in education? Examining its technological, pedagogical, and social affordances. *Educational Research Review, 21*, 85–104.

Thamjaiwanankitwannasin, A. & et al. (2011). *Populist analysis: Effect on economic justice and financial status.* Faculty of Economics, Economy and Business for Reform Research Center.

Wonganannont, S. (2012). *Thailand's One Tablet PC Per Child Policy.* Retrieved from http://library.senate.go.th/document/Ext3217/3217017_0002.PDF.

Ethics education, pro-social motivation, and moral disengagement among entrepreneurs

A. Margiono & P. Heriyati
Bina Nusantara University, Jakarta, Indonesia

ABSTRACT: This preliminary study aims to investigate the role of pro-social motivation and ethics education, especially informal religious-based ethics education, on the moral disengagement's tendency of entrepreneurs. Using 95 survey data of entrepreneurs in greater Jakarta areas, this preliminary study analyzes the moderating role of informal religious-based ethics education on the relationship between pro-social motivation and moral disengagement. This study finds that pro-business entrepreneurs tend to have lower moral disengagement when they receive informal religious-based ethics education. In contrast to popular beliefs, this study finds that pro-social entrepreneurs have lower moral disengagement only when they do not receive informal religious-based ethics education.

1 INTRODUCTION

Scholars have recently started to put their attention to ethics issues in entrepreneurship (Hannafey, 2003; Harris, Sapienza & Bowie 2009; Brenkert, 2009). Studying entrepreneurship ethics is important because entrepreneurs often break rules and conduct unethical behavior in recognizing and exploiting business opportunities. A recent longitudinal study in a European country shows that successful entrepreneurs broke the rules and were involved in "petty" crime in their youth (Obschonka, Andersson, Silbereisen & Sverke, 2013). Similarly, the stories that are told around successful entrepreneurs, such as Mark Zuckerberg and Steve Jobs, are illustrated with narratives of the entrepreneurs engaging in many kinds of unethical activities.

Many extant studies on entrepreneurship ethics focus on three broad areas: entrepreneurial ethics, social venturing, and entrepreneurship and society (Harris et al., 2009). Research on entrepreneurial ethics focus on the micro level, with the emphasis on the entrepreneurs. Others focus on social venturing study on aspects related to ethical entrepreneurial activities in the social context, such as ethics of social ventures (Smith, Kistruck & Cannatelli, 2016). Further, a few research pays attention to a more macro view, such as the contribution of entrepreneurial activities towards societies (Newbert, 2003).

Despite the growing attention to ethics in entrepreneurship literature, limited studies focus on the role of ethics education among entrepreneurs. Much research on ethics education focuses on business ethics of large organizations. If there were studies paying attention to entrepreneurship ethics education, much of the attention is given to ethics education in the formal setting (e.g. Tesfayohannes & Driscoll, 2010). Extant entrepreneurship ethics studies focus on how formal education, such as universities and schools, incorporate ethics components in their teachings. As a result, the role of the informal, especially religious-based, ethics education towards the behavior of entrepreneurs is underexplored despite recent calls to consider religions into entrepreneurship teachings (Calkins, 2000; Griebel, Park & Neubert, 2014).

An understanding of the role of informal institutions in ethics education is essential. Informal institutions, such as religious congregations, shape an individual's sense of right and wrong and influence the ethical behavior of a person (Epstein, 2002; Rashid & Ibrahim, 2008). A recent study highlights the role of religions in education; especially on the use of the religious narratives in entrepreneurship education (Toledano & Karanda, 2017). In many occasions, religious narratives are often delivered in societies through various means, such as in informal congregational gatherings, or in community events. In this light, the limited understanding of the role of informal ethics education, especially those that are religious-based, towards the behavior of entrepreneurs presents a significant gap in the entrepreneurship literature.

Therefore, in this paper we ask: does informal, religious-based, ethics education affect how entrepreneurs justify their unethical behavior?

We utilize moral disengagement theory (Bandura, 1986; Bandura, Barbaranelli, Caprara & Pastorelli, 1996) to make sense of the role of informal, religious-based, ethics education in the justification of unethical behavior among entrepreneurs. Moral disengagement refers to the ways persons "deactivate" moral compass that usually prevents them in doing unethical behavior (Bandura, 1986). Moral disengagement consists of several mechanisms (Bandura et al., 1996), yet the one that may be relatively more relevant to entrepreneurs is the displacement of responsibility. Displacement of responsibility refers to a justification of unethical behavior by shifting personal responsibility to others. Entrepreneurs tend to break rules by displacing their responsibilities to uphold the existing moral codes for the sake of higher or larger social benefits (e.g. creating jobs, etc). This rule-breaking behavior is considered ethical since this particular activity is done on behalf of the better future or for the sake of the betterment of societies that they aim to achieve; in contrast, rule breaking for the sake of individual benefit is not tolerable and therefore it is often considered not ethical (Brenkert, 2009).

In this light, the relatively high pro-social motivation of entrepreneurs becomes important element that "guard" the ethical principles that these entrepreneurs have. Pro-social motivation refers to the desire to benefit other people (Batson, 1987). Thus, entrepreneurs who have high pro-social motivation may break the rules, but they may do so because of the drive to benefit people in general.

This paper makes several contributions to the literature. First, this paper contributes to the entrepreneurship ethics literature by offering insights on the role of informal, religious-based education towards the potential unethical behavior of entrepreneurs. We extend the extant discussion on entrepreneurship ethics in the literature by providing empirical insights that takes account the important role of informal ethics education. Second, this paper contributes to the entrepreneurship education literature by presenting empirical insights on the role of informal ethics education in the entrepreneurship context.

In the next section, we will outline the literature review and the hypotheses. We will continue to discuss the method that we use to answer the research question and to present the result of the analysis. At the end, we will conclude with a discussion of contributions, limitations, and potential future research.

2 THEORETICAL FRAMEWORK

2.1 *Entrepreneurship ethics and education*

Entrepreneurship literature has recently embraced discussion on ethics. Entrepreneurship ethics have been underexplored since much research on this literature focuses on non-ethic topics, such as opportunities (Davidsson, 2015). In contrast to many mainstream entrepreneurship literature, Hannafey (2003) argues that entrepreneurs, as moral agents, face complex moral problems, such as fairness, personnel and customer relationship, distribution issues, and many other aspects in their day to day activities. Understanding their behavior in relations to ethics is therefore an important part of understanding the role of entrepreneurs in society. Harris et al. (2009) highlights the emerging streams of discussions of ethics in the entrepreneurship literature.

The first stream is research that discusses entrepreneurship ethics at the micro-level, for example the search of the difference between entrepreneurs and non-entrepreneurs in terms of ethics (Xu & Ruef, 2004; Bucar & Hisrich, 2001; Teal & Caroll, 1999). The second stream addresses the social context of entrepreneurship. More popularly known as social entrepreneurship, this stream of literature focuses on entrepreneurship that prioritizes social value creation (Mair & Marti, 2006; Santos, 2012). This stream of entrepreneurship ethics addresses, among others, social innovation, social ventures, and how they can facilitate social change (Zahra, Gedajlovic, Neubaum & Shulman, 2009; Choi & Majumdar, 2014). The third stream of entrepreneurship ethics discusses the role of entrepreneurship in society. In contrast to the second stream, the literature in this area focuses on macro level of analysis, such as the role of entrepreneurship in macro-economy (Birch, 1989; Kirchhoff, 1991).

Despite this emerging body of literature, the discussion on education in entrepreneurship ethics is still scant. Most studies in the entrepreneurship education literature pay attention to general entrepreneurship education. For example, they are focusing on the impact of entrepreneurship education in the higher education (Nabi, Linan, Fayolle, Krueger & Walmsley, 2017). Ethics entrepreneurship education is still underexplored. If any, extant literature on ethics education for entrepreneurs mostly addresses this in the formal education setting. For example, a study to examine whether existing small business and entrepreneurship textbooks incorporate ethics components.

As a result, there is a lack of research that focuses on informal ethics education for entrepreneurs. An understanding of informal ethics education for entrepreneurs is important because informal institutions, such as religions, play an important role in determining the ethical foundation of a person. Calkins (2000) argues that business ethics have neglected the foundation that they have been built from. Fortunately, business ethics is now turning to philosophy instead of acknowledging its traditional root in religions. In a recent study, Rashid and Ibrahim (2008) argues that ethics education should also include religion because religions and morality cannot be separated; ignoring the role of religions in people's judgement of right and wrong may derail ethics education because in real life students have their own religious predispositions (Rashid & Ibrahim, 2008).

In summary, informal ethics education, especially those that are religion-based, serve to play important roles in entrepreneurship ethics and education. In the next section, we will outline the mechanisms that entrepreneurs embrace to "disconnect" their moral positions as well as the ways in which pro-social motivation of entrepreneurs affect these mechanisms to further understand the role of informal ethics education in entrepreneurship.

2.2 *Moral disengagement*

Moral disengagement, refers to a set of mechanisms that a person applies to deactivate moral principles that he/she normally adheres to. Moral disengagement extends social cognitive theory that explains the self-regulatory processes that individuals have over their thoughts and behaviors.

Social cognitive theory has been used to explain how moral self-regulation of an individual influence a person's behavior that he/she has (Bandura, 1986). Yet, this moral self-regulation only applies when it is activated by the person. When it is deactivated, an individual is capable to engage in behavior that contradict his/her moral self-regulation. Bandura et al. (1999) highlights eight mechanisms that persons use to deactivate their moral self-regulation: moral justification, euphemistic labeling, advantageous comparison, displacement of responsibility, diffusion of responsibility, disregarding or distorting the consequences, dehumanization, and attribution of blame.

In this paper, we focus on a particular mechanism that may often be conducted by entrepreneurs: displacement of responsibility. The displacement of responsibility in moral disengagement occurs when individuals would like to distort the effects of harmful actions resulting from their unethical behavior (Bandura, 1986). Entrepreneurs break the rules because they are not satisfied with the existing conditions or with the existing distribution of wealth. Schumpeter (2013) argues that entrepreneurs conduct "creative destruction" to change the existing equilibrium. Applying "creative destruction" and altering existing equilibrium in the economy will create harmful effects to others. As an example, the success of Apple computer in launching iPhone led to lay-off in the Nokia's side. In this case, entrepreneurs apply displacement of responsibility by blaming their competitors because they are unable to maintain their businesses to survive.

2.3 Pro-social motivation

Just like any other persons, entrepreneurs also exhibit various degrees of pro-social motivation. Pro-social motivation refers to the desire to benefit other people (Batson, 1987). Being other-regarding, a person with pro-social motivation is assumed to exhibit more ethical behavior. Altruistic persons like to help other people and show high moral standards. In other words, a person with high pro-social motivation may therefore keep their moral self-regulation activated and therefore he/she may avoid moral disengagement. In contrast, persons with low pro-social motivation, or in our context they are more pro-business/pro-profit motivation, may be quicker to deactivate their moral self-regulation to justify their profit maximization interest. As a result, persons with lower pro-social motivation may be prone to moral disengagement.

2.4 Hypotheses

Based on the theoretical framework outlined above, we develop the following hypotheses:

H1: Entrepreneurs with higher pro-social motivation tend to have lower moral disengagement

H2: Informal, religious-based, ethics education moderates the relationship between pro-social motivation and moral disengagement

3 METHOD

We utilize quantitative method to test the hypotheses using data collected from a survey of 95 entrepreneurs in greater Jakarta area, Indonesia.

3.1 Participants and procedures

The participants in this research are nascent entrepreneurs who have started their business for at least two years. They are part of entrepreneurship association groups that bring together various entrepreneurs in a geographical area. Data was collected after they conducted trainings facilitated by the associations. The trainings were business-related training in general and there were no ethics components involved in the training; and therefore the participants were not conditioned to answer the questionnaires. Participants were asked to fill in survey questionnaires in Bahasa Indonesia.

3.2 Measure and pre-test

Dependent variable. We measured moral disengagement using validated scale of the construct in the literature. The construct is multidimensional and we only focus on one particular mechanism of moral disengagement: displacement of responsibility. In this paper, we used 3 items that measured displacement of responsibility taken from 32 validated items of moral disengagement presented in Detert, Trevino, and Sweitzer (2008). These items were translated and adapted into Bahasa Indonesia. The items were measured in 6-point likert scales. We asked questions such as: "it is all right to lie as long as my objectives are achieved".

Independent variable. We measured pro-social motivation using validated scale in the literature (Grant & Berry, 2011); 2 items of pro-social motivations were used and adapted into Bahasa Indonesia. We asked questions such as "I would like to help people through my work". The items were measured in 6-point Likert scales. Further, we measured informal, religious-based, ethics education by asking the respondents whether they have received ethics education from the following sources: (a) religious congregations; (b) school; (c) family; or (d) government. They were asked to select the most influential one. We then dummy coded the categorical variable into a binary variable: one that consists of respondents who answered (a) religious congregations as those who received informal, religious-based, ethics education (1); and the other that consists of respondents who answered (b), (c), and (d) as those who did not received informal, religious-based, ethics education (0).

Control variable. We used gender and education level as control variables. Gender was measured as a categorical variable and we dummy coded the gender variable with 1 represents male and 0 represents female. We measured education level in five categories. We also dummy coded the categorical variable into a binary variable to control the effect of people with formal, especially high education (1) and low education (0), in the analysis.

Factor analysis using principal component analysis was conducted as a pre-test of the continuous items. All items load above >.3 cut off into two factors. Reliability tests were further conducted with good Cronbach's alpha(α) scores for each variable (>.7). Composite variables were created after the EFA.

3.3 *Data analysis*

Data was analyzed using Ordinary Least Square regression method in statistical package SPSS ver. 23. As suggested in the literature (Aiken & West, 1991), we mean-centered pro-social motivation composite variable and develop an interaction variable between pro-social motivation and the informal, religious-based, ethics education variable to conduct moderation analysis. Using the graph, we reported the result of moderation analysis.

4 RESULTS AND DISCUSSION

4.1 *Results*

Correlation analysis of the moral disengagement and pro-social motivation variables ($r = -.170$) shows non-significant relationship and no correlation; indicating that there is no multicollinearity among the continuous variables involved in this analysis. The regression analysis in table 1 shows that the control variables, male and respondents with high education, are both significant towards moral disengagement.

Our data indicate that male participants in our sample corresponds to more moral disengagement, indicating that the male participants in our sample tend to justify their unethical behavior more than the female participants. This is consistent to the extant literature that finds gender differences in moral disengagement (Almeida, Correia & Marinho, 2009). Moreover, the high education of the participants also positively corresponds to moral disengagement indicating that people with higher formal education in our sample are relatively more susceptible to moral disengagement.

In model 2, we analyzed the linear relationship between pro-social motivation, informal ethics education and moral disengagement. While the control variables are significant, pro-social

Table 1. Regression analysis results.

Variables	Model 1		Model 2		Model 3	
	B	SE	B	SE	B	SE
Male	.322*	.132	.318*	.131	.356*	.131
High Education	.398*	.196	.402*	.199	.339	.198
Pro-social motivation (PSM)			−.136	.099	−.220*	.106
Informal Ethics Education (EE)			−.145	.163	−.270	.177
PSM*EE					.576*	.285
Adjusted R^2	.105*		.116		.145*	
ΔR^2			.029		.037	

* p < .05.

215

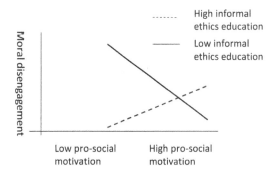

Figure 1. Interaction between pro-social motivation, informal, religious based ethics education, and moral disengagement.

motivation and informal ethics education do not individually affect moral disengagement, showing that they have no individual effect towards moral disengagement. The overall model is not significant.

We further analyzed the relationship and the interaction of the variables in model 3. The model 3 is significant and this may be due to the interaction of the variables. Again, our finding indicates that gender significantly affects moral disengagement; yet in this model high education is no longer significant. Informal, religious-based, ethics education is also not significant towards moral disengagement, indicating that by itself ethics education does not affect the ways entrepreneurs disengage their moral self-regulation.

However, in this model the relationship of pro-social motivation towards moral disengagement is significantly negative indicating that the hypothesis 1 is accepted. Pro-social entrepreneurs tend to less deactivate their moral self-regulation.

Inspection of the interaction variable (between pro-social motivation and informal, religious-based, ethics education) shows significant effect on moral disengagement, indicating that the presence of moderating role of informal, religious-based, ethics education in the relationship between pro-social motivation and moral disengagement. Following Aiken and West (1991) we further developed a diagram that shows interaction between the variables in figure 1.

The figure reveals that participants who received high informal, religious-based, ethics education tend to have lower moral disengagement if they have low pro-social motivation. This implies that the more pro-business our participants are, the more they avoid moral disengagement if they receive high informal, religious-based, ethics education. In other words, the more pro-business entrepreneurs attend religious congregation, the less morally disengage they are. Further, the less they receive informal, religious-based, ethics education the more they tend to do moral disengagement.

In contrast, participants who received low informal ethics, religious-based, education tend to have low moral disengagement if they have high pro-social motivation. This indicates that among pro-social entrepreneurs, the less informal, religious-based, ethics education they receive the less they deactivate their moral self-regulation mechanism. In other words, the less they go to religious congregation, the more they adhere to their moral principles. Further, our data shows that the more they receive informal, religious-based, ethics education, the more they are prone to moral disengagement. In other words, the more they go to religious congregation, the more they tend to justify their unethical behavior. Thus, based on the regression result and the analysis of the interaction diagram we accept the hypothesis 2.

4.2 *Discussion*

This paper started by a gap in the entrepreneurship ethics and education literature in relations to the study of informal, religious-based, ethics education and moral disengagement. Research on entrepreneurship ethics is growing, however limited study focuses on the role of informal ethics education, especially those that are religious-based, on the tendency of entrepreneurs to justify their unethical behavior. Using moral disengagement theory as a framework of analysis, this paper explored the moderating role of informal, religious-based, ethics education in the relationship between pro-social motivation and moral disengagement among 95 entrepreneurs in greater Jakarta area.

This study is a preliminary research on entrepreneurship ethics in Indonesia. We found that all our hypothesized relationships were accepted. Our analysis indicated the negative relationship between pro-social motivation and moral disengagement. This relationship reflects a recent discussion on moral disengagement in the literature. Moral disengagement scholars have indicated that moral disengagement contradicts with pro-social behaviors of individual (Bandura et al., 1999). Our findings further extend this argument by showing that pro-social motivation, in addition to pro-social behaviour, also negatively corresponds to moral disengagement.

Our analysis indicated that pro-business participants tend to have lower moral disengagement when they receive informal, religious-based ethics education. This finding is consistent with extant literature that forefront the importance of religions in ethics education (Rashid & Ibrahim, 2008; Calkins, 2000; Griebel, Park & Neuebert, 2014). This body of literature argues that moral education without religious perspective is "incompatible" with the religious predisposition of the students and therefore advancing business ethics in the entrepreneurship context require the incorporation of religions.

However, in contrast to the other findings in the literature, we found that pro-social entrepreneurs tend to have higher moral disengagement when they receive informal, religious-based, ethics education. This is to say that the more social entrepreneurs go to the religious congregation, the more they are able to justify their unethical behavior. Although this finding is surprising at the outset because most people in Indonesia assume that more religious activities should correlate with good, ethical behavior, we suspect this is related to the rule breaking and innovative nature of entrepreneurs (Brenkert, 2009). Social entrepreneurs are innovative (Mair & Marti, 2006) and many of them attempt to change the existing system (Zahra et al., 2009). Our findings may imply that pro-social entrepreneurs in our sample justify rule breaking and the introduction of novel activities – despite some harms done – on behalf of larger purposes.

According to Brenkert (2009), rule breaking in this context is related to the larger pro-social intention that these social entrepreneurs aim to achieve and therefore moral disengagement does not necessarily correspond to unethical behavior. Yet, the ethical and moral consequences and the implications of this particular tendency is still underexplored in the social entrepreneurship literature and therefore further research and investigations around this matter is essential.

5 CONCLUSION

Our findings contribute to the literature in the following ways. First, we extend the discussion in the entrepreneurship ethics literature by providing insights on the role of informal, religious-based, ethics education towards moral disengagement. We provided preliminary evidence that shows how pro-social and pro-business entrepreneurs differ in their orientation towards moral disengagement. Our findings, therefore, also support the separation of "moral" and "ethics" as outlined in Brenkert (2009). Second, we also extended the discussion in the entrepreneurship education literature by offering insights of informal ethics education. Our finding shows that informal institutions, especially religious-based informal institutions, play an important role in ethics education.

We recognize several limitations in our research. First, the measures are limited. Our research used a particular dimension of moral disengagement: displacement of responsibility. In doing so, this research ignores other aspects of moral disengagement that may be relevant in research on informal ethics education. Therefore, future research should attempt to include all dimensions or mechanisms of moral disengagement to generate richer analysis on the moral self-regulation deactivation mechanisms, especially in relations to informal ethics education.

Second, our way of measuring informal, religious-based, ethics education is also limited. Using dummy coded measure to capture informal ethics education may be insufficient. However, since this is a preliminary study, this measure should give initial indication of the role of informal, religious-based, ethics education in the entrepreneurship context. Future studies should apply more advance measure to capture the role of informal, religious-based, ethics education. Alternative methods may include better self-report measure, as well as, experience sampling methods (ESM) that can be used to collect real-time data when the entrepreneurs attend informal religious congregational gatherings.

Third, we also have a limitation in our study design. This study only captures a snapshot of different entrepreneurs in a particular time due to its cross sectional design. Future studies may need to have more appropriate methods, such as longitudinal studies, to see the difference in the role of informal ethics education across different time periods. In terms of the overall research paradigm, future studies may also use person-centered approach to investigate sub-population differences. Using recent profiling methods such as Latent Class Analysis (LCA) may be useful.

REFERENCES

Aiken, L. S., West, S. G., & Reno, R. R. 1991. *Multiple regression: Testing and interpreting interactions*. Sage.
Almeida, A., Correia, I., & Marinho, S. 2009. Moral disengagement, normative beliefs of peer group, and attitudes regarding roles in bullying. *Journal of School Violence* 9 (1): 23–36.
Bandura, A. 1986. The explanatory and predictive scope of self-efficacy theory. *Journal of Social and Clinical Psychology* 4 (3): 359–373.
Bandura, A. 1999. Moral disengagement in the perpetration of inhumanities. *Personality and Social Psychology Review* 3 (3): 193–209.
Bandura, A., Barbaranelli, C., Caprara, G. V., & Pastorelli, C. 1996. Mechanisms of moral disengagement in the exercise of moral agency. *Journal of Personality and Social Psychology* 71 (2): 364.
Batson, C. D. 1987. Prosocial motivation: Is it ever truly altruistic? *Advances in Experimental Social Psychology* 20: 65–122.
Birch, D. L. 1989. Change, innovation, and job generation. *Journal of Labor Research* 10 (1): 33–38.
Brenkert, G. G. 2009. Innovation, rule breaking and the ethics of entrepreneurship. *Journal of Business Venturing* 24(5): 448–464.
Bucar, B., & Hisrich, R. D. 2001. Ethics of business managers vs. entrepreneurs. *Journal of Developmental Entrepreneurship* 6 (1): 59.
Calkins, M. S. 2000. Recovering religion's prophetic voice for business ethics. *Journal of Business Ethics* 23 (4): 339–352.
Choi, N., & Majumdar, S. 2014. Social entrepreneurship as an essentially contested concept: Opening a new avenue for systematic future research. *Journal of Business Venturing* 29 (3): 363–376.
Davidsson, P. 2015. Entrepreneurial opportunities and the entrepreneurship nexus: A re-conceptualization. *Journal of Business Venturing* 30 (5): 674–695.
Detert, J. R., Treviño, L. K., & Sweitzer, V. L. 2008. Moral disengagement in ethical decision making: a study of antecedents and outcomes. *Journal of Applied Psychology* 93(2): 374.
Epstein, E. M. 2002. Religion and business–the critical role of religious traditions in management education. *Journal of Business Ethics* 38 (1): 91–96.
Grant, A. M., & Berry, J. W. 2011. The necessity of others is the mother of invention: Intrinsic and prosocial motivations, perspective taking, and creativity. *Academy of Management Journal* 54 (1): 73–96.
Griebel, J. M., Park, J. Z., & Neubert, M. J. 2014. Faith and work: An exploratory study of religious entrepreneurs. *Religions*, 5 (3), 780–800.
Hannafey, F. T. 2003. Entrepreneurship and ethics: A literature review. *Journal of Business Ethics* 46 (2): 99–110.
Harris, J. D., Sapienza, H. J., & Bowie, N. E. 2009. Ethics and entrepreneurship. *Journal of Business Venturing* 24(5): 407–418.
Kirchhoff, B. A. 1991. Entrepreneurship's contribution to economics. *Entrepreneurship Theory and Practice* 16(2): 93–112.

Mair, J., & Marti, I. 2006. Social entrepreneurship research: A source of explanation, prediction, and delight. *Journal of World Business* 41(1): 36–44.

Nabi, G., Liñán, F., Fayolle, A., Krueger, N., & Walmsley, A. 2017. The impact of entrepreneurship education in higher education: A systematic review and research agenda. *Academy of Management Learning & Education* 16 (2): 277–299.

Newbert, S. L. 2003. Realizing the spirit and impact of Adam Smith's capitalism through entrepreneurship. *Journal of Business Ethics* 46 (3): 251–258.

Obschonka, M., Andersson, H., Silbereisen, R. K., & Sverke, M. 2013. Rule-breaking, crime, and entrepreneurship: A replication and extension study with 37-year longitudinal data. *Journal of Vocational Behavior* 83 (3): 386–396.

Rashid, M. Z., & Ibrahim, S. 2008. The effect of culture and religiosity on business ethics: A cross-cultural comparison. *Journal of Business Ethics* 82 (4): 907–917.

Santos, F. M. 2012. A positive theory of social entrepreneurship. *Journal of Business Ethics* 111 (3): 335–351.

Schumpeter, J. A. 2013. *Capitalism, Socialism and Democracy*. Routledge.

Smith, B. R., Kistruck, G. M., & Cannatelli, B. 2016. The impact of moral intensity and desire for control on scaling decisions in social entrepreneurship. *Journal of Business Ethics* 133 (4): 677–689.

Teal, E. J., & Carroll, A. B. 1999. Moral reasoning skills: are entrepreneurs different? *Journal of Business Ethics*, 19 (3), 229–240.

Tesfayohannes, M., & Driscoll, C. 2010. Integrating ethics into entrepreneurship education: An exploratory textbook analysis. *Journal of Entrepreneurship Education* 13: 85.

Toledano, N., & Karanda, C. 2017. Morality, religious writings, and entrepreneurship education: An integrative proposal using the example of Christian narratives. *Journal of Moral Education*: 1–17.

Xu, H., & Ruef, M. 2004. The myth of the risk-tolerant entrepreneur. *Strategic Organization* 2 (4): 331–355.

Zahra, S. A., Gedajlovic, E., Neubaum, D. O., & Shulman, J. M. 2009. A typology of social entrepreneurs: Motives, search processes and ethical challenges. *Journal of Business Venturing* 24 (5): 519–532.

Educational Administration Innovation for Sustainable Development – Komariah et al. (Eds)
© 2018 Taylor & Francis Group, London, ISBN 978-1-138-57341-3

Headmaster leadership styles in elementary schools in Jambi city, Indonesia

S. Marmoah & T. Rahayu
Universitas Batanghari, Jambi, Indonesia

A. Ratmani
STKIP Muhamadiyah Kerinci, Indonesia

ABSTRACT: The headteacher is the leader and the manager in the school. There are many successful ways of leading and managing and how people actually behave in practice is a mixture of their ideas and personality. A headmaster has to decide how far to be democratic and how far autocratic. The purpose of this research was to find out about the type of leadership that is used by headmasters of elementary schools. The design of this research was descriptive qualitative research. The data for this research was collected through questionnaires and documentation. The research was carried in 32 state elementary schools in Telanaipura, Jambi city. A total of 128 individuals participated in the research. Among them, 96 teachers were included as a sample through a simple random sampling technique. Questionnaires on communication, decision-making, and delegation of duties were used to ascribe the headmaster leadership styles. Based on analysis of the questionnaires and documentation that related to the leadership style of the headmaster, this research revealed three important common styles of leadership: autocratic, democratic, and laissez-faire. In conclusion, the democratic style was the most commonly used to practice leadership in the state elementary schools of Telanaipura, Jambi city. Based on the findings, it is recommended that the headmasters of state elementary schools should adopt a mixture of autocratic and democratic styles of leadership.

1 INTRODUCTION

Most schools are gradually moving towards a more collegiate mode of operation and few headteachers now work in isolation. The leadership of schools is usually in the hands of a senior management team rather than a single person. Democratic forms of leadership offer good staff development opportunities, because in order to make a sensible decision a group needs to study the situation carefully. It is also valuable to involve students in some decision-making, because part of the school's task is to train young people for life in a democratic society.

According to Dean (2002, p. 9), when people move into leadership and management roles in schools, their experience of possible styles of management is usually limited. Most people have seen only a small number of headteachers or senior staff at work and these may represent a limited range of models. The new leader has to apply abilities, personal qualities, views of the role and the circumstances in which she or he is working, to the performance of leadership and management tasks. The particular mixture of approaches and behavior becomes a style of management which develops slowly as the manager becomes more experienced.

Smith (2016, p. 78) stated that leadership styles play an integral role in positive educational outcomes and the creation of a positive school culture. Transformational transactional, inspirational, and instructional leadership styles all have characteristics that are critical in effective leaders and can be effectively integrated in order to maximize the human resource potential of school administration. Lee and Li (2015, p. 57) conducted research that aimed: (1) to describe a school principal's leadership and the context of the school's overall teacher culture that cultivated an award-winning team at an elementary school; (2) to analyze the award-winning team's learning behaviors, shared goals, values, beliefs, mutual interactions or dialogs, and sharing of experiences; (3) to unveil the key factors that shape excellent teaching team culture and its functions. Mehrad and Fallahi (2014, p. 47) concluded that improper leadership style is a problem for every public educational organization. The most important abnormal response is the dissatisfaction that appears among staff at educational organizations, which considerably reduces the level of their performance. A manager's role is to recognize the right style of leadership based on various conditions and relations for application at an educational organization.

A headteacher has to decide how far to be democratic and how far autocratic. The democratic process can be slow and people may become impatient, particularly if they have been used to an autocratic style of leadership. It may, in some circumstances, be better for a person to be more autocratic at the beginning of a headship than he or she may wish to be later, if this is what people expect and are used to.

School management is the most important factor in education. Teaching in schools where success is measured by the achievements obtained, therefore, should use a system in providing leadership. That is to say, the administration of education in schools in which there are related components such as teacher-teacher, administration staff, parents, community, government, students, and others, must function optimally influenced by policy and performance management. The headteacher is the leader and the manager in the school. There are many successful ways of leading and managing and how people actually behave in practice is a mixture of their ideas and personality.

On this basis, the principal question is what type of leadership is commonly used by headmasters of the elementary schools in Jambi city, Indonesia. The aim of this research was to address this question.

2 METHOD

The purpose of this research was to analyze the type of leadership that is commonly used by the headmasters of elementary schools. The design of this research was descriptive qualitative research. Bogdan and Biklen (1982) suggest that qualitative research considers several aspects, including: (1) natural environment as source of data; (2) researcher as key instrument; (3) process as more important aspect than result; (4) inductive data analysis; (5) participants' backgrounds to respond to a phenomenon as essential aspect.

The data for this research was collected through questionnaire and documentation. The research was conducted in 32 state elementary schools of Telanaipura, Jambi city. The subjects in this research were the elementary school teachers in Telanaipura, Jambi city; a total of 170 teachers and 32 headmasters participated in the research. The first questionnaires for teachers on communication, decision-making, and delegation of duties were used to describe the headmaster leadership styles. The second questionnaires for headmasters on autocratic, democratic, and laissez-faire styles were used to describe the headmaster leadership styles.

3 RESULTS AND DISCUSSION

3.1 *Headmaster involvement of teachers in decision-making*

Involvement in decision-making refers to a practice by which both superiors and subordinates jointly sit together to discuss the way to run the organization. According to Okumbe (1998, p. 39), involvement in decision-making is a typical characteristic of a participatory type of leadership. Lack of involvement in decision-making portrays an autocratic leadership style, and a laissez-faire style is portrayed when leaders may reluctantly involve subordinates in decision-making processes.

In this sub-section, the opinions of those respondents who disagreed and strongly disagreed were combined to represent *disagreement* and this was interpreted as indicating an autocratic leadership style. On the other hand, neither agreement nor disagreement would indicate that a leader had a laissez-faire style. Those who agreed and strongly agreed were combined to represent *agreement*, which was interpreted as indicative of a leader that was democratic in leadership style.

Based on the questionnaire results of teachers' opinions in the elementary schools of Telanaipura, Jambi city – about the approach of principals to considering teachers' suggestions and thoughts, final decision-making in the school, passing final resolutions in school, innovativeness, initiative and creativity in decision-making processes of the school, teaching staff involvement during the decision-making process of the school, and promotion in staff meetings – the majority of elementary school headmasters are uncomfortable with the views of teachers in meetings; this is an indication that an autocratic leadership style is practiced by the elementary school headmasters.

3.2   *Headmaster communication to teachers*

The importance of communication in institutions of learning has in many cases been undermined, especially in state elementary schools. According to Armstrong (2003, p. 52), the advantages of communication in the leadership process were derived from a survey conducted in relation to performance management. The advantages identified included individuals obtaining a broader perspective of how they are perceived by others than previously possible. From the above reviews, it is important to recognize that the idea of communication is important in leadership; where communication is truly practiced, the leadership tends to be democratic, while where it is denied to the subordinates, the leadership style becomes autocratic.

According to a question about the principal sending memos, the majority ($n = 40$; 42%) of the teachers were in agreement that their headmasters send them memos when they want to communicate to them. This reveals a democratic style of leadership where headmasters find it easy to pass information to teachers through memos. A question about the principal making telephone calls indicated that 41 (43%) of the elementary school teachers in the research area are communicated to by their headmasters through telephone calls. This suggests that proper communication to teaching staff by headmasters is a characteristic of a democratic leadership style. A question about the headmasters organizing meetings showed 60 (62%) of the respondents agreeing that their headmasters organize meetings when they want to communicate to them. This indicates that headmasters use a democratic style of leadership where staff meetings are organized for teachers to exchange their views with their superiors. A question about the headmasters writing a note indicated that 56 (58%) teachers were in agreement that their headmasters write notices on the staff noticeboard when they want to talk to them. This indicates that most elementary school teachers in the research area are communicated to by their headmasters through notices written on the staff noticeboards.

3.3   *Headmaster delegation of duties to teachers*

Blair (2002) defines delegation as a management skill that underpins a style of leadership which allow the staff to use and develop their skills and knowledge to their full potential, and as a dynamic tool for motivating and training the team to realize their full potential. The above definitions show that delegation exists at both organizational and individual or personal level. At the organizational level, it has to do with the location of decision-making and it is reflected in the organizational chart, that is, it provides the structure of the organization.

As viewed from the question about duties delegated by the school headmaster – whether the headmaster delegated duties by directing, guiding, supervising, rewarding, principle, considering the knowledge, skill, talent, and/or experience of the employee – the majority of elementary school headmasters delegated duties to teachers, as indicated by the 55% of elementary school teachers in the region agreeing that they are delegated duties by their headmasters (see Table 1). This means that both autocratic and democratic leadership styles are almost equally practiced by elementary school headmasters in Telanaipura, Jambi city.

Table 1. Summary of distribution of respondents' opinion on headmasters' involvement of teachers in decision-making, communication to teachers, and delegation of duties to teachers.

| Question | | Teachers' opinion | | | |
		Agree	Neither agree nor disagree	Disagree	Total
Headmasters' involvement of	n	56	25	15	96
teachers in decision-making	%	58	26	16	100
Headmasters' communication	n	49	24	23	96
to teachers	%	51	25	24	100
Headmasters' delegation of	n	53	20	23	96
duties to teachers	%	55	21	24	100

The summary of respondents' opinions on headmasters' involvement of teachers in decision-making, headmasters' communication to teachers, and headmasters' delegation of duties to teachers is presented in Table 1.

The information in Table 1 about headmasters' involvement of teachers in decision-making indicates that the majority ($n = 56$; 58%) of the respondents were in agreement that their headmasters involved them in the decision-making of the school. This was accompanied by 15 (16%) respondents who disagreed, and 25 (26%) respondents who neither agreed nor disagreed with the notion that their headmasters involved them in the decision-making of the school. This means that a large number ($n = 56$; 58%) of the elementary schoolteachers in the research areas were involved by their headmasters in the decision-making of their schools. This suggests that many elementary school headmasters in Telanaipura, Jambi city, practice a democratic leadership style, although some headmasters appear to practice a more laissez-faire leadership style.

Information about headmasters' communication to teachers reveals that 49 (51%) teachers were in agreement that their headmasters communicate to them, while 23 (24%) teachers were in disagreement in their opinion of the question asked. However, 24 (25%) teachers neither agreed nor disagreed with the view that their headmasters communicated to them. This means that most of the elementary schoolteachers in the research area are communicated to by their headmasters, and indicates that a sizable number of elementary school headmasters practice a democratic leadership style.

The overall results concerning headmasters' delegation of duties to teachers indicate that 53 (55%) respondents were agreed in their opinion of the view that headmasters delegated duties to teachers, while 23 (24%) respondents disagreed. This left 20 (21%) respondents who neither agreed nor disagreed with the view that they are delegated duties by their headteachers. This indicates that a majority of elementary schoolteachers in the region are delegated duties by their headmasters, and suggests that both autocratic and democratic leadership styles are almost equally practiced by elementary school headmasters in Telanaipura, Jambi city. Table 2 shows the average of teachers' opinions in terms of associated leadership styles.

The results in Table 2 indicate that the majority ($n = 53$; 55%) of the teachers' opinions revealed that their headmasters practiced a democratic leadership style, while 20 (21%) respondents indicated that their headmasters were autocratic in their leadership style. This left 23 (24%) respondents revealing that their headmasters were laissez-faire in approach. This means that most of the elementary school headmasters practiced a democratic leadership style.

3.4 Headmasters' leadership style in the elementary school

3.4.1 Autocratic leadership style
The autocratic leadership style is also known as the authoritarian style of leadership. Power and decision-making reside in the autocratic leader. Autocratic leaders make decisions on their own

Table 2. Average distribution of teacher respondents' opinion on leadership styles practiced by state elementary school headmasters.

| Leadership style | Average teachers' opinion | | | |
	Democratic, represented by agreement	Laissez-faire, represented by neither agreement nor disagreement	Autocratic, represented by disagreement	Total
n	53	23	20	96
%	55	24	21	100

Table 3. Headmasters' opinions of autocratic style.

| Elements of autocratic leadership style | | Responses | | |
		Yes	No	Total
1 Employees need to be supervised closely, or they are not likely to do their work.	n	5	27	32
	%	16	84	100
2 It is fair to say that most employees in the general population are lazy.	n	2	30	32
	%	6	94	100
3 As a rule, employees must be given rewards or punishments in order to motivate them to achieve organizational objectives.	n	31	1	32
	%	97	3	100
4 Most employees feel insecure about their work and need direction.	n	4	28	32
	%	12	88	100
5 The leader is the chief judge of the achievements of the members of the group.	n	1	31	32
	%	3	97	100
6 Effective leaders give orders and clarify procedures.	n	31	1	32
	%	97	3	100
Average	n	12.3	19.7	32
	%	38.5	61.5	100

without consulting others. According to Pareek, (2010, p. 71), the autocratic leadership style involves the head administering the school virtually by decree because children, staff and parents often abandon autocratic heads. The decisions that autocrats make often face resistance because they are made single-handedly. An autocratic head resists the role of school development committees and may find it difficult to operate in an environment which demands collective decision-making. According to Hoy and Miskel (1992, p. 32), such a leader directs group members on the way things should be done and does not maintain clear channels of communication between himself or herself and subordinates. He or she does not delegate authority nor permit subordinates to participate in policy-making.

Table 3 shows the questionnaire results of headmasters' opinions of autocratic style in the elementary schools of Telanaipura, Jambi city.

According to the overall distribution of headmasters' opinion on autocratic style, the information in Table 6 relating to question 1 indicates that 27 (84%) of the elementary school headmasters disagreed that their employees needed to be supervised closely or they were not likely to do their work, while five (16%) headmasters were in agreement with this view. It can be deduced from this information that headmasters in the selected elementary schools of the research area are generally democratic in leadership style because they practice appropriate supervision closely, which is an element embodied in democratic style.

In analyzing whether headmasters are of the view that most employees in the general population are lazy, the overall results for question 2 indicate that two (6%) headmasters were in agreement with such a view, while 30 (94%) respondents disagreed that it was fair to say that most of the population are lazy. That the headmasters say most employees in the general population are not lazy is an element found in a democratic style of leadership.

Responses to questions 3 and 6 indicate that a majority ($n = 31$; 97%) of the headmasters were in agreement that their teachers must be given rewards or punishments in order to motivate them to achieve, and that effective leaders give orders and clarify procedures. This was accompanied by one (3%) headmaster who disagreed with these opinions. This result indicated that an autocratic leadership style is highly practiced by headmasters of state elementary schools in Telanaipura, Jambi city.

According to question 4, a minority of four (12%) of the headmasters were in agreement that most employees feel insecure about their work and need direction, whereas 28 (88%) respondents disagreed in their response to the question asked. It can be concluded that appropriate direction by headmasters is a characteristic of a democratic leadership style.

As can be viewed from the responses to question 5, a majority ($n = 31$; 97%) of the headmasters disagreed with the view that the leader is the chief judge of the achievements of the members of the group, with just one (3%) headmaster in agreement with this view. This indicates a democratic style of leadership being practiced by the majority of headmasters.

3.4.2 *Democratic leadership style*

The democratic style of leadership emphasizes group and leader participation in the making of policies. Heenan and Bennis (1999, p. 28) describe how decisions about organizational matters are arrived at after consultation and communication with various people in the organization. The leader attempts as much as possible to make each individual feel that he is an important member of the organization. Communication is multidirectional while ideas are exchanged between employees and the leader. As described by Pareek (2010, p. 62), democratic leaders involve employees in decision-making. Democratic leaders, however, may have difficulties when opinions differ widely and it is difficult to arrive at a consensus. The democratic style of leadership includes administration by consensus through consultation with staff and parents, and leads to informed decisions because of the experience and wisdom of other professionals inside and outside the organization. It can be concluded that the democratic style of leadership emphasizes group and leader participation in the making of policies. The leader attempts as much as possible to make each individual feel that he is an important member of the organization.

Table 4 shows the questionnaire results of headmasters' opinions of democratic style in the elementary schools of Telanaipura, Jambi city.

According to question 1 in Table 4, all ($n = 32$; 100%) of the headmasters were in agreement that employees want to be a part of the decision-making process.

This reveals a democratic style of leadership where headmasters recognize that employees want to be a part of the decision-making process.

With regard to question 2, 30 (94%) headmasters agreed that providing guidance without pressure is the key to being a good leader, with just two (6%) headmasters disagreeing. This implies that (94%) of the elementary schoolteachers in Telanaipura, Jambi city, are provided with guidance without pressure. The provision of guidance without pressure by headmasters is characteristic of a democratic leadership style.

Responses to question 3 showed 31 (97%) of the headmasters agreeing that most workers want frequent and supportive communication from their leaders, and only one (3%) headmaster disagreeing. This suggests that the majority (97%) of elementary school headmasters in Telanaipura, Jambi city, are communicating supportively, and indicates headmasters are using a democratic leadership style.

The responses to question 4 indicate that 29 (91%) of the headmasters were in agreement that they as leaders need to help subordinates accept responsibility for completing their work, with three

Table 4. Headmasters' opinions of democratic style.

Elements of democratic leadership style		Responses		
		Yes	No	Total
1 Employees want to be a part of the decision-making process.	n	32	0	32
	%	100	0	100
2 Providing guidance without pressure is the key to being a good leader.	n	30	2	32
	%	94	6	100
3 Most workers want frequent and supportive communication from their leaders.	n	31	1	32
	%	97	3	100
4 Leaders need to help subordinates accept responsibility for completing their work.	n	29	3	32
	%	91	9	100
5 It is the leader's job to help subordinates find their "passion".	n	28	4	32
	%	88	12	100
6 People are basically competent and if given a task will do a good job.	n	27	5	32
	%	84	16	100
Average	n	29.5	2.5	32
	%	92.3	7.7	100

(9%) headmasters in disagreement. This suggests that most of the headmasters in the research area practice a democratic leadership style.

Question 5 concerned the leader's role in helping subordinates find their passion. The responses gathered indicate that the majority ($n = 28$; 88%) of headmasters were in agreement that the leader's job includes helping subordinates to find their passion. However, four (12%) headmasters were in disagreement with this view. This clearly indicates that most 28 (88%) of the elementary school headmasters see the leader's job as helping subordinates find their passion. Such headmasters who helped teaching staff are democratic in leadership style.

Question 6 responses indicate that five (16%) headmasters disagreed with the view that people are basically competent and if given a task will do a good job, while 27 (84%) headmasters agreed with this notion. This indicates that headmasters in the research area practice a democratic leadership style.

3.4.3 *Laissez-faire leadership style*

Laissez-faire leadership style is one that advocates minimal supervision and moderate involvement in the instructional process. According to Lewin et al. (1939, p. 16), the laissez-faire leadership style is one where all the rights and power to make decisions are fully given to the worker. Laissez-faire leaders allow followers to have complete freedom to make decisions concerning the completion of their work.

Table 5 shows the questionnaire results of headmasters' opinions on laissez-faire leadership style in the elementary schools of Telanaipura, Jambi city.

The data for question 1 in Table 5 indicates that three (9%) of the headmasters were in agreement that in complex situations, leaders should let subordinates work problems out on their own, while 29 (91%) headmasters disagreed with this view. This showed that a laissez-faire leadership style is not highly practiced by headmasters of state elementary schools in Telanaipura, Jambi city.

Responses to question 2 indicate that 18 (56%) headmasters agreed that leadership requires staying out of the way of subordinates as they do their work, but 14 (44%) headmasters disagreed with this view. This suggests that requiring headmasters to stay out of the way of subordinates as they do their work is a characteristic of a laissez-faire leadership style.

Information from question 3 responses indicated that 30 (94%) headmasters were in disagreement that, as a rule, leaders should allow subordinates to appraise their own work. This is an indication of a democratic leadership style that does not consider the views of the followers. Just two (6%)

Table 5. Headmasters' opinions of laissez-faire style.

Elements of laissez-faire leadership style		Responses		
		Yes	No	Total
1 In complex situations, leaders should let subordinates work problems out on their own.	n	3	29	32
	%	9	91	100
2 Leadership requires staying out of the way of subordinates as they do their work	n	18	14	32
	%	56	44	100
3 As a rule, leaders should allow subordinates to appraise their own work.	n	2	30	32
	%	6	94	100
4 Leaders should give subordinates complete freedom to solve problems on their own.	n	12	20	32
	%	37	63	100
5 In most situations, workers prefer little input from the leader.	n	10	22	32
	%	31	69	100
6 In general, it is best to leave subordinates alone.	n	0	32	32
	%	0	100	100
Average	n	7.5	24.5	32
	%	23.2	76.8	100

Table 6. Summary distribution of headmaster leadership in autocratic, democratic, and laissez-faire styles.

Questions on leadership style elements		Average headmasters' opinion		
		Yes	No	Total
Autocratic	n	12.3	19.7	32
	%	38.5	61.5	100
Democratic	n	29.5	2.5	32
	%	92.3	7.7	100
Laissez-faire	n	7.5	24.5	32
	%	23.2	76.8	100

headmasters were in agreement with the premise: an indication of laissez-faire leadership style. This means the majority of the headmasters in the research area practiced a democratic leadership style.

Question 4 explored the headmasters' opinions on whether leaders should give subordinates complete freedom to solve problems on their own. The result reveals that 12 (37%) headmasters were in agreement with this, while 20 (63%) headmasters disagreed. Thus, right to conclude that this type of headmasters demonstrate democratic leadership style.

Question 5 explored the view that in most situations, workers prefer little input from the leader. The responses indicate that a minority ($n = 10$; 31%) of headmasters were in agreement with this view, whereas 22 (69%) headmasters were in disagreement. This showed that a laissez-faire leadership style is not highly practiced by headmasters in state elementary schools in this research area.

The responses to question 6 reveal that all 32 (100%) of the headmasters disagreed that, in general, it is best to leave subordinates alone. This suggests that all of the headmasters (100%) in the state elementary schools in the research area reject a laissez-faire leadership style.

A summary of results in relation to headmaster leadership style is presented in Table 6.

Table 6 indicates that a majority ($n = 19.7$; 61.5%) of the headmasters disagreed that they used an autocratic leadership style, whereas an average of 12.3 (38.5%) headmasters agreed with the view that they had an autocratic leadership style. This clearly shows that many elementary school headmasters in Telanaipura, Jambi city, practice a democratic leadership style, although some practiced elements of a laissez-faire leadership style.

Opinions about a democratic leadership style reveal that, on average, 29.5 (92.3%) headmasters agreed that they had a democratic leadership style while 2.5 (7.7%) headmasters disagreed with this notion. This suggests that the majority of elementary school headmasters in Telanaipura, Jambi city, practice a democratic leadership style.

In terms of a laissez-faire leadership style, an average of 7.5 (23.2%) headmasters agreed that they had such a style, whereas 24.5 (76.8%) headmasters disagreed. This means that both laissez-faire and autocratic leadership styles are almost equally practiced by elementary school headmasters in Telanaipura, Jambi city.

The overall results in relation to headmaster leadership style in the state elementary schools of Telanaipura, Jambi city, showed that the most commonly used was a democratic leadership style. This clearly shows that many elementary school headmasters in Telanaipura, Jambi city, were consistent with the views that: employees want to be a part of the decision-making process; providing guidance without pressure is the key to being a good leader; most workers want frequent and supportive communication from their leaders; leaders need to help subordinates accept responsibility for completing their work; the leader's job is to help subordinates find their passion; people are basically competent and if given a task will do a good job.

4 CONCLUSION

First, the results indicated that the headmaster leadership style through communication, decision-making, and delegation in the state elementary schools of Telanaipura, Jambi city, was found to be moderate. *Second*, the overall results concerning headmaster leadership style in the state elementary schools of Telanaipura, Jambi city, showed that a democratic leadership style was most commonly used.

REFERENCES

Adeyemi, T.O. (2006). *Fundamentals of educational management.* Lagos, Nigeria: Atlantic Associated Publishers.

Arikunto, S. (2012). *Manajemen Penelitian.* Jakarta, Indonesia: Rineka Cipta.

Armstrong, M. (2003). *Team rewards.* London, UK: Chartered Institute of Personnel and Development.

Bender, P.U. (2001). *Leadership from within.* Toronto, Canada: Stoddart Publishing.

Bush, T. (2005). *Leading and managing people in education.* London, UK: SAGE Publications.

Dean, J. (2002). *Managing the secondary school.* London, UK: SAGE Publications.

El Widdah, M., Suryana, A. & Musyaddad, K. (2012). *Kepemimpinan Berbasis Nilai dan Pengembangan Mutu Madrasah.* Bandung, Indonesia: Alfabeta.

Goldman, E. (2002). The significance of leadership style. *Educational Leadership*, 55(7), 20–22.

Hackman, M.Z. & Johnson, C.E. (2009). *Leadership: A communication perspective* (5th ed.). Long Grove, IL: Waveland Press.

Hannagan, T. (2002). *Management: Concepts and practice.* London, UK: Pitman.

Heenan, D.A. & Bennis, W. (1999). *Co-leaders. The power of great partnership.* New York, NY: John Wiley and Sons.

Hoy, W.K. & Miskel, C.G. (1992). *Educational administration: Theory, research and practice* (2nd ed.). New York, NY: Random House.

Hoy, W.K. & Miskel, C.G. (2008). *Educational administration: Theory, research, and practice* (8th ed.). New York, NY: McGraw-Hill.

Husaini, U. (2009). *Manajemen Teori, Praktik, dan Riset Pendidikan.* Rawamangun, Indonesia: Bumi Aksara.

Ivancevich, J.M., Konopaske, R. & Matteson, M.T. (2007). *Organizational behavior and management* (8th ed.). New York, NY: McGraw-Hill.

Lee, H.-H. & Li, M.-N.F. (2015). Principal leadership and its link to the development of a school's teacher culture and teaching effectiveness: A case study of an award-winning teaching team at an elementary school. *International Journal of Education Policy and Leadership*, 10(4).

Mehrad, A. & Fallahi, B. (2014). The role of leadership styles on staff's job satisfaction in public organizations. *Acta Universitaria* 24(5), 27–32.

Mulyasa, E. (2007). *Menjadi Kepala Sekolah Profesional.* Bandung, Indonesia: PT Remaja Rosdakarya.

Northouse, P.G. (2015). *Introduction to leadership*: *Concepts and practice* (3rd ed.). Thousand Oaks, CA: SAGE Publications.

OUP. (2005). *Advanced learner's dictionary.* Oxford, UK: Oxford University Press.

Pareek, U. (2010). *Leadership and team building.* Oxford, UK: Oxford University Press.

Ramaiah, A.I. (2003). *Kepimpinan pendidikan: Cabaran masa kini.* Petaling Jaya. IBS Buku Sdn. Bhd. Somech et.al.

Smith, B.S. (2016). The role of leadership style in creating a great school. *SELU Research Review Journal, 1*(1), 65–78.

Syaiful, S. (2008). *Administrasi Pendidikan Kontemporer.* Bandung, Indonesia: CV Alfabeta.

Sweeney, P.D. & McFarlin, D.B. (2002). *Organizational behavior: Solutions for management.* New York, NY: McGraw-Hill/Irwin.

Yukl, G.A. (1989). *Leadership in organizations* (2nd ed.). Englewood Cliffs, NJ: Prentice-Hall International.

Yukl, G.A. (1994). *Leadership in organizations* (3rd ed.). Englewood Cliffs, NJ: Prentice-Hall.

Educational Administration Innovation for Sustainable Development – Komariah et al. (Eds)
© 2018 Taylor & Francis Group, London, ISBN 978-1-138-57341-3

Commitment, performance and service quality of civil servants

N. Mugiasih
Universitas Pendidikan Indonesia, Bandung, West Java, Indonesia

ABSTRACT: This study examined the organizational commitment, performance, and service quality in government education and training institutions 37 respondents were selected by a random sampling technique. Data were analyzed by using multiple linear regression in SPSS 20 application. The result of this research are, first, employees' response to organizational commitment variable, performance, and service quality are in good category. Second, the variables of commitment and performance of employees simultaneously have a significant effect on the quality of service employees. Less than 50% of service quality is affected by commitment and employee performance variables and the rest is influenced by other variables not investigated in this study.

1 INTRODUCTION

Civil servants working at government agencies are required to provide quality services to their customers. Quality is agreed as something that meets customer expectations and needs. A service is an activity or benefit offered by one party to another that is essentially intangible and produces no ownership whatsoever. Customers are divided into: internal customers and external customers. Internal customers are people within an organization and have an influence on the performance of that person or organization, while the external customer is the end user of the product (Nasution, 2015). Center for the Development and Empowerment of Teachers and Education Personnel Kindergarten and Special Education (PPPPTK TK and PLB) Bandung serves teachers of Kindergarten and Special Education from all over Indonesia as external customers. The internal customers are the employees of the institution itself. Organizational commitment describes how a person identifies himself with an organization and is tied to its goals (Kreitner & Kinicki, 2013). (Jex & Britt, 2014) views organizational commitment as the level of dedication of employees to the organization of work and the willingness to work for the benefit of the organization, and maintains its presence in the organization. (Kaswan, 2015) concludes from the definition of some experts that organizational commitment is a work attitude in the form of desire, willingness, dedication, loyalty, and/or strong beliefs that indicate the desire to remain part of the organization members by accepting the value and goals of the organization, and work for the benefit of the organization.

A highly committed employee will devote all his or her ability and time to achieve the desired results of the institution. Commitment begins from the heart, tested by action and opens the way to the door of attainment. Therefore, the emergence of commitment takes a long time but gives a big impact. Performance can be seen from the work process of employees. Employees who have a strong desire or committed to achievement will show good results with full responsibility.

(Meyer & Allen, 1997) divides the organizational commitment dimension into three: 1) affective commitment ie an emotionally strong desire to conform to existing values in order to achieve the organization's goals as well as its existence within the organization; 2) a continuing commitment that is a commitment based on an individual's concerns about losing something he or she has gained from the organization so far; and 3) normative commitment describes the employee's moral responsibility to remain within his organization. (Wirawan, 2014) refined these three dimensions by adding a fourth dimension, the intermediate dimension, also called jumpstart commitment. This dimension describes a person who is inside an organization only as a stepping stone to get a job or a better position. So, its existence only for a while.

Performance is basically the ability of employees to carry out their duties to produce something that reflects the knowledge and skills it has. (Mangkunegara, 2013) states that performance or work performance is the result of work in quality and quantity achieved by an employee in performing their duties in accordance with the responsibilities given to him. Mathis and Jackson (2006) state that performance is how much they contribute to organizations that include: 1) Quality of output; 2) Quantity of output; 3) Timeline of settlement; 4) Workplace attendance; and 5) Cooperative attitude.

Commitment strongly affects performance. A committed employee will be serious in doing his job. This has an impact on the quality of the work it produces. Many studies have proven the close relationship between commitment and performance. (Sudarma, 2012) in his research proves that organizational commitment has a positive effect on performance. (Setiawan & Amar, 2016) also found that high commitment to the organization will have a positive impact on its performance. (Az, 2017) in his research found that the three dimensions of organizational commitment are important factors in developing the performance of bank employees.

Performance is one element that can be used to distinguish the quality of a product. Goods and services differentiated in good or bad terms in performing their duties. Product quality is developed through improved product performance (Wijaya, 2011). Performance has also received important attention in improving service quality through customer survey methods and feedback and complaints forms. Successful service companies generally communicate their concern about the quality of service to employees and provide performance feedback method.

2 METHOD

This research uses descriptive method, which is a study aimed at describing or explaining ongoing events or events at the time of the research regardless of before and after (Riduwan, 2015).

The location of this research took place in PPPPTK TK and PLB Bandung. The reason for choosing the location because this place is where researchers follow the apprentice program for 3 months from March to May 2017. Population used in this study is 37 people Civil Servants (PNS) working in the General Section. Data collection techniques used a questionnaire containing the dimensions mentioned in the previous sub section. Questionnaires for commitment variables consist of three dimensions developed by Meyer and Allen that are affective commitment, continuity commitment, and normative commitment. For performance variables using five dimensions of output quality, output quantity, settlement period, attendance at work, and cooperative attitude. While the service quality variable using SERVQUAL model that consists of five dimensions are tangible, reliability, responsiveness, assurance and emphaty.

(Yarimoglu, 2014) in his research found that several different service quality measurement models have a very close relationship with the SERVQUAL model. This model is therefore still the most widely used model for measuring service quality.

Hypothesis testing is done by multiple linear regression with the formula:

$$Y = a + b_1 X_1 + b_2 X_2 + \cdots + e$$

Y   = dependent variable
a   = constants
b1 ... bn = regression coefficient
X1 ... Xn = independent variable
e   = error

3 RESULTS AND DISCUSSION

In general, respondents gave good responses to the variables of commitment, performance, and service quality. The mean values obtained from the data processing are shown in Table 1.

Table 1. The highest and lowest mean value of each variable.

No.	Question Items	Mean
	Commitment	
1	Workplace institutions have a very big meaning	3.72
2	Being faithful to the institution is a moral obligation	3.72
3	Prefer another better institution	2.11
	Performance	
1	Cooperative in work	4.31
2	Mementingkan quality in completing the job	2.85
	Quality of Service	
1	Able to maintain organizational trust in working	4.31
2	Able to provide services to all customers fairly	2.43

Table 2. Results of multiple linear regression.

R	R Square	Adjusted R Square	Std. Error of the Estimate
.688[a]	.473	.442	3.76357

The frequency distribution of the respondents' responses to the commitment variables shows the largest mean value is in the 3rd question item and the 8th question item (3.72) which means the respondent considers the institution of work to have a very big meaning. In addition, loyal to the institution is considered a moral obligation. While the lowest mean value reaches 2.11 on the 10th question item which means the respondent still chooses another institution which is felt better. The mean of the mean obtained is quite high (3.06).

The frequency distribution of the respondents' responses to the performance variables shows that the civil servants in PPPPTK TK and PLB Bandung give a very big contribution in the form of cooperative attitude in work. This is indicated by the largest mean value being on the 10th question item (4.31). However, respondents assume that the quality in completing their work is not so important, as indicated by the lowest mean value (2.85) in the 3rd question item. Overall, the performance of civil servants in the General Section is very good, as indicated by the average obtained reached 3.55, including in the high category.

Frequency distribution of staff responses of General Section PPPPTK Kindergarten and PLB Bandung showed average of good acquisition (3.30). The highest mean is obtained on the 6th question item that respondents are able to maintain the trust of the organization in carrying out its duties. The lowest mean is obtained on the 8th item (2.43) indicating that the staff has not been able to provide fair service to all customers. The overall quality of service has an average of 3.30, including the category is quite high.

Multiple linear regression analysis is a tool of forecasting analysis of the value of the influence of two independent variables or more on the dependent variable to prove the presence or absence of functional relation or causal relation between two independent variables or more (X1, X2, X3, ... Xn) with one dependent variable (Riduwan, 2015). In this research, Multiple Linear Regression is used to measure the influence of commitment (X1) and employee performance (X2) on service quality in PPPPTK TK and PLB Bandung (Y).

The results of multiple linear regression analysis obtained with the help of SPSS 20 software can be seen in Table 2. It is seen that the value of R = 0.688 means that the influence of Commitment and Performance of Employee to Service Quality is 68.8%. However, if the R Square value of 0.473 indicates that there is a disturbance value so that the correlation value between the two independent variables is only 47.3%. For a more accurate correlation value can be seen in the value Adjusted R

Table 3. Output of linear regression result model 1 (commitment to performance relationship).

Independent Variable	t	Significancy
Commitment	2.542	0.016

Table 4. Output of linear regression result model 2 (performance relationship with quality of service).

Independent Variable	t	Significancy
Performance	4.534	0.000

Table 5. F-test results (commitment and performance relationship with service quality simultaneously).

Independent Variables	F	Significancy
Commitment Performance	15.280	0.000^b

Table 6. Output of linear regression result model 3 (performance relationship, commitment to quality of service).

Variabel bebas	t_{hitung}	Signifikansi
X_1 (komitmen)	1.116	0.272
X_2 (kinerja)	4.534	0.000

Square 0.442. Thus, the influence of Commitment and Employee Performance variable to Quality of Service is $0.442 \times 100\% = 44.2\%$. Std Value. Error of the Estimate of 3.764, indicating that the accuracy of the regression model is $100\% - 3.764 = 96.24\%$.

Hypothesis testing

The first hypothesis states that commitment has a positive effect on performance.

Based on the T-Test whose results are shown in Table 3, the value of ttable $= 1.69 <$ tcal $= 2.542$ then H0 is rejected. This means commitment has been shown to have a significant effect on performance.

The second hypothesis states that performance has a positive effect on service quality. Based on the T-Test in Table 4, the value of ttable $= 1.69 <$ tcal $= 4.534$ then H0 is rejected. This means performance has been shown to have a significant effect on service quality

If F-Test is done, from Table 5 it can be seen that the significance value of $0.016 <$ significance level α 0.05, in addition, Ftable $4.12 <$ Fcount 15.280, in the third hypothesis H0 was rejected, it means that the variable commitment and employee performance simultaneously affect the quality of service.

However, relationship of each independent variable with service quality partially the following results are obtained. Based on the t-test the results can be seen in table 6, the value of ttable $= 1.69 >$ tcount $= 1.116$. Then H0 is accepted, meaning commitment (X1) does not partially affect the quality of service (Y). The second hypothesis states that: the performance of employees positively affect the quality of service. Based on the t-Test whose results are tabulated in table 6, ttable $= 1.69 <$ tcal 4.534 at significance level $\alpha = 0.05$. This means that employee performance (X2) has a partial effect on service quality (Y).

4 CONCLUSION

Organizational commitment significantly influences employee performance. Then, employee performance significantly influences the quality of service. Organizational commitment and employee performance have an effect simultaneously on service quality. Based on the descriptive analysis found that in general the three variables fall into either category although there are certain aspects that are still not good.

The results found in this study indicate that the theory of service quality by civil servants cannot be simply generalized. A deeper study needs to be taken into account with more complex aspects.

Based on the findings of this study, researchers provide suggestions as input for PPPPTK TK and PLB Bandung and other parties concerned in improving the quality of service and human resources development of civil servants are as follows.

Based on the findings of this study, researchers provide suggestions as input for PPPPTK TK and PLB Bandung and other parties concerned in improving the quality of service and human resource development of civil servants are as follows; guidance should be made to the commitment of employees in terms of loyalty to keep working in institutions today, although based on the results of research on the commitment of employees did not significantly affect the quality of service; another research is needed to measure the influence of employee commitment to other variables such as employee performance in PPPPTK TK and PLB Bandung; need to do coaching in terms of quality improvement work done by employees PPPPTK TK and PLB Bandung; and need to do coaching in terms of improving the quality of work performed by employees PPPPTK TK and PLB Bandung.

REFERENCES

Az, H. 2017. Relationship between Organizational Commitment and Employee's Performance Evidence from Banking Sector of Lahore, 7(2). https://doi.org/10.4172/2223-5833.1000304
Jex, S. M., & Britt, T. W. 2014. *Organizational Psychology: A Scientist-Practitioner Approach* (Third). New Kersey: John Wiley & Sons, Inc.
Kaswan. 2015. *Sikap Kerja: Dari Teori dan Implementasi Sampai Bukt* (Cetakan ke). Bandung: Alfabeta.
Kreitner, R., & Kinicki, A. 2013. *Organizational Behavior* (10th edition). New York: McGraw-Hill/Irwin.
Mangkunegara, A. A. A. P. (2013). *Manajemen Sumber Daya Manusia Perusahaan.* (S. Sandiasih, Ed.) (Sebelas). Bandung: PT Remaja Rosdakarya.
Mathis, R. L. & Jackson, J. H. 2006. *Manajemen Sumber Daya Manusia.* (J. Sadely & B. P. Hie, Trans). Jakarta: Salemba Empat.
Meyer, J. P., & Allen, N. J. 1997. *Commitment in the Workplace: Theory, Research, and Application.* (M. Flemming, Ed.). SAGE Publications.
Nasution, M. N. 2015. *Manajemen Mutu Terpadu (Total Quality Management).* Bogor: Ghalia Indonesia.
Riduwan. 2015. *Belajar Mudah Penelitian untuk Guru-Karyawan dan Peneliti Pemula.* (J. S. Husdarta, Akdon, N. Mulyono, & Subandi, Eds.) (Cetakan ke). Bandung: Alfabeta.
Setiawan, S., & Amar, K. 2016. Hubungan Gaya Kepemimpinan Transformasional, Komitmen Organisasional dengan Kinerja Pustakawan, 4(1), 14–21.
Sudarma, K. 2012. Mencapai Sumber Daya Manusia Unggul (Analisis Kinerja dan Kualitas Pelayanan). *Jurnal Dinamika Manajemen,* 3(1), 76–83.
Wirawan. 2014. *Kepemimpinan: Teori, Psikologi, Perilaku Organisasi, Aplikasi dan Penelitian.* Jakarta: PT Rajagrafindo Persada.
Yarimoglu, E. K. 2014. A Review on Dimensions of Service Quality Models. *Journal of Marketing Management,* 2(2), 79–93.
Wijaya, T. 2011. *Manajemen Kualitas Jasa: Desain Servqual, QFD, dan Kano: Disertai Contoh Aplikasi dalam Kasus Penelitian.* Jakarta: PT Indeks.
Wirawan. 2014. *Kepemimpinan: Teori, Psikologi, Perilaku Organisasi, Aplikasi dan Penelitian.* Jakarta: PT Rajagrafindo Persada.

Inclusive kindergarten leadership in a rural setting

S. Purwanti & A. Komariah
Universitas Pendidikan Indonesia, Bandung, Indonesia

ABSTRACT: The aim of this study is to establish: (1) an overview of a principal's transformational leadership and teachers' pedagogic competence in a rural inclusive kindergarten; (2) the effect of a principal's transformational leadership on teachers' pedagogic competence in an inclusive kindergarten in a rural setting. The research method implemented in the present study is a descriptive one, using a quantitative approach. The primary data is collected through questionnaire, while secondary data is gathered using interviews and observation. Respondents for this study were the principal, teachers, staff, and students' parents of an inclusive kindergarten in a rural area. The result of the study showed that there was a positive and significant correlation between the principal's transformational leadership and the teachers' pedagogic competence. It implies that transformational leadership is an effective leadership style in managing an inclusive kindergarten in a rural setting.

1   INTRODUCTION

The Salamanca Statement on inclusive education (UNESCO, 1994) has had a significant effect on education systems all around the world. The statement avers that all children, including children with special needs, have equal rights to quality education. An educational system that facilitates diversity and respects the needs of every child is called inclusive education (Mwangi & Orodho, 2014). Inclusive education should begin in early age, as a study (Odom, 2016) on the effect of inclusive education on children's development found. Inclusive education for early-age children is a strategy to develop the key competencies that determine a child's success in the future. In addition, through inclusive education, children with disability will be able to adapt and engage themselves fully with the social environment in their inclusive class.

The overview of inclusive education implementation in Indonesia, particularly in rural areas, shows that there are still some problems, including a scarcity of competent educators and education staff, a lack of facilities, and a lack of support from society (Lestariningrum, 2017). In another rural area of Indonesia, there is a kindergarten that has successfully delivered inclusive education, despite its limitations in educators and facilities. Every year, this institution accepts regular students and students with special needs, such as those with Attention-Deficit Hyperactivity Disorder (ADHD), autism, or Down's syndrome. Its success in implementing inclusive education is due to the role of its principal, who has a clear vision and mission and works hard to realize them. Such leadership is assumed to be an influential factor in changing educators' and parents' paradigms to implement inclusive education successfully. As found in studies such as Irvine et al. (2010) and Bush (2013), a principal's leadership is an important factor in successfully implementing inclusive education in early childhood educational settings. The principal has full responsibility in answering to the school components, parents, and other school administrators, especially teachers. The principal of an inclusive school has to provide more support and attention to teachers, compared to the principal of a regular school. The principal of an inclusive school should implement the following important components: (1) building a shared vision and commitment; (2) sharing responsibility for the learning of all students by developing a professional community; (3) redesigning the school; (4) sharing responsibility for inclusive education (Billingsley et al., 2014). These components are reflected in the characteristics of transformational leadership. Johnsen and Skjorten (2004) state that to achieve inclusive education requires a change of heart and attitude. Such change should be experienced by students in an inclusive class through teachers' pedagogic competence.

The present study aims to obtain an overview of: (1) a principal's transformational leadership in an inclusive kindergarten in a rural setting; (2) teachers' pedagogic competence in an inclusive kindergarten in a rural setting; (3) the effect of a principal's transformational leadership on teachers' pedagogic competence in an inclusive kindergarten in a rural setting.

2 METHODOLOGY

The hypothesis in the present study is: there is a significant correlation between a principal's transformational leadership and teachers' pedagogic competence in an inclusive kindergarten in a rural setting.

Based on this hypothesis, the research methodology employed in this study is the descriptive method, using a quantitative approach. The sample in the present study is 23 people, consisting of principal, school management, teachers, and students' parents. The primary data is obtained through questionnaire, while the secondary data is gathered from interviews and observation. The instrument used in this study is a questionnaire, which has been tested in terms of its validity and reliability, adapted from the instrument used in the studies of Cucu and Herawan (2016) and Kurniawan (2013), adjusted for the context of an inclusive kindergarten.

The data collection technique employed in the present study is a close-ended questionnaire. Data analysis begins with data selection, followed by calculation of the general tendency of respondents' scores for each variable using a Weighted Mean Score (WMS) formula, normality testing to determine whether data processing will use parametric or non-parametric analysis, and hypothesis testing through several stages: correlation analysis, significance testing, coefficient of determination testing, and regression analysis.

3 RESULTS AND DISCUSSION

The findings are obtained from processing the questionnaires completed by the respondents. The findings are processed using Microsoft Excel 2013 and IBM SPSS for Windows Version 22 to derive the correlation of the independent X variable (principal's transformational leadership) and the dependent Y variable (teachers' pedagogic competence). The data is obtained from questionnaires administered to 23 respondents, containing 25 items for the X variable and 20 items for the Y variable. WMS calculation results in a mean score of 3.62 for all X variable (transformational leadership) items. In other words, principals' transformational leadership, based on respondents' perception, belongs in the 'very good' category. Meanwhile, for the Y variable (teachers' pedagogic competence), the WMS calculation results in a mean score of 3.53, which means that teachers' pedagogic competence is also in the 'very good' category.

Then, hypothesis testing is conducted by calculating the correlation coefficient using SPSS. The calculation uses Spearman's non-parametric statistical technique because the number of samples is below 30 ($n = 23$), the data distribution is not normal, and the data is in ordinal form. Hypothesis testing aims to determine whether the formulated hypothesis is accepted or rejected. The calculation of correlation between the X and Y variables finds a correlation coefficient of 0.479. This means that the correlation between the two variables is of a 'medium' classification. In other words, there is a medium correlation between the principal's transformational leadership and teachers' pedagogic competence.

The next step is a significance test, aiming to measure the significance of the correlation between the X and Y variables. This measurement results in a significance value of 0.021. Because 0.021 < 0.05, we can conclude that the coefficient correlation between the X and Y variables is significant. Hence, the hypothesis is accepted.

To understand the extent of the influence of the X variable on the Y variable, the coefficient of determination is calculated, resulting in a value of 0.353. This means that 35.3% of the teachers' pedagogic competence is accounted for by the principal's transformational leadership, while the remaining 64.7% is determined by other factors.

The next data processing is regression analysis. Based on the SPSS output, a constant of $-$11.199 and a regression coefficient of 0.901 are found. The analysis shows that t_{calc} is 3.381 and the p-value is $0.003/2 = 0.0015$, which is lower than 0.05. This means that transformational leadership has a positive effect on teachers' pedagogic competence. The regression equation is $Y = -11.199 + 0.901X$, signifying that every change of one unit in the X variable is accompanied by a 0.901 change in the Y variable.

The next stage of this paper is the discussion of these data analysis results, supported by the results of interviews with the principal, teachers, and students' parents, and the results of field observation.

The principal's transformational leadership in managing an inclusive kindergarten is an effective leadership style, as proven by the very good perceptions of the respondents in this study. This is in line with Yukl (2005), who states that the general indicator of an effective leader is the attitude and behavior of their followers. The behavior of followers in the present study is represented by the teachers' pedagogic competence. The positive correlation between the principal's transformational leadership and the teachers' pedagogic competence demonstrates that leadership contributes towards the improvement of teachers' pedagogic competence. According to Komariah and Triatna (2008), transformational leadership is a catalyst because it plays a role in improving all human resources. A transformational leader provides responses that motivate and encourage maximum efficiency because he or she always acts as a pioneer.

Based on the interviews and literature review, it is found that the academic qualifications of teachers in the inclusive kindergarten is not merely a result of education in schools for kindergarten teachers, but also a product of the principal's transformational leadership, which contributes 35.3% of the teachers' pedagogic competence. With such a contribution, teachers' pedagogic competence in the institution is very good. This supports the finding of Komariah and Triatna (2008) that transformational leadership is a catalyst in improving all human resources. The four dimensions of transformational leadership proposed by Komariah and Triatna (2008) are shown in the principal's behavior: (1) idealized influence, reflected in the respect that students, teachers, students' parents, and school staff show towards the principal; (2) inspirational motivation, reflected in the principal's behavior and attitude in motivating students, teachers, students' parents, and school staff; (3) intellectual stimulation, reflected through the principal's efforts to involve a psychologist to improve teachers' and students' parents' knowledge of inclusiveness; (4) individualized consideration, reflected through the principal's behavior in listening to and responding to complaints, ideas, and expectations of students, teachers, and students' parents.

4 CONCLUSION

The principal's transformational leadership and the teachers' pedagogic competence in an inclusive kindergarten in a rural setting were found to be very good, and the principal's transformational leadership was proven to have a significant effect on the teachers' pedagogic competence, even though the influence was in the 'medium' category. Specifically, the present study found that the principal's transformational leadership contributed a 35.3% influence on the teachers' pedagogic competence.

It is recommended that further studies focus on other factors that affect teachers' pedagogic competence in an inclusive kindergarten. In addition, future studies should be conducted using a larger population and more samples to produce a more significant and more general conclusion, not limited to only one area as in the present study.

The implication of this study is that a principal's transformational leadership is proven to be an effective leadership style in managing an inclusive kindergarten in a rural setting.

REFERENCES

Billingsley, B., McLeskey, J. & Crockett, J. (2014). *Principal leadership: Moving toward inclusive and high-achieving schools for students with disabilities*. Gainesville, FL: CEEDAR Center. Retrieved from http://ceedar.education.ufl.edu/wp-content/uploads/2014/09/IC-8_FINAL_08-29-14.pdf

Bush, T. (2013). Leadership in early childhood education. *Educational Management Administration & Leadership*, 41(1), 3–4. doi:10.1177/1741143212462968

Cucu & Herawan, E. (2016). Kontribusi Perilaku Kepemimpinan Transformasional Kepala Sekolah dan Kinerja Komite Sekolah Terhadap Efektivitas Implementasi Manajemen Berbasis Sekolah. *Jurnal Administrasi Pendidikan*, 23(1), 40–48.

Irvine, A., Lupart, J., Loreman, T. & McGhie-Richmond, D. (2010). Educational leadership to create authentic inclusive schools: The experiences of principals in a Canadian rural school district. *Exceptionality Education International*, 20(2), 70–88. Retrieved from https://ir.lib.uwo.ca/eei/vol20/iss2/7/

Johnsen, B.H. & Skjorten, M.D. (Eds.). (2004). *Menuju Inklusi: Pendidikan Kebutuhan Khusus Sebuah Pengantar* (S. Rakhmawati, Trans.). Bandung, Indonesia: Unipub Forlag.

Komariah, A. & Triatna, C. (2008). *Visionary Leadership Menuju Sekolah Efektif*. Jakarta, Indonesia: PT Bumi Aksara.

Kurniawan, T. (2013). *Pengaruh Kompetensi Pedagogik dan Kompetensi Profesional Guru Terhadap Kinerja Guru di SMK* (Unpublished thesis, Technology and Vocational Education Program, Postgraduate School, Universitas Pendidikan Indonesia, Bandung, Indonesia). Retrieved from http://repository.upi.edu/id/eprint/3723

Lestariningrum, A. (2017). Implementasi Pendidikan Inklusif Anak Usia Dini di Kota Kediri (Studi Pada PAUD Inklusif YBPK Semampir, Kecamatan Kota, Kediri). *Jurnal CARE*, 4(2), 53–68.

Mwangi, E.M. & Orodho, J.A. (2014). Challenges facing implementation of inclusive education in public primary schools in Nyeri Town, Nyeri County, Kenya. *Journal of Education and Practice*, 5(16), 118–126. Retrieved from http://www.iiste.org/Journals/index.php/JEP/article/view/13081

Odom, S. (2016). Preschool inclusion. *Topics in Early Childhood Special Education*, 20(1), 20–27.

Sugiyono. (2016). *Metode Penelitian Kuantitatif, Kualitatif dan R&D*. Bandung, Indonesia: CV Alfabeta.

UNESCO. (1994). *The Salamanca Statement and Framework For Action on Special Needs Education*. Paris, France: UNESCO.

Yukl, G.A. (2005). *Kepemimpinan dalam Organisasi* (5th ed.). Jakarta, Indonesia: PT Indeks.

Educational Administration Innovation for Sustainable Development – Komariah et al. (Eds)
© 2018 Taylor & Francis Group, London, ISBN 978-1-138-57341-3

The application of knowledge management to academic services in higher education

L. Raspatiningrum, U.S. Sa'ud, Sumarto & A. Komariah
Universitas Pendidikan Indonesia, Bandung, West Java, Indonesia

ABSTRACT: The purpose of this research was to analyze and develop a hypothetical model of a more effective application of knowledge management to academic services. This research employed a qualitative method by using a case study approach. Data collection was conducted through in-depth interviews, observation, and documentation study. Data analysis was administered by refining and presenting the data, drawing conclusions, and verification. This study indicated that the people component is the main source of knowledge flow and cannot be separated from aspects such as people's competence, leadership, knowledge sharing, innovation, and teamwork. The availability of human resources who enjoy learning and sharing their knowledge enables the creation of knowledge-processing channels, knowledge creation and capture, and the use of knowledge sharing to facilitate the implementation of academic services activities. The application of technology is a supporting element in optimizing knowledge flow and extends the reach and increases the speed of knowledge transfer.

1 INTRODUCTION

The university is a science-based professional education organization. If knowledge is not managed properly, it will become decayed and useless. In order to make knowledge function optimally in human lives, it is necessary to have particular management that is able to handle knowledge, which is known as Knowledge Management (KM).

Some experts define knowledge management as the art of adding value through the use of non-physical assets that enable an organization to absorb its knowledge, experience, and creativity to improve organizational performance (Sveiby, 1997; Davidson & Voss, 2002). Organizations and companies, including universities, are encouraged to manage their knowledge as it contributes to improving organizational performance in achieving missions and goals (Jane, 2009; Darudiato & Setiawan, 2013; Petrides & Nguyen, 2006). The research of Kidwell et al. (2000) and Prabowo (2010) suggests that universities can use KM for five main processes: (1) research; (2) curriculum development; (3) student and alumni services; (4) administrative service; (5) strategic planning. In order to apply KM properly, universities need to pay attention to involving people, process, and technology as important elements that can determine the successful implementation of a KM system (Bhatt, 2000; Tobing, 2007; Lee & Choi in Suharti & Hartanto, 2009).

Figure 1 illustrates that KM is the integration of people and process, which is then enabled by technology, to facilitate the exchange of information, knowledge, and expertise in an effort to improve organizational performance.

In Indonesia, the universities that recognize the need to apply KM are still very few in number (Sopandi, 2015), despite the government publishing guidelines in 2011 for the implementation of knowledge management programs through the Regulation of the Minister of State for Administrative Reform and Bureaucratic Reform No. 14/2011. Based on this regulation, every institution, including universities under the Ministry of Research, Technology and Higher Education should have been applying KM. This study aims to give a more in-depth description of the contribution

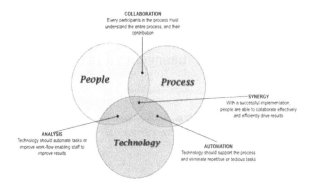

Figure 1. Knowledge management components.

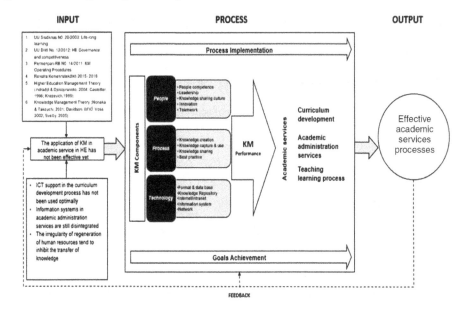

Figure 2. Research framework.

of KM to organizational and institutional management systems, especially in academic services in universities.

As shown in Figure 2, in order to realize knowledge management that can improve the quality and performance of higher education institutions, this study will examine and analyze the application of knowledge management at the university in curriculum development, academic administration services, and teaching and learning processes. Management theories, educational administration, and knowledge management are used as the basis for the review of issues related to the knowledge management components, such as the people, processes, and technology used in academic services. Defining the framework or problem-solving steps before problem-solving is conducted will facilitate the researchers in carrying out the series of tracking and data collection activities.

2 RESEARCH METHODS

The research was conducted in one university in Indonesia, Bogor Agricultural Institute (IPB), because IPB has determined to strengthen KM as one of the elements in the drafting of the IPB strategic plan for 2014–2018. IPB consciously identifies the knowledge that it possesses and utilizes it to improve performance and generate innovations. Through the I-MHERE program, IPB has built a Knowledge Management System (KMS) as a forum to identify and document various sources of knowledge, as well as make ways to acquire existing knowledge and associate it with strategic component processes.

We used a qualitative approach with case studies to examine the information about KM implementation involving people, process, and technology components in academic services, consisting of curriculum development, academic administration services, and the teaching and learning processes at undergraduate level. The type of data used is primary data obtained from interviews and observations and secondary data from the study of documentation. Interviews were conducted with the respondents, namely, the heads of the rectorate, directorate, sub-directorate, study program, and lecturers. Observations were conducted through open observation technique, where the object of the study is observed. Data analysis techniques were performed through several stages of categorization, involving data collection, data reduction, issue categorization, data interpretation, data display, conclusion drawing, and verification. In completing the data analysis process, the validity of the research data was also considered by extending the observation time by increasing the frequency of meetings with the data source, increasing the persistence, and triangulation.

3 RESEARCH FINDINGS

3.1 *"People" in the application of knowledge management to academic services*

Lecturers and staff are the people components in academic services in IPB who participate in managing and developing knowledge by contributing their knowledge in accordance with their respective duties and functions. To ensure that their knowledge is not obsolete, IPB enhances their competence through further studies, pedagogical training, training on updating course content and teaching methods, teaching clinic activities, and update training in the online IPB Academic Information System (IPAK). The limitations on education personnel when it comes to attending such a variety of training has encouraged the leaders of IPB to develop their people through "learning by doing" and overcoming problems that arise every day. It cannot be denied that learning through problem-solving represents the best teacher and the best practice.

Leadership roles ranging from the senior management down to the level of a study program are needed in the implementation of KM. Activities that have been undertaken by IPB leaders at various levels include: (1) the establishment of foundation and policy for the access, extension, and strengthening of KM (IPB, 2013); (2) the development of a KMS through the I-MHERE program; (3) awarding 'tributes' to innovators and authors; (4) the establishment of cooperative connections; (5) the development of new methods of organizational problem-solving; (6) facilitation in dealing with and solving various problems; (7) the identification of knowledge gaps; (8) the preparation of those who are sensitive to knowledge-processing behaviors.

To develop a knowledge-sharing culture in academic service, IPB encourages an "interactive knowledge café" culture among lecturers and an informal approach for staff. The foundation of the knowledge-sharing culture in IPB is trust. Leaders trust lecturers and staff to be able to create *know how* such that everyone has an opportunity and is free to determine new ways to complete tasks and innovate, subject to IPB regulations.

In curriculum development activities, the emergence of innovation is motivated by the challenge to answer crucial problems in education. Innovation in academic administration services is formed through the interaction and knowledge sharing of educational personnel when facing problems. Innovation in the undergraduate learning process in IPB is done by utilizing information and communication technology, which contribute to e-learning development.

Working in groups encourages everyone to work better together in accomplishing academic service tasks. In order for the curriculum development team to work together, each individual is required to have a pedagogic competence and be interested in pedagogy, especially curriculum development. The communication aspect in the collaboration of educational personnel in the Directorate of Educational Administration provides individual effectiveness and produces good teamwork. In the process of learning, teamwork shaped team teaching to build togetherness between the lecturers.

3.2 *"Process" in the application of knowledge management to academic services*

The process component focuses on optimizing the flow of knowledge within the organization and supporting activities that facilitate the transfer of knowledge in academic services at IPB. The creation of new knowledge in curriculum development is conducted through regular meetings, discussions or by sharing new ideas/thoughts. In academic administration services, knowledge creation happens through direct observation and informal interaction, and spontaneous communication between students, faculties, and education personnel. Classroom knowledge creation occurs through teaching–learning activities, the practices of tracking scientific information and field data collection, thesis writing or scientific paper supervision, and exposure to tasks, research papers or scientific papers. The use of the Internet and information technology messaging systems, such as SMS, WhatsApp, Line, BBM, Facebook, and Twitter, also make a significant contribution to the process of creating knowledge.

Lecturers and education staff acquire new knowledge through scanning and interest in the external environment, accepting complaints, criticisms, suggestions and inputs from various parties, and research and development. In curriculum development activities and teaching–learning processes, the process of knowledge capture occurs when a lecturer conducts a study, or develops models or learning media. By growing knowledge through research, it is possible for knowledge capture to occur. In order to reuse knowledge, IPB is building a KMS that supports the capture and reuse of knowledge, as well as becoming a medium for electronic knowledge sharing.

Sharing knowledge about the curriculum, academic administration services, and teaching–learning processes between IPB academic lecturers is done through face-to-face meetings, documentation, websites, electronic discussions, and publications (scientific repository, electronic journals, IPB Green TV, IPB online magazine), which enable easy and low-cost information communication.

In improving the quality of curriculum development, academic administration services, and teaching–learning processes, both lecturers and educational staff carry out benchmarking, in which they can identify, adopt and apply the best practices gained. The results of benchmarking activities are in the form of data and information transfer that later becomes new reference knowledge for improving the quality of academic services, expanding knowledge insights, improving the running systems, determining new policies, and improving rules and regulations.

3.3 *"Technology" in the application of knowledge management to academic services*

Up until now, IPB has made use of several data servers, namely, the SIMAK (academic) database server, SIMPEG (personnel), employee attendance data, scientific works, DUPAK, and the IPB website. IPB realized that the management of digital documents is much easier than that of printed documents. Dissemination and access to the documents is faster. Therefore, a repository of local content is increasingly felt important by IPB. The repository developed contains academic documents in the form of dissertations, theses, research articles, scientific journals, guidebooks, student papers, professorial speeches, and final assignments of diploma students. "My Curriculum" repositories and academic administration services are enabled by academic information applications (KRS online and SIMAK). To support the teaching service, IPB has built LMS (LMS) and Lecture Content Management System (LCMS), based on open source software, as a center for the storage and management of teaching data.

IPB is connected to the Internet through Telkom and Indosat service providers, with 800 Mbps international bandwidth, 400 Mbps domestic bandwidth, and an interconnection between IPB campuses of 1.6 Gbps bandwidth. IPB network facilities can be accessed by anyone with the right user access. However, some information systems still exist that stand alone, so the network has not been wholly effective and efficient in its implementation. Nevertheless, the role of networking in supporting KM implementation allows IPB to disseminate research results more quickly and facilitates the stimulation of the creation of new knowledge and learning.

4 DISCUSSION

As organizations, universities are very conducive to the development of knowledge. By considering the role and the main tasks of transferring, transforming, and translating knowledge according to the needs of universities in the fields of teaching, research, and community service, a hypothetical model of KM application to academic services in the context of higher education institution should be developed. The senior management of universities, with the rector as the top manager (or Chief Executive Officer), has a big role in the preparation of a KM implementation plan in academic services, which then explicitly informs the vision, mission and objectives, to conical on statute, RIP, the strategic plan, the operational plan, and quality policy (Kikoski & Kikoski, 2004; Anna, 2009). The utilization and management of knowledge in planning, organizing, implementing and controlling processes can be a valuable and strategic resource in optimizing the achievement of objectives in academic services. The three components of KM, which are people, process, and technology, have an important role in every academic services process because these can determine the successful implementation of KM systems. KM is built from the knowledge associated with the people in the form of lecturers and staff (Lee & Choi, 2003; Probst et al., 2000; Gillingham & Roberts, 2006). In this case, lecturers and staff share their knowledge, manage knowledge in a sustainable cycle, and use knowledge in analyzing and solving various problems. Here the role of leaders is needed to foster mutual trust between lecturers and educational staff because this becomes the key to the existence of a knowledge-sharing culture such that great teamwork is possible.

The activities of creating, capturing, reusing, transferring and sharing knowledge will only be effective if the processes implemented in the organization support them (Kahreh et al., 2014; Duran et al., 2014). Without clear processes, it will not be possible to create a culture of knowledge sharing, innovation and best practice within the organization.

As the glue for the two elements of people and process, technology is the other important element that makes the sharing of knowledge as efficient as possible. All academic services data is stored in the form of knowledge repositories, KMSs, and other application systems to support curriculum development activities, and academic and teaching administration services. The improvement of Internet and intranet access also supports the implementation of KM because academic faculties then find it easier to obtain knowledge and media from a variety of sources. Finally, universities' ability to build networks can trigger creativity, and strengthen collaboration and knowledge-processing because networking for universities can not only be a source of new knowledge, but also be a facility to spur the creation of new knowledge and learning.

In Figure 3, a hypothetical model is presented that is tailored to the characteristics of universities in order for the application of knowledge management in academic services in universities to run effectively. Every component of people, process, and technology has requirements that must be met by the relevant universities so that this hypothetical model can be implemented. An interface between the people and process components fosters collaboration in which every person involved should understand the whole set of processes that occur and contribute positively to them. The interface between process and technology components produces automation in the form of technological support to the process to reduce the work that is otherwise done over and over again. The interface of people with technology allows people to conduct analysis to improve their performance with the help of technology. Thus, the successful application of knowledge management in universities will increase the ability of people to collaborate and be more effective, thus achieving efficient results. It will complement and become the driving force of the university management process to achieve the organizational objectives and improve the quality of the implementation of

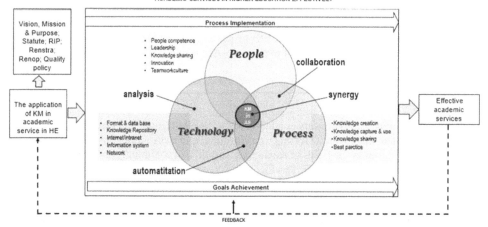

Figure 3. Hypothetical model for effective KM application to academic services (AS) in higher education (HE).

Tridharma Perguruan Tinggi (three-principle higher education: education, research, and societal contribution), creating organizations with competitive advantage.

5 CONCLUSIONS

The KM components of people, process, and technology have an important role in academic services in higher education. The availability of people with excellent competencies supported by technology will facilitate the implementation of KM; knowledge itself is associated with the people component within the organization. Meanwhile, universities explore the richness of knowledge that exists in every lecturer and member of education staff, and then assemble it into a knowledge base, before utilizing it effectively to help the acceleration of the planning, organizing, implementing and monitoring functions that are applied in strategic academic services components. As the unifier of the people and process elements, technology is used to make the sharing of knowledge into an activity that is conducted as efficiently as possible, and KM implementation in universities will complement and become the impetus for the university management process for improving the quality of implementation of *Tridharma Perguruan Tinggi*, creating organizational competitive advantage.

REFERENCES

Anna, N.E.V. (2009). *Peran Pemimpin dalam Menciptakan Knowledge-Sharing di organisasi* [*Leader's role in creating knowledge-sharing in organizations*] (Seminar, Faculty of Social and Political Science, Universitas Airlangga, Surabaya, Indonesia). Retrieved from http://journal.unair.ac.id/download-fullpapers-palim0b5dd2eaf9full.pdf

Bhatt, D. (2000). *EFQM: Excellence model and knowledge management implications*. Retrieved from http://citeseerx.ist.psu.edu/viewdoc/summary?doi=10.1.1.573.6798

Darudiato, S. & Setiawan, K. (2013). Knowledge management: Concepts and methodology. *ULTIMA InfoSys*, 4(1), 11–17.

Davidson, C. & Voss, P. (2002). *Knowledge management: An introduction to creating competitive advantage from intellectual capital*. Auckland, New Zealand: Tandem Press.

Duran, C., Çetindere, A. & Şahan, Ö. (2014). An analysis on the relationship between Total Quality Management practices and knowledge management: The case of Eskişehir. *Procedia – Social and Behavioral Sciences*, 109, 65–77.

Gillingham, H. & Roberts, B. (2006). Implementing knowledge management: A practical approach. *Journal of Knowledge Management Practice*, 7(1).

IPB. (2013). *Bogor Agricultural University Strategic Planning 2014–2018*. Bogor, Indonesia: Institut Pertannian Bogor.

Jane, O. (2009). The role of knowledge management in improving the performance of higher education. *Journal of Business Administration*, 5(1), 30–43.

Kahreh, Z.S., Shirmohammadi, A. & Kahreh, M.S. (2014). Explanatory study towards analysis the relationship between Total Quality Management and knowledge management. *Procedia – Social and Behavioral Sciences*, 109, 600–604.

Kidwell, J.J., Vander Linde, K.M. & Sandra, L.J. (2000). Applying corporate knowledge management practices in higher education. *Educause Quarterly*, 23(4), 28–33.

Kikoski, C.K. & Kikoski, J.F. (2004). *The enquiring organization: Tacit knowledge, conversation, and knowledge creation: Skills for 21st-century organizations*. Westport, CT: Praeger.

Lee, H. & Choi, B. (2003). Knowledge management enablers, processes, and organizational performance: An integrative view and empirical examination. *Journal of Management Information Systems*, 20(1), 179–228.

Petrides, L. & Nguyen, L. (2006). Knowledge management challenges and opportunities for education institutions. In A.S. Metcalfe (Ed.), *Knowledge management and higher education: A critical analysis* (pp. 21–33). Hershey, PA: IGI Global. doi:10.4018/978-1-59140-509-2.ch002

Prabowo, H. (2010). Knowledge management in higher education. *Binus Business Review*, 1(2), 407–415.

Probst, G.J.B., Raub, S. & Romhardt, K. (2000). *Managing knowledge: Building for success*. New York, NY: John Wiley & Sons

Sopandi, O.D. (2015). *Implementation of knowledge management at higher education: Case study at Bandung Institute of Technology* (Dissertation, Graduate School, Universitas Pendidikan Indonesia, Bandung, Indonesia).

Suharti, L. & Hartanto, I. (2009). Identifikasi Kesiapan Penerapan Knowledge Management di Perguruan Tinggi [Identification of knowledge management implementation readiness in higher education]. *Jurnal Ekonomi dan Bisnis*, 15(2), 181–196.

Sveiby, K.-E. (1997). *The new organizational wealth: Managing and measuring knowledge based assets*. San Francisco, CA: Berret Koehler.

Tobing, P.L. (2007). *Knowledge management: Concepts, architecture and implementation* (1st ed.). Yogyakarta, Indonesia: Graha Ilmu.

Educational Administration Innovation for Sustainable Development – Komariah et al. (Eds)
© 2018 Taylor & Francis Group, London, ISBN 978-1-138-57341-3

Development of a spirituality-based leadership model for senior high school principals

Ridhwansyah, Gusril, J. Jama, Rusdinal & N. Gistituati
Universitas Negeri Padang, Padang, West Sumatra, Indonesia

ABSTRACT: The purpose of this study is to develop a leadership model for principals of senior high schools based on spiritual intelligence, practicality and effectiveness. The research method used a staged development procedure, based on an ADDIE (Analysis, Design, Development, Implementation and Evaluation) model. The subjects of the research were headmasters of senior high schools in Merangin district, Indonesia. Data were analyzed using qualitative and quantitative methods. As a result of this study, a leadership model for headmasters based on spiritual intelligence was successfully built and declared valid by experts with a validation value of 86.67% (very good) in relation to the principal leadership material. Furthermore, the validation of the principal leadership program scored an average of 4.03, equating to an achievement level of 80.62%, placing it in the 'good' category. Validation of leadership design based on spiritual intelligence with an average score of 4.0 with achievement 87.80% with very valid category.

1 INTRODUCTION

Effective, high-quality and popular schools cannot be separated from the role of the principal. In general, if a school is led by an effective principal, the success of the organization in achieving its goals reflects this more determined leader. Thus, a successful leader is able to utilize all of their abilities in managing all supporting resources and is able to understand the advantages and disadvantages of themselves as an individual, as part of various groups, and in their wider social environment.

The government is now stepping up its efforts to renew national education and create a more harmonious system that supports national development programs. The entire education system is undergoing change and readjustment. What is sought is effectiveness, productivity, relevance, and efficiency in the implementation of education. With a better and directed national education system, it is expected to produce improved Indonesian human resources that are able to compete with those of other nations In the context of these education system changes, the study of headmaster leadership is interesting and valuable, because: (1) school success is determined by leadership; (2) a school is a complex and unique organization requiring a leader with a distinctive leadership style.

The issue of headmaster leadership today is very interesting in terms of the role, function and the different issues facing those with the responsibility of such a position. As the main leader of a school, the headmaster has been shown to play a key role in improving school quality. The principal plays a very important role in implementing the quality of education as well as individuals who are above the components within the organization of the school.

Bezy (2011) reported on a Delphi study designed to identify the characteristics, behaviors, and work environments of spiritual leaders. Likewise, Frisdiantara and Sahertian (2012) emphasized the importance of spiritual leadership in relation to other theories of leadership, and the purpose of this article is to further explore the concept of spiritual leadership in an academic setting.

From the analysis of the organizational structure from the central level to the school level, as well as the decision-making mechanisms and authority possessed, the principals of senior high schools are still waiting for the above guidelines, resulting in ineffective and inefficient school management. Whereas the implementation of education becomes the responsibility of the principal, namely: (1) management functions; (2) administrative functions; (3) supervision functions; (4) teaching and special service functions.

In fact, as supreme leader figures, many school principals are not equipped with good leadership skills and managerial knowledge, due to lack of training and an appointment process for principals that overstates ranking sequences and ignores other important factors such as insight and ability to lead institutions.

A leader is someone who is able to actualize their power capacity intelligently. Leaders must be able to combine soft power through persuasion, encouragement and motivation with hard power, which may include sanctions, assertiveness and threats. Leadership qualities, good performance and the ability to use power intelligently should immediately replace the wailing declamation and bad prose that has been inscribed.

There is a selection of various alternative models of leadership styles to choose from. The election of leadership by the principal of senior high school through various actions as a model, or leadership to carry out his or her actions, which consist of (1) mission, (2) meaning, (3) existence, (4) resources, (5) structure, (6) power, and (7) completeness. Leadership during the senior high school conflict. Principals can use their leadership to ensure the sustainability of schools amidst the intense competition between schools and the efforts of certain parties to fight for the trust of the community in conducting education.

Nevertheless, the success of the actions undertaken by the principal cannot be separated from teacher support and the stern and transparent attitude of the principal. The ambience of the School Circle being sought remains conducive. So the image of an effective, high-quality and popular school cannot be separated from the role of a school's head.

Fry et al. (2007) describe spiritual leadership as an emerging paradigm that has the potential to guide organizational transformation and positive organizational development in which human well-being and organizational performance can not only coexist, but can be maximized.

2 METHODOLOGY

The research method used was a staged development procedure, based on the ADDIE model: Analysis, Design, Development, Implementation and Evaluation. The subjects of research were, overall, the headmasters of senior high schools in Merangin district who are members of the principals' meeting workgroup. Data were analyzed using a qualitative and quantitative descriptive data approach with percentage formulas.

3 RESULTS AND DISCUSSION

Based on the research conducted, the following is a description of the results of the development of a model of leadership-based spiritual intelligence in principals of senior high schools.

The leadership of the principals in Merangin senior high schools is generally in the low category, especially in terms of exerting influence on subordinates, with praise rarely given to subordinates or teachers, and exemplary personality including less category. The spiritual intelligence of the principal can be seen in Table 1, which presents the results of observation of the principals' performance.

Based on Table 1, it can be concluded that the lower level of spiritual intelligence of the principal results from a lack of high levels of awareness in performing flexible duties and abilities, as well as the ability to deal with and overcome pain. However, overall, all spiritual intelligence needs development.

In the analysis, we conducted needs analysis, contextual analysis, and theory analysis. From the data found through questionnaires involving needs analysis, it can be concluded that the respondents

Table 1. Principal performance observation.

No.	Principal performance capability	Average	Achievement	Criteria
1	Personality and social	19.22	76.82	Enough
2	Leadership learning	39.17	78.35	Enough
3	School development	23.39	66.83	Low
4	Resource management	28.93	72.34	Enough
5	Entrepreneurship	20.87	69.57	Low
6	Entrepreneurship	13.60	68.00	Low

Table 2. Tests of validity of headmaster leadership model.

Product	No. of validators	Average	ICC
Model book	4	3.46	0.860
Guidebook	4	3.23	0.719
Program	4	4.32	0.726
Design model	4	4.00	

really need against the purpose of this model. Table 2 presents the needs of respondents in relation to the purpose of the model being assessed.

Table 2 generally describes the validation of products assessed by experts, including the validation of the model book, manual, program and design model. Based on spiritual intelligence, including very practical categories, the principal model obtained an average score of 4.33 which equates to an achievement rate of 86.67% in relation to the evaluation model. At each stage, we carried out evaluation, assessing the suitability between analysis and design, between design and development, and between development and implementation. In the implementation phase, we evaluated the learning in terms of both process and result, to see the suitability of the implementation of the model in comparison with its design. We evaluated the results using a pretest and a post-test to assess the achievement levels of respondents before and after training in this model.

Field findings among the respondents concluded that the principals of senior high schools in Merangin district had not incorporated the material being studied. This is evidence of the need to present a model book of principal leadership with the aim of improving the principals' competence in leadership, based on spiritual intelligence, and as a coaching tool that can assist principals in providing guidance to teachers. From the results of the study, we concluded that the model developed in this study was valid, practical and effective in accordance with the development of leadership models based on spiritual intelligence.

First, the area of positive knowledge of the organization and workplace spirituality are discussed as two areas in the field of organizational study that have important implications for servant leadership. Tabroni (2005) states that the principal (leader) is required to have an ethical attitude toward God in realizing spirituality-based leadership, namely: (1) faith, (2) taqwa (piety), (3) sincerity, (4) tawakkal (trust in God), (5), (6) patience, (7) repentance, (8) remembrance, and (9) ridho. While Kardhawi (in Faith, 2003) states the purpose of spiritual leaders is as follows: (1) faith (belief in God), which is the nature of man; (2) the faithful have a true purpose in life; (3) faith will give birth; (4) faith will generate optimism. Based on the opinions expressed by some of the experts above, this research focuses on the aspects of thought that are fitrah (faith), wisdom in performing duties, and tolerance of others, as indicators of spiritual intelligence.

Leadership can be seen namely leadership-oriented task and leadership style oriented subordinates (Wahjosumidjo, 2002). Ohio University divides leadership into two dimensions: initiation and consideration structures. The initiation structure refers to the leader's behavior in describing the relationship between themselves and their staff in establishing a well-defined channel of communication and procedure, whereas consideration refers to behaviors that show friendship, mutual trust, respect, and warmth in the relationship between the principal and their teachers.

The findings in this study are supported by a study from Ginanjar (2001). Spiritual intelligence involves the ability to live the deepest truth. That is, to manifest the best, whole, and most human in the mind that produces ideas, energy, values, visions and the call of life that flows from within. Further, it gives meaning to the worship of every behavior and activity, through the steps and thoughts towards the whole human, and has a pattern of thinking monotheism: "just because God Almighty".

The study was also supported by the research of Sariakin (2005) who reported a significant relationship between spiritual intelligence and the leadership style of senior high school headmasters in the city of Batu. Sariakin concluded that the higher the spiritual intelligence of the high school principal in Batu, the better and more mature their style of leadership, especially in terms of understanding. Being fast and responsive in implementing the rules or existing norms made for a better leadership style. In addition, the principal who lacks the ability to optimize elements of spiritual intelligence, such as responsibility, and high working morale, has only an adequate leadership style. The best leadership model is oriented towards others, where the principal tends to pay attention to team maintenance and ensures that all people get satisfaction in every job.

Employment and leadership-oriented employees or people with various coaching actions and tend to pay less attention to necessary work procedures (Sule & Saefullah, 2008).

In addition, the principal prioritizes the leadership style of coaching, where the leader coaches by showing the goals to be achieved and ways to achieve the target by involving followers in solving the problems that are being faced (Siagian, 2001). The approach to coaching uses a religious path, with immersion in Islamic values. So the leadership that skewed with a collaborative style of coaching, democracy and free control. This is in contrast to a study which states that the benchmarks used for a leader have four dimensions: cognitive skills, interpersonal skills, business skills, and strategic skills.

To implement the expertise possessed by a leader, the leadership must be able to organize the available human resources, organize the implementation of activities, and organize the available infrastructure facilities. However, in this research, to implement the expertise possessed by a leader, the leadership must understand religion well.

The school administration activities that must be managed by the principal include preparing teachers for workshops, developing syllabus and lesson plans, creating and developing curricula, creating UN value analysis, creating remedial and enrichment programs, creating textbooks, scheduling supervision programs, socializing with teachers, conducting overall socialization, following up supervision findings with personal/group coaching, and providing evaluation/supervision implementation schedules, all conducted with friendly and patient individual approach. This shows that in influencing others the headmaster has shown a sense of love and defends and protects his subordinates, which is one of the characteristics of Islamic leadership: the leader who defends the *ummah* (community).

By conducting gatherings with other schools or comparative studies of MOUs with educational institutions, creating a model of learning, creating training, grouping students at the middle and lower levels, the principal shows that they want real change, which is in accordance with the principal's role as an innovator. By providing motivation to teachers, staff and students through regular coaching, official meetings, family meetings, flag ceremonies and modeling of good deeds, the principal demonstrates his or her role as a motivator.

Based on these ideas, it can be seen that in their leadership practice of Muhammadiyah 1 Surakarta Junior High School, the principal has performed their role as Educator, Manager, Administrator, Supervisor, Leader, Innovator, and Motivator (EMASLIM), and all these roles are done by the principal with patience, showing good relationships and protecting subordinates, in an effort to improve the professionalism of the teachers through coaching. Thus the results of this study support research conducted by Patterson (2008), who concluded that in an effort to improve teacher professionalism, the principal must develop strategic planning activities when coaching teachers.

To develop the professionalism of teachers the principal must have an agenda that addresses teacher preparation; these preparations include an explanation of the teacher preparation process with reference to several studies conducted in a classroom that strongly influence teacher training both as a teacher and a student.

Leaders are at the core of management, meaning that management will achieve its goal if there is a leader. Leadership can only be executed by a leader. A leader is a person who has the ability to influence the opinion of a person or group of people without being asked the reasons. A leader is someone who actively makes plans, coordinates, conducts experiments and leads the work to achieve goals together. George R. Terry, as quoted by Thoha (2010), defines leadership as an activity to influence people toward the goals of an organization. Robbins, as quoted by Danim and Suparno (2009), defines leadership as the ability to influence groups towards the achievement of goals. Owens defines leadership as an interaction between the leader and those being led, while James Lipham, as followed by M. Ngalim Purwanto, defines leadership as the beginning of a new structure or procedure for achieving or changing the goals and objectives of an organization. Mulyasa (2004) defines leadership as an activity to influence people who are directed towards achievement of organizational goals.

Anita E. Woolfolk argues that according to the old theories, intelligence incorporates three things, namely: (1) the ability to learn; (2) overall knowledge gained; (3) ability to adapt successfully to new situations or the environment in general. Furthermore, Woolfolk argues that intelligence involves one or more abilities to acquire and use knowledge in order to solve problems and adapt to the environment. Therefore, intelligence is not an object that can be seen or counted; intelligence is potential – it can be considered a potential at a cell level – which may or may not be activated, depending on the values of a particular culture, the opportunities available in that culture, and the decisions made by the person and/or family, the schoolteacher and others. Likewise, spiritual emotional intelligence is the potential that exists within man to shape his character with fellow creatures of God to face and solve the problems of meaning and value, placing human behavior and life in the context of a wider and richer meaning; judging that the actions or way of life of one person is more meaningful than another.

Within this framework, it can be concluded that the Emotional Spiritual Quotient (ESQ) model is the ability of human reason according to the sensitivity of the heart that its existence is always in contact with other people, other creatures, and the natural surroundings based on the strength of faith in God. Ginanjar (2001) defines the ESQ model as an emotional and spiritual dilation with a universal concept capable of delivering satisfactory predicates for himself and others, and can inhibit everything counterproductive to the progress of mankind. Thus, the ESQ model is the human ability that includes the emotional and spiritual intelligence that can construct things and can also inhibit counterproductive things for himself and for others based on the strength of faith in God.

This research was conducted in relation to principals of senior high schools of Merangin district by applying a leadership model based on spiritual intelligence. This study has several limitations, including: (1) the implementation of a leadership guidance model based on spiritual intelligence is still limited because the only respondents to date have been high school principals; (2) the development of a leadership model based on spiritual intelligence is limited to the improvement of school headmaster competence in implementing leadership; (3) the principals' mastery as described in this study is limited to mastery in terms of exercising spirituality-based leadership.

4 CONCLUSION

The development and application of a leadership model based on spiritual intelligence creates a requirement for principals to change their pattern of leadership. As the director of activities in a school, the principal must have a high commitment and earnestly improve the quality of school-based spirituality. This model can provide supplements to help principals in spirituality-based leadership. In this case, of course, teachers should be more confident in carrying out leadership.

Based on the conclusions of this study, we provide the following suggestions:

(1) For the principal of senior high schools of Merangin district, it is better to study this model because this model can be used as a supplement in assisting the principal in carrying out their leadership. This model can also be studied independently and repeatedly according to the ability of the principal.
(2) For the high school supervisors of Merangin district, this model should be used as a reference in the guidance given to principals.
(3) For the government and city Education Office, this model should be used as material for the development and improvement of principals' competence, especially in leadership.
(4) For Quality Assurance Institution School and madrasah education, it is recommended that this model be developed in the future according to technological developments and the needs of principals.

REFERENCES

Ary, D., Jacobs, L.C. & Razavieh, A. (1985). *Introduction to research in education.* New York, NY: Holt, Rinehart and Winston.
Bezy, K.G. (2011). *An operational definition of spiritual leadership* (Unpublished doctoral thesis). Educational Leadership and Policy Studies, Virginia Polytechnic Institute and State University, Blacksburg, VA. Retrieved from https://vtechworks.lib.vt.edu/handle/10919/26865
Boyatzis, R.E., Goleman, D. & Rhee, K. (1999). Clustering competence in emotional intelligence: Insights from the Emotional Competence Inventory (ECI). In R. Bar-On and J.D.A. Parker (Eds.), *Handbook of emotional intelligence* (pp. 343–362). San Francisco, CA: Jossey-Bass.
Burke, W.W. (1965). Leadership behavior as a function of the leader, the follower, and the situation. *Journal of Personality*, 33, 60–81.
Danim, S. & Suparno. (2009). *Manajemen dan Kepemimpinan Transformasional Kekepala Sekolahan.* Jakarta, Indonesia: Rineka Cipta.
Freeman, G.T. (2011). Spirituality and servant leadership: A conceptual model and research proposal. *Emerging Leadership Journeys*, 4(1), 120–140.
Frisdiantara, C. & Sahertian, P. (2012). The spiritual leadership dimension in relation to other value-based leadership in organization. *International Journal of Humanities and Social Science*, 2(15), 285–290.
Fry, L.W., Matherly, L.L., Whittington, J.L. & Winston, B.E. (2007). Spiritual leadership as an integrating paradigm for servant leadership. In S. Singh-Sengupta & D. Fields (Eds.) *Integrating spirituality and organizational leadership* (pp. 70–82). Noida, India: Macmillan India.
Ginanjar, A. (2001). *Rahasia Sukses Membangun Kecerdasan Emosi dan Spiritual (ESQ)* (Vol. 1). Jakarta, Indonesia: Arga Wijaya Persada.
Malone, P.N. & Fry, L.W. (2003). *Transforming schools through spiritual leadership: A field experiment.* Paper presented at the 2003 Meeting of the Academy of Management, Seattle, WA. Retrieved from http://iispiritualleadership.com/transforming-schools-through-spiritual-leadership-a-field-experiment/
Siagian, S.P. (2001). *Manajemen Sumber Daya Manusia.* Jakarta, Indonesia: Bumi Aksara.
Sternberg, R.J. (2005). WICS: A model of positive educational leadership comprising wisdom, intelligence, and creativity synthesized. *Educational Psychology Review*, 17(3), 191–262.
Sule, E.T. & Saefullah, K. (2008). *Pengantar Manajemen* (1st ed.). Jakarta, Indonesia: Kencana Predana Media Group.
Szu-Fang, C. (2013). Essential skills for leadership effectiveness in diverse workplace development. *Online Journal for Workforce Education and Development*, 6(1).
Tabroni. (2005). *The spiritual leadership.* Malang, Indonesia: UMM Press.
Thoha, M. (2010). *Perilaku organisasi: Konsep Dasar dan Aplikasinya.* Jakarta, Indonesia: Grafindo Persona.
Wahjosumidjo. (2002). *Kepemimpinan Kepala Sekolah.* Jakarta, Indonesia: PT Raja Grafindo Persad.

Educational Administration Innovation for Sustainable Development – Komariah et al. (Eds)
© 2018 Taylor & Francis Group, London, ISBN 978-1-138-57341-3

Educational service ethics index of undergraduate programs in private universities

E. Rusyani & Y. Arifin
Universitas Pasundan, Bandung, West Java, Indonesia

T.C. Kurniatun
Universitas Pendidikan Indonesia, Bandung, Indonesia

ABSTRACT: This study aims to measure an ethical index of educational services in undergraduate programs in private universities. The research method applied is a quantitative approach, using an indexed measurement and students as respondents. Overall, the ethical index of services in the undergraduate programs of private universities in Bandung, Indonesia, is categorized as good but there are still several weaknesses.

1 INTRODUCTION

The challenges faced by private universities have been widely discussed. The challenge for private universities in China is related to how to build trust, ownership and supervision (Lin et al., 2005). In Africa, the challenge for private universities is the increase in the number of applicants as well as the constraints in providing good facilities and services. Further research in Australia shows attention being paid to aspects of ethics in services at the university. These ethical issues are, among others, related to dishonesty and non-compliance in staff and student behavior, and ethical conflicts within the organization.

In higher education services, the ethical aspect is very important due to increasing awareness of the importance of ethical education (Siegel & Watson, 2003; Keenan, 2015). Concern among students about ethical aspects is also increasing in relation to learning. This is related to criticisms of the implementation of education that education services currently face: (1) low curriculum relevance; (2) low lecturers' commitment to teaching; (3) lowered institutional responsibilities to the wider community. In addition, universities also face challenges of accessibility, and expansion in the community, and universities are beginning to face the issue of service non-conformity (Bennis & O'Toole, 2005). Indicators in education service ethics are: honesty, clarity, fulfillment of program commitment promises, service recovery systems, service encounter education services, lecturer ethics, program ethics, and customer service ethics (Kurniatun & Heriyati, 2011). Another study on ethics in college was conducted by Au et al. (2006) who reviewed the business ethics at the faculty level. Although research on ethics in universities has been done, research on the measurement of a service ethics index is still rarely done.

The purpose of this study is to create an educational service ethics index for private universities, especially in relation to undergraduate programs. This measurement can then provide guidance for understanding the character of ethical implementations in universities, as well as providing direction on which aspects of their ethics should be improved.

2 RESEARCH METHOD

This research uses a quantitative approach by employing an ethical index measurement tool. The research was conducted at private universities in Bandung city, West Java, Indonesia. The value of

Table 1. Higher education service ethics indicators.

No.	Higher education service ethics indicator
1	Honesty
2	Clarity
3	Fulfillment of program commitment promises
4	Service recovery systems
5	Lecturers' ethics
6	Program ethics
7	Customer service ethics

Table 2. Perception values, EI intervals, value of service ethics, and ethics performance of higher education units.

Perception value	EI interval	Interval value of EI conversion	Value of service ethics	Ethics performance of higher education units
1	1.00–2.25	25–56.4	D	Not Good
2	2.26–3.51	56.5–87.9	C	Less Good
3	3.52–4.77	88–119.4	B	Good
4	4.78–6.00	119.5–150	A	Very Good

the higher education service Ethics Index (EI) is calculated using a "weighted average score" of each service ethical indicator, as listed in Table 1.

For the calculation of a student service ethical index of the service ethics indicators studied, each service ethics indicator is assigned the same weighting according to the following formula:

$$\text{Weighted average value} = \frac{amount\ of\ weight}{number\ of\ indicators}$$

$$= \frac{1}{7}$$

$$= 0.14$$

To obtain the value of EI for private higher education, a weighted average value approach with the following formula is used:

$$EI = \frac{Total\ of\ Perception\ Values\ Per\ Indicator}{Total\ Indicator\ filled} \times \text{Value scale}$$

To facilitate the interpretation of EI assessment with values between 25 and 100, the result of the valuation above is converted to a base value of 25 with the following formula:

$$\text{EI higher education unit} \times 25$$

The resulting perceptions of ethical index achievement are categorized as shown in Table 2.

3 RESULTS AND DISCUSSION

This research identifies ethical indicators in educational services at universities and then formulates an index of higher education service ethics that can be used to identify the level of service ethics in the implementation of education in universities. The findings of the education services ethics index for five private universities (A–E) are shown in Table 3.

Table 3. Ethics index of private universities.

No.	Indicator	Description	Private university index					Average private university ethics index
			A	B	C	D	E	
1	Honesty	Consists of 6 questions that identify the suitability of physical condition of campus buildings, study rooms, library rooms, and teaching and learning methods based on information.	0.53	0.52	0.67	0.48	0.60	0.56
2	Clarity	Consists of 6 questions that identify information received about campus building & infrastructure conditions, study spaces, library rooms, learning facilities, curricula, and teaching methods.	0.54	0.53	0.67	0.61	0.62	0.57
3	Program fulfills its promised commitments	Consists of 7 questions that identify seriousness in providing good campus buildings, building facilities, and learning facilities, as well as concern for academic issues, responsibility in the implementation of education, and improving teaching and learning processes.	0.58	0.53	0.71	0.51	0.60	0.59
4	Service recovery systems	Consists of 5 questions that identify the level of failure recovery in user facility services, libraries, study spaces, and academic and educational administration.	0.54	0.51	0.68	0.51	0.59	0.57
5	Lecturers' ethics	Consists of 8 questions that identify whether lecturers provide opportunities for students to ask questions, discuss and convey opinions, treat students objectively, speak politely and wisely, motivate, and do not prioritize personal interests.	0.66	0.60	0.70	0.58	0.63	0.63
6	Program ethics	Consists of 4 questions that identify program/department/program information in respect of student rights, treating students fairly, maintaining the confidentiality of academic information, and providing information related to the learning process.	0.63	0.58	0.70	0.57	0.63	0.62
7	Customer service ethics	Consists of 2 questions that identify whether staff interact politely and keep academic information confidential.	0.58	0.55	0.71	0.56	0.65	0.61
	Total ethics of private universities index							4.16

Based on Table 3 we can identify the overall value of the EI of these private universities as 4.16. This means that the value of education services of private higher education, or the EI performance, is categorized as "B" or 'Good'. The highest-scoring average indicator is for lecturers' ethics, while the lowest relates to honesty. The aspects of honesty in question are the correlation between the physical facilities promised on promotional materials and the existing conditions on the ground.

The implementation of this ethics index suggests that universities have sought to adhere to ethical principles as part of educational practice in college. This is in line with community expectations that universities need to show responsibility to the community (Ferrell, 2001). It is important to build a college value (Bennis & O'Toole, 2005; Galloway & Wearn, 2005). Furthermore, values are a very important aspect for universities in building trust and image in the community, and improving their competitiveness (Mennon, 1997, 2008; Hubber & Herman, 2001; Chung & Ho, 2010). Some aspects of ethics that still have lower scores are clarity and honesty. This indicates that conformity between the initial promotional information and existing conditions is a concern for students when assessing the ethics of a university.

4 CONCLUSION

Indicators of service ethics in the educational services of higher education consist of honesty, clarity, fulfillment of program commitments, service recovery systems, lecturer ethics, program ethics, and customer service ethics. An ethics index of private university services can be used to identify the level of service ethics in the implementation of education in universities. Based on the findings obtained, the service ethics of private universities in Bandung are in the good category. However, there are still some weaknesses, particularly in the aspects of honesty and clarity, where honesty concerns the correlation between the facilities offered and those actually delivered, and clarity concerns the completeness of information at every stage of the educational services.

REFERENCES

Au, A.K.M, Chan, A.K.K. & Tse, A.C.B. (2006). Business ethics of university professors in China: A preliminary analysis. *Journal of Asia Entrepreneurship and Sustainability*, 2(3), 63–71.
Bennis, W.G & O'Toole, J. (2005). How business schools lost their way. *Harvard Business Review, May*, 96–104.
Chung, F.-S., Hung, Y.-P. & Ho, E.S.-C. (2010). To work or to continue to higher education? The choice of senior secondary students in Shenzhen China. *Higher Education*, 39, 455–467.
Ferrell, O.C. (2001). Marketing ethics and social responsibility. In S. Dibb, L. Simkin, W.M. Pride & O.C. Ferrell (Eds.), *Marketing: Concepts & strategies* (pp. 755–779). Boston, MA: Houghton Mifflin.
Galloway, R.L. & Wearn, K. (1998). Determinant of quality perception in educational administration. *Educational Management and Administration*, 26(1), 35–48.
Keenan, J.F. (2015). *University ethics: How colleges can build and benefit from a culture of ethics*. Lanham, MD: Rowman & Littlefield.
Kurniatun, T. & Heriyati, P. (2011). The ethics of the promise in the Service Marketing Triangle and its effect on value and customer intention. *Acta Universitatis Bohemiae Meridionales*, 15(1), 43–53.
Lin, J., Zhang, Y., Gao, L. & Liu, Y. (2005). Trust, ownership, and autonomy: Challenges facing private higher education in China. *China Review*, 5(1), 61–81.
Siegel, B.L. & Watson, S.C. (2003). Terms of the contract: The role of ethics in higher education. *Journal of Executive Education*, 2(1), 11–16. Retrieved from http://digitalcommons.kennesaw.edu/jee/vol2/iss1/7

Implementation of organization development of public elementary schools according to school management standards

R. Rusdinal & Y. Santoso

Universitas Negeri Padang, Padang, West Sumatra, Indonesia

ABSTRACT: This article discusses the implementation of organization development of public elementary schools based on management standards according to government regulation of the Indonesia Republic number 19 of 2005, which looked at five aspects: program planning, program implementation, supervision and evaluation, leadership, and management information systems. The population of this research is all public elementary schools in West Sumatera Province, which amounted to 392 schools with total sample of 124 schools. The respondents were the principals. Samples were taken using the proportional technique of stratified random sampling. The data was collected using questionnaires that have been tested for their validity and reliability. Data was analyzed using the descriptive statistic technique. The results of this study describe that in general the implementation of the organization development in public elementary schools based on the school management standard has been done well, but there are some indicators of school management standards that it has not been implemented properly.

1 INTRODUCTION

The purpose of organization development generally is to achieve the goals of the organization. In addition, the organizational development goal is to improve the quality, effectiveness, and accountability of the organization for its stakeholders (Grint, 1997). This means that the organization's development is inseparable from efforts to improve organizational performance.

The development of school organizations is undertaken by adopting new ideas, models, ways, or methods to improve organizational effectiveness (Owen, 1991). The ideas, models, methods or new ways of being adopted may be derived from the analysis of the organization itself or they may apply a policy and approach developed by others. It is based on the consideration that adoption can improve the best quality of school organization effectiveness. Implementation of school management standards as part of the national education standard policy in Indonesia requires an organizational development process so that the policy is implemented effectively.

The meaning of the national standard of education is the minimum criteria of the Indonesian Republic education system based on (Government Regulation number 19, 2005). This research is related to the implementation of one of the national education standards in Indonesia consisting of five aspects/indicators, (1) program planning, (2) program implementation, (3) supervision and evaluation, (4) leadership, and (5) management information system (Government Regulation number 19 of 2005).

The development of school organizations based on the standards of school management is still a massive debate among educational actors. This is demonstrated by various evaluations from the public that education in Indonesia has not fulfilled the specified quality assurance although there are already mandated management standards.

This study is intended to prove whether elementary schools have been undertaking school organizational development based on National Education Standards, by making efforts to ensure the quality of national education that has the purpose to educate the nation's life and shape the character and civilization of a dignified nation.

Thus, this research should be able to provide input to the stakeholders of education in other institutions about the effort that must be done in developing the school organization based on the national standard of education instructed by the government.

2 RESEARCH METHOD

This study uses quantitative methods that aim to describe the implementation of school organizational development seen from education management standards based on national standards of education that has been established by the government. This research was conducted at a public elementary school in Pesisir Selatan Regency of Sumatera Barat Province, which has a total of 392 schools. The respondents are the principals. Given the large number of schools, this study just used a sample of 124 schools. The size of this sample is determined by using the Cohran's formula with the Stratified Proportional Random Sampling technique (Cochran, 1977).

The data of this study was collected using questionnaires that have been tested for their validity and reliability. The data collected was analyzed using the descriptive statistical technique using SPSS.

3 RESEARCH RESULT

The results of research on the implementation of organizational development in public elementary schools based on management standards was reviewed from five indicators as follows.

The results of the analysis of school program planning showed that it is done well. The analysis of 124 respondents showed, 37 respondents (56.45%) stated that it was good, 15 respondents (12.10%) stated that it was enough, 1 respondent (0.81%) stated it was less than enough and 1 respondent (0.81%) stated that it was not good. Based on the above description it can be concluded that the school program planning is done well.

Likewise, the results of the analysis of the implementation of the school program showed that it performed well. Given the results of the analysis of 124 respondents, 44 respondents (35.48%) stated very well, 66 respondents (53.23%) stated good, 13 respondents (10.48%) stated that it was enough, and 1 respondent (0.81%) stated that it was not good. It can be therefore concluded that the implementation of school activities performed well.

The results of the analysis on monitoring and evaluation of the program showed that it performed well. The result of analysis shows that from 124 respondents obtained as many as 51 respondents (41.13%) stated that it was very good, 65 respondents (52.42%) stated good, 7 respondents (12.10%) stated enough, and 1 respondent (0.81%) stated not good. Based on the above description it can be concluded that the supervision and evaluation of the program performed well.

The analysis of the school leadership is that it is done very well. From the analysis of 124 respondents, 64 respondents (51.61%) stated very well, 53 respondents (42.74%) stated good, 5 respondents (4.03%) stated enough, and the remaining 1 respondent (0.81%) stated that it was not good. Based on the above description it can be concluded that the school program planning is done very well.

The result of the analysis of the management information system indicator on elementary education level showed that from the 124 respondents, as many as 35 respondents (33.06%) stated very good, 61 respondents (49.19%) stated good, 22 respondents (17.74%) stated enough, 4 respondents (3.23%) stated less than enough and 2 respondents (1.61%) stated that it was not good. Based on the above description it can be concluded that the management information system is done well.

4 DISCUSSION

According to the results of data analysis on the organizational development of public elementary school based on school management standards reviewed from 5 indicators namely: (1) program planning, (2) program implementation, (3) monitoring and evaluation, (4) leadership, and (5) management information system, generally it can be concluded that is in the good category. Although it has been going well, there are still some aspects that should be brought to the attention of the principal in order to develop the school organization. For example, the availability of facilities and infrastructure for students' extracurricular activities, which has not met the specified standards. The implementation of extracurricular activities requires the support of the availability of facilities and infrastructure. This includes the all the physical, social, and cultural facilities that are required to realize the educational process in an educational unit (Rifai & Murni, 2009). In addition, the elements of infrastructure such as land, buildings, sports infrastructure and arts infrastructure, and other infrastructures must be considered.

Furthermore, related to the active role of the community in supporting non-academic activities conducted by the school should also be improved by the school. Schools are expected to be able to explore and manage all kinds of parent and community participation in supporting the success of school programs in accordance with their respective needs, in the form of the participation of mind, energy, property, skills and social participation. Educational leadership is key to addressing the persistent inequities in low-income urban schools, but most principals struggle to work with parents and communities around those schools to create socially just learning environments (Ann, 2013). Efforts are needed to increase parents and community participation, in order to create a harmonious relationship and cooperation between schools and communities. Surely this is supported by the principal's managerial skills and professional staff to create quality school programs to increase community participation.

The availability of adequate and accessible management information system facilities still needs to be improved by schools. This certainly affects the principal decision-making process. Completeness of this information system facility can help the policy makers in education area to decide upon the right strategy to be applied in the control and monitoring of education components.

5 CONCLUSSION

Based on data analysis and discussion, it can be concluded that the implementation of the development of school organizations based on management standards at the level of primary school in general runs well. However, from some management indicators there are still some things that should be the focus of attention for improvement. For example, it is necessary for the role of the principal to always provide input and encourage teachers to further increase their attention to teacher achievement motivation by improving teacher commitment to tasks and improving collaboration between teachers and all school staff so that the implementation of school programs runs well (Northouse, 2007).

Besides that it is necessary to improve teachers' commitment to the task through qualifications enhancing in order to improve the successful implementation of school programs, to develop professional teachers by organizing and attending trainings and seminars (Kouzes & Posner, 2004). Teachers working group and deliberation of principal's work activities are an important role in improving the competence of teacher. Professional development is the catalyst for transforming theory into current best teaching practices. In order to provide effective professional development, there are many variables that must he considered by the school principal including teacher beliefs and receptivity, the school climate, and available local school support. Ultimately, administrators must focus on linking effective professional development to teacher quality in order to yield student success (Kent, 2004).

REFERENCES

Ann, Ishimaru. (2013). Principals and education organizing in urban school reform. *Sage Journals, 49*(1), 3–5.
Cochran, W.G. (1977). *Sampling technique*. Translation by Rudiansyah. 1991. Jakarta: UI Press.

Government Regulation of the Republic of Indonesia Number 19 of 2005. About National Education Standards.

Grint, K. (1997). Leadership (classical, contemporary and critical approaches). New York, NY: Oxford University Press.

Kent, A.M. (2004). Improving teacher quality through professional development. *Education*, 124(3), 427–435. Retrieved from https://login.e.bibl.liu.se/login?url=https://search.ebscohost.com/login.aspx?direct=true&db=aph&AN=13186498&site=eds-live&scope=site

Kouzes & Posner (2004). *The leadership challenge*. Jakarta, Indonesia: Erlangga.

Northouse, P. (2007). *Leadership theory and practice*. California: Sage Publications Inc.

Owen S.R.G (1991). *Organizational behavior in education* (4th ed.). Gould Street Needham Heights, MA: Prentice Hall Inc.

Rifai, V. & Murni, S. (2009). *Education management*. Jakarta, Indonesia: Raja Gravindo Persada.

Educational Administration Innovation for Sustainable Development – Komariah et al. (Eds)
© 2018 Taylor & Francis Group, London, ISBN 978-1-138-57341-3

E-leadership of Thailand's higher education leaders in 2027

K. Sathithada
Mahidol University, Bangkok, Thailand

ABSTRACT: E-leadership is the technology for communication between leaders and followers in the new environment. The new technology-based work processes are needed in order for virtual teams to succeed. Administrators need to effectively develop both leadership skills and knowledge of technology. The Thailand Information and Communication Technology (ICT) Policy Framework (2001–2010) has guided the development of Thailand's ICT in the first decade of the 21st century, aiming to enhance the economy and quality of life for Thai people toward the 5 E's strategy. In Thailand moving toward 2020, ICT may aid in developing academic content both formally and informally. It can also be used to uplift the management capacity of local education administrators. This research is studied by mix-method methodology with the research objectives to develop e-leadership and to build up future scenarios of e-leadership in Thailand's higher education in 2027.

1 INTRODUCTION

The effective use of technology in the educational field can provide many benefits. Technology has a wide range of uses in such diverse areas as professional development, curriculum alterations, distance learning, and the teaching of skills necessary to have a positive career in our technologically integrated world. Educational technology leaders performing as strong supporters lead the education able to successfully integrate technology into a school system, local school site, or classroom. There is a need for expert individuals to undertake leadership roles and promote technology for educational purposes in order to earn the benefits of technology usage. The research objectives are to develop e-leadership and to build up future scenarios of e-leadership in Thailand's higher education in 2027.

2 DEFINITION

There are many words refer to e-leadership, such as virtual leadership, digital leadership, distance leadership, technological leadership, global virtual team leadership. In this research, the author will use e-leadership, which is defined as form of leading across time, space, and organizational boundaries, usually supported by networks of communication as well as technology. Organizations and their leaders must be ready to deal with globalization and with the exponential explosion of Information and Communication Technology (ICT) (Zaccaro & Bader, 2003). The virtual leaders must acquire new skills that enable them to create and maintain high performance groups, as well as being able to develop a leadership style that takes advantage of the available technologies and minimizes the face-to-face (f2f) environments (Colfax et al., 2009). Because of the exponential increase in technology and its global reach, in the near future e-leadership will become a routine, not an exception (Zaccaro & Bader, 2003). ICT (Information and Communication Technology) today implements these same organization structures electronically across time and space, where it is not only the communication between leader and follower that takes place via information technology, but also the collection and dissemination of information required to support organizational work is discharged via the electronic media (Avolio & Kahai, 2003). Technological leadership is vital for the effective use of technology (Anderson & Dexter, 2005), and therefore, efforts to change and prepare schools and students for the information age demand effective technological leadership from principals (Ross & Bailey, 1996). As described above, in this period of digital technology, e-leadership is gaining significance. Thus, in pursuit of the crucial goal of improving students' abilities, principals aiming to simplify school reform should have technological leadership capabilities.

The emergent of e-leadership has occurred since 1950 and many researchers have discussed the e-leadership concept as follows.

E-leadership builds on the socio-technical systems approach (Trist, 1950, 1993). Avolio et al. (2000) reviewed the literature and noted that "we chose the term e-leadership to incorporate the new emerging context for examining leadership". The authors defined e-leadership as a social influence process mediated by AIT (Advanced Information Technology) to produce a change in attitudes, feelings, thinking, behavior and/or performance with individuals, groups and/or organizations. Pulley and Sessa (2001) explored the impact of digital technology on leadership and identified e-leadership as a complex challenge. According to the authors, perhaps the greatest e-leadership challenge is how to make individuals work cooperatively to create a culture. Zaccaro and Bader (2003) noted that in view of the rapid technology growth in organizations and their increasingly global reach, in the near future e-leadership will be the routine rather than the exception in our thinking about what constitutes organizational leadership. Hambleya et al. (2007) explored the new paradigm of work that can now be conducted anytime, anywhere, in real space or through technology. Carreno, 2008 studied e-mentoring with reference to the virtual leader. The author focused on the use of information and communication technology in an educational settings. The author discussed the main strengths and skills of the virtual leader and their importance in the management of education at a distance. Carreno concluded by formulating a research question on providing leadership to the virtual or distance learning.

E-leadership is the technology for communication between leaders and his or her followers in the new emerging social environment. The technology communication is the related occupations between them. E-leaders should focus on the sustained communication also have and suitable e-environment that accompanied everyplace at any time. The technology is easily accessible and not limited by place and time. E-leadership is able to be accustomed with technologies and technology to current and balance the information during the operation.

3 VIRTUAL TEAMS

Changes in working environments have implied a tendency from individual-based work performance towards a team performance, and an increase in global teams where working methods are claimed to differ from the traditional teams because of their reliance on technology for communicating and disseminating information and knowledge (Jarvempaa & Tanriverdi, 2003). The most common reason for forming virtual teams is to overcome geographical or temporal separations while at the same time reducing office space, travel and time-related costs (Cascio & Shurygailo, 2003). A virtual team is group of people who work interdependently with a shared purpose across space, time, and organizational boundaries using technology (Lipnack & Stamps, 1997). Virtual teams can also be defined as groups of geographically and/or organizationally dispersed co-workers that are assembled using a combination of telecommunications and information technologies to accomplish an organizational task (Townsend et al., 1998). It is also claimed that as virtual teamwork differs from face-to-face teamwork, new technology-based work processes are needed in order to make virtual teams succeed (Nunamaker et al., 2009).

4 COMPONENTS FOR E-LEADERSHIP

There are many dimensions of e-leadership from the view of theorists. Since the theory is very new, these have mostly been discussed in the research.

The research of Matthews (2002) mentioned that effective principals should be (a) actively involved with technology, (b) maintain and model personal technology skills, (c) consult knowledgeable people about technology, (d) use school-level shared decision-making such as a technology committee, and (e) serve as a catalyst to motivate low-use teachers.

Schiller (2000) stated that executives who have e-leadership is expressed in many ways, such as 1) to support technology 2) facilitate changes 3) strategies for teaching and learning 4) resources 5) teacher development.

Kozloski (2006) stated that current technology has become a critical component of management education. School administrators need to effectively develop both leadership skills and knowledge of the technology.

Leaders who are effective in leading across different cultures have relational competence to build common grounds and trust in relationships (Black & Gregersen, 1999; Gregersen et al., 1998; Manning, 2003). "Successful virtual team facilitators must be able to manage the whole spectrum of communication strategies as well as human and social processes and perform these tasks across organizational and cultural boundaries via new (information and communication technologies)" (Pauleen & Yoong, 2001).

5 E-LEADERSHIP IN HIGHER EDUCATION

The university is one of the oldest formal organizations. Leadership of the university therefore has been for centuries grounded on the mutual agreements of the "academics communities". Unlike other organizations that were affected by the industrial revolution in the 19th century, the university maintained its stable core and its primary purpose of providing an environment for teaching, research and scholarly service (Balderston, 1995; Clarke, 1998). In his description of organizational types, Mintzberg (1979, 1983) described the university as a professional bureaucracy. The professional bureaucracy has key features that can be associated with the typical university organization: standardized products and services, high levels of control over the core functions of the organization by the professionals (university faculty), highly democratic and decentralized decision-making processes. The leadership and power reside in the professoriate and there is a small administrative core that services the professoriate (Mintzberg, 1983).

Franciosi (2012) argued that limited attention has been given to leadership frameworks at the school, district, or government level. In a field characterized by technological innovation and change, leadership style is critical to facilitating the successful use of technology that contributes to positive learning outcomes. According to Franciosi (2012), educational leadership should be more flexible to cope with technology-driven changes and developments. Higher education leaders play crucial roles in the adoption of ICT. In a study on the use of ICT in education in Norway researchers found that distributed forms of leadership led to an increased willingness by staff to incorporate ICT into their teaching (Ottestad, 2013).

6 THAILAND HIGHER EDUCATIONAL POLICIES

University caught in a time of rapid technological change need Thai higher education administrators to motivate the use of ICT to operate the influence of computer and internet technology on call operation in Thailand. The technology leader should have the capability to take full advantage of the use and impact of technology. The behavior of leaders is symbolized by a visionary technology that is encouraging stakeholders to participate in the development of technology applications and captivating vision that immensely. Technology is used in the administration daily. Moreover, e-leadership means having the skills of team building and teaching organizations to apply the technology for administration development, to create productive jobs, and to create opportunities to advance the professional development of those technologies used for teaching. A new generation of leaders should understand and recognize the significance of technology now and in the future.

The Commission on Higher Education (2013) reported the policies as follows:

1. To develop people both academically and professionally with skills necessary for the country, community, and local development. Higher education has to encourage students to be intellectual, moralistic and ethical while having creative thinking and pursuing a life-long learning in order to boost the competitiveness of the country.
2. To formulate a body of knowledge and local wisdom for capacity building and encourage research and innovation that supports the country, community, and local development, and also to maintain economic, social and environmental stabilization. Higher education plays a significant role in solving the country's problems and crises, and also promoting Thailand as a regional hub for education.
3. To build a solid foundation for the local and community development that encourages self-reliance and responsibility, and to be able to catch up with the changing world.
4. To improve higher education administration systems both at government and institutional levels that will allow more flexibility and efficiency, and also enhance the quality of higher education and be able to cope with economic, social, political and technological changes. In addition, the private sector and communities are encouraged to play a greater role in delivering higher education.

The Thailand Information and Communication Technology (ICT) Policy Framework (2001–2010) or IT2010 has guided the development of Thailand's ICT in the first decade of the 21st century up to the present. The flagships (the "5 E's strategy") emphasize the development and application of ICTs in five strategic areas, namely, e-Government, e-Industry, e-Commerce, e-Education and e-Society, aiming to enhance the economy and quality of life of the Thai people and lead Thailand towards a knowledge-based economy and society. Furthermore, the development of the policy framework has also considered the technological changes that will occur in this period, in order to assess the impacts of these technological changes on individuals, the economy, industry and social transformation in the country. (The National Information Technology Committee Secretariat, 2002).

The Thailand Information and Communication Technology (ICT) Policy Framework (2011–2020), According to the Ministry of Science and Technology (2011), it noted that Thailand towards 2020 as pertains to the Directions for ICT Development in the second decade of educational reform: The ultimate goal of the education reform is to instill learners with skills that are essential to success in the 21st Century society, i.e. creativity, higher-order thinking, and citizenship. The ICT will have a role in the second phase of education reform in various ways. For instance, computer equipment and internet access will be a necessity in schools and at home. ICT may aid in developing academic content both formally and informally. It can also be used to help uplift the capacity of local education administrators in managing schools. Technology can help upgrade skills in producing quality vocational workers. It can enhance linkages among university information networks toward improved teaching, learning and research. Online, distance education for the disadvantaged and technology-enabled education for People with Disability (PWD) in various ways can be strengthened. Finally, it can also help in enhancing knowledge and skills for youth so that they will become good citizens, by acting with wisdom, morality and ethics, and avoiding bad behavior.

7 CONCLUSION

The current technology has become a critical component of management education. Higher education should take into account the impact of globalization, the development of information and advance communicative technologies, the rapid change in demand in employment, and the critical need for highly qualified educators who have practical experience in their discipline. As higher education continues to realize enrollment expansion, educators, state governments, and business should begin working in a partnership atmosphere (Alexander, 2000). School administrators need to effectively develop both leadership skills and knowledge of the technology. Leaders of institutions of higher education need to comprehend the situation and provide visions of the changes and directions that will be necessary to achieve this current trend.

Hence, the policy of Thailand's higher education is to develop people both academically and professionally with the skills necessary for the country, community, and local development. Higher education plays a significant role in solving the country's crises and also promoting Thailand as a regional hub for education. Thailand's higher education administrators need to motivate the use of ICT to operate the influence of computer and internet technology on call in operation. ICT will have a role in the education reform in various ways. It can also help in enhancing knowledge and skills for the youth so that they will become good citizens, by acting with wisdom, morality and ethics, and avoiding bad behavior. A new generation of leaders should be those who understand and see the significance of technology now and in the future.

There is very little literature on e-leadership in higher education and there is little knowledge and research about e-leadership among Thailand's higher educational leaders. The future research will identify the frontier knowledge of e-leadership that is appropriate for Thai universities. It is because future research can encourage the use of concepts, tools and processes that researcher can think long-term, and consequentially imaginatively. It generally helps researchers to conceptualize more just and sustainable human and planetary futures, develop knowledge and skills in exploring probable and preferred futures, understand the dynamics and influence human, social and ecological systems that have alternative futures, conscientize responsibility and action on the part of researcher toward creating better futures.

REFERENCES

Alexander, F.K. (2000). The changing face of accountability. *The Journal of Higher Education, 71*(4), 411–431.

Anderson, R.E. & Dexter, S.L. (2005). School technology leadership: An empirical investigation of prevalence and effect. *Educational Administration Quarterly, 41*(1), 49–82.

Avolio, B.J. & Kahai, S. (2003). Adding the – "e" to e-leadership: How it may impact your leadership. *Organizational Dynamics, 31*(4).

Avolio, B.J., Kahai, S. & Dodge, G.E. (2000). E-leadership: Implications for theory, research, and practice. *The Leadership Quarterly, 11*(4).

Balderston, F. (1995). *Managing today's universities. Strategies for viability, change and excellence.* San Francisco, CA: Jossey-Bass.

Black, J.S. & Gregersen, H.B. (1999). The right way to manage expats. *Harvard Business Review, 77*(2), 52–57.

Bureau of International Cooperation Strategy: BICS, office of The Higher Education Commission, Thailand. (2013). *Higher Education Policies.* Retrieved from http://inter.mua.go.th/

Carreno, I.G. (2008). *E-mentoring and e-leadership importance in the quality of distance and virtual education Century XXI.* Paper from m-ICTE 2009: Research, Reflections and Innovations in Integrating ICT in Education. Retrieved from http://www.formatex.org/micte2009/book/728-732.pdf

Cascio, W.F. & Shurygailo, S. (2003). E-leadership and virtual teams. *Organizational Dynamics, 31*, 362–367. Retrieved from http://dx.doi.org/10.1016/S0090-2616(02)00130-4

Clarke, B. (1998). *Creating entrepreneurial universities: Organisational pathways of transformation.* New Jersey: Agathon.

Colfax, R.S., Santos, A.T. & Diego, J. (2009). Virtual leadership: A green possibility in critical times but can it really work? *Journal of International Business Research, 8*(2).

Franciosi, S.J. (2012). Transformational leadership for education in a digital culture. *Digital Culture and Education, 4*(2), 235–247.

Gregersen, H.B., Morrison, A.J. & Black, J.S. (1998). Developing leaders for the global frontier. *Sloan Management Review, Fall*, 21–32.

Hambley, L.A., O'Neill, T.A. & Kline, T.J.B. (2007). Virtual team leadership: The effects of leadership style and communication medium on team interaction styles and outcomes, *Organizational Behavior and Human Decision Processes, 103*, 1–20.

Jarvempaa, S.L & Tanriverdi, H. (2003). Leading virtual knowledge networks. *Organizational Dynamics, 31*, 403–412. doi:10.1016/S0090-2616(02)00127-4

Klein, H.K. & Hirschheim, R. (1983). "Issues and Approaches to Appraising Technological Change in the Office: A Consequential Perspective," Office. *Technology and People*, 2, 1524.

Kozloski, C.K. (2006). *Principal leadership for technology integration: A study of principal technology leadership.* (Unpublished PhD Thesis), Drexel University.

Lipnack, J.S., & Stamps, J. (1997). *Virtual teams – Reaching across space, time, and organizations with technology.* New York, NY: Wiley.

Manning, T.T. (2003). Leadership across cultures: Attachment style influences (Electronic Version). *Journal of Leadership & Organizational Studies, 9*(20). Retrieved from LIRN ProQuest.

Matthews, A.W. (2002). *Technology leadership at a junior high school: A qualitative case study.* (Unpublished doctoral dissertation), University of Nevada-Las Vegas, USA.

Ministry of Science and Technology. (2011). *Executive summary Thailand Information and Communication Technology Policy Framework (2011-2020),* Bangkok.

Mintzberg, H. (1979). *The structuring of organizations.* Englewood Cliffs: Prentice-Hall.

Mintzberg, H. (1983). *Structure in fives: Designing effective organizations.* Englewood Cliffs: Prentice- Hall.

Nunamaker, J.F., Reinig, B.A. & Brigg, R.O. (2009). *Principles for effective virtual teamwork. Communications of the acm, 52,* 113–117. doi:10.1145/1498767

Ottestad, G. (2013). School leadership for ICT and teachers' use of digital tools. *Nordic Journal of Digital Literacy, 8*(01–02), 107–125.

Pauleen, D. & Yoong, P. (2001). Facilitating virtual team relationships via Internet and conventional communication channels. *Internet Research: Electronic Networking Applications and Policies 11*(3), 190–202.

Pulley, M.L. & Sessa, V.I. (2001). "E-leadership: tackling complex challenges", *Industrial and commercial Training, 33*(6), 225–230.

Ross, T.W. & Bailey, G.D. (1996). *Technology-based learning: A handbook for teachers and technology leaders (Rev. ed.).* Arlington Heights, IL: IRI/Skylight.

Schiller, J. (2000). *Implementation of computing in schools by primary principals: A longitudinal perspective.* Paper presented at AARE in Sydney, December 8th, 2000. Retrieved from http://www.aare.edu.arc/oopap/sch00254.htm

The National Information Technology Committee Secretariat. (2002). *Information technology policy framework 2001-2010: Thailand vision towards a knowledge-based economy.* Retrived from http://www.nectec.or.th/pld/documents_pris/IT2010eng.pdf

Trist, E.L. (1950). *The relations of social and technical systems in coal-mining.* Paper presented to the British Psychological Society, Industrial Section.

Trist, E.L. (1993). *Guilty of enthusiasm.* In A.G. Bedeiam (ed.), Management laureates: A collection of autobiographical essays (pp. 1991–221). Greenwich, CT: JAI press.

Townsend, A.M., DeMarie, S.M. & Hendrickson, A.R. (1998). Virtual teams: Technology and the workplace of the future. *Academy of Management Executive, 12,* 17–29.

Webber, C.F. (2003). New technologies and educative leadership. *Journal of Educational Administration, 41*(2), 119–123.

Zaccaro, S.J. & Bader, P. (2003). E-leadership and the challenges of leading e-teams: Minimizing the bad and maximizing the good. *Organizational Dynamics, 31*(4), 377–387.

Educational Administration Innovation for Sustainable Development – Komariah et al. (Eds)
© 2018 Taylor & Francis Group, London, ISBN 978-1-138-57341-3

National education quality assurance analysis

D. Satori
Universitas Pendidikan Indonesia, Bandung West Java, Indonesia

ABSTRACT: Quality assurance is becoming essential to ensure the best educational services in meeting or even exceeding the established standards as designed by the system. Guarantee and improvement of the quality of national education is directed at the realization of the implementation of well-designed education, in this case will be focusing on schooling, which provides assurance to generate a well-educated person. Therefore, in order to meet the purpose of quality improvement, data and information on quality assurance must be well-managed, carefully analyzed, accessible, used to encourage planning, decision-making, resource allocation and improvement programs. The quality assurance system should ultimately build a culture of continuous quality improvement in schools and structures that facilitate the delivery of education.

1 EDUCATIONAL QUALITY ASSURANCE AND IMPROVEMENT FOCUS

International studies indicate that educational human resources, especially teachers, are the ones who make the greatest contribution to the educational process and outcomes of learners (Best & Kahn, 2016; Cochran-Smith, et al., 2016; Eisner, 2017). For the above reasons, the scope of the Education Assurance and Quality Improvement System should be directed to guaranteeing and improving quality performance for teachers, principals, and school supervisors, and other personnel in schools (librarians and labors for example) and systems that support their work. School as an organization is a container of professionals and support staff to serve learners to learn (Grannäs & Frelin, 2017). Education Offices at the District and Provincial levels in Indonesia are the tools of local government to facilitate the implementation of education. Similarly, the Office of the Ministry of Religious Affairs in the Regencies/Municipalities and Provincial Offices have same responsibility to facilitate the implementation of education in madrasah.

The current educational development policy shows strong intention to improve the quality of national education (Liu, 2015). The National Education System Act No. 20 of 2003 stipulates that the reconciliation of the quality of the national education is the National Education Standard. In Government Regulation no. 19 of 2005 which has been refined in 2013 on National Education Standards it is stated that 8 (eight) National Standards of education as refer to the development of quality performance of educational unit. Eight National Education Standards (NES) provide a reference for assessing educational attainment, quality of education and areas requiring improved quality of education. The intended NES includes: (1) the content standard, (2) the process standard, (3) the competency standard of the graduate, (3) the standard of the educator and the educational staff, (5) the standard of facilities and infrastructure, (6) school management standards, (7) financing standards, and (8) educational assessment standards. This explains that the Government as the party responsible for organizing national education has set the national standard of education as referring to quality improvement of education.

Assurance and improvement of the quality of education (basic and secondary) is formulated as a series of related processes and actions to collect, analyze and report data on the performance and quality of educators, programs, and institutions. The quality assurance process identifies aspects of achievement and improvement priorities, provides data as a basis for planning and decision making and helps build a culture of continuous improvement. The achievement of education quality for

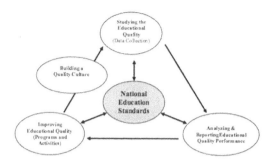

Figure 1.   Educational quality assurance and improvement.

primary and secondary education is assessed based on eight National Education Standards. Quality assurance will contribute to quality improvement. Thus, the essence of quality assurance and improvement for primary and secondary education in Indonesia is related to activities as follow:

1. Assessment of education quality
2. Analysis and reporting of education quality
3. Improving the quality of education
4. Continuous quality improvement

Eight National Education Standards (NES) become a reference for assessing the achievement of education quality performance.

Primary and secondary education in Indonesia operates within a government management context that delegates most of its implementation responsibilities to provinces, districts and schools. To be effective in this policy and management context, the education and quality improvement system needs to provide sufficient flexibility that will allow provincial, district, and school governments to assess and improve quality with priorities reflecting contextual factors and local characteristics.

The diagram above provides a general overview of the relationship cycle of guaranteeing and improving the quality of education.

2   EDUCATIONAL QUALITY ASSURANCE AND IMPROVEMENT CYCLE

One model is offered with the following cycle stages: (1) Program planning, (2) Development of data collection instruments, (3) The design of quality assurance and monitoring program, (4) Data collection and recording, (5) Data verification and analysis, (6) Findings report, (7) Study results of improvement program implementation, (8) Identification of achievements and aspects of development, (9) Develop further quality improvement program, and then back to the initial stage again the program planning. The stages can be seen in figure 2.

It should be reminded here that if applied to educational units, improving the quality of education should be based on the realization of the vision, mission and objectives of the educational unit. With regard to the above cycle can be explained as follows.

2.1   *Program planning*

The program is an elaboration of the vision, mission, and goals of the educational unit. The program is the design of the implementation of activities to realize better conditions in the future. The program contains a series of activities in which clarity of achievement targets, implementing personnel, facilities, costs, time and stages of implementation are included. Program planning begins with the identification of needs which in nature needs to be realistic and contextual.

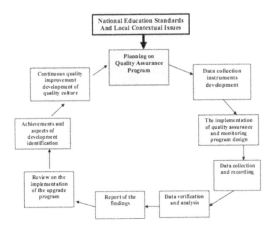

Figure 2. Educational quality assurance and improvement cycle.

2.2 *Development of data collection instruments*

Instruments for measuring the quality of education performance (educational unit) are arranged according to quality standards. Internally, School Self Evaluation (SSE) instruments have been developed for the collection of quality performance data in annual cycles. Externally, National Accreditation Board employs School Accreditation Instruments.

2.3 *The design of quality assurance and program monitoring*

Quality assurance as the needs of educational unit is prepared and implemented by each educational unit. To implement SSE, the school established a Team consisting of teacher representation, School Committee, Principal as coordinator, and School Supervisor as facilitator/resourcefull person. The time for SSE implementation is prepared in accordance with the school calendar. School accreditation is conducted by National Accreditation Board for School/Madrasah, Provincial School/Madrasah Accreditation Board, and Implementing Unit of School/Madrasah Accreditation in regency/municipality. Schools prepare for accreditation needs in such a way as to be in accordance with the terms and procedures in the five-year cycle.

2.4 *Data collection and recording*

In accordance with the instruments used, quality performance data needs to be supported by evidence of quality performance. Empirical evidence that reflects quality performance is grouped according to National Education Standards.

2.5 *Verification and analysis of data*

The data collected consists of qualitative and quantitative data. The verification of the data is formulated with the review team based on the parameters that have been agreed previously.

2.6 *Finding report*

The report of findings reflects the gap of achievement of standards between the position of conformity with performance achievement. For example, the implementation of process standards that should be demonstrated in active, creative, and fun learning, in fact still shows more conventional practices oriented to teacher activity.

2.7 Study result

Study results of improvement program implementation. The gaps found in the sixth stage above require honest acceptance in the context of the reality of performance achievement. Specification of action with achievement must be well understood so that it can be assessed the accuracy of treatment of improvement and improvement of quality performed.

2.8 Identification

Identification of achievements and aspects of development. The achievement of the seventh stage by itself can know the positive changes toward the position of achievement, which is also known the accuracy of actions taken. In this phase it is not impossible to find inhibiting factors caused by low motivation and ability of executor, not only caused by facility availability factor.

2.9 Further development

Further development of quality improvement program, and then back to the initial stage again that is planning program. The identification of factors that support the success or non-achievement of the quality performance positions is an input for the further development of the quality improvement program.

Based on the above description which is accompanied by two picture illustrations, it can be concluded that in the effort of guaranteeing and improving the quality of education, all ranks of education providers should pay attention to the main reference that is the national standard of education.

3 EDUCATIONAL QUALITY ASSURANCE AND IMPROVEMENT STRATEGY

The assurance and quality improvement system uses a variety of data assessment strategies, which, if implemented properly, will provide qualitative and quantitative data on educational performance. The main purposes of collecting quality data, quality data analysis, and reporting phases are as follow:

- Obtained valid and reliable data on the performance of educational institutions and education personnel based on National Education Standards (NESs) for users at all levels.
- Supporting quality improvement initiatives and programs at the school, district/city, provincial and national levels

Where possible, data collection strategies used in the underwriting and quality improvement systems are attempted to reduce complexity, cost, and resources. In the institutional environment many data about education have been collected. Unfortunately the validity and reliability of the data is still in doubt and its use is also not fully effective. Taking into account the problem, two key principles that encourage the development of a guarantee and quality improvement system are as follow:

- Improving data collection strategies so that the data collected becomes relevant, valid, and reliable.
- Ensure a management information system that can maintain up-to-date data.
- Ensure that data are used more effectively for planning purposes, decision-making in planning and resource allocation to improve the quality of education.

To meet the above three principles, it is necessary to develop ways that have clarity in the validity of the contents and construction of data collection instruments and the clarity of processing and utilization of the results of data processing. Below are shown some complementary quality assurance methods. Each method of collecting data and data sources collected in this system has the potential to provide valuable quality assurance information about the performance of educational institutions and education personnel. Different data collection methods can be more appropriately used for collecting data on national educational standards than single assessment methods. Some data collection methods are deemed not always suitable for collecting educational data for certain national education standards. For example, teacher performance appraisal and continuous improvement of the profession emphasizes the effort to build teacher competence comprehensively. This method involves educator standards. The teacher certification program is temporarily believed to support improving well-being which is expected to be conducive to the improvement of professionalism and teacher performance quality. Even if accompanied by a continuous program of professional upgrading (updating) will strengthen its impact on education quality assurance and upgrading. The Center for the Development and Empowerment of Teachers and Education Personnel (CDETEP) and the Institute for Quality Assurance (EQAI) is an institution that has a strategic role in improving and ensuring the quality of education. District Education Offices, Provincial Education Offices, and Data and Information Centers, The Research and Development Agency of the Ministry of Education and Culture collects annual data in accordance with the needs of policy implementation assessments. School/Madrasah accreditation collects data concerning school performance related to eight National Education Standards. The result of accreditation is used as the basis for determining the feasibility of the education unit and the programs stated in the A, B, and C assessment categories. The result of accreditation is very beneficial for the improvement of the quality of educational unit and the education investment planning of the district/city. The school/madrasah accreditation program implemented by the Provincial Accreditation Board gradually encourages schools/madrasah to complement the demands and quality of performance in accordance with 8 (eight) NESs.

School self-evaluation (SSE) is a process of quality improvement driven from within the school. SSE teams collect data with evidence relating to achievement of performance to meet NES achievement. Special studies are especially concerned with their impact on improving educational outcomes of learners (Content Standards, Processes, Graduate Competencies, and Assessments). Likewise, matters that are closely related to quality improvement in schools (Teacher and Education Personnel Standards, Infrastructure, Financing, and Management).

Additional information on school achievement compared with eight NESs is collected from schools through other school data collection strategies ie school monitoring programs undertaken by the District/City and Provincial Education Offices. Selective school assessments were selected and determined on the basis of school performance of self-evaluation and monitoring by District Education Offices. The target school of study is selectively determined to determine the contextual conditions that are the main drivers of prominent achievement, or the inhibiting factors for schools that do not perform and show no significant progress. As it can be seen in figure 3.

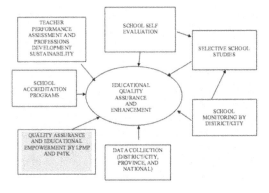

Figure 3.   Data collection strategies for quality assurance and improvement.

Development of Pilot Schools show better orientation on strengthening the program of guarantee and improvement of education quality. A number of well-organized private schools run by the governing body (Educational Foundation), also strengthen efforts to guarantee and improve the quality of education.

Collecting data on quality assurance itself will not lead to an improvement in the quality of education. Therefore, in order to be useful for the purpose of quality improvement, data and information on quality assurance should be:

- Well managed
- Analyzed carefully
- Accessible
- Used to encourage planning, decision-making, resource allocation, and improvement programs
- Used to build a culture of sustainable quality improvement in schools and work units that facilitate the provision of education.

The Education Quality Assurance Agency (EQAI), the Center for Development and Empowerment for Teachers and Educational Personnel (CDETEP), Education Statistics Centers, the District/City Education Office and the Office of the Ministry of Religious Affairs, the Provincial Education Office and the Regional Office of the Ministry of Religious Affairs hold a great responsibility in implementing these activities to ensure that educational data are used for the purpose of improving the quality of education.

The diagram above illustrates the data collection strategy that can be used in the implementation of the stages of the quality assurance system. Each Quality Assurance activity illustrated in the diagram above has relevance for achieving the quality standard (NES). The Quality Guarantee Strategy shown in the diagram above is an integrative effort. Where possible, it is necessary to refine and develop existing data collection strategies, not creating new data collection strategies. This process is done by:

1. gaining agreement on the objectives, scope and manner of implementation of each quality assurance strategy.
2. linking data collection process with National Education Standards.
3. building process flexibility to help provinces, districts and schools collect information related to local contexts by referring to the National Education Standards.
4. developing and training personnel in the use of data collection instruments that can be applied with standard reporting systems.
5. developing the capacity of the District/City Education Office to manage and analyze data.
6. developing a consistent process and providing training for data entry, analysis, access and use of data.

All these quality improvement strategies need to be carried out in a synergy involving school institutions, supervisors, District/City Education Offices and Provinces, School/Madrasah Accreditation Bodies, Education Quality Assurance Institutions (EQAI), Center for Development and Empowerment for Teachers and Educational Personnel (CDETEP) and Higher Education Institution for Teacher' Training (HEITT).

Changing from quality control to quality assurance and development requires a change management strategy. Understanding the present conditions raises the idea of a need for a change in the working order of compliance to simply enforcing regulations into professional compliance awareness, where educators and education personnel make improvements on the basis of self-professional management. At the school level, for example, there is a need to develop work that enables schools to gain support and have the tools to achieve the expected performance. Schools are given the opportunity to elaborate national education standards in the context of their need to move forward. Meanwhile, the supervisors and district/municipality Education Officers must provide support that enable the school to undertake its performance improvement program. Research shows that student achievement is not solely related to the availability of facilities and teacher qualifications, but rather relates to serious teaching planning that facilitate active, creative, effective and fun learning approaches, and an assessment of various techniques.

EQAI in its new role implies empowerment steps with main tasks and functions include: (1) mapping of education quality, (2) supervision in the framework of quality development, (3) development of quality education information system, and (4) facilitation for better performance of educators and education personnel. In carrying out the roles and responsibilities of Quality Assurance and Improvement, EQAI empowerment is focused on guidance, direction and advice/technical assistance. In the system of assurance and improvement of educational quality as proposed in this paper, EQAI as a service institution of human resources empowerment and quality assurance of education must build strong network amongst institution involved to guarantee quality improvement of education. This involves education unit (schools), school superintendent, and district education office.

The development of quality assurance and improvement system within the framework of the national education system requires institutional investment by focusing on changes in mind set and work culture amongst people, especially those who occupy managerial positions. The change strategy must be implemented starting from what, for what, why, and how about capacity building in the form of training, designing, case analysis, and simulation.

4 CONCLUSION

Quality assurance is a set of related processes and systems for collecting, analyzing, and reporting data on the performance and quality of educators and education personnel, programs and institutions. The quality assurance process identifies aspects of achievement and improvement priorities, provides data as a basis for planning and decision making and helps build a culture of continuous improvement. The achievement of education quality for primary and secondary education in Indonesia is reviewed based on eight National Standards of Education. In an implemantation perspective, the assurance and improvement system will reveal the reliability of the NES as referring to the quality of education and performance of the education manager. Thus there will be an attempt or process of empirical validation of the NES that includes mapping of all standards to identify overlaps and gaps, and further improving it so that the NES can be accessed, understood, and used easily, developing a number of achievement indicators for all standards that can be used to help educational personnel identify whether a particular standard has been achieved. Indicators of achievement are things or evidences have been achieved. Indicators of achievement are used to guide the development of assessment instruments for quality assurance. Last but not least, each standard that indicates the level of performance required for a standard or aspect of a particular standard to be achieved.

These efforts are published in the form of an educational unit profile for District/City, Provincial and National Reports on the achievement of the National Education Standards. This framework will be the core document to guide the efforts of National Education Standard achievement done by education personnel in educational units and within management structure of the education system.

REFERENCES

Best, J.W., & Kahn, J.V. 2016. *Research in Education.* India: Pearson Education.
Cochran-Smith, et al. 2016. Initial teacher education: What does it take to put equity at the center? *Journal of Teaching and Teacher Education.* Vol 57 pp. 67–78, https://doi.org/10.1016/j.tate.2016.03.006.
Eisner, E.W. 2017. *The Enlightened Eye, Qualitative Inquiry and the Enhancement of Educational Practice.* New York: Teachers College Press.
Grannäs, J., & Frelin, A. 2017. Spaces of student support – Comparing educational environments from two time periods. *Journal of Improving Schools* Vol 20(2) pp. 127–142. https://doi.org/10.1177/1365480216688547.

Liu. 2017. Professional standards and performance evaluation for principals in China, a policy analysis of the development of principal standards. *Journal of Educational Management Administration & Leadership.* Vol. 45(2) pp. 238–259. https://doi.org/10.1177/1741143215587304.

Tim Pengembang Penjaminan Mutu Sekolah (2003). Konsep Dasar Program Penjaminan Mutu Sekolah. Lembaga Penelitian, Universitas Pendidikan Indonesia. *(School Quality Assurance Development Team (2003). Basic Concepts of School Quality Assurance Program. Research Institute, Universitas Pendidikan Indonesia).*

Undang-Undang No. 20 Tahun 2003 tentang Sistem Pendidikan Nasional *(Indonesian Law no. 20 of 2003 on National Education System).*

Entrepreneurial university in Thailand's higher education institutions

W. Siriteerawasu
Mahidol University, Thailand

ABSTRACT: This article aims to present the concept of entrepreneurial university used as a basis of developing the education and learning system of Thailand's higher education institutions. The initial development model focusing on solving problems could not be potentially effective. Thus, the foresight methods are needed to help enhance the quality of education service due to globally changes. Besides, the entrepreneurial concept is, at present, used for strategic planning including developing specific issues in certain contexts in some countries. To Thailand's Higher Education Institutions and Entrepreneurial Behaviors, forefront universities are highly expected to effectively respond to the nation's demands with New Public Management (NPM) introduced as a result of the state decentralization and the transfer of authority from state to universities. This article benefits for Thailand's Higher Education Institutions to develop human resources consistent to Thailand educational reform, educational strategic planning, and sustainable growth in the future.

1 INTRODUCTION

Regarding Thailand's higher education institutions (OHEC, 2016), it dates back to the latter part of the nineteenth century when King Chulalongkorn (Rama V) introduced visionary education reforms after he assumed the throne in 1868. Centers of higher education incorporating elements of western influence were established and subsequently flourished. The history of higher education in Thailand can be divided into three periods: The Early Modernization Period (1889–1931), the Post Revolution Period (1932–1949), and the Development Planning Period (1950–present). Each type of higher education institution in Thailand has certain governing bodies that are responsible for academic administration: the maintenance and supervision of the institution. These types of institutions include public and private higher education institutions, as well as autonomous universities. In addition, the Council of University Presidents of Thailand and the Association of Private Higher Education Institutions of Thailand play a significant role in university administration and serve as advisory bodies to public and private institutions respectively (OHEC, 2016).

However, Thailand's higher education institutions have been encountering a variety of challenges and obstacles such as aging society contributing to the quality of student selection; majority of the undergraduates have been left unemployed since they are undesirable for the global market needs which anticipate and concern with the educational quality and effectiveness. For all of these reasons, it is necessary for many higher education institutions to develop the curriculum of community enterprises allowing private sectors and bodies to participate in goal-setting leading to a curriculum development, teaching and instruction, in search of research, interdependence between universities and industries. This ultimately results in developing capability of competition of the nation (OHEC, 2016).

Accordingly, to attain these purposes, entrepreneurial university concept would be applied to higher education institutions across Thailand, targeting to provide more opportunities for knowledge and technology transfer to better the economy and society specifically entrepreneurial start-up. Also, higher education institutions more or less had better be adjustable to a wide range of dimensions: a research approach, instruction focusing on experiential learning, including academic integration of entrepreneurship and innovation.

2 THE CONCEPT OF ENTREPRENEURIAL UNIVERSITY

Like any other conceptual theories, the concept of the entrepreneurial university originated from its root. Henry Etzkowitz credited with coining the term entrepreneurial universities in the 1980s. He first noticed at the time that certain universities in the United States, such as MIT, were gravitating towards the entrepreneurial model. He decided to do further research on this model while at MIT. Terming it a second academic revolution, Etzkowitz notes that entrepreneurial universities are transforming the traditional teaching and research universities by encouraging interactions among university, industry, and government, which is the key to improving the conditions for innovation in a knowledge-based society (UN, 2017).

The distinctive principle of the entrepreneurial university is that it empowers all staff, students, external stakeholders and communities to effect meaningful change in the world around them, and does so by directly engaging in such change through its own activities. The focus is on creating organizational DNA which enables the organization to act entrepreneurially across all disciplines, at all levels and in all functions.

The emergence of an entrepreneurial university represents a transformational opportunity to develop a truly relevant and innovative organization capable of responding flexibly to the needs of stakeholders and society in ways that have real and lasting impact while enhancing the graduate attributes the student experience.

The challenge is to re-conceptualize higher education institutions (HEI) as an academic enterprise, one that is agile, competitive, adaptable and responsive to the changing needs of stakeholders and society alike. The adoption of an academic entrepreneurial mind-set may be useful as an organizing principle, both organizationally and conceptually. However, instilling the spirit and application of enterprise into the institutional culture of a public HEI is a major challenge, not least of which is coping with legacy administrative and management systems. The creation of HEI that combines academic excellence, maximum societal impact and inclusiveness to as broad a demographic as possible requires the conceptualization of a new HEI paradigm for the entrepreneurial university.

Being or becoming an entrepreneurial HEI is a response to the many challenges which raise questions about the current shape and constitution of the educational sector. Some scholars are calling for a "deep, radical and urgent transformation" (HEInnovate, 2012), questioning in particular the relevance of traditional conceptual and organizational models (HEInnovate, 2012). Moreover, HEIs are complex pluralistic organizations with each department and discipline facing different stakeholder environments with varying degrees of complexity and actual or potential involvement in knowledge creation, exchange and utilization processes (HEInnovate, 2012). Successfully managing such complexity is dependent upon the motivated commitment of engaged individuals enabled through the intelligent design of systems, structures and processes aligned to the organizational mission and strategy. Within such complex organizations and their networked environments, entrepreneurship as a process can promote change and development through enhancing the capacity to recognize and act upon new opportunities (OECD Guiding Framework for Entrepreneurial Universities, 2012).

Being an entrepreneurial HEI depends, to a large extent, upon individuals and innovative ways of doing things. It is the creation of informal personal networks between academics and entrepreneurs that seems to hold the key (Gibb & Hannon, 2006). Promoting the entrepreneurial HEI is not about relabeling existing systems and structures; it is about recognizing and building, in innovative ways, on what already exists.

Becoming an entrepreneurial university may involve difficult institutional change towards a position of intellectual entrepreneurship (Cherwitz, 2002, 2005) where each and every individual and unit within the organization internalizes entrepreneurial characteristics and implement entrepreneurial practices within their area of influence, creating a living entrepreneurial culture. Institutional change can be defined broadly in terms of both changes in formal and informal ways of doing things. It therefore embraces not only changes in organizations and organizational relationships but also changes in the governance systems and underpinning culture (Gibb & Hannon, 2006). Organization theory suggests that for progress to be made the pressures for change need to be clearly understood, felt and owned within the organization (Schein, 1992). It is imperative that the entrepreneurial university has clarity and coherence in its mission, vision, values, and strategy, and that its people, systems and structures are enabled to support the entrepreneurial mission of the organization.

Coyle, Gibb, & Haskins (2013), in a major work for The University Leaders Program, 'Entrepreneurial University: From Concept to Action' found that essentially entrepreneurial organizations are designed to encourage and support bottom-up initiative and reward and empower such initiative. Such organizations facilitate informal relationships and network building as a necessary condition for the promotion of innovation via the building of individual and collective social capital. They are held together more by shared values and culture than by formal control systems and more by informal flexible strategic thinking and awareness than by highly formal planning systems (Coyle, et al., 2013). The greatest challenge remains in 'how' universities become entrepreneurial institutions and how they create effective environments for developing entrepreneurial capacities in their staff and students (Hannon, 2013). The model outlined below is a framework for evaluating the broad entrepreneurial challenges to university organization design (Gibb, Haskins & Robertson, 2009). The challenges point to the operational and cultural adjustments required for an organization to be truly entrepreneurial.

The strategic concept of an entrepreneurial university typically focuses on reinforcing activities which transform the university from a state-led to an own-led institution. As a result, the university should be able to move fast, with high ambitions of its own, in the globalized environment of the 21st century. Of course, universities differ and, as a consequence, strategies need to also address the specialties of the institution. In addition, universities used the emerging entrepreneurialism to create spin-offs and start-ups, thereby bringing entrepreneurship into society. In order to transform an originally state-led university into an entrepreneurial one, the strategic plan should concentrate on strengthening factors which act as catalysts for change. There are key factors to consider: diversify the funding sources, develop the strong capacity of the university administration, build up new units for modern areas of teaching and research, and support for entrepreneurial actions and changes. The concept of an entrepreneurial university contains a strategic plan for change, from a bureaucratic and slow-moving institution to a university being able to steer itself and to move fast. The objective is to strengthen university autonomy and their world standings.

3   ENTREPRENEURIAL UNIVERSITY IN ASIA

Altbach and Umakoshi stated that "No Asian university is truly Asian in origin – All are based on European academic models and traditions, in many cases imposed by colonial rulers, and in others (e.g., Japan and Thailand) on voluntarily adopted Western models" (Altbach & Umakoshi, 2004). The authors mentioned the undeniable western influence on Asian university feature including academic freedom, institution autonomy and the relationship of the university to society as well as other factors. At present, the clear traces of western influence on higher education policies in Asian countries still appear in the form of national policy documents, study visits of university policy makers, historical data collection, developed frameworks in higher education research and even the rationales used to justify the existing university behaviors.

Yokohama (2006), who studied the organizational change in Japanese and UK universities that engaged in entrepreneurial activities, argued that being an entrepreneurial type of university, a university does not necessarily have to be profit making, risk taking or commercialized. Instead, the researcher proposed in her research that entrepreneurial universities are those strive to be self-reliant and would want to be seen as being responsible for society as a whole (Yokoyama, 2006). Therefore, she proposed that an entrepreneurial university emerges from the need to respond to changing internal and external demands and universities have different degrees of entrepreneurial behaviors. There are two types of institutional response: (1) to be based upon business like and commercialized or (2) self-reliant and autonomous. Research on entrepreneurial university in Asia has already existed mostly in East Asia. In 2010, Guerrero and Urbano did their research on "The development of an entrepreneurial university". They tracked empirical studies about entrepreneurial university from 1995–2008 and some Asian countries appeared to be on the list including Korea, China, Japan, and Singapore (Guerrero & Urbano, 2012). Until 2016, there are more research from Asian countries contributed to the knowledge pool about entrepreneurship in Asian higher education including Malaysia, Taiwan, Indonesia and Thailand (Reyes, 2016). Some scholars have been observing changes in Asian higher education context and used analytical frameworks which developed from western contexts to analyze Asian universities.

4   THAILAND'S HIGHER EDUCATION INSTITUTIONS AND ENTREPRENEURIAL BEHAVIORS

According to national research universities report, research universities are promoted to enhance academic excellence and Thailand's competiveness as well as support economic and social development of the country (OHEC, 2011). Therefore, they are expected to be the forefront universities to effectively respond to the nation's demands. According to Office of higher education commission (OHEC), there are nine research universities in Thailand. Since 1999, a number of research public universities in Thailand have been granted autonomy in the area of financial, personnel, and academics affair. While private universities mostly focus on teaching and learning 13 out of 65 public universities are promoted to support the country's social and economic development by engaging themselves with research mission (Irawati & Rutten, 2013). Less dependence on the government budget and the need to gain external financial support push the universities to become more entrepreneurial (Intarakumnerd & Schiller, 2009) while trying to respond to societal and industrial demand.

To excel in research priority has long been challenging for Thai research universities. Apart from public support, industry and companies are considered as main potential external stakeholders and private funders. Although government, universities and research agencies have worked to improve the effectiveness of economy by promoting university-industry linkages, universities do not contribute enough to the industry (Intarakumnerd & Schiller, 2009). Thai universities are considered as knowledge sources, key innovators and economic development drivers (Intarakumnerd & Schiller, 2009; Mongkhonvanit, 2014). According to Schiller (2007), university-industry linkage in Thailand is still limited. Massive Thai and foreign companies tend to develop in-house R&D capacities instead of asking for support from universities (Schiller & Diez, 2007). However, small and medium-sized enterprises (SMEs), which are the majority or 99.8 percent of local firms, still have to conduct R&D through collaboration with universities (Irawati & Rutten, 2013). Schiller (2007) suggested that to benefit from their research discoveries, universities should focus more on university-industry linkages by providing researchers more support (Schiller & Diez, 2007).

Regarding to the analysis of Etzkowitz about entrepreneurial university, there is always some possible conflicts when a university maintains both teaching and research roles (Etzkowitz, 2013). However, the irrelevance between Thai research university missions and the quality of research and graduates expected from industry raises concern about the capability of Thai research universities in dealing with teaching and research missions and how universities are being operated in response to the demand of industry and society.

5   NEW PUBLIC MANAGEMENT AND ENTREPRENEURIAL BEHAVIORS OF THAILAND'S HIGHER EDUCATION INSTITUTIONS

New public management (NPM) is a mode of governance which have influenced public sector in many countries (De Boer, Enders, & Schimank, 2007). NPM has been used as a new way to improve European public organizations to be more effective and efficient (Sporn, 2003). The principles of NPM have brought governance and management reforms in European higher education institutions (HEIs). In Thai higher education context, NPM was introduced as a result of the state decentralization and the transfer of authority from state to universities (Sae-Lao, 2013). The Asian financial crisis in 1997 influenced greatly on the idea of promoting autonomy and the existence of entrepreneurial activities among Thai universities (Rungfamai, 2011). Sae Lao (2013) pointed out that the emergence of NPM can be seen through the efforts of Thai government in promoting autonomous universities to instill private sector values and expecting those universities to have greater institutional autonomy, administrative management, and financial flexibility. The establishment of ONESQA, the Thailand's only external assurance agency which was expected to be run like private organization, was influenced by NPM (Sae-Lao, 2013). Some scholars agree that the greater autonomy generates Entrepreneurial behaviors among some Thai universities. Rungfamai (2011) argues that Thai universities have changed its behaviors to be more market driven after the Asian financial crisis and from that the introduction of the new behaviors facilitates entrepreneurial culture especially the increasing funding channels of universities (Rungfamai, 2011). As Intarakumnerd and Schiller (2009) reported, a number of public research universities in Thailand have been granted autonomy in the areas of financial, personnel, and academics affair. Therefore, the universities become less depending on the governmental funding, gain external financial support and push the universities to become more entrepreneurial while responding to society and economic demands (Intarakumnerd & Schiller, 2009). OHEC restructures Thai autonomous universities by granting autonomous status through the legal framework for universities to have more institutional autonomy, flexibility, and self-management. After receiving the autonomous power, universities are controlled by university councils with their own institutional legal framework (Asian Development Bank, 2012). The governance of Thai public universities at institutional level can be seen mainly in two different ways based on the type of institutions: public universities under state's control and autonomous universities (OHEC, 2016).

6 CONCLUSION

On account of the crisis and global changes, several universities are required to be more adaptive in order to keep pace of such an uncontrolled dramatic alteration. Thailand's higher education institutions have also been impacted from these critical circumstances. To efficiently tackle these problems, entrepreneurial concept has been incessantly applied to reinforce and improve the quality of education services together with strategic planning for some certain higher education institutions in Thailand. Further, entrepreneurial university is highly recommended to empower the linkage of university, industry, and government through university activities and behaviors across all disciplines. It can be seen that many Asian universities including Thailand base their practical approaches upon western concepts. Additionally, there have been high levels of expectations from forefront higher education institutions to have workable responses to meet the nation's requirements. Therefore, this article benefits for Thailand's Higher Education Institutions to develop human resources consistent to Thailand educational reform, educational strategic planning in education, and sustainable growth in the future.

REFERENCES

Asian Development Bank. 2012. *Administration and Governance of Higher Education in Asia Patterns and Implications*. Retrieved from Asian Development Bank: https://www.adb.org/sites/default/files/publication/29956/administration-governance-higher-education.pdf.
Altbach, P. G. & Umakoshi, T. 2004. Asian universities: *Historical perspectives and contemporary challenges*. USA: Johns Hopkins University Press.
Cherwitz, R. 2002. *Intellectual Entrepreneurship Program (IE)*. The University of Texas at Austin.

Cherwitz, R. 2005. *Intellectual entrepreneurship*: The new social compact. Inside Higher Ed.

Coyle, P., Gibb, A. & Haskins, G. 2013. *The Entrepreneurial University: From Concept to Action, the Entrepreneurial Leaders Programme*. Entrepreneurial University Leaders Programme, National Centre For Entrepreneurship in Education. December.

De Boer, H., Enders, J. & Schimank, U. 2007. *On the way towards new public management? The governance of university systems in England, the Netherlands, Austria, and Germany New forms of governance in research organizations*: 137–152: Springer.

Etzkowitz, H. 2013. *Anatomy of the entrepreneurial university*. Social Science Information, 52(3): 486–511. doi:10.1177/0539018413485832

Gibb, A.A. & Hannon, P. 2006. *"Towards the entrepreneurial university"*, International Journal of Entrepreneurship Education, Vol. 4:73–110.

Gibb, A., G. Haskins & I. Robertson. 2009. *Leading the entrepreneurial university: Meeting the entrepreneurial development needs of higher education institutions.* http://www.ncge.org.uk/publiction/leading_the_entrepreneurial_university.pdf.

Guerrero, M. & Urbano, D. 2012. *The development of an entrepreneurial university.* The journal of technology transfer, 37(1):43–74. doi:10.1007/s10961–010-9171-x

Hannon, D. P. 2013. *Why is the Entrepreneurial University Important?* Journal of Innovation Management, 1(2): 10–17.

HEInnovate. 2012. *The Entrepreneurial Higher Education Institution: A Review of the Concept and its Relevance Today*. https://heinnovate.eu/intranet/tef/downloads/HEInnovate_Analytical%20paper.pdf

Intarakumnerd, P. & Schiller, D. 2009. *University-industry linkages in Thailand: Successes, failures, and lessons learned for other developing countries*. Seoul Journal of Economics, 22(4): 551. doi:10.1080/19761597. 2017.1302399

Irawati, D. & Rutten, R. 2013. *Emerging Knowledge Economies in Asia*: Current Trends in ASEAN-5 (Vol. 122). New York, USA: Routledge.

Mongkhonvanit, J. 2014. *Coopetition for Regional Competitiveness: The Role of Academe in Knowledge-Based Industrial Clustering*. Singapore: Springer.

OECD. 2012. *A Guiding Framework for Entrepreneurial Universities*. European Commision.

OHEC. 2011. *Thailand's National Research Universities: Enhancing Academic Excellence and Competitiveness*. Bangkok, Thailand: Amarin Printing and Publishing.

OHEC. 2016. *Type of Thai Higher Education Institutions*. Retrieved from http://www.mua.go.th/muaold/

Reyes, C. N. 2016. *Framing the entrepreneurial university: the case of the National University of Singapore*. Journal of Entrepreneurship in Emerging Economies, 8(2):134–161. doi:10.1108/JEEE-09–2015-0046

Rungfamai, K. 2011. *Research universities in Thailand*. (Doctoral thesis), University of Hong Kong, Hong Kong.

Schiller, D. & Diez, J. R. 2007. *University–industry linkages: potential and realization in developing countries*: Thai experiences. Tech Monitor, 38: 38–44.

Sae-Lao, R. 2013. *The Logic of the Thai Higher Education Sector on Quality Assessment Policy*. (Doctoral thesis), Columbia University, New York, USA.

Schein, E.H. 1992. *Organizational Culture and Leadership* (2nd ed.). San Francisco: Jossey-Bass.

Schiller, D. 2007. *Higher education funding reform and university: industry links in developing countries—the case of Thailand*. High Educ 54(4):543–556.

Sporn, B. 2003. *Convergence or Divergence in International Higher Education Policy*: Lessons from Europe. Retrieved from https://net.educause.edu/ir/library/pdf/ffpfp0305.pdf

Yokoyama, K. 2006. *Entrepreneurialism in Japanese and UK universities: Governance, management, leadership, and funding*. HigherEducation, 52(3):523–555. doi:10.1007/s10734-005-1168-2

Educational Administration Innovation for Sustainable Development – Komariah et al. (Eds)
© 2018 Taylor & Francis Group, London, ISBN 978-1-138-57341-3

The efficiency of the ICT-based instructions

Slameto
Universitas Kristen Satya Wacana, Salatiga, Central Java, Indonesia

ABSTRACT: This research is aimed at measuring the efficiency of the ICT-based instructions at the Elementary School Teacher Education Program (ESTEP) and at identifying determinant factors which affect the program efficiency. The factors concerned are the instructional sequence, student's learning motivation, and the quality of instructional planning. The data source is 1 class of students of Open/Distance Education (O/DL), ESTEP, Satya Wacana Christian University (SWCU) selected out of 4 classes, as many as 32 alumni. Data were screened by using self-rating scale which consists 40 items. The O/DL ESTEP, SWCU, Salatiga has a high degree of efficiency. Three efficiency determinant models were obtained; 1) the quality of instructional planning, 2) sequence, and 3) student's learning motivation. This new finding will be very useful for educational quality management concerning its efficiency, effectivity, and productivity of Higher Education.

1 INTRODUCTION

In the twenty first century education plays a very important role to develop a nation (Basak, 2014). The development of Information and Communication Technology (ICT) moves very quickly and is cheaper to access. ICT has influenced all aspects of life. Processing the knowledge of ICT is really the need of the hour (Philomina & Amutha, 2016). The role of ICT in education is becoming more and more important and this importance will continue to grow and develop in the 21st century (Beena & Mathur, 2012). There are many barriers and enhance factors that effect on the adoption and use of ICT for teachers (Basak, 2014). However, its practice in the field shows that a lot of students are still unskillful in using the computer and the internet. On the other hand, many teachers are unable to integrate ICT into their instructions because of the various myths they possess (Rahmawati & Diatmika, 2011).

The implementation of the educational program at the Elementary School Teacher Education Program (ESTEP), Satya Wacana Christian University (SWCU) is carried out in an ICT-based Open/Distance Learning (O/DL) mode. The instructions are deemed appropriate to produce first degree (S-1) graduates equal to the regular on-campus programs. This program is an acceleration program to upgrade teachers' academic qualification to the S-1 degree. Since 2009 this program has been executed by 55 universities in Indonesia. In order to decide and measure appropriateness and success of the program, monitoring and evaluation were administered in 2010, 2011, 2012, and 2013. One of the results of the monitoring and evaluation is that there has been no significant increase in the number of participants, which later led to the thought that questioned about the acknowledgement of the program in its effort of upgrading the academic qualification to the S-1 degree.

The ICT-based ESTEP offers educational program especially for the permanently employed Elementary School (ES) teachers on their job to get the degree of Bachelor (S-1). The program enables teachers to get a bigger opportunity not to interfere with their job and responsibility. It is expected that the program may provide a more efficient, effective, and accountable teacher education as well as a wider access to educational services without sacrificing its quality. The completion of the ICT-based O/DL is regulated and determined by SWCU on the basis of the academic rules and regulations in effect.

Teaching efficiency in higher education is an argumentative concept (Skeleton, 2004); The results of the studies by Suydam, (2007) and Young, (2006) indicate that organization of materials, classroom management, use of students' ideas, task-orientedness, flexibility, use of different teaching methods and respecting students are the most important characteristics of efficient teachers.

Rüütmann & Vanaveski (2009) have reported four different types of knowledge for teaching efficiency, including knowledge of content, pedagogical content knowledge, general pedagogical knowledge and knowledge of learning and learners. The dimensions of teaching efficiency were: lesson plan development, control over content, content presentation skills, learning evaluation and class management (Shohoudi et al, 2015).

The development of website-based instructions is meant to support efficient instructions (Mukminan & Muhammad, 2013). ICT increased efficiency of school administrations and effectiveness of school management (Fredriksson et al, 2008). The management of efficient education is one that utilizes limited number of resources to produce optimal productivity (Dharmadi, 2013).

Since 2009, SWCU has started to manage ICT-based ESTEP using Open/Distance learning (O/DL) system. Despite the monitoring and evaluation carried out by the Education Department, there are still doubts on the program effectiveness. So far, there has been no particular research that explores factors related to the success of the program. That is why a research on this topic is needed.

Although it is not yet developed, the management of the ICT-based O/DL should emphasize its efficiency and enable teachers to make a reflection on the instructional processes, both individually and in groups (for example, in a conference or a joint product on the on-line, electronic self assessment). Encouraging teachers and students to think about the process of ICT-based teaching-learning may make the teacher's pedagogy more accurate, effective, and efficient (Slameto, 2016).

This research is aimed at studying the efficiency of the ICT-based ESTEP in upgrading Elementary School teachers (EST) to get the first degree (S-1) qualification without leaving their daily duty. It is also to identify determinant/factors which affect the efficiency of the program. In the educational perspective as a system, the success (i.e., efficiency) of the ICT-based ESTEP is directly affected by the learning process: it is not only students and teachers who play a primary role — and that needs attention, but also by the input. The process factor in this research is the sequence of instructions (X_1), the student factor is learning motivation (X_2), and the teacher factor is the quality of planning the instructions (X_3).

ICT-based instructional management should focus on the teacher in developing the plan and implementation of quality instructions while keeping the sequence of teaching materials which is able to motivate student's learning. The new finding in this research will someday be useful for educational quality management and for the efficiency of Higher Education as an executor of the ICT-based ESTEP.

2 METHOD

This quantitative research belongs to the causality ex-post facto research. The ex-post facto research is designed to explain the cause-effect relationship among variables by testing the effect of learning sequence (X1), student's learning motivation (X2), and the quality of teacher's instructional planning (X3) on the ICT-based instructional efficiency (Y) of ESTEP, UKSW, Salatiga. The data source is 1 class of O/DL students, ESTEP, UKSW who were chosen out of 4 classes, consisting of 32 alumni in the academic year 2015/2016. Data were screened using self-rating scale, having 40 items which were then reduced to 4 variables. The self-rating scale has been tested valid (0.206–0.720) and reliable (0.860). The data were then analyzed descriptively and inferentially using the SPSS program for windows version 20.

3 RESULTS AND DISCUSSION

After data screening by self-rating scale which consist of 40 items, which were reduced to 4, they were then analyzed descriptively with the help of the SPSS program for windows version 20. The result is shown in table 1 Statistics.

Based on the descriptive analysis as shown in Table 1 above, most respondents put the quality of instructional material sequence (X_1) in the medium rate, learning motivation (X_2) in the medium rate, and quality of instructional planning (X_3) is rated fair. Most of them see the ICT-based ESTEP have high efficiency (Y).

The next analysis is to know whether the three independent variables (X) give effects to the degree of efficiency of the ICT-based ESTEP (Y). The result of the regression analysis using the stepwise model is in table 2.

Based on table 2 the result of regression test as presented in Table 2 above, 3 models are found. Model 1: R = 0814 and Adjusted R Square = 0.646 or 6460%. Model 2: R = 0886 and Adjusted R Square = 0.763 or 76.30%. Model 3: R = 0938 and Adjusted R Square = 0.859 or 85.90%. To make sure whether the size of R is significant, it can be seen in table 3.

Based on Table 3 Anova, in Model 1: F = 39.330 at the significance level 0000; in Model 2: F = 34.789 at the significance level 0000; in Model 3: F = 43.703 at the significance level 0.000. The size of significance level in Model 3 is smaller than 0.05. Therefore, the quality of instructional planning (X_3), sequence (X_1), learning motivation (X_2) altogether affect positively and significantly on the ICT-based ESTEP efficiency at 85.90%. Next, to know each role of the predictor variable, it can be seen Table 4.

Based on table 4 the coefficient in Table 4 below, it is clear that each variable X to be investigated has significance level less than 0.05, meaning that the quality if instructional planning (X_3),

Table 1. Statistics.

Variables	Mean	Med.	Sd.	Min.	Max.
Sequence	2.4545	2.0000	0.50965	2.00	3.00
Learning Motivation	2.7273	3.0000	0.55048	2.00	4.00
Quality of Inst Planning	2.5455	3.0000	0.73855	0.00	3.00
Efficiency of ICT-based ESTEP	2.7727	3.0000	0.61193	1.00	4.00

Table 2. Model summary.

Model	R	R Square	Adjusted R Square	Std. Error of the Estimate
1	0.814[a]	0.663	0.646	0.36406
2	0.886[b]	0.786	0.763	0.29795
3	0.938[c]	0.879	0.859	0.22965

Table 3. ANOVA.

	Model	Sum of Squares	df	Mean Square	F	Sig.
1	Regression	5.213	1	5.213	39.330	0.000[b]
	Residual	2.651	20	0.133		
	Total	7.864	21			
2	Regression	6.177	2	3.088	34.789	0.000[c]
	Residual	1.687	19	0.089		
	Total	7.864	21			
3	Regression	6.914	3	2.305	43.703	0.000[d]
	Residual	.949	18	0.053		
	Total	7.864	21			

Table 4. Coefficients.

	Model	Unstandardized Coefficients		Standard Coef.		
		B	S. E.	Beta	t	Sig.
1	(Constant)	1.056	0.285		3.709	0.001
	Quality of Ins. Planning	0.675	0.108	0.814	6.271	0.000
2	(Constant)	−0.133	0.429		−0.309	0.761
	Quality of Ins. Planning	0.729	0.090	0.880	8.138	0.000
	Sequence	0.428	0.130	0.356	3.295	0.004
3	(Constant)	−1.367	0.467		−2.925	0.009
	Quality of Ins. Planning	0.672	0.071	0.811	9.507	0.000
	Sequence,	0.570	0.107	0.475	5.326	0.000
	Learning Motivation	0.378	0.101	0.340	3.740	0.002

sequence (X_1) and learning motivation (X_2) altogether affect positively and significantly on the efficiency of the ICT-based ESTEP.

The sequence of the teaching materials should systematic to make the learning process run fluently. A stepwise arrangement of instructions means that the teaching materials must be arranged according to the levels of complexity or difficulty, for example, starting from easy materials to more difficult ones, from simple to more complicated, and from factual to more abstract teaching materials (Romansyah, K., 2016).

Based on the findings in table 1 it turns out that the students' assessment of organizing the content of lectures or sequences in high level tends to be very high; in contrast to the findings of Weng, (2012) which states most respondents (55.5%) rate clear the clarity of the sequence of the teaching materials

Motivation is part of what makes a student successful, it affects how they respond to materials presented in a learning environment (Edori, 2014). It is found that the motivation of students on their instructional material is slightly above average. In contrast to the subjects who scribe meticulous, it turns their learning motivation is generally only on the bottom of the average.

Instructional planning is an interconnecting and supporting series of existing elements and components in learning or, a process of arranging, coordinating, and deciding learning elements and components. It includes an activity in formulating objectives to be achieved in a learning activity, in deciding what method to be used to assess the achievement of the objective, what method will be taught, what method of delivery to be used, and what tools or media to be needed (Bachri, 2010). Instructional planning plays an important role in the teaching-learning process. The researcher also determined the elements of instructional content, behavioral objectives, instructional strategies, mass media, educational activities, cognitive activators, and evaluation procedures, along with the loop of feedback (Darwazeh, 2008). Based on the results of the analysis in table 1 it turns out that the quality of learning planning is assessed by the students at the middle level; A good learning strategy depends on the quality of the planning, which is made systematically in a program by the teacher. Although it is not the only factor, instructional planning always determines the success of the transferring process of knowledge and skills. The student's achievement is related to the instructional planning made by the teacher.

Based on the analysis result in table 1, it turns out that the efficiency of ICT-based learning is in the middle level; Different found by Shohoudi et al, 2015): with regard to teaching efficiency an average level.

The determinant factor for instructional efficiency is teacher's age, work experience, academic achievement, and education and training (Marbaniang et al, 2013). He found that teacher's mastery on knowledge/main teaching materials, teacher's academic qualification, teacher's sympathetic attitude on students' mastery, teaching methods, sincerity in teaching, correct use of media in teaching, art of interrogation menjadi become determinants of efficiency (Bakhru et al, 2013). Of course, all will be realized if the teacher concerned has a quality instructional planning. This research found that the quality of instructional planning becomes determinant for the efficiency of the ICT-based ESTEP; 65% of the program efficiency depends on the quality of the teacher's instructional planning. A good learning strategy is very much dependent on the quality of instructional planning, which is prepared systematically and in a programmed way by the teacher. Student's learning achievement is related significantly with the teacher's instructional planning. Although it is not the only factor, instructional planning always determines the success of learning itself.

This research also found that sequence becomes a determinant for the efficiency of the ICT-based ESTEP. The contribution rate of sequence after the quality of instructional planning is from 64.60% to 76.30%, or around 12%. As far as Google Schoolar is concerned, both in Indonesian and in English, there is no information that sequence becomes a determinant for the learning efficiency in the ICT-based ESTEP. When it is looked into more deeply, sequence originates from creative skills as an initiative in which someone manifests his or her ability in describing according to his or her thinking order appropriately into a varied thinking pattern (Rao, 2016).

Based on the result of the descriptive analysis on the research findings, most of the respondents have learning motivation (X_2) at the medium level, unlike the result of the research by Sovia, A. (2016), who found that the level of student's motivation in learning after taking classes belongs to a high category.

University managers should realize the importance of efficiency in their own university; the action of the management should be orientated on excellence in teaching and research (Sellers et al, 2010). This new finding is very useful for the educational quality management for the sake of efficiency, effectiveness, and productivity of Higher Education. The management of ICT-based instructions, although is not yet developed, should be focused on the teacher in developing quality instructional planning without neglecting sequence or order of learning materials which can motivate the teacher to make a reflection on the process of his or her instructions, both individually and in groups (for example, in conferences and joint product on the on-line elektronic selfassessment). Encouraging teachers and students to think about the process of teaching-learning (ICT-based instructions) may give quality assurance in relation to efficiency and effectiveness (Slameto, 2016). The new finding will be very useful for the educational quality management for the sake of efficiency, effectiveness, and productivity of Higher Education as the executor of the ICT-based O/DL Program.

4 CONCLUSION

This research has measured the efficiency of the ICT-based ESTEP, SWCU, Salatiga. It was found that the ICT-based ESTEP, SWCU, Salatiga has a high rate of efficiency. Three determinant models for the efficiency of the ICT-based ESTEP, SWCU, Salatiga were also found. Model 1: the quality of instructional planning contributes as much as 64.60%; Model 2: sequence contributes 76.30%; and Model 3: learning motivation 85.90%. University managers should realize the importance of efficiency for their own university. Their actions should also be orientated to the excellence in teaching instructions and research. For this purpose, the management should focus on the teachers in developing quality instructional planning by keeping in mind the sequence or order of instructional materials which can motivate students. This new finding will be very useful for educational quality management for the sake of efficiency, effectiveness, and productivity of Higher Education as an executor of the ICT-based ESTEP, O/DL instructions.

REFERENCES

Bachri, B. S. 2010. Implementasi Pengembangan Content Curriculum dalam Proses Perencanaan Pembelajaran. *Jurnal Teknologi Pendidikan,* 10(2), 1–11.
Bakhru, K. M., Sanghi, S., & Medury, Y. 2013. Ranking Teaching Competencies: Teachers and Administrators Perception. *International Journal of Organizational Behaviour & Management Perspectives*, 2(3), 540.

Basak, S. K. 2014. A comparison of barriers and enhance factors on the adoption and use of ICT into teaching and learning for teachers. In *Information Society (i-Society), 2014 International Conference*. IEEE (244–247).

Beena, M., & Mathur, M. 2012. A study on the ICT awareness of M. Ed. trainees. *International Journal of Business Management & Economic Research*, 3(4), 573–578.

Darwazeh, A. 2008. Adequacy and Consistency in Instructional Planning Processes as a Means for Evaluating and Developing Teacher's performance. *An-Najah University Journal for Research*, 22(2), 643–667.

Dharmadi, G. G. M. 2013. Strategi Pemberdayaan Fungsi Perencanaan Pendidikan Pada Kantor Dinas Pendidikan Tingkat Kabupaten Dalam Rangka Pelaksanaan Otonomi Daerah. *Doctoral dissertation*, Universitas Pendidikan Indonesia.

Edori, P. G. 2014. *Students' Motivation and the Challenges Instructors Face Incorporating ICT Based Instructional Materials* (*Doctoral dissertation*, Eastern Mediterranean University (EMU)-Doğu Akdeniz Üniversitesi (DAÜ).

Fredriksson, U., Jedeskog, G., & Plomp, T. 2008. Innovative use of ICT in schools based on the findings in ELFE project. *Education and Information Technologies*, 13(2), 83.

Marbaniang, S., Mishra, P., & Khuhly, B. L. 2013. Socio-personal, Professional and Psychological characteristics of Agricultural University Teachers: A study in Assam Agricultural University. *Journal of Academia and Industrial Research (JAIR)*, 2(4), 235.

Mukminan, D., & Muhammad, N. B. 2013. *Pengembangan Media Perkuliahan Berbasis WEB Untuk Menentukan Pola Hubungan Regulasi Diri dan Proses Kognitif Mahasiswa* eprints.uny.ac.id

Philomina, M. J., & Amutha, S. 2016. Information and communication technology awareness among teacher educators. *International Journal of Information and Education Technology*, 6(8), 603.

Rahmawati, P. I., & Diatmika, I. P. G. 2011. Pembelajaran Berbasis ICT Dalam Perkuliahan Jurusan Pariwisata dan Perhotelan: Peran, Peluang, dan Tantangannya. *Jurnal Pendidikan dan Pengajaran*, 44(1).

Rao, K. S. 2016. *A Study of Teacher Effectiveness in Relation to Creativity and Accountability of Secondary School Teachers*. Lulu.com.

Romansyah, K. 2016. Pedoman Pemilihan dan Penyajian Bahan Ajar Mata Pelajaran Bahasa dan Sastra Indonesia. *Logika*, 17(2), 59–66.

Rüütmann T. & Vanaveski J. 2009. Effective strategies and models for teaching thinking skills and capitalizing deep understanding in engineering education. *Problems of Education in the 21st Century.* 17: 176–187.

Sellers-Rubio, R., Mas-Ruiz, F. J., & Casado-Díaz, A. B. 2010. University Efficiency: Complementariness versus Trade-off between Teaching, Research and Administrative Activities. *Higher Education Quarterly*, 64(4), 373–391.

Shohoudi, M., Zandi, K., Faridi, M. R., Fathi, G., & Safari, Z. 2015. Relationship of Teaching Efficiency with Academic Self-Efficacy and Self-Directed Learning among English Language Students: University Students' Perspectives. *Educational Research in Medical Sciences Journal*, 4(2), 68–77.

Skeleton, A. 2004. Understanding 'teaching excellence' in higher education: A critical evaluation of the National Teaching Fellowships Scheme 2004. *Studies in Higher Education.* 29(4): 451–468.

Slameto, 2016. The Determinants of the ICT-Based O/DL Program to Encourage and Support the Country's Economy. *Proceeding of International Conference on Teacher Training and Education (ICTTE) FKIP UNS 2015.* vol 1 no 1, Universitas Sebelas Maret.

Sovia, A. 2016. Motivasi Belajar Mahasiswa Dengan Strategi Question Student Have Disertai Pemberian Modul Pada Perkuliahan Kalkulus Vektor. *LEMMA*, 2(1).

Suydam, M. 2007. Teaching effectiveness. *Arithmetic Teacher*. 31(2): 30–35.

Weng, T. S. 2012. Using Fairy Pitta as a case study for multimedia ecological learning materials. *African Journal of Agricultural Research*, 7(2), 311–319.

Young, M. 2006. Characteristics of high potential and at-risk teachers. *Action in Teacher Education.* 11(4): 35–39.

Educational Administration Innovation for Sustainable Development – Komariah et al. (Eds)
© 2018 Taylor & Francis Group, London, ISBN 978-1-138-57341-3

Utilization of standard procedures and workflow according to the school vision and mission

D. Sukaningtyas, D. Satori & U.S. Sa'ud
Universitas Pendidikan Indonesia, Bandung, West Java, Indonesia

ABSTRACT: Many school documents are not utilized as work guidelines for program management. How do schools develop the management capacities by utilizing standard procedures and workflow according to the school's vision and mission? This study aims to utilize standard procedures and workflow in line with the school's vision and mission to develop the capacity of program management. The research used a qualitative approach, with a case study method. Case studies were conducted at two sites, focusing on the design of standardized procedures and workflows. Data collection methods used were interviews, field observations, document studies and artifacts. The data validity test was carried out with credibility, transferability, dependability, and confirmability. The results and discussion show that the standard procedures and workflows are understood, visualized and used by teachers and staff, making management performance more organized and focused.

1 INTRODUCTION

The achievement of the quality of school services is assessed by the quality of the school management services. Effective school management performance can improve the quality of school services. It is important for schools to carry out their responsibilities to the highest standards of performance by providing quality services. Schools are said to be qualified if they meet and exceed the customer expectations or satisfaction (Evans & Lindsay, 2005; Hoy & Miskel, 2008; Brown & Mevs, 2012). Schools should be able to provide assistance to build capacity to provide better educational services, and must improve the quality and quantity of their performance, especially the achievement of learners. This means building capacity at the school's organizational level. Organizational capacity is described as the knowledge and resources needed by an organization to be effective, with interrelated components. Organizational capacity is a collection of individual capacity supported resources. Capacity is related to the capabilities, competencies, and services of the organization that are needed to improve performance (Goldkuhl & Nilsson, 2000; Coates & Associates, 2008; Edgar & Lockwood, 2008; PricewaterhouseCooper Canada Foundation, 2011; Bryan, 2011).

Conceptually, the approach in school service quality requires the improvement of school capacity to provide better services. School capacity in the context of a performance-based school accountability system is a service to improve learners' performance (Hatch, 2009; Beaver & Weinbaum, 2012). It is generally assumed that schools without adequate capacity will have difficulty making effective continuous improvement efforts, such as the inadequate role of teachers and education personnel in completing their tasks and solving problems that schools are facing (Sumintono, 2013; Triatna, 2015).

Maximum utilization of school capacity is aligned for successful implementation of School-Based Management (SBM), and improves the learning environment and achievement of learners. Maximized school capacities are, among others, related to the following aspects: the objectives, policies and commitments of school management, school budgets, human resources and school infrastructure, and participation of parents (Yat & Oek, 2008; Robinson, et al., 2011; Bandur, 2012). Other studies mention the development of school capacity for the achievement of superior schools or to improve the quality of school performance, improve teaching and learning, and encourage the development of professional teachers (Sarrico, et al., 2012; Sumintono, 2013; Triatna, 2015; Bush & Glover, 2016; Li & Ko, 2016).

Based on some of these studies, it is clear that building capacity at the school organizational level is beneficial to improving the quality of school services. Development of management capacity is required for schools, as it is assumed to improve school performance, which has an impact on the achievement of expected quality. Various studies focusing on school capacity building have also been conducted with key development dimensions, including, teacher professional development (knowledge and skills) (King & Newmann, 2001; Stocklin, 2010; King & Bouchard, 2011), development of learner/professional educators (King & Newmann, 2001; Stocklin, 2010; Triatna, 2015), policy changes and strategic directions (Watterston & Caldwell, 2011); self-organization (Bain et al., 2011).

In this study, the focus is on the development of school management capacity, especially program management. How can the performance of program management work effectively? Many school documents have not been used as guidelines for management work. This study aims to utilize standard procedures and workflow in developing the management capacity of school programs according to the vision and mission. Performance effectiveness through school program management can be seen at the implementation stage. Implementation strategy is prepared so that the program runs according to its procedures and success criteria.

2   METHOD

This study used a qualitative approach, with a type of case study method. The study was conducted on two sites/locations, with consideration: both sites have similar background conditions, with differences in quantity, number of study groups and teachers/staff. The data was collected through in-depth interviews and daily observation, and study of the documents and artifacts was conducted at two schools, Nasima High School (school A) and Sultan Agung 1 High School (school B) Semarang.

Preparation for this approach was carried out by setting up the research framework that contains the focus of the study, the used data collection methods, and the participants involved. Then the research framework was elaborated according to the instrument containing the aspects studied. Next, the instruments were elaborated in the form of detail as the guidelines to all methods of data collection. Each contained a guide to interviews, observations and documents/artifacts.

The process of collecting and processing the data, as well as displaying the results of the qualitative approach, was carried out in approximately eight months. This sequence of stages was intended to examine the condition of the school management capacity. Detailed data about the condition of the school management capacity was evaluated and analyzed to determine the pattern of developing the capacity of school management in building the vision and mission.

Observations were conducted to determine the routine activities undertaken related to the school community programs, which were intended to build the vision and mission. Besides, the researchers also made the observation on some meetings in discussing and establishing policies or guiding teachers and education personnel. Interviews were conducted based on the outline instrument of literature review in the form of questions with open answers. The interviews were conducted with one or more participants in the form of Focus Group Discussion (FGD).

The FGD was conducted in a design program and evaluation session because at that stage the teachers and the education personnel worked as a team. Interviews were also conducted with unstructured or informal techniques by doing "conversational"/daily conversation. Participants involved in the interview were selected through the snowball method. Researchers determined the first participant as the key informant, and then he/she selected the next participant. The context of this study is related to the basic values of the institutions that were usually developed early by the founders of the school. In that context, the researchers chose the founder or the chairman of the foundation and the school principal as the key informants for each school. The other participants involved were the educators and education personnel, students/prospective students, and parents/expectant parents. Each of these various roles were involved in the administration of the school. Selection of this method was expected to produce a sufficient range of sample to describe the condition in a variety of perspectives. The researchers were the main instrument (key instrument). Researchers also took on the role as participant observers.

The study of the school documents was carried out by collecting relevant school documents within the context of the research. These documents were in the form of the school development plan, the annual work plan, the school activities documents, learning documents (teaching planning, implementation agenda, as well as plans and assessments), the budget plan of the school, and so on. While the artifacts studies were carried out by documenting them in the form of images. An artifact is any object made by human beings, especially with a purpose for subsequent use. Examples of artifacts in schools include flags, institutional symbols and wall displays.

The collection was intended to connect the existence of the artifact with their benefits in the process of developing the capacity of school management. The entire process of data collection was carried out in a manner based on the qualitative data collection procedures.

The validity of the data was tested with its degree of credibility, transferability, dependability, and conformability. Based on the data collection, researchers obtained the rational conditions that occur in the field. The description of the condition was the result of the rational credibility (internal validity) using member checking and triangulation techniques.

Member checking was the result of the interpretation and conclusion of the researchers' data presented to participants for gaining approval. While triangulation was carried out by comparing and checking the level of trust of the information obtained from multiple sources (participants involved in formal and informal interviews), methods for collecting the data (such as interviews, observation, and study of documents/artifacts). The data collected was analyzed qualitatively; the analysis of a single case and multicast.

3 RESULT AND DISCUSSION

The study was conducted by researchers to answer the following question: how do schools develop the management capacities by utilizing standard procedures and workflow according to vision and mission?

Focusing on the research question the assessment included the aspect of formulating operational standard procedures consisting of five question indicators. Here are the results of both locations according to the aspects of the code.

In concept, the implementation of the program requires a strategy to run in accordance with the policies and needs that are expected. According to David (2011), the implementation of the program strategy requires the setting of annual goals, policy formulation, staff motivation, and resource management, so that the formulated strategy can be implemented. Implementation of the program strategy includes developing a culture that supports strategy, designing effective organizational structures, directing marketing or publication efforts, preparing budgets, developing and utilizing information technology systems, and linking teacher/staff compensation to organizational performance.

School programs in both are repetitive programs in that each year they are carried out under relatively similar conditions. This is an efficient way to do the job so that it is done exactly as the expectation, reducing errors and ensuring that work or tasks can be done consistently and repeatedly (Manich, 2015). One of the program implementation strategies used is standardized program activity. Standardization is defined as activities that bring up solutions for repetitive applications or programs, which may be problematic, and may be used for all disciplines (Akyar, 2012). In general, the activities consist of compiling and implementing standards.

School A has prepared Standard Operating Procedures (SOP) as part of the ISO 9001: 2008 documents. Meanwhile, school B is not accustomed to using procedural documents. Based on document studies it was found that program procedures and workflows were created, but not yet

Table 1. Results of data collection.

| Rational/Conditions Empirical | |
| School A | School B |

Aspect Code: RMa03.01.02
Aspect: Preparation of Standard Operating Procedure

Code: RMa03.01.02.01

• School prepares Standard Operating Procedures (SOP).	• School B has not been using standard procedure documents.
• Preparation of SOPs in school are related to the preparation of ISO 9001: 2008 documents.	• However, the results of the document studies mention that standard procedure for typical school programs, such as BuSI program procedures are available.
• School program SOPs are only made public, as there is no demand for details.	• Document procedures other than typical school programs do not exist.

Code: RMa03.01.02.02

• Each year, standard procedures for annual routine programs tend to be unchanged, because it is repeated.	• BuSI program procedures are prepared with reference to predefined policies.
• SOPs are prepared based on the context of needs, including adjusted policies in schools and institutions.	• A description of the tasks as the work guidelines for teachers and staff is also structured on the basis of institutional and school policies.

Code: RMa03.01.02.03

• Based on the result of document study, almost all ISO document files are related to school programs, in which there are SOPs for each program.	• Every year, more programs are repetitive, so that the implementation strategy stages have been memorized by teachers/staff.
• Standard document procedures are more often in place but not being used as the reference at any time. Even some of the teachers/staff have never seen the documents.	• Yet, it is one of the weaknesses of the program because there are still things that are not effective in the implementation.
• The assumption of the participants was that if there SOP and is it is implemented accordingly, then it is very possible it could form an effective culture.	• Some participants have started to implement an effective culture, but there is no clear backup rules or procedures. The assumption is that if there are such backups, then an effective culture can be created.
Parties involved in the preparation of SOPs are school leaders, principals and vice principals.	The flow and procedure of BuSI are prepared by a special team that includes the leaders from the early days when the program started. They are principals and the representatives.
Currently, school A is doing an adjustment of the existing ISO documents with the accreditation component. It also involves a flow procedure that is the flow and procedure of all school programs. It means that SOPs can change in accordance with the existing policies.	• In 2016, the school initiated the preparation of ISO documents. Automatically, all program procedures began to be arranged.
	• In 2017, precisely at the beginning of August, school B has also gained the ISO 9001 certificate.

used properly. For both schools, the preparation of standardized procedures and workflow is one of the strategies used as a standard for good program implementation. Amare (2012) stated that the standard procedure is part of an effective management system, one which can be a strategic pattern to prevent inconsistent service quality. A Standard Operating Procedure (SOP) is a set of written instructions that document a routine or repetitive activity followed by an organization. The development and use of SOPs are an integral part of a successful quality system as it provides individuals with the information to perform a job properly, and facilitates consistency in the quality and integrity of a product or end result (Environmental Protection Agency, 2007). Lin and Green (2016) also referred to a SOP as a safeguard or rescue for pre-analysis plans.

In both schools, the understanding of procedural documents has not been done, resulting in different perceptions of each task. It also causes misrepresentation that results in ineffective work execution. The same is mentioned in other studies, that discussing the shortcomings associated with the absence of standard procedures leads to inconsistent service quality, performance variations, mixed procedures, misinterpretation or misinformation (Amare 2012). SOPs detail the regularly recurring work processes that are to be conducted or followed within an organization (Environmental Protection Agency, 2007). An understanding of procedural documents is required in order for SOPs to become documents that facilitate consistent appropriateness with technical requirements and service quality. The development and use of SOPs minimizes variation and promotes quality through consistent implementation of a process or procedure within the organization, even if there are temporary or permanent personnel changes (Department Cooperative Governance Republic of South Africa, 2016; Environmental Protection Agency, 2007).

At both schools, standardized procedures and workflows are structured according to the context of needs that are especially suited to school or agency policies.

However, not all standard procedures and workflows of the programs have been developed. The standard procedure that is always been prepared is the large capacity school program, with a high degree of complexity. The school acknowledges that if the standard procedure is utilized according to its function, then it is possible that an effective culture can be formed. Participants explain examples that occur for specific programs, that by building an understanding of the operational standards of workplace procedures, it always keeps the focus that SOPs can reduce nonconformities, improve workplace efficiency, and streamline work processes (Manich, 2015; Environmental Protection Agency, 2007).

SOPs and workflows are arranged based on the existing policies. The policy meant here is the school policy based on the performance of management in accordance with the achievements of vision and mission; as in several studies conducted to examine the relationship between corporate performance with vision/mission statement (Kantabutra & Avery, 2010; Kantabutra, 2010; Kantabutra, & Vimolratana, 2009; Bart, et al., 2001). In his research, Kantabutra and Avery (2010) found that in fact many factors have the potential to affect organizational performance and need to be taken into account by researchers. They call this as the "vision realization factor". The following factors greatly influence realizing the vision: communicating the vision, aligning organizational processes and systems according to vision, empowering others to act in order to achieve the vision, and motivating staff. Factors aligning the process and organizational system according to vision are guidelines for the preparation of standard procedures and workflows. Standard procedures and workflows that fit the vision and mission also serve as a control mechanism by identifying limits that prevent an organization from engaging in unrelated or inappropriate business activities (Bart, et al., 2001; Bartkus, et al., 2006).

In schools A and B, the preparation of standard procedures is the responsibility of the school leaders. Existing standard procedures have changed according to school or institution policy. For example, when the school decides, it synchronizes the school accreditation component with ISO documents, then the standard procedure is automatically adjusted. The role of leaders in SOP implementation is to ensure the process is carried out accurately (Department of Cooperative Governance Republic of South Africa, 2016). According to Lin and Green (2016), the SOP should be a living document developed over time. The results also found some standard benefits of procedures against pre-analysis plans.

4 CONCLUSION

The implementation of the school program requires a strategy to run in accordance with the expected policies and needs. The policy meant here is the school policy based on the performance of management in accordance with the achievements of the vision and mission. Implementing strategies includes developing a culture that supports strategy.

The school program is a recurring program, carried out under relatively similar conditions each year.

One program implementation strategy that can be used is standardizing program activity. The standardization is to compile and implement a standard operating procedure (SOP) and workflow. SOPs and workflows that are developed and implemented are part of an effective management system and solution for repeatable school programs. The existence of SOPs and workflows allow the development of a consistent culture, as well as sufficient information to implement the program.

Understanding of procedural documents is required for SOPs and workflows that facilitate consistent appropriateness with technical requirements and service quality. The development and use of SOPs minimizes variation and improves quality through the application of consistent processes or procedures within the organization. If the standard procedure is utilized according to its function, then it is possible that there can be an effective culture. By building the understanding of SOPs in the workplace, always keep in focus that SOPs can reduce incompatibility, improve workplace efficiency, and streamline work processes.

The preparation of SOPs and workflows is the responsibility of school leaders. In addition to writing them, leaders also have a role to ensure the implementation of the SOP and workflow is done accurately. Therefore, the SOP document should be a living document developed over time. Having standard procedures and workflows that are understood, visualized, and used by all teachers and staff, management performance becomes more organized and well directed.

REFERENCES

Akyar, I. (2012). Standard operating procedures (what are they good for?). *Licensee InTech*, 367–391.

Amare, G. (2012). Reviewing the values of a Standard Operating Procedure. *Ethiop J. Health Sci.* 22(3), 205–208.

Bain, A., Walker, A., & Chan, A. (2011). Self-organisation and capacity building: Sustaining the change. *Journal of Educational Administration, 49*(6), 701–719.

Bandur, A. (2012). School-based management developments: Challenges and impacts. *Journal of Educational Administration*, 50(6), 845–873.

Bartkus, B., Glassman, M., & McAfee, B. (2006). Mission statement quality and financial performance. *European Management Journal, 24*(1), 86–94.

Bart, C.K. 2001. Measuring the mission effect in human intellectual capital. *Journal of Intellectual Capital*, 2(3), 320–330.

Bart, C.K., Bontis, N. & Taggar, S. (2001). A model of the impact of mission statements on firm performance, *Management Decision, 39*(1), 19–35.

Beaver, J.K. & Weinbaum, E.H. (2012). *Measuring school capacity, maximizing school improvement.* Philadelphia: The Consortium for Policy Research in Education (CPRE), Graduate School of Education, University of Pennsylvania.

Brown, C. & Mevs, P. (2012). *Quality performance assessment: Harnessing the power of teacher and student learning.* Boston, MA: The Center for Collaborative Education & Quicy: Nellie Mae Education Foundation.

Bryan, T.K. (2011). *Exploring the dimensions of organizational capacity for local social service delivery organizations using a multi-method* (Dissertation). The Virginia Polytechnic Institute and State University, Alexandria, Virginia.

Bush, T., & Glover, D. (2016). School leadership and management in South Africa: Findings from a systematic literature review. *International Journal of Educational Management*, 30(2), 211–231.

Coates, C. & Associates. (2008). *Organizational Competencies.*

David, F.R. (2011). *Strategic management: Concepts and Cases* (13th ed.). New Jersey: Pearson Education, Inc., publishing as Prentice Hall.

Department of Cooperative Governance Republic of South Africa. (2016). *Standard Operating Procedure (SOP) Manual.* South Africa: PAIA Requests.

Edgar, W.B. & Lockwood, C.A. (2008). *Organizational Competencies: Clarifying the Construct.* USA: University of Arizona and Northern Arizona University.

Environmental Protection Agency (EPA). (2007). Guidance for preparing *Standard Operating Procedures (SOPs)*. United States: Environmental Protection Agency.

Evans, J.R. & Lindsay, W.M. (2005). *The management and control of quality* (6th ed.). Ohio: South-Western.

Goldkuhl, G. & Nilsson, E. (2000). Organizational ability, constituents and congruencies. *Proceedings of the OR42 Conference: Stream 'Knowledge and Learning – a Socio-technical Perspective'.* (pp. 1–15), Swansea, Wales.

Hatch, T. (2009). *Managing to change: How schools can survive (and sometimes thrive) in turbulent times.* New York, NY: Teachers College Press.

Hoy, W.K. & Miskel, C.G. (2008). Educational administration, theory, research, and practice (8th ed.). New York, NY: The McGraw-hill Companies, Inc.

Kantabutra, S. & Avery, G.C. (2010). The power of vision: Statements that resonate. *Journal of Business Strategy, 31*(1), 37–45.

Kantabutra, S. & Vimolratana, P. (2009). Vision-based leadership: Relationships and consequences in Thai and Australian retail stores. *Asia-Pacific Journal of Business Administration, 1*(2), 165–188.

Kantabutra, S. (2010). Vision effects: A critical gap in educational leadership research. *International Journal of Educational Management, 24*(5), 376–390.

King, M.B. & Bouchard, K. (2011). The capacity to build organizational capacity in schools. *Journal of Educational Administration,* 49(6), 653–669.

King, M.B. & Newmann, F.M. (2001). Building school capacity through professional development: Conceptual and empirical considerations. *International Journal of Educational Management,* 15(2), 86–94.

Li, L., Hallinger, P. & Ko, J. (2016). Principal leadership and school capacity effects on teacher learning in Hong Kong. *International Journal of Educational Management,* 30(1), 76–100.

Lin, W. & Green, D.P. (2016). Standard operating procedures: A safety net for pre-analysis plans. *American Political Science Association: The Profession,* 495–499.

Manich, K. (2015). Developing, maintaining standard operating procedures: Part three. *Shop Management 8*(12). Retrieved from https://www.autotraining.net/articles/

PricewaterhouseCooper Canada Foundation. (2011). *Capacity building investing in not-for-profit effectiveness. Discussion paper on strengthening the dialogue between the not-for-profit and corporate sectors.* Toronto, Canada: Author.

Robinson, V.M.J., McNaughton, S. & Timperley, H. (2011). Building capacity in a self-managing schooling system: The New Zealand experience. *Journal of Educational Administration,* 49(6), 720–738.

Sarrico, C.S., Rosa, M.J. & Manatos, M.J. (2012). School performance management practices and school achievement. *International Journal of Productivity and Performance Management,* 61(3), 272–289.

Sumintono, B. (2013). Sekolah Unggulan: Pendekatan Pengembangan Kapasitas Sekolah. JMP, 2(1).

Stocklin, S. (2010). The initial stage of a school's capacity building. *Educational Management Administration and Leadership 38*(4), 443–453.

Triatna, C. (2015). Pengembangan Kapasitas Manajemen Sekolah untuk Meningkatkan Mutu Pendidikan di Sekolah, Studi Kasus di SMA Negeri 2 Kota Bandung dan SMA Negeri 2 Kota Tasikmalaya. *Disertasi.* Bandung: Program Studi Administrasi Pendidikan, Sekolah Pascasarjana, Universitas Pendidikan Indonesia.

Watterston, J. & Caldwell, B. (2011). System alignment as a key strategy in building capacity for school transformation. *Journal of Educational Administration,* 49(6), 637–652.

Yat Wai Lo, W. & Oek Gu, J. (2008). Reforming school governance in Taiwan and South Korea: Empowerment and autonomization in school-based management. *International Journal of Educational Management,* 22(6), 506–526.

Educational Administration Innovation for Sustainable Development – Komariah et al. (Eds)
© 2018 Taylor & Francis Group, London, ISBN 978-1-138-57341-3

Authentic leadership in embedding pedagogic values of teachers

Suryadi, J. Permana & A. Komariah
Universitas Pendidikan Indonesia, Bandung, Indonesia

ABSTRACT: Changes in science technology make the competition between schools more stringent, this condition requires every school has a competent teacher. Teacher pedagogic competence becomes one of the keys to success in facing change. This study aims to examine the relationship of authentic leadership with pedagogic competence of teachers and test the multidimensionality of authentic leadership constructs. This study employs a quantitative approach. Data are collected using the survey method. This method is used to obtain data from a natural setting; however, when collecting data using the survey from 225 participants, the researcher employed the questionnaire techniques. Data collected were analysed using multiple-regression techniques with the aid of Ms. Excel 2016, IBM SPSS Statistic 22.0. for Windows The results showed that authentic leadership underpins the pedagogic competency values of teachers significantly. This implies the importance of cultivating the values of authentic leadership that are multidimensional to the pedagogic character of the teacher.

1 INTRODUCTION

Development of education includes a systemic unity with an open and multimakna system, both on the path of formal education, non formal, and informal. Therefore, in the context of educational development, education should be seen as a human investment that has a multidimensional perspective of social, cultural, economic and political. Schools are a place to learn in which resources are available with a high capacity to educate, provided a deliberate process of preparing for education so as to be the first and foremost choice to be effective.

Reveal various problems and constraints relating to the condition of teachers, among others related to quality, justice, teacher welfare and teacher management (Surya, 2007). The results of teacher competency test in November 2015 which shows the average national teacher competency test results are still low, while the government targets the standards. This can be seen from the still low value of professional competence and pedagogic teachers.

States that principal leadership is second only to classroom teaching as an influence on student learning. This implies that a principal is the second spearhead in successful classroom learning after the teacher (Leithwood & Day, 2007). The success of a leader in influencing members of the organization to be willing to work together, to have high discipline, to work passionately, and to be more productive in working for the achievement of organizational goals is influenced by the behaviors that leaders show to members of the organization and the power base they possess.

Leadership, until now believed to be an important factor that affects people's behavior, makes the organization become very popular, growing and progressing. but not a few also some organizations that have been very advanced, gradually become dim even dropped. Leadership through a long process is able to conjure up the passion of the people who are in it, or otherwise become very depressed and restless.

Islamic High School in Tasikmalaya city and district shows that pedagogic competence in making learning interesting and fun and making assessment (affective and psychomotor sphere) and assignment is in low category (Saripudin, 2015).

Teacher pedagogic competence can be influenced by the principal's leadership, one of the results of the study Nasrum (2013), shown that (1) dimensions of self-awareness have a positive and significant effect on teacher performance. The higher the self-awareness dimension shown by the principal's behavior the teacher's performance will also be higher; (2) balanced processing dimensions have a positive and significant effect on teacher performance.

The purpose of this study was to find relationship between the principal's authentic behavior and teacher pedagogic values.

2 METHODS

This study employs a quantitative approach. Data are collected using the survey method. This method is used to obtain data from a natural setting; however, when collecting data using the survey, the researcher employed several techniques, including the questionnaire, a test and structured interviews (Sugiyono, 2009). Using this descriptive method, the following steps will be carried out: 1) conducting literature studies on various references related to the research conducted, 2) focusing on solving existing problems in the present, 3) collecting data, collating data that has been collected , explained and then analyzed.

The source of data is responses to a questionnaire about the effect of Authentic Leadership at Islamic High School on school principals of pedagogic competences; these questionnaires were administered at teacher on islamic senior high school, which the researcher regards as representing the diversity of teachers. In order to obtain research data, a survey was conducted to collect large amounts of data and correlational studies were conducted to test whether a variable correlated, as well as how it correlated with other variables, either singular or plural.

The population in this study are the teachers who are on Islamic High School. Given a population of 512 teachers and a prescribed precision level of 5%. Thus, based on the formula obtained the number of samples (n) teachers on Islamic High School is as follows:

$$n = \frac{N}{1+N.e^2}$$
$$n = \frac{512}{1+512.(0,05)^2} = \frac{512}{1+512.(0,0025)} = 224,56$$

Proportional sampling random sampling is then sought by the formula: $n_i = \frac{N_i}{N} \times n$.

From the results of the above sample calculations, it can be concluded that the number of samples in this study with a precision of 5% is as many as 225 teachers.

The study used two types of data, namely primary data and secondary data. Primary data contains the understanding of data obtained by researchers directly from the main source. Primary data in this study comes from the answers given respondents through a given questionnaire/instrument. In this study, researchers used a questionnaire in obtaining primary data. Questionnaire given in the form of a closed questionnaire where the researcher provides options or answer options by using the scale of measurement, the Likert Scale. The second data comes from the review of documents derived from peer assessment documents from principals present in Islamic high schools and school supervisors.

To determine the reliability of the instruments used, the researchers tested the validity of the instrument so that the data obtained can answer the formulation of the problems raised. A valid instrument means that the measuring instrument used to get the data (measure) is valid.

Testing the validity can be known through the calculation by using the formula Pearson Product Moment to the values on each item question variable with a probability of 5%. Researchers in the test validity using IBM SPSS 22 applications as a means of testing. To calculate the reliability test, this research uses Cronbach alpha formula. Cronbach alpha is a reliability coefficient that shows how the parts of a set are positively correlated with each other.

After conducting validity test, instrument reliability and dissemination of instruments to respondents. Data processing is done by basing on statistical calculation procedure, in the form of: (1) calculation of respondent's score and descriptive analysis, (2) testing requirements analysis; data normality test, homogeneity test data, and data linearity test, and (3) hypothesis testing; correlation test, coefficient of determination test, regression test. In data processing, the researcher uses an application tool/data processing program in the form of Ms. Excel 2016, IBM SPSS Statistic 22.0.

3 RESULTS

The general description for each dimension of the authentic leadership variable can be seen in Figure 1.

Based on Figure 1, above can be seen that the value dimension has the highest score, the next dimension of purpose, relationship dimension, heart dimension and the lowest dimension of the authentic leadership variable of the madrasah head is in self dicipline dimension.

The general description of the pedagogic competence dimension can be seen in Figure 2.

Based on Figure 2, it can be seen that known pedagogical variables Teachers enter in high category. The highest score is in the "Assessment" dimension included in the high and low category in the medium-term "Learning" category.

Based on the picture above can be seen that each indicator on teacher teaching performance variables are in the high and medium category.

From table 2, it is known that in column B in constant (a) is 66.514, while the authentic leadership value (b1) is 0.875, so the regression equation can be written as follows:

$\hat{Y} = a + bX1$ or $66{,}514 + 0{,}875X\_1$

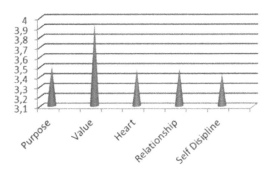

Figure 1. Authentic leadership overview.

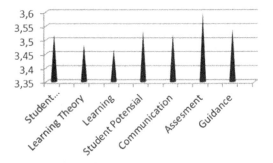

Figure 2. Description of pedagogic competence.

Table 1. Correlation of Variable AL to PC.

		Authentic leadership	Pedagogic competencies
Authentic leadership	Pearson Correlation	1	.859**
	Sig. (2-tailed)		.000
	N	225	225
Pedagogic competencies	Pearson Correlation	.859**	1
	Sig. (2-tailed)	.000	
	N	225	225

**. Correlation is significant at the 0.01 level (2-tailed).

Table 2. Regression variable AL to variable PC.

Model		Unstandardized Coefficients		Standardized Coefficients	t	Sig.
		B	Std. Error	Beta		
1	(Constant)	66.514	1.774		3.672	.000
	Authentic leadership	.875	.035	.859	25.041	.000

a. Dependent Variable: pedagogic competencies.
(source: suryadi, 2017)

Table 3. Correlation coefficients and coefficient of determination.

Model	R	R Square	Adjusted R Square	Std. Error of the Estimate	Durbin-Watson
1	.859^a	.738	.736	5.122	1.791

a. Predictors: (Constant), authentic leadership.

The above regression equation can be interpreted that if the constant of 66.514 states that if there is no authentic leadership value then the value of teacher's teaching performance is 66.514. The regression coefficient of X_1 is 0.875 means that every addition of one authentic leadership value, the teacher's performance value increases by 0.875.

From table 4, above it is clear that the value of the correlation coefficient (R) of 0.859 and the correlation coefficient value is included in very high category. The table above also describes the effect of independent variable (X) to the dependent variable (Y) or also called the coefficient of determination (R2) which is the result of squaring R. From the above table it is known that the coefficient of determination (R2) is 0.738 which means that the influence Authentic leadership on teacher's teaching performance is 73.8% while the remaining 26.2% is influenced by other variables.

Based on the above table (model summaryb) obtained value of R2x1y or Rsquare value = 0.738. To find the value of ρyε1 (epsilon/residual variable) is determined by the following formula.

ρ41ε1 = √(1-R2yx1) = √(1 − 0.738)√0.262 = 0.512 the empirical causal relationship between X1 to Y can be made the following structural equations:

ρx1ε1 = ρ21 + ρ21ε1 = 0.738 + 0.512ε1

Figure 3 describes the influence of authentic leadership principal's variables Authentic leadership (AL) against pedagogic competence Pedagogic competencies (PC) is 73.8% while the rest 26.2% influenced by other factors.

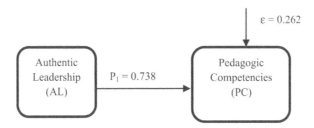

Figure 3. Authentic leadership influence on teachers' pedagogy.

4 DISCUSSIONS

In leading the principal refers to shared moral values or *value based* which is embraced by the citizens of the school as a reference in thinking, acting and acting, and the principal upholds these moral values and implements them in leading teachers to achieve common goals and make schools more productive based on the moral values it embraces.

Authentic leadership was a suitable type of leadership model to effectively instill value system (Komariah, 2012). Principals who have good moral and ethical values will reflect good attitudes and behaviors as well, along with the attitudes and behaviors that the principal must have in his leadership according to Mulyasa (2012): (1) has responsibility for the position entrusted to him; (2) has a high level of concern and commitment to achieve something meaningful during his tenure; (3) enforcing time discipline with full awareness that discipline is the key to success; (4) carry out every task and activity with passionate responsibility and enthusiasm and must always be clear meaning (*value*) of each activity in relation to improving the quality of graduate and school productivity; (5) proactive (initiative to do something that is believed to be good) to improve the quality of education in schools, not just reactive (just carry out activities as directed); (6) has a strong will and courage to decide every problem faced by his school; (7) become a communicative leader and a motivator for his staff to be more accomplished and not behave *bossy* (officials who only want to be respected and obeyed); (8) have sensitivity and feel guilty about something that is not quite right, and try to correct it; (9) dare to correct every mistake firmly and act wisely and not permissive (easy to understand, understand and forgive mistakes).

Authentic leadership conditions in schools on the dimensions of values in this moral form of leadership, in accordance with the concept of authentic leadership. Bento (2013), developed transparency of the relationship by Avalio, Walumba & Weber in Northouse (2013). While according to Bill Gorge in Northouse (2013). Authentic leadership is a leader who has a passion for leadership and he is free to lead by virtue of his core values, and his features have five aspects: goals, values, relationships and hearts. Further authentic leadership according to Robber Terry in Northouse (2013) the leader who must try to do what is right is based on the practice and the formulation that has been made which is called the authentic action wheel consisting of six aspects namely the meaning, mission, existence, resources, strength and structure. Authentic leadership and authentic followership with follower basic need satisfaction in a crosslevel model where authentic leadership was aggregated to the group level of analysis. Crosslevel interaction results indicated that authentic leadership strengthened the relationship Leroy (2015).

Principal as a leader's efforts to keep his awareness remains focused on reality, rationality and sincere intention to move his followers to achieve the goals of the school he leads in accordance with the vision and mission set. There are many tests and trials a leader must face throughout his career. The higher the position as a leader, the higher the depth and extent of the exam or problems it faces. The opposite of self-awareness is that a leader loses control over him therefore an authentic principal will not lose control of him.

In the event of a problem or failure to achieve the goal of the school, a person who served as principals should be able to revive his motivation and enthusiasm and pass it on to all the citizens of the school. In addition to that, the relationship between team leaders' authenticity and creativity is mediated by perception of support for innovation (Ccrnc, 2013).

If the principal has no self-motivation and discouragement then all of his members will be lethargic and his organization is on the verge of destruction. A principal who leads authentically will not lose his or her awareness of being overwhelmed by various calamities or problems. He is well aware that he is the model and source of the spirit of all his followers. At the time the school is down, all members will pay attention to the leader. The authentic school principal must show his strength, his optimism, and his ability to build his future vision in order to have the strength to stand in the face of the times with full optimism and confidence.

self awareness also helps the principal to know the extent to which he knows his own self, to know the advantages and disadvantages he has. One way to raise the headmaster's personal awareness is to understand how exactly the concept of himself, with more and more what can be understood and done, will increasingly understand who he really. There are several ways to improve *self awareness*: (1) asking himself about himself; (2) listen to others (members or colleagues); (3) actively seeking information about yourself; (4) look at yourself with a different perspective; (5) increase self-disclosure.

This condition indicates that most of aliyah headmaster in Bandung have good relationship, with internal environment that is teacher and staff and board of foundation, but still need effort braided with external party. The ability of the principal to establish relationships with others, especially in building productive relationships with teachers and staff of tenders based on commitment and belief in organizational life and personal life. In developing relationships with others this requires the ability to adapt to the norms of society, accept and bridge differences (diversity), controlling emotions in managing conflicts that occur in schools.

In relation to this relationship, it is necessary to develop the values of openness between the school principal and the leader in order for the principal to gain recognition and respected as a leader in the school, then also develop opportunities for teachers to enable the future to take a leadership role as part of the regeneration of leadership in take decisions that have consequences or risks of small, medium and large with alternatives developed in accordance with their own creativity.

In the development of this dimension, the principal is willing to provide input in the application of new things to the success of the teaching and learning process, the willingness to accept constructive criticism and suggestions from various groups, especially from the teachers, and to carry out tasks with no burden, such activities demonstrating the ability in self-discipline as a manifestation of positive values in consistent action towards success.

In addition, the principal has a high competitive spirit as a manifestation of the quality of a leader by providing opportunities for teachers to excel and develop and be able to cope with stress and job pressure. In relation to the development of the teacher profession, the principal knows the procedures for professional development of teachers by implementing professional teacher development procedures and encourages teachers and staff to improve learning outcomes overall learners and to control principal leadership activities to monitor and evaluate the implementation of learning programs and also assess the potential shortcomings and advantages of teachers by revealing two advantages, one deficiency and two alternative solutions (2:1:2 Model).

In this study, pedagogic competence variables are divided into seven dimensions consisting of knowing the characteristics of learners, mastering learning theories and principles of educational learning, educational learning, development of potential learners, communication with learners, assessment and guidance of learners.

Teachers tend to use pedagogical competences occasionally rather than regularly. Planning education is where this activity becomes more regular, which is in line with what other research has indicated (Alba & Carballo, 2005; Empirica, 2006; Wastiau et al., 2013). These results are still better than the research undertaken by (Saripudin, 2015) in the city and district of Tasikmalaya which illustrates that pedagogic competence in the dimension makes the lesson interesting and fun, and make assessment and assignment in low category, while in carrying out the guidance activities including enough category.

This research on pedagogic competence, in line with Mohammad Ali's opinion that "based on various quality education studies determined by 60% quality of teachers, the quality of teachers can be seen from the performance of teaching" (Hayat & Ali, 2012). Usman (2010) explains that, the task of teachers as a profession requires the teacher to develop professionalism in accordance with the science and technology. Educating, teaching and training students is a teacher's job as a profession. (Engkoswara, 1992) further said that the performance of employees is necessary and absolutely improved in accordance with the demands and development of society.

High performance of employees depends on the factors that influence it. In this case Jones (2002) say that "Many things cause poor performance, among others: (1) personal ability, (2) ability of manager, (3) process gap, (4) environmental issues, (5) personal situation, (6) motivation". Wood, et al. (2001) look at the factors that affect individual performance (*job performance*) as a function of the interaction of individual attributes, business work effort. Meanwhile (Zainun, 1989) suggests "there are three factors that can affect the performance of employees, namely: (1) characteristic of a person, (2) the outside environment, and (3) attitude towards the employee profession". Performance is a multidimensional construct that includes the factors that influence it.

Factors that influence performance by Mahmudi (2015) is: (1) Individual factors, including: knowledge, skills, abilities, confidence, motivation and commitment that each individual; (2) Leadership factors include: quality in providing encouragement, encouragement, direction, and support provided by managers and *team leader*; (3) Team Factors, including: the quality of support and encouragement provided by peers in a team, trust in team members, cohesiveness and closeness of team members; (4) System factors, including: work systems, work facilities or infrastructure provided by organizations, organizational processes, and performance culture within the organization; (5) Contextual factors, including: pressure and changes in the external and internal environment.

Performance can be seen from several criteria, according to Castetter (1996) suggests there are four performance criteria that is: (1) Individual characteristics; (2) Procces; (3) result; and (4) The combination of individual characters, processes and results.

Assessing the quality of performance can be reviewed from several indicators that include: (1) Work method; (2) Mastery of Material; (3) Mastery of professional proficiency and education; (4) Mastery of ways of adjustment; (5) Personality to carry out their duties properly (Sulistiyono, 2001). Leadership is important because it serves as an anchor, provides guidance on changing times, and is responsible for organizational effectiveness (Hoy & Miskel, 2014). With good leadership and authentic it is expected to trigger the level of pedagogic competence for the better. With regard to the effect of authentic leadership aspects on pedagogic competence, (Leithwood & Day, 2007) states that the principal's leadership as the second part after classroom teaching influences learning. While an important aspect of the leadership role in education is empowering teachers and giving them broad powers to improve learners' learning (Sallis, 2005).

From this authentic leadership influence, Moeljono (2008) adding to the need for generous, loving, caring, forgiving leaders, promoting humanity and faith and sincere loyalty. Superior authentic leadership is built one of them with the value dimension (value). The principal as a leader needs to carry out his roles and tasks based on values that can lead to ideal conditions. Thus the aspect of values underlying the leadership of the principal will have an impact on the behavior and style of leadership applied in carrying out his duties as the person responsible in building the school. Internalized moral perspective refers to an internalized and integrated form of self-regulation (Ryan & Deci, 2003). This sort of self-regulation is guided by internal moral standards and values versus group, organizational, and societal pressures, and it results in expressed decision making and behaviour that is consistent with these internalized values (Avolio & Gardner, 2005; Gardner et al., 2005; Walumba et al., 2008). Covey (1997) introduces a principle-centered leadership, Goleman (2002) introduce the ultimate leadership, likewise with Maxwell (2004) which includes the individual values of the leader in one of the laws of leadership. This is as stated by Maxwell (2004) that one must first believe in the leader, his new vision.

5 CONCLUSIONS

Authentic leadership of the principal is in the high category, sequentially influential aspects include value, purpose, relationship, heart and the last dimensions of self-discipline are categorized being.

Thus the principal in an effort to improve pedagogic competence must: (1) set learning achievement goals of learners by communicating directly to learners, teachers and parents; (2) establish clear rules on the use of classroom time; (3) establishing, implementing and evaluating guidelines and rules to address and enforce disciplinary issues with teachers and learners.

The things that make the principal's authentic leadership affect the pedagogic competence are the principal in the lead: (1) using the sincerity in serving as a form of responsibility of the office duties in his embannya, for that the need of a leader in understanding the true duties and functions of the position given to him; (2) oriented to the school objectives formulated in the form of school vision and mission that are derived from the national education objectives, then the school objectives are incorporated into the school work plan; (3) does not exclude positive moral values that are shared or can be said to be value based, positive moral values are used as a reference in leading and in taking a policy; (4) in dealing with its members and also with the community sufficiently transparent to the various problems experienced and faced by the school and trying to find solutions to these issues collectively and openly; (5) there is a two-way communication between the principal and the teacher in many ways, which makes the school more democratic and a balance process which will have a good impact on school productivity; (6) show the spirit to the teachers in leading the school and able to make the teachers also to more spirit in teaching to produce qualified graduates.

REFERENCES

Alba, C., & Carballo, R. 2005. Viabilidad de las propuestas para la aplicaci_on el cr_edito europeo por parte del profesorado de las universidades espa~nolas,bvinculadas a labutilizaci_on de las TIC en la docencia y la investigaci_on. *Revista de Educaci_*on, 337,b71e97.

Avolio, B.J., Gardner, W.L., Walumba, F. O., Luthans, F., & May, D.R. 2004. Unlocking the mask: a look at the process by which authentic transformational leaders impact follower attitudes and behaviors. *Leadership Quarterly* (15): 801–823.

Bento, A.V. & Ribeiro, M.I. 2013. Authentic Leadership in School Organizations. *European Scientific Journal* 9(3): 121–130.

Castetter, W. B. 1996. *The Human Resource Function in Educational Administration, 6th ed.* New Jersey: Prentice-Hall, Inc.

Cerne, M., Jaklic, M. & Miha Škerlavaj. 2013. Authentic leadership, creativity, and innovation: A multilevel perspective. *Leadership* 9 (1); 63–85.

Covey, S. R. 1997. *Principle Centered Leadership: Kepemimpinan yang Berprinsip.* Jakarta: Dunamis Intermaster.

Empirica. 2006. Benchmarking access and use of ICT in European schools 2006. Bonn: Empirica. Retrieved from http://www.empirica.de/publikationen/ documents/No08–2006_learnInd.pdf.

Engkoswara. 1992. Pengembangan Performance Guru. *Jurnal Pendidikan*, 39–40.

Goleman, D. 2002. *Working with Emotional Intelligence.* Jakarta: Gramedia Pustaka Utama.

Hayat, B., & Ali, M. 2012. *Khazanah dan Praksis Pendidikan Islam di Indonesia.* Bandung: CV Pustaka Cendekia Utama.

Hoy, W.K., & Miskel, C.G. 2014. *Educational Administration: Theory, Research, and Practice.* New York: McGraw-Hill

Jones, P. 2002. Buku Pintar Manajemen Kinerja. Jakarta: Metalexia Publishing & Qreator Tata Qarakter.

Leithwood, K., & Day, C. 2007. *Seven Strong Claims about Succesful School Leadership.* London: England NSCL.

Leroy, H., Anseel, F., Gardner, W.I. & Sels, L. 2015. Authentic Leadership, Authentic Followership, Basic Need Satisfaction, and Work Role Performance: A Cross-Level Study. *Journal of Management* 41 (6): 1677–1697.

Komariah, A. 2012. The Authentic Leadership of School Principals in Inculcating Value System. *Jurnal Ilmu Pendidikan* 18 (2):194–200.

Mahmudi. 2015. *Manajemen Kinerja Sektor Publik, ed 3.* Yogyakarta: UPP STIM YKPN.

Maxwell, J. C. 2004. *Berpikir lain dari yang Biasanya.* Jakarta: Karisma Press.

Moeljono, D. 2008. *More About Beyond Leadership.* Jakarta: Elex Media Komputindo.

Mulyasa, E. 2012. *Manajemen dan Kepemimpinan Kepala Sekolah.* Jakarta: Bumi Aksara.

Nasrum, Andi. 2013. *Kinerja Guru Kepemimpinan Aiutentik – Pengaruh Pada Kinerja Guru SMA Negeri 1 Bulukumba.* (Thesis). School of Postgraduate, Universitas Gadjah Mada, Yogyakarta.

Northouse, P. G. 2013. *Leadership: Theory and Practices, 6th ed.* California: Sage Publication Inc.

Ryan, R. M., & Deci, E. L. 2003. On assimilating identities to the self: A self-determination theory perspective on internalization and integrity within cultures. In M. R. Leary & J. P. Tangney (Eds.), Handbook *of self and identity*: 253–272. New York: Guilford.

Sallis, E. 2005. *Total Quality Management in Education.* New York: Prentice-Hall.

Saripudin. 2015. *Studi tentang Pengaruh Kepemimpinan Kepala Sekolah, Kompetensi pedagogik dan Budaya Madrasah terhadap Kepuasan Siswa dan Dampaknya pada Prestasi Belajar di MA kota dan kabupaten Tasikmalaya.* Bandung: SPS UPI.

Sugiyono (2009) *Metode penelitian kuantitatif dan kualitatif.* Bandung, Indonesia: CV. Alfabeta.

Sulistiyono, A. 2001. *Manajemen Penyelenggaraan Hotel.* Bandung: Alfabeta.

Surya, M. 2007. *Bunga Rampai Guru dan Pendidikan.* Jakarta: Balai Pustaka.

Usman, M. U. 2010. *Menjadi Guru Profesional.* Bandung: Remaja Rosda Karya

Wastiau, P., Blamire, R., Kearney, C., Quittre, V., Van de Gaer, E., & Monseur, C. 2013. The use of ICT in education: a survey of schools in Europe. *European Journal of Education*, 48, 11e27. http://dx.doi.org/10.1111/ejed.12020.

Wood, J., Wallace, J., & Zeffani, R. M. 2001. *Organization Behavior a Global Prespectives.* Australia: John Wiley & Sons.

Zainun, B. 1989. *Manajemen dan Motivasi.* Jakarta: Bumi Aksara.

Educational Administration Innovation for Sustainable Development – Komariah et al. (Eds)
© 2018 Taylor & Francis Group, London, ISBN 978-1-138-57341-3

The effectivity of principal performance appraisal instruments

Sururi & A. Suryana
Universitas Pendidikan Indonesia, Bandung, West Java, Indonesia

ABSTRACT: Inaccurate performance appraisal instruments might lead to imprecise performance evaluation. The effectivity of principal performance appraisal depends a lot on the effectiveness of the evaluation instrument. Based on this issue, this research aimed at analyzing the effectiveness of the instruments for evaluating the performance of state senior high schools' principals within the area of the Education Agency of Bandung Barat West Java Indonesia. This research uses descriptive analysis method based on opinion from respondents. Result of this research, the effectivity of principal performance appraisal instruments can be recognized from the following aspects relevancy, sensitivity, reliability, acceptability, and practicality. Furthermore, the use of this instrument principal performance appraisal could be utilized for many purposes such as clarifying the principals' roles and changing the current policy. The fact showed that the benefits of this evaluation had not completely reached these principals.

1 INTRODUCTION

A principal of a school has an important role in the success and the effectiveness of the school (Susanto, 2015; Gurr et al, 2005; Akinola, 2013). To measure how well principals run their responsibility, their performance needs to be assessed. Many education supervisors believe that principal performance appraisal is the most effective way to see the effectiveness of principals' performance at schools, although numerous principals perceive it as a waste of time (Gaziel, 2008). This appraisal is essential to be conducted even though many principals still question the objectivity and the follow-up to this assessment (Muenich, 2014; Goldring et al, 2014; Hadi, 2008).

One of the crucial matters in a schools' management of human resources is evaluating how successful the principal accomplishes his/her jobs since he/she is also part of the school community. Through such evaluation, everyone, particularly policy makers can see how well the principal has worked (Catano, 2006). It is very reasonable that principal's performance affects the entire school. Thus, the upshot of the appraisal can give a clear picture of real condition for the sake of the schools' and the principal's development. In reality, inappropriate and inaccurate evaluation might happen due to many reasons. These are the vagueness of the meaning of the implemented performance, the misapprehension of the supervisors about the expected performance, the inaccurate performance appraisal instrument, and the ignorance of the head of the organization about the performance management.

Reflecting from the essential objective of the evaluation as well as the existing evaluation problems above, it will work best if during the performance appraisal, the vision, missions and the strategy of the organization are translated into an operational objective (Fathoni & Inda, 2011; Abbas, 2014; Ahmed, 2013). Derived from this notion, a research on the effectiveness of principal performance appraisal instrument as a means of evaluation is worth conducted. It is expected that the evaluation will accurately assess the principals' performance and the results will bring benefits for the related education agency.

Performance appraisal instrument to be effective should meet the following criteria (Dhewi et al, 2006; Susanto, 2015:

a. Reliability: It means that the instrument should have consistent assessment for any employee (principal) anywhere. The appraisal which is made by independent assessors should have correspondence between one another. For examples: the supervisor, colleagues, and the principal can have different interpretation about that principal's performance by seeing the instrument.
b. Relevancy: The instrument reflects an obvious connection between the standard of performance and the objective of the organization as well as among the job elements. For this purpose, a clear identification on the job covering its elements needs to be created.
c. Sensitivity: Sensitivity requirement is met when a performance appraisal instrument can clearly distinguish between excellent and poor performance of the principals.
d. Acceptability: When the principal performanceappraisal instrument has been created and the implementation is supported by the assessor team, it means acceptability is fulfilled.
e. Practicality: An appraisal instrument is considered effective when it can be easily understood and implemented either by the supervisors or the principals.

2 METHOD

The design of this research was qualitative descriptive research. The method of this research is qualitative descriptive format by conducting documentation research, interview and observation to schools about the instrument used in performance assessment of principal. Data analysis used is qualitative data analysis verifikatif. This design was chosen with a deep consideration that this research is classified as a social research which aimed at describing the effectiveness of the instrument employed to evaluate junior high schools' principal performance in West Bandung Regency. The focus of this research was the content of the instrument as well as the management of the evaluation results.

3 FINDINGS AND DISCUSSION

The effectiveness of principal performance appraisal instruments can be recognized from the following aspects: (1) Reliability; the reliability of an instrument is essential in collecting consistent data and information, regarding both time and place consistency. It is obvious that all principals expect that the evaluation system can be applied for different person independently but is still corresponding with one another. A reliable evaluation is an appraisal which is far from significant flaws in it. There is no significant problem in determining quantitative assessment as the measurement is quite clear. However, bias and subjectivity might occur in qualitative measurement because the quality of one principal is different from another one. Hence, the accuracy of the qualitative measurement depends a lot on the quality and the quantity of the given information of the principals' performance. In this case, the assessors' ability in making fair and objective judgment is highly required. In other words, the use of consistent evaluation criteria for the performance appraisal is fundamental. In terms of reliability, based on the answers of respondents of this research, the instruments used for principal performance appraisal had high reliability. This finding was supported by the following data: (a) the assessors were competent in accomplishing their task and so far there were no significant differences between the performance appraisal results of one assessor with the other's; (b) in order to minimize subjectivity, the appraisal was executed by a supervisor(s) from a cluster other than that currently visited area, and accompanied by a supervisor(s) the education authority. This system would result in more accurate evaluation. It was revealed hitherto insignificant differences in the evaluation results among different assessors. Each assessor had fairly the same appraisal result of a principal performance. (c) the researcher did not find any significant differences among the assessors' evaluation result because the assessor team always discuss their evaluation before the made a final judgment. These statements uttered by the respondents above matched with the reliability criterion of an instrument, in which the evaluation from different assessors is corresponding with one another and showed objective as well as fair measurement (Dhewi et al, 2006).

(2) Relevancy; relevancy deals with the correlation between the principals' jobs (input, process, and output) and the measured aspects of their performance. It implies that the criteria for evaluating principal performance should be relevant with their actual job descriptions. Therefore, clear information on the jobs should be specified for an optimum performance. It was found on the field that the instruments used for principal performance appraisal were reasonably effective. Some of the respondents stated as follows: (a) this appraisal was relevant to the job descriptions of the principals at schools. Ultimately, it was also related to the schools' objectives and quality; (b) the instruments already covered all the matters regarding principals' responsibilities as the leader of a school; (c) the implemented instruments were also related to the objectives of the organizations. These assertions were suitable with the criteria of a relevant instrument, in which there is an apparent correlation between the standard of performance and the objective of the organization, and there is an obvious connection between the job elements with the assessed indicators in the instruments (Dhewi et al, 2006).

(3) Sensitivity; sensitivity of an instrument enables she assessors to distinguish between effective performance and ineffective performance. If an instrument does not have this criterion, it is not recommended for any administrative objectives. Such instruments will not give considerable meaning for principals' professional development; besides, this instrument might discourage both the assessors and the assessee It was observed that the instruments used for junior high school principal performance appraisal in West Bandung Regency in 2014 were fairly sensitive. It just needed more objectivity of the assessors, particularly when the assessors wanted simplicity during the evaluation, or if the principals had a close relationship with the assessor(s), the score would tend to be higher. These fraudulent behaviours affected the ability of the instruments to distinguish between productive principals and mordant principals. This reality was revealed from the respondents' avowals: (a) if the assessors were objective, this appraisal was able to differentiate principals with excellent performance from those with poor performance; (b) generally, the instruments were able to measure the principals' performance but it greatly depended on the way of the evaluation. If the assessors truly referred to the instruments and evaluate the principal performance as the way it was, the performance could be objectively measured. However, sometimes the feeling of compassion to the principals led to subjective evaluation; (c) the instruments which were used at present merely measured the principals' competencies; (d) the most competence parties to distinguish between outstanding and poor principals was actually education supervisors; and thus supervisors should take part as the assessors. These reports were in line with the criteria of a sensitive instrument (Dhewi, 2006), in which the sensitivity of an instrument is related to the accuracy of the performance appraisal system so that it is able to differentiate between outstanding and poor employees as well as related to its utility for personnel administration purposes.

(4) Acceptability; acceptability becomes the most important matter among the other criteria of a good instrument for any program for human resources development, including performance appraisal needs an approval as well as support from the related parties. This acceptance is an indirect form of support from the associated parties and also a kind of participation of people who will use this appraisal system. Principal performance appraisal instruments which are accepted by the related parties can be used for evaluating principals' performance for the following reasons: (a) the implementation of the evaluation is somewhat easy for usually Principal Performance Appraisal program (PPKS) has been created in the form of an application (Microsoft Excel), so the assessors could easily and directly fill it and see the result; (b) before the appraisal is carried out, there will be a briefing or socialization, led by a couch supervisor. Finally, the researcher drew a conclusion that the instruments used for evaluating junior high schools' principal performance were highly acceptable based on the following reasons: (a) there was a socialization of performance appraisal system; (b) the results of performance appraisal towards the assesses had got an approval from the assessors; (c) the instruments were acceptable since the way to fill these was very practical and easy.

(5) Practicality; practicality means that an appraisal instrument should be able to be understood and utilized by both the assessors and assesses. Derived from this definition, the researcher concluded that the instruments used for evaluating the performance of junior high school principals were quite practical. There were some statements of the respondents which supported this

conclusion as follows: (a) generally this instrument could be easily comprehended and this was also practical because it was designed in the form of a computer application/program; (b) the program was developed in Microsoft Excel format, so that the assessors could easily input the score and see the results. To sum up, the researcher concluded that the junior high school principal performance appraisal instruments in West Bandung Regency were practical as they covered most of the practicality criteria. The fulfilment of these criteria enabled the assessors to evaluate the principals and the principals to understand the results.

4 CONCLUSION

Based on the criteria of an effective performance appraisal instruments – reliability, sensitivity, relevancy, acceptability, and practicality, the researcher drew a conclusion that the implemented instruments were effective in terms of their reliability, sensitivity, relevancy, acceptability, and practicality. When the assessors wanted simplicity during the evaluation, or if the principals had a close relationship with the assessor(s), the score would tend to be higher. In other words, the instruments failed to distinguish between outstanding and poor principals. From the perspective of the effectiveness of the achievement of the objectives of the performance appraisal, including promotion, demotion, compensation administration, coaching and development, it could be concluded that this performance appraisal was not effective and could not be a strong foundation of decision making.

REFERENCES

Abbas M Z. 2014. Effectiveness of Performance Appraisal on Performance of Employees. IOSR *Journal of Business and Management.* (IOSR-JBM) e-ISSN: 2278–487X, p-ISSN: 2319–7668. Volume 16, Issue 6. Ver. II (Jun. 2014), pp. 173–178.

Ahmed, I et al. 2013. Employee performance evaluation: a fuzzy approach. *International Journal of Productivity and Performance Management.* Vol. 62, No. 7, 2013 pp. 718–734, Emerald Group Publishing Limited 1741–0401.

Akinola O B. 2013. Principals' Leadership Skills and School Effectiveness: The Case of South Western Nigeria, www.sciedu.ca/wje *World Journal of Education* Vol. 3, No. 5; 2013.

Catano, et al. 2006. What are Principals Expected to Do? Congruence between Principal Evaluation and Performance Standards, *NASSP Bulletin,* September 2006; vol. 90, 3: pp. 221–237, SAGE Pub Journal.

Dhewi, R M et al. 2006. Analisis Pengaruh Efektivitas Sistem Penilaian Kinerja Terhadap Motivasi Kerja, Kepuasan Kerja dan Kinerja Karyawan PT Coats Rejo Indonesia. *Jurnal Manajamen dan Agribisnis*, MB-IPB, ISSN 1693–5853 halaman 1–5.

Fathoni & Inda K S. 2011. Analisis Penilaian Kinerja Rumah Sakit Dengan Penerapan Balanced Scorecard (Studi Kasus Rumah "ABC"), *Jurnal Sistem Informasi* (JSI), Vol. 3, No. 1, April 2011.

Gaziel, H. 2008. Principals' Performance Assessment: Empirical Evidence from an Israeli Case Research. *Educational Management Administration & Leadership*. July 2008; vol. 36, 3: pp. 337–351. SAGE Pub Journal.

Goldring E B et al. 2014. Multisource Principal Evaluation Data: Principals' Orientations and Reactions to Teacher Feedback Regarding Their Leadership Effectiveness. *Journal Educational Administration* Quarterly 1–28.

Gurr et al. 2005. Successful Principal Leadership: Australian Case Studies. *Journal of Educational Administration*: The International Successful School Principalship Project Vol 43 (6) 539–551.

Hadi, S. 2008. Konstruk Kinerja Kepala Sekolah Dasar Di Daerah Istimewa Yogyakarta. *Jurnal Penelitian dan Evaluasi Pendidikan* Nomor 1 tahun XI hal 20–37 ISSN: 1410–4725 Akreditasi no: 167/DIKTI/Kep/2007, Yogyakarta.

Muenich, J A. 2014. A Research of How Secondary School Principals in Minnesota Perceive the Evaluation of Their Performance, *NASSP Bulletin*. December 2014; vol. 98, 4: pp. 280–309, first published on November 23, 2014, SAGE Pub Journal.

Susanto. 2015. Pengaruh Kepemimpinan Kepala Sekolah, Kinerja Guru, Komite SekolahTerhadapKeefektifan SDN Se-Kecamatan Mlati, *Jurnal Akuntabilitas Manajemen Pendidikan* Volume 3, No 2, September 2015 hlm 250–263, Universitas Negeri Yogyakarta.

Educational Administration Innovation for Sustainable Development – Komariah et al. (Eds)
© 2018 Taylor & Francis Group, London, ISBN 978-1-138-57341-3

College students' intention to become entrepreneurs

R.A. Syathari, A. Rahayu & R. Huriyati
Universitas Pendidikan Indonesia, Bandung, West Java, Indonesia

ABSTRACT: Entrepreneurship is concerned with business and innovation with regard to changing the prosperity status quo. From a macroeconomic perspective, the increasing number of educated entrepreneurs would make a significant contribution to the nation's economic stability and growth. This study addresses the problem of the extent to which the Bandung city's college male and female students intend to choose entrepreneurship as their career. Employing a survey method, the data from structured questionnaires of 360 sample students was analyzed by using percentage calculation and the contingency table of chi square. The result of the analysis indicates that only a limited number of the Bandung city's college students, particularly female, had the intention of becoming entrepreneurs and only a small number of them had tended not to implement entrepreneurship. This study specifies the important need to promote entrepreneurship in the Bandung colleges by providing the students with entrepreneurship-related course.

1 INTRODUCTION

The high number of the unemployed educated workforce, including unemployed college graduates, in Indonesia is one of the country's serious issues. This may cause various national development problems and influences social and individual productivity.

As the fourth most populated country in the world, it is not easy to eliminate the unemployment problem. Along with the increase in the population number, unemployment, including those who hold a college diploma, is also increasing. The Indonesian's Central Bureau of Statistic (2014), noted that the share of higher education graduates to the country's unemployment data was 15%. This means that around 1.1 million out of the 7,240,000 workforce were unemployed. This number increases every year along with the increasing population.

In regard to taking care of this particular issue it is important to consider encouraging youngsters aged 18–24 years old, including those who are already in the higher education system, to choose entrepreneurship as their alternative career choice. This may shift their paradigm when they have graduated from becoming a job seeker to becoming a job creator, thereby increasing the number of entrepreneurs in the country.

Entrepreneurship has various definitions. Kuratko (2009) defines it as an integrated concept that permeates an individual business in an innovative manner. Beckman and Cherwitz (2009), define entrepreneurship as an intrinsic human right to change the status quo. This means the concept of entrepreneurship concerns business and innovation with regard to changing the status quo. Acs (2006) defines it as a process through which an individual or group of individuals identify opportunities, allocate resources, and create value. The creation of value is often done through the identification of unmet needs or through the identification of opportunities for change. Entrepreneurs see "problems" as "opportunities," by taking action to identify the solutions to those problems and the customers who will pay to have those problems solved. Referring to those concepts, entrepreneurship can be an alternative solution to the nation's unemployment problem.

An entrepreneur is someone who is specialized in making judgmental decisions about the coordination of scare sources. This is because entrepreneurial activity involves the discovery, evaluation and exploitation of opportunity within the framework of an individual-opportunity nexus. This is in line with what the United Nations Conference on Trade and Development (2015) mentions in that three of the most frequently mentioned functional roles of entrepreneurs are associated with major schools of thought to an entrepreneurship, namely risk taking, innovativeness, and opportunity seeking.

The United States of America is one of the risk taker nations and the dominant force in entrepreneurial activities. Entrepreneurial firms are the essential mechanism by which millions of people enter the economic and social mainstream of American society. In the US, entrepreneurship enables millions of people, including women, minorities, and immigrants, to access the American Dream. In the evolutionary process, entrepreneurship plays the crucial and indispensable role of providing the "social glue" that binds together both high-tech and mainstream activities.

According to Drucker (2005), an entrepreneur can be perceived as someone who actually searches for change, responds to it, and exploits change as an opportunity. Entrepreneurs share certain personal attributes, such as creativity, dedication, determination, flexibility, leadership, passion, self-confidence and smarts.

Entrepreneurship makes a significant contribution to the Gross Domestic Product (GDP) and to employment (Oosterbeek et al., 2008). Its contribution to GDP, however, was still lower than community service which contributed 9.7%, mining which contributed 10.4%, trade, hotels and restaurants which contributed 12.1%, agriculture which contributed 14.0%, and manufacturing industry which contributed 24.2%.

Accordingly, entrepreneurship is an alternative solution that can be made to overcome the unemployment problem by bringing back the power of real economic sector. It is agreed that entrepreneurship becomes necessary to stimulate economic growth and employment opportunities. For a developing country like Indonesia, micro, small and medium enterprises have their parts in creating jobs, growing income, and reducing poverty. It is proven that a monetary crisis does not have any impact on micro, small and medium enterprises. Therefore, millions of entrepreneurs are needed to boost the economy.

Extensification of entrepreneurship is considered as a reasonable effort in regard to increasing the numbers of entrepreneurs in the country. This is because entrepreneurship has an impact on strengthening the country's economic foundation and increasing its economic stability. It also makes a significant contribution to the country's economic growth. Therefore, an attempt of its extensification would be very important.

The ideal ratio between the number of entrepreneurs and the population should be equal or more than 2%. It means that if the number of entrepreneurs in a country reaches 2% or more, the economic growth will be high and the unemployment rate will stay low. Kuratko (2009) noted that there are as many as 5.6 million Americans below the age of 34 who are actively trying to start their own business today. One third of new entrepreneurs are 30 years old and more than 60% of them are 18 to 29 years old whom people say they want to own their own business, and nearly 80% of them who would become entrepreneurs in the US are between the age of 18 and 34.

In producing new entrepreneurs, education should not only consider the quantity of entrepreneurs but also their quality (Kourilsky, 1995). It should, therefore, perform the role of educating them to be more creative and innovative so that they can identify, follow, control and also apply the latest developments in science and technology (Aidis, 2003). This can have a large impact on the profile of entrepreneurs in understanding the importance of the advantages of new technologies and becoming competitive. To support this, education curricula should be comprehensive and should emphasize the importance of creativity, innovative, awareness on science and technology, and of fostering the soul and spirit of entrepreneurship (van Grundy, 2007). In other words, education is expected to be the solution and tool for the improvement of living standards. At the macro level, it increases economic growth and at the micro level there are only certain activities and functions of entrepreneurs that may stimulate economic growth (Wong et al., 2005).

During the last decades, the rise of entrepreneurship education at universities around the globe is significant (Hamidi et al., 2008). It can be concluded that in an attempt to increase the number of entrepreneurs it is important to raise entrepreneurship intention among college students and to consider encouraging them to think, to plan, and to start an entrepreneurship or business enterprise.

Indonesia might need to improve the quality of the entrepreneurial environment. According to Acs (2006), a nation's economic development depends on successful entrepreneurship. In line with this thesis, the Ministry of Cooperative and Small and Medium Business Enterprise has launched a National Entrepreneurship Movement or *Gerakan Kewirausahaan Nasional* (GKN). This is a program where the government grants an amount of funding to college students to start up their own business with the intention of promoting entrepreneurship in the country. Those who are interested in taking this opportunity are mandated to write their business plans. Once they are selected, they have to present the plans to the judges.

The city of Bandung is one of the most populated cities in the country with a large number of higher education institutions. As the city with a large number of higher education institutions, it attracts senior high schools graduates from various part of the country to study at its colleges or the higher education institutions.

Theoretically, education improves the students' capacity and capability as well as enhancing their employability prospects. The increasing well-educated workforce contributes to the country's economy (Aidis, 2003). For example, in American and Japanese cases, within 10 years, the number of university graduates in the US were contributing to the country's Gross Domestic Product (GDP) per capita at around 42%, whereas the increase in the number of university graduates in Japan could achieve 35% of the country's GDP per capita (Ali, 2015).

It is believed that higher education institutions could play an important role in preparing young-sters to become entrepreneurs as well as providing them with the relevant competencies for undertaking entrepreneurship activity (Fayole et al., 2006). Therefore, it needs to encourage them to take entrepreneurship as their career choice. Further, every college needs to have a commitment of providing their students with a proper and relevant entrepreneurship education program. The relevancy between colleges' commitment and the students' intention will increase the number of entrepreneurs in the country and it is expected to have the effect of decreasing number of the educated unemployment.

This study addresses a problematic question of the extent to which the Bandung city's college students have an intention to choose entrepreneurship as their career choice. Their intention can be identified from their understanding, interest, and action of entrepreneurship. To make it more specific, the study discusses the intention based on the gender. Therefore, the study addresses the following research problems:

1. To what extent do Bandung city's colleges provide entrepreneurship courses?
2. To what extent do Bandung city's colleges' male and female students have an understanding of entrepreneurship?
3. To what extent do Bandung city's colleges' male and female students have interest in choosing entrepreneurship as their career?
4. To what extent do Bandung city's colleges' male and female students implement entrepreneurship?

By answering the aforementioned research questions, the study is expected to make a contribution to the government program of increasing the number of educated entrepreneurs, to attempt to provide the educated youngsters with an entrepreneurship empowerment program, and to contribute toward enriching the related concept and its application.

2 RESEARCH METHOD

This study employed a survey method conducted using a sample of Bandung city public and private higher education students. The subjects were randomly selected from the total population of 225,000 students in 150 higher education institutions in Bandung. In detail, the study involved 360 subjects consisting of 162 male and 178 female students from six higher education institutions (three public, two private universities and one pubic institute).

The data was collected by using a structured questionnaire that generally captured the students' understanding, perception and preferences about entrepreneurship. The questionnaire had been confirmed and its content validity by three expert judges. The data was then analyzed using percentage calculation and the contingency table of chi square (χ^2) in order to analyze whether or not the difference in the sample's response is dependent on the male or female category.

3 RESULTS AND DISCUSSION

3.1 Data description and findings

As mentioned earlier, this study tries to answer the research questions covering the availability of entrepreneurship courses in the colleges, the male and female students' understanding, interests, and implementation of entrepreneurship.

Based on the data, the subject's response to the questions on whether or not the colleges where they study provide the students with entrepreneurship as a specific course indicates that 16.1% of them responded that it was an elective course, only 7.3% responded that it was a mandatory course, 17.9% responded that it was an elective training instead of a specific course and 58.6% responded that there was no specific course or training on entrepreneurship.

Meanwhile, regarding the information about entrepreneurship they acquired, 33.9% acquired it from friends and the neighborhood community, 37.8% acquired it from the internet and media including the social media, 17.2% acquired it from their instructors, and 11.1% did not acquire any information about entrepreneurship.

Their perception on the importance of entrepreneurship is indicated in Table 1.

Based on Table 1, the students' perception on the importance of entrepreneurship for economic stability and growth does not indicate variation between the male and female students. 71.7% of them perceived entrepreneurship as important for economic stability and growth, and 28.3% perceived it as not important. Looking at the male and female categories, 36.7% of the male students perceived it as important and 17% perceived it as unimportant. On the other hand, 35.0% of the female students perceived it as important, while 11.1% perceived it as unimportant. Chi square analysis of the data indicates the statistic of $\chi^2 = 1.830$, which is insignificant at $\alpha = 0.05$, which means that the male and female students tend to perceive entrepreneurship as important for economic stability and growth.

Meanwhile, the data on the students' understanding of entrepreneurship is depicted in Table 2.

Table 2 shows that 86.9% of the students, both male and female, understand entrepreneurship and only 13% of them do not. 41.9% of the male students and 45.0% of the female students understand it. Only 3.6% of the male students and 9.4% of female students do not understand it. Chi square

Table 1. Perception of the importance of entrepreneurship.

Response	Male (Percentage)	Female (Percentage)	Total (Percentage)
It is important for economic growth	132 (36.7%)	126 (35.0%)	258 (71.7%)
It is not important	62 (17.2%)	40 (11.1%)	102 (28.3%)
Total	194 (53.9%)	166 (46.1)%	360 (100%)

Table 2. Degree of understanding of entrepreneurship.

Response	Male (Percentage)	Female (Percentage)	Total (Percentage)
Understand entrepreneurship	151 (41.9%)	162 (45.0%)	313 (86.9%)
Do not understand	13 (3.6%)	34 (9.4%)	47 (13.1%)
Total	164 (44.5%)	196 (54.4%)	360 (100%)

Table 3. Degree of interest in entrepreneurship.

Response	Male (Percentage)	Female (Percentage)	Total (Percentage)
Intersted in	86 (23.9%)	84 (23.3%)	170 (47.2%)
Uninterested in	76 (21.1%)	114 (31.7%)	190 (52.8%)
Total	152 (45.0%)	198 (55.0%)	360 (100%)

Table 4. Being employed or entrepreneurship preference.

Response	Male (Percentage)	Female (Percentage)	Total (Percentage)
Being employed	121 (33.6%)	137 (38.1%)	258 (71.7%)
Becoming an entrepreneur	76 (21.1%)	26 (7.2%)	102 (28.3%)
Total	197 (54.7%)	163 (45.3%)	360 (100%)

Table 5. The implementation of entrepreneurship.

Response	Male (Percentage)	Female (Percentage)	Total (Percentage)
Yes, have put into action	17 (16.7%)	9 (8.8%)	26 (25.5%)
No, have not put into action	43 (42.2%)	33 (32.3%)	76 (74.5%)
Total	60 (58.8%)	42 (41.2%)	102 (100%)

analysis of the data indicates the statistic of $\chi^2 = 2.555$, which is insignificant at $\alpha = 0.05$, which means that the difference between male and female in their understanding of entrepreneurship is independent on the category of male and female.

Next, the data about the students' interest in entrepreneurship is described in Table 3.

Based on Table 3, 47.2% of the students are interested in entrepreneurship, while 52% of them are not interested in it. Of those who are interested in it, the percentages of male and female students are not significantly different. 23.9% of male students and 23.3% of female students are interested in entrepreneurship. Looking at those who are uninterested in entrepreneurship, the male students is 21.1%, which is lower than that of the female students, which is 31.7%. Chi square analysis indicates the result of $\chi^2 = 4.064$, which is significant at $\alpha = 0.05$ and df = 1 ($\chi^2_{\alpha,df} = 3.041$). This means that the difference in the response to the question is dependent on the category of male and female. However, the female students tend to be less interested in entrepreneurship compared with the male students.

Meanwhile, students that are willing to choose a career either as an employee or as an entrepreneur is indicated in Table 4.

Table 4 describes the Bandung city's college students' preference for either being employed (become an employee) or becoming an entrepreneur, indicating that 71.7% prefer being employed to becoming entrepreneurs and only 28.3% prefer becoming entrepreneurs. Of those who prefer being entrepreneurs, the male students percentage is are a bit higher at 21.1%, than the female at 7.2%. The analysis of chi square, however, indicates $\chi^2 = 2.530$, which is insignificant at $\alpha = 0.05$, meaning that male and female students preference for being employed or becoming entrepreneurs is not different, that is, they tend to prefer being employee.

Among those who prefer being entrepreneurs, as indicated in Table 4, there are those who have, and those who have not put it into action, as described in Table 5.

Based on Table 5, 26.5% of those who prefer being entrepreneurs have put into action running an entrepreneurship and 74.5% have not. Of those who have put it into action, 16.7% of them are male students and 8.8% are female. On the other hand, among those who prefer becoming entrepreneurs but have not put into action, 42.2% of them are male students and 32,3% are female. Chi square analysis of this data indicates the result of $\chi^2 = 14.124$, which is significant at $\alpha = 0.05$ and df = 1

$(\chi^2_{\alpha,df} = 3.041)$. This is interpreted that those who are interested in entrepreneurship indicate that male students tend to have put into action in entrepreneurship. The data also indicates more male students than female have put it into action.

All in all, the findings of this study can be concluded as follows:

1. Most of the Bandung city's colleges do not provide their undergraduate students with a specific course on entrepreneurship either as a mandatory or as an elective one.
2. Most of the students do not acquire information about entrepreneurship from the colleges where they are studying or from their instructors but instead from friends, their neighborhood community, the internet, and/or media.
3. The college students, both male and female, tend to perceive entrepreneurship as important for economic stability and growth.
4. The college students, both male and female, tend to have a proper understanding of entrepreneurship.
5. The college students tend to be less interested in entrepreneurship particularly the female students.
6. The college students tend to have a preference for being employees rather than becoming entrepreneurs.
7. Only a limited number of the college students, particularly the female students, prefer becoming entrepreneurs, but they tend not to have put it into action.

3.2 *Discussion*

As discussed earlier, the data about the first research question dealing with the availability of entrepreneurship courses in the colleges indicates that most of the Bandung city's colleges do not provide their undergraduate students with any specific courses on entrepreneurship, either as a mandatory or as an elective one. This situation could be assumed as one of the causes that leads to a situation where most of the college students in Bandung city do not acquire information about entrepreneurship from the colleges or their instructors but instead from friends, the community, the internet, and/or media. They also tend to be less interested in entrepreneurship.

In regard to supporting the government program related to the National Entrepreneurship Movement, an effort is needed to encourage colleges to provide their students with a specific course or education program on entrepreneurship. This is because entrepreneurship plays an important role in macroeconomic stability and growth. In Indonesia, entrepreneurship makes a significant contribution to the GDP. The related data indicated within the six year period 2002–2008, the average contribution of entrepreneurship to the GDP was 7.8%, which was higher than the 7.4% contribution by the construction industry, 7.1% by financial, real estate and service, 6.4% by transportation and communication, and 0.9% made by electricity, natural gas and water. Its contribution to the GDP, however, was still lower than that of the community service which was 9.7%, mining which was 10.4%, trade, hotels and restaurants which was 12.1%, agriculture which was 14.0%, and manufacturing industry which was 24.2% (Department of Trade, 2009). For the purposes of accelerating economic growth and achieving its stability, encouraging more Indonesian youngsters, particularly the college graduates, is considered as one of the urgent programs.

In addition, the findings of the rest of the research question indicate that the Bandung city's college students, both male and female, tend to perceive entrepreneurship as important for economic stability and growth and they also tend to have a proper understanding of entrepreneurship along with its importance. They, particularly the female students, tend to be less interested in entrepreneurship and they prefer being employees rather than becoming entrepreneurs. Only a limited number of them prefer becoming entrepreneurs but most of them have not put into action any entrepreneurship activities. According to Kerr and Nanda (2009), financial constraints are among the reasons.

The important implication of this study is that every higher education institution in Bandung needs to encourage the students to have an intention to put into action an entrepreneurship so that they can make more of a contribution to the economic stability and growth. This is due to the needs to increase the number of entrepreneurs in the situation of which the college students tend to have less intention to become entrepreneurs.

This study only involved prominent universities and institutes, which are in fact only a small portion of the total number of universities, institutes, polytechnics, higher academic schools and academies that offer the undergraduate program. Therefore, the validity of its findings is considered questionable. This implies that in regard to enhancing this particular validity the study needs to be repeated and involve other college types, a greater number of students and a larger regional scope.

4 CONCLUSIONS

Based on the findings, the study can conclude that the Bandung city's college students acquired an understanding of entrepreneurship from several resources, although only a limited number of them acquired it from a specific class provided by their college. Both male and female students tend to perceive entrepreneurship as important for the macroeconomic stability and growth. They also tend to have an adequate understanding of entrepreneurship. The female students tend to be less interested in entrepreneurship and tend to have a preference for being employees rather than becoming entrepreneurs. The small number of those who prefer becoming entrepreneurs, particularly the female students, tend to have not put it into action.

REFERENCES

Acs, Z. (2006). How is entrepreneurship good for economic growth. *Innovation, (Winter)* 97–107.
Aidis, R., (2003). *Entrepreneurship and economic transition*. Tinbergen Institute Discussion Paper. Retrieved from http://www.timbergen.nl
Ali, M., (2015). *Education for national development: A case study of Indonesia*. Bandung, Indonesia: Imperial Bhakti Utama Publishing Company.
Beckman, G.D. & Cherwitz, R.A. (2009). Intellectual entrepreneurship: An authentic foundation for higher education reform. *Society for College and University Planning (SCUP)*. Retrieved from www.scup.org/phe.html
Central Bureau of Statistic, (2014). *Data on Indonesian Economy and Workforce*. Jakarta, Indonesia: BPS.
Drucker, P.F. (2005). *Management challenges for the 21st century*. Oxford, UK: Butterworth-Heinemann.
Fayole, A., Gailly, B. & Lassas, C.N. (2006). Assessing the impact of entrepreneurship education programmes: A new methodology. *Journal of European Industrial Training 39*(9), 7001–7020.
Hamidi, D.Y., Wennberg, K. & Berglund, H. (2008). Creativity in entrepreneurship education. *Journal of Small Business and Enterprise Development 15*(2), 304–320.
Kerr, W. & Nanda, R. (2009). *Financing constraints and entrepreneurship*. National Bureau of Economic Research (NBER) Working Paper Series. Retrieved from http://www.nber.org/papers/w15498
Kourilsky, M.L. (1995). *Entrepreneurship education: Opportunity: In search of curriculum*. Kansas City, MO: Kauffman Center for Entrepreneurial Leadership.
Kuratko, D.F. (2009). Entrepreneurship education in the 21th century: From legitimization to leadership. *A Coleman foundation White paper USASBE National conference*. January 16, 2004.
Oosterbeek, H., van Praag, M.C. & Usselstein, A. (2008). *The impact of entrepreneurship education on entrepreneurship competencies and intentions*. Tinbergen Institute Discussion Paper. Retrieved from http://www.timbergen.nl
United Nations Conference on Trade and Development, (2005). *Entrepreneurship and economic development: The empretec showcase*. Geneva.
van Grundy, A.B. (2007). *Getting to innovation: How asking the right questions generates the great ideas your company needs*. New York, NY: American Management Association.
Wong, P.K., Ho, Y.P. & Autio, E. (2005). Entrepreneurship, innovation and economic growth: Evidence from GEM data. *Small Business Economics 24*, 335–350.

Educational Administration Innovation for Sustainable Development – Komariah et al. (Eds)
© 2018 Taylor & Francis Group, London, ISBN 978-1-138-57341-3

The effectiveness of school self-evaluation practices

Y. Triana, D. Satori, U.S. Sa'ud & A. Komariah
Universitas Pendidikan Indonesia, Bandung, West Java, Indonesia

ABSTRACT: This study aims to investigate the School Self-Evaluation (SSE) process and asks how beneficial it has been in encouraging schools to continuously improve. The research was conducted at Gresik, East Java, and six schools have been involved in the study. Research data was collected qualitatively by means of document analysis, focus group discussions and interviews. The results of the findings have shown that most schools have adequate knowledge and understanding of SSE, but that the process is still perceived as an obligation task imposed by the ministry. The implementation is not yet effective enough to be utilized as a management tool for school improvement. The study has emphasized that a major challenge is the lack of leadership capacity, which implies the need for supportive supervision or moderation from outsiders.

1 INTRODUCTION

Policymakers around the world have drawn on the research findings to develop policies regarding intervention in schools in order to raise educational standards. The evaluation of the quality of education provision on a whole school basis in Indonesian schools has been conducted through school accreditation, an external mechanism with a focus on compliance and on eight national education standards. Policymakers have also listened to the arguments of academics and researchers, who have called for improvements to be made within schools (Barth, 1990; Hopkins & West, 1996; Stoll & Fink, 1996). Within the context of the decentralization of decision making and the increased levels of autonomy given to schools, greater attention is paid to quality assurance (Maslowsky, 2007). Consistent with international trends, the role and function of evaluation in Indonesian schools has been the subject of much debate among policymakers and school practitioners since the School Self-Evaluation (SSE) initiative was introduced to all schools in 2010. This debate has been of interest to the researcher after the government take into account to support the self-evaluation process in schools and the quality of school development planning as a follow-up product. The effectiveness of the conduct of self-evaluation and how it ensures the quality of education in schools is of particular interest.

Undertakings of self-evaluation require knowledge and skills from schools that are not self-evident. This is particularly true of the role that self-evaluation plays in the current requirement to include quality assurance as part of school policy. Both schools and governments are now adopting initiatives aimed at achieving systematic forms of school self-evaluation. In recent years, a series of frameworks have been developed in order to help to make these self-evaluations as successful as possible and self-evaluation instruments have been developed for various functions of the school. It is apparent, however, that it is no easy matter for schools to initiate and implement a systematic and cyclical process of self-evaluation within their own context.

2 METHOD

Before embarking on a study of school self-evaluation, the concept of 'school self-evaluation' must be defined. Vanhoof et al. (2009) define school self-evaluation as 'the process, generally initiated by the school itself, and involving well-chosen participants, who systematically describe and judge the functioning of the school in order to take decisions relating to general school (policy) development'. This definition furnishes us with certain criteria that can be used to describe and assess the quality of school self-evaluations. These are: has the self-evaluation been conducted systematically; were the participants chosen correctly; did the school both describe and assess its functioning; and did the self-evaluation result in decisions relating to quality development (MacBeath, 1999; MacBeath, 2007).

A number of research findings support the expectation that the quality of a self-evaluation process is strongly determined by how that self-evaluation is carried out. The process of this self-evaluation can be investigated using the concept of 'self-evaluation as a school Quality Assurance (QA) policy action'. Empirical evidence tells us that self-evaluation processes are more effective when they are more closely linked with the following characteristics: offering professional and personal support for team members (SICI Report, 2005); ensuring stakeholder input in decision-making processes (Vanhoof et al., 2009); co-ordinating the actions to be undertaken with activities in other policy areas; using effective communication strategies (MacBeath, 2007); and having shared objectives as a team. It should also be stressed that self-evaluation can only work if team members have a positive attitude toward it (MacBeath, 1999). Creating an awareness of the usefulness and value of self-evaluation is, therefore, a precondition for achieving a successful self-evaluation (MacBeath, 2007). SSE is believed to be one of the management tools of internal school quality assurance that contributes to creating a school's climate, and also to engaging commitments and quality culture within schools in order to implement QA continuously. Since 2008, the Indonesian government has initiated SSE implementation in three districts as a pilot project, one of which is Gresik. This initiation then spread to other schools throughout Indonesia. However, the extent to which it contributes to the QA implementation is limited. Some researchers worldwide agree that, although many welcome these school self-evaluations, there is considerable doubt regarding their quality (Nevo, 2002; Vanhoof et al., 2009; Shirley, 2010).

This study aims to investigate the SSE process and asks how beneficial it has been in encouraging schools to continuously improve. For the purpose of this study, in order to describe and analyze the conduct and results of self-evaluation in schools, the research was conducted at Gresik, East of Java and six schools, representing schools belonging to the group of government piloted schools and Gresik District piloted schools, were involved in the study. Research data was collected qualitatively by means of document analysis, focus group discussions and in-depth interviews.

Heads and teachers cannot be expected to engage in successful school self-evaluations unless they have the necessary capacities to do so (MacBeath, 2007; Stöcklin, 2010). These capacities will only develop and be sustained if participants receive a sufficient degree of personal and professional support. Professional support means, in essence, that participants do not have the impression of being left to carry out their (self-evaluation) tasks entirely on their own and it involves active follow-up and guidance by colleagues (heads and teachers) and supervisors. While head teachers clearly have a central role to play in the management of school self-evaluations, leadership during the process is not a matter for the head teacher alone (Harris, 2002). Effective leaders are aware of the importance of investing in other people in order to get the best results from self-evaluation activities (Neil, 2013). Therefore, two perspectives are fundamental to the research in this paper. The first perspective observes school (self) evaluation from the viewpoint of the actors involved. It distinguishes two main actors in a school evaluation: an internal actor (schools – heads and teachers) and an external actor (the school supervisor). The second perspective focuses on the actual practices, processes and viewpoints on school (self) evaluation.

The description of the results, below, is written based on the research questions, which start from the standpoint of how self-evaluation as a school quality assurance policy action is perceived and understood by the local actors, both inside and outside the school. The results are then followed by an explanation of the self-evaluation processes in practice; the follow-up action from the self-evaluation report in relation with the quality of school development planning; and how self-evaluation as a management tool leads to quality improvements in school culture.

3 RESULTS AND DISCUSSION

3.1 *Perceptions on school self-evaluation*

It is apparent from the literature that the purpose of evaluation needs to be clearly understood by all those involved in the process (Devos et al, 2003; MacBeath, 2007; Meureut & Morlaix, 2003). School Self-Evaluation (SSE) is the process by which a school undertakes its own initiative to assess the extent to which it meets the expectations of its stakeholders; by systematically gathering and analyzing information about itself to make a value judgment. Thomas and Telper (2012) define it as the type of evaluation that is done internally by its members. In line with this, respondents commonly defined self-evaluation as a term used to describe all the processes by which a school gets to know itself better regarding its own strengths and weaknesses. Head teachers or managers tended to perceive the purpose of SSE as mainly for school improvement, especially in primary schools, while head teachers in secondary schools perceived there to be an accountability purpose of SSE. Therefore, when SSE was introduced to schools as a policy, school heads soon related it to QA and believed that SSE was merely a tool for evaluating the implementation of QA and other government policies in schools. Most teachers generally responded that SSE has helped them to find out the strengths and weaknesses of the school. Other teachers stated that they have learned more about how the school functions. In secondary schools, many teachers regarded the primary purpose of SSE as improving the school, whether it was voluntary or not. By identifying its strengths, SSE helps a school to prioritize areas for development. It is interesting to find that, although the teachers strongly supported the implementation of the policy in the school, it seems that they had no faith in it, although this is not to suggest that teachers rejected the notion of SSE. Most of the respondents agreed that the school could benefit from SSE through teachers engaging in school self-evaluation, which was like a 'school report' to help them see clearly 'what the school falls short of and needs to improve'.

An Effective School Self-Evaluation (ESSE) project undertaken by SICI (2005) concluded that effective school self-evaluation requires external support, guidance and training and that the blend between self-evaluation and external evaluation needs to be right. In a quality assurance system, a distinction has to be made between an expected quality, a perceived quality and an actual quality (MacBeath, 2004). However, there are indications that head teachers and teaching staff hold different views on self-evaluation and its qualities. Teachers are, on the whole, not really convinced of the importance of self-evaluation, while head teachers are. As shown by the work of Vanhoof et al. (2009), head teachers are more positive with respect to self-evaluation and are more convinced of its usefulness. However, this is the case in primary schools, while in secondary schools it is vice versa. The way in which school self-evaluation is implemented can either facilitate or frustrate its effectiveness. Teachers are crucial players in the process of school self-evaluation; they can make significant impacts on the success of the policy. Examining teachers' perceptions can possibly shed some light on the strategies for effecting changes that suit the local context. The purposes of SSE seemed to be vague to teachers. Although they appeared to accept that SSE was intended to serve the purposes of both school development and accountability, they became skeptical about the intent of SSE as they implemented it. It was found that those teachers who had not clearly construed the meaning of SSE had doubts about its potential benefits. SSE was perceived to be of greatest benefit to the school, but less so to teachers, and was apparently viewed as having no impact on their students. Lack of time and resources and lack of professional experience and skills were constraints that confronted the teachers.

3.2 *Implementation of self-evaluation in schools*

Research found that when schools conduct self-evaluation, this is often interpreted to mean school management and is typically a top-down process within a school. A less risky and more pragmatic approach is for the process to be undertaken by a team that is drawn from a range of teachers and staff within the school. This may be a group of teachers or teachers and staff, ideally also including the school committee or parents. Where there is top-down pressure and time is a scarce commodity, off-the-shelf products have considerable appeal. This is likely, however, to lead both to a mechanistic approach and a disempowering of teachers. This is not surprising as they had no part in its development and no engagement in the process, but were simply presented with a ready-made product.

The study shows that if self-evaluation focuses on aspects on which team members are likely to have strong views, then the school management needs to consider involving them in the self-evaluation process. Senior managers (secondary schools) generally agreed that setting up the systems and processes of self-evaluation had been very time consuming. In one primary school, it had taken longer due to a lack of staff. However, in one case of a 'good' primary school, this was seen as time well spent; it ensured that staff at every level understood why and how the systems were being introduced, as well as their roles and contributions.

Hofman et al. (2005) suggest that instruments can be assessed for their focus on school accountability and on school improvement, and that school leaders should select an instrument that is fitting for the situation of their school. However, in the school visited, the instruments have been ready made by the government and local district. This is to answer that the development of indicators in Hong Kong (Moore et al., 2006) and of suitable methods to determine value added in China (Peng et al., 2006) are not a simple one. Moore et al. (2006) highlight the complexity of selecting performance indicators, particularly in the affective and social aspects of education, and in norming these in the context of a rapidly developing world. The collection of data in SSE is a practical task that needs to be accommodated within the routines of a school day. However, it will not happen without support. Data analysis sounds like a technical process, and sometimes it is. Schools themselves should have the capacity to carry out some complex analyses, but this was not the case in the schools that were visited, since the data collection method and analysis was also ready made by the government. The issue of capacity is likely to be concentrated on how schools can complete further analysis in order to see their 'school report'.

The conduct of self-evaluation plays a deservedly important role in the government's equal educational opportunities policy and a great deal is expected from equal educational opportunities schools. Yet this study has indeed shown that conducting self-evaluations may not be an activity that schools necessarily want to, or are able to, implement. Most schools do not take the concept of 'self-evaluation' very far in the implementation stage. Some respondents recognized that SSE requires teamwork but felt that teachers were not equally committed to the task. This can be a major issue in the case of primary schools here due to the absenteeism of school managers except school heads only in their structure.

3.3 *School development planning as follow-up action*

A crucial element in school self-evaluation is the step following data analysis, which is taking action based on its key messages. The link between evaluation and action is clearly highlighted in the guidance, particularly the way that the rigorous analysis of strengths and weaknesses in teaching and learning can lead to the clear identification of priorities for improvement. It is also crucial that participants are kept informed of any action taken following an evaluation process to which they have contributed. The lack of detailed information on pupils' progress in schools detracted from the rigor and quality of schools' self-evaluation. In almost all of the schools visited, there was an unclear link between self-evaluation and school development planning. However, schools are indeed aware about the linkage. The use of internal evaluation, originally seen as a tool in the school development process, is increasingly regarded as an aspect of the evaluation system in European countries and beyond (SICI, 2005). Self-evaluation as part of a cyclical school planning process enabled schools to manage change and engage in innovation practices to improve quality.

The teachers and heads interviewed gave the impression that communication regarding self-evaluation in schools is often limited to informing people about what is going on without involving them in interactive sessions and discussions. This is largely due to the fact that school principals and coordinators often feel that more extensive communication is unnecessary, or they did not have enough spare time, since SSE implementation is still 'steered' by a national agenda. They tend to assume that their schools do not have any fundamental objections or questions about the implementation of the self-evaluation process. If they do, they are often skeptical about getting valuable answers or support. This finding implies the importance of improving the willingness and the capacities of schools to achieve high quality self-evaluations, and that this is not only a matter of giving them the necessary tools and technical self-evaluation skills. Enhancing the capacity of schools is also an appropriate strategy in order to improve the quality of self-evaluations. The informants felt that no significant change had taken place in the school due to the implementation of SSE, except that there was an increased awareness on the part of teachers, especially the manager and the middle managers. They became more aware of the requirements of the national standards, yet not every teacher had raised their awareness to the same extent. It means that the practice of SSE only ends on the recommendation since schools admitted that the result are not yet link to the policy in school development plan (SDP) policy. Most of the respondents agreed that SSE was still at an early stage in the school. Teachers had been collecting information and making sense of whatever data they had to hand, but there were not yet any plans stemming from the evaluation. Schools are running their daily business with their 'real' SDP.

3.4 *School self-evaluation as a management tool for building quality culture*

Self-evaluations provide a valuable opportunity for learning in organizations. But time is scarce and results must be at hand quickly and easily. Simple and inexpensive tools are needed. The schools visited in this study tended to underestimate the extent to which team members wanted to make their own tools, due to the capacity issue. This became a problem when schools were relatively poorly informed about the objectives, conduct and results of the self-evaluation instruments, which was suggested by complaints received during the research. Schools face trouble in owning the tools, so some team members will find it hard to be convinced that this is something worth doing. The reflective capacity of schools is arguably the most crucial factor in achieving a high quality self-evaluation (Vanhoof et al., 2009). Self-evaluation is, in effect, a systematic form of reflection. The dominant culture in many schools, however, is one of 'getting things done' with little or no attention paid to reflection and learning. By the reflective capacity of schools, we mean the personal willingness of the team members to reflect upon and improve their own approaches and professional practices (MacBeath, 2009). Although SSE is considered as an important component of schools under the model of school-based management, the rhetoric of school development and the improvement of learning outcomes that SSE is purported to bring about seems inexplicable. They see self-evaluation more as a component of the school's quality assurance system. It is clear that the kind of SSE that the policy documents communicate embodies the characteristics of technical and bureaucratic school self-evaluation. The focus for evaluation is on school characteristics rather than the situated practice of individuals. The teachers interviewed generally expressed negative feelings toward the implementation of SSE. They wondered if the way in which the school was conducting SSE would really help the school to improve. Further, the results of SSE were only circulated to those in the higher positions of the school hierarchy, without immediately being made available to class teachers. The findings from SSE were not readily used to help the teachers to plan for school development. This situation was found in most of the schools visited, which makes it clear that SSE has not yet been used as a management tool for the improvement of the school. Head teachers seemed to have failed to build collaboration among teachers and school staff for the purpose of professional development as an implication of 'effective' self-evaluation.

4 CONCLUSION AND IMPLICATIONS

In conclusion, the results of the findings have shown that: 1) Most schools have an adequate knowledge and understanding of SSE and its implementation, but seem to be vague about linking it with the QA concept; 2) SSE was implemented based on the guidelines provided, but its process is still perceived as an obligation task imposed by the ministry and schools have to adapt and use different instruments every year with little help or support from outside; 3) In general, a school development plan (SDP) as a follow-up action of SSE has yet to be optimized in writing in schools due to various factors such as lack of ability, time constraints and the SDP criteria used; and 4) The implementation is still not able to be utilized by schools as one of the tools that can activate the school community in relation to the improvement of school quality. The result implies that a major challenge is the lack of capacity, particularly a lack of leadership capacity from the head teacher, which suggests the need for supportive supervision or moderation from an outsider.

The evidence within this study has shown that the current initiative of SSE is regarded as technical, bureaucratic and top-down, and it suggests that if individual schools can create supportive environments, then school self-evaluation has an important role to play in supporting their own quality assurance and professional learning.

The conclusion reached is that schools ought to have their own say on development and accountability, which should be done systematically with agreed criteria and some help from external supports. One problem is that this top-down approach to self-evaluation flows from top to bottom, rather than going laterally or from bottom to top. As schools, especially primary schools, are not likely to confess their difficulties to the local authorities, and likewise to the local policymaker to the school, those in the higher positions may not fully understand the difficulties encountered by the school's members and often fail to offer assistance in time. Another problem of this externally initiated and top-down policy is that teachers lack ownership and commitment. During its implementation, teachers were confronted with constraints of time and resources, and also a lack of professional experience and skills. These constraints, together with the problems caused by the technical, bureaucratic nature and top-down approach, undermined the effectiveness of SSE in causing real change. As a consequence, SSE had not been incorporated into the routines of the school and the practices of the teachers. This implies that, if SSE is to serve the purpose of school improvement and development, then changes need to take place in schools and individual teachers need to understand what this means to them. In this case, leadership capacity at every level of the school is a basic requirement.

Schools must have the necessary support base in order to carry out a successful self-evaluation. This can only be developed (and maintained) if there is a sufficiently large and broad body of people behind the initiative. This refers to supportive professional relationships where those involved have the feeling that they are not carrying out their allotted self-evaluation tasks entirely on their own, but are (actively) supported by colleagues (management and teachers) and/or external bodies. Self-evaluations can only work properly if there is sufficient collaboration, support, trust, openness and involvement (MacBeath & McGlynn, 2002).

REFERENCES

Barth, R. (1990). *Improving schools from within: Teachers, parents and principals can make a difference.* San Francisco, CA: Jossey-Bass.

Cranston, N. (2013). School leaders leading: Professional responsibility not accountability as the key focus. *Educational Management Administration & Leadership* published online 1 February 2013. doi: 10.1177/1741143212468348.

Devos, G. & Verhouven, J. (2003). School self evaluation: Conditions and caveats. The case of secondary school. *Educational Administration and Management*, 31(4), 404–420.

Harris, A. (2002). School improvement: What's in it for schools? In J. MacBeath (Ed.), *A new relationship with schools: Inspection and self evaluation.* InFORM September, 5, 1–7.

Hofman, R.H., Dukstra, N.J. & Hofman, W.H.A. (2005). School self-evaluation instruments: An assessment framework. *International Journal of Leadership in Education*, 8(3), 253–272.

Hopkins, D. & West, M. (1996). *Improving the quality of education for all: Progress and challenge.* London, UK: David Fulton Publishers.

MacBeath, J. (1999). *Schools must speak for themselves: The case for school self evaluation.* London, UK: Routledge.

MacBeath, J. (2004). A new relationship with schools: Inspection and self evaluation. *InFORM*, September, 5, 1–7.

MacBeath, J. (2007). *The impact study on the effectiveness of external school review in enhancing school improvement through self evaluation in Hong Kong*. Hong Kong: Education Bureu.

MacBeath, J. & McGlynn, A. (2002). *Self evaluation: What's in it for schools*? London, UK: Routledge.

Maslowski, R. (2007). *School culture and school performance* (Ph.D dissertation). Netherlands: University of Twente Press. Acessed at http://www.tup.utwente.nl. Tanggal 20 September 2014.

Meureut, D. & Morlaix, S. (2003). Condition of success of a school's self evaluation: Some lessons of an European experience. *School Effectiveness and School Improvement*, 14((1), 53–71.

Moore, P.J., Mo, C.M.M., Chan, L.K.S. & Yin Lai, P. (2006). The development of an indikator systems for the effective and social schooling outcomes for primary and secondary student in Hong Kong. *Educational Psychology*, 26(2), 273–301.

Nevo, D. (Ed.). (2002). *School-based evaluation: An international perspective* (vol. 8, pp. 17–34). Elsevier Science Ltd.

Peng, W.J., Thomas S.M., Yang, X. & Li. J. (2006). Developing school evaluation method to improve the quality of schooling in China: A pilot 'value added' study. *Assessment in Education, 13*(2), 135–154.

Shirley, S. Y. (2010). Using school evaluation policy to effect curriculum change? A reflection on the SSE and ESR exercise in Hong Kong. *Educational Research Journal*, 25(2).

SICI Report. (2005, January). The effective school self-evaluation project, Standing International Conference of Central and General Inspectorates of Europe, Brussels European Commission. In *SICI workshop on effective self-evaluation (ESSE)*. Report of the SICI workshop held in Copenhagen January 2005.

Stöcklin, S. (2010). The initial stage of a school's capacity building. *Educational Management Administration & Leadership, 38*, 443. doi: 10.1177/1741143210368263

Stoll, L. & Fink, D. (1996). *Changing our schools. Linking school effectiveness and school improvement*. Buckingham, UK: Open University Press.

Thomas G.R. & Leslie, T. (2012). A review of (elementary) school self-assessment processes: Ontario and beyond. *Studies in Educational Evaluation*. 38(1), 15–23.

Vanhoof J., Petegem, P., Verhoeven, J. C. & Buvens, I. (2009). Self-evaluations: The view of school leaders linking the policymaking capacities of schools and the quality of school. *Educational Management Administration & Leadership*, 37, 667.

Educational Administration Innovation for Sustainable Development – Komariah et al. (Eds)
© 2018 Taylor & Francis Group, London, ISBN 978-1-138-57341-3

Investigation of organizational learning perception and readiness through information systems

J.A. Turi & S. Sorooshian
University Malaysia Pahang, Pahang, Malaysia

M.F.A. Ghani
University of Malaya, Kuala Lumpur, Malaysia

Y. Javid
COMSATS Institute of Information Technology, Abbottabad, Pakistan

ABSTRACT: This study examined the perception and readiness of employees working in a learning organization. Organizational learning is a form of learning in which a person utilizes their unique capabilities, including information systems, in order to get an insight into organizational problems and opportunities. In this study, a conceptual model is used based on the theory of planned behavior, which explains how workers in a learning organization conceive organizational learning using information systems. Structural equation modeling was used to analyze data from 200 workers, including knowledge workers, faculty members, students, administrators and software house employees and internees in a university. The results show that, based on the theory of planned behavior, employees acceptance of organizational learning is reasonably good. More specifically, attitudes and behavioral controls positively influenced their intention to accept organizational learning through information systems. The research shows that both the perceived ease of use and the perceived usefulness affected the workers' and students' attitudes toward the adaptation of information systems for organizational learning.

1 INTRODUCTION

The role of Information Systems (IS) in any organization is like that of the heart in the body, it plays the role of providing pure blood to all of the elements of the body, including the brain. Information systems guarantee that the required data is collected from the various sources, processed under the control of stored programs and sent to all of the required destinations. The system fulfills the information needs of individuals, groups and management functionaries, including line and top management, in order to improve the decision-making process and performance of the organization.

Learning is a dynamic, integral, social, psychological, and natural process and product; it starts with the inception and remains active until death (Law & Chuah, 2015; Savolainen & Haikonen, 2016). According to learning theories (Alzahrani & Woollard, 2011; Bandura, 1989; Belle, 2016), both humans and non-humans learn from environmental happenings, disasters, practices, and experiences; consciously, subconsciously, and unconsciously through formal, non-formal, and informal sources. Learning is a conscious and deliberate attempt on an organization's part to maintain and improve its effectiveness, competitiveness, productivity, and innovativeness in uncertain technological and market circumstances. Experiential Learning Theory (ELT) supports organizational learning through experiencing organizational projects and problems that organizations learns through grasping and transforming of experiences. The cognitive and adoptive learning theory supports organizational learning through seeking continuous improvement, based on the construct of exploitation and exploration. Similarly, the assimilation theory focuses on action-based learning through individual performance with the help of rational observations (Leavitt, 2011).

2 LITERATURE REVIEW

2.1 *Definitions and explanations of organizational learning*

Organizations are considered to be biological entities; they can adapt purposefully and exist in a fluctuating setting (Spender, 2009). They learn in the most feasible, optimal, and economical ways due to internal and external pressures (Spender, 2009). In the same way, it is defined by Simon (1969) in (Fiol & A, 1985) as a growing insight and successful restructuring of organizational problems and opportunities by individuals and organizations. It adds to the mission, vision, structure, and memory of the organizations. It is a change in the organizational knowledge repository that comes from the circulation of experiences, practices, and policies (Lalli, 2014). It is a multilevel process where individuals acquire, reflect, create, transfer, share, and store knowledge in the organizational memory (Scott, 2011). Organizational learning occurs in an organizational context that is focused on targets and problems, containing organizational structures, procedures, norms, cultures, memory, and information systems (Levitt & March, 1988; Yousef et al, 2016). Therefore, organizational knowledge has been named as relative, provisional, and context-bound knowledge (Visser, 2010). It is a twofold process, where individual knowledge is captured and made part of the organizational repository and, in return, shared among new workers as a guideline for organizational processes (Scott, 2011). It is a source of developing organizational capacities and capabilities, gaining competitive sustainable development, supporting innovation, and bringing competitive advantages, from an economic prospective, through repeated and newly learned skills and knowledge (Kalmuk & Acar, 2015).

Organizational learning and Information Systems (IS). Information systems are integrated user-machine systems for capturing and providing information in order to support operations, management functions, and decision making in an organization. Information systems include not only a computer's hardware and software, but also people, manuals, models, techniques, and well-defined procedures. Different IT-based systems, such as Enterprise Resource Planning (ERP), Customer Relationship Management (CRM), Supply Chain Management (SCM), Decision Support System (DSS), Expert Systems (EX), Integrated Learning System (ILS), and Learning Management System (LMS) are used by different organizations for effective planning, decision making, and management functions. ERP helps in reducing operational costs and time by making available organizational data repositories and logs, which further help in analysis, report generation, and answering any queries (Seo, 2013). It connects all of the stakeholders and causes the functions of the different departments to become synchronized and coherent (Sadrzadehrafiei, 2013). CRM provides the cross-functional integration of processes, people, operations, and marketing, which may not be possible without an IT integrated system, and helps in organizational learning by updating the organizational memory with its best practices, removing the failed ones (Peltier, 2013), making the most successful projects and programs the benchmark, and also focusing on the weaknesses found from past experiences (Chen, 2003). DSS provides help in complex and uncertain situations, paved basis for integrated organizational learning (Zack, 2013), and plays the role of enabler for organizational learning (Bhatt, 2002). Knowledge management systems overcome the inborn deficiency of the human for the retaining, recalling, and full utilization of its skills, knowledge, and experiences, by providing opportunities to acquire, create, and distribute potential knowledge and to make it available for individual and organizational learning by providing a developmental perspective (Hovland, 2003). ILS provides support for both individual and organizational learning beyond instructional content through management practices, tracking, personalized instructions, and the integration of all the organizational functions, processes, and procedures across the systems and organizations (William & Watson, 2007).

2.2 *Information system and theory of planned behavior*

The theory of planned behavior explains individual engagement in certain behaviors, in certain spaces and at certain times. Further, it states that behaviors are driven by their intensions, which are further based on three constructs: of an individual's attitude toward behavior, subjective norms, and perceived behavioral control (Ajzen, 1991). It guides individual intensions to actions positive attitude and behaviors, supported by favorable social norms and high level of perceived behavioral control are the best predictors for behavioral intensions and planned behaviors. It is in human nature that <u>he</u> adopts all those objects, which are productive, facilitative, provide them better behavioral command and control. Therefore, many external stimuli exert their forces in order to change our behaviors, either voluntarily or involuntarily, by stating their assumed usability, utility, and better control mechanism. We act due to certain reasons, and logics, and because of a construct that influences our decisions (Rise et al., 2010; Knabe, 2012; Cameron, 2010). Information systems have pervaded workplaces in every walk of life, and every day computer scientists strive to make user-machine interaction easier and more comfortable. It is now evident from the prevailing practices that even novice users are able to operate information systems smoothly. Information systems, due to their utility, have made the environment eye-catching, interesting, and relaxing. A good simulated environment has increased learning intensions and readiness. Augmented and virtual realities have reshaped the working and learning environment. Similarly, it has made our assignments easier and faster, and has lessened memory load (Sato, 2006; Fallman, 2007). All three construct's objectives of TPB are mat therefore has proved its predictions and intentions for adopting information system (Truong, 2009; Yi et al., 2006). In addition to the theory of planned behavior, technology adoption is also supported by the Theory of Reason Action (TRA), Socio-technical Theory, Complementary Theory (CT), and the Technology Acceptance Model (TAM) (Shareef et al., 2009).

2.3 *Hypothesis*

This study tested the nine hypotheses, as shown in Figure 1.

H1: Employees' attitudes toward organizational learning positively influence their intention to adopt information systems for organizational learning.

H2: Employees' subjective norm toward organizational learning positively influences their intention to use information systems for organizational learning.

H3: Employees perceived behavioral control on information systems positively influences their intention to adopt information systems for organizational learning.

H4: Employees' perceived ease of use of information systems positively influences their attitude to adopting information systems for organizational learning.

H5: Employees' perceived usefulness of information systems positively influences their attitude toward organizational learning.

H6: The instructors' perceived readiness for information systems positively influences the subjective norm for organizational learning.

H7: The learners' perceived readiness for information systems positively influences the subjective norm for organizational learning.

H8: Employees' perceived general ability to operate information systems positively influences their behavioral control toward organizational learning.

H9: Employees' perceived learning autonomy toward organizational learning positively influences their behavioral control toward information students.

3 METHOD

3.1 *Participants*

Quota sampling techniques were used to gain the correct proportion of all categories of workers for the collection of data. There were 200 participants, including workers in a support office, the office of planning and development, and the project management office, Deans of faculties, directors and deputy directors, knowledge workers among the support staff, teaching faculty members, and

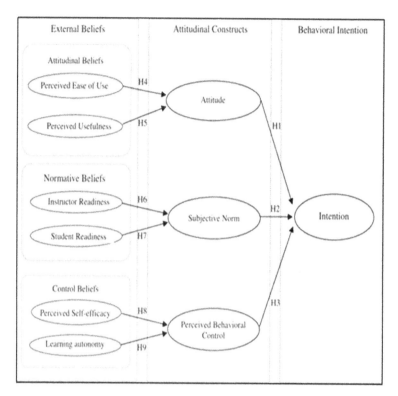

Figure 1. Hypothesis.
Source: Cheon et al. (2012).

graduate and post-graduate students who were working as research associates or teaching assistants (internship).

3.2 *Data collection*

Data was collected by a self-administered questionnaire, using quota sampling techniques to get the correct proportion of participants from all departments and levels. The assessment contains 30 queries: 3 questions for each of the 10 constructs. For the inquiry form, due to the sensitivity of the study, a 7-point Likert Scale is used, ranging from totally disagree to totally agree. High scores indicated a more positive perception toward m-learning.

3.3 *Data analysis*

Data analysis was done by using both SPSS and AMOS. First of all, the mean and standard deviation of each item was discovered, followed by the mean, standard deviation and Cronbach alpha of each construct and then the Cronbach alpha of all the constructs as a whole, using SPSS. The structural equation modeling was then done in AMOS, as shown in Table 1.

4 RESULTS

The mean results show that data is not dispersed but is concentrated to the center of the constructs, which shows data validity and meaningfulness. At the same time, the values for the dispersions are

Table 1. Descriptive statistics, Cronbach alpha and standardized factor loading.

	Mean	Standard deviation	Cronbach alpha	Standardized factor loading
P_E_O_U	5.03	1.63	0.84	
q1	5.35	2.03		0.85
q2	4.39	1.94		0.80
q3	5.15	1.85		0.83
P_U	4.65	1.61	0.85	
q4	4.54	1.93		0.76
q5	4.63	1.91		0.72
q6	4.65	1.82		0.84
A_T_D	4.44	1.54	0.88	
q7	4.24	1.83		0.79
q8	4.45	1.74		0.84
q9	4.46	1.76		0.77
I_R	4.25	1.64	0.84	
q10	4.13	1.95		0.72
q11	4.25	1.97		0.78
q12	4.26	1.85		0.71
S_R	4.56	1.54	0.86	
q13	4.54	1.85		0.78
q14	4.62	1.86		0.75
q15	4.45	1.77		0.78
S_N	4.44	1.44	0.77	
q16	4.44	1.85		0.73
q17	4.65	1.85		0.80
q18	4.26	1.83		0.73
P_S_E	4.35	1.55	0.86	
q19	4.34	1.76		0.84
q20	4.65	1.77		0.71
q21	4.76	1.73		0.84
L_A	4.35	1.55	0.74	
q22	4.46	1.73		0.75
q23	4.57	1.85		0.78
q24	4.53	1.73		0.74
B_C	4.46	1.55	0.83	
q25	4.56	1.73		0.82
q26	4.34	1.76		0.83
q27	4.46	1.76		0.85
I_N_T	4.46	1.52	0.85	
q28	4.48	1.74		0.81
q29	4.54	1.85		0.76
q30	4.45	1.95		0.81
Total Cronbach alpha			0.97	

very small, which supports our first argument. Most of the values are higher than the mid-point and have scored near to agree and strongly agree, which indicates that most of the respondents have the intention of accepting information systems in their working environment. They considered it useful and easy to use and operate. Similarly, reliability analysis values fall into an acceptable range and all of the values are larger than 0.70 for all variables and constructs, showing validity of instrument. Table 2 shows model fitness, and the values show best model fitness. The model was a best fit for all variables except X2. So, all of the conditions were fulfilled for the path analysis

Table 2.   Model fit indices.

Fit indices	Values	Recommended guidelines	References
x2	1341.9	Non-significant	Klima, 2001; Kline, 2004
x2/df	2.8	<3	Kline, 2004; Teaneck & Fidel, 2008
CFI	0.923	>=0.90	Hu & Bandler, 1998
TLI	0.911	>=0.90	Hu & Bandler, 1998; Kline, 2004
RMSEA	0.066	<0.08(good fit)	Kline, 2004; Donald & Ho, 2002
Standardized RMR	0.147	0.15	Byrne, 1997; Hu & Bentley, 1998; Kline, 2004

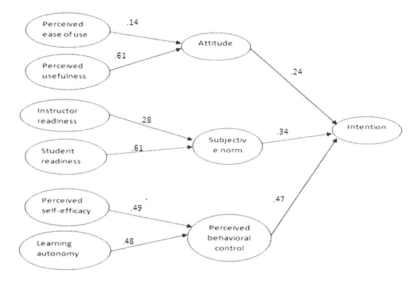

Figure 2.   Path analysis.

in Figure 2. All of the hypotheses were accepted, which means that there is a greater impact of the independent variable in the dependent variable or results.

4.1 *Hypothesis testing*

From the consequences of path coefficient, hypothesis 1, 2 and 3 that attitude (0.24), subjective norm (0.34), perceived behavioral control (0.47), essentially affect expectation to utilize m-learning. Perceived behavioral control has the most noteworthy effect, followed by subjective norm and attitude. Perceived ease of use and perceived usefulness were both observed to be identified with attitude, with 0.14 and 0.61 respectively. Hypotheses 4 and 5, concerning regularizing convictions, understudy availability, and teacher status, essentially affected subjective standards with (0.61) and (0.28) respectively. So, theories 6 and 7 were acknowledged. Finally, for behavioral control, both perceived self-adequacy and learning self-sufficiency were essentially identified with seen behavioral control, with 0.49 and 0.48 respectively. Accordingly, the outcome bolsters hypotheses 8 and 9.

4.2 *Discussion*

The purpose of this study was to identify the factors that affect organizational learning, supported by information systems, and to understand the relationships between these factors by using the theory of planned behavior. Results show that employees and graduate students of all levels have an accepting and favorable attitude to using and deploying information systems for organizational learning. The study found that the attitudes of employees' and students' toward organizational learning, with the support of information systems, are greatly affected by factors such as subjective norms and behavioral control. Multiple prospective factors are involved in the adaptation of information systems for organizational learning. The research shows that perceived ease of use and perceived usefulness affects workers' and students' attitudes toward the adaptation of information systems for organizational learning. One of the key contributors was the perception of good commands and controls over the use of information systems, which is measured here by the workers' and students' behavioral control. Similarly, the self-efficacy and learning autonomy of the employees significantly affects behavioral control.

5 CONCLUSION

This study found major contributing factors that affect the perception and readiness of employees and working graduate students to adopt organizational learning with the help of information systems. The significant factors were attitude, subjective norm, and behavioral control. It is important for practitioners and researchers to understand what makes end users either accept or resist information systems and how to improve employees' acceptance of information systems for organizational learning. To deploy information systems in any organization, especially the learning organizations, the organization should consider long-term implementation projects, develop ready–to-use manuals and guidelines, and provide standard operating procedures for the use of the information system in the different developmental stages. Policies regarding the prevailing organizational system and information system usage should be developed and articulated among workers and working graduates, and they should be given orientation and usage training, so that they find it easy to operate, find it useful, and find it easier to command and control them. Their efficiency and effectiveness can be increased by the orientation of the information system. As sudden change is not welcomed by every user, information systems for organizational learning should, therefore, be completed in phases and its utility should be shown to the workers. New information systems should be within a worker's comfort level and they should feel confident, and even proud, of using the latest information system or tool for the organizational process. In this digital age, we are left with no other option except accepting information systems as tools, moderators and mediators for organizational learning.

REFERENCES

Ajzen, I. (1991). The theory of planned behavior. *Organizational Behavior and Human Decision Processes,* 179–211.

Alzahrani, I. & Woollard, J. (2011). The role of the constructivist learning theory and collaborative learning environment on wiki classroom, and the relationship between them. *International Conference for e-learning & Distance Education* (pp. 1–9). UK: University of Southampton.

Bandura, A. (1989). Social cognitve theory. *Annals of Child Development.* 1–60.

Belle, S. (2016). Organizational learning? Look again. *The Learning Organization.* 332–341.

Cameron, R. R. (2010). *Ajzen's theory of planned behavior applied to the use of social networking by college students* (Unpublished thesis). Texas State University-San Marcos, Texas.

Fallman, D. (2007). Persuade into what? Why human-computer interaction needs a philosophy of technology. (pp. 295–306). Berlin, Germany: Springer-Verlag.

Fiol, L. C. & A, M. (1985). Organizational learning. *Academy of Management Review, 10*(4), 803–813.

Kalmuk, G. & Acar, A. (2015). The mediating role of organizational learning capability on the relationship between innovation and firm's performance: A conceptual framework. *Procedia – Social and Behavioral Sciences,* 164–169.

Knabe, A. (2012). *Applying Ajzen's theory of planned behavior to a study of online course adoption in public relations education* (Unpublished dissertation). Marquette University, Milwaukee.

Lalli, A. (2014). *Organizational learning theorectical framework.* Islamabad, Pakistan: University of Lahore.

Law, K. M. & Chuah, K. B. (2015). *Organizational learning as a continuous.* DELO.

Levitt, B. & March, J. G. (1988). Organizational learning. *Annual Review of Sociology, 14,* 319–340.

Rise, J., Sheeran, P. & Hukkelberg, S. (2010). The role of self-identity in the theory of planned behavior: A meta-analysis. *Journal of Applied Social Psychology*, 1085–1105.

Sato, M. (2006). *Human-computer interaction from philosophical viewpoint.* Telecommunications Software and Multimedia Laboratory, Helsinki University of Technology.

Savolainen, T. & Haikonen, A. (2016). Dynamics of organizational. *Siteseer.*

Scott, B. B. (2011). *Organizational learning: A literature review.* Australia: IRC.

Shareef, M. A., Kumar, V., Kumar, U. & Hasin, A. A. (2009). *Theory of planned behavior and reasoned action in predicting technology adoption behavior.* Canada: IGI Global.

Snyder, W. M. (1996). *Organization learning and performance: An exploration of the linkages between organization learning, knowledge, and performance.* California: University of Southern California.

Spender. (2009). Organizational learning and knowledge management. *Management Learning*, 159–178.

Spender. (2009). Organizational learning and knowledge management: Whence and whither? *Management Learning*, 159–178.

Truong, Y. (2009). An evaluation of the theory of planned behaviour in consumer acceptance of online video and television services. *The Electronic Journal Information Systems Evaluation, 12*(2), 177–186.

Yi, M. Y., Jackson, J. D., Park, J. S. & Probst, J. C. (2006). Understanding information technology acceptance by individual professionals: Toward an integrative view. *Information & Management, 43,* 350–363.

Yousef, B., Mai, O., Ra'ed, M. A.-S. & Tarhini, M. A. (2016). Knowledge management, innovation and firm performance. *Journal of Knowledge Management, 9*(3), 101–115.

Educational Administration Innovation for Sustainable Development – Komariah et al. (Eds)
© 2018 Taylor & Francis Group, London, ISBN 978-1-138-57341-3

Leadership and Total Quality Management (TQM) for sustainability in *Madrasahs Aliyah* (MAs)

N. Waruwu
Universitas Negeri Jakarta, Jakarta, Indonesia

D. Hermana
Universitas Padjadjaran, Bandung, Jawa Barat, Indonesia

A.K. Hia
Universitas Pendidikan Indonesia, Bandung, Jawa Barat, Indonesia

ABSTRACT: One of the challenges for madrasah leaders is ensuring sustainability in a Total Quality Management (TQM) system. Leaders have the responsibility to encourage the development of total quality practices in *Madrasahs Aliyah* (MAs). The implementation of the sustainability concept in the quality management system requires the presence of a leader who inspires and motivates with authenticity. The aim of this study is to analysis the influence of authentic transformational leadership on TQM for sustainability in *madrasahs aliyah*. This research used a descriptive research approach with a verification survey. Findings showed that authentic transformational leaders who motivate and inspire can encourage innovation in TQM for sustainability in MAs – both radical and incremental innovation.

1 INTRODUCTION

The concept of authentic transformational leadership was developed by Bass and Steidlmeier (1999). Both of authentic and transformational leadership as if separated included in formal educational institutions. Gardner et al. (2011) and Banks et al. (2016) suggested that research on authentic leadership has been a focus of attention for the past ten years. Begley (2006) suggests what authentic leadership is within a school. Walker and Shuangye (2007) examine its relation to cultural diversity. Stoten (2014) describes leadership at the university level. Dudka and Griswold (2016) explore authentic leadership topics in popular education. Unfortunately, literature on authentic leadership in educational institutions with distinctive characteristics, such as madrasahs, is limited. Gardner et al. (2011) state that leadership rooted in authenticity has the potential to foster sustainability.

The same thing happens in transformational leadership research. McCleskey (2014) suggested additional research on preferred self-regulatory orientation and other organizational outcome variables. Berkovich and Eyal (2017) examine the transformational leadership of educational institutions and their impact on teachers in terms of the emotional aspects of leaders. Ibrahim et al. (2014) examine transformational leadership in education as well as its impact on teachers and students. Day et al. (2013) highlight the issue of individual leaders.

There is a research direction that focuses on individual leaders, values, awareness of sustainability in the system, and the process of transforming leadership in the next generation. Price (2003) examines aspects of the ethics of authentic transformational leadership. Zhu et al. (2011) examine the effect of authentic transformational leadership on follower and group ethics. Research on authentic transformational leadership in educational institutions is still limited; this means that research on transformational and authentic leadership in madrasahs for the development and improvement of sustainable systems is still an open field.

One type of educational institution that is less able to compete than vocational school or senior high school is the *Madrasah Aliyah* (MA). Only a small number of madrasahs have the capability to provide quality education. Most of them are unable to optimize the functioning of a quality management system in their management and are also unable to guarantee the availability of resources, especially the teachers who realize the quality of MAs. Anggraeni (2017) stated that quality has become a consideration in madrasahs, including West Java as well as other provinces. The results of MA accreditation were reiterated by the Ministry of Religion in the provincial offices of West Java Province in 2015 and showed that there are still some problems that hinder efforts to improve the quality of MAs. They have many advantages, especially in terms of their image of moral character with respect to *sidiq* (righteous), *amanah* (trustworthy), *fathonah* (intelligent) and *tableg* (convey a revelation), which can be seen from the curriculum and learning process. These advantages have not been fully optimized as benefits of MAs. The values have not been used as a means of action orientation to optimize the madrasah quality system and their moral character has not become the basis for strengthening the quality of the madrasah system.

One important factor in increasing the strategic capability of organizations is leadership. Leadership with vision and dissemination of this vision to the entire organization – inspiring subordinates to focus on customers, as well as prioritizing continuous improvement of excellence – requires a systematic process. Organizational capacity is strongly influenced by authentic leadership and organizational leaders. The successful implementation of internal service quality management is determined by organizational capabilities: vision, stakeholders as change agents, school culture, and professional development that emphasizes the importance of the resulting context and practices.

Most of the madrasahs in Bekasi are not satisfying both parent and student, with the exception of MAs that have the capability to undertake activities such as monitoring quality in the learning process. MAs have no substructure in the organization that has the effect of addressing the needs of both students and teachers. There has been no radical change in the organizational structure aimed at optimizing education services to parents. Principals focus on administrative issues rather than encouraging radical changes, either structurally or culturally.

Leadership, in managing changes to compete, has not been manifested in leadership skills such as: 1) developing a shared sense of goals with colleagues; 2) facilitating group processes for internal service performance, especially staff groups to compete; 3) good communication to build understanding; 4) understanding the transition period, the changes and impacts on members of the organization; 5) mediating conflict to develop positive relationships based on customer orientation.

Leaders have not encouraged radical change for the division of service-oriented service, the development of roles and responsibilities in implementing quality management. Examples of aspects of leadership that are a manifestation of poor quality management include:

1) The principal has not optimized the function of a school vision and its dissemination. Implementation of the principal's work focuses on administration and lacks encouragement of innovation and creativity to prioritise sustainable quality.
2) There has been little partnership with outsiders to carry out the mission of effective quality management. The principal did not have the ability to ensure the general conditions for a successful quality system.
3) The mission was not understood by staff, students or the community.
4) There was no commitment statement relating to quality.

Aseltine et al. (2006) described three principal tasks to enhance student learning, through a plan that focuses on improving teaching and learning, providing instructional leadership to teachers and students, and gaining strategic professional development relevant to job responsibilities. Goestch and Davis (2003) describe the leadership position as "a commitment to leading people with continous improvement and communications".

Concerning the concept of leadership, Harris and Lambert (2003) stated that the main idea of leadership is to learn together, build meaning and knowledge collectively, and develop collaborative Total Quality Management (TQM). The leader performs a function as a communicator – communicating strategic issues in order to realize the vision and to ensure that quality management functions such as planning, organizing, implementing, and evaluating systems and policies on quality follow the direction of the vision. Concerning the leadership at the school, Krüger and Scheerens (2012) described the principal's leadership in terms of personality and values.

The concept of a transformational leader was introduced by Burns (1978). Bass et al. (1987) stated that the transformational leader attempts to elevate the needs of the follower in line with the leader's own goals and objectives. Transformational leadership factors include: 1) charisma; 2) individualized consideration; 3) intellectual stimulation. Bass (1995) stated that transformational leaders inspire, energize, and intellectually stimulate their employees. Avolio and Bass (2002) determined that transformational leadership is an expansion of transactional leadership. Bass and Riggio (2006) state that an important aspect of transformational leadership is developing, maintaining and enhancing this alignment.

According to Gardner et al. (2005), authentic leadership consists of four components: 1) self-awareness; 2) transparency; 3) morality; 4) balanced processing. Walker and Shuangye (2007) described authentic leadership as a result of clarification from following a set of personal beliefs. The authentic leader demonstrates values, principles, morals and ethics. Begley (2006) reviewed the metaphors for effective, professional, ethical and conscious practice in educational administration. Branson (2007) stated that authentic leadership has a self-reflective structure of reality based on values. Walumbwa et al. (2007) described authentic leadership as leadership that displays the characteristics of individuals who understand morals. Kruse (2013) argued that authentic leaders are:

1) Self-aware and sincere. An authentic leader encourages individuals to have self-awareness (consciousness).
2) Mission-driven and focused on results.
3) Led by the heart, not just the mind. They are not afraid to show the emotions they have and their vulnerability to employees.
4) Focused on the long term. Authentic transformational MA leadership models have a spiritual and personality dimension.

Authentic transformational leadership, according to Bass and Steidlmeier (2006), "…must be grounded in moral foundations. A moral foundation of legitimate values. Authentic transformational leadership fosters the moral values of honesty, loyalty and fairness and the end values of justice, equality, and human rights." Fundamentally, the authentic transformational leader must forge a path of congruence of values and interests among stakeholders, while avoiding the pseudo-transformational land mines of deceit, manipulation, self-aggrandizement, and power abuse. According to Bass and Steidlmeier (1999), the components of moral analysis are conscience, a degree of freedom, the ends sought, the means employed, and the consequences. Price (2003) stated that authentic transformational leaders are not tempted to deviate from the requirements of morality because of self-interest alone; the search for potential sources of immorality thus fixes on the beliefs that these leaders hold about the normative force of their altruistic values.

According to Sallis (2005), quality is a philosophical and methodological concept that helps institutions to plan change and set the agenda in the face of excessive external pressures. Gaspersz (2005, p. 5) suggests that quality management can be regarded as an overall activity, goal, and management function that determines quality policy, objectives, and responsibilities, implemented through quality management tools such as quality planning, quality control, quality assurance, and quality improvement.

Sustainability has become a focus of attention. Reed et al. (2000) suggested that using TQM for sustainability confers a competitive advantage. Zairi (2002) pointed out the essence of TQM for sustainability is a paradigm shift in product, service, customer, and market orientation. Zink (2007) developed a TQM approach to sustainability with a stakeholder approach.

Kuei and Lu (2012) suggested the implementation of sustainability principles in TQM, using the conceptual frameworks that are derived from quality management principles as building blocks for the implementation of Sustainability Management (SM) systems. To develop a sustainable quality management system, it is necessary to develop the operating system of each unit so they are: 1) engaging in project works; 2) developing an integrated assessment framework for sustainability performance measurement; 3) creating a platform for learning.

The concepts and dimensions of leadership are too general. Empiric reference as an indicator in the concept has not yet considered the meaning associated with educational institutions such as madrasahs. Based on leadership practices in madrasahs, especially in Indonesia, the principal's leadership emphasizes the moral aspect that characterizes authentic leadership. There are a small number of published studies on authentic leadership in madrasahs, such as Komariah (2016), who focused on individuals.

Rodriguez et al. (2017) describe authentic leadership as a predictor of job satisfaction, motivation, and intellectual stimulation. Lambrechts and Van Petegem (2016) examine the integration of competence with sustainable development in college.

Duignan (2014) stated there is a general tendency in the concept of authentic leadership to focus on oneself, defining oneself in relationships, accepting the moral force behind ideas and acknowledging authentic leaders in real terms.

The concepts of transformational and authentic leadership are correlated. Leadership is not just based on the individual aspect nor can it be viewed in isolation from its relationship with the system. Research presents it as an integrated concept of authentic transformational leadership. Its relationship with the systems of educational institutions that have distinctive characteristics will be discussed. The proposed concept can serve as a basis for solving quality sustainability problems in MAs. It is related to leadership.

This study offers a theory about authentic leadership in the context of educational institutions that have distinctive characteristics. Unfortunately, the concept of leadership in madrasahs is weak. Authentic leadership in madrasahs is not connected to the system. Finally, the leadership function of supporting sustainability in organizational life is very limited.

The aim of this research is to analyze the influence of authentic transformational leadership on TQM sustainability.

2 METHOD

This study was a field study using a quantitative methodology. Questionnaires on a five-scale model were used to collect data on principals and TQM sustainability from 58 MAs chosen randomly in Bekasi. The units of observation were teachers and school staff. The statistical calculation for data analysis was performed by using multiple regression analysis. The measurement of authentic transformational leadership was based on the concept proposed by Bass and Steidlmeier (2006) (moral agent and moral action), reinforced by Komariah (2016) (spiritual intelligence) according to the characteristics of MAs. Following Sallis (2005), the quality indicators are communicating a vision, developing a quality culture, and empowering teachers. Zairi and Liburd (2001) stated them on essentially TQM sustainability, Collaborated as TQM sustainability indicators in education.

3 RESULTS AND DISCUSSION

The results showed that the characteristics of madrasah leaders can show a strong moral foundation. On the other hand, management practices that are oriented towards sustainability were still low, as can be seen in Table 1.

The findings showed that moral agent, moral action, spiritual intelligence, and communicating a vision are in the moderate category. The dimensions of teacher empowerment, and transformational change paradigms are in the low category. TQM for sustainability in the balanced perspective is also in the low category. This shows the conditions in the madrasahs are not of the level expected.

Strong headmaster leadership on the moral dimensions of agents and moral actions shows the principal has a sense of identity as a role model. The principal shows "authentic character" based on

Table 1. The value of characteristics of madrasah leaders.

	Mean	Std. dev.	Variance	Category
Moral agent	3.73	.45300	.206	Moderate
Moral action	3.84	.59400	.353	Moderate
Spiritual intelligence	3.82	.49099	.241	Moderate
Communicating a vision	3.27	.64327	.414	Low
Empowering teachers	3.13	.29155	.085	Low
Transformational change paradigms	3.22	.65676	.431	Low
Balanced perspective	3.33	.59022	.348	Low

sincerity, as someone who is appointed as caliph to organize spiritual education. Aspects become the mainstay of the growing awareness of school as a moral agent both for teachers and students. The moral action shown was a form of awareness based on the business *aniyah dhamirul akhlaqi* (spirit of conscience) (Sobar, 1994). *Syakhshiyak-muqimah* as true (personal integrity and independence, having a system based on the value of individual devotions). Moral action is the realization of an action full of divine value, an activity that contains the dimension of *dhamirul aniyah akhlaqi*. The spiritual intelligence shown was a reflection of the self from his world; this is in accordance with that proposed by Bass and Steidlmeier (2006). The other dimension measured according to the characteristics of MA was the spiritual dimension. The results for basic dimensions such as *fitrah* (clear thought) and wisdom in performing tasks that show spiritual intelligence were at moderate levels. Actions as the principle of divine value requirements. MAs were regarded as distinctive educational institutions with religious values. Therefore, the expression of principals in the execution of nature relied on religion as a value system. In contrast to the scores for TQM for sustainability in MAs, the results showed that in the dimensions of communicating a vision to applied teacher transformation paradigm was low. This situation is different from that described by Sallis (2005) in relation to quality schools, and also by Zairi and Liburd (2001). It means that the sustainability of TQM in MAs is still low. It is therefore not surprising that MAs find it difficult to compete with high schools or vocational schools. Referring to Reed et al. (2000), MAs that have a sustainable TQM system are competitive MAs.

Practices such as communicating a vision to serve as a foundation for optimizing customer-focused services were still at a low level. Developing and creating a culture of continuous improvement was also lacking. These conditions were due to weaknesses, including the lack of development of mechanisms for monitoring and critically evaluating success. Empowered teachers in the MAs were still at a low level. This means that teachers had not been involved in solving quality problems, in professional rejuvenation, or in ensuring a balance between the needs of internal customers and external customers as part of sustainability. In line with Koch (2003), the weakness of TQM was due to the fact that schools are not focused on the important issues that both internal and external customers require. Sirvanci (2004) stated that customer identification is an issue in TQM implementation.

The results showed the correlation between authentic transformational leadership and TQM for sustainability was 0.673 with an effect of 0.453 (Figure 1). The weak influence of leadership on sustainable TQM was affected by the relative condition of the MAs, which were quite diverse. MAs that have accreditation of 'A' are very different from those that have 'C' accreditation and are located on the edge of town. The quality management system that applied was very weak and it could be concluded that TQM has not become a philosophy or method for MAs.

TQM sustainability is a system, as well as a philosophy, that provides a good value orientation tool for schools, allowing them to conduct customer-oriented education both internally and externally. The integration of sustainable TQM into the school governance system, as well as the foundation of its philosophy, requires structural and cultural support, including budgetary considerations. Most MAs have a weak balance in terms of finance, growth, and ways of learning about the sustainable meaning of TQM for MAs.

Table 2. Summary of model.

Model	R	R Square	Adjusted R Squre	Std. Error of the Estimate	R Square Change	F Change	df1	df2	Sig F Change
					Change Statistics				
1	.673[a]	.453	.443	7.228	.453	46.114	1	56	.000

a. Predictors (Constant), Transformational authentic Leadership
b. Dependent Variable: TQM Sustainability

As shown in Table 2, the correlation between transformational authentic leadership and TQM for sustainability was 0.673. The value of significance was 0.000, showing that authentic transformational leadership can predict the sustainability of the TQM system in madrasahs. The effect of authentic transformational leadership on TQM sustainability was 0.443. The regression equation for the model is formulated as follows: $\hat{Y} = 31.922 + 1.020X_1$.

Realizing TQM as a philosophy, method, to direct TQM sustainability that leaders must have an obligation to optimize their function in the framework of realizing the sustainability of the quality management system. The leader ensures that the principles are implemented in the TQM operating system. This reflects the opinion of Zairi (2002) that it is the responsibility of leaders to create and communicate the idea of the movement of the organization toward continuous improvement, and also to be supportive, in order to enable the creation and sustenance of an organizational system that is receptive to process management practices.

Leadership conditions in MAs and TQM for sustainability were paradoxes. Both variables have a relationship at moderate levels. Leadership shown by the principals has not been accompanied by the implementation of a sustainable TQM system. A weak TQM system was influenced by several factors, especially financial problems. The results of the research showed that the financial indicator for the balance dimension was low, including the paradigm change in relation to the services of MAs in the era of competition and the paradigm change about who the madrasah customers are, whether internal or external. Teachers perceived that schools did not view them as internal customers with a high need for education and learning, and the needs of teachers have not been addressed by schools.

The strong leadership of the MA principal is a key asset in driving sustainable quality improvement. Zhu et al. (2011) proposed that authentic transformational leadership develops the ethical climate group, which in turn contributes to enhancing ethics groups and to developing the followers' moral identities and emotions. The moral action shown by the principal can influence the climate and moral identity. The teacher has orientation facilities in his actions. The problem is that schools have no focus and are unable to identify who their customers are. Ultimately, the actions of teachers become less effective in supporting the realization of TQM sustainability.

Principals with structural support, especially related to the MA budget, can optimize their function as moral agents that communicate the vision of the MA to teachers and students, whether this is in relation to external parties or to determine how teachers are empowered through the structure. MAs require the presence of principals who can demonstrate authentic leadership and inspire teachers' moral actions in optimizing the function of teachers to realize a sustainable TQM – as Gonzales and Guillén (2002) put it when discussing the ethical dimensions of leaders in TQM implementation. The ethical dimension is a powerful enabler in sustaining TQM efforts, together with systematic management. Ethics are an orientation tool for teachers and principals to develop a sustainable TQM. Bass and Steidlmeier (1999) asserted that "Ethical content focuses upon values, which highlight the issue of standards and criteria of ethical behavior." Price (2003) suggested that "...it would be a mistake to deny the moral acceptability of a requirement that leadership behavior line up with values that reflect the interests of others. This means that authentic transformational leadership is needed by educational institutions to encourage TQM sustainability."

4 CONCLUSION

Authentic transformational leadership at a moderate level in MAs has not been accompanied by TQM sustainability. The moral foundations, acts and spiritual intelligence of the principal as the leader of the Supreme Court have not been followed by increased vision, empowered teachers, or paradigm changes in relation to education services and MA customers. A balance between service to internal and external customers has not yet been achieved. Authentic transformational leadership can predict TQM sustainability.

TQM integration is needed, because a system that gets structural support for authentic transformational leadership is more effective. Future research is expected to focus on implementation and operation of TQM sustainability.

REFERENCES

Anggraeni, F. (2017). *The impact of instructional leadership and communities professional learning to teacher's ability in order to achieve learning effectiveness (Studies in madrasah teachers in Bandung Raya)* (Unpublished dissertation, Universitas Pendidikan Indonesia, Bandung, Indonesia).

Aseltine, J.M., Faryniarz, J.O. & Rigazio-DiGilio, A.J. (2006). *Supervision for learning: A performance-based approach to teacher development and school improvement.* Alexandria, VA: Association for Supervision and Curriculum Development.

Avolio, B.J. & Bass, B.M. (2002). *Developing potential across a full range of leadership: Cases on transactional and transformational leadership.* Mahwah, NJ: Lawrence Erlbaum Associates.

Banks, G.C., McCauley, K.D., Gardner, W.L. & Guler, C.E. (2016). A meta-analytic review of authentic and transformational leadership: A test for redundancy. *Leadership Quarterly*, 27(4), 634–652.

Bass, B.M. (1995). Transformational leadership redux. *Leadership Quarterly*, 6, 463–485.

Bass, B.M. & Riggio, R.E. (2006). *Transformational leadership.* Mahwah, NJ: Lawrence Erlbaum Associates.

Bass, B.M. & Steidlmeier, P. (1999). Ethics, character, and authentic transformational leadership behavior. *The Leadership Quarterly*, 10(2), 181–217.

Bass, B.M. & Steidlmeier, P. (2006). *Ethics, character, and authentic transformational leadership.* New York, NY: Binghamton University.

Bass, B.M., Waldman, D.A., Avolio, B.J. & Bebb, M. (1987). Transformational leadership and the falling dominoes effect. *Group & Organization Management*, 12(1), 73–87.

Begley, P.T. (2006). Self knowledge, capacity and sensitivity: Prerequisites to authentic leadership by school principals. *Journal of Educational Administration*, 44, 570–589.

Berkovich, I. & Eyal, O. (2017). The mediating role of principals' transformational leadership behaviors in promoting teachers' emotional wellness at work: A study in Israeli primary schools. *Educational Management Administration & Leadership*, 45(2), 316–335.

Branson, C. (2007). Effects of structured self-reflection on the development of authentic leadership practices among Queensland primary school principals. *Educational Management Administration & Leadership*, 35(2), 225–246.

Burns, J.M. (1978). *Leadership.* New York, NY: Harper & Row.

Day, D.V., Fleenor, J.W., Atwater, L.E., Sturm, R.E. & McKee, R.A. (2013). Advances in leader and leadership development: A review of 25 years of research and theory. *Leadership Quarterly*, 25(1), 63–82.

Dudka, G.M. & Griswold, W. (2016). Embodying authentic leadership through popular education at Highlander Research and Education Center: A qualitative case study. *Adult Learning*, 27(3), 105–112.

Duignan, A.P. (2014). Authenticity in educational leadership: History, ideal, reality. *Journal of Educational Administration*, 52(2), 152–172.

Gardner, W.L., Avolio, B.J., Luthans, F., May, D.R. & Walumbwa, F. (2005). Can you see the real me? A self-based model of authentic leader and follower development. *Leadership Quarterly*, 16(3), 343–372.

Gardner, W.L., Cogliser, C.C., Davis, K.M. & Dickens, M.P. (2011). Authentic leadership: A review of the literature and research agenda. *Leadership Quarterly*, 22(6), 1120–1145.

Gaspersz, V. (2005). *Total quality management*. Jakarta, Indonesia: Gramedia.

Gocstch, D.L. & Davis, S.B. (2003). *Quality management. Introduction to TQM for production, processing and services*. Upper Saddle River, NJ: Pearson Prentice Hall.

Gonzales, T.F. & Guillén, M. (2002). Leadership ethical dimension: A requirement in TQM implementation. *The TQM Magazine*, 14(3), 150–164.

Harris, A. & Lambert (2003). *Building leadership capacity for school improvement*. Philadelphia, PA: Open University Press.

Ibrahim, M.S., Ghavifekr, S., Ling, S., Siraj, S. & Azeez, M.I.K. (2014). Can transformational leadership influence on teachers' commitment towards organization, teaching profession, and students learning? A quantitative analysis. *Asia Pacific Education Review*, 15(2), 177–190.

Koch, J.V. (2003). TQM: Why is its impact in higher education so small. *The TQM Magazine*, 15(5), 325–333.

Komariah, A. (2016). Authentic leadership behaviour in madrasah aliyah in Tasikmalaya Regency. *Jurnal Pendidikan Islam*, 1(3), 407–422.

Krüger, M. & Scheerens, J. (2012). Conceptual perspectives on school leadership. In J. Scheerens (Ed.), *School leadership effects revisited*. Dordrecht, The Netherlands: Springer.

Kruse, K. (2013, May 12). What is authentic leadership? *Forbes*. Retrieved from https://www.forbes.com/sites/kevinkruse/2013/05/12/what-is-authentic-leadership/

Kuei, C. & Lu, M.H. (2012). Integrating quality management principles into sustainability management. *Total Quality Management & Business Excellence*, 3363, 1–17.

Lambrechts, W. & Van Petegem, P. (2016). The interrelations between competences for sustainable development and research competences. *International Journal of Sustainability in Higher Education*, 17(6), 776–795.

McCleskey, J.A. (2014). Situational, transformational, and transactional leadership and leadership development. *Journal of Business Studies Quarterly*, 5(4), 117.

Price, T.L. (2003). The ethics of transformational leadership. *The Leadership Quarterly*, 14, 67–81.

Reed, R., Lemak, D.J. & Mero, N.P. (2000). Total Quality Management and sustainable competitive advantage. *Journal of Quality Management*, 5, 5–26.

Rodriguez, R.A. et al. (2017). Authentic leadership and transformational leadership: An incremental approach. *Journal of Leadership Studies*, 11(1), 20–35.

Sallis, E. (2005). *Total Quality Management in education*. London, UK: Kogan Page.

Sirvanci, M.B. (2004). Critical issues for TQM implementation in higher education. *The TQM Magazine*, 16(6), 382–386.

Sobar. (1994). *Khalifah di Bumi sebagai Tujuan Pendidikan Umum* (Unpublished doctoral dissertation, Universitas Pendidikan Indonesia, Bandung, Indonesia).

Stoten, W.D. (2014). Authentic leadership in English education: What do college teachers tell us? *International Journal of Educational Management*, 28(5), 510–522.

Walker, A. & Shuangye, C. (2007). Leader authenticity in intercultural school contexts. *Educational Management Administration & Leadership*, 35(2), 185–204.

Walumbwa, F.O., Avolio, B.J., Gardner, W.L., Wernsing, T.S. & Peterson, S.J. (2007). Authentic leadership: Development and validation of a theory-based measure. *Journal of Management*, 34(1), 89–126.

Zairi, M. (2001). Driving strategy with quality. *International Journal of Applied Strategic Management*, 2(2).

Zairi, M. (2002). Beyond TQM implementation: The new paradigm of TQM sustainability. *Total Quality Management & Business Excellence*, 13, 1161–1172.

Zairi, M. & Liburd, I.M. (2001) TQM sustainability – A roadmap for creating competitive advantage. In *Integrated Management, Proceedings of the 6th International Conference on ISO 9000 and TQM* (pp. 452–461).

Zhu, W., Avolio, B.J., Riggio, R.E. & Sosik, J.J. (2011). The effect of authentic transformational leadership on follower and group ethics. *Leadership Quarterly*, 22(5), 801–817.

Zink, K.J. (2007). From total quality management to corporate sustainability based on a stakeholder management. *Journal of Management History*, 13(4), 394–401.

Educational Administration Innovation for Sustainable Development – Komariah et al. (Eds)
© 2018 Taylor & Francis Group, London, ISBN 978-1-138-57341-3

Repackaging welfare services to improve teacher productivity in Nigeria

S.M. Warrah
University Pendidikan Sultan Idris, Malaysia

S. Nurlatifah & A.T. Ismail
Universitas Pendidikan Indonesia, Bandung, Jawa Barat, Indonesia

ABSTRACT: This paper examines the potential for teacher welfare services to improve teacher productivity in Nigeria. Teachers have been regarded as the engine of transformation of a country, nurturing learners to become useful to society. The academic performance of students has been declining to the extent that parents blame secondary schools for a lack of qualified teachers. The government, which is the policymaker, contributes immensely to the low productivity of teachers in the classroom. Hence, this paper attempts to introduce the repackaging of teacher welfare services to improve the productivity of teachers in the school system. This repackaging will be a signal by the government of Nigeria in an area vital to assisting teachers in increasing their productivity. Based on this discourse, it is recommended that teachers' salaries need to increase in line with employees in other sectors, and encouraging the development of teachers through attendance at conferences and workshops was also suggested.

1 INTRODUCTION

Education is vital to the political and economic development of any country. Most countries earmark half of their national income to the education sector (Olujuwon & Perumal, 2017). Education is the process of transmitting the culture of a society from one generation to the next generation (Adeyinka, 2000). It is the process by which the older members of society bring up the younger ones. As a result of this, education should be the number one priority for any nation that wants to develop both human and material resources. It would not be an over-statement to say that the survival of anyone is futile without education. Furthermore, education tends to close the gap between the rich and the poor as well as giving freedom and emancipation.

In order to have meaningful education, the contribution of teachers to national transformation is worthy of recognition by all nations. Teachers have been regarded as contributing factors to the success of any education system – even when there are learning materials, we still need a qualified teacher who will orchestrate the meaningful transmission of such materials to learners. The pillar of the Nigerian educational system is the teacher, who controls the whole process (Amasuomo & Ozurumba, 2017). Teachers prepare lesson plans, organize the class and use relevant teaching methods. The teacher will certainly continue to be the major factor, both at primary and secondary level, and the determinant of the quality of education (Akinsolu, 2010). Teachers are mentioned more than any of the other factors that contribute to the quality of education at all levels (Darling-Hammond, 2000). Teaching and learning occur with the assistance of teachers. The teachers of today have special qualities that made them teachers, and these qualities help them in fulfilling their duties. It is clear that qualified, committed and dedicated teachers are important tools for achieving educational goals as well as national development (Ekpiken & Edet, 2014).

Despite these countless roles in society, teachers have been complaining about the neglect of their welfare by the government in Nigeria, affecting their ability to compete globally

(Fadeyi et al., 2015). The minister of education in Nigeria had urged the federal government to implement the approved national minimum wage and teacher enhancement allowance. He further expressed sadness over the deteriorating economic and social conditions of teachers in view of government failure to commence implementation of this wage.

The living conditions of teachers are seriously affected and this is having direct consequences on productivity in the sector (Nbina, 2010). Arikewuyo (1999, 2004) noted that living conditions of teachers in secondary schools had deteriorated, they showed poor productivity and were afforded little value in society. In relation to this, the present study aimed to examine the effect of the repackaging of components of teacher welfare, such as increments in salary, promotion, incentives, and leave allowance, on productivity in the service.

2 THEORETICAL FRAMEWORKS

Motivational theory was the underpinning theory for this current study. According to motivational theorists, motivation refers to the intrinsic force within a human being that will make employees play a vital role in the accomplishment of organizational objectives. Herzberg's two-factor theory was suitable for this study, in the sense that teacher welfare is fundamental to achieving educational objectives. It is when teachers are motivated in their work that they will contribute effectively to the academic performance of the learners.

There were two distinct factors that influenced workers' performance: motivator factors and hygiene factors. The motivator factor simply means that workers can be motivated to work harder to achieve their objectives if they enjoy their work and are recognized in their work, while the hygiene factor stipulated that salary, bonus, promotion and relationship between employer and employees could lead to actualization of organizational goals. Conversely, the lack of these factors can lead to dissatisfaction and lack of motivation among workers.

In simple terms, this theory suggests that employers must make teachers happy and build on both motivator and hygiene factors to improve productivity. Workers must be motivated and appreciated, and providing them with feedback is essential. The theory further found that to prevent workers' absenteeism, they needed to be provided with good conditions of work, better pay, attention and support.

2.1 *Teacher welfare services*

Teacher welfare is a vital stimulus that could facilitate good performance at a workplace. Teacher welfare needs to be seen as a motivational factor for the sustenance and survival of educational systems. Teacher welfare packages cover recognition, car loan, leave bonus, and free education for teachers and their children (Mokshein et al., 2009). If these are provided, teachers are productive. Teacher welfare is anything that could make teachers more committed, dedicated, satisfied and motivated to work harder in the system.

Teaching in Nigeria needs to be upgraded in order to meet international standards (Arikewuyo, 2004). The government did not support the teachers because they are treated in a hands-off way and with disdain. Ozigi (1992) found that teachers were unhappy, uninspired, unmotivated, and frustrated. The government must place the same value on teachers as their counterparts in other sectors (Fadeyi et al., 2015). To support this argument, Jamil (2014) stated that the Malaysian government had doubled their efforts in this regard, by providing the necessary services to teachers to improve their productivity in the system. Teachers have been the focus of government in recognition of the roles they play in society.

2.2 *Teacher productivity*

Many definitions of teacher productivity are given by different scholars. Productivity is the measure of job performance. Indeed, teacher productivity could be determined by how well the objectives of an organization are being attained, as a result of their commitment to learners and performance at work (Nakpodia, 2011). In the same vein, productivity can be determined by an assessment of the extent to which the objectives of an educational system have been achieved. Teacher productivity can be assessed in areas like critical thinking, their relationship with learners, their communication skills, the way they teach the learners, and their management of the classroom.

Productivity of teachers is treated as one of the leading predetermined objectives of educational system attainment. This is why it is imperative for the government to employ qualified teachers that will transform the learners as well as the country (Duze & Ogbah, 2013). Good working conditions are very important in encouraging productivity among teachers. Attending workshops and conferences would allow teachers in the system to improve their productivity.

Teachers are vital agents in any educational system and there are no substitutes for teachers (Ijov et al., 2016). Skills that can make teachers productive in performing their services are the knowledge of how to understand the students, the ability to improve students' competence, good leadership capacity, resourcefulness and self-discipline. Indeed, the quality of teachers employed determines the productivity of the teachers. The levels of teachers' knowledge and skills are the factors that affect teacher performance at work (Wilson & Rumuolumeni, 2016).

2.3 *Instructional role of teachers in education*

The role of teacher is vital to the development of an individual, and without teachers it seems that a person's life will be futile. In this light, the plethora of functions of teachers are highlighted and discussed below.

(a) Teacher as counselor. The teacher acts as a counselor for the learners within the school environment. Through the interaction that takes place in the school, the teacher renders counseling services to the learners in the areas of sexual behavior, health issues, choice of subjects, behavioral adjustment and reading habits.

(b) Teacher as parent figure. It is believed that the teacher plays the role of parent to the learners, especially in boarding schools. Learners feel comfortable when they have a good relationship with their teachers; they express their problems and feelings and these are solved or addressed by the teachers living in the school environment. Udo (2003) supported the idea that learning will be lively when students view the interaction that occurs between them and their teacher as warm, caring and non-threatening.

(c) Teacher as role model. Most scholars, and most people, see the teacher as a role model in the sense that students look to them for how to behave and how knowledge is transferred. Students can emulate the teacher who has good behavior and attends classes, as well as being brilliant in their field. Most of what learners become has been determined by the teacher who has been monitoring them since they entered school.

(d) Teacher as spokesperson for their immediate community. The teacher is considered as a knowledgeable person in society in terms of knowledge transfer to children. Teachers represent the community on many occasions to discuss issues that affect them.

2.4 *Teacher challenges in Nigeria*

It has been observed that teachers in Nigeria face challenges in their work that affect their productivity. Some of the challenges confronted are as follows:

(a) Poor motivation. Lack of motivation has affected teachers greatly and contributed to the low academic performance of students. This lack of motivation affected the attitude of teachers towards their normal duty. Teachers had no respect and value in society. Poor motivation of teachers had left the educational system in bad shape (Wilson & Rumuolumeni, 2016). This caused teachers to set up other businesses, resulting in less commitment to the teaching profession.

(b) Dearth of workshop attendance. The majority of teachers in Nigeria did not attend workshops and conferences to increase their knowledge. This dearth of workshop attendance indirectly affected the job performance of teachers (Wilson, 2016; Wilson & Rumuolumeni, 2016). New knowledge,

methods of teaching, and skills would be gained in attending workshops and conferences. Lack of conference attendance to improve knowledge posed a challenge to teachers (Nwabochi, 2013).

(c) Ill-equipped classrooms. Ill-equipped classrooms affected the productivity levels of teachers. Some classes were dilapidated and not in a good condition for either teachers or students. In these situations, teachers' productivity could never be at its best. In addition, there is a shortage of classes and teachers in remote areas.

(d) Problems of teacher employment. The employment of teachers was another topical issue that affected the productivity of teachers in Nigeria. Politicians had hijacked much of the employment in the teaching profession, serving personal interests when it came to employing teachers in schools. In this case, good-quality teachers were not necessarily employed and appointments were based on favoritism and nepotism. This affected the productivity levels of teachers in the classroom because poor quality teachers were employed.

2.5 *Repackaging of teacher welfare to improve productivity*

(a) Salary increment and other remuneration. Salary is one of the key factors impacting the performance of teachers. When salaries are paid at the appropriate time, teachers' productivity will tend to increase. Nakpodia (2011) asserted that when salaries of teachers are not paid at the right time, the level of their commitment and dedication to work will be affected. Most of the incessant strikes we are experiencing in the teaching profession today, in both primary and secondary schools, are caused by dearth of payment. Many teachers of today have resorted to other businesses, because the salaries paid to them were more commensurate with what they buy in the market. This has indirectly affected the level of teachers' commitment to the teaching profession. It is believed that when these anomalies are corrected, the productivity of teachers will increase and students' academic performance will increase. According to Mokshein et al. (2009), the Malaysian government has created a special package for teachers teaching critical subjects such as English, technology, science, and mathematics. Incentives and allowances are of great benefit as means of improving productivity and retaining and rewarding excellence (Petras et al., 2012). This technique is effective in attracting and retaining teachers.

(b) Teacher motivation. Motivation is also regarded as a contributor to the overall performance of teachers in secondary schools. In addition, it is key to the attainment of a quality educational system. Teacher motivation is regarded by the government as a way of empowering teachers in the field for the benefit of providing a quality service. In many schools, efforts had been put in place to accomplish workers' satisfaction (Ofojebe & Ezugoh, 2010). When teachers are demotivated, they will resort to developing businesses elsewhere. This is because a motivated teacher will work harder to achieve the aims and objectives of the school. There is hope that if the government can increase teachers' motivation through providing job security, loans and other services, teacher performance will increase. Giving hardship allowances and special incentives for teaching in remote village areas will also serve as motivational techniques to retain quality teachers (Mokshein, et al., 2009). It is believed that if this could be done in Nigeria, the productivity of teachers would improve.

(c) Good-quality working conditions. Good working conditions for teachers translate to good productivity at work. It is believed that a good environment facilitates effective teaching and learning (Adelabu, 2005; Mokshein et al., 2009). Teachers' offices were in bad shape and poorly equipped for effective teaching and learning. Effective teaching could not take place in such an area. If teachers' offices are well furnished with quality teaching materials, the productivity of teachers will increase. Such facilities will help to redeem the image of teachers in society, and incoming generations will be more likely to want to be part of the teaching profession.

(d) Prompt promotion. Teacher promotion contributed immensely to the productivity of teachers. When teachers are promoted on a regular and timely basis, productivity tends to increase (Adelabu, 2005). Dissatisfaction and lack of interest will set in when promotion is not given at an appropriate time. Petras et al. (2012) argued that special rewards could be given to teachers

who performed excellently in the promotion scheme and they would provide a role model for other teachers.

3 CONCLUSION

Ultimately, the literature reviewed for this paper has supported the idea that for any nation to transform both human and material resources, quality teachers are required to impart knowledge. The productivity of teachers is determined by the quality of incentives and remuneration, as well as the quality of teaching aids available for teachers from the government. In this paper, we have identified that poor conditions of service, problems in the employment of teachers, a dearth of workshops and remuneration, and ill-equipped classrooms, among other factors, had contributed to the low productivity of Nigerian teachers. It is hoped that if these anomalies are corrected, the productivity of teachers will improve both locally and globally.

REFERENCES

Adelabu, M.A. (2005). *Teacher motivation and incentives in Nigeria.* London, UK: Department for International Development. Retrieved from https://www.gov.uk/dfid-research-outputs/teacher-motivation-and-incentives-in-nigeria

Adeyinka, A.A. (2000). Current problems of educational development in Nigeria. *Journal of Education.*

Akinsolu, A.O. (2010). Teachers and students' academic performance in Nigerian secondary schools: Implications for planning. *Florida Journal of Educational Administration & Policy*, 3(2), 86–103.

Amasuomo, J.O. & Ozurumba, C.N. (2017). A comparative study of provision of primary schools and teachers supply between rural and urban local government areas in Bayelsa State, Nigeria. *Balkan Journal of Interdisciplinary Research*, 404.

Arikewuyo, M.O. (2004). Stress management strategies of secondary school teachers in Nigeria. *Educational Research*, 46(2), 195–207.

Arikewuyo, O. (1999). Job attitude profiles of managers of secondary schools in Nigeria. *IFE PsychologIA: An International Journal*, 7(2), 69–84.

Darling-Hammond, L. (2000). Teacher quality and student achievement. *Education Policy Analysis Archives*, 8, 1.

Duze, C.O. & Ogbah, R. (2013). Retaining and developing quality teachers: Critical issues for administrators in Nigeria secondary schools. *Journal of Sociological Research*, 4(1), 145–161.

Ekpiken, W.E. & Edet, A.O. (2014). The role of teacher education and Nigerian teachers in national development: The way forward. *Higher Education of Social Science*, 7(1), 139–143.

Fadeyi, V.T., Sofoluwe, A.O. & Gbadeyan, R.A. (2015). Influence of teachers' welfare scheme on job performance in selected Kwara State secondary schools. *Asia Pacific Journal of Education, Arts and Sciences*, 2(4).

Ijov, M.T., Hemen, M.T., Austin, A.O. & Akinyemi, M.A. (2016). Human resource management and teachers' job performance in secondary schools in north west senatorial district of Benue State, Nigeria. *Journal of Teacher Perspective*, 10(2).

Jamil, H. (2014). Teacher is matter for education quality: A transformation of policy for enhancing the teaching profession in Malaysia. *Journal of International Cooperation in Education*, 16(2), 181–196.

Mokshein, S.E., Ahmad, H.H. & Vongalis-Macrow, A. (2009). *Towards providing quality secondary education: Training and retaining quality teachers in Malaysia.* Bangkok, Thailand: UNESCO.

Nakpodia, E.D. (2011). Work environment and productivity among primary school teachers in Nigeria. *African Research Review*, 5(5), 367–381.

Nbina, J. (2010). Re-visiting secondary school science teachers motivation strategies to face the challenges of the 21st Century. *Journal of Emerging Trends in Educational Research and Policy Studies*, 2(6), 413–417.

Nwabochi, F.N. (2013). Teacher quality and professional challenges in the expectancy of universal basic education programme in Rivers State. *Siren Journals*, 5(4).

Ofojebe, W.N. & Ezugoh, C. (2010). Teachers' motivation and its influence on quality assurance in the Nigerian educational system. *African Research Review*, 4(2).

Olujuwon, O. & Perumal, J. (2017). Nigerian teachers' understanding of school.

Ozigi, A. (1992, December). Keynote address for the national conference on financing teacher's education at N.I.C.E, Owerri.

Petras, Y., Jamil, H. & Mohamed, A.R. (2012). How do teachers learn? A study on the policy and practice of teacher professional development in Malaysia. *KEDI Journal of Educational Policy*, 9(1).

Wilson, G. (2016). Teachers' challenges and job performance under the Universal Basic Education Scheme in Rivers State, Nigeria (2007–2015). *Covenant University Journal of Politics and International Affairs*, 4(1).

Wilson, G. & Rumuolumeni, P.H. (2016). Teachers' challenges and job performance in Rivers State, Nigeria Universal Basic Education. *Journal of Research in National Development*, 14.

Educational Administration Innovation for Sustainable Development – Komariah et al. (Eds)
© 2018 Taylor & Francis Group, London, ISBN 978-1-138-57341-3

Consensus on an ideal leadership style in relation to school effectiveness

Z. Yasni
Queen's University of Belfast, UK

H. Wathoni
Hamzanwadi University, West Nusa Tenggara, Indonesia

ABSTRACT: An array of studies in the literature on educational leadership and school effectiveness have placed school leadership at the center of school effectiveness and school improvement. This research delves into the concensus of the ideal leadership styles of school principals regarding their roles in relation to school leadership and school effectiveness. Taking a qualitative approach, data was aggregated through semi-structured interviews with the selected principals of A-accredited schools located on Lombok Island, Indonesia. The study suggests that the inter-relationship between a principal's style and their role strongly impacts on the effectiveness of a school. This research is also asserted that attempts to promote school effectiveness have been linked with ideas of democratic leadership, strong academic emphasis, the strong involvement of teach-ers, staff and students within the school context, and the principals had a shared management style and responsibilities.

1 INTRODUCTION

Leadership is vital to effective schools but which model of leadership is most frequently employed by principals? In addition, the everyday practices of school leadership has been correlated with school effectiveness. It follows that the main goal of a school leader is to develop self-renewal and betterment processes that are able to lead school change (Moos & Huber, 2007). To do so, school leaders are pivotal agents of change who play a significant role in whether the school will improve or not.

A series of studies on school effectiveness has concentrated on the forms of different variables that might be examined with respect to how influencial a particular style of leadership is. Recent literature in the USA, UK and European countries has focused on the pivotal role of school principals in influencing a school's effectiveness (Harris *et al.*, 2013; Day *et al.*, 2009; Robbins *et al.*, 2009; Robinson, 2007). In other words, the search for better school quality is now widely concentrated on the leadership of school principals (Hallinger & Bryant, 2013).

This article reports on research inquiries which explored the making of a 'good' school and strategies to make all schools 'good'. The context is the efforts being made to accelerate the quality of education in Indonesia by searching for approaches to leadership that influence school effectiveness.

2 LITERATURE REVIEW

2.1 *Preliminary study on educational leadership: Indonesian context*

In the past, leadership was developed within the field of business, while today, leadership is being widely augmented into educational setting to aide transformative reforms in education.

Consideration is also occurring in terms of differences between leaders by examining trends in the thinking of leaders (Hallinger & Huber, 2012).

A preliminary study of principal leadership in Indonesia by Jones & Hagul (2001) noted that school principals had low authority in operating their school and the allocated resources. This context showed the insufficient support and training for managing and leading the school effectively. Similarly, Bjork's research (2005) confirmed the finding that school principals had an inadequate capacity, expertise and experiences to deal with opportunities and challenges to their educational autonomy. Both studies revealed that shared-decision making and empowering teachers are acknowledged as favorable practices. This acknowledgement did not occur frequently because the principals generally relied on an autocratic leadership style.

Research conducted by Raihani (2008) piloted in the International Successful School Principalship Project (ISSPP), suggested some familiar practices of successful school leadership from earlier studies regarding beliefs and values of leadership within three Islamic successful schools in Jogjakarta, Indonesia. Principals' leadership and strategy articulated were strongly influenced by Islamic values and cultural beliefs. It suggests that meeting school improvement, the principals should exhibit capability in developing school vision and strategy, building capacity, and expanding a wider network. Two quantitative research completed in two different regions in Indonesia; in Lampung (Hariri *et al.*, 2014) and in Padang (Damanik, 2014) revealed respectively that teachers' and staffs' job satisfaction could be raised if the principal's style of decision making was more democratic and less coercive.

In addition, research related to principal leadership in Indonesia was completed by Yasin *et al.* (2013) which analysed relationships between the level of principal competency and the school performance in practicing the national education standard of Indonesia. These research findings suggest a significant relationship between the competency level of leadership and management of the school principal and the achievement of the National Education Standard of Indonesia. The research noted that the higher levels of leadership and management by the principals, the higher the achievement of national education standard could be met.

However, Lee & Hallinger's (2012) noticed a different finding that Indonesian principals put their main emphasis on school management and administration rather than leadership and development. Principals were much paying attention on the daily routine administration rather than developing leadership activities as their main role.

2.2 *Research on school effectiveness and the leadership of the principal*

School effectiveness can be based on the attainment of students and the evidence of transformative school changes (Reynolds *et al.*, 2001). This research suggests that effective schools focus on improving students' achievements and capacity to lead changes. Effectiveness is linked to a school's capability to run its operation efficiently. Likewise, Morrison (2004) measures effective school based on several features of school effectiveness, such as teachers and teaching, curriculum, management, students, and community feature. Research completed by Creemers and Kyriakides (2009) suggest that school effectiveness can be seen from the leader and teacher attitudes, curriculum, school organisation, and school policy.

One of key factors which cause school effectiveness is the activity of strong leadership.

2.3 *Effective leadership for effective schooling*

The effectiveness of leadership roles played by the principal could potentially influence all school members at all levels such as teachers, staff, students and even the students' parents or society. Principals are responsible for creating a collaborative school culture by coordinating individual work during the school improvement process for continuous development and to improve achievements and staff and teacher professionalism (Southworth, 2003).

In several countries, the endeavours toward school change have confirmed that neither top-down measures nor the use of bottom-up approaches exclusively have the effects expected. Instead, a combination and systematic harmonisation of both has been shown to be most effective. Moreover, improvement is noted as a continuous process with diverse stages, which follows the individual's rules. Innovation also need to be established after their creation and implementation at the individual school level, so that they will become a perpetual part of the school's culture, that is, part of the structures, atmosphere and regular routine (Moos & Huber, 2007).

A second identification of effective leadership notes a participative approach, ensuring that significant others are involved in the process. Mortimore et *al.* (1988) suggest it is the essence of involving staff in the life of the school system and in decision making. It is important to make sure that teachers feel they are represented and their ideas have been considered.

The third and fourth characteristics identified as aspects of effective leadership comprise two direct interactions within school life, as argued by Reynolds & Teddlie (2002): the personal monitoring of staff accomplishment and proactive staff recruitment and replacement. The former has been included as an important variable in this study as a sense-making process, and being an advisor or helper in making decisions. The latter has also been picked out in this study as involving the principal's recruitment of good teachers, and pressing teachers who are low in competencies to either progress or leave to another institution. The principal knows how to manage and dismiss incompetent teachers if necessary.

2.4 *Relating the ideal leadership styles to school effectiveness*

Simply, leadership style is a matter of utilising a degree of power to lead a group of people (Northouse, 2015). In educational practice, school principals are known as educational leaders who are given responsibilities to lead schools and achieve the goals of the school (Lokman *et al.*, 2013). The important role of principals as a factor of school effectiveness has been suggested by the findings of school effectiveness studies conducted in the UK and European countries (Huber & Muijs, 2010; Moos and Huber, 2007) in recent decades to provide a critical overview. The findings of all of these studies agree that the correlation between school effectiveness and the role of school principals is highly significant. Therefore, Robbins *et al.* (2009) and Eberlin and Tatum (2008) emphasised that the principal's role as a school leader must be prioritised to improve school effectiveness. They are legitimate as Moos and Huber (2007) state that 'school leaders matter, they are educationally significant, school leaders do make a difference'.

3 RESEARCH METHOD

This study employed a qualitative approach of face-to-face interviews with participants because it enabled them to be directly observed. This also led to an in-depth understanding of each participant's response, attitudes and behaviours, body language and gestures, multi-sensory data, non-verbal reactions, all of which influenced their answers and their roles employed within their school as recorded (Cohen *et al.,* 2013).

Qualitative research was adopted to employ an anti-positivist stance in this research rather than using a quantitative approach. Data obtained from participants by asking open questions, gathering information in the form of interviews and examining the collected data from their views to summarise and analyse the problem (Creswell, 2014).

The benefit of using a qualitative approach was emphasised by Cohen *et al.* (2013, p. 146), that 'it is concerned with precision and accuracy'. Using a qualitative method allowed the researcher to obtain information about the leadership style of the principals in different A-accredited schools.

This study used interviews to collect the data. The type of interview used was semi-structured due to its flexibility. During interviewing the participants, the researcher was guided by the research questions about leadership style and school effectiveness. What common aspects lead to successful school leadership and what common pitfalls appear to lead to a failed school leadership in Indonesian's schools. By employing a less formal interview method it also provided more opportunities to clarify and inquire with follow-up questions to explore more about a situation or invisible problems and clarify any misunderstandings.

Twelve principals were involved as participants in this study. The twelve A-accredited school principals were taken purposively from different levels of education on Lombok Island, Indonesia. Surprisingly, the twelve chosen participants come from diverse types of schools such as general schools, vocational schools and religious schools. Some are overseen by the government and the rest are private. This diversity gives benefits in terms of the complexity of data sources. The participants presented diverse views and perspectives based on the type of school they lead along with their leadership experiences.

4   RESULTS & DISCUSSIONS

A school principal has multi-faceted tasks with a complexity on responsibilities. For example, management and administration, professional autonomy and accountability, personal and social education, collaboration and competition, meet students' needs and the narrow implementation of required government standards (Kemendikbud, 2007).

> The principal's role is too complex. As a leader, we should be responsible from A to Z. Meaning that, it's not only in terms of administration, but also all of the things within the school are our responsibility (PA2).

4.1   *Principal leadership in practice: Transformational leadership*

In the 'average' levels of effective schools, the principals operate effective leadership styles, which are appropriately employed in accordance with their school (Reynolds & Teddlie, 2002). Indeed, it is agreed that there is no single style of leadership which is best for all types of school (Northouse, 2015). A senior principal commented in comparing their experience as a principal in two different schools:

> My style of leadership is diverse, depending on the character of the subordinates I lead. My style here is different from my style in my previous school. The people are different. I lead them with a different style as well (PA3).

This would suggest that the leadership which principals practice is adjusted depending on whom they interact with. This is confirmed by another principal of an elementary school who believes that a principal should be friendly without any pressure, and not be frightening:

> When I deliver instructions to my subordinates, I do it while smiling and joking with no pressure to supervise them in detail. I ask for their readiness while smiling. If they find some difficulties, I help them without any enforcement (PA4).

School principals make changes and improve effectiveness by eliminating pressures in order to remove any fear and give space to develop. Effective leadership desire to create supportive working conditions within a school. It is important to be 'accepted by those they lead' (PA4).

This is justifiable, not because it was stated by experienced school principals, but because the majority of principals interviewed had the same view that with the lack of a principal-teachers gap and a positive atmosphere it would be easier to achieve effectiveness because they are accepted and deserve to be followed as a leader.

Collaborative work and teamwork could possibly occur if the leader is accepted by their colleagues. The majority of principals agreed that the acceptance by teachers of their leader can significantly maximise the quality of collaborative work between the principal and teachers. Therefore, reducing the gap in the principal-teacher relationship is one way to improve results. As stated in the following comment:

> When the gap is still high between the principal and teachers and staff, the working results are never excellent. Thus, my concern is how to reduce the gap between the principal and teachers and staff to get a more satisfying result (PB4).

This statement would suggest that reducing the interaction gap can open spaces for the subordinates to get involved in school life and decision making. With 'warm communication' (PA4) that is 'not too rigid' (PC2) and there is 'no dividing fence regarding interaction' (PA1). This can generate a positive atmosphere among staff.

The way principals articulate ideas confidently indicates that they knew what they wanted to do and what the school needed to progress. Their intonation and gestures also showed that they clearly understood where the school will be led. However, this kind of style would potentially cause criticism and resistance. They realised that:

> There are some friends resisting it, if the programs I offer felt difficult to meet after their consideration (PA3).

Consequently, conflict resolution could happen between the principal and their colleagues if they are not able to reach agreement each other, or the programme would not be achieved as expected because of the principal's enforcement. Staff may feel that it seems like coercion.

Thus, the principal gives spaces for everyone to talk if they do not agree with what the principal offers: 'If you disagree with it, it is better to discuss it here now' (PA3). These words show that the principals want to make their desires clear in the hope that everyone could share some understandings about the growth of the school. The Principal's expression of what they want does not imply enforcing teachers to accept their ideas. The principal still deliberates on their colleagues' ideas and together they seek to reach agreement.

Practicing a combination of 'top-down nest' and 'bottom-up nest' simultaneously is considered a more effective way than applying one and ignoring another (Murphy & Louis, 1994). Systematic harmonisation of both top-down and bottom-up nest as part of the principal's role to lead change has been shown by Moos and Huber (2007).

4.2 *Principal leadership in practice: Democratic leadership*

Although the principals believed that their ideas for the school were great, they were still democratic and did not want to be a dictator to enforce others to agree. Effective principal leadership is identified as a participative approach, of assuring others engage in the process. It is important to make sure that all staff feel represented and their opinions have been taken into account. This is articulated by one principal, 'I always figure out how we can feel fine with each other. A joint decision is welcomed by all. (PA3)'.

This also illustrates that the principals preferred to accommodate other ideas and suggestions in order to be more participative and strengthen the organisational team. It is recognised that ignoring other voices will potentially lead to negative effects such as cracks in the team, particularly in decision making where the principals should involve their staff in making a decision.

> Although I have authority, I must involve others in deciding. I avoid cliques which would talk about the team and potentially cause cracks in our teamwork (PB2).

By involving the teachers, it can reduce the weight of a leaders responsibilities. As noted, 'when the decision is made together, whatever the consequences will be handled together and all the needs will be shared together (PB3)'.

This approach is good for the sake of democracy. They say that 'it is much safer and better' (PA2). 'Everyone will be satisfied because whatever the agreement it is a joint decision' (PB2). Most of the participants admitted that engaging teachers adequately created more benefits in decision making.

> We often find solutions through sharing and discussions. Everyone feels more involved. If the solutions are coming from them, they will be in favour of being more responsible (PB4).

This implies that when decisions are made democratically by involving others, conflict among the team can be avoided and the satisfaction which results would serve the interests of the stakeholders. As a result, the responsibility to implement the decision is not only given to the principal, but also to others. Indeed, a principal echoed that, 'everything must be decided in the meeting by involving everyone (PA1).

This suggests that although the school principal is the key in decision making, other staff must be involved as well because the principal's role as a leader is also to be responsible for fostering a strong teamwork within the school.

Further, a school principal should seek to 'strengthen teamwork and respect' (PA1) as much as possible among staff within the school. The principal tends to be more inclusive, even in an emergency situation. As a principal from a secondary junior high school stated, 'if I find an emergency issue, I call others to meet as soon as possible to find the solution together (PB2).

This implies a strong commitment to teamwork by the principals who are often low in personal power and authority. This is in contrast with a senior principal pronouncing:

> If an unexpected problem appears which requires immediate decision, I decide it soon (PA4).

This principal is showing their style of leadership in a more flexible way, not strictly committing to the team's agreement, but still considering the issues they face to ensure the school runs effectively. They recognised how important a leader's power is in making a decision in compelling and distressing situations without being influenced by others.

4.3 *Emphasizing on academic achievement*

Almost all of principals mentioned characteristics of school effectiveness set by researchers noted earlier in this article. In terms of academic emphasis as part of school effectiveness, nine out of twelve principals confirmed this saying:

> Successful school effectiveness can be seen from student activities in the classroom, the roles of the teacher, academic results and products they generate from the learning process. It should be judged from student achievement, satisfactory results in final examinations, or from student achievement at the national competition level in the Science Olympiad (the most prestigious science competition in Indonesia) (PC2).

The principals clearly emphasise academic process and achievement. The way they articulate their views on school effectiveness as resulting from academic emphasis showed that their focus is on the quality of the educational process.

5 CONCLUSION

Beginning from a simple curiosity which became the central issue, what makes a school good and how do we make all schools good? This led the researcher to explore one key factor of school effectiveness that being the school leader's leadership role and style. It is noted that none of the educational leadership and school effectiveness literature reviewed denies the significant of the principal's roles and styles in achieving school effectiveness.

The data suggested consistently that a principals' leadership style can make a difference in school effectiveness in the way they undertake their role in practice. It is clear that the interrelation between a principals' leadership role and style strongly influences the effectiveness within a school. A-accredited school principals' leadership role and style is in line with what effective leadership should be for an effective school. The improvement of student attainment and educational quality by policy makers and practitioners would be helped by the findings of this study. A way to improve educational quality, then, can be achieved by improving the quality of principals professionalism and leadership skills.

Efforts to create school effectiveness have been linked with ideas of transformational and democratic leadership, strong academic emphasis, the strong involvement of teachers, staff and students within the school context, and the principals had a shared-management style and shared responsibilities. This suggestion could contribute to developing principal training and frameworks to provide better continuous professional development for principals. Effective leadership characteristics which are internationally accepted could be implemented to make 'good' schools.

REFERENCES

Bjork, C., 2005. Indonesian education: Teachers, schools and central bureaucracy. New York, NY: Routledge

Cohen, L., Manion, L. & Morrison, K., 2013. *Research methods in education*. Routledge.

Creemers, B. & Kyriakides, L. 2009. Situational effects of the school factors included in the dynamic model of educational effectiveness. *South African Journal of Education*, 29(3), pp. 293–315.

Creswell, J.W. 2014. *Research design: Qualitative, quantitative, and mixed methods* approaches. California: Sage Publications.

Damanik, E. 2014. Principal Leadership Styles and Its Impact on School Climate and Teacher Self-Efficacy in Indonesian Schools (*Unpublished doctoral dissertation*). Curtin University of Technology, Australia.

Day, C., Hopkins, D., Harris, A. & Ahtaridou, E. 2009. The impact of school leadership on pupil outcomes. Final report.

Eberlin, R. J., & B. C. Tatum. 2008. Making Just Decisions: Organizational Justice, Decisionmaking, and Leadership. Management Decision 46 (2): 310–329.

Hallinger, P. & Bryant, D. 2013. Mapping the terrain of educational leadership and management in East Asia. *Journal of Educational Administration* 51(5): 618–637.

Hallinger, P & Huber, S. 2012. School leadership that makes a difference: international perspectives.

Hariri, H., Monypenny, R. & Prideaux, M. 2014. Leadership styles and decision-making styles in an Indonesian school context. *School Leadership & Management* 34 (3): 284–298.

Harris, A., Day, C., Hopkins, D., Hadfield, M., Hargreaves, A. & Chapman, C. 2013. *Effective leadership* for *school improvement*. Routledge.

Huber, S.G. & Muijs, D. 2010. School leadership effectiveness: The growing insight in the importance of school leadership for the quality and development of schools and their pupils. In *School leadership-international perspectives* (pp. 57–77). Springer Netherlands.

Jones, G. W., & Hagul, P. 2001. Schooling in Indonesia: Crisis-related and longer-term issues. Bulletin of Indonesian Economic Studies, 37(2): 207–231.

Lee, M., & Hallinger, P., 2012. National contexts influencing principals' time use and allocation: Economic development, societal culture, and education system. School Effectiveness and School Improvement, 23(4): 461–482.

Lokman, M.T., Yasin, M., & Salleh, M. 2013. Impak Strategi Politik terhadap Amalan Kepemimpinan Pengajaran Pengetua Sekolah Semerlang. *Jurnal Teknologi, 60(2013):* 1–10. [Impacts of Politic Strategy towards Teaching Leadership Practice of School Principal in Semerlang].

Ministry of National Education and Culture of Republic of Indonesia. 2007. *Peraturan Pemerintah nomor 13 tahun 2007 tentang Standard Nasional Kepala* Sekolah. [Decree number 13 of 2007 on National Standards for Principals]. Jakarta: Ministry of National Education and Culture of Republic of Indonesia.

Moos, L. & Huber, S. 2007. School leadership, school effectiveness and school improvement: democratic and integrative leadership. In *International* handbook *of school effectiveness and improvement*: 579–596.

Morrison, K. 2004. *A Guide to Teaching Practice* [Online]. Routledge Falmer. Retrieved from http://cw.routledge.com/textbooks/0415306752/resources/pdf/09DefiningEffectiveSchools.pdf

Mortimore, P., Sammons, P., Stol, L., Lewis, D. & Ecob, R. 1988. *School Matters: The junior years*. Open Books

Murphy, J. & Louis, K.S. 1994. *Reshaping the principalship: Insights from* transformational *reform efforts*. Corwin Press, Inc., 2455 Teller Road, Thousand Oaks.

Northouse, P.G. 2015. *Leadership: Theory and practice*. Sage publications.

Raihani, 2008. An Indonesian model of successful school leadership. Journal *of Educational Administration* 46(4): 481–496.

Reynolds, D. & Teddlie, C. 2002. *The international* handbook *of* school *effectiveness research*. Routledge.

Reynolds, D., Hopkins, D., Potter, D. & Chapman, C. 2001. *School Improvement for Schools Facing Challenging Circumstances*. London: DES.

Robbins, S., Bergman, R., Stagg, I. & Coulter, M. 2009. *Management*. 5th ed. Frenchs Forest, NSW: Pearson Prentice Hall.

Robinson, V.M., 2007. *School leadership and student* outcomes*: Identifying what works and why* (Vol. 41). Melbourne: Australian Council for Educational Leaders.

Southworth, G., 2003. Learning-centered leadership: the only way to go.

Yasin, M., Mustamin, Tahir, L.M. 2013. Principal Competencies and Achievement of National Education Standard in Indonesia. *International Journal of Humanities and Social Science Invention* 8(2): 31–36.

Author index